# UNIVERSITY CASEBOOK SERIES

### EDITORIAL BOARD

**ROBERT C. CLARK**
*DIRECTING EDITOR*
Dean & Royall Professor of Law
Harvard University

**DANIEL A. FARBER**
Henry J. Fletcher Professor of Law
University of Minnesota

**OWEN M. FISS**
Sterling Professor of Law
Yale University

**GERALD GUNTHER**
William Nelson Cromwell Professor of Law, Emeritus
Stanford University

**THOMAS H. JACKSON**
President
University of Rochester

**HERMA HILL KAY**
Dean & Barbara Nachtrieb Armstrong Professor of Law
University of California, Berkeley

**DAVID W. LEEBRON**
Dean & Lucy G. Moses Professor of Law
Columbia University

**SAUL LEVMORE**
William B. Graham Professor of Law
University of Chicago

**ROBERT L. RABIN**
A. Calder Mackay Professor of Law
Stanford University

**CAROL M. ROSE**
Gordon Bradford Tweedy Professor of Law & Organization
Yale University

**DAVID L. SHAPIRO**
William Nelson Cromwell Professor of Law
Harvard University

# CORPORATE REORGANIZATION AND BANKRUPTCY

## LEGAL AND FINANCIAL MATERIALS

By
**MARK J. ROE**
Columbia University, School of Law
Milton Handler Professor of Business Regulation

**New York, New York**
**FOUNDATION PRESS**
**2000**

Foundation Press, a division of West Group, has created this publication to provide you with accurate and authoritative information concerning the subject matter covered. However, this publication was not necessarily prepared by persons licensed to practice law in a particular jurisdiction. Foundation Press is not engaged in rendering legal or other professional advice, and this publication is not a substitute for the advice of an attorney. If you require legal or other expert advice, you should seek the services of a competent attorney or other professional.

COPYRIGHT © 2000 By FOUNDATION PRESS
                          11 Penn Plaza, Tenth Floor
                          New York, NY 10001
                          Phone Toll Free 1–877–888–1330
                          Fax (212) 760–8705
                          fdpress.com

All rights reserved
Printed in the United States of America

ISBN 1–56662–966–7

TEXT IS PRINTED ON 10% POST CONSUMER RECYCLED PAPER

# PREFACE

With these materials I hope the student will learn not only the major elements of corporate reorganization in chapter 11 of the Bankruptcy Code, but also the major facets of bankruptcy that influence financing transactions. After all, what counts in a financing transaction is what will happen if the firm does badly and cannot repay its debt, because for the most part a simple I.O.U. would suffice otherwise. Much of the documentation that accompanies complex financing transactions is drafted and negotiated in anticipation of a possible reorganization in chapter 11, or a private reorganization accomplished in its shadow.

I hope the student will acquire another skill while mastering these materials. Good lawyers can advise clients about financial complexity and these financial skills aren't always front and center in law school courses. Indeed, if we can over-generalize, the hidden message in many first-year (and upper-year) law school courses is that students need to understand how to distinguish one judicial decision from another. And the hidden message in some upper-level courses, like taxation and maybe securities regulation or a commercial law course, is to teach the student how to read and construct a complex regulatory or statutory system. The message behind these materials is how to understand complex financial deal-making and how to integrate finance with law, in the context of bankruptcy. These deal-making skills are usually picked up (or not) by the young lawyer working in the law firm, but there's no reason, in my view, why young lawyers shouldn't get a head start in law school.

With these financial and deal-making skills in mind, I've approached the subject of bankruptcy quite differently than how it's approached in many, perhaps most, bankruptcy casebooks. Most bankruptcy courses provide an anatomy-of-a-bankruptcy. That is probably the better way to approach a course designed primarily for budding bankruptcy practitioners, but a less useful approach for budding deal-makers and financiers (or young advisors to deal-makers and financiers). An anatomy-of-a-bankruptcy course might begin with the requirements for a petition and end with the confirmation of a plan of reorganization. But to a financier, the contents of the plan—how can my contract be affected by bankruptcy?—are probably more important than the largely formal prerequisites to filing a petition, so early on in these materials we focus on the contents of a plan, the bargaining context of plan formation, and the principal warps in the bargaining process.

The goals here also affect the type of materials I've chosen to include. When feasible, I've used not just judicial opinions, but materials that financing lawyers use day-to-day: bond indentures, prospectuses, materials about drafting loan agreements, and SEC submissions. The result is that the materials are less black-letter law oriented, more conceptual and more deal-oriented than is typical. And, although finance theory might be thought the province of academics, I believe that the student or young lawyer who understands the basic concepts from finance theory—not just the sine qua non basics of discounting, present value, risk, and diversification, but also principal-agent theory, monitoring, information incompleteness, and so on—will be a better lawyer, will be better able to advise clients, and will be better able to structure deals.

Mark Roe<br>
January 2000

# TABLE OF CONTENTS

**Preface** ............................................................................................................. iii
**Table of Contents** ............................................................................................. v
**Table of Authorities** ...................................................................................... xvii

## Chapter 1: Introduction ..................................................................................... 1

¶101: Introductory note .................................................................................... 1
¶102: Glenn Porter & Harold Livesay, Merchants and Manufacturers: Studies in the Changing Structure of Nineteenth Century Marketing 63-65 (1971) ...... 4
¶103: The shift in business at the end of the 19th century ............................... 6
¶104: The equity receivership ........................................................................... 7
¶105: A brief anatomy of a bankruptcy ............................................................. 9

## Chapter 2: Reorganization and Valuation ...................................................... 13

### A. Why valuation is important ....................................................................... 13

¶201: Schematic of controls on the corporation ............................................. 13
¶202: Sample balance sheet ............................................................................ 15
¶203: Seniority, security, and valuation .......................................................... 15
¶204: Who gets what when things go wrong? ................................................ 17
¶205: A brief introduction to reorganization in chapter 11 ............................ 17
¶206: Winners and losers ................................................................................ 19
¶207: The limits of judicial expertise: reliance on the parties? ...................... 19
¶208: In re New York, New Haven and Hartford RR Co., 4 Bankr. 758 (D. Conn. 1980) ...................................................................................... 20
¶209: The implications of valuation ................................................................ 24

### B. Basic valuation ........................................................................................... 24

¶210: Discounting to present value ................................................................. 24
¶211: Present values in more detail: Richard A. Brealey & Stewart C. Myers, Principles of Corporate Finance 35-40 (6th ed. 2000) ......................... 26
¶212: Present value problem ........................................................................... 28
¶213: Risk .......................................................................................................... 29
¶214: Variance and diversification .................................................................. 32

## Chapter 3: Judicial Valuation ........................................................................... 35

### A. Failure .......................................................................................................... 35

¶301: The distinction between financial failure and economic failure .......... 35
¶302: Background to *Atlas Pipeline* ............................................................... 37

## B. Liquidation vs. reorganization .................................................................. 38

¶303: Questions on *Atlas Pipeline*: Liquidation vs. reorganization ................... 38
¶304: In re Atlas Pipeline Corporation, SEC Advisory Opinion Release No. 42, 9 S.E.C. 416 (1941) ............................................................................... 39
¶305: Liquidating or reorganizing: Who should decide? ................................. 45
¶306: Eastern Air Lines .................................................................................. 47

## C. Valuation of Atlas Pipeline ........................................................................ 49

¶307: Valuing the firm: *Atlas Pipeline* ............................................................ 49
¶308: *Atlas Pipeline* (continued): Valuation .................................................. 50
¶309: Financial risk vs. operational risk ......................................................... 55
¶310: Walter J. Blum & Wilbur G. Katz, Depreciation and Enterprise Valuation, 32 U. Chi. L. Rev. 236 (1965) ............................................... 58
¶311: The concept of depreciation ................................................................. 61
¶312: *Atlas Pipeline* (continued) ................................................................... 63
¶313: In re Atlas Pipeline Corp., 39 F. Supp. 846 (W.D. La. 1941) (July 15, 1941) ...... 71
¶314: Earlier in the Proceeding: First Trust Co. of Philadelphia v. Atlas Pipeline Corp., 29 F. Supp. 32 (W.D. La. 1939) .................................. 73
¶315: After the reorganization ........................................................................ 74

## D. The capital layers .................................................................................... 74

¶316: Henry B. Gardner, The SEC and Valuation Under Chapter X, 91 U. Pa. L. Rev. 440 (1947) ............................................................................. 74
¶317: Questions on Gardner ........................................................................... 77
¶318: *Atlas Pipeline* and decapitalization ..................................................... 78

## E. Advisors and conflicts ............................................................................. 79

¶319: Joseph Kennedy, Big Business, What Now?, Saturday Evening Post, Jan. 16, 1937, at 10 ................................................................................ 79
¶320: Modern variations ................................................................................. 80

## F. Valuation of Duplan ................................................................................. 83

¶321: Price-earnings ratios: In re The Duplan Corporation, Advisory Report of the SEC, 20 S.E.C. Docket 189 (May 2, 1980) ................................. 83
¶322: Questions on *Duplan* ........................................................................... 88
¶323: Using price/earnings multiples in *Duplan* ........................................... 90
¶324: *Duplan* problem .................................................................................. 93

# TABLE OF CONTENTS

**Chapter 4: Priority** .................................................................................................. 95

**A. The concepts: absolute priority** ......................................................................... 95

¶401: Priorities in reorganization ............................................................................ 95
¶402: The setting of reorganization ......................................................................... 96
¶403: Case v. Los Angeles Lumber Prods. Co., 308 U.S. 106 (1939) ........................ 97
¶404: Notes on *Los Angeles Lumber* ..................................................................... 101

**B. The statute today** ............................................................................................. 104

¶405: Background to the 1978 Act: Report of the Commission on the Bankruptcy Laws of the United States, House Doc. 93-137, 93d Cong., 1st Sess 255 et seq. (1973) .......................................................................... 104
¶406: Statement By The Hon. Dennis DeConcini, Chairman of the Subcommittee on Improvements in Judicial Machinery of the Sen. Judiciary Committee, Upon Introducing the Senate Amendment to the House Amendment to H.R. 8200, 124 Congressional Record S 17406 (Oct. 6, 1978) ..................... 105
¶407: Absolute priority under the half-century old Bankruptcy Act of 1938 ............. 106
¶408: The 1978 Bankruptcy Code changes ............................................................. 106
¶409: Priority today: understanding § 1129(a)(8) ................................................... 108
¶410: Reorganization statutory provisions for ¶409 ................................................ 109
¶411: Trade creditors and unfair discrimination ..................................................... 112
¶412: Unfair discrimination and trade creditors (H.R. Rep. No. 95-595) ................. 114
¶413: Dieglom problem ........................................................................................ 116
¶414: Reinstatement in Dieglom ........................................................................... 120
¶415: Section 1129(a)(7)—The best interests test .................................................. 122
¶416: Fairness ...................................................................................................... 123
¶417: Other creditors with priority ........................................................................ 124

**C. The reality of delay in chapter 11** ................................................................... 125

¶418: Value rising: The Cotton Belt Railroad: Walter Blum & Stanley Kaplan, Corporate Readjustments and Reorganizations 485-86 (1976) ........................ 125

**D. The lawyers** .................................................................................................. 126

¶419: Value uncertain: Practical lawyers, modern delay, and the advantages of the valuation hearing for shareholders ................................................................ 126
¶420: Rule 11 ....................................................................................................... 128
¶421: Standards of professional responsibility ....................................................... 128
¶422: Psychology ................................................................................................. 129

**E. The managers** ............................................................................................... 131

¶423: The role of managers in chapter 11 .............................................................. 131

## F. The costs of delay .................................................................................................. 131

¶424: Value declining: cutbacks and bankruptcy costs ................................................. 131
¶425: Some costs of delay: Summers & Cutler, Texaco and Pennzoil Both Lost Big, N.Y. Times, Feb. 14, 1988, at 3, cols. 1–3 ................................................................. 132
¶426: Questions on Summers & Cutler ............................................................................ 134
¶427: The common pool problem in general .................................................................... 135
¶428: Bankruptcy as a common pool problem: Thomas H. Jackson, The Logic and Limits of Bankruptcy Law 10-19 (1986) ................................................................ 136
¶429: Miscellaneous Code provisions ............................................................................... 140

## G. A note on purposes ............................................................................................. 141

¶430: Fresh starts ............................................................................................................... 141
¶431: Priority and pre-bankruptcy investments ............................................................... 142

# Chapter 5: Alternatives to Chapter 11: Selling .......................................................... 145

## A. Selling? .................................................................................................................. 145

¶501: Sale of the firm to provide a value? ....................................................................... 145
¶502: Conversion to chapter 7? ....................................................................................... 145
¶503: Sales under § 363 .................................................................................................... 147
¶504: Statutory provisions ................................................................................................ 148
¶505: In re The Lionel Corp, 722 F.2d 1063 (2d Cir. 1983) ........................................... 148
¶506: Questions on *Lionel* ............................................................................................... 156
¶507: Side deals under § 363 ............................................................................................ 157
¶508: Selling under § 363? ............................................................................................... 159
¶509: The best interests test ............................................................................................. 159
¶510: Alternatives: Some kind of sale? ............................................................................ 161
¶511: Some kind of sale?: J. Bonbright, The Valuation of Property, ch. xii (1937) ..... 162
¶512: Buying up claims? ................................................................................................... 163
¶513: Selling: James White, Bankruptcy and Creditors' Rights 288 (1985) (summarizing Roe, Bankruptcy and Debt, 83 Colum. L. Rev. (1983)) ....................... 164
¶514: A chapter 11 mismatch? ......................................................................................... 165

## B. The judiciary and valuation ................................................................................. 166

¶515: In re Equity Funding Corp. of America, 391 F. Supp. 768 (1975) ..................... 166
¶516: In re New York, New Haven and Hartford RR. Co., 632 F.2d 955 (1980) ......... 166
¶517: James Lorie, Peter Dodd & Mary Hamilton, The Stock Market: Theories and Evidence (2d ed. 1985) ................................................................................... 168
¶518: Efficient markets for a bankrupt's securities? ...................................................... 169
¶519: Edward Altman, Bankrupt Firms' Equity Securities as an Investment Alternative, Fin. Analysts J., July–Aug. 1969, at 129 ................................................. 170
¶520: Walter Blum, The Law and Language of Corporate Reorganization, 17 U. Chi. L. Rev. 505, 571-580 (1950) ......................................................................... 171
¶521: Overvaluation and undervaluation in reorganization .......................................... 173

# TABLE OF CONTENTS

## Chapter 6: Junk Bonds .................... 175

### A. Characteristics of bond indentures .................... 176

¶601: Background to the bond indenture .................... 176
¶602: Dewing, The Financial Policy of Corporations (5th ed. 1953) .................... 178

### B. The junk bond .................... 180

¶603: Drum Financial prospectus .................... 180
¶604: Questions on the Drum Financial Indenture .................... 186
¶605: American Bar Foundation, Corporate Debt Financing Project, Commentaries on Model Debenture Indenture Provisions (1971) .................... 187

### C. Financial markets and junk bonds .................... 190

¶606: Jan Loeys, Low-Grade Bonds: A Growing Source of Corporate Funding, Fed. Res. Bank of Phil., Bus. Rev., Nov./Dec. 1986 .................... 190

### D. Negative pledge clauses .................... 195

¶607: The negative pledge clause .................... 195
¶608: Chrysler solicitation of consents .................... 196
¶609: Questions about Chrysler's negative pledge .................... 201
¶610: Kelly v. Central Hanover Bank & Trust Co., 11 F. Supp. 497, rev'd 85 F.2d 61 (2d Cir. 1936) .................... 203
¶611: The UCC, *Kelly* and the negative pledge clause .................... 207

### E. Secured credit and finance theory .................... 209

¶612: Secured Transactions: Donald W. Baker, A Lawyer's Guide to Secured Transactions (1983) .................... 211
¶613: The avoiding power .................... 215
¶614: Secured interests and finance theory .................... 216
¶615: A note on marshalling .................... 218

### F. Morality, markets, and practicing law with bond indentures .................... 219

¶616: Harry M. Markowitz, Markets and Morality: Or Arbitragers Get No Respect, Wall St. J., May 14, 1991 .................... 219
¶617: Data on the growth of the junk bond market .................... 223

### G. Low priority .................... 225

¶618: Agency costs and monitoring: Mitchell Berlin, Bank Loans and Marketable Securities: How Do Financial Contracts Control Borrowing Firms?, Fed. Res. Bank of Phil., Bus. Rev., July–Aug. 1987, at 9 .................... 225
¶619: Bases for subordination .................... 229
¶620: Drafting a bond indenture .................... 233

## Chapter 7: Reranking in the Holding Company: Substantive Consolidation, Fraudulent Conveyances, and Preferences .................... 235

**A. Substantive consolidation of the holding company** .................... 236

¶701: Holding companies .................... 236
¶702: Consolidated Rock Prods. Co. v. DuBois, 312 U.S. 510 (1941) .................... 237
¶703: Questions on *Consolidated Rock* .................... 242
¶704: Fraudulent conveyances, veil-piercing, illegal dividends, improper use of control, and substantive consolidation .................... 244
¶705: Disclosure and consolidation: Regulation S-X .................... 245
¶706: Richard Posner, The Rights of Creditors of Affiliated Corporations, 43 U. Chi. L. Rev. 449, 507 (1976) .................... 245
¶707: Questions on complex corporate structures and seniority .................... 247
¶708: Administrative consolidation: In re Commercial Envelope Mfg. Co., 14 Collier Bankr. Cas. (MB) 191 (Bankr. S.D.N.Y. Aug. 22, 1977) .................... 248

**B. Fraudulent conveyances and the holding company** .................... 253

¶709: Holding companies and effective seniority .................... 253
¶710: Fraudulent conveyances and finance companies .................... 254
¶711: Fraudulent conveyances under the Bankruptcy Code .................... 256
¶712: The origins of fraudulent conveyance law: Garrard Glenn, Fraudulent Conveyances and Preferences 79-87 (1940) .................... 257
¶713: The creditor of the subsidiary .................... 259

**C. Preferences and the holding company** .................... 261

¶714: Deprizio Construction Co. v. Ingersoll Rand Financial Corp., 874 F.2d 1186 (7th Cir. 1989) .................... 261
¶715: Preferences .................... 270
¶716: Questions on *Deprizio* .................... 273
¶717: Priority equalizations across time: Preferences; Lynn LoPucki, Strategies for Creditors in Bankruptcy Proceedings 41 (1985) .................... 275

**D. Intercorporate payments in the holding company** .................... 278

¶718: Sinclair Oil and intercorporate payments .................... 278
¶719: Questions on *Sinven* .................... 281

## Chapter 8: Equitable Subordination .................... 283

**A. General** .................... 283

¶801: Introduction: Equitable subordination and rescission .................... 283

# TABLE OF CONTENTS

**B. Equitable subordination of a stockholder's debt claim** .......................................................... 284

¶802: Taylor v. Standard Gas & Electric Co., 306 U.S. 307 (1939) ............................. 284
¶803: *Deep Rock* problems ............................................................................................ 289
¶804: *Deep Rock* and corporate planning ...................................................................... 290
¶805: Partnership liability ............................................................................................... 293

**C. Subordination of securities law claims** ................................................................................. 297

¶806: Oppenheimer v. Harriman National Bank & Trust Co., 301 U.S. 206 (1937) .... 297
¶807: John Slain & Homer Kripke, The Interface Between Securities Regulation and Bankruptcy—Allocating the Risk of Illegal Securities Issuance Between Securityholders and the Issuer's Creditors, 48 N.Y.U. L. Rev. 261 (1973) ......... 298
¶808: Bankruptcy Code, § 510 ...................................................................................... 303
¶809: *Oppenheimer*, Slain & Kripke, § 510, rescission and fraud .................................. 303
¶810: Does subordination make the rescission or damages claim useless, always? ..... 305
¶811: Reranking ............................................................................................................. 306
¶812: Transition problem ............................................................................................... 307

## Chapter 9: More on Creditors' Conduct .................................................................................. 309

**A. Equitable subordination of a creditor's claim** ..................................................................... 310

¶901: In re American Lumber Co., 7 Bankr. 519 (1979) .............................................. 310
¶902: Questions on *American Lumber* .......................................................................... 317
¶903: Note re Washington Plate Glass Co., 27 Bankr. 550 (D.D.C. 1982), 3 Bankruptcy News Letter (WGL), No. 6 (June 1986), at 1 ......................................... 322
¶904: The collapse of W.T. Grant Company ................................................................. 322
¶905: In re W.T. Grant Co., 699 F.2d 599 (1983) ........................................................ 324
¶906: Questions on *W.T. Grant* ..................................................................................... 331
¶907: In re Clark Pipe & Supply Co., Inc., 870 F.2d 1022 (5th Cir. 1989) .................. 332
¶908: Cross-collateralization .......................................................................................... 340

**B. Lender liability** ........................................................................................................................ 341

¶909: Sources of lender liability ..................................................................................... 341
¶910: State National Bank of El Paso v. Farah Mfg. Co., 678 S.W.2d 661 (Tex. Ct. App. 1984) .............................................................................................. 341
¶911: Questions on lender liability in *Farah* ................................................................. 352
¶912: A comparative note ............................................................................................... 354

## Chapter 10: Rejecting Pre-bankruptcy Contracts ................................................................... 357

**A. The trustee's right to reject or assume** ................................................................................. 357
**B. Social costs** ............................................................................................................................... 360
**C. Specific performance** .............................................................................................................. 361
**D. Labor** ........................................................................................................................................ 362
**E. Assignment** .............................................................................................................................. 363
**F. Environmental clean-up obligations** ..................................................................................... 363

## Chapter 11: Interest .................................................. 367

### A. The statute .................................................. 367

¶1101: Interest accruals and nonaccruals in bankruptcy for unsecured creditors ........... 367
¶1102: Interest accruals .................................................. 368

### B. Creditors versus stockholders .................................................. 371

¶1103: Chaim Fortgang & Lawrence King, The 1978 Code: Some Wrong Policy Decisions, 56 N.Y.U. L. Rev. 1148 (1981) .................................................. 371
¶1104: Case law, and then Congress acts .................................................. 375

### C. Seniors versus juniors .................................................. 376

¶1105: Subordination .................................................. 376
¶1106: In re King Resources, Inc., 528 F.2d 789 (10th Cir. 1976) .................................................. 377

### D. Guarantors versus guaranteed .................................................. 380

¶1107: In re Bruno, [1984 Transfer Binder] Bankr. L. Rep. (CCH) ¶70,084 (1st Cir. Nov. 2, 1984) .................................................. 380
¶1108: The lawyers .................................................. 382

### E. Secured versus unsecured .................................................. 382

¶1109: Adequate protection for secured creditors .................................................. 382
¶1110: United Savings Ass'n v. Timbers of Inwood Forest Assoc., 484 U.S. 365 (1988) .................................................. 385

### F. What rate? .................................................. 390

¶1111: Unsecureds with high interest rates versus those with low rates .................................................. 390

### G. General and miscellaneous .................................................. 391

¶1112: Interest on interest .................................................. 391
¶1113: A relational theory of bankruptcy? .................................................. 392
¶1114: Oscillations: Roe, Bankruptcy, Priority and Economics, 75 Va. L. Rev. 219, 234-40 (1989) .................................................. 393

## Chapter 12: Workouts to Avoid a Bankruptcy .................................................. 399

### A. General .................................................. 399

¶1201: Workouts to avoid bankruptcy .................................................. 399
¶1202: Arthur S. Dewing, The Financial Policy of Corporations (5th ed. 1953) .................................................. 399

## B. Modification of the indenture ... 400

¶1203: Aladdin Hotel Co. v. Bloom, 200 F.2d 627 (8th Cir. 1953) ... 400
¶1204: Questions on *Aladdin* ... 404
¶1205: Trust Indenture Act of 1939, § 316(b) (15 U.S.C. § 77ppp) ... 405

## C. Holding out and buoying up ... 405

¶1206: Collapse of a workout ... 405
¶1207: The economics of holding out ... 409
¶1208: Case v. Los Angeles Lumber Prods. Co., 308 U.S. 106 (1939) ... 412
¶1209: Notes on *Los Angeles Lumber* ... 416

## D. Exit consents ... 418

¶1210: Exit consents ... 418
¶1211: Katz v. Oak Industries, Inc., 508 A.2d 873 (Del. Ch. 1986) ... 421
¶1212: *Katz* and the Trust Indenture Act ... 428
¶1213: Fidelity Investments petition to the SEC ... 432
¶1214: Questions on Fidelity application ... 437
¶1215: Exchange offer problem ... 438
¶1216: Exchange offer prospectus (the *Chateaugay* problem) ... 440
¶1217: Original issue discount ... 443
¶1218: Subsequent developments (*Chateaugay* on appeal) ... 444
¶1219: Exchange offers and original issue discount ... 449
¶1220: On the possible inability to raise capital during financial stress: Chrysler on the verge of shut-down, 1978–1979 ... 451
¶1221: Mergers ... 456

# Chapter 13: Duties to Creditors? ... 459

## A. The trustee ... 459

¶1301: Trustees under the Trust Indenture Act ... 459
¶1302: The depression-era SEC investigation into trustees ... 461
¶1303: The notion of trustee: fiduciary or contracted-for agent? ... 462
¶1304: Morris v. Cantor, 390 F.Supp. 817 (S.D.N.Y. 1975) ... 463
¶1305: Passage of the Trust Indenture Act ... 466
¶1306: Broad v. Rockwell Int'l Corp., 642 F.2d 929-30 (5th Cir. 1981) ... 467
¶1307: Questions on *Rockwell* ... 468
¶1308: Excerpt from *Grant* opinion ... 469
¶1309: Edward Fleischman, Proposed Amendments to the Trust Indenture Act of 1939 (SEC memorandum Aug. 10, 1987) ... 470
¶1310: Amendments to the Trust Indenture Act ... 473
¶1311: The Trust Indenture Act's new conflicts provision ... 473

## B. Duties of the company ... 475

¶1312: MetLife v. RJR Nabisco ... 475
¶1313: Gary Hector, The Bondholders' Cold New World, Fortune, Feb. 27, 1989 ... 485
¶1314: When is there a fiduciary duty? In re MortgageAmerica Corp., 714 F.2d 1266 (5th Cir. 1983) ... 487
¶1315: Credit Lyonnais Bank Nederland, N.V. v. Pathe Communications Corp., 1991 Del.Ch. LEXIS 215 at n.55 (Dec. 30, 1991) ... 491
¶1316: Questions on *Credit Lyonnais* ... 493
¶1317: Fiduciary theory: Andrew Bogen, David Kennedy & Bradley Schwartz, Landmarks on an Unmapped Terrain: Defining the Rights of Debtholders, 5 Insights, Jan. 1991, at 19 ... 494

## C. Contract theory ... 495

¶1318: Charles Goetz & Robert Scott, Principles of Relational Contracts, 67 Va. L. Rev. 1089-91, 1149-50 (1981) ... 495
¶1319: Allan Farnsworth, Disputes Over Omission in Contracts, 68 Colum. L. Rev. 860, 891 (1968) ... 498

## Chapter 14: Finance Theory and Debt: Modigliani-Miller, Bankruptcy Costs and Taxes ... 501

¶1401: Why then debt? ... 501
¶1402: Richard Brealey & Stewart Myers, Principles of Corporate Finance 473-91 (6th ed. 2000) ... 505
¶1403: Leverage, value and Modigliani-Miller ... 512
¶1404: With risk ... 513
¶1405: With corporate taxes ... 514
¶1406: With owner-level taxes ... 514
¶1407: With individual taxes and long-term capital gains ... 515
¶1408: With tax-favored institutions ... 517
¶1409: Some stages of analysis ... 518
¶1410: Perspectives on the firm, capital structure, and some policy implications ... 518
¶1411: Tax consequences of recapitalizations in bankruptcy ... 520
¶1412: Could the market produce a bankruptcy-avoiding security? ... 523

## Chapter 15: Chapter 11 as a Mechanism of Corporate Governance ... 529

¶1501: Operating the business in general ... 529
¶1502: Operating the business, getting inventory ... 530
¶1503: Credit outside the ordinary course of business ... 531
¶1504: Cross-collateralization ... 532
¶1505: Using cash to operate the business ... 533
¶1506: Displacing management with a trustee ... 534

# TABLE OF CONTENTS

## Chapter 16: The LBO ... 535

### A. The leveraged buyout ... 535

¶1601: LBO's and the prospect of fraudulent conveyance liability ... 535
¶1602: United States v. Tabor Court Realty Corp., 803 F.2d 1288 (3d Cir. 1986) ... 537
¶1603: Questions on *Gleneagles* ... 546
¶1604: Wieboldt Stores, Inc. v. Jerome M. Schottenstein, 94 Bankr. 488 (Bankr. N.D. Ill. 1988) ... 549
¶1605: Questions on *Wieboldt* ... 560
¶1606: A note on Kaiser Steel Corp. v. Charles Schwab ... 562
¶1607: Benjamin Stein, Shooting Fish in a Barrel—Why Management Always Makes a Bundle in an LBO, Barron's, Jan. 12, 1987, at 6 ... 563

### B. Margin regulations ... 568

¶1608: Margin regulations and other issues relating to debt ... 568
¶1609: Federal Reserve Interpretive Rule: Securities Credit by Persons Other Than Banks, Brokers, or Dealers; Purchase of Debt Securities to Finance Corporate Takeovers, 12 C.F.R. Part 207 [Regulation G] ... 569

## Chapter 17: Markets and Chapter 11 ... 577

¶1701: Robert C. Clark, The Interdisciplinary Study of Legal Evolution, 90 Yale L. J. 1238 (1981) ... 577
¶1702: Mark J. Roe, Bankruptcy and Debt: A New Model for Corporate Reorganization (1983, 1987) ... 578
¶1703: Questions on Roe ... 590
¶1704: Douglas Baird, The Uneasy Case for Corporate Reorganization, 15 Journal of Legal Studies 127 (1986) ... 591
¶1705: Questions on Baird ... 594
¶1706: Lucian Arye Bebchuk, A New Approach to Corporate Reorganizations, 101 Harv. L. Rev. 775 (1988) ... 595
¶1707: Questions on Bebchuk ... 600
¶1708: Advantages and disadvantages of each market-based alternative ... 600
¶1709: General problems with using the market to replace chapter 11 ... 604

**Appendix A: Present Value** ... 607

**Appendix B: The Statutes** ... 611

**Index** ... 631

# TABLE OF AUTHORITIES

## STATUTES

### BANKRUPTCY CODE

| | |
|---|---|
| § 101(5) | 264 |
| § 101(10) | 264 |
| § 101(14) | 81, 82 |
| § 101(31) | 264 |
| § 101(32) | 275 |
| § 101(41) | 263 |
| § 101(54) | 276 |
| § 307 | 81 |
| § 327(a) | 82 |
| § 361 | 383 |
| § 362 | 18, 19, 96, 320, 367, 383 |
| § 362(a) | 364, 385, 386 |
| § 362(b) | 321, 364 |
| § 362(d) | 383, 385, 386 |
| § 363 | 147, 148, 156, 159, 163, 533 |
| § 364 | 530, 531, 532 |
| § 365 | 111, 357, 363, 524 |
| § 502(b) | 140, 367, 375, 376, 380, 392, 394, 446 |
| § 502(c) | 362 |
| § 502(g) | 358 |
| § 503(b) | 530, 531 |
| § 506 | 118, 382, 387, 389 |
| § 507 | 124, 360, 530, 531, 532 |
| § 510 | 341, 379 |
| § 510(b) | 303 |
| § 510(c) | 309, 322 |
| § 544 | 216, 256, 320, 549, 559 |
| § 546 | 321, 562 |
| § 546(b) | 321 |
| § 547 | 261, 264, 265, 275, 283, 316, 319 |
| § 548 | 256, 549, 557 |
| § 550 | 260, 261, 264, 270, 274, 549, 554, 560, 561 |
| § 726 | 368, 370, 373, 375, 390 |
| § 1104 | 96, 147 |
| § 1107 | 82, 529, 530 |
| § 1108 | 530 |
| § 1112 | 146 |
| § 1113 | 362 |
| § 1121 | 131, 374 |
| § 1123 | 2, 391 |

| | |
|---|---|
| § 1124 | 108, 109, 111, 119, 121, 123, 124, 160, 363, 391 |
| § 1125 | 140, 159 |
| § 1126 | 109, 111, 112, 152, 159, 163, 452 |
| § 1126(c) | 108 |
| § 1126(e) | 159 |
| § 1129 | 110, 215, 368, 370, 372, 373, 375, 417, 558 |
| § 1129(a) | 109, 114 |
| § 1129(a)(7) | 108, 109, 122, 123, 159, 417 |
| § 1129(a)(8) | 108, 109, 112, 127 |
| § 1129(a)(11) | 109 |
| § 1129(b) | 108, 109, 112, 120, 127, 128, 391 |
| § 1141 | 2 |

## OTHER STATUTES

| | |
|---|---|
| IRC § 1014 | 516 |
| IRC § 108(e) | 521 |
| IRC § 108(e)(11) | 522 |
| IRC § 382 | 522 |
| IRC § 1202 | 516 |
| TIA § 77ddd(d) | 473 |
| TIA § 77jjj | 465 |
| TIA § 77kkk | 465 |
| TIA § 77vvv | 464 |
| TIA § 310 | 473 |
| TIA § 315(a) | 460 |
| TIA § 316(a) | 429 |
| TIA § 316(b) | 405, 429, 526 |
| UCC § 1-201(37) | 213 |
| UCC § 3-302 | 418 |
| UCC § 3-305 | 418 |
| UCC § 9-102 | 207 |
| UCC § 9-102(2) | 213 |
| UCC § 9-203 | 208 |
| UCC § 9-303 | 214 |
| UFCA § 3 | 537, 541 |
| UFCA § 4 | 254, 541 |
| UFCA § 6 | 254 |
| UFCA § 7 | 244, 254, 536, 546 |
| UFCA § 9 | 255, 536 |
| UPA § 6 | 294 |

## CASES

| | |
|---|---|
| Aladdin Hotel v. Bloom | 400 |
| Associates Commercial Corp. v. Rash | 118 |

# TABLE OF AUTHORITIES

Broad v. Rockwell Int'l Corp. .................................................................... 467, 469, 470
Burger King Corp. v. Rovine Corp. ..................................................................... 361
Case v. Los Angeles Lumber Products Co. ........................... 97, 103, 240, 412, 417, 429
Chemical Bank, N.Y. Trust v. Kheel ..................................................................... 251
Christian Life Center Litigation Defense Comm. v. Silva .................................. 306
Consolidated Rock Products Co. v. DuBois ........................................... 88, 237, 603
Continental Supply Co. v. Marshall ..................................................................... 218
Cox v. Hickman ..................................................................................................... 296
Credit Lyonnais Bank Nederland, N.V. v. Pathe Communications Corporation ... 491
Crozier v. Bradford ................................................................................................ 391
Dabney v. Chase Nat'l Bank ................................................................................. 469
Deprizio Construction Co. v. Ingersoll Rand Financial Corp. ............................ 261
E.I. Dupont de Nemours Co. v. Collins ................................................................ 167
Erie Railroad v. Tompkins .................................................................................... 490
First Trust Co. of Philadelphia v. Atlas Pipeline Corp. ........................................ 73
Geyer v. Ingersoll Publications Co. ..................................................................... 491
Gosoff v. Rodman .................................................................................................. 322
Group of Institutional Investors v. Chicago, Milwaukee, St. Paul & Pacific R. Co. ...... 166
Hazzard v. Chase National Bank of the City of New York .................................. 462
In re Allegheny Int'l .................................................................................... 163, 164
In re American Lumber Co. ........................................................................ 310, 334
In re American Mariner Indus., Inc. .................................................................... 384
In re Atlas Pipeline Corporation .............................................................. 39, 50, 63, 71
In re Augie/Restivo Baking Company, Ltd. .......................................................... 247
In re Braniff Airways ............................................................................................ 157
In re Bruno ............................................................................................................ 380
In re Chateaugay Corporation ...................................................................... 443, 444
In re CHG Int'l, Inc. .............................................................................................. 274
In re Clark Pipe & Supply Co., Inc. ..................................................................... 332
In re Clark Pipe & Supply Co., Inc. (Rehearing) ................................................. 336
In re Commercial Envelope Mfg. Co. ............................................................ 248, 603
In re Duplan Corporation ............................................................................... 83, 87
In re Eagle-Picher Indus., Inc. ............................................................................... 80
In re Equity Funding Corporation of America ............................................ 151, 166
In re Flora Mir Candy Corporation ...................................................................... 251
In re Forest Hills Assocs. ..................................................................................... 396
In re Georgian Villa Inc. ....................................................................................... 307
In re Investors Funding Corp. .............................................................................. 307
In re Ionosphere ................................................................................................... 379
In re Johns-Manville Corp. .................................................................................. 524
In re King Resources, Inc. ........................................................................... 377, 396
In re Kingsboro Mortgage Corp. .......................................................................... 396
In re Kizzac Management Corp. .......................................................................... 396
In re Lionel Corp. ................................................................................................. 148
In re Manville Forest Prods. Corp. ............................................................. 375, 396
In re MortgageAmerica Corp. .............................................................................. 487

In re New Valley Corp. .................................................................................................. 375
In re New York, New Haven and Hartford RR ............................................................ 20
In re Prescott ................................................................................................................. 269
In re Sire Plan, Inc. ...................................................................................................... 151
In re Solar Mfg. Corp. .................................................................................................. 150
In re Southeast Banking ................................................................................................ 379
In re Sufolla .................................................................................................................. 274
In re Texlon Corp. ......................................................................................................... 340
In re Vecchione ............................................................................................................. 558
In re Washington Communications Group, Inc. ............................................................ 294
In re W.T. Grant Co. .............................................................................................. 324, 339
In re Yale Express ......................................................................................................... 384
Kaiser Steel Corp. v. Charles Schwab & Co. ................................................................ 562
Kansas City Terminal Ry. Co. v. Central Union Trust Co. ............................................ 99
Kass v. Eastern Air Lines ........................................................................................ 430, 436
Katz v. Oak Industries, Inc. ...................................................................................... 421, 436
Kelly v. Central Hanover Bank & Trust Co. .................................................................. 203
Levien v. Sinclair Oil Corp. .......................................................................................... 278
MacAndrews & Forbes Holdings, Inc. v. Revlon, Inc. .................................................. 570
Martin v. Peyton ............................................................................................................ 296
Matter of SeaTrade Corporation ..................................................................................... 251
Meechan v. Valentine .................................................................................................... 296
MetLife v. RJR Nabisco ................................................................................................ 475
Minute Maid Corp. v. United Foods, Inc. ..................................................................... 295
Morris v. Cantor ..................................................................................................... 463, 469
Munford v. Valuation Research Corp. ........................................................................... 563
NLRB v. Bildisco & Bildisco ........................................................................................ 363
Official Committee of Unsecured Creditors v. PaineWebber Inc. ................................ 306
Oppenheimer v. Harriman National Bank & Trust Co. ................................................ 297
Pisik v. BCI Holdings Corp. ......................................................................................... 430
Rake v. Wade ................................................................................................................ 392
Seaboard World Airlines, Inc. v. Tiger International, Inc. ............................................. 167
Shapiro v. Saybrook Mfg. Co. ................................................................................ 340, 533
Spier v. Lang ................................................................................................................. 296
State National Bank of El Paso v. Farah Mfg. Co. ........................................................ 341
Tanzer v. Int'l General Indus. ........................................................................................ 281
Taylor v. Standard Gas and Electric Company ....................................................... 240, 284
U.S. v. Kirby Lumber .................................................................................................... 520
U.S. v. Ron Pair Enterprises Inc. ................................................................................... 391
Union Bank v. Herbert Wolas ....................................................................................... 274
United Savings Ass'n v. Timbers of Inwood Forest Assoc. .......................................... 385
United States v. Tabor Court Realty Corp. .............................................................. 536, 537
Vanston Bondholders Protective Committee v. Green ............................................ 378, 380
Washington Plate Glass Co. .......................................................................................... 322
Wieboldt Stores, Inc. v. Jerome M. Schottenstein .......................................................... 549

# TABLE OF AUTHORITIES

## OTHER OFFICIAL MATERIALS

| | |
|---|---|
| American Bar Association's Model Rules of Professional Responsibility; Rule 3.1: Meritorious Claims and Contentions | 128 |
| Bankruptcy Rule 9011 | 128 |
| Board of Governors of the Federal Reserve System, Flow of Funds Accounts First Quarter 1986, at 34 (1986) | 103 |
| Board of Governors of the Federal Reserve System, Interpretive Rule: Securities Credit by Persons Other Than Banks, Brokers, or Dealers; Purchase of Debt Securities to Finance Corporate Takeovers, 12 C.F.R. Part 207 [Regulation G; Docket No. R-0562] | 569 |
| Federal Rules of Civil Procedure, Rule 11 | 128 |
| H.R. Report No. 595, 95th Cong., 1st Sess (1977) | 109, 114 |
| Report of the Commission on the Bankruptcy Laws of the United States, House Doc. 93-137, 93d Cong., 1st Sess (1973) | 104, 106 |
| Restatement (Second) of Agency (1958) | 331 |
| Restatement (Second) of Contracts (1979, 1981) | 425, 426 |
| SEC, Report on the Study of Protective and Reorganization Committees, Vol. 7, § IIB (1940) | 161 |
| SEC, Form and Content of Financial Statements, Securities Act of 1933, Securities Exchange Act of 1934 | 245 |
| SEC, Report on the Study and Investigation of the Work, Activities, Personnel and Functions of Protective and Reorganization Committees—Part VI, at 2–6 (1936) | 461 |
| Statement By The Hon. Dennis DeConcini, Chairman of the Subcommittee on Improvements in Judicial Machinery..., Upon Introducing the Senate Amendment to the House Amendment to H.R. 8200, 124 Congressional Record S 17406 (Oct. 6, 1978) | 105 |

## ARTICLES, BOOKS, AND OTHER COMMENTARY

| | |
|---|---|
| Adler, Barry E. *An Equity-Agency Solution to the Bankruptcy-Priority Puzzle*, 22 J. Legal Stud. 73 (1993) | 217 |
| Adler, Barry E. *A Theory of Corporate Insolvency*, 72 NYU L. Rev. 343 (1997) | 600 |
| Aghion, Philippe, Oliver Hart & John Moore. *The Economics of Bankruptcy Reform*, 8 J.L. Econ. & Org. 523 (1992) | 600 |
| Altman, Edward. *Bankrupt Firms' Equity Securities as an Investment Alternative*, Fin. Analysts' J., July–Aug. (1969) | 170 |
| Altman, Edward. The Anatomy of the High Yield Bond Market: After Two Decades of Activity-Implications for Europe 5 (NYU Center for Law and Business Working Paper #CLB-98-021) | 224 |
| American Bar Foundation, Corporate Debt Financing Project. Commentaries on Model Debenture Indenture Provisions (1971) | 187 |
| Andrade, Gregor & Steven N. Kaplan. *How Costly is Financial (not Economic) Distress?—Evidence from Highly Leveraged Transactions that Became Distressed*, 53 J. Fin. 1443 (1998) | 134, 581, 601 |

Aoki, Masahiko. *Ex Post Monitoring by the Main Bank* (1992) .......................................... 355

Aoki, Masahiko & Paul Sheard. *The Role of the Japanese Main Bank in the Corporate Governance Structure in Japan* (1991) ................................................................ 355

Babcock, Linda & George Loewenstein. *Explaining Bargaining Impasse: The Role of Self-Serving Biases*, 11 J. Econ. Perspectives 109 (1997) ........................................ 131

Baird, Douglas. *The Hidden Virtues of Chapter 11: An Overview of the Law and Economics of Financially Distressed Firms*, Chicago Law School, John M. Olin Program in Law & Economics, Working Paper No. 43 (2d Series) (March 1997) ............................................................................................................... 7

Baird, Douglas. *The Uneasy Case for Corporate Reorganizations*, 15 Journal of Legal Studies 127 (1986) ........................................................................................................ 591

Baird, Douglas & Thomas Jackson. *Security Interests in Personal Property* (1984) ........ 208

Baird, Douglas & Thomas Jackson. *Fraudulent Conveyance Law and Its Proper Domain*, 38 Vand. L. Rev. 829 (1985) ........................................................... 542, 554

Baird, Douglas & Thomas Jackson. *Corporate Reorganization and the Treatment of Diverse Ownership Interest: A Comment on Adequate Protection of Secured Creditors in Bankruptcy*, 51 U. Chi. L. Rev. 97 (1984) ............................................... 393

Baker, Donald. *A Lawyer's Guide to Secured Transactions* (1983) ................................... 211

Bebchuk, Lucian. *A New Approach to Corporate Reorganizations,* 101 Harv. L. Rev. 775 (1986) ................................................................................................................... 595

Bebchuk, Lucian & Jesse M. Fried. *The Uneasy Case for the Priority of Secured Claims in Bankruptcy*, 105 Yale. L.J. 857 (1996) ................................................... 218

Berle, Adolf & Gardiner Means. *The Modern Corporation and Private Property* (1932) ........................................................................................................................ 462

Berlin, Mitchell. *Bank Loans and Marketable Securities: How Do Financial Contracts Control Borrowing Firms?*, Fed. Res. Bank of Phil., Bus. Rev., July–Aug. 1987 ............................................................................................................ 225

Blum, Walter & Stanley Kaplan. *Corporate Readjustments and Reorganizations* (1976) .................................................................................................................. 35, 125

Blum, Walter, & Wilbur Katz. *Depreciation and Enterprise Valuation*, 32 U. Chi. L. Rev. 236 (1965) ............................................................................................................ 58

Blum, Walter. *Some Marginal Notes on TMT Ferry Reorganization: The New Math?*, 1968 Sup. Ct. Rev. 77 ................................................................................................ 173

Blum, Walter. *The Law and Language of Corporate Reorganization*, 17 U. Chi. L. Rev. 565 (1950) ........................................................................................................ 165

Bogdanoff, Lee R. *The Purchase and Sale of Assets in Reorganization Cases*, 47 Bus. Law. 1367 (1992) ................................................................................................ 156

Bogen, Andrew E., David H. Kennedy & Bradley D. Schwartz. *Landmarks on an Unmapped Terrain: Defining the Rights of Debtholders,* 5 Insights, Jan. 1991 ............................................................................................................................. 494

Bonbright, James. *The Valuation of Property* (1937) ........................................................ 162

Bradley, Michael & Michael Rosenzweig. *The Untenable Case for Chapter 11*, 101 Yale L.J. 1043 (1992) ................................................................................................. 600

Bratton, William. *The Economics and Jurisprudence of Convertible Bonds,* Wis. L. Rev. 667 (1984) ........................................................................................................... 425

# TABLE OF AUTHORITIES

Brealey, Richard & Stewart Myers. Principles of Corporate Finance (6th ed. 2000) ............ 26, 505
Brudney, Victor & Marvin Chirelstein. Cases and Materials on Corporate Finance (3d ed. 1987) ............ 29, 35, 45, 74, 88, 179, 202, 462
Brudney, Victor. *The Bankruptcy Commission's Proposed "Modifications" of the Absolute Priority Rule*, 48 Bankr. L. J. 305 (1974) ............ 165
Buchanan, Norman S. The Economics of Corporate Enterprise (1940) ............ 45
Buckley, Frank. *The Bankruptcy Priority Puzzle*, 72 Va. L. Rev. 1392 (1986) ............ 218
Bulow, Jeremy I., & John B. Shoven. *The Bankruptcy Decision*, 9 Bell J. Econ. 437 (1978) ............ 523
Callison, William. Partnership Law and Practice: General and Limited Partnership (1997) ............ 294
Clark, Robert C. *The Duties of the Corporate Debtor to Its Creditors*, 90 Harv. L. Rev. 505 (1977) ............ 289, 318
Clark, Robert C. *The Interdisciplinary Study of Legal Evolution*, 90 Yale L.J. 1238 (1981) ............ 577
Coase, Ronald. *The Problem of Social Cost*, 3 J.L. & Econ. 1 (1960) ............ 406, 523
Comment. *The Proper Application of Marshaling on Behalf of Unsecured Creditors*, 1983 Brigham Young U.L. Rev. 639 ............ 219
Coogan, Peter F., Richard Broude & Herman Glatt. *Comments on Some Reorganization Provisions of the Pending Bankruptcy Bills*, 30 Bus. Law. 1149 (1974) ............ 318
Cravath, Paul D. *The Reorganization of Corporations, in* Some Legal Phases of Corporate Financing, Reorganization and Regulation 153 (1917) ............ 233
Davis, Kenneth B., Jr. *The Status of Defrauded Security Holders in Corporate Bankruptcy*, 1983 Duke L.J. 1 (1983) ............ 305
Dewey, Donald. *Mergers and Cartels: Some Reservations about Policy*, 51 Market Econ. Rev. 257 (1961) ............ 456
Dewing, Arthur S. The Financial Policy of Corporations (3d ed. 1939) ............ 43
Dewing, Arthur S. The Financial Policy of Corporations (5th ed. 1953) ............ 178, 399
Douglas, William. Democracy and Finance (1940) ............ 584
Douglas-Hamilton, Margaret. ALI-ABA Resource Materials: Banking and Commercial Lending Law—1980, Some Problems Associated with Creditor Control of Debtor Companies 330 (1980) ............ 324
Easterbrook, Frank. *Is corporate bankruptcy efficient?* 27 J. Fin. Econ. 411 (1990) ............ 134, 590
Eberhart, Allan, Edward Altman & Reena Aggarwal. *The Equity Performance of Firms Emerging from Bankruptcy*, 54 J. Fin. 1855 (1999) ............ 171
Farnsworth, Alan. *Disputes Over Omission in Contracts*, 68 Colum. L. Rev. 860 (1968) ............ 498
Fleischman, Edward H. Proposed Amendments to the Trust Indenture Act of 1939 (SEC memorandum Aug. 10, 1987) ............ 470
Fortgang, Chaim & Lawrence King. *The 1978 Code: Some Wrong Policy Decisions*, 56 N.Y.U. L. Rev. 1148 (1981) ............ 371, 394
Fortgang, Chaim J. & Thomas Mayer. *Trading Claims and Taking Control of Corporations in Chapter* 11, 12 Cardozo L. Rev. 1 (1990) ............ 163

Frank, Jerome. *Epithetical Jurisprudence and the Work of the Securities and Exchange Commission*, 18 N.Y.U.L.Q. Rev. 317 (1941). ............................... 85, 106

Friendly, Henry. *Some Comments on the Corporate Reorganizations Act*, 48 Harv. L. Rev. 39 (1934) .................................................................................... 106

Gaffney, Donald L. *Bankruptcy Petitions Filed in Bad Faith: What Actions Can Creditor's Counsel Take?*, 12 U.C.C. L. J. 205 (1980) ........................................ 524

Gardner, Henry. *The SEC and Valuation Under Chapter X*, 91 U. Pa. L. Rev. 440, (1947) ........................................................................................................ 74

Gilson, Stuart. *Bankruptcy, boards, banks, and blockholders: Evidence on changes in ownership and control when firms default*, 27 J. Fin. Econ. 355 (1987) ........................................................................................................ 131, 534

Glenn, Garrard. Fraudulent Conveyances and Preferences (1940) ........................... 257

Goetz, Charles J. and Robert E. Scott. *Principles of Relational Contracts*, 67 Va. L. Rev. 1089 (1981) .................................................................................... 495

Gordon, Roger H. & Burton G. Malkiel. *Corporation Finance, in* How Taxes Affect Economic Behavior 161 (Henry Aaron & Joseph Pechman eds. 1981) ............. 510

Graham, Benjamin. The Intelligent Investor (1949) ................................................. 126

Grayson, Charles J. The Use of Statistical Techniques in Capital Budgeting, Financial Research and Management Decisions 98 (Alexander A. Robicheck ed. 1967) .... 29

Hector, Gary. *The Bondholders' Cold New World*, Fortune, Feb. 27, 1989 ..................... 485

Heidt, Kathy. *The Automatic Stay in Environmental Bankruptcies*, 67 Am. Bankr. L.J. 69 (1993) ............................................................................................ 365

Heymann, Philip B. *The Problem of Coordination: Bargaining and Rules*, 86 Harv. L. Rev. 797 (1973) ..................................................................................... 165

Jackson, Thomas & Anthony Kronman. *Secured Financing and Priorities Among Creditors*, 88 Yale L.J. 1143 (1979) ............................................................ 218

Jackson, Thomas & Robert Scott. *On the Nature of Bankruptcy*, 75 Va. L. Rev. 155 (1989) ........................................................................................................ 392

Jackson, Thomas. *Avoiding Powers in Bankruptcy*, 36 Stan. L. Rev. 725 (1984) ............. 265

Jackson, Thomas. The Logic and Limits of Bankruptcy Law (1986) ........................... 136

Kahan, Marcel & Bruce Tuckman. *Do Bondholders Lose from Junk Bond Covenant Changes?*, 66 J. Bus. 499 (1993) .................................................................. 430

Kaplan, Steven N. *Federated's Acquisition and Bankruptcy: Lessons and Implications*, 72 Wash. U.L.Q. 1103 (1994) .......................................... 134, 581, 601

Kassin, Saul M. An Empirical Study of Rule 11 Sanctions (Federal Judicial Center 1985) ........................................................................................................ 128

Kennedy, Joseph. *Big Business, What Now?*, Saturday Evening Post, Jan. 16, 1937, at 10 ........................................................................................................... 79

Kim, E. Han, John J. McConnell & Paul R. Greenwood. *Capital Structure Rearrangements and Me-first Rules in an Efficient Capital Market*, 32 J. Fin. 789 (1977) ........................................................................................................ 256

Kindleberger, Charles. Manias, Panics and Crashes: A History of Financial Crises (1980) ........................................................................................................ 397

Kirschner, Marc. *Prepackaged Bankruptcy Plans: The Deleveraging Tool of the '90s in the Wake of OID and Tax Concerns*, 21 Seton Hall L. Rev. 643 (1991) ......... 447

# TABLE OF AUTHORITIES

Koch, James. *Bankruptcy Planning for the Secured Lender*, 99 Banking L.J. 788 (1982) .................................................................................................................. 341
Korobkin, Donald R. *The Role of Normative Theory in Bankruptcy Debates*, 82 Iowa L. Rev. 75 (1996) ............................................................................................. 142
Kripke, Homer. *Law and Economics: Measuring the Economic Efficiency of Commercial Law in a Vacuum of Fact*, 133 U. Pa. L. Rev. 929 (1985) ............... 218
Levmore, Saul. *Monitors and Freeriders in Commercial and Corporate Settings*, 92 Yale L.J. 49 (1982) ............................................................................................. 218
Libecap, Gary D. & Steven N. Wiggins. *Contractual Responses to the Common Pool: Prorationing of Crude Oil Production*, 74 Am. Econ. Rev. 87 (1984) ........................................................................................................ 135, 136, 581
Loeys, Jan. *Low-Grade Bonds: A Growing Source of Corporate Funding*, Fed. Res. Bank of Phil., Bus. Rev., Nov./Dec. 1986 ........................................................... 190
LoPucki, Lynn & William Whitford. *Corporate Governance in the Bankruptcy Reorganization of Large, Publicly Held Companies*, 141 U. Pa. L. Rev. 669 (1993) .......................................................................................................... 534
LoPucki, Lynn & William Whitford. *Preemptive Cram Down*, 65 Am. Bankr. L.J. 625 (1991) ........................................................................................................... 127
LoPucki, Lynn. *Strange Visions in a Strange World*, 91 Mich. L. Rev. 79 (1991) .... 131, 600
LoPucki, Lynn. Strategies for Creditors in Bankruptcy Proceedings (1985) .................... 275
Lorie, James, Peter Dodd & Mary Hamilton. The Stock Market: Theories and Evidence (2d ed. 1985) ......................................................................................... 168
Luehrman, Timothy A. & Lance L. Hirt. *Highly Leveraged Transactions and Fraudulent Conveyance Law*, 6 J. App. Corp. Fin. 104 (1993) .......................... 547
Macey, Morris. *No Fault Subordination of Loans in Bankruptcy*, 85 Com. L.J. 44 (1980) .................................................................................................................. 341
Malitz, Ileen B. *A Re-Examination of the Wealth Expropriation Hypothesis: The Case of Captive Finance Subsidiaries*, 44 J. Fin. 1039 (1989) .................................. 256
Manne, Henry. *Mergers and the Market for Corporate Control*, 73 Journal of Political Economy 110 (1965) ........................................................................................... 456
Markowitz, Harry. *Markets and Morality: Or Arbitragers Get No Respect*, Wall St. J., May 14, 1991 ....................................................................................................... 219
McDaniel, Morey W. *Are Negative Pledge Clauses in Public Debt Issues Obsolete?*, 38 Bus. Law. 867 (1983) ..................................................................................... 217
Meckling, William. *Financial Markets, Default, and Bankruptcy: The Role of the State*, 41 Law & Contemp. Probs. 13 (Autumn 1977) ........................................ 138
Miller, Merton & Myron Scholes. *Dividends and Taxes*, 6 Journal of Financial Economics 333 (1978) ......................................................................................... 517
Miller, Merton. *Debt and Taxes*, 32 J. Fin. 261 (1977) ..................................................... 516
Mnookin, Robert H. & Robert B. Wilson. Rational Bargaining and Market Efficiency: Understanding Pennzoil v. Texaco, 75 Va. L. Rev. 295 (1989) ................... 135, 581
Modigliani, Franco & Merton H. Miller. *The Cost of Capital, Corporation Finance and the Theory of Investment*, 48 American Economic Review 261 (1958) ....... 505
Nelson, Richard & Sidney Winter. An Evolutionary Theory of Economic Change (1982) .................................................................................................................. 395

Note. *Plausible Pleadings: Developing Standards for Rule 11 Sanctions*, 100 Harv. L. Rev. 630 (1987) ............................................................................................ 128
Opler, Tim & Sheridan Titman. *Financial Distress and Corporate Performance*, 49 Journal of Finance 1015 (1994) ......................................................................... 501
Ouchi, William. The M-Form Society (1984) ................................................................. 355
Picker, Randal C. Designing Verifiability: Boyd's Implications for Modern Bankruptcy Law (U. Chi. Law School Working Paper 1997) ..................................... 104
Porter, Glenn & Harold Livesay. Merchants and Manufacturers: Studies in the Changing Structure of Nineteenth Century Marketing (1971) ......................... 4
Posner, Richard. *The Rights of Creditors of Affiliated Corporations*, 43 U. Chi. L. Rev. 449 (1976) ..................................................................................................... 245
Rachlinski, Jeffrey J. Prospect Theory and Civil Negotiation, Stanford Center on Conflict and Negotiation, Working Paper No. 17 (Oct. 1990) ............................ 130
Radick, Barry G. & Stephen J. Blauner. *Shareholders, Unite!—What To Do When a Firm Goes Bankrupt*, Barron's, Apr. 14, 1986 ........................................... 127
Rasmussen, Robert. *Bankruptcy and the Administrative State*, 42 Hastings L.J. 1567 (1991) ..................................................................................................................... 365
Reich, Robert & John Donahue. New Deals: The Chrysler Revival and the American System (1985) ....................................................................................................... 355
Roe, Mark. *Backlash*, 98 Colum. L. Rev. 217 (1998) ..................................................... 605
Roe, Mark. *Bankruptcy and Debt: A New Model for Corporate Reorganization*, 83 Colum. L. Rev. 527 (1983) ......................................................... 164, 578, 599
Roe, Mark. *Bankruptcy, Priority and Economics*, 75 Va. L. Rev. 219 (1989) ................ 393
Roe, Mark. *The Voting Prohibition in Bond Workouts*, 97 Yale L. J. 232 (1987) ............ 412
Salpukas, Agis. *Court Gives Eastern Air $135 Million: Trustee Is Allowed Use of Escrow Funds to Keep Line Going*, N.Y. Times, Nov. 28, 1990, at D1, col. 1 ..... 48
Schwartz, Alan. *Bankruptcy Workouts and Debt Contracts*, 36 J.L. & Econ. 595 (1993) ..................................................................................................................... 600
Schwartz, Alan. *Security Interests and Bankruptcy Priorities: A Review of Current Theories*, 10 J. Legal Stud. 1 (1981) ..................................................................... 218
Schwartz, Alan. *The Continuing Puzzle of Secured Debt*, 37 Vand. L. Rev. 1051 (1984) ..................................................................................................................... 218
Scott, Robert. *A Relational Theory of Secured Financing*, 86 Colum. L. Rev. 901 (1986) ..................................................................................................................... 218
Seligman, Joel. The Transformation of Wall Street (1982) ............................................. 466
Shleifer, Andrei & Robert Vishny. *Liquidation values and debt capacity: A market equilibrium approach*, 47 J. Fin. 1343 (1992) ...................................................... 601
Simon, Herbert A. Administrative Behavior (3d ed. 1976) ............................................ 496
Simon, Herbert A. Models of Man: Social and Rational (1957) .................................... 395
Skeel, David. *Markets, Courts, and the Brave New World of Bankruptcy Theory*, 1993 Wisc. L. Rev. 465 ..................................................................................................... 605
Slain, John J. & Homer Kripke. *The Interface Between Securities Regulation and Bankruptcy—Allocating the Risk of Illegal Securities Issuance Between Securityholders and the Issuer's Creditors*, 48 N.Y.U. L. Rev. 261 (1973) ........ 298
Smith, Clifford W. & Jerold B. Warner. *On Financial Contracting: An Analysis of Bond Covenants*, 7 J. Fin. Econ. 117 (1979) ........................................................ 177

# TABLE OF AUTHORITIES

Stein, Benjamin J. *Shooting Fish in a Barrel—Why Management Always Makes a Bundle in an LBO*, Barron's, Jan. 12, 1987 .......................................................... 563
Summers, Lawrence & William Cutler. *Texaco and Pennzoil Both Lost Big*, The New York Times, Feb. 14, 1988 .......................................................... 132
Tashjian, Elizabeth, Ronald C. Lease & John J. McConnell. Prepacks: An Empirical Analysis of Prepackaged Bankruptcies (unpublished manuscript) (April 1994) .......................................................... 431
Van Horne, James C. *Of Financial Innovations and Excesses*, 40 J. Fin. 621 (1985) ...... 525
Wahl, Fritz. A New Technique for Evaluating Exchange Offers (1986) .......................... 409
Warren, Elizabeth. *Bankruptcy Policy*, 54 U. Chi. L. Rev. 775 (1987) ............................ 605
Warren, Elizabeth. *The Untenable Case for Repeal of Chapter 11*, 102 Yale L.J. 437 (1992) .......................................................... 600
Weintraub, Benjamin & Alan Resnick. *Subordination of the Guarantor's Subrogation Rights—The Marshalling Doctrine Revisited*, 18 U.C.C. L.J. 364 (1986) .......... 219
Weiss, Lawrence A. *Bankruptcy Resolution: Direct costs and violation of priority of claims,* 27 J. Fin. Econ. 285 (1990) .......................................................... 134, 590
Weiss, Melvyn, William S. Lerach & Jan M. Adler. *Obtaining Adequate Monetary Relief for Shareholders of Bankrupt Public Companies: The Nearly Impossible Dream, in* Complex Litigation in the Context of the Bankruptcy Laws 11 (Michael F. Perlis ed. 1984) .......................................................... 306
Westbrook, Jay. *A Functional Analysis of Executory Contracts,* 74 Minn. L. Rev. 227 (1989) .......................................................... 362
Weston, J. Fred. *Some Economic Fundamentals for an Analysis of Bankruptcy*, 41 Law & Contemp. Probs. 47 (Autumn 1977) .......................................................... 138
White, James. Bankruptcy and Creditors' Rights 288 (1985) .......................................... 164

# Chapter 1

# INTRODUCTION

## ¶101: **Introductory note**

This course is about debt.

Companies borrow money to finance capital expansion of factories and machines, to purchase inventory and raw materials, to pay workers to produce goods, to replace cash lost in poor operations when goods do not sell profitably, and to refinance assets already in place.

Oftentimes the borrowing, especially when of a significant sum of money, will be documented by more than a simple IOU. Equally frequently, the lender will seek protection beyond a handshake and a firm's promise of repayment. Oftentimes lawyers become involved, drafting and negotiating the documents and advising lender and borrower of risks and pitfalls.

When the company fails to produce sufficient cash to repay the loan, lenders can invoke legal institutions. Lenders and their lawyers scrutinize the loan document, the basic lending contract, for its terms and conditions. What remedies does the lender have? Can it sue for not only repayment of the missed installments but also for payment of the future obligations from the debtor? Can the lender seize the debtor's assets? The loan may be renegotiated on mutually agreeable terms. Or the creditor might want to seize property or get immediate repayment. A legal super-structure atop the loan document governs the means of repayment. The lender may try to have the court allow the lender to take the company's machinery in satisfaction of the debt, selling the machinery to get cash to apply to repaying the loan. The creditor may sue in local courts to recover the money due under its contract. A further super-structure, the bankruptcy system, affects how (and whether) that contract will be enforced.

Bankruptcy comes in two varieties, liquidation and reorganization. In a liquidation, the bankruptcy trustee sells the firm, usually piecemeal. The trustee collects the cash and then disburses the cash to the creditors. When the usual liquidation (which turns the firm's solid assets into "liquid" cash) is completed, the business ceases to exist. The second variety, reorganization, is more complex and, for businesses of any significant size, more common. In a reorganization, debt payments are deferred or reduced, stock redivided, and the firm continues to operate. These—liquidation and reorganization—are the two polar pure cases; hybrids exist as well.

The reorganization statute vitally affects the nature, meaning and enforceability of basic contract terms of any business financing. Accordingly, although some corporate finance lawyers might see bankruptcy as a specialist's task, most quickly learn that the lawyers who draft and negotiate financing documents must be familiar with the ramifications of their drafting and negotiating should a reorganization come to pass. Bankruptcy overrides contracts and corporate charters; the statute gives the court authority to rewrite financial (and other contracts) and to re-do the bankrupt corporation's charter:

### § 1141. Effect of confirmation

(a) ... the provisions of a confirmed plan bind ... any entity ... acquiring property under the plan, and any creditor, equity security holder, or general partner in the debtor, whether or not the claim or interest of such creditor, equity security holder, or general partner is impaired under the plan *and whether or not such creditor, equity security holder, or general partner has accepted the plan.*[1]

(b) Except as otherwise provided in the plan or the order confirming the plan, the confirmation of a plan vests all of the property of the estate in the debtor.

(c) ... the property dealt with by the plan is free and clear of all claims and interests of creditors, equity security holders, and of general partners in the debtor.

(d) (1) Except as otherwise provided in this subsection, in the plan, or in the order confirming the plan, the confirmation of a plan—

(A) discharges the debtor from any debt that arose before the date of such confirmation ... whether or not ... the holder of such claim has accepted the plan; and

(B) terminates all rights and interests of equity security holders and general partners provided for by the plan.

### § 1123. Contents of plan

(a) Notwithstanding any otherwise applicable nonbankruptcy law, a plan shall—

(1) ...

(2) specify any class of claims or interests that is not impaired under the plan;

(3) specify the treatment of any class of claims or interests that is impaired under the plan;

(4) ...

(5) provide adequate means for the plan's implementation, such as—

---

[1] [Emphasis supplied.—Roe.]

(A)...

(B)...

(C) merger or consolidation of the debtor with one or more persons;

(D)...

(E) satisfaction or modification of any lien;

(F) cancellation or modification of any indenture or similar instrument;

(G) curing or waiving of any default;

(H) extension of a maturity date or a change in an interest rate or other term of outstanding securities;

(I) amendment of the debtor's charter; or

(J) ...

(6) [amend the corporate charter in several respects]; and

(7) contain only provisions that are consistent with the interests of creditors and equity security holders and with public policy with respect to the manner of selection of any officer, director, or trustee under the plan and any successor to such officer, director, or trustee.

(b) Subject to subsection (a) of this section, a plan may—

(1) impair or leave unimpaired any class of claims, secured or unsecured, or of interests;

(2) ... provide for the assumption, rejection, or assignment of any executory contract or unexpired lease of the debtor not previously rejected under such section;

(3) provide for—

(A) the settlement or adjustment of any claim or interest belonging to the debtor or to the estate; or

(B)...

(4) provide for the sale of all or substantially all of the property of the estate, and the distribution of the proceeds of such sale among holders of claims or interests;

(5) modify the rights of holders of secured claims, ... or of holders of unsecured claims, or leave unaffected the rights of holders of any class of claims; and

(6) include any other appropriate provision not inconsistent with the applicable provisions of this title.

Chapter 11 obviously anticipates re-writing of bankrupt debtor's contracts, re-drafting of the corporate charter, selling assets of the debtor, and modifying the rights of the parties contracting with the bankrupt corporation. Why do we want a system of reorganization that over-rides contract?

While reorganization is obviously relevant to practicing law today—in 1997 corporations issued $125 billion of high-risk junk bonds, more than American firms issued during the entire debt-happy 1980s, when the junk bond became famous in financing takeovers—it is helpful to first put the problem of corporate finance and reorganization into historical perspective.

Reorganization problems link to technological and engineering changes that became prevalent at the end of the 19th century. Early in the 19th century, business finance and reorganization were simple when an entrepreneur typically financed his or her own operations from savings and earnings. But by the end of the century, large enterprises required commitments of capital larger than that which any single saver (or small group of savers) could provide. The capital built not simple operations that could be shut down nearly costlessly, but long-lived assets such as steel mills, refineries and railroads, which even when currently unprofitable might have long-run value. The long-lived nature of large-scale capital assets, and the complex arrangements needed to finance the assets, formed the basis for complex reorganization institutions that arose toward the end of the 19th century—called equity receiverships at the time—and that developed (and are still developing) during the 20th.

## ¶102: Glenn Porter & Harold Livesay, Merchants and Manufacturers: Studies in the Changing Structure of Nineteenth Century Marketing 63-65 (1971)

### LONG-TERM CAPITAL

Most early manufacturing firms were proprietorships or small partnerships. The owners were usually [people] of limited means. Assembling the fixed assets to commence or expand production often absorbed all the proprietors' resources. Additional fixed capital was extremely difficult to raise. Equity financing through the mass sale of securities did not begin in the United States until the introduction of the railroads, and it did not play a significant role in manufacturing finance before the Civil War.

The legal foundation for equity financing existed long before it found widespread employment in manufacturing. Prior to the Civil War many states had general incorporation laws embodying limited liability; however, for a variety of reasons, manufacturers seldom took advantage of them. Among the reasons were lack of precedent, public skepticism toward such investments, lack of institutions to market shares, and entrepreneurial unwillingness to share ownership and control with "outsiders." Indeed, the correspondence and autobiographies of early American businessmen document the intensity with which the [business people] identified themselves with their firms. Driven by pride, they labored continually to keep their affairs under their own control. This attitude often manifested itself in a reluctance to accept partners, and it certainly was not conducive to the adoption of financing methods that would have diluted ownership even further by selling shares in the business to the general public.

Financial institutions such as banks and insurance companies were of limited utility as sources of long-term capital. Banks would occasionally make long-term loans to manufacturers, but only on strong collateral. They did not make unsecured loans to business prospects, however glowing ....

A mortgage on real estate was another acceptable form of security. In the 1820s and 1830s, Washburn and Godard obtained long-term capital from a Worcester savings bank. The bank in turn held a mortgage on the firm's machine shop and on the millowners' real estate. In 1856 the Baltimore ironmaster S.S. Keyser obtained funds to build a warehouse by mortgaging his family's property to a local bank. Such conservative lending polices seem to have been typical of most sound eastern banks throughout the period ....

Insurance companies, like savings banks, were in the business of pooling individuals' savings and investing them at a profit. Insurance firms were, however, even less inclined than banks to make manufacturing loans. Refusing a loan request submitted by the Shawmut Fibre Company of Shawmut, Massachusetts, an officer of the Union Mutual Life Insurance Company commented that[:] "It is the custom of our company, which has become practically a law with us, that we do not loan on manufacturing establishments."

Massachusetts Hospital Life Insurance Company, which opened for business in 1818, invested heavily in the stock of New England textile mills and made large loans to individual stockholders in textile firms, but it made few other investments in manufacturing. Massachusetts Life's participation in textile financing is doubtless explained by the fact that its list of stockholders consisted of names such as Lawrence, Lowell, Jackson, Cabot, Appleton, and other prominent New England merchants. These were, of course, the same families that owned controlling interests in the textile mills, and the merchants were, in effect, lending to themselves by siphoning funds from one family enterprise into another. This pattern of a merchant-controlled financial institution underwriting its stockholders' industrial investments while refusing loans to other manufacturing proprietors and partners was common-place in the period. It was one of the principal ways in which merchants were able to control antebellum manufacturing developments.

Modern industrial firms secure long-term capital for expansion or modernization by tapping the savings of the general public. They do so through mass sales of securities, or through loans from financial institutions such as banks and insurance companies. Since neither of these methods was open to pre-Civil War entrepreneurs, growth depended upon personal resources and retained earnings (both of which were usually inadequate), or upon financial assistance from wealthy merchants. In such circumstances it is not surprising that many of the most successful firms were either those founded by the merchants themselves or those in which the entrepreneur was able to secure funds for fixed capital assets through an alliance with members of the mercantile community.

The outstanding examples of the first case were the Waltham and Lowell textile mills and such integrated rail mills as Cambria and Bethlehem—the largest manufacturing enterprises of their times. All of these firms were originally created through merchants' initiative. The merchants raised fixed capital by forming a corporation and selling stock privately to limited numbers of their colleagues.[2] .... [3]

The second case, in which an established manufacturer financed expansion through an alliance with wealthy merchants, occurred far more often. Sometimes these alliances took the form of a closely held stock corporation; often they were a formal or informal partnership ....

## ¶103: The shift in business at the end of the 19th century

When manufacturing firms were small proprietorships with generic machinery, such as a simple lathe or a forge, the essential problems of modern reorganization had yet to appear. The firm's creditors were few: a local bank, a few suppliers, and several employees. A firm might fail, but closing it was simple. The entrepreneur collected its assets, received and held all the payments due him or her, and then distributed the receipts to the creditors. (Sometimes a court-appointed official, aptly named a "receiver," gathered the debtor's receipts for the bankrupt's creditors, who feared what the debtor might do with the cash.) With the ordinary assets sold and the cash due to the debtor collected, the fund could then be distributed to the debtor's creditors. Because the firm usually had very few creditors, the creditors had little problem coordinating their collection actions.

Businesses changed in scale and scope towards the end of the 19th century. Advances in engineering technologies made it possible to manufacture goods much more cheaply in huge enterprises than in small ones. Steel mills and oil refineries were built, and railroads criss-crossed the nation. These large specialized assets—mills, refineries, railroad tracks—had no obvious alternative use to their intended use as a mill, refinery, or railroad, unlike the simple lathe or forge. The difference between their scrap value and their value in a reorganized firm was seen to be large and worth preserving. Moreover, the large enterprises were financed by many creditors, who had trouble coordinating their actions when their debtor failed. Lastly, the large failures at the end of the 19th century were the railroads, which were seen as critical to regional economies. Courts developed a reorganization apparatus to keep the railroads running, even when the railroads failed to make as much money as anticipated and could no longer pay off their creditors.

---

[2] A firm in which all the stock is closely held by a few individuals is called a "close corporation."

[3] Victor S. Clark commented: "Commerce supplied capital to manufacturing in two ways: by direct investment and by credits to industrial companies. The latter way, although less conspicuous, was probably the more important of the two." (History of Manufactures in the United States, I: 368).

**¶104: The equity receivership**

The first large scale bankruptcies in the United States were major railroads, which grew rapidly and then collapsed financially during the deep depression of the 1890s. Until 1898, there was no continuing American bankruptcy statute; yet, during this period companies owning a majority of the railroad tracks in America were reorganized. The receivership, however, was a long-standing common law device, originally designed for simpler times and simpler companies. Federal judges adapted the receivership to reorganize the railroads. Over the next century the equity receivership developed into chapter 11.

**Douglas Baird, The Hidden Virtues of Chapter 11: An Overview of the Law and Economics of Financially Distressed Firms, Chicago Law School, John M. Olin Program in Law & Economics, Working Paper No. 43 (2d Series) (March 1997).**

\* \* \*

The equity receivership emerged in courts of equity. In these courts, a judge has the equitable power to appoint a receiver to take control of a litigant's assets. In recent years, federal courts have used the equity receivership to take control of a prison system that violated the Eighth Amendment rights of the inmates or a school system that ignored the 14th Amendment. In the typical case, the plaintiffs are creditors and the receiver comes into control of the property of the debtor. As these other examples suggest, the procedure is flexible. Lawyers for the creditors of troubled railroads, with the blessing of sympathetic judges, took advantage of the equity receivership. As they used it over time, their practices became more fixed as judges set limits on how these receiverships could be used and how they could change the rights of the various affected parties. What emerged in the end were the basic features of Chapter 11.

The following is a stylized example of an equity receivership. A railroad has 100,000 shares of stock outstanding. It owes $150 million, $50 million to three different groups of bondholders. The first loan of $50 million was used to build the main line, the second to build the terminal, and the third to build a line connecting the terminal to a port. The remaining creditors are suppliers and a few others whose loans are unsecured. The railroad cannot meet payments on the $150 million of debt. Indeed, the railroad is worth less than $100 million. The railroad defaults on its fixed obligations and the investment bankers representing the three groups of bondholders realize that the time has come to restructure the firm.

The investors call upon their lawyers and their investment bankers. The lawyers persuade a general creditor to ask a federal court to appoint a receiver for the railroad. The receiver the court appoints is often the group of manager-shareholders that has been running the railroad. The receiver pays off all the suppliers in full and keeps the railroad running. In the meantime, lawyers and the investment bankers form four committees, representing the three classes of bondholders and the equityholders[. The bondholding classes] deposit their bonds with [their committee] and give it the power to assert all the rights of the bondholders in the reorganization. Let us assume that, in our case, 90 percent of the bondholders in each class give their bonds to their committee.

The four committees then meet and create a new committee, the reorganization committee, on which members of each of the other committees sit and which is empowered to act on behalf of the other committees. The reorganization committee now controls 90 percent of all outstanding securities. It then proceeds to form a plan of reorganization. In this case, the reorganization committee must decide first how much each group of bondholders should receive and then what a new capital structure should look like.

In our case, each group might insist on an equal share, given that each invested $50 million. On the other hand, some of the investments might have been less successful. For example, if the line connecting the terminal to the port had not brought much business, the representatives of the two other committees might be able to insist on a larger share. In the typical case, the plan might reduce the rate of interest, make interest payments contingent upon income, convert debt to preferred stock, reduce the amount of principal, or extend the term of the loan.

To keep things simple, let us assume that this plan provided that each group of bondholders reduce their claims by 40% and for the new bonds to be secured by all three assets. Each $1,000 bond secured by one of the three assets will be exchanged for a $600 bond secured by all of the railroad's assets. The shareholders who turned over their shares to the committee are given the option to exchange an old share of stock and $15 for a new share of stock. Through their representatives on the reorganization committee, the participating creditors and shareholders consent to this plan.

The reorganization committee then borrows $15 million from a bank on a short-term basis. At this point, the receiver conducts a foreclosure sale in which the assets of the railroad are sold to the highest bidder. Although the foreclosure sale is nominally open to anyone, in practice the reorganization committee usually turns out to be the only bidder. It bids $15 million, $5 million for [each of] the main line, the terminal, and the connecting line respectively. The receiver takes the $15 million and distributes it to the bondholders. Because the reorganization committee itself owns 90 percent of the bonds, the receiver gives back to the reorganization committee $13.5 million of the $15 million the committee paid to buy the railroad. The receiver pays the other $1.5 million to the nonparticipating bondholders who did not give their bonds to the reorganization committee.[4] The shareholders get none of the proceeds because the sale price was not enough to pay the bondholders, who enjoyed a higher priority, in full.

---

[4] Recall that ten percent of the bondholders did not participate. Hence, each of the bondholders who did not participate receives only 10 cents on the dollar, much less than they would have received if they had participated in the reorganization in which they would have received 60 cents on the dollar. The device of the nominally open foreclosure sale in the equity receivership is what allowed freezing out the nonparticipating bondholders and hence largely eliminated the holdout problem of the common law composition.

After the foreclosure sale, the old corporation is a hollow shell and the old shareholders dissolve it under state law. Because the legal entity that was the railroad now no longer exists, all claims against it are worthless. Hence any shareholders who did not turn over their rights to the relevant committee are out of luck, as are any general creditors.

At this point, the reorganization committee has the assets of the railroad and the $13.5 million it received from the receiver. The committee now forms a new corporation and transfers all the assets of the railroad to it. The new corporation creates $90 million in bonds and gives them to the old participating bondholders as promised in the reorganization plan. All the stock in the new firm is given to the old shareholders when they come up with the $1.5 million in cash they promised in the reorganization plan. With this $1.5 million and the $13.5 million the receiver gave it, the committee repays the $15 million bank loan. The reorganization committee now goes out of existence.

If we focus entirely on legal forms, we see a new corporation with a new set of ownership claims against it. In substance, however, the story is quite different. If one collapses the various steps in this elaborate dance, most of the bondholders and shareholders have simply exchanged their old claims against the firm for new ones that take better account of the condition in which the railroad finds itself. We have exactly the same railroad with the same managers and the same investors, but the ownership rights of the investors have been adjusted so that they are in line with the revenue that the railroad actually earns.

## ¶105: A brief anatomy of a bankruptcy

These materials are not organized to replicate the legal path of a bankruptcy, a path that begins with the debtor filing a bankruptcy petition, continues with the trustee gathering the bankruptcy property, culminates with the debtor and its creditors forming a plan of reorganization, and then ends with the court confirming a plan of reorganization.

Nor are these materials designed as a tour of the Bankruptcy Code, beginning, say, with chapter 1 of the Code (which contains the definitions and general provisions), then proceeding to chapters 3 (which deals with the administration of bankruptcy proceedings) and 5 (which establishes creditors' claims and defines what goes into the debtor's bankrupt estate), footnoting chapters 9 (which deals with the bankruptcy of municipalities), 12 (for farmers), and 13 (for individuals), and then concluding with the finale: chapters 7 (which liquidates a bankrupt firm) and 11 (which reorganizes a bankrupt firm).

Instead, these materials allow the student to analyze deeply the financially salient features of bankruptcy, mostly relating to priority, that are critical both inside a bankruptcy *and* to financiers and managers (and, most importantly, their lawyers) when they finance enterprises. Hence, we will begin at the end, with the priority system set out in chapter 11, asking who gets what and who comes first under the Bankruptcy Code. From there we will work backwards to fill-in the definitions and concepts needed to understand priority. The topics are designed to do double-duty: to be important to those of us who will practice bankruptcy *and* to be important to those of us who work on financing transactions and other business deals.

Still, an overview of the modern reorganization of a public firm is useful to get us started. The pre-bankruptcy scenario will have the firm borrowing to finance its operations, to build new factories, to acquire other enterprises and to expand. Then the firm earns less than expected from its operations and cannot service its debt. Markets for its products fall, or operating expenses go up. Or both. Sometimes the firm's financial decline happens due to no fault of its own; it was unlucky. Sometimes the firm is mismanaged.

If the cash pinch gets severe enough, the company files for bankruptcy in chapter 11. Although the Bankruptcy Code allows *creditors* to force the bankruptcy, it's rare for creditors to force a firm into bankruptcy. Overall, the Code's provisions help the debtor and its managers, so chapter 11 is usually used defensively by debtors, not offensively by creditors.

Chapter 11's central organizing feature is that it gathers all of the firm's assets and debts, and then allows a global reorganization plan to be formulated and implemented. This global settlement contrasts with what happens under most state law, before bankruptcy: Each creditor outside of bankruptcy has an incentive to rush to sue the debtor, get a judgment, and levy on that judgment, because state law favors the first to the courthouse.

But as soon as the petition for bankruptcy is filed, all lawsuits against the debtor are automatically stayed. No one can sue the bankrupt debtor, levy on a judgment against the debtor, or seize security from the debtor under a state law security agreement. The bankrupt's managers, who were harassed before the filing, now can breathe more easily, because creditors are no longer breathing down the managers' necks, demanding immediate repayment. The Bankruptcy Code allows the judge to "lift" the bankruptcy stay, and a good deal of bankruptcy litigation arises from creditors seeking to get the stay lifted, so that they can sue the debtor, or more frequently, so that they can seize assets securing their loans.

A new bankrupt typically needs fresh cash to keep operating. It needs to pay its employees and its suppliers. Occasionally, it gets enough from operations to pay them, but more typically it must borrow yet more. Just before the bankruptcy, that borrowing was often impossible because of infighting among the creditors about who would come first. The Bankruptcy Code resolves the infighting that could stymie new credit; it permits the *new* financing, usually called debtor-in-possession financing, to be paid first, before (nearly) all creditors are paid when the plan of reorganization is made final.

Who runs the bankrupt firm? Typically incumbent managers and not a bankruptcy trustee run the firm. The court could appoint a bankruptcy trustee to run the firm for the benefit of the firm's creditors; the firm's managers could be ousted. But this kind of ouster is rare. When the incumbent managers run the firm, as is usual, the debtor is said to remain in possession of its own assets, hence the term "debtor-in-possession."

Creditors form committees, which hire lawyers, to negotiate a plan of reorganization with the debtor. Creditors are grouped into classes, roughly based on the similarity of their claims.

The committees, the debtor, and the court look at pre-bankruptcy grabs, to bring assets back into reorganization. That is, to further defeat the state law tendency to "race to the courthouse" to be the first to seize a weakened firm's assets (either by getting a judgment and levying, or by seizing and selling collateral), the Bankruptcy Code allows the bankrupt to recover assets dissipated on the eve of bankruptcy. The two critical recovery provisions are *fraudulent conveyance* liability (which exists under state law as well as the Bankruptcy Code) and *preference* law. When a debtor transfers an asset to another party without adequate consideration, or with intent to hinder its other creditors, then (if the other conditions for fraudulent conveyance liability are met), the bankrupt can recover this "fraudulent" transfer for itself and for the benefit of all of the bankrupt's creditors. Preference law allows the bankrupt company to recover payments made to creditors (or assets taken by secured creditors) within 90 days *before* the bankruptcy, to allow all creditors to share the payment (and to discourage races to seize the debtor's assets). Another remedy, *equitable subordination,* sends misbehaving, over-reaching creditors, to the end of the bankruptcy priority line.

The bankrupt can reject many of its unperformed contracts. While the contracting party can "sue" the bankrupt (if the court lifts the stay against suing the bankrupt), it becomes just another unsecured creditor in the bankruptcy, with the amount of its claim equal to the damages from the debtor's breach of the contract. In effect, parties with unperformed contracts can be made into creditors of the firm. And most creditors are not paid in full in a bankruptcy reorganization.

The bankrupt firm and its managers get to propose the first plan of reorganization. A court will not listen to others proposing reorganization plans until management gets to show the court its plan; nor can others formally solicit agreement to their own plan until management has revealed and sought formal acceptance of its own plan. This ability to control the bankruptcy agenda puts great power in the hands of the incumbent managers.

The formal terms of the Bankruptcy Code are not, in terms of agenda control, however, as pro-management as the practice has been, because the Code gives management a *period of exclusivity* of only 120 days. But in practice the managerial agenda control has lasted much longer, because courts have extended that period of exclusivity, often for years. (The 1994 amendments to the Bankruptcy Code sought to tighten up on repeated extensions of managers' exclusivity periods, but it's yet to be seen how effective the procedural changes will be.)

A chapter 11 proceeding for a public firm takes typically two or three years. The creditors grasp to come first in priority and to conclude the proceeding quickly (so that they can get their money back); the debtor and its managers seek to survive. They all usually settle their disputes after a couple of years; if they don't, the judge can "cram-down" a plan of reorganization. A "cram-down" typically requires a valuation of the firm—to see how much value there is in the firm to distribute. Because the cram-down is the "ultimate" judicial weapon in chapter 11 and affects renegotiations even in the many reorganizations in which the debtor and its creditors settle, it will be the first feature of bankruptcy we will examine, despite that it is nearly the last act in the bankruptcy play. Although the bankruptcy players usually make a deal, and usually don't invoke bankruptcy's ultimate weapon, their fears (or hopes) of how a judicial cram-down would be employed will influence what they will accept, or what they will insist on, when making a deal.

## Chapter 2

# REORGANIZATION AND VALUATION

A. Why valuation is important
B. Basic valuation

...........................................................................................................................................

A. Why valuation is important

**¶201: <u>Schematic of controls on the corporation</u>**

One can think of the corporation as a collection of cash flows. Creditors provide funds and goods to the corporation. Banks, bondholders, and debentureholders lend funds and expect to be repaid, with interest. Trade creditors ship goods into the corporation and expect to be paid for them. A secured creditor gets a promise from the corporation that it, the secured creditor, can collect its payments by seizing specific assets of the corporation if the corporation cannot get the cash together to pay the secured creditor. The security might be real estate, governed by mortgage laws in the state; or the security might be the machines, inventory, or accounts receivable of the corporation, governed typically by the Uniform Commercial Code. Not all debtors use security, and general, unsecured creditors collect from the company out of the company's unencumbered assets (or from what's leftover after the secured creditors get paid). The company normally produces cash to pay the creditors by using its factory and machines to produce products to sell. The sale generates an account receivable from a customer; when the customer pays the firm, the firm has cash to pay its creditors. If there's any cash left over, the firm might pay a dividend to its stockholders.

These cash relationships can be represented with a schematic, which follows below. A more standard way to represent the relationships is with financial statements, which follow on the next page.

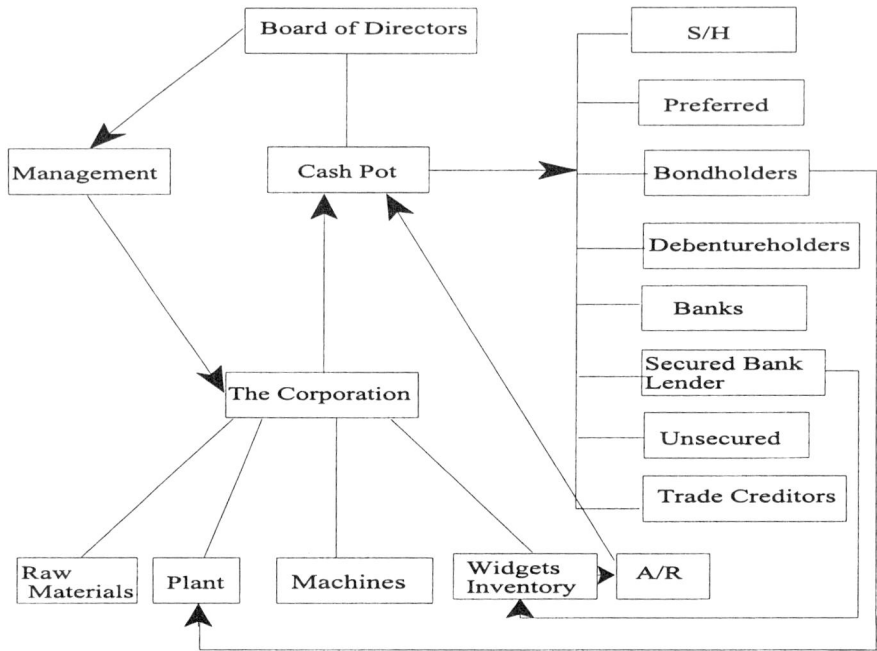

A pre-bankruptcy scenario:

1. Bondholders attempt to seize plant if payment not received from cash pot.
2. Secured banks attempt to seize Accounts Receivable ("A/R") and inventory if not paid.
3. All creditors hope to displace board of directors with their trustee in bankruptcy if not paid.
4. All creditors believe they should be preferred and be paid earlier than the others.
5. Stockholders seek to get dividends paid or stock repurchased before creditors are paid.
6. Contractual arrangements with creditors or suppliers may limit disposition of cash pot or limit other decision-making authority of board and management.

## ¶202: Sample balance sheet

**Balance Sheet of XYZ Corp. at 12/31/98**

| Assets | | | Liabilities | | |
|---|---|---|---|---|---|
| Current | | | Current | | |
| Cash | $1M | | Accounts Payable | $1M | |
| Accounts Receivable | 1M | | Bank Demand Note | <u>1M</u> | |
| Raw materials | 1M | | | | |
| Inventory & work in-progress | <u>2M</u> | | | | |
| | | 5M | | | |
| Plant and equipment | 2M | | Long-term debt | | |
| Plant | 3M | | 1st mortgage bond | 2M | |
| Machines | <u>2M</u> | | 2nd mortgage bonds | 1M | |
| | | 5M | Debentures | 1M | |
| | | | Equipment financing | <u>1M</u> | |
| | | | | | 5M |
| | | | Shareholder's equity | | |
| | | | Preferred | 1M | |
| | | | Common | <u>2M</u> | |
| | | | | 3M | |
| | | <u>10M</u> | | | <u>10M</u> |

## ¶203: Seniority, security, and valuation

As shall be clear as we go through the readings, the two central variables in determining a financier's "take" in a bankruptcy are the value of the enterprise and the "ranking" of the financier's claim.

Priority in chapter 11 will command several weeks of our attention after we discuss valuation. But we ought first to know a little about how ranking is determined and preserved. Financiers seek to have borrowers provide contractual terms that will best assure the financiers of repayment if disaster strikes. If the financier cannot assure itself of repayment, it would seek to have the borrower pay (usually in the form of higher interest) for any increased risk that the financier bears. Financiers will sometimes seek security: if the borrower cannot repay, the financier can seize and sell this or that asset that belongs to the borrower. In its pure form the financier will be paid out of the security that the borrower gave. If the security is worth enough to cover the loan, the financier is paid in full and the remainder is returned to the bankrupt estate to satisfy its other creditors.

Creditors seek to use loan agreements to protect themselves. The core obligation of the company is to pay back the loan, with interest. Lenders to a company that makes enough money to pay all of its creditors need little protection. Not all companies will make enough money; anticipating that possibility, creditors seek various protections. The most common protection usually known to law students is security: the lender gets the company's commitment that if the company cannot pay off the loan, the lender can seize a specific asset of the company. The filing and notice provisions in the Uniform Commercial Code and in real estate mortgage laws protect other lenders from secret deals; these are the subject of commercial transactions, debtor-creditor and secured transactions courses.

But security is far from the exclusive protection that lenders seek. Many lenders seek to limit (1) the amount of dividends that the company can pay (money paid out as dividends is usually unavailable to the lender when things get tight), (2) the amount of other debts that the debtor company can incur, (3) various ratios of debt to assets, and (4) who will pick up the debtor company's obligations if the debtor merges with another company.

Debentures are certificates representing loans to the company. They are typically unsecured and long-term. The debentureholders' "loan agreement" is called an indenture. The indenture specifies the obligations of the company to the debentureholders and the circumstances under which the debentureholders may sue the company. A trustee, which is usually a bank, acts on behalf of all debentureholders, ideally as if it were itself the lender. The trustee enforces the company's obligations to the debentureholders. The trustee is usually the entity that brings suit on behalf of wronged debentureholders. When the indenture trustee takes security from the company on behalf of the creditors, the debt instruments are often called bonds instead of debentures, although the two terms, bonds and debentures, are tending to become interchangeable.[1]

Financiers will rank order themselves. Some will insist on being paid first. They would usually get a lower interest rate (because they are taking less risk of nonpayment) than those who agree to be paid second. Some will insist that the borrower not issue new debt, or issue no debt beyond a specified amount, or issue no debt if an agreed upon formula would not be satisfied, or never give security to any other creditors. A creditor who agrees to come last usually is compensated for that risk, with a higher interest rate. More precisely, the creditor agrees to wait under this or that condition. This agreement, called a subordination agreement, became a central financial instrument in the 1980s: most "junk" bonds were subordinated to other creditors. The subordinated creditor agreed not to accept any payment in the event of a bankruptcy, or, occasionally, in any event, until the specified "senior" creditors were repaid.

---

[1] The vocabulary we have here is impoverished. Two types of trustees concern us, the trustee for the bondholders, who operates outside (and inside) bankruptcy, and the trustee of the bankrupt debtor's estate, who, if the judge appoints one, runs the bankrupt company for the creditors.

These arrangements can be complex. Hybrids are possible. One secured creditor can obtain the "first" mortgage in this property. Other creditors can obtain the "second" mortgage in the same property. They agree that the first mortgage holder will be paid first out of the value of the mortgaged property; the second mortgage holder will get whatever is left over. One creditor can be subordinated to that set of loans, but not to another set. Another creditor may be subordinated to a creditor that is itself subordinated to other loans. A subordinated creditor may agree to be subordinated only in the event of a bankruptcy or other reorganization, expecting to receive payments in the interim; other subordination agreements may be "complete": the creditor agrees not to receive a dime until the "senior" creditor—to which the "junior" creditor has subordinated itself—is paid off in full.

Several difficulties arise in reorganization. The property may be worth less if severed from the enterprise than if kept embedded in the enterprise. Imagine a mortgage covering some of the track of a railroad system. Ripping the track out may have little value to the mortgage holder: the cost of ripping old track out may exceed the sale value of the track. But the value to the enterprise could be very high: if the track is ripped out, the railroad cannot run. Is the track "worth" its scrap value or its value to the running railroad? And are the financier's rights to seize the security determined solely by the contract or by the overarching bankruptcy law? Defining the limits of what secured creditors can do with their security, and determining the value of the security under such circumstances is critical in bankruptcy reorganization. Such problems justify the creation of a government apparatus to reorganize companies under a framework that is not always that which the parties—financier and borrower—agreed to in their contract.

## ¶204: Who gets what when things go wrong?

Company was worth $1 billion. It borrowed $100 million, secured by a mortgage on its principal factory. It also borrowed $100 million of unsecured debt. The company fails and goes bankrupt. It is now worth only $150 million. Its factory could be sold for $50 million. Who gets what? Reconsider after reading *Atlas Pipeline*. What if the company were deemed worth $250 million at the time of reorganization?

## ¶205: A brief introduction to reorganization in chapter 11

When the firm is unable to meet its financial obligations or owes more than it owns, it may declare bankruptcy. The form of that bankruptcy might be a liquidation. The business could be discontinued. Its assets could be sold off, piecemeal or in operating units if the units have some value. Although this could be accomplished by arrangement among the creditors, it is understandable that judicial supervision could provide a more orderly liquidation than an arrangement among the parties. Supervision for such a liquidation occurs today under chapter 7 of the Bankruptcy Code: Assets are sold, the cash gathered, and then the cash is distributed to the creditors in the order of their priorities.

But in some instances the firm, although unable to meet current financial obligations, will in time be worthwhile as a continued enterprise. (Or at least that prospect of continuance is a question for exploration and litigation.) The scrap value of the steel mill is low: what else can be done with the mill anyway? But once the economy pulls out of the recession, the company will earn (or at least it is so hoped) a good return. The company owes $100 million, the mill is worth (in terms of its expected net cash flows) $50 million, but the next best use for the mill (scrap and real estate with an unsightly structure) is only $25 million. The $100 million debt burden is unsupportable, but liquidation (in the sense of scrapping and closing the $50 million mill) is wasteful because scrapping it would garner only $25 million.

The legal mechanism in which to reorganize the company is now chapter 11 of the Bankruptcy Code. The firm will be held together, neither liquidated piecemeal under judicial supervision nor ripped apart in creditors' seizure of parts of the firm, but the ownership interests in the firm will be reallocated. Two considerations will be primary: Should some of the ownership interests be eliminated or cut-down? After all, the firm has come to be worth so much less than was originally thought. And should the ownership interests be reallocated? After all, the immediate problem that led to the bankruptcy reorganization in chapter 11 was (almost always) the inability of the firm to generate sufficient cash to pay off creditors currently. Should the creditors change the nature of their obligation to stock, or delay receipt of the payments that they would otherwise be entitled to receive under their contract?

These questions will not be immediately answerable and could be expected to be litigated. But the reorganization process could be thwarted if creditors could seize their security or obtain default judgments and have the sheriff levy on the bankrupt's assets. The chapter 11 reorganization would then quickly descend into a free-for-all liquidation as the creditors rip apart the firm. This destructive prospect provides the rationale for the bankruptcy stay (really an injunction on the creditors), prohibiting the creditors from trying to collect from the firm when it is in chapter 11. The current form of the stay can be found in the Bankruptcy Code, § 362.

The stay is automatic, quite broad and very effective. It is as if the firm could, upon filing of a petition in chapter 11, operate for a time without a liability side to its balance sheet. No one from the liability side can insist upon payment of interest or repayment of loans. The firm that has such a benefit can operate with such forbearance for a long time. For example, in the *Atlas Pipeline* proceedings, which we will soon read, under predecessor forms to § 362 the creditors apparently began their collection proceedings in 1934, continued them in a failed effort to sell the company's principal assets in 1939, and were still in the final stages of approving a reorganization plan in the autumn of 1941. Except for a brief period when the company was out of receivership/bankruptcy proceedings during this seven-year period, the creditors received neither their interest on their original loan nor any return of the principal of their original loan. In the 1990s a chapter 11 proceeding typically lasts about two or three years, during which most creditors typically wait to be paid.

The modern form of the bankruptcy stay is found in § 362 of the Bankruptcy Code:

**11 U.S.C. § 362. Automatic stay**

> (a) [A] [bankruptcy] petition operates as a stay, applicable to all entities, of—
>
> (1) the commencement or continuation, including the issuance or employment of process, of a judicial, administrative, or other action or proceeding against the debtor that was or could have been commenced before the commencement of the case under this title, or to recover a claim against the debtor that arose before the commencement of the case under this title;
>
> (2) the enforcement, against the debtor or against property of the estate, of a judgment obtained before the commencement of the case under this title;
>
> (3) any act to obtain possession of property of the estate or ... to exercise control over property of the estate;
>
> (4) any act to create, perfect, or enforce any lien against property of the estate;
>
> (5) any act to create, perfect, or enforce against property of the debtor any lien to the extent that such lien secures a claim that arose before the commencement of the case under this title;
>
> (6) any act to collect, assess, or recover a claim against the debtor that arose before the commencement of the case under this title;
>
> (7) the setoff of any debt owing to the debtor that arose before the commencement of the case under this title against any claim against the debtor; and
>
> (8) the commencement or continuation of a proceeding before the United States Tax Court concerning the debtor.

## ¶206: Winners and losers

Who wins and who loses in chapter 11? The initial answer will turn on how much the firm is worth. The more value there is in the firm, the further down the capital structure pecking order the court can move.

The distributional question will depend on estimates of the future cash flows of the bankrupt. That is why we must master the basic concepts of present value and why we will examine the valuation proceedings in *Atlas Pipeline*.

## ¶207: The limits of judicial expertise: reliance on the parties?

The bankruptcy judge will not ordinarily be expert at valuation techniques. Indeed as shall be seen upon examination of the *Atlas Pipeline* SEC advisory opinion, there is some basis to fear that expert agencies, even those whose personnel will have a finance background, will issue opinions that are internally inconsistent. Judges are not usually trained for valuation; financiers are.

The problem may be deeper than a question of technical expertise. Since valuation is a guess about future states of the economy, future prices of the company's product, and future costs of the company's production, knowledge of the tools for valuation (discounting, variance, diversification, etc.) may not be enough. Knowledge or a feel for the particular industry and sometimes the particular company is required. Is an adversary proceeding the best place to get it?

Financial analysts will themselves come up with differing valuation figures. The economic analysts at Merrill Lynch might tell the industry analyst to assume a 2% growth rate in the gross national product. The economists at Goldman, Sachs might be more optimistic and assume a 3% growth rate. Merrill Lynch's oil analyst could conclude oil will go to $15 per barrel next year, while Goldman's is projecting $20 per barrel. These differences would lead Goldman (or its client) to buy the oil property from Merrill Lynch's client. Who is right? Usually we have no need for a judicial second guess; in a market economy, the project goes to the higher bidder. Is the deeper problem with judicial valuation that the court is not spending its own money and accordingly might more easily make a mistake or let nonfinancial considerations infect its valuation determination?

Could the court rely on the parties to bring forth experts who will present the relevant valuation data? Consider the district court opinion in In re New York, New Haven and Hartford RR, 4 Bankr. 758 (D. Conn. 1980). The Second Circuit affirmation is reproduced infra at ¶516. (Note, by the way, the year of bankruptcy and the year of valuation.)

## ¶208: In re New York, New Haven and Hartford RR Co., 4 Bankr. 758 (D. Conn. 1980) (Zampano, J.)

[The New Haven Railroad went bankrupt in 1961 and was later absorbed into Penn Central. Years later, at the time of confirmation of the New Haven plan of reorganization, the principal assets of New Haven were securities of Penn Central, which itself had recently emerged from reorganization. At issue in the plan of reorganization was the value of the New Haven Railroad.]

...

### A. THE PARTIES' VALUATION OF THE NEW HAVEN ESTATE

A valuation of the assets of the New Haven in a necessary prerequisite to the design of a fair and equitable plan of reorganization for the enterprise. Once that valuation is ascertained, it is then translated into a new set of securities of the reorganized New Haven which, in turn, is distributed to creditors in accordance with the absolute priority rule. As Collier explains:

> If the court is to pass upon the proposed distribution of the debtor's assets, the classes of creditors and stockholders to be granted participation, the allocation of new securities or other compensation, the allocation of voting control, and the like, as well as upon the soundness of the proposed capital structure of the rehabilitated enterprise with regard to its ability to meet future charges and to furnish an adequate return to creditors, the court obviously must have before it a complete and reliable evaluation of the debtor's assets. Absent the requisite valuation data, the court is in no position to exercise the informed judgment required of it in assessing the fairness, equity and feasibility of a plan, either upon approval or confirmation thereof.

6A Collier on Bankruptcy, P11.05 at 184-85 (1977); see also Consolidated Rock, [312 U.S. 510, 524 (1941), infra these materials, at ¶702] (a determination of the value of the debtor's assets is required so that criteria will be available to determine an appropriate allocation of new securities between bondholders and stockholders).

The main controversy in this case focuses on the proper methodology to be applied by the Court in valuing the assets of the New Haven, which [now] consist solely of cash and Penn Central securities. *The parties urge acceptance of the valuation procedures for the securities* which best conform to their views of the applicable law and *which, coincidentally, establish the most favorable standing with respect to their own cause.* In support of their positions, the parties have submitted considerable evidence by way of affidavits, expert testimony, exhibits, moving papers, and briefs. *Each of the varied and conflicting opinions of the experts was the subject of extensive and, at times, exhaustive cross-examination; hardly a material representation on valuation submitted by one party went unchallenged by another party. The voluminous record in the proceedings speaks eloquently of the tireless efforts of counsel on behalf of their clients.*[2]

### The Trustee's Methodology

The trustee contends that, for reorganization purposes, the Court is required to measure the worth of the New Haven by evaluating its earning power as a going concern. Under this methodology, the securities held by the New Haven must be appraised by estimating their "intrinsic" or "reorganization" value, rather than by reference to their current market value ....

\* \* \*

... [The trustee] argues that the current market value of the Penn Central securities is not a reliable indicator of the worth of the New Haven's holdings because the investing public's perception of the true value of the securities has been distorted by various factors.

---

[2] [Emphasis supplied.—Roe.]

First, the Penn Central has just recently emerged from a lengthy and complex reorganization and the "stigma of bankruptcy" necessarily results in a serious depression in the market value of its securities ....

Second, the market place is unable to make sound business judgments concerning Penn Central at this time because of the major legal complexities of the Valuation Case. The Valuation Case ... has an indeterminable value; therefore, its uncertainty may adversely affect the market values of all the securities of Penn Central which are ... tied to the ultimate receipt of the award in that case.

Third, the Penn Central securities at this time lack "seasoning" and "stability" because they are generally in the hands of large institutions and have not been sufficiently traded over a long period of time to reflect their true value. Finally, the trustee contends that the investing public's lack of knowledge about and confidence in certain features peculiar to Penn Central—the results and timing of the Asset Disposition Program, its unusual capital structure and debt cascades, its new management—make it highly unlikely that the market place has correctly appraised the value of the securities.

Utilizing the intrinsic value concept for the securities held by the New Haven, the trustee concludes that, with the cash on hand, the value of the New Haven estate for reorganization purposes is within a range of $120 million to $150 million, and that the value of the equity of the reorganized New Haven is commensurate with this value. At the high end, this valuation would provide compensation to the First Mortgage Bondholders to the full extent of their claim, as computed by the trustee, i.e., approximately $135.7 million ($76,819,900 in principal plus $58,895,251 in interest to date), as well as affording a present equity in the estate for the Income Bondholders. In practical effect, the Amended Plan affords the First Mortgage Bondholders 93.1%, and the Income Bondholders 6.9%, of the reorganized New Haven.

\* \* \*

**The First Mortgage Bondholders' Methodology**

In marked contrast to the trustee's position, the basic argument of the First Mortgage Bondholders is that fair market value, almost wholly derived from market price, constitutes the primary criterion for determining the reorganization value of the New Haven. They argue that it is logical and practical for the Court to calculate the net asset value of the New Haven and the reorganized company mathematically by reference to the opinion of investors in the open market because, except for cash, the estate consists solely of marketable securities.

While recognizing the intrinsic value concept in principle, they contend it is inapplicable as employed by the trustee because there is and has been broad, active, and orderly sales of the Penn Central securities over an extended period of time which establishes the market place as the primary and most reliable indicator of value.

\* \* \*

[Based on market value, the First Mortgage Bondholders' expert testified that the New Haven Railroad was worth $71 million.]

\* \* \*

### The Income Bondholders' Methodology

The Income Bondholders and their experts contend, as does the trustee and his experts, that intrinsic value rather than market price is the appropriate measure of value for the securities.

\* \* \*

The Income Bondholders [expert] ... testified that in his view the reorganization value of the New Haven is in the range of $174.5 million to $246 million, that the trustee's Amended Plan was not fair and equitable, and that the Income Bondholders' proposed plan of reorganization was the only one feasible and equitable.

## B. THE COURT'S RULINGS ON VALUATION

The disputed issues of fact and law relating to the applicable methodology for the valuation of the assets of the New Haven have been fully litigated in a trial on the merits. *The validity of every opinion expressed on the subject was contested to the minutest detail.*[3] After a careful review and consideration of the extensive evidence and voluminous briefs, the Court is of the opinion that no party's valuation procedures can be accepted in toto as the basis for a fair, equitable and feasible plan of reorganization.

\* \* \*

In the instant case, the Court finds that the market in general is somewhat unsettled because of the social, political, and economic stresses current on the domestic and international scenes. Yet, it is neither in disarray nor in a panic state which in and of itself would warrant a rejection of the investors' perceptions of the value of securities ...

Use of a substitute "reorganization value" [instead of the market value of the firm's assets] may under the circumstances be the only fair means of determining the value of the securities distributed.

In addition, it is reasonable to assume that much more time is necessary for the marketplace to absorb, digest and react rationally to the available information concerning the Asset Disposition Program, the Valuation Case, and the complex capital structure of the Penn Central with its tiers of securities, cascades, lien priorities and the utilization of tax losses. It is evident that traditional methods employed by inves-

---

[3] [Emphasis supplied.—Roe.]

tors in valuing securities cannot be readily applied to the securities in question. As pointed out by Judge Fullam: "The actual dollar value of the [Penn Central] securities ... could not be fixed with even the minimal degree of precision encountered in ordinary reorganization plans until the Valuation Case litigation is concluded." 458 F. Supp. at 1301.

[The court then valued New Haven as worth $150 million.]

### ¶209: The implications of valuation

1. How does valuation of the firm in reorganization determine who gets what? Imagine that the New Haven Railroad will be recapitalized with 100 shares of common stock. If the judge values the railroad at $71 million, as the First Mortgage Bondholders contended was proper, how would the shares of stock be divided? (How much were the Firsts owed?)

   If the judge values the railroad at $246 million, as the Income Bondholders contended was proper, how would the shares of stock be divided?

   The judge concluded that the railroad was worth $150 million. How would a new 100-share capital structure be divided up?

2. The judge noted that the players in the New Haven Railroad reorganization contested "the validity of every opinion expressed on the subject ... to the minutest detail." See p. 23. Why did the parties fight so vociferously over the railroad's valuation, a number that is, after all, just the judge's opinion of the railroad's value?

3. Is valuation solely a matter of concern as it determines the allocation of the bankrupt pie? How does (or could) valuation determine the operational decision of whether to liquidate or reorganize the firm? Must the bankruptcy system explicitly or implicitly find the value of the firm if liquidated, find the value if reorganized, and then compare the two?

4. To answer these questions well, to represent clients well in a bankruptcy, to judge a bankruptcy well, and to evaluate the success of a reorganization system, the lawyer will have to understand the basic techniques of valuation.

## B. Basic valuation

Discounting to present value, the variance of different possible outcomes, and diminishing marginal utility are the three core concepts of valuation.

### ¶210: Discounting to present value

The value of a firm to a financier will usually be the value of cash the firm can throw off. Because the firm will throw the cash off in the future, some method to find the value of that future cash in today's dollars must be found. Money to be received years from now is not as valuable as the same dollar amount received today, not just because of the risks of non-receipt but because money today can be put into a bank, which will pay interest. So a sure $1000 a year from now will be worth less than $1000, because a smaller sum of money can be put into the bank and yield the $1000 a year from now. At 10% interest, the question is: How much must be deposited today, so that the money deposited today, plus 10% interest for the year, will yield $1000 a year from now. Or:

(1) X+10% of X = $1000

Or:

(2) 1.1 X = $1000

(3) X = $1000/1.1

(4) X = $ 909.09

$909, deposited today at 10% interest, will give the depositor about $1000 in the bank a year from now.

Another way of looking at present value problems, one that is useful for understanding *Atlas Pipeline,* the first big case that we'll study, is to value a perpetuity. Here we are told that the firm will produce a certainty equivalent of $100 per year, forever. The question then is: How much must be deposited in the bank to yield $100 per year at 10%. The value of this firm must be $1000, the amount that would yield $100 per year.

This perpetuity is equivalent to taking the value of $100 a year from now, discounting it to present value, then taking the value of $100 two years from now, discounting it to present value, then taking the value of $100 three years from now, discounting it to present value, etc. When this infinite process is completed, the present values of $100 in each year would be added up, giving us the present value of this firm.

The process of discounting the perpetual income stream is usually called "capitalizing" an income stream, and the discount rate is the inverse of the capitalization rate. So a stream of $100 per year, discounted at 5%, yields a present value of $2000 for the perpetuity. The "capitalization rate" (sometimes called the capitalization multiplier) for the income is 20 times the expected income.

As will be apparent once we get a feel for the numbers, the choice of a discount rate, or its inverse, the capitalization rate, can be crucial. The same expected income can yield widely variant present values, depending on the choice of the discount rate. As we've just seen, $100 at 10% yields a present value of $1000; $100 at 5% yields a present value of $2000. If the discount rate were 20%, the present value would plummet to $500.

Lastly, while discounting a perpetuity to present value has an unreal air to it—we can barely predict income for next year, so how can we have any assurance of income twenty years down the road?—the problem is less critical than it might seem. In most valuations, all of the income from twenty years on out in perpetuity will be a small part of the present value of most industrial firms.

## ¶211: Present values in more detail: Richard A. Brealey & Stewart C. Myers, Principles of Corporate Finance 35-40 (6th ed. 2000)[4]

In ¶210 we saw how to work out the value of an asset that produces cash exactly 1 year from now. But we did not explain how to value assets that produce cash 2 years from now or in several future years. That is the first thing that we must do in ¶211. We will then have a look at some shortcut methods for calculating present values and at some specialized present value formulas.

\* \* \*

### Valuing Long-Lived Assets

Do you remember how to calculate the present value (PV) of an asset that produces a cash flow ($C_1$) one year from now? [If not, re-read ¶210.]

$$PV = DF_1 \times C_1 = \frac{C_1}{1 + r_1}$$

The discount factor for the year-1 cash flow is $DF_1$, and $r_1$ is the opportunity cost of investing your money for one year. [The subscript 1 signifies that the term relates to year 1. Subscript 2 will relate to year 2.] Suppose you will receive a certain cash inflow of $100 next year ($C_1=100$) and the rate of interest on one-year U.S. Treasury bills is 7 percent ($r_1=.07$). Then present value equals

$$PV = \frac{C_1}{1 + r_1} = \frac{100}{1.07} = \$93.46$$

The present value of a cash flow two years hence can be written in a similar way as

---

[4] Reproduced with permission of The McGraw-Hill Companies.

$$PV = DF_2 \times C_2 = \frac{C_2}{(1+r_2)^2}$$

$C_2$ is the year-2 cash flow, $DF_2$ is the discount factor for the year-2 cash flow, and $r_2$ is the annual rate of interest on money invested for two years. Suppose you get another cash flow of $100 in year 2 ($C_2$=100). The rate of interest on two-year Treasury notes is 7.7 percent per year ($r_2$=.077); [meaning] that a dollar invested in two-year notes will grow to $1.077^2$=\$1.16 by the end of two years. The present value of your year-2 cash flow equals

$$PV = \frac{C_2}{(1+r_2)^2} = \frac{100}{(1.077)^2} = \$86.21$$

**Valuing Cash Flows in Several Periods**

One of the nice things about present values is that they are all expressed in current dollars—so that you can add them up. In other words, the present value of cash flow A + B is equal to the present value of cash flow A plus the present value of cash flow B. This happy result has important implications for investments that produce cash flows in several periods.

[An extended series of annual cash flows would look like:]

$$PV = \frac{C_1}{1+r_1} + \frac{C_2}{(1+r_2)^2} + \frac{C_3}{(1+r_3)^3} + \ldots$$

\* \* \*

[In principle there can be a different interest rate for each future period.] This relationship between the interest rate and the maturity of the cash flow is called the **term structure of interest rates**. [We will assume that the interest rate in each period is the same.]

**How Present Value Tables Help the Lazy**

So far all our examples can be worked out fairly easily by hand. Real problems are often much more complicated and require the use of an electronic calculator that is specifically programmed for present value calculations, a spreadsheet program on a personal computer, or present value tables.

\* \* \*

### Looking for Shortcuts—Perpetuities and Annuities

Sometimes there are shortcuts that make it easy to calculate the present value of an asset that pays off in different periods. Let us look at some examples.

Among the securities that have been issued by the British government are so-called **perpetuities.** These are bonds that the government is under no obligation to repay but that offer a fixed income for each year to perpetuity. The rate of return on a perpetuity is equal to the promised annual payment divided by the present value:

$$\text{Return} = \frac{\text{cash flow}}{\text{present value}}$$

$$r = \frac{C}{PV}$$

We can obviously twist this around and find the present value of a perpetuity given the discount rate $r$ and the cash payment C. For example, suppose that some worthy person wishes to endow a [university] chair[.] If the rate of interest is 10 percent and if the aim is to provide $100,000 a year in perpetuity, the amount that must be set aside today is

$$\text{Present value of perpetuity} = \frac{C}{r} = \frac{100,000}{.10} = \$1,000,000$$

## ¶212: Present value problem

Your client, a construction company, is in bankruptcy. It has one available project. The project is covered by a draft contract, which has been drafted by counsel for the manufacturing company. You review the draft of the contract. Your client will build an addition to a factory at a price of $550,000. The manufacturer will pay $50,000 down, when construction will commence. Construction will take five years. The completed factory will be delivered at the very end of five years; and the buyer will make the final payment of $500,000 on the next day, which would be five years from the signing of the contract.

Your client expects construction to cost $500,000 and take 5 years. Your client, the bankrupt construction company, has $500,000 cash, an asset which is somewhat unusual for a bankrupt firm. (But this is a hypothetical.) Expenses (which to simplify will include the normal profits the client would expect) will be incurred annually at a rate of about $100,000 per year. So, the bankrupt will incur $100,000 of expenses in the first year. Another $100,000 of expenses will be incurred in the second year, and then $100,000 again in the third year. (We'll assume that the expenses are incurred at the very end of each year so that we can keep the arithmetic tractable.)

The client says "$550,000 is coming in; $500,000 is going out. Fifty thousand dollars profit on a project like this one isn't bad. Sure, I'll make less than $50,000, because of the timing discrepancies. But how much less?"

Do you have any further comments for your client? Assuming the risk of non-payment by the manufacturer upon completion is nil and assuming that your client's next best use of funds is 10% per year, how might you outline the terms to your client, or to the valuing authority?

| | | Value of Construction Project | | | | | |
|---|---|---|---|---|---|---|---|
| | Now | End of Year 1 | End of Year 2 | End of Year 3 | End of Year 4 | End of Year 5 | Total |
| Receipts (actual) | ? | ? | ? | ? | ? | ? | ? |
| Expenses (actual) | ? | ? | ? | ? | ? | ? | ? |
| Receipts (present value) | ? | ? | ? | ? | ? | ? | ? |
| Receipts (present value) | ? | ? | ? | ? | ? | ? | ? |

After valuing the company, would you have an operating recommendation to make to the construction company? If you were the judge making the valuation in bankruptcy, might you consider whether the bankrupt should go ahead and finish the deal to construct the factory?

## ¶213: Risk

To understand discounting, we've assumed that the future returns are fixed and certain, and the only issue is how much it's worth to delay their realization. The problem in ¶212 requires the discounting of a sum certain back to present value.

But investments are fraught with risk. The economy might change, the debtor's business might change, management might be unsuccessful.

The following excerpt helps illustrate the problem. It's Grayson, The Use of Statistical Techniques in Capital Budgeting, Financial Research and Management Decisions 98-107 (Robicheck ed. 1967), as reproduced in Victor Brudney & Marvin Chirelstein, Corporate Finance 52 (3d ed. 1987).

> Let's take a closer look at the [best estimate of future income.] How confident is the forecaster of that figure? Is he very certain, very uncertain, or somewhere in between? And what does he really mean by the words, best estimate or most likely? ... Is he truly giving us the most likely figure, which is the *mode*? Is he really thinking through some internal calculus of a weighted average figure, the *mean*? Or, [did] he ... select the middle figure, the *median*? ... [W]hich measure is inferred can make quite a difference ....

... First, we do not know the uncertainty surrounding that figure[.] [T]hat is, we do not know the "probability distribution"—the range of the forecast and the probability estimates associated with figures within that range. Second, we do not know for sure whether his best estimate is really the mode, median, or mean. For both reasons, we would like therefore, to have the forecaster give us not just one estimate, but a *range* of estimates and associated *probabilities* ....

A probability distribution, in its simplest form, could consist of only a few estimates. One popular form consists of three figures: the "optimistic, most likely, and pessimistic," or the "high, low, and best guess" estimates.

| Annual sales | |
|---|---|
| Forecast | (units) |
| Optimistic | 100,000 |
| Most likely | 75,000 |
| Pessimistic | 50,000 |

Some improvement has been made over the single forecast figure .... [And] how likely is the "most likely" estimate in the forecaster's mind? Is the optimistic forecast very improbable, or close to the most likely forecast? Or, are all three forecast equally likely? [How confident is the forecaster?]

| Annual sales | | |
|---|---|---|
| Forecast | (units) | Probability |
| Optimistic | 100,000 | .30 |
| Most likely | 75,000 | .60 |
| Pessimistic | 50,000 | .10 |

Clearly, more information is available now .... [It] is an appealing [next] step to ask our forecaster to give us his estimates of the entire range of figures that might occur—the entire probability distribution as shown in Figure 5.1.

[But] how can such a probability distribution[ ] be obtained? This is a subject to which theorists have been devoting a great deal of attention in recent years, and with some success.

What has restrained the use of probability theory in business decision making for many years has been the classical "frequency" concept of probability. Briefly, this concept indicates that no statement *whatsoever* can be made about the probability of any single event. In fact, the classical view holds that one can only talk about probability in a very long-run sense, given that the occurrence or non-occurrence of the event can be repeatedly observed over a *very large number of times under independent identical conditions.*

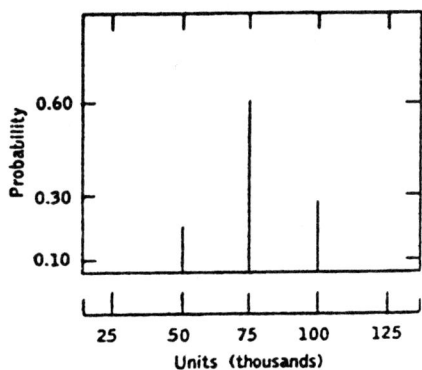 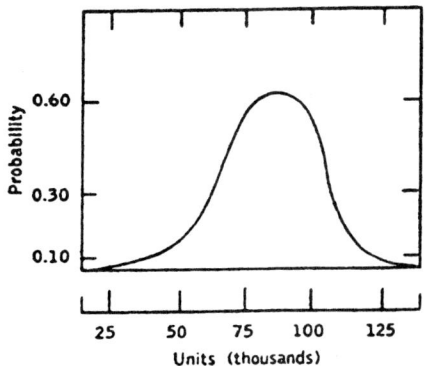

FIG. 5.1. *Left:* three-figure estimate; *right:* entire probability distribution.

Diminishing marginal utility is a third concept that must be understood. (Discounting to present value (¶¶210–211 and Appendix A) and risk from variant possible outcomes were the first two.) Application is straightforward, although at first puzzling, because we are forced to conclude that $10,000 is not always worth $10,000. The basic idea is that we spend our first $10,000 on things worth quite a bit to us: medicine, shelter, food. Our next $10,000 goes to things worth a bit less, like, say, law school tuition. Our third $10,000 goes to luxuries, like a vacation or a car. The more money we have the better off we are, but the successively equal increments of money yield smaller increments of happiness.

The consequence of the diminishing marginal value is that the value of a risky project is not the same as a riskless one with the same expected valued. (Expected value is the sum of the outcomes times their probabilities.) Consider the student with $20,000, asked to invest in a project expected to yield a sure $10,000, plus a small profit. The distribution of that profit, or in another vocabulary, the shape of the probability distribution (see Figure 5.1 from the Grayson reading above) will be of intense interest to the student. If the project will yield $10,000 with certainty (plus the small profit), the project will allow continued enrollment in law school. If the project yields zero or $20,000 (plus a small profit), then the expected monetary value is still $10,000 [from (.5 x $20,000) + (.5 x 0)].

But the usefulness (or expected utility, in the economic jargon) of the double or nothing bet with an expected dollar value of $10,000, is less than that of the sure thing $10,000. Why? Because the risky project means there's a 50% chance that the student will be forced to drop out of law school. But the upside, the good outcome, yields $10,000, which will enable the student to take a vacation or buy a car, which the student finds less worthwhile than going to law school.

The net effect is that the risky investment will be worth less than $10,000 to the student. A 50-50 chance of $20,000 or nothing, is not worth $10,000, but something less, perhaps considerably less.

Financial markets work similarly. Financiers expend great energy in discovering the dispersion of risks and in finding ways to eliminate or offset these risks. When the risk cannot be shed, the investor will insist on a "premium" to absorb these risks. The premium is another way of saying that the $20,000 or zero bet is not worth $10,000, but something less.

One short-cut to value projects with noticeable variance and diminishing marginal utility is to adjust the discount rate to account for the variance and diminished utility attached to it. So, a sure $10,000 a year from now might be discounted at 10% (and therefore be worth $9,091). The risky, double or nothing, $20,000 or zero outcome still has an expected outcome of $10,000, but the expected outcome is discounted at, say, 20%, yielding a value of $8,333. The discount rate does double duty: paying for the time delay in receiving money and accounting for the diminishing utility of low outcomes.

## ¶214: Variance and diversification

Risky returns will demand a premium. How does this play out when there are many risky investments in the economy? The answer lies in the next key concept for valuation: diversification.

*The sure-thing railroad.* A riskless railroad, originally worth more, has fallen on hard times, but still has a solid core business. It is expected to have certain income of $1 million per year. The riskless rate of interest is 10%. Accordingly, this railroad, Railroad A, the sure-thing railroad, would be worth $10 million. The judge accepts the $1 million projection, the 10% discount rate, and turns the whole railroad over to the railroad's one creditor, owed $10 million.

*The risky railroad.* Now with risk: Another railroad goes bankrupt, but we don't know how good the railroad will be. On average, we expect the railroad to yield $1,000,000. But we don't know for sure. It could earn $2 million per year. Or it might earn nothing every year.

The problem is that the railroad runs from the oil fields to the munitions plants. If there's war, the railroad makes a lot of money, $2,000,000 per year. If there's peace, the railroad is useless and makes nothing. If there's tension, the railroad makes $1,000,000 per year.

| **Risky Warco Railroad** | | |
|---|---|---|
| Peace | Tension | War |
| .33 | .33 | .33 |
| -0- | $1 million | $2 million |

The expected income in any year will still be $1 million. To establish the present value of this risky income stream would presumably require a higher discount rate than 10%. Say that market participants insist on an extra 2%, as a risk premium for this kind of variance. Use of a 12% discount rate would yield an enterprise value of $8.3 million. This is no different than the law school student worried that the investment will, if it turns out badly, force withdrawal from law school.

So, now this railroad, railroad B, the risky warrior railroad has an expected average income of $1 million and a value of $8.3 million, because the income is uncertain. Accordingly, the judge values the railroad at $8.3 million and still gives it to the $10 million creditor.

Diversification. Railroad A, the sure-thing railroad, also has an expected income of $1 million, but because its assured income will not force any investor to face diminishing marginal returns and a decision to drop out of law school, its value is $10 million. After emerging from bankruptcy, both railroads have publicly offered their stock to law school students and recent law school graduates. One thousand law school students invest $10,000 in the sure-thing railroad, which will yield each of the them $1000 in the next year. They sell their stock when they have to meet tuition bills. Stock of Railroad B, the risky railroad, sells for $8300, but it's taken up by recent law school graduates, with salaried jobs, people who can handle some of the risk.

Railroad C and an uncorrelated income stream. Bored with schoolwork and looking at investment reports, you discover a third railroad, railroad C. Railroad C's road runs from wheat fields and infrastructure factories to cities. If there's war, it will be worthless, because the products it transports will not be made in the factories or sold in the cities if there's war. If there's tension, some of its products will be made, shipped, and sold. But if there's peace, it will boom, because demand for the products it ships will zoom and it will be able to raise its rates.

If there's peace, the railroad makes a lot of money, $2,000,000 per year. If there's war, the railroad is useless and makes nothing. If there's tension, the railroad makes $1,000,000 per year.

| Risky Peaceco Railroad | | |
|---|---|---|
| Peace | Tension | War |
| .33 | .33 | .33 |
| $2 million | $1 million | -0- |

Again, although the expected income in any year will still be $1 million, investors insist on an extra 2% premium for this kind of variance. Use of a 12% discount rate would yield an enterprise value of $8.3 million. You notice that each of the 1,000 shares of Railroad C, the Infrastructure Express, sells for $8300. Recent law school graduates, your friends, own the stock.

Are you on your way to making a fortune? How?[5]

---

[5] Measuring firm-specific, unsystematic risk, and the techniques of constructing a portfolio to reduce its impact is a key financial goal. Some risks, like those to which the whole economic system is subject to, such as from a general decline in the economy, are called systematic risks, and, in the financial formulas are measured by a term "beta," which you will hear about from time to time in financial circles, but is not critical for this course. Beta is a measure of how sensitive a particular company, or its stock, is to general changes in economic conditions. To get the story on beta and systematic risk, consult any good Corporate Finance book, like Brealey and Myers.

## Chapter 3

# JUDICIAL VALUATION

**A. Failure**
**B. Liquidation vs. reorganization**
**C. Valuation of Atlas Pipeline**
**D. Capital layers**
**E. Advisers and conflicts**
**F. Valuation of Duplan**

..................................................................................................

### A. Failure

¶301: <u>**The distinction between financial failure and economic failure**</u>

The problems of reorganization in bankruptcy tend toward intractability. To understand them it is necessary to see the complexities entailed in a full-scale judicial reorganization of a bankrupt company. A modern case might have some advantages. A series of cases might build toward the ultimate problems of judicial reorganization slowly. But few cases are as good at revealing the difficulties of judicial valuation as is the SEC's advisory opinion for Atlas Pipeline in 1940. Moreover, the case for quite some time has been at the heart of finance-oriented law school casebooks, such as Victor Brudney & Marvin Chirelstein, Corporate Finance (3d ed., 1987) and Walter Blum & Stanley A. Kaplan, Corporate Readjustments and Reorganizations (1976), both of which came in earlier, and, in Brudney and Chirelstein's case, later, editions. So we will start examining the problems of valuation with the SEC's Advisory Opinion in *Atlas Pipeline,* an opinion that for several decades now has become part of the collective consciousness of law school students studying corporate reorganization.

1. *Atlas Pipeline* is a factually complex case. To begin with, it is useful to introduce us (or remind us, if we have already been introduced) to a variety of terms and

corporate financial actors. What is an indenture trustee?[1] a first mortgage bond?[2] a second mortgage bond?[3] a trade creditor?[4] a sinking fund? preferred stock? liquidation value?[5] going concern value?[6]

2. In March 1941, was Atlas Pipeline an economic failure, a financial failure, both, neither? An economic failure makes less from its operations than expected. A financial failure (in this setting) is unable to pay back its creditors. Will an economic failure always go bankrupt? Will a financial failure? Are economic failures always, sometimes, or never worth saving? Are financial failures always, sometimes, or never worth saving? Is destruction of either, sometimes, always or never worth expediting? Consider two identical firms, each of whose operations are expected to be worth about $25 million. Firm A is financed completely with common stock; Firm B borrows $10 million and raises the rest with common stock. Both firms unexpectedly decline in value to $10 million. Which one needs to reorganize? Which one is a financial failure (in a bankruptcy sense)? Are both economic failures?

3. How do you conceptualize the corporation? What images, metaphors or similes come to mind when you think of the word "corporation"? A businessperson? An entrepreneur? A board of directors? A bundle of sticks?

4. Who owned Atlas Pipeline?

---

[1] The entity, usually a bank, that acts for the many bondholders.

[2] A bond secured by a mortgage. If the debtor firm defaults on its borrowing, the bondholders can then, usually acting through their trustee, seize the mortgaged properties from the debtor under state law, sell the mortgaged properties, and use the proceeds to satisfy their loan.

[3] A second mortgage bond gets paid out of the mortgaged property after the first mortgage bondholder is paid.

[4] A supplier sells merchandise to the firm; the firm pays the supplier after the supplier has delivered the merchandise to the firm. During the gap between delivery and payment, the supplier is a trade creditor.

[5] Usually the value from the quick sale of pieces of the firm, occurring as the firm's operations are shut-down. However, it's plausible to imagine the quick sale of the firm, intact, with the buyer then deciding after the sale what to shut-down and what to keep in business. The former owners would have "liquidated" their position in the firm, by turning their ownership interests into liquid cash (or other consideration). The firm would be kept intact, but with a new owner.

[6] Going concern value, or reorganization value, would be the value of the firm if reorganized and kept in business. The standard way to find going concern value is to estimate the firm's future net cash flow and discount that cash flow to present value.

A good place to look for explanations for unfamiliar financial terms is in the glossary of the Corporate Finance textbook written by Brealey and Myers.

## ¶302: Background to *Atlas Pipeline*

The next long reading is the SEC's advisory opinion in the reorganization of Atlas Pipeline. Atlas was an oil refiner and transporter, which failed in a series of reorganizations in the 1930s. It went bankrupt under chapter X of the Bankruptcy Act of 1938. In 1978, the new chapter 11 of the Bankruptcy Code replaced chapter X, whose features differed somewhat from those of the current chapter 11. Under chapter X, the bankrupt filed a petition, the court appointed a trustee, and the trustee ran the company and proposed a plan of reorganization.[7] Then the court valued the bankrupt firm, decided (implicitly or explicitly) whether to liquidate or reorganize, and distributed claims on the reorganized firm to (some of) the bankrupt's creditors. The court determined whether the plan of reorganization proposed by the trustee was "fair and equitable"—a term that, we shall see, is loaded with detail—and "feasible."

Under the old chapter X, the trustee proposed a plan of reorganization and the SEC wrote an advisory opinion to the court administering the proceeding, a process that gave the court the benefit of the SEC's financial expertise. Creditors organized themselves in committees to assist, or contest with, the trustee.

While this plan development was going on—a process that in the 1930s took years (and whose modern correlate of chapter 11 in the 1990s takes years)—the bankruptcy stay (an injunction) stopped the creditors from suing the bankrupt firm to collect on their loans.

These features of chapter X are reordered in today's chapter 11, but they are still present. Valuation can arise when the creditors vote against the plan. Usually in chapter 11 the court does not appoint an independent trustee. The role of the trustee in chapter 11 typically turns out to be taken over by the managers of the debtor, who are given the first crack at proposing a plan of reorganization. Lastly, the new chapter 11 gives several alternatives to a court finding that a plan is "fair and equitable." There are "deemed" creditor approvals, and if there are enough deemed and actual creditor approvals, the court can confirm the reorganization plan without valuing the firm.

But the details of chapter 11 can wait. A great deal of the current chapter 11 was designed to suppress and avoid valuation hearings such as that seen in *Atlas Pipeline*. To see what Congress and the reorganization establishment were trying to avoid in 1978, and to see the valuation hearing cloud that the parties to today's chapter 11 fear, and under which they negotiate, we must first read and understand *Atlas Pipeline*.

---

[7] Once again note our impoverished vocabulary. An indenture *trustee* works for bondholders (in and out of bankruptcy). The trustee in bankruptcy runs the bankrupt company. They're two different entities, with different functions.

## B. Liquidation vs. reorganization

### ¶303: Questions on *Atlas Pipeline:* Liquidation vs. reorganization

1. One critical decision in *Atlas Pipeline* is whether to liquidate the firm or reorganize it. Liquidation—typically the piecemeal sale of the firm's assets—would end its existence. Reorganization lets it try again. In reading *Atlas Pipeline*, consider the reasons why a court should decide whether to liquidate or reorganize Atlas Pipeline.

2. Usually such business decisions are made in the American economy by those running the enterprise, without significant judicial intervention. If US Steel is losing money on a steel mill, once it satisfies whatever contractual and statutory obligations it may (but often does not) have to its employees, it can decide to close the unprofitable mill. What are the justifications for the business judgment rule from corporate law? Are they inapplicable to the reorganization of Atlas Pipeline?

3. Is judicial intervention solely an act of sympathy for the bankrupt firm's satellite interests? If so, why intervene only for bankrupts? Why not intervene when factories close, whether inside or outside of bankruptcy? Do any of the opinions evince such sympathy for the bankrupt firm's satellite interests?

4. Will each party to the reorganization make a scientific calculation along the lines of valuing the firm if liquidated, valuing it if reorganized, and then presenting that valuation to the judge?

5. What if the first mortgagee in *Atlas Pipeline* knew the pipeline and refinery could be scrapped for $1 million. It also knows, we hypothesize, that the firm's going concern value is $1.2 million (equal chances of earning enough to be worth $.6 million, $1.2 million or $1.8 million). What operational decision does the first mortgagee want? To what extent does the operational decision depend upon the type of compensation given the first mortgagee (stock, debt or some hybrid)? Does it also depend on the ease of negotiating terms with the second mortgagee and the other parties to the reorganization?

6. Is the second mortgagee necessarily more trustworthy? What if Atlas Pipeline's liquidation value was $1 million, but its going concern value was $800 million, made from equal chances of 0, $800 million and $1.6 million, what does the second mortgagee want (assuming that reorganization would keep the first mortgagee's debt in place)?

7. Is there any party to the reorganization to whom the judge can turn?

8. After working through the prior two paragraphs carefully, consider whether the judge in the Eastern Air Lines bankruptcy (¶306) could have had any confidence in deferring to any of the financial parties.

**¶304: In re Atlas Pipeline Corporation, Debtor, Securities and Exchange Commission, Advisory Opinion Release No. 42, under the Corporate Reorganization Act, June 7, 1941, 9 S.E.C. 416 (1941)**

In Proceedings for Reorganization of a Corporation:

REPORT OF THE SECURITIES AND EXCHANGE COMMISSION ON PROPOSED PLAN OF REORGANIZATION

## HISTORY AND BUSINESS OF DEBTOR

### A. Debtor's Business and Principal Assets

The Debtor is presently engaged in refining petroleum and marketing the products thereof. It owns an inland refinery located near Shreveport, Louisiana, and an oil pipeline system connecting its refinery with oil fields in East Texas, Arkansas and Louisiana. In the past the Debtor has operated as a pipeline carrier transporting oil for other companies, but at the present time it is not carrying any oil through its East Texas line and is using its Arkansas-Louisiana line only to transport the crude oil requirements of its own refinery.

\* \* \*

### B. History of Debtor and Predecessor Corporations

\* \* \*

In November 1934 Atlas Pipeline Company, Inc., and its subsidiary, Spartan, both went into receivership.[8] This was followed by a reorganization proceeding under Section 77B of the Bankruptcy Act. A plan was confirmed in that proceeding which provided, in brief, for a new $1,000,000 first mortgage bond issue, the proceeds of which were used to pay receiver's certificates ($225,000) and other cash requirements of the plan, and to provide increased working capital. The plan further provided for the issuance of $1,312,000 of second mortgage bonds, of which $712,000 went to Alco Products, Inc., a subsidiary of American Locomotive Company, in final settlement of the amount owing for cracking units which had been built in 1934. The remaining $600,000 of second mortgage bonds were issued to the holders of Shreveport-El Dorado bonds then outstanding in that amount.

---

[8] [In a receivership, a court appoints a person, or occasionally a bank, to gather a weak firm's assets for the benefit of the firm's creditors. The receiver "receives" payments due the firm, holds the receipts for the creditors, and prevents unwise disbursement of these receipts. The modern reorganization apparatus—chapter 11 of the Bankruptcy Code and its pre-1978 predecessor, chapter X—grew out of the receivership mechanism.—Roe.]

... Thereafter the Debtor defaulted on the interest payments due November 1, 1938 on both the first and second mortgage bonds, and a receivership proceeding was instituted on May 26, 1939 by the indenture trustee for the first mortgage bondholders. *On August 17, 1939 the court directed a public sale of the mortgaged properties, and fixed an upset price of $1,200,000. No bids were received*[9] and on September 20, 1939 the present proceeding was instituted by the filing of the Debtor's petition for reorganization under Chapter X.

## PRESENT CAPITALIZATION

The present capitalization of the Debtor is as follows:

| | |
|---|---:|
| First Mortgage 6% Sinking Fund Convertible Bonds | $836,000 |
| Accrued interest to May 1, 1941 | 125,400 |
| | $961,400 |
| | |
| Second Mortgage 6% Sinking Fund Convertible Bonds | $1,305,000 |
| Accrued interest to May 1, 1941 | 195,750 |
| | $1,500,750 |
| | |
| Common Stock, par value $10 | 268,800 Shs. |

\* \* \*

## VALUATION [AND LIQUIDATION VS. REORGANIZATION]

In valuing this marginal enterprise it is necessary to consider what may be obtained from the Debtor's assets on the basis of two alternative courses of action, a) liquidation and sale of the property and b) continuation of the Debtor as an operating entity.

### A. Liquidating Value

\* \* \*

... [T]he net liquidating value of the Debtor's assets after allowance for $356,000 of Trustee's liabilities as of March 31, 1941, is $1,189,600 and is summarized in Table III.

### B. Value as Operating Entity

The value derivable from this Debtor as an operating entity is dependent in large part upon the amount of earnings to be obtained from the property as reorganized and the length of time for which such earnings will be available .... We turn now to a consideration of the remaining economic life of the enterprise.

---

[9] [Emphasis supplied here and elsewhere where italicized.—Roe.]

### TABLE III
### Estimated Liquidating Value of Debtor's Assets
### (As of March 31, 1941)

1) Fixed Assets

| | |
|---|---|
| Pipe, Tanks, Pumping and Refinery Equipment | $628,000 |
| Office Building | 83,000 |
| Refinery Land | <u>43,000</u> |
| Total Fixed Assets | $754,000 |

2) Current Assets

| | |
|---|---|
| Cash on hand | $211,000 |
| Cash on deposit with Indenture Trustee | 150,600 |
| Notes and Accounts Receivable | 123,000 |
| Inventories—Crude | 54,000 |
| Inventories—Refined | 155,000 |
| Inventories—Materials and Supplies | <u>85,000</u> |
| Total Current Assets | $778,600 |
| Less: Trustee's Liabilities | <u>356,000</u> |
| Net Current Assets | $422,600 |
| 3) Other Assets Sparco Gasoline Co., Inc., Stock | <u>13,000</u> |
| Total Net Liquidating Value | $1,189,600 |

1) Economic Life

The [Trustee's estimate] of the remaining life of the present plant facilities [as 10 years and] he computed annual depreciation for the reorganized company['s present facilities] on th[at] basis[.]

\* \* \*

[But in] view of the age of the equipment and the trend of technological advance in the industry it is our opinion that substantial investment in plant facilities will be required before the end of the 10 year period in order to keep the enterprise competitive. If this point is reached in 3 to 5 years as it very well may, the Debtor's earnings would have provided for this purpose a total of $190,000 at the end of three years, and $328,000 at the end of five years. These figures are based on estimated earnings of $130,000 before depreciation and assume that no income taxes will be paid, no preferred dividends will be paid, and that the annual sinking fund requirements will be met by the purchase of $50,000 face amount of bonds at $25,000.

Even though the Debtor could continue to operate for the next five years there is substantial reason to doubt that $328,000 should be adequate to make competitive the cracking units, which cost $900,000 and which at that time will be 11–12 years old, and the other equipment most of which will be over 20 years old. If at the end of the economic life of the present facilities, the Debtor has been unable to earn sufficient funds above its debt service requirements to re-equip its plant and maintain its competitive position the Debtor's existence as an operating entity will cease.[10] Under these circumstances the proposed plan will in effect have provided for a deferred liquidation of the Debtor's assets.

2) Determination of Value

**[Choosing a capitalization rate]**

The Trustee has estimated the going concern value of the reorganized Debtor at approximately $1,700,000 .... In arriving at this value the Trustee deducted an annual depreciation charge of $90,000 from his estimated prospective earnings of $262,000. The balance of $170,000, representing his estimated prospective earnings before bond interest and income taxes, was capitalized at 10%.

In our opinion this value is predicated on an estimate of prospective earnings which is overstated by $135,000, [on] the depreciation charge[11] [which] is calculated on the assumption of a 10 year remaining life for the present facilities which we believe excessive, and for the reasons set forth subsequently, [on a] 10% [capitalization rate which] is too low a rate of capitalization in the light of the risks inherent in this enterprise.

*We believe a more appropriate approach to the valuation of this Debtor would be one which recognized the company's uncertain tenure of existence as an operating entity. In our opinion, it is improbable that this Debtor will be able during the remaining economic life of its present properties to obtain sufficient funds from earnings to meet its debt service and to make the necessary plant replacements to maintain its competitive position.* On this basis the elements of value derivable from the reorganized company consist of the present worth, at an appropriate discount rate, of the cash profits that may be produced during its remaining operating life and the present worth of the values realizable at the end of that life from the disposition of its assets.

The Trustee has testified that in his opinion the proper rate of return to apply in valuing the Debtor ranged from 8% to 20%. The General Manager testified that in his opinion the rate should be 8% to 12% or possibly 14%. The rate used by them was 10%.

---

[10] Because of the excessive issuance of debt and preferred stock provided for in the proposed plan, the Debtor will be effectively foreclosed from entering the capital markets for the necessary funds. [Why would this be so even if the firm had a good, profitable project? See the discussion of Chrysler in Chapter 12, at ¶1220.—Roe.]

[11] The depreciation charge of $90,000 compares with an average depreciation charge of $236,000 for the last five years.

The determination of an appropriate rate must be predicated on the risks inherent in the enterprise.[12] The Debtor is operating in a highly competitive field. Furthermore it has the weaknesses characteristic of a small inland refinery. In addition to the general risks arising from the nature of the industry and the Debtor's position in it, there are numerous hazards affecting the realization by the Debtor of the prospective earnings estimated herein. These have been set forth earlier in the report.[13] *In the light of the risks inherent in the enterprise[14] it is our opinion that the proper rate of return to be applied to the Debtor's prospective earnings before income taxes would be 15%, certainly not less than 12%.*[15]

### [Estimating future earnings for Atlas' expected life]

We have already indicated that in our opinion reasonably prospective earnings do not exceed $130,000 annually before depreciation and bond interest. There remain to be considered the values that may be realizable at the end of the Debtor's operating life and the period over which this life may extend.

### [Scrap value at the end of Atlas' expected life]

In a previous section we have shown the liquidating value of the Debtor's assets as indicated by the record. This value is applicable only to a liquidation undertaken by the Debtor at the present time. The realization that may be obtained in a liquidation several years hence is a speculative and uncertain matter. The testimony is clear that present conditions provide an *unusually favorable opportunity* for the disposal of the Debtor's fixed assets. *There is a scarcity of new and used pipe, and prices advanced considerably in the 60 or 90 days preceding the hearing on the proposed plan. How long these unusual conditions may be expected to continue is a matter of speculation.*

Although a precise determination cannot be made of value obtainable in a subsequent liquidation, there is ample ground for the belief that such values would not exceed those presently obtainable and may well be less because of changed market

---

[12] Dewing, The Financial Policy of Corporations (3d ed. 6th reprinting 1939) at 145: "... the rate at which a business shall be capitalized, to obtain its value, will depend on the relative uncertainty or certainty, the relative risk, of the continuation of the earnings. The greater the risk, the greater the doubt of continued earnings and the lower is the capitalized value of these earnings; and conversely, the lower the risk, the greater the value."

[13] [An edited version of this portion of the opinion is in ¶308.]

[14] The Debtor was characterized as a "sick baby" by a member of the Producers Group.

[15] The only reference in the record to rates of return at which other companies are selling indicates that General Motors is selling (after taxes) on a 10% basis. Despite the distinction between selling price and value which was attempted in the testimony, the contrast between General Motors and the Debtor points up the inadequacy of the Trustee's rate.

## TABLE IV
### Value of Reorganized Debtor as Operating Entity

|  | High | | Low | |
|---|---|---|---|---|
|  | Rate | Amount | Rate | Amount |
| ... | | | | |
| Prospective Earnings | 12% | $469,000 | 15% | $436,000 |
| Salvage Value, Fixed Assets | 12 | 428,000 | 10 | 375,000 |
| Net Current Assets[16] | 6 | 320,000 | 6 | 320,000 |
| Sparco Gasoline Co. Stock | | 13,000 | | 13,000 |
|  | | $1,230,000 | | $1,144,000 |
| Less-Cost of Capital Improvements | | 110,000 | | 110,000 |
| Value of Reorganized Debtor As Operating Entity | | $1,120,000 | | $1,034,000 |

conditions and the continued aging of the equipment and pipe. We may therefore adopt [an] estimate of present liquidating value as a maximum measure of the realization available at the end of the Debtor's operating life. However, because of the uncertainties of realization on the fixed assets we believe that the rate of discount to be applied in reducing this realization to present worth should be as high as the rate applicable to prospective earnings. With respect to current assets we believe a 6% rate is appropriate.

### [Conclusion on liquidation vs. reorganization value, and the 28-mile extension]

In our opinion, a reasonable estimate of the operating life of the reorganized company should be taken at approximately five years for purposes of valuation. As indicated in Table IV the value of the reorganized company as an operating entity, on the basis of a five-year life and the other factors set forth above, ranges between $1,144,000 and $1,230,000 before allowance for capital improvements and reorganization expenses. From this must be deducted $110,000 representing the cost of necessary capital improvements. This sum includes $60,000 as the cost of the proposed 28-mile pipeline extension and $50,000 to be extended in connection with the rehabilitation program begun in August, 1940. The net value remaining after this deduction ranges between $1,034,000 and $1,120,000 before reorganization expenses.

[I]t appears that the value of the reorganized Debtor ... would be $1,100,000 before reorganization expenses, provided that the property is managed in the best interests of its security holders as such and that any renewal of the oil purchase contract will be on equitable terms.

---

[16] Based on Trustee's pro forma balance sheet as of March 31, 1941, before deduction of reorganization expenses.

## ¶305: Liquidating or reorganizing: Who should decide?

Now is a good time to break off our reading of *Atlas Pipeline* and think through the questions in ¶303, about why the judge decides whether Atlas should be liquidated or reorganized.

The SEC's advisory opinion notes at p. 40 that on August 17, 1939 the court directed a public sale of the pipeline properties, but required that the minimum bid be $1.2 million. It refused to consider bids that were any lower. No bids came and the reorganization began.

Should the judge have taken the best bid it could have found?

Does the fact that Atlas staggered through the 1930s, unable to repay its debt, strongly suggest that it was a candidate for liquidation? Or does it, in theory, tell us very little about whether Atlas's operations should have been liquidated in 1939?

..................................................................................................................

## Victor Brudney & Marvin Chirelstein, Corporate Finance 31-33 (3d ed. 1987): Value of an Unprofitable Concern

How can a firm claim to have value as a going concern if its net operating income falls short of its fixed interest obligations, and why under such circumstances should it continue (or be continued) in business? If a company which cannot meet its interest obligations is in some sense running at a loss, as it surely is, then does not the decision to continue production have the effect of extending or increasing the loss, and if so, why should such a decision ever be made?

Putting these questions in still another way, if reorganization under chapter 11 permits insolvent corporations to continue in operation instead of winding up, is this simply an act of mercy directed at unfortunate investors, or is there some impersonal, economic justification for it? The following excerpt from [Norman S.] Buchanan, The Economics of Corporate Enterprise, Ch. XII (1940) pp. 332–335 should help to suggest an answer:

> "*Failure in the economic sense and withdrawal of productive capacity.* An examination of the theoretical literature in economics reveals that its authors have apparently not thought it necessary to define 'failure' or scarcely even to employ the term. One reads of the withdrawal of firms from an industry but usually there is no indication of whether failure is taken to be synonymous with withdrawal or antecedent to it. For the broader problems of economic adjustment the important thing is withdrawal of productive capacity, and perhaps for that reason the departure of particular firms which yet leave productive capacity behind has been slighted.

\* \* \*

"If a new enterprise is brought into existence, it is presumptive evidence that those supplying the capital believe that the net returns thereon in this opportunity are greater than those elsewhere available, due allowance being made, of course, for risk and uncertainty elements. On the basis of these prospective returns money capital is invested, real capital goods come into being, and the financial structure of the corporation is reared. If it be granted that new enterprises come into existence because of a prospective return to invested capital here greater than the then going rate, it is perhaps less difficult to indicate what we mean by failure. In the narrow economic sense failure means simply that the returns to capital invested in the opportunity that the promotion was designed to exploit have in fact so fallen short of those expected that, instead of the realized returns being greater than those that were elsewhere available, they have actually proven to be less. Otherwise expressed, we might say that costs being computed on an alternative opportunity basis at the time the enterprise began, costs are in excess of returns.[17] In diagrammatical terms average total cost is in excess of average revenue. The enterprise is a failure in the sense that had this state of affairs been expected or anticipated the firm would not have been brought into being. Hence economically speaking there has been misdirected capital investment; the enterprise is a failure.

"Failure in this sense, however, does not necessarily mean that the resources will be withdrawn from the industry and that production will cease. Whether or not this result will follow will depend upon the degree to which it is possible in the instant case to disinvest the capital entirely or adapt it to the production of alternative products or services. Many capital goods are technologically so highly specialized that they are not adaptable to uses other than those for which they were designed. In this instance the unfortunate circumstance of returns less than those anticipated when the commitment was made is not a sufficient reason for ceasing production. If the alternative to continuing the production of this product is to sell the equipment for scrap, the returns currently secured may be relatively quite high on such scrap value. In that instance the best of the available alternatives is to continue on with the manufacture of the original product; the liquid funds obtained from selling the equipment for scrap if invested in something else will yield a smaller return than that obtainable from using the assets here. The income from production and sale of the product must of course be greater than the direct cost outlays incurred, for otherwise the return on the specialized equipment is zero or negative. But the returns may in some instances fall a good deal before this situation is encountered.[18]

---

[17] This amounts almost to saying that the rate of return on past historical outlay cost has been less than the going rate of interest. Indeed for practical purposes this does well enough for a first approximation.

[18] This is a matter of common observation familiar to everyone. For instance, most street railway companies in the United States earn a negligible return on the basis of past historical capital investment. Yet the equipment being highly specialized in the form of tracks, cars, wires, etc., it is next to impossible to adapt it to other uses and its scrap value net after disinvestment costs is very small. As a consequence such enterprises continue to operate so long as they succeed in securing an income from selling transportation service greater than the direct out-of-pocket costs involved in producing that service by an amount at least equal to a fair return on the net scrap value of the equipment. When the returns fall below that the tracks are torn up and cars sold for kindling wood and scrap iron.

"It is worth noting, however, that failure in this economic sense of an excess of average total cost above average revenue through historical time need not be accompanied at once by financial difficulties, such as a poor credit rating, an inability to meet cash obligations as they mature, etc. That is to say, an enterprise may be a failure in the economic sense defined and yet neither receivership, bankruptcy, nor liquidation follow as a result. Moreover, as we have just indicated, a business enterprise may be a failure in the economic sense (or for that matter in the legal sense too) without a withdrawal of capital equipment from the industry. If the capital equipment is highly specialized and has a small net scrap value a whole succession of enterprises may come into being and pass out of existence before the specialized capital goods are withdrawn from production. Notice also that this statement holds regardless of whether we interpret the term 'enterprise' or 'firm' in its economic sense or in its legal sense. This fact has important economic consequences in that a comparatively long time interval may be required before needed adjustments within a particular industry can be brought about. If the capital goods are comparatively durable, and are not soon rendered hopelessly obsolete by great technological improvements, many years may elapse before the misdirected capital investment will cease to exert its influence on the conditions of supply.

"To attempt to summarize: from the point of view of economic analysis failure means an excess of average costs (in the sense of historical outlay cost) over average receipts; but failure in this sense need not necessarily cause the firm in question to cease operations or default on any of its obligations. Many a firm is a failure in the economic sense and yet neither withdraws from business nor acquires a poor credit rating. Finally, even though financial difficulties do lead to default, and certain well-known legal consequences ensue, the capital goods may nonetheless continue in production for a considerable time interval, and thereby affect the price and total output of the commodity concerned."

## ¶306: Eastern Air Lines

Bankruptcy courts often make what are in effect liquidation versus reorganization decisions at several points during the proceeding. One is obvious: a creditor may ask that the company be liquidated, usually by requesting that the chapter 11 proceeding (a reorganization) be converted to chapter 7 (a liquidation). One creditor group did so in the Eastern Air Lines bankruptcy.

A second is less obvious: when the typical bankrupt enters chapter 11, it has run out of cash. If it doesn't get new money soon, it will be unable to pay its employees on their next pay-date, and if it fails to meet its payroll (or fails to get new inventory, or fails to buy the necessary new machine, etc.), it will be forced to self-liquidate. The firm can, under the Bankruptcy Code, borrow by giving a new creditor a super-priority, but must get court approval. If the court doesn't approve, the firm would usually then have to liquidate.

A third possibility: some firms do find themselves with cash but need court approval to use it. If they cannot use their cash, they will typically be forced to liquidate.

Consider the following news summary of part of the Eastern Air Lines bankruptcy. The unsecured creditors asked that the firm be liquidated, which would have yielded them 2 cents on each dollar of debt they were owed (according to Eastern's trustee). Should the judge have been reluctant to turn them down, if he were only interested in maximizing the value to Eastern's financial owners?

........................................................................................................................

### Agis Salpukas, Court Gives Eastern Air $135 Million: Trustee Is Allowed Use Of Escrow Funds To Keep Line Going, N.Y. Times, Nov. 28, 1990, at D1, col. 1

A Bankruptcy Court judge yesterday allowed Eastern Airlines to draw up to $135 million in escrow funds to help assure that the airline can keep operating through early next year.

In his decision, Judge Burton R. Lifland backed up the business judgment of Martin R. Shugrue, the trustee appointed by the judge in April to try to make the airline viable.

A relieved Mr. Shugrue said the money would enable Eastern to attract advance bookings again. In his testimony yesterday Mr. Shugrue said it was impossible to run an airline by being kept on such a short financial leash.

### "Through the floor"

He said advance bookings went "through the floor" after Nov. 14, when a committee of unsecured creditors urged Judge Lifland to shut the airline down and liquidate it.

At the hearing the judge granted Eastern $30 million out of the funds being held in escrow, with $15 million being made available right away to keep the airline operating.

Mr. Shugrue said many customers took the step as meaning that Eastern could operate for only 15 days unless more cash was allotted. The trustee testified yesterday at the Federal Bankruptcy Court in Manhattan that he could not operate the airline if he was given small amounts of cash that would last only a short time. He said $135 million was what Eastern needed to survive until it could break even, and he said he needed it in one lump sum to reassure customers, suppliers and travel agents that it would keep operating for the long term.

### Warning to Creditors

The unsecured creditors, in this round, did not specifically urge a liquidation; although in their motion they said Eastern "is not and cannot be a viable stand-alone airline." They also warned that "further withdrawal of the magnitude now requested throws into doubt the ability of the estate to conduct an orderly liquidation."

Of the $135 million granted yesterday, $120 million can be used at the discretion of Mr. Shugrue, while $15 million would be set aside by the court as a fund to reassure suppliers. Eastern would have to get the court's permission to use the $15 million.

Mr. Shugrue has predicted that Eastern could begin to break even by March if fuel prices moderated and if its program to attract business passengers continued to work.

Joel Zweibel, the attorney representing the unsecured creditors, repeated many of the same arguments presented at the last hearing, when the committee had urged a liquidation. He said Mr. Shugrue was attempting a turnaround at a time of great Mideast uncertainty. Jet fuel prices have skyrocketed since Iraq's invasion of Kuwait in August, although they have declined recently.

He added that Eastern had continually been unable to meet its own projections and has had to come back to the court for more money from the escrow fund to keep operating.

Mr. Zweibel also said that Mr. Shugrue had estimated that only $40 million, or about 2 cents for every dollar of debt, would go to the unsecured creditors if the airline was liquidated. He said that at the current rate of losses this could be wiped out in less than a month.

Another reason Judge Lifland decided to grant a large lump sum was that in the Nov. 14 hearing the publicity about liquidation hurt Eastern bookings severely. Estimating that the airline lost about $36 million in revenue and costs to counter the negative publicity, Mr. Shugrue said that Eastern customers who wanted to travel in, say, February were booking with competitors since they did not believe that the line would be operating much longer.

Mr. Shugrue said Eastern would have enough funds to carry out a liquidation if that was the only option. He added that the company had set aside for the unsecured creditors more than $252 million in the escrow account, which was accumulated through the sale of Eastern assets like the shuttle and Latin American routes.

## C. Valuation of Atlas Pipeline

### ¶307: <u>Valuing the firm: Atlas Pipeline</u>

1. How much was Atlas Pipeline worth? On August 17, 1939? In September 1941? On December 8, 1941? After 1945?
2. Can we find out what Atlas Pipeline is worth by looking for market bids for its stock? For the whole company? On August 17, 1939, Judge Dawkins put the company up for sale. No bids came in. (P. 40.) Why? Did Dawkins want too much for Atlas?

3. If the market price is deemed unreliable or is rejected for other reasons, what must be done?

4. If expected earnings are discounted to present value, where does the discount rate come from? Must it come from the market, which was rejected in the prior two sets of questions?

5. Return to the question of the projected earnings. How do you project earnings? If you use the past as a guide to the future, which past earnings do you use? The last five years? The last year? The last month? Are past earnings very helpful?

Review ¶214.

## ¶308: *Atlas Pipeline* (continued): Valuation

**In re Atlas Pipeline Corporation, Debtor, Securities and Exchange Commission, Advisory Opinion Release No. 42, under the Corporate Reorganization Act, June 7, 1941, 9 S.E.C. 416 (1941)**

In Proceedings for Reorganization of a Corporation:

### REPORT OF THE SECURITIES AND EXCHANGE COMMISSION ON PROPOSED PLAN OF REORGANIZATION

\* \* \*

### EARNINGS

In order to pass on the fairness and feasibility of a plan of reorganization [and thereby ascertain whether the reorganized Atlas will be able to pay the debts contemplated in the reorganization plan and survive as a going concern], it is necessary to determine the prospective earnings and value of the reorganized property. The capitalization of prospective earnings is the basic element in the latter determination.[19] In estimating prospective earnings we may turn to the past earnings record of the Debtor which, after adjustment for unusual conditions and reasonably foreseeable changes, here provides a guide to what may be anticipated in the future.

### A. Debtor's Past Earnings

Table I presents the Debtor's net income by divisions before and after depreciation for the five years following previous reorganization. In none of these years did the Debtor earn a profit after depreciation, and losses even before depreciation were

---

[19] The United States Supreme Court has recently so held. Consolidated Rock Products Co. v. DuBois, [312 U.S. 510 (1941), infra these materials, at ¶702].

## TABLE I
### Earnings 1936–1940
### By Major Divisions

|  | Net Income Before Depreciation and Non-Operating Expenses | Depreciation | Net Income After Depreciation Before Non-Operating Expenses |
|---|---|---|---|
| | Refinery Division | | |
| 1936 | $(44,472.99) | $143,049.04 | $(187,522.03) |
| 1937 | (357,884.31) | 143,524.58 | (501,408.89) |
| 1938 | (240,776.12) | 145,709.10 | (386,485.22) |
| 1939 | (3,612.17) | 148,090.94 | (151,703.11) |
| 1940 | (60,714.98) | 148,378.80 | (209,093.78) |
| | Pipeline Division | | |
| 1936 | 183,778.05 | 85,092.23 | 98,685.82 |
| 1937 | 316,379.91 | 77,506.48 | 238,873.43 |
| 1938 | 175,692.42 | 80,553.70 | 95,136.72 |
| 1939 | 114,988.32 | 78,117.20 | 36,871.12 |
| 1940 | 108,846.53 | 73,957.25 | 34,889.28 |
| | Other Income (Net) | | |
| 1936 | 32,184.40 | 27,131.23 | 5,053.17 |
| 1937 | 41,391.59 | 26,928.48 | 14,463.11 |
| 1938 | 1,450.00 | | 1,450.00 |
| 1939 | 8,950.33 | 1,414.82 | 5,535.51 |
| 1940 | (25,117.64) | 1,414.80 | (26,532.44) |
| | Total, All Divisions | | |
| 1936 | 171,489.46 | 255,272.50 | (83,783.04) |
| 1937 | (112.81) | 247,959.54 | (248,072.35) |
| 1938 | (63,633.70) | 226,262.80 | (289,896.50) |
| 1939 | 118,326.48 | 227,622.96 | (109,296.48) |
| 1940 | 23,013.91 | 223,750.85 | (200,736.94) |

( ) Loss

shown in two of the five years. It is to be noted also that the refining division reported a deficit before depreciation every year and that such profits as were shown by the Debtor were contributed by the pipeline division.

[Shutdown of Pipeline]

It is against this background of unprofitable operations that the Debtor's prospective earnings must be judged. However, a number of major changes have occurred during this 5-year period. Among the more significant of these is the loss of the Debtor's former business in the transportation of crude oil for the account of others. This pipeline business, which previously had contributed substantial revenues, ceased in September 1940 with the expiration of a contract with the Pure Oil Company. The Debtor's system of gathering lines and the major part of its trunk line are not now in operation.

Since 1936 the Debtor's source of crude oil supply has shifted frequently with the result that it has purchased oil from 10 different fields at varying prices. This has involved changes in the type of oil processed, in the yield of refined products and in operating costs. The most important change that has occurred in this respect resulted from the bringing in of production in 1938 in the Magnolia and Schuler fields of Southern Arkansas. Since these fields are located close to the Debtor's pipe line and since Shreveport is now a natural outlet for some of this production large supplies of lower priced crude have become available to the Debtor.

During the period refinery [capacity has] also changed considerably both in volume and character ..., [rising and falling as its facilities wore out and were rehabilitated].

As a result of the significant changes in the character of the Debtor's operations and in the conditions affecting them, it appears that the five year record of earnings as such does not constitute a satisfactory basis for the calculation of prospective earnings.

## B. Trustee's Estimate of Prospective Earnings

As the basis of his estimates the Trustee has adopted the 5-month period from November 1940 through March 1941. To the Debtor's earnings of this period he has applied various adjustments in arriving at his determination of prospective earnings. The use of this period as a base has certain advantages; it is a recent period, it follows the increase in refinery capacity and in operating efficiency which occurred in October 1940, it gives effect to the cessation of pipeline transportation for the account of others and reflects the predominant use of Magnolia crude on which the refinery would operate during the life of the proposed purchase agreement. It appears therefore that although 5 months is a short record on which to predicate future earnings, the period selected by the Trustee may here constitute an acceptable base period.

As indicated in Appendix A, actual earnings during the five months ended March 31, 1941, were $11,042 before depreciation, bond interest and discount. Without allowance for seasonal variation these earnings are at the rate of $26,500 for a full year. To these earnings the Trustee has applied a number of adjustments as set forth in the following table.

**[Freight Reductions]**

We turn now to [consider] the Trustee's adjustments. The increase of $90,314 in "Sales of Refined Products" represents the Trustee's estimate of the amount by which the Debtor's [profits on] gasoline sales will be increased by certain freight rate reductions ordered by the Interstate Commerce Commission effective June 11, 1941. These rate reductions apply to shipments of refined petroleum products from all the points in the midcontinent field to western trunk-line territory.

The question of how much of this reduction will be retained by the refiner and how much will be passed on to jobbers and wholesalers depends .... [T]he marketing of gasoline in the western trunk-line territory is highly competitive [and] there is a substantial possibility that midcontinent refiners will reduce their prices ..., thus passing on ... part of the savings in transportation costs. [O]f the average rate reduction of .305 per gallon [that the Debtor will receive], only [about].125 will be retained by the Debtor in [profit].

This results in a total increase in sales of refined products of $51,469, or $38,845 less than the Trustee's estimate of $90,314.

Of the remaining adjustments made by the Trustee and shown in Table II, the items "Purchases: Crude Oil" and "Pipeline Operation" are related. The adjustment of $78,733 for "Purchases: Crude Oil" represents the Trustee's estimate of the reduction in the cost of obtaining crude oil which will result from the elimination of a transportation charge of 4 cents a barrel for oil from the Magnolia field. This charge is now made by Standard Oil Company of Louisiana for transporting oil from that field for delivery to the Debtor's pipeline at Gilark, Louisiana. The plan provides for the construction of a twenty-eight mile extension to the Debtor's line at Cornie, Arkansas, which will enable it to reach the gathering lines of the Purchasing Group. This will eliminate the 4 cent transportation charge and will be only partly offset by increased cost of operation of the Debtor's pipeline. Accordingly the Trustee has made an adjustment to actual earnings to reflect this economy. He has also calculated the estimated increase in pipeline expenses incident to the operation of the new extension at 4 cents per barrel. This amounts to $7,873 which the Trustee has shown as an adjustment to "Pipeline Operation." The Trustee's estimate of increased pipeline expense is in accord with the Debtor's experience in the operation of its line and we believe that both this adjustment and the adjustment to "Purchases: Crude Oil" are reasonable.

\* \* \*

## TABLE II
### Trustee's Estimate of Prospective Earnings
### (Before Bond Interest, Bond Discount and Depreciation)

| | |
|---|---|
| Actual Earnings (12 Months Basis) | $26,500 |
| Adjustments Increasing Earnings | |
|     Sales of Refined Products | $90,314 |
|     Purchases: Crude Oil | 78,733 |
|     Purchases: Ethyl Lead | 45,444 |
|     Refinery Fuel | 29,798 |
| Total Adjustments Increasing Earnings | $244,289 |
| Adjustment Decreasing Earnings | |
|     Pipeline Operation | 7,873 |
| Net Adjustments Increasing Earnings | 236,416 |
| Trustee's Estimated Earnings (12 Months Basis) | $262,916 |

## C. Other Adjustments to Earnings

\* \* \*

The Trustee has also adopted without adjustment the average refining margin .... The record indicates that [margins] during the base period were the lowest in the Debtor's history but also indicates that earnings during the period showed substantial improvement as compared with the preceding 18 months.

Since the close of the base period on March 31, 1941, ... advances [have] occurred in the prices of crude oil and gasoline .... [T]here have been wide fluctuations in the refining margins, and although at the present time they show improvement it is not possible to determine what they will be when prices of crude and refined products become more stable. Furthermore, the recent fluctuations do not appear to be of great significance in a consideration of the Debtor's prospective earnings over the remaining economic life of its refinery. The immediate cause of the advance in gasoline prices has been a *"record breaking increase in gasoline demand"*[20] *reflecting*, at least in part, *the stimulus of the defense program.* Although the initial effect has been favorable to the Debtor's operations, the extension of the defense program may result in offsetting developments such as diversion by the Government of means of oil transportation, reduction in automobile output and measures affecting prices. Under all the circumstances, we believe that the Trustee's adoption of the Debtor's refining margin during the base period is reasonable.

\* \* \*

---

[20] Oil and Gas Journal, April 17, 1941, p. 39.

## D. Summary

In arriving at his estimate of prospective earnings the Trustee has taken the actual earnings of the five months period which were at the annual rate of $26,500. To this he has added certain net adjustments in the amount of $236,416 representing estimated improvements which have not yet been realized. Total estimated earnings so arrived at amount to $262,916 before depreciation [of $90,000] and bond interest. It is pertinent to note that these unrealized estimates represent 90% of the earnings forecast and only 10% consists of the actual earnings of the base period.

For the reasons indicated earlier, we believe that the Trustee's adjustment to "Sales of Refined Products" is excessive by about $39,000 and that his estimate of prospective earnings should be reduced by $95,000 to reflect the unusual situation ... that prevailed during the base period. We have also pointed out the degree of uncertainty attaching to the Trustee's estimated reduction of $29,798 in cost of refinery fuel. Taking into account these various factors, it is our opinion that the Trustee's forecast is excessive by at least $135,000 and that the Debtor's reasonably prospective earnings for reorganization purposes do not exceed $130,000 annually before depreciation and bond interest.

Even such an estimate, however, requires substantial qualification. Initially it is to be noted that the Debtor's operation is a marginal one. Prospective earnings of $130,000 represent a profit of only 5.2 [cents] per barrel of crude processed before allowance for depreciation. Thus, *a continued decline in refining margin equivalent to 3/16 cents per gallon of gasoline sold would come near to eliminating all earnings*, before depreciation, reducing them by $115,000. Because of the small margin of profit any such estimate of earnings is subject to a high degree of uncertainty.

[S]avings resulting from the reduction in price of ethyl lead and the lowering of freight rates are available to a great many other refiners[, and competition may force price cuts].

\* \* \*

[T]he estimate of prospective earnings in the amount of $130,000 if applied to an extended period of time is [uncertain]. This uncertainty may be only partially offset by such possibilities as may exist for obtaining pipeline revenues. Therefore, in the light of the foregoing it appears that the estimate of prospective earnings of $130,000 before depreciation and bond interest must be regarded as a maximum.

---

### ¶309: Financial risk vs. operational risk

1. What role does risk play in choosing a discount rate in *Atlas Pipeline*?
2. What are the principal risks the opinion enumerates?
3. Do all of these risks attach to every year of Atlas Pipeline's projected future earnings?

4. A coin flip will pay $100 if it turns out to be heads. The expected value of the flip is surely not $100, since tails do come up sometimes. Thus the expected value must be reduced from $100. Or you could discount the $100 maximum payoff by a rate of 50%. Should you reduce the expected value from the highest potential value ($100) *and* use a steep discount rate of 50%? What happens in *Atlas Pipeline*?

5. A riskless railroad is expected to have certain income of $1 million per year. The riskless rate of interest is 10%. Accordingly, the railroad would be worth $10 million.

Now with risk: The railroad has a 50% chance of realizing the $1 million but has a 25% chance of realizing $2 million and a 25% chance of total disaster, in which it will realize no income.

|  .25  |  .5  |  .25  |
|-------|------|-------|
|  -0-  | $1 million | $2 million |

The expected income in any year will still be $1 million. To establish the present value of this risky income stream would presumably require a higher discount rate than 10%. Say that market participants usually insist on a 2% risk premium for this kind of variance. Use of a 12% discount rate would yield an enterprise value of $8.3 million.

Alternatively, the risky railroad could be viewed as a sequence of two coin flips. In the first flip, the betting investor has a 50–50 chance of getting the $1 million and a 50–50 chance of having to play the double or nothing, zero or $2 million game.

The second game would presumably be worth less than $1 million, because of money's diminishing utility. Say a 0 vs. $2 million bet is viewed in the market as being worth not its expected value of $1 million, but only $660,000. (The risks of this railroad cannot be diversified away, and investors are very risk-averse.) So the second bet is worth only $660,000.

The first bet could then be seen as a bet with a 50–50 chance of a $660,000 or $1,000,000 pay-off. Expected value of the first bet (including the risk adjustment to the second bet, but not to the first bet) would be $830,000. (This result comes from trading off $1,000,000 against a second bet worth $660,000, and ignoring further risk aversion for this first bet.) We have arrived at the enterprise's value via an alternative (but substantively identical) method to manipulating the discount rate.[21]

---

[21] If *another* enterprise has an expected income stream that is perfectly negatively correlated with the railroad subject to valuation and if securities of that enterprise are readily available, then what result in valuing the securities of the subject railroad? I.e., railroad B has an expected income stream that will yield $2 million whenever the first railroad would yield zero, will yield $1 million whenever the first

Which method does the SEC use in *Atlas Pipeline*?

6. The trustee valued Atlas Pipeline as a perpetuity. P. 42. The SEC disagreed. Why? How did the SEC's view affect its valuation of Atlas Pipeline. See p. 45 of the opinion ("improbable [Atlas will] obtain sufficient funds from earnings" to renew itself). What "risks inherent in the enterprise" (p. 43) led the SEC to reject the trustee's 10% capitalization rate and choose a 12%–15% rate?

7. The trustee thought Atlas would obtain $90,000 in freight savings. P. 53. What did the SEC think? What did the SEC do? To the earnings estimate? To the discount rate?

8. Atlas will have to build a 28-mile extension that will cost $60,000 if it is to gain access to new oil. P. 44. How does that affect valuation?

9. A decline in gasoline refining margins of only 3/16 of a cent will reduce Atlas Pipeline's profitability by $115,000. See page 55. What effect on valuation? What effect of an increase in refining margin of 3/16 of a cent?

10. In March 1941, Atlas had crude and refined products in inventory, carried at a value of $194,000. In November 1940, a neighboring refinery took a loss of 20% in disposing of its crude inventory. Yet after the close of the trustee's base period, at the end of March 1941, the price of crude and gasoline had risen; indeed there is a "record breaking increase in gasoline demand." P. 54. In estimating Atlas' liquidation value, the SEC preferred the November 1940 loss as a better indicator of the value of Atlas' inventory in June 1941 than the post-March 1941 advance in prices. Comments?

11. Is the SEC's methodology sound?

12. Did the SEC just pick a low number, reflecting the depression-era economy and then justify the number inadequately? Did the SEC fail to anticipate the subsequent success of Atlas Pipeline? Should it be faulted for doing so? Is there any evidence in the case that people familiar with the oil market at the time of the advisory opinion had reason to believe that those with oil distribution and refining facilities had what was becoming a scarce resource? Why was there "an unusually favorable opportunity for the disposal of the Debtor's fixed assets"? (P. 43.) Why was there a "record breaking increase in gasoline demand" after March 1941? (P. 54.)

13. Consider how Blum & Katz would have dealt with valuing the facilities that were wearing out. And if Atlas's facilities would have been worthless and worn out after five years, how would Blum & Katz value the income from rebuilding and continuing in the sixth year?

---

railroad would yield $1 million, and would yield nothing when the first railroad would yield $2 million. If the securities of both types of railroads are generally available for investors to mix and match, how would risk affect the valuation of the railroad? (As a slightly more realistic matter, no two enterprises could be perfectly negatively correlated in this way. Presumably both would be affected by the general level of economic activity in the country, by war, and by technological change. But they may be uncorrelated in at least some attributes. The railroads could be in different regions of the country; each would be relatively immune to a regional downturn in the other's locale.)

**¶310: Walter J. Blum and Wilbur G. Katz, Depreciation and Enterprise Valuation, 32 U. Chi. L. Rev. 236, 236-41 (1965)**

What function should prospective depreciation of assets serve in valuing an enterprise, especially for purposes of constructing a fair plan of corporate reorganization?

The answer which in the past gained wide acceptance in legal literature can be stated rather simply. Value of an enterprise is to be arrived at by estimating its earnings in future years, on the basis of its assets and prospects as of the time of reorganization, and capitalizing the projected earnings at an appropriate rate. If the firm is viewed as having an earnings capability for an unlimited time, the estimate of annual earnings is to be capitalized in perpetuity. The projection of earnings then must reflect the need to replace major operating assets where it is foreseen that they will lose value through use and that at some predictable date their retention by the firm will become uneconomic in the sense that in operation their worth to the firm will be less than their resale or scrap value. Replacement in this common situation has to be presumed in order to validate the basic assumption that the estimated annual earnings will continue undiminished in perpetuity. The projection of an annual charge for depreciation adjusts estimated earnings to accommodate such replacement in valuing an enterprise.

Under the generally accepted approach to valuation, the total of depreciation charges over the forecasted life of an asset reduces estimated earnings by the expected diminution in the value of that asset resulting from its consumption. The total usually has no connection with the foreseeable cost of replacing the asset with a new or better model. The main reason for tying depreciation to existing asset values is that earnings estimates are usually geared to assets of the firm as of the time of reorganization. It would be incorrect to reduce such estimates by the anticipated cost of higher quality replacements inasmuch as, all other things being equal, these improvements can be expected to enhance the earnings picture.

In placing a value on a perpetual firm, the accepted approach usually entails calculating depreciation charges on the simple straight line annual basis—that is, dividing the total foreseeable charges for an asset by its estimated life. For some assets a case might be made for using an accelerated or retarded pattern of annual charges. But it is sufficient to observe that in reaching valuations there is a strong pull towards using a constant charge. In the typical situation the estimate of earnings, which is to be capitalized, takes the form of a constant figure that represents the most probable annual earnings for the foreseeable future. The quest for a constant annual estimate of earnings tends to be served by constant depreciation and to be thwarted by other patterns.

For purposes of valuing a perpetual enterprise, nothing turns on whether depreciation is thought of as reflecting anticipated declines in values or as reflecting costs which are to be amortized by charges against future operations. The two conceptions produce like results because in valuing an enterprise the total cost of depreciable assets to be amortized is, as previously stated, equal to the total anticipated deterioration in value.

Not all firms are viewed as perpetuities; in various situations it is anticipated that the enterprise will be liquidated at some foreseeable future date and it is not contemplated that major assets are to be replaced. In arriving at valuation in these cases, the prescription which has gained general acceptance is different. Estimated values obtainable on liquidation and estimated annual earnings for the finite period of predicted operation are to be discounted to present value without depreciation being taken into account in computing those earnings. Depreciation can be ignored because the prediction of earnings does not turn on replacing the existing assets of the enterprise. It is only necessary to take account of the estimated cost of maintaining and operating the existing assets until the date assumed for liquidation of the firm.

These principles for valuing perpetual and limited life enterprises were given official expression in corporate reorganization proceedings in the late thirties and early forties.[22] They appear still to receive general acceptance in reorganization literature. However, a reconsideration of the treatment of depreciation seems to be in order. More recent trends in financial analysis suggest that the old standard way of handling depreciation in valuing enterprises viewed as perpetuities is too simple and often leads to incorrect results.

The clue to the source of oversimplification is found in the accepted treatment of an enterprise of limited life. Assume for purposes of analysis that an enterprise is composed of a single asset, a commercial building, which was completed today at a total cost of $1,000,000; assume further that it is estimated to have a [5] year useful life and no scrap value thereafter, and that it is expected to produce an annual net cash inflow of $[300,000] before depreciation; and finally assume that ... there is no income tax, and that all agree that [10]% is the appropriate rate for converting the projected net cash inflow into a statement of present value. If the venture is treated as a perpetuity—meaning that it is assumed that every [5] years the structure will be replaced by an identical building costing $1,000,000—the standard approach would operate as follows: Straight line depreciation of $1,000,000 spread over [5] years would call for an annual charge of $[200,000]; this would bring net cash inflow down to $[100,000] year; and capitalizing that amount in perpetuity at [10]% would result in a valuation of $1,000,000. Suppose, however, it is assumed that the enterprise has a life limited to [5] years and that the building will not be replaced. Under the accepted approach, depreciation would not be taken into account, the $[300,000] of estimated net cash inflow would be valued as a [5] year annuity on an [10]% basis, and the result would be a present value of not $1,000,000 but [a higher value, which calculation will uncover].

Why, against all the dictates of common sense, is the same profitable enterprise found to be worth more as one of limited duration than as a perpetuity? A moment's reflection will point to the treatment of depreciation in the perpetuity calculation as

---

[22] What is referred to as the generally accepted approach is well illustrated in Matter of Atlas Pipeline Corp., 9 S.E.C. 416 (1941).

the root of trouble. The straight line assumption produces an improper timing of earnings and therefore an understatement of value. Depreciation covered by earnings can be thought of as capital which has been disinvested from the depreciated asset and which is now available for other purposes: it can be left at risk generally in the operation of the enterprise; it can be accumulated in a savings account type of sinking fund for replacing the building; or it can be used to reduce outstanding indebtedness of the firm. Under any of these programs the value of the $[200,000] a year taken as depreciation would at the end of [5] years exceed $1,000,000. If the savings account rate of interest were [10]% per annum, the sinking fund would accumulate to [well over $1,00,000] in [5] years ... .[23] Obviously ... the allowance for depreciation is far too generous. What is needed is not $1,000,000 in total charges over [5] years, but charges which, compounded at the proper earnings rate assigned to the disinvested amounts, will grow to a total of $1,000,000 in that time.

It might now be asked whether the straight line approach to depreciation on the basis of existing values always results in an incorrect valuation of the firm. ... The reason why the straight line approach is inappropriate is that it fails to take account of the time schedules for disinvestment and reinvestment. In the illustration, the $1,000,000 of anticipated disinvestment spread over [5] years through earned depreciation of course has a higher present value than anticipated reinvestment of $1,000,000 in a lump sum [5] years from date. A disparity of sufficient proportions between time of disinvestment and of reinvestment always causes straight line depreciation on existing values to produce distorted results; and this is equally true where reinvestment is expected to take place earlier than disinvestment through earned depreciation. Only where such disinvestment and reinvestment are expected to occur on substantially the same schedules—so that the two are in equilibrium—will straight line depreciation based on existing values produce a proper result in valuing the enterprise.

These reflections suggest that an enterprise can be valued without taking *annual* depreciation into account. ...

... The alternative would treat the cost of anticipated asset replacements merely as cash outflows and would offset their negative present values against the valuation otherwise obtained by capitalizing anticipated positive annual net cash inflows. The commercial building case can be used as an illustration once again. The estimated an-

---

[23] $200,000 is set aside at the beginning of each year. If put in the bank at 10% interest, what will the bank account accumulate for each $200,000 set aside.

For year 5: $200,000 x 1.1 = $220,000
For year 4: $200,000 x $(1.1)^2$ = 242,000
For year 3: $200,000 x $(1.1)^3$ = 266,200
For year 2: $200,000 x $(1.1)^4$ = 292,820
For year 1: $200,000 x $(1.1)^5$ = 322,102
$1,343,122

nual net cash inflow of $[300,000] (ignoring depreciation) would be capitalized in perpetuity at [10]%, giving a present value of $[3,000,000]; the negative present value of $1,000,000 to be spent every [5] years to keep the enterprise operating in perpetuity [would be calculated and then subtracted from the present value of the net revenues].

### ¶311: **The concept of depreciation**

A corporation in reorganization expects to have gross revenues of $1 million per year for the next five years. Capital plant will become useless on the last day of the fifth year after reorganization (at which time it will have no scrap value). For five years of expected operation the capital plant will work "like new." It will then collapse in a heap of dust and be worthless. The accounting book value of the plant is $1 million. The ordinary cost of operating the enterprise will be $700,000 per year. (To make the arithmetic simpler, assume that revenues are received, and expenses are incurred, at the end of each year.)

Investors expect an enterprise in this risk class to return 10% per year. There are no taxes or inflation.

What is the value the trustee in *Atlas Pipeline* might accord this company? What would Blum and Katz say?

What would the value of the enterprise be if it were to continue for another 5 years (10 years in all) and the capital plant were expected to be replaced at the end of year 5 for $1 million with a 5 year expected life? The plant's operating expenses will still be $700,000 annually. If the enterprise fails to "save" $1 million from the first 5 years of operations will it be precluded from renewing itself? What does the SEC say about Atlas Pipeline's similar situation? (SEC: "[I]mprobable [that Atlas] will obtain sufficient funds from earnings[.]" p. 42.) What does that presume about capital markets for firms in general or a least for firms emerging from bankruptcy? Should the inability to renew itself affect the capitalization rate for the second five years of operation? For the first five years? What does the SEC say about Atlas' similar problem?

1. <u>Five year life, trustee's methodology, truncated.</u>

|  | 1 | 2 | 3 | 4 | 5 |
|---|---|---|---|---|---|
| Revenues | ? | ? | ? | ? | ? |
| Expenses | (?) | (?) | (?) | (?) | (?) |
| Depreciation | (?) | (?) | (?) | (?) | (?) |
| Net Earnings | ? | ? | ? | ? | ? |
| PV | ? | ? | ? | ? | ? |

Total Present Value=?

## 2. Perpetuity as per trustee.

The trustee takes the expected annual income and turns it into a perpetuity. What is the value of $100,000 per year, forever, at 10% capitalization rate? That's the trustee's valuation.

## 3. The SEC and Blum & Katz.

The SEC says that the trustee's methodology is wrong. The enterprise is not going to live forever and the timing of the depreciation charges is incorrect.

Look at the enterprise as a five year enterprise.

|              | 1   | 2   | 3   | 4   | 5   |
|--------------|-----|-----|-----|-----|-----|
| Revenues     | ?   | ?   | ?   | ?   | ?   |
| Expenses     | (?) | (?) | (?) | (?) | (?) |
| Depreciation | (?) | (?) | (?) | (?) | (?) |
| Net Earnings | ?   | ?   | ?   | ?   | ?   |
| PV           | ?   | ?   | ?   | ?   | ?   |

Total Present Value=?

To paraphrase Blum & Katz, how against the dictates of common sense could the enterprise be worth more dead after five years, than alive?

## 4. Blum & Katz, if the enterprise were continued past year five.

How would Blum & Katz value the enterprise if it were expected to live until year 10?

First take the operating cash flows:

|              | 6   | 7   | 8   | 9   | 10  |
|--------------|-----|-----|-----|-----|-----|
| Revenues     | ?   | ?   | ?   | ?   | ?   |
| Expenses     | (?) | (?) | (?) | (?) | (?) |
| Depreciation |     |     |     |     |     |
| Net Earnings | ?   | ?   | ?   | ?   | ?   |
| PV, **year 6** | ? | ?   | ?   | ?   | ?   |

Total Present Value=?, **in year 6**.

Is the project viable in year 6? Looking from today's perspective, how much is it worth? What if the chance that the firm would be able to re-new itself in year 6 was low? (I.e., the opportunity might not be there, or financing or managerial assets might be unavailable.) Would the risk of non-renewal affect the discount rate to be applied to the net cash flows in years 1-5, or in years 6-10?

## ¶312: *Atlas Pipeline* (continued)

[Now back to *Atlas Pipeline* to see whether the SEC advises the court that the trustee's plan is feasible and fair and then to see what the court does:]

In Proceedings for Reorganization of a Corporation:

REPORT OF THE SECURITIES AND EXCHANGE COMMISSION ON PROPOSED PLAN OF REORGANIZATION

\* \* \*

## SUMMARY OF PLAN

### A. Distribution of Cash and Securities

The [trustee's] proposed plan provides for the organization of a new company to take over the assets of the Debtor. The new company will have the following capitalization:

| | |
|---|---:|
| 4½% First Mortgage Bonds | $1,011,400 |
| 4% Preferred Stock | 435,000 |
| Common Stock ($20 par value) | 100,000 |

Under the plan Federal [and state] tax claims aggregating approximately [$105,000] will be paid in cash .... General unsecured claims aggregating approximately $400,000 will receive 10% in cash without interest ....

The first mortgage bondholders will receive $961,400 of the new 4½% first mortgage bonds, which corresponds to the principal amount of their claims plus accrued interest to May 1, 1941. The remaining $50,000 of new first mortgage bonds will be sold at par to the American Locomotive Company[24] subject to a purchase agreement with the Producers Group hereinafter described. The second mortgage bondholders will receive the new $435,000 issue of preferred stock, corresponding to one-third of the principal amount of their claims, "in exchange not only for the security of their mortgage but for their interest as ordinary creditors in the unmortgaged

---

[24] This company holds $765,000 of the Debtor's second mortgage bonds ....

assets."²⁵ In view of the Debtor's insolvency, as found by the Court, its common stockholders are excluded from participation in the plan.

The common stock of the new company is to be purchased for $100,000 by a group of oil producers (hereinafter called the "Producers Group" or "Group") who own or control substantial oil production in the Magnolia Oil field in Arkansas. As will be noted below, the common stock cannot be divested of control for at least the first 3 years of the company's existence because of failure to pay preferred stock dividends. The plan further provides that the new company shall enter into an oil purchase contract with the Producers Group under which it will agree to purchase all of its crude oil requirements from the group, up to a maximum of 8,000 barrels per day, for a period of 3 years. For such oil the contract provides that the company will pay the price posted in the Magnolia field by the major companies provided, however, that in no event shall the price payable under the contract be more than 5 cents above or more than 5 cents below 93/110ths of the posted price for crude oil in the East Texas field .... The contract ... may not be modified or extended during its life without the consent of those directors who are to represent the bondholders and preferred stockholders on the board.

In addition to their $100,000 payment for the common stock the new company the Producers Group, in order to induce the American Locomotive Company to subscribe to $50,000 of new first mortgage bonds, agree to purchase such bonds from the latter at par plus accrued interest at the rate of $10,000 of bonds each year after consummation of the plan. The Producers Group further agrees that during the life of the 3-year oil purchase contract they will advance the company short-term credit not to exceed $200,000 in the event that additional working capital is needed.²⁶

## B. Terms and Voting Rights of New Securities

The new bonds will be dated May 1, 1941, and will mature in 15 years. They will bear interest at the rate of 4½%. Sinking fund payments are required at the rate of $50,000 per year but it is provided that for the first 3 years this requirement may be met by expenditures for construction and deferred maintenance. It is also provided that the bonds may be purchased by the company in the open market ... and used at

---

[25] ... It appears to be generally agreed that the first and second mortgages do not cover any of the current assets of the Debtor, except for certain materials and supplies with a book value of $41,573. It has also been held in this proceeding that the 10-mile pipeline from Gilark, Louisiana to the Cotton Valley Oil Field is not subject to either lien. State of Louisiana v. Atlas Pipeline Corporation, supra.

[26] Such credit may take the form of cash, commercial credit or crude oil and the Group "may require that the cash, credit or oil so furnished may be secured by an act of pledge, lien or chattel mortgage on the oil in storage and on the refined or manufactured products owned by the company on the basis of one hundred percent (100%) of the lower of cost or market value and together with the face amount of accounts receivable." The plan further provides that such $200,000 loan or credit "may be declared due at any time that the company defaults in the payment for any oil purchased." ...

par in lieu of cash in meeting sinking fund requirements. The lien securing the bonds will extend to the assets covered by the present first mortgage .... The bondholders will be entitled to elect one out of 11 directors.

The preferred stock will carry a dividend rate of 4%. If, after the first year, eight successive quarterly preferred dividends are omitted, the entire voting rights pass to the preferred stock subject to the right of the common stockholders and the bondholders to elect two directors (one for each class).

### C. Summary

The plan, in brief, gives all the common stock and virtually complete control of the Debtor to a group of oil producers who will have a 3-year contract to sell crude oil to the Debtor, under which the latter is obligated to purchase all of its requirements. This group will pay $100,000 for the common stock of the company and will in effect guarantee the $50,000 investment in the new bonds by American Locomotive Company. In addition the group will to the extent required finance the sale of its crude to the new company up to $200,000 by secured short-term credit.

The first mortgage bondholders are required to take a reduction in interest from 6% to 4½%, to extend the maturity of their bonds for 15 years and to give up their lien on approximately $150,600 in cash held by the indenture trustee. The sinking fund requirements in connection with their bonds are also reduced, and their conversion privilege is eliminated. The second mortgage bondholders are required to accept new 4% preferred stock having a par value equal to one-third of the principal amount of their claims.

\* \* \*

## FEASIBILITY AND FAIRNESS

The soundness of any plan of reorganization for the Debtor must be weighed in light of the facts adduced in the proceeding section of this report. To recapitulate, the salient facts are that (a) the Debtor's value upon present liquidation may well equal, if not exceed, its value as a continued operating entity; (b) its earnings prospects are subject to substantial fluctuation, and as a going concern it would operate as a marginal enterprise; (c) its remaining economic life is limited by reason of advancing obsolescence of its refining facilities and its apparent inability to earn the substantial investment to be required within a few years if the enterprise is to be kept competitive.

Especially when viewed against this background, the terms of the proposed plan do not meet the statutory requirement of feasibility. A company emerging from reorganization as a going concern should possess a sound capital structure. The amount and character of the new securities proposed to be issued should be properly related to the value of the property, and adequate provision must be made for working capital and the maintenance of a sound credit status. In a number of respects the proposed plan violates these elementary requirements.

The plan provides for a total capitalization of $1,546,400, consisting of $1,011,400 of 4½% first mortgage bonds, $435,000 of 4% preferred stock and $100,000 par amount of common stock. It has been estimated in the preceding section of this report that the going concern value of the Debtor does not exceed $1,100,000, before reorganization expenses. The proposed new bond issue alone approximates that amount, and it is obvious that the total capitalization proposed in the plan is excessive. The new bond issue would represent 92% of the going concern value; the bonds and new preferred stock would represent 131% of such value; and the total capitalization 140%.

Even if a valuation is assumed equal to the total capitalization proposed in the plan, the capital structure would be unsound, with over 93% of the total capitalization in senior securities and approximately 65% in fixed-interest bearing debt. The plan sets up a capital structure which would be unsound even for a company with a long established record of stable earnings, and we have demonstrated that the Debtor has not been and will not be such a company. In this connection, Mr. Boenning, Chairman of the First Mortgage Bondholders' Committee, testified that "if we were approaching this on a basis of original financing we would certainly not set up the financing as it is set up in this proposed reorganization."[27]

We have emphasized in the preceding section that the company will have an uncertain tenure of existence as an operating unit. In our opinion, for the reasons set out above, it is improbable that the new company will be able during the remaining economic life of its present properties to obtain sufficient funds from earnings to meet its debt service and make the necessary plant replacements to maintain its competitive position. The effort to do so alternatively from the sale of securities would appear doomed to failure, in view of the nature of the proposed capitalization. With its property grossly overbonded and subject to the other deficiencies we have discussed, the plan thus contains the seeds of another early reorganization, or liquidation. In this connection it should be emphasized that the Debtor was reorganized as recently as 1935 (when $880,000 of new money was brought into the enterprise). The present reorganization (the second within 5 years) was precipitated by the high charges and heavy debt structure provided for in the previous reorganization plan. The present plan

---

[27] The creation of an excessive and top-heavy capitalization for the new company (especially in view of its probable limited life) also involves the issuance of deceptive securities worth only a fraction of their face amount. There has been judicial recognition of the added responsibility which the exemption from the requirements of the Securities Act imposes upon the courts to reject any plan which provides for the issuance of unsound securities. In re American Department Stores Corporation, 16 F. Supp. 977, 979–80 (D. Del. 1936), the court, in dealing with this question in a Section 77B case, said: "It is the duty of the court to pass upon the feasibility of the plan of reorganization. Although the plan [was] unopposed, the court should not approve any feature fundamentally unsound. * * *"

may well return the Debtor to this court for a third reorganization, or liquidation, in the near future.

In view of the new company's relatively short prospective life and the marginal nature of its operations, it is important to the Debtor's security holders that the terms and quality of the new securities they are to receive should constitute payment to them as certain and as much as liquidation would produce. In the event of present liquidation, whether or not it produces the estimated [value] discussed earlier, the fact remains that [nearly] all the fixed assets of the debtor ... are subject to the lien of the first mortgage bonds. The proceeds derived from the sale of those assets would therefore be applied to the $961,400 claim of the first mortgage bondholders. The second mortgage bondholders would participate in the proceeds realized from the disposition of all the unpledged assets of the Debtor, together with the first mortgage bondholders to the extent of their deficiency claim, and with general unsecured creditors.

The proposed plan purports to protect the first mortgage bondholders in the event of any early liquidation of the new company, by preserving their creditor position in the full face amount of their present claim. But the security behind the new bonds is diluted by the plan.

Thus, under this plan the property which the first mortgage bondholders may look to at the end of the Debtor's economic life would be less than the property to which they can look for satisfaction of their claims today, and the price which that property would bring at such future date might well be less than present prices. Furthermore, the new bonds which they are to receive upon consummation of the plan will be worth, as estimated by the chairman of the First Mortgage Bondholders Committee, only about half their face amount. The second mortgage bondholders, who are to receive new preferred stock for only one-third of the face amount of their outstanding claims exclusive of accrued interest, give up their creditor position altogether, and on a subsequent liquidation they may well find that they have been deprived of the value of their presently realizable claim against the Debtor's free assets.[28]

To summarize, the plan allocates to the first mortgage bondholders new bonds which, it was testified, will have a value materially less than their face amount, and their security is diluted. In addition, the bondholders' interest rate is reduced from 6% to 4½%, their annual fixed sinking fund requirements are reduced from $100,000 to $50,000,[29] and they surrender the cash deposit of $150,600 now held by the indenture

---

[28] Moreover, they are not to receive the cash payment to be made to other unsecured creditors with claims in the amount of $400,000. This variance in the treatment provided for the deficiency claims of the second mortgage bondholders from the treatment granted the other unsecured claimants appears to violate the principle that all substantial claims having the same legal status should receive the same treatment.

[29] In this respect, moreover, the plan provides, not that $50,000 a year must be applied in retiring bonds, but only that $50,000 face amount of bonds be retired yearly.

trustee for their benefit. If the operating life of the enterprise terminates in three years, bondholders will have received in interest no more than the cash held by the indenture trustee which is presently available to them, and they will face the prospects of liquidation under circumstances which may be less favorable than those at present. The bondholders, moreover, are to be made participants in an excessive and top-heavy capital structure which plainly does not meet the requirements of the Act as to feasibility. In addition, as next discussed, they are to place the fate of their investment in the hands of the Producers Group despite the latter's conflicting interests, and the benefits, if any, which they are to obtain are not shown to be adequate to compensate them for the sacrifices and risks entailed by the plan, leading in our opinion to the conclusion that the plan cannot be considered fair.

As earlier described, the Group, which owns or controls substantial oil production in the Magnolia oil field, will purchase the common stock of the new company for $100,000 (with virtually complete control of the new company for at least the first three years after reorganization), and will agree to advance the new company credit if needed not to exceed $200,000, which may be secured by a lien on inventories and certain current assets. In addition, the new company will enter into a three-year oil purchase contract with the Producers Group.

The contract obligates the Debtor to purchase its crude oil requirements from the group up to a maximum of 8,000 barrels per day, for a period of three years. This makes the new company dependent upon the Producers Group exclusively for its entire supply of crude oil for that period, thereby depriving it of possible advantages accruing from use of diversified sources of supply. The Debtor is so located that it has access to the crude oil production of many fields in addition to Magnolia, and as recently as March 1941 it obtained its crude oil from as many as five different fields. Certain of the fields which the Debtor is in a position to tap, e.g., Cotton Valley, produce a higher grade crude than Magnolia. If it should prove advantageous for the Debtor to use such higher grade crudes, that would be impossible under the terms of the contract which constitutes part of the proposed plan. If the comparable price to the Debtor of crude oil in other fields should drop below the price of Magnolia crude, the Debtor would be prevented by this contract from taking advantage of that fact. As recently as November 1940 the Debtor found it possible to purchase a substantial quantity of distress crude oil at a price 20% below the prevailing market.

Another feature of the contract which may operate to the detriment of the new company is the provision prescribing the price which the new company is to pay the Producers Group for its crude oil. This is fixed by the contract at the price posted in the Magnolia field unless the posted price of Magnolia crude is lower than 93/110 of the East Texas posted price less 5 cents, or is higher than 93/110 of the East Texas posted price plus 5 cents. In the first contingency the company would pay 93/110 of the East Texas posted price less 5 cents. This would be more than the Magnolia posted price and therefore to the disadvantage of the company. In the other contingency, however, the company would pay 93/110 of the East Texas posted price plus 5 cents.

This would be less than the posted price and therefore to the advantage of the company. On the basis of the posted prices May 21, 1941, of $1.25 for East Texas and $1.04 for 38 degrees Magnolia, the company would pay the Magnolia posted price. At the time the plan was filed East Texas crude was selling at $1.10 a barrel, and Magnolia 38 degrees crude was selling at 87. If the contract had been in effect at that time, the new company would have had to pay 88 cents a barrel for this grade, or 1 cent more than the posted price. On March 29, 1941, Magnolia 38 degrees crude was selling at 87 cents and 39 degrees crude was selling at 88 cents, and the price that Atlas would have had to pay under the contract would have been 92.22 cents for either. Thus the operation of the price provisions of the contract throughout the 5 months ended March 31, 1941 would have been disadvantageous to the Debtor.

It is contended, however, that the contract does contain advantages for the new company in providing it with an assured supply of crude oil of uniform grade. Although there was testimony at the hearing on the plan to the effect that the Debtor would benefit from having an assured supply of crude oil it does not appear from the record that the Debtor has ever had any difficulty in obtaining as much crude oil as it needed and could pay for. The Debtor's difficulties have not been with sources of supply, which appear to be ample.[30]

The Producers Group, however, needs the Debtor because without the Debtor they do not have sufficient outlet for their production.[31] Thus, a spokesman for the Producers Group testified: "more or less we are buying a market for our crude which from time to time you have trouble in selling because of the pipeline situation." The interest of the Producers Group in maintaining the outlet for their crude oil production will prompt continued operation of the refinery during the three years even if it is adverse to the interests of the other security holders of the new company. The problem will exist in aggravated form at the end of the three year period. During that time the Producers Group will have received what primarily they are now paying $100,000 for; namely, "a market for our crude." At the end of the period, if operations are to be continued, the position of the other security holders will be materially affected by the arrangements made for further purchases of crude from the Producers Group, which will have obvious conflicting interests. Although the present contract will have expired the

---

[30] There is expert testimony by a member of the Producers Group, who is also a geologist, to the effect that the underground oil reserves in the Magnolia field are equivalent to 23 years production at the present rate.

[31] "Because of the bottleneck in the marketing and pipeline situation in Arkansas. There are no refineries in Arkansas to speak of. The oil there must get out of Arkansas. The refineries there have too much. Even with the small production, it has been top-heavy. So this is a natural home right here for this oil now and I think it will continue unless something—well, there is no other way for it to go. You could not send it to Chicago. With this oil in Oklahoma you could send it north to Chicago or south to the Coast or refine it there. You have a variety of things you could do with it, but that is not true with Magnolia. It has to come down this way or stay there. It could go to Eldorado, but the refineries there own more oil there of their own than they can refine."

Producers Group will still hold 100% of the stock of this corporation, and the decision as to whether the Producers Group will continue to sell crude oil to the company, and upon what terms, will be negotiated by the Producers Group, as vendors, with themselves as directors of the company.

The plan proposes that the Producers Group, who will own all the stock of the new corporation, will finance the latter's purchases of crude oil from the Producers Group to the extent of $200,000, and it is provided that this credit may be secured by a lien on the crude oil so purchased and on the refined products and accounts receivable. Because of the failure of the Producers Group to provide an adequate equity investment, the Debtor must obtain a loan to supply necessary current assets. The Producers Group proposes to make this loan. ...[32]

## CONCLUSION

We believe that the proposed plan cannot be approved as feasible or fair. It has been suggested that the interests of the Debtor's security holders require an agreement with the Producers Group, and that the plan embodies the most favorable terms which could be obtained from them. It is our view that the risks to the Debtor's security holders entailed by disapproval of the plan are outweighed by the sacrifices they are asked to make under the plan, and by the probable existence of alternative courses of action which are not subject to these same objections.

(a) On the assumption that continuation of the Debtor's operations would be in the interests of its security holders, and should rest on a sound capital structure, it does not appear that recent and prospective improvements in the Debtor's earnings will not produce a substantial part of the funds needed for expenses and working capital within a short period as a result of the Trustee's operations, and that the Debtor could not borrow its remaining requirements directly from banks, or similar sources, or indeed borrow all of its requirements from such sources immediately. On that basis the Producers Group's contribution is not shown to be essential to continuation of operations... .[33]

(b) The record contains evidence that there has been interest in the Debtor's property on the part of producers other than the Producers Group as well as on the part of integrated companies.[34] If developed, such possibilities might actually achieve for

---

[32] The inadequacy of equity investment is here shown by the fact that the par value of the new common stock represents only 7% of the total face amount of the securities to be issued under the plan. And on the basis of the going concern value discussed earlier, the new senior securities to be issued (bonds and preferred stock) alone exceed the going concern value by 31%.

[33] In any event, a device such as an underwriting instead of a subscription, by the Producers Group would at least permit the bondholders to retain an interest in the equity, if they so desire while permitting contribution of additional money required for operations.

[34] It appears that Lion Oil Company in December of 1939 was "willing to negotiate an agreement for the purchase of the [Debtor's] properties" on a basis involving issuance by Lion of its own obligations

the present bondholders the benefits of integration which this plan fails to give them. The fact that the record discloses negotiations, in most instances not described, with a number of different interests falls far short of demonstrating that the possibilities along these lines have been exhausted, particularly in view of indications that the parties have unduly restricted their efforts by attempting to work out a plan which would produce a maximum face amount of new fixed obligations for the bondholders.

(c) Finally, if it develops that no reorganization can be effected on a fair and feasible basis, a liquidation of the enterprise may be necessary. In our opinion it is entirely possible that the Debtor's bondholders will fare as well, if not better, in such event than they would under the present plan. We have already considered at length the factors which point in that direction, such as the marginal nature of the enterprise, its necessarily limited life in view of the age of its equipment and the technological advances in the industry, the fact that liquidation will be probable in a relatively few years, and the indications that favorable liquidation possibilities exist at the present time which may not be present later.

By the Commission (Chairman Eicher, Commissioners Healy, Henderson and Pike).

---

## ¶313: In re Atlas Pipeline Corp., 39 F. Supp. 846 (W.D. La. 1941) (July 15, 1941) (Dawkins, District Judge)

The Trustee has presented to the court for tentative approval and *submission to creditors a plan of reorganization for this corporation, which already has the approval of representatives of all classes of creditors.* However, the Securities and Exchange Commission, to whom it was submitted under provisions of the Bankruptcy Act, 11 U.S.C.A. § 1 et seq., has filed a report to the effect that the plan is neither fair nor feasible.

\* \* \*

Since it has been in the hands of this court, first through receivership beginning in May 1939, and then a Trustee in the present proceeding, its operations have experienced a decided improvement. The court has judicially declared it insolvent, eliminated participation of common stock and the proposed plan therefore attempts to provide for the claims of creditors only. The plan will not be quoted or stated in detail.

\* \* \*

---

to the first mortgage bondholders of the Debtor for the full amount of their claims, such obligations of Lion to be secured by all the assets now securing the Debtor's first mortgage bonds. Other Lion obligations were to be allotted to the Debtor's second mortgage bondholders for their claims. Mr. Boenning described this plan as "a very satisfactory deal from the viewpoint of the bondholders."

*The report of the Commission consisting of some sixty odd pages,* criticized the figures of the Trustee in calculating or estimating the prospective earnings and consequent success of the new company in numerous respects, and of course, speaks for itself. I shall not undertake to discuss these in detail, but think it sufficient to say that while no one can be certain as to such matters, I believe that the Trustee has adopted a reasonable and conservative basis for his calculations, which are being borne out by his own experience over the period since certain improvements and changes in operations were instituted in the fall of 1940. The feasibility of the plan would seem to be further attested, if not assured, by the fact that the Purchasing Group, who will have charge of the new management, are men of large means with an assured supply of crude oil, which they agree to furnish upon a reasonable basis, so as to keep the refinery operating at something near capacity. Their investment of $100,000 in the common stock and willingness to extend addition credit or cash for another $200,000 is very tangible evidence of the faith of these experienced operators in the success of the undertaking. When this is considered, along with the fact that bankers and business men of wide experience acting for and interested with the present first and second mortgage bondholders, have unqualifiedly approved the plan, the court would hesitate to turn it down and adopt the suggestion of the Commission that the properties be scrapped and liquidated as junk.

I am impressed that the views of the Commission are somewhat cold blooded and are based on the theory that no new security should be issued which is not worth, at the time, its face value. If the organization of a new enterprise was involved that view might be justified, but when you have a situation such as is presented here, where it is the duty of the court to try to protect the interest of all creditors as far as the assets and circumstances of the debtor permit, a more practical view should be taken. Liquidation, according to the Commission's own calculation, would wipe out the second mortgage creditors entirely, except to the extent that they might participate along with the ordinary creditors in the free assets.

It seems to me that the proposal is fair in that it preserves the position of the first mortgage creditors to the full amount of their principal and accrued interest, and the only sacrifice they are making is in the reduction of the interest rate from 6 to 4½% for the future. At the present time, the latter is more than can be obtained on a reasonably safe investment and the very spirit of the law which permits reorganization of embarrassed corporations appears to contemplate that there shall be some giving and taking by all concerned. If it is probable that the plan will realize a greater portion of the equity of any class of creditors in the assets of the corporation, then this is a sufficient consideration for the sacrifices that may be made to that end ....

Under all the circumstances, I think that the plan is both fair and feasible, and should be submitted to the creditors for their consideration.

Proper decree should be presented.

**¶314: Earlier in the Proceeding: First Trust Co. of Philadelphia v. Atlas Pipeline Corp., 29 F. Supp. 32 (W.D. La. 1939) (August 7, 1939) (Dawkins, District Judge)**

Upon the application of the First Trust Company of Philadelphia, Trustee, under the first bond mortgage, on May 26, 1939, a temporary receiver for all property and effects of the Atlas Pipeline Corporation was appointed, and upon contradictory hearing held later, the appointment was made permanent.

The property has been administered and the business carried on as a going concern since that time. Subsequently, *the said Trustee applied to have the receiver sell the entire assets as a going concern*, publication was made and notice sent out to all creditors, and on July 26, 1939, hearing was had, at which, informal or oral objections to granting the order of sale and for an adjournment or postponement of thirty days was made in open court by counsel representing some of the second mortgage creditors. At the same time, counsel for the Atlas Pipeline Corporation excepted to the procedure ....[35]

The Court declined to grant the postponement, allowed the proof to be offered by the applicant in support of its petition for the order and at the conclusion, granted attorneys who had appeared for the second mortgage bond holders twenty days or until August 15 to continue and complete the arrangements for an adjustment of matters between the two groups, that is, first and second mortgage bond holders. The exception of the Atlas Pipeline Corporation was taken under advisement.

\* \* \*

The property and affairs of the Atlas Pipeline Corporation are under the control of this Court through a general receiver, and any bona fide creditor whose interest might warrant, could apply for the sale of the property. At the hearing on such application, the Court might, as the circumstances justified, order a sale, and refer to a master the liquidating or establishing claims to the proceeds. On the other hand, it could permit the proving of such claims after sale ....

\* \* \*

The exception of the Atlas Pipeline Corporation will be over-ruled and the Receiver is directed to notify the holders and representatives of both first and second mortgage bond holders that on August 15, if amicable disposition of this matter is not had in the meantime, the Court will determine the amounts due or outstanding under the second bond mortgage issues, as well as the sum necessary to be deposited in cash in bidding upon said properties.

---

[35] [Why would Atlas oppose a sale? Could stockholders be expected to oppose a sale?—Roe.]

## ¶315: After the reorganization

**Victor Brudney & Marvin Chirelstein, Corporate Finance 57 (3d ed. 1987): The Aftermath of the Atlas Pipeline Case**

Atlas Pipeline Corporation emerged from reorganization as Atlas Oil and Refining Company in January 1942. The prices at which its bonds sold are as follows:

|      | 1942 | 1943 | 1944   | 1945   | 1946    | 1947    |
|------|------|------|--------|--------|---------|---------|
| High | 88   | 95   | 100    | 99-1/2 | 103-3/4 | 102-1/2 |
| Low  | 62   | 80   | 92-1/2 | 90     | 98      | 92      |

The enterprise apparently succeeded beyond all expectations. The following are its earnings before taxes and interest, after taxes and interest and per share of preferred stock and of common stock for the years ended November 30, 1943 and 1944, the only years for which figures are available:

|                                        | 1943      | 1944      |
|----------------------------------------|-----------|-----------|
| Before taxes & interest                | $515,422  | $966,955  |
| After tax & interest                   | 134,818   | 242,093   |
| Per preferred (4350 shares outstanding)| 30.99     | 60.06     |
| Per common (5000 outstanding)          | 23.48     | 45.19     |

Atlas' common stock was purchased by Standard Oil (Ohio) periodically; by the end of 1945 Standard Oil owned 28% of the common stock, by the end of 1946 it owned 57% of the common stock, and in 1948 the bonds and the preferred stock were retired. As of the end of 1943 only $513,200 principal amount of the bonds was outstanding. The bonds in Atlas' treasury had been acquired by the company at a discount of approximately 11%.

### D. The capital layers

## ¶316: Henry B. Gardner, The SEC and Valuation Under Chapter X, 91 U. Pa. L. Rev. 440, 460–64 (1947)

... Suppose that an industrial [company] in a relatively stable industry with a good record of earnings and a reasonably bright future is capitalized as follows:

| | | |
|---|---|---|
| 4% | $5,000,000 (face) | |
| 6% preferred | 3,000,000 (par) | |
| common | 1,000,000 | |

Assume that a bond maturity coincides with a temporary financial panic so that refunding is impossible, the bonds are defaulted and the company files under Chapter X. Assume further that reasonably prospective earnings are found to be $900,000, and that these are capitalized at 10 per cent, giving a going concern value of $9,000,000. As the bondholders' and preferred stockholders' claims are $5,000,000 and $3,000,000, respectively, the common stockholders would be entitled to receive no more than $1,000,000 in assets value, or one ninth of the total. For purposes of illustration suppose the enterprise emerged from reorganization with a capital structure patterned upon the old, as follows:

|   |   |
|---|---|
| 4% bonds | $5,000,000 (face) |
| 6% preferred | 3,000,000 (par) |
| No par common | 1,000,000 |

On the annual earnings, $200,000 would be consumed in interest on the bonds, and $180,000 in dividends on the preferred. As the bond interest would be covered 4½ times, it would seem not unreasonable to suppose that the bonds would sell at par in a normal market, and as there would be overall coverage on the preferred of 2⅓ times, it would seem that it too might normally command par. The plan would hence appear feasible as well as fair to the bondholders and preferred stockholders. It will be observed, however, that of the prospective earnings of $900,000, the sum of $520,000, or nearly 60 per cent, would be left for the common, which according to our computation had a maximum going concern value of only $1,000,000. This hardly makes sense.[36] The apparent absurdity of holding that stock which will receive over half the company's total earnings represents only one-ninth of the value of the enterprise would be of little practical consequence provided the company should emerge from reorganization with the foregoing structure. If the common stock is to realize $520,000 in earnings, it will make little difference to its holders that it has been found to have a going concern value of only a million. If, however, the company was reorganized under an all common stock plan, the consequence to the old common stockholders of holding their interest to represent a going concern value of only a million would be very great, for they would then be entitled to receive a maximum of only one-ninth of the new common, upon which they could expect to realize annual earnings of no more than $100,000. ... The bondholders, on the other hand, would receive a minimum of five-ninths of the common, upon which they would realize annual earnings of $500,000 as against their former interest of $200,000, and the preferred stockholders at least three-ninths of the common, upon which they would realize earnings of $300,000 as against their former dividend of $180,000.

It may be suggested that the apparent absurdity and unfairness encountered in the foregoing examples result from the use of a flat 10 per cent capitalization which

---

[36] The market would certainly consider the common worth more than a million dollars; that is, it would apply to earnings a less conservative capitalization rate than 52%.

on its face fails to recognize that different segments of earnings are subject to varying degrees of risk that they will not be realized. This suggests the propriety of capitalizing each segment of earnings at a rate which will fairly reflect the risk attached to its realization. For example, if the company has a stable record of earnings and indicated prospective earnings of $900,000, it would seem that the risk that it will not earn at least $200,000 is relatively slight. This might then safely be treated as a fixed charge and capitalized at, say, 4 per cent into 4 per cent bonds for the old bondholders, which, interest being covered 4½ times, might reasonably be expected to sell at par in a normal market. If we take $180,000 as the next segment of earnings, it is clear that the chance that it will not be earned, while somewhat greater, is still comparatively slight. This segment might safely be treated as a preferred stock dividend and capitalized at, say, 6 per cent into 6 per cent preferred for the old preferred stockholders, which, since there would be overall coverage on its dividend of 2⅓ times, might be expected to be worth par in a normal market. If we take as our last segment the remaining earnings of $520,000, it is apparent that the chance that it will not be realized is comparatively great, and that a considerably higher capitalization rate, say 15 per cent, should be employed. Use of a 15 per cent rate would give a going concern value of about 3½ million to this last segment, which might reasonably be capitalized as common stock for the old common stockholders. The result would be a going concern value of about 11½ million.[37]

Whatever merit the varying rate technique may possess lies in the fact that it, as does the market, recognizes that different degrees of uncertainty attach to the realization of different segments of earnings. In the foregoing example, for simplicity's sake, the first two segments chosen corresponded exactly to the interest and dividend requirements of the old bonds and preferred. It is apparent, however, that other segments might have been used, appropriate adjustments being made, where necessary, in the allocation of securities for changes of position. For example, it might appear desirable to simplify the corporate structure and to capitalize the first $400,000 of prospective earnings into new preferred, which, being the senior security, might reasonably be capitalized at 5 per cent, and be expected to sell at par in a normal market. If the remaining earnings were capitalized into common at 15 per cent, approximately the

---

[37] If, in the example given, prospective earnings had been $800,000 instead of $900,000, capitaliz[ing the earnings] at a flat 10% rate would shut out the common completely, although under the old set-up $420,000, or over 50% of earnings, could have been left for the common. Application of a varying rate might work out somewhat as follows: the first $200,000 of earnings capitalized at 4% into 4% bonds for the old bondholders; the remaining earnings capitalized into common, the first $300,000 segment at, say 10% and the second $300,000 segment at, say, 15%. This would result in a going concern value of $10,000,000. Of the new common shares representing $5,000,000 of going concern value the old preferred stockholders would be entitled to receive the fair equivalent of their old stock. Just how much new common would be a fair equivalent would depend upon a balancing of their higher income and perhaps increased voting power against their loss of position. The important point, however, is that, irrespective of the precise division, use of a varying rate would seem to justify substantial participation by the old common stockholders.

same total value would result. Even were the new capitalization to be in common alone, it would seem appropriate in computing total value to take into account the fact that the realization of different segments of earnings is subject to different risks.

In opposition to use of the varying rate it may be urged that it multiplies questions soluble only in terms of business judgment. In lieu of the determination of one flat rate, it requires not only the determination of earnings segments but also the fixing of a different rate for each segment. Furthermore, its use will normally result in a determination of the capital structure before enterprise value is determined, but this, while somewhat unconventional, does not seem open to serious objection. Finally, it may be urged that if in our illustration we had used a flat rate of 8 per cent instead of 10 per cent we would have reached approximately the same value that was obtained by employing varying rates. In other words, it may be argued that the flat rate should be a composite of the varying rates, and that there is, therefore, no need for departure from the conventional flat rate method. This would seem, theoretically at least, to be so. There would seem to be less chance of serious error, however, in taking several small jumps, guided in each by reference to what appears to be a fitting financial structure and subject more or less to market check in fixing segment risk, than in taking one relatively unguided big jump. Hence, at the very least, employment of the varying rate would appear to be a useful means of discovering what the composite rate ought to be.

## ¶317: Questions on Gardner

1. Use Gardner's approach to segment the trustee's expected earnings of Atlas and his proposed capital structure. What are the implicit capitalization rates for each layer in the proposed capital structure? Does the trustee's proposal make sense? What explanations are there for the result?

    |  | Value | Income | Percentage return |
    |---|---|---|---|
    | Bondholder | ? | ? | ? |
    | Preferred | ? | ? | ? |
    | New shareholders | ? | ? | ? |
    | Overall company | ? | ? | ? |

2. Could these results, particularly the percentage return you just came up with for the new shareholders, explain the SEC's opposition to the trustee's plan? But why don't the Firsts, or their representatives, object? Why are the Seconds (American Locomotive) throwing more money into the enterprise? What conflicts of interest are there?

3. How much does the trustee expect the First's new bonds to trade at after the reorganization? See pp. 41, 66 (footnote).

4. Is there any way to justify the plan as beneficial to the Firsts? If the Firsts reject the trustee's plan, what follows? Another plan? Another two years of process? Another SEC advisory opinion? A court confirmation hearing? Appeals? When was the last time the Firsts received interest on their bonds? Could well-informed bondholders rationally approve the trustee's plan?

## ¶318: *Atlas Pipeline* and decapitalization

The SEC argues Atlas will not be able to renew itself because it will not be able to obtain sufficient cash from operating profits, given the obligations under the trustee's plan, to pay for a new pipeline and refinery. P. 42. Where is the cash going during the first five years? Does that explain (a lot of) the operational problem?[38]

(The SEC says that the plan is excessively top-heavy. "[T]he [proposed] capital structure [is] unsound, with over 93% of the total capitalization [in] senior securities and approximately 65% in fixed-interest bearing debt." Does Gardner's segmentation analysis provoke us toward a different view?)

Let's accept the SEC's view that the plan is excessively top-heavy. Can we solve it by requiring new sacrifices from bondholders?

The SEC assumed that Atlas Pipeline would not have access to the capital markets to finance worthwhile projects at the end of the five-year period. What if parties to a reorganization recognize and agree with that perspective? How could they remedy the decapitalization problem? Must the old capital structure (with its attendant debt) be preserved?

Consider the following hypothetical: Company A is in reorganization. It owes $1 million at 6% interest per year to a creditor. It has no current cash and its operations will produce none for at least five years. In year 5 it will need $350,000 for crucial new capital expenditures for the factory. Neither the SEC, the creditor, nor the stockholders expect the company to be able to go successfully to the capital markets in, or before, the fifth and critical year.

The SEC (or the trustee, or the judge, or one of the parties—the stockholders' representative or the creditor's representative) suggests that the company pay no cash for the next five years to the creditor. The creditor says she will agree, but not if the elimination of the cash payment is simply a gift to the stockholders. The creditor will agree only if paid the $1 million otherwise. How? asks the common stockholders' representative? In common stock, she replies.

What result? Assume the company is worth $1.5 million in the creditor's view. Common stockholders, however, think the stock is worth $3 million (or could well be

---

[38] The cash drain from the sinking fund is more than $50,000 per year. For three years improvements to plant can satisfy the requirement. Thereafter, says the SEC at p. 41, "the annual sinking fund requirements will be met by the purchase of $50,000 face amount of bonds at $25,000."

worth $3 million when the court gets around to a valuation hearing). Can the parties reach agreement on an all common stock plan? What percentage of the stock will the creditor insist she receive? What percentage of the stock will the stockholder insist upon? The first recapitalization proposal has the company recapitalizing with only 300 shares of common stock. Can the parties agree how many shares each will get? Would a plan that essentially reconfirms the debt, but just tinkers at the edges with it (i.e., reduces interest a little, moves or keeps the maturity date for the debt short-term (only a few years), and/or gives the debtor only a little stock) face the same valuation tension? Resolvable? If so, how?[39]

| Recapitalizing a 300 share bankrupt company | | | |
|---|---|---|---|
| | Value of company | Bondholders' stock entitlement | Common SH's stock entitlement |
| Bondholder's opinion | ? | ? | ? |
| Common Stockholder's opinion | ? | ? | ? |

### E. Advisers and conflicts

### ¶319: Joseph Kennedy, Big Business, What Now?, Saturday Evening Post, Jan. 16, 1937, at 10, 11, 80

The activities of protective committees constitutes one of the most dismal chapters in the annals of American finance. The theory of a protective committee is very simple. A company gets in financial difficulties. A single security holder cannot act effectively for himself. Hence a committee seeks to secure authority to act for the security holders. But in practice it has resulted in the most vicious kind of imposition, double-dealing and downright fraud. The investigation by the SEC has revealed two general types of protective committees, and in their practices there is little to choose between them. The first, and by far the more common, is the investment-banker committee, and the second is what might be called the entrepreneur type, which is sponsored, usually, by a lawyer and is seldom but a racket for fees.

The investment banker who sponsors a protective committee usually justifies his conduct on the ground that he is protecting the investor to whom he sold securities. This is seldom, if ever, true.

The investment banker, excepting rare cases, organizes these committees for selfish purposes, and the interests of the security holders are a secondary consideration at

---

[39] More complex securities, such as the exchangeable bonds and options discussed in Chapters 15 and 17, might reduce the problem.

best. The record of the commission's investigation teems with instances where there existed major conflict of interest. In many cases, the investment bankers organized committees to act for one class of security holders when they themselves held large blocks of a different class of securities. There was bound to be a conflict, to the detriment of the hapless and helpless investor.

In many instances, the bankers organized a committee for the express purpose of taking command of the reorganization and, by covering up the evidence of their past wrongdoings, insulat[ed] themselves against liability. In practically every case, the bankers were motivated by a greedy desire to preserve or secure control, so that they might enjoy the perquisites thereof. This is the equivalent of what we call "graft" in public life.

In addition to all these factors, the legal fraternity have distorted, by the most ingenious phraseology, a simple relation of principal and agent into a status where the agent lays down all the conditions and the principal who owns the security and does the hiring has nothing to say.

After signing on the dotted line, the principal finds himself bound hand and foot by his protective committee.

........................................................................................................

Joseph Kennedy, the author of the article, was the first chair of the SEC. Boenning and Company, a Philadelphia investment bank, underwrote some of Atlas' bonds and represented the First Mortgagee bondholders in the reorganization proceedings.

## ¶320: Modern variations

If investment bankers' conflicts of interest, due to previous relations with the company and its bondholders, are a problem, are there ways other than those pursued in *Atlas Pipeline* of dealing with those problems? The following case deals with the issue of whether an investment banker's prior dealings with the bankrupt disqualified it from working for the bankrupt company. (Note the difference with *Atlas*: Boenning and Company represented the creditors in the reorganization, not the company itself.)

### In re Eagle-Picher Indus., Inc., 999 F.2d 969 (6th Cir. 1993)

RYAN, Circuit Judge. The United States Trustee, M. Scott Michel, appeals an order of the district court that affirmed a bankruptcy court order allowing the debtors to employ the investment banking firm of Goldman, Sachs & Co. as a financial adviser. The appeal's sole issue is whether the bankruptcy court erred in concluding that Goldman, Sachs is a disinterested party within the meaning of the bankruptcy code, and so properly able to serve as the debtors' financial adviser.

Concluding that the bankruptcy code makes it quite clear that Goldman, Sachs is not a disinterested party, we reverse.

I.

The debtors, all currently operating their businesses as debtors in possession,[40] moved the bankruptcy court for leave to employ Goldman, Sachs to advise them financially in connection with their reorganization under Chapter 11 of the bankruptcy code. The United States Trustee[41] objected to the employment of Goldman, Sachs because of a preexisting affiliation between the parties—principally because Goldman, Sachs served as managing underwriter for [the bankrupt] on a number of outstanding revenue bonds.

The bankruptcy court rejected the Trustee's objections to the appointment, finding that the preexisting affiliation between the debtors and their proposed financial advisor is precisely the reason why Goldman, Sachs should be appointed; Goldman, Sachs, the court reasoned, "will need less time to familiarize itself with the Debtors' business and affairs than another financial adviser." Noting that [Goldman] does not hold or represent an interest actually adverse to the debtors, the bankruptcy court concluded that the prior relationship does not preclude the firm from being employed as the debtors' financial adviser, especially because "the retention of Goldman Sachs is the most efficient and economical way in which to proceed with the administration of the Chapter 11 cases."

In short, the bankruptcy court concluded that for the purposes of the bankruptcy code, "Goldman Sachs is a 'disinterested person.'" The district court affirmed, and the U.S. Trustee timely appeals.

II.

A.

The debtors concede, in the brief they filed with this court, that "Goldman Sachs technically is not a 'disinterested person' under 11 U.S.C. § 101(14)(B) because Goldman Sachs was an investment banker for outstanding securities of the Debtor." They go on to argue, however, that it is necessary for the U.S. Trustee to show facts that demonstrate the existence of an "actual conflict" of interest in order for Goldman, Sachs to be considered a non-disinterested party within the meaning of the bankruptcy code.

---

[40] [Under today's Bankruptcy Code, management of the company usually can assume the role of trustee and run the firm in bankruptcy. When a trustee is not appointed to replace incumbent management, the debtor is said to remain "in possession" of its property, which does not pass into the hands of a trustee.—Roe.]

[41] The U.S. Trustee, a Department of Justice official responsible for the oversight of bankruptcy cases, "may raise and be heard on any issue in any case or proceeding." 11 U.S.C. § 307.

In response, the government simply points out 1) that Goldman, Sachs is an investment banker; 2) that it served as an underwriter for outstanding securities; and 3) that it continues to serve as a remarketing agent for one outstanding bond issue. It is these factors, the government argues, that disqualify Goldman, Sachs from serving now as the debtors' financial adviser.

B.

The bankruptcy code prescribes certain standards for the employment of professional persons to assist in a reorganization:

> (a) Except as otherwise provided in this section, the trustee,[42] with the court's approval, may employ one or more attorneys, accountants, appraisers, auctioneers, or other professional persons, that do not hold or represent an interest adverse to the estate, and that are disinterested persons, to represent or assist the trustee in carrying out the trustee's duties under this title.

11 U.S.C. § 327(a).[43] The employed person, it is clear, must be both without an interest adverse to the estate and disinterested. The bankruptcy code defines the term "disinterested person" as follows:

> (14) "disinterested person" means a person that—
> ...
> (B) is not and was not an investment banker for any outstanding security of the debtor; [or]
> (C) has not been, within three years before the date of the filing of the petition, an investment banker for a security of the debtor.

11 U.S.C. § 101(14). The code carves out, however, a narrow exception to section 327(a)'s requirement of disinterestedness [for those who were merely employed by the debtor-in-possession. 11 U.S.C. § 1107(b)].

III.

The language of section 327(a), when read in conjunction with the definitions set out in section 101(14), does not leave room for debate: Goldman, Sachs is and was an investment banker for outstanding securities of the debtors, and as such, is not a disinterested person within the meaning of the statute. To read section 1107(b) as providing

---

[42] [Again, recall that when incumbent management run the bankrupt as a debtor-in-possession, they assume the statutory responsibilities of the trustee.—Roe.]

[43] This section refers to the powers of a "trustee," but under 11 U.S.C. § 1107(a), a debtor in possession has the same rights, powers, and duties as a trustee.

an exception to this case would be to rob sections 101(14)(B) and (C) of any meaning in cases with debtors-in-possession .... [S]ection 1107(b) is a narrow exception, meant to apply only when the sole reason for disqualification is former employment. Goldman, Sachs was formerly employed as Eagle-Picher's investment banker—but, moreover, was the investment banker for an outstanding security. This is more than "mere" employment.

It is, moreover, clear from both the statute that a person can be not "disinterested," yet without an adverse interest. Although it may make little sense to the bankruptcy court and the debtors—or, for that matter, to this court—that Goldman, Sachs is not permitted to serve as financial adviser, the statute requires that result. This court is bound to apply the plain meaning of the statute even when the application apparently results in an apparent anomaly.[44]

IV.

In short, irrespective of whether one understands the rationale behind the statute's mandate, there is simply no reasonable basis for ignoring it. Goldman, Sachs is not a disinterested person within the meaning of the bankruptcy code. The bankruptcy code accordingly directs that Eagle-Picher may not hire Goldman, Sachs. We, therefore, REVERSE.

## F. Valuation of Duplan

### ¶321: Price-earnings ratios: In re The Duplan Corporation, Advisory Report of the Securities and Exchange Commission on Proposed Plan of Reorganization, 20 S.E.C. Docket 189 (May 2, 1980)

[The Duplan Corporation was from its inception in 1917 until the mid-1970s, an innovator and leader in the development of textile products. In the late 1960s, Duplan began a program of diversification by acquiring several corporations in businesses related to the textile industry. After a sharp decline in the double knit industry in the mid-1970s, Duplan was forced into bankruptcy under Chapter X in August 1976. During the bankruptcy, the trustee sold many of the unprofitable subsidiaries. The trustee promulgated a plan of reorganization in late 1979 which called for Duplan to retain two primary operating divisions, Wundies, Inc. and Rochester Button Division (RBD). Wundies manufactured sleepwear and thermal undergarments. RBD was the largest domestic manufacturer of buttons. Both divisions operated on a "substantially autonomous basis" from the parent company.]

---

[44] ... [T]o the extent that the bankruptcy and district courts based their decisions in this case on equitable considerations—namely, the familiarity of Goldman, Sachs with the debtors' business operations—their reasoning was, inappropriate. [The statute is clear.]

Total funded debt[45] was as follows:

|  | Principal (000 omitted) |
|---|---|
| Term bank loans | $38,500 |
| Subordinated notes | 6,045 |
| 5½% convertible subordinated debentures | 19,198 |

The subordinated notes are subordinated to the bank debt. The debentures are subordinated to both. Claims of trade creditors are estimated at $2.6 million .... The notes and debentures are not subordinated to the trade claims, and the trade claims are not subordinated to anyone.[46]

As the debtor is insolvent, the plan makes no provision for the preferred and common shares.

[The trustee's plan proposed to pay the bank $24 million in cash, leaving the bank $14 million in additional claims. The bank's claims and the other creditors' claims would be satisfied by dividing up the remaining value of Duplan via common stock.]

**Table III**
The Duplan Corporation
Distribution Pursuant to Trustee's Plan [abridged]

|  | Amount of claim (after cash payments) | Stock issued (at $10 per share) |
|---|---|---|
| Bank | $14,124 | $9,124 |
| Sub. notes | 6,104 | 6,104 |
| Sub. deb. | 19,814 | 8,093 |
| [Other claims | ———— | 4,000 (approx.)] |
| Total |  | 27,200 |

## A. Valuation

The "value" of a business or property is based on expectations of profit. As the late Judge Frank of the United States Court of Appeals for the Second Circuit observed, "Value is the present worth of future anticipated earnings. It is not directly dependent on past earnings; these latter are important only as a guide in the prediction of

---

[45] [Debt with a maturity of more than one year.]

[46] [This structure, a common one, will be examined in more detail in Chapter 4.—Roe.]

future earnings."[47] Thus, to arrive at the value of a debtor's business, prospective earnings are capitalized at a rate derived from market yields on comparable businesses.

Bear Stearns & Co. ("Bear Sterns"), an investment banking firm, was employed by the estate in valuing the debtors.

All of the testimony relating to going concern value and tax loss was based on forecasts, discussed in Appendix B, of the two operating divisions, Wundies and RBD, prepared by their respective managements.

[An analyst employed by the estate] also questioned whether the forecasts for 1980 correctly gauged the duration of the recession and pointed out that costs for the additional facilities which Wundies will require to meet its expected enlarged business after 1981, have not been allowed for. [That firm] similarly criticized the omission of interest costs for Wundies recurrent inventory loans. [The subordinated noteholders' investment banker] was of the view that the forecasts should not be considered. It valued the going businesses by multiplying 1979 projected earnings, $2,120,000 by five, producing a value of $10.6 million rather than $14.4 million.

\* \* \*

**B. ...**

**C. Value of Duplan (Reorganized)**

The following table shows the value of the reorganized company as arrived at by Bear Stearns and [the noteholders' banker].

| | [Edited table] (000 omitted) | | |
|---|---|---|---|
| | Bear Stearns | Adjusted | [Noteholders] |
| Capitalized Earnings | $14,450 | $14,450 | $10,600 |

*[Our corrections, which increased Duplan's value by $12,740,000, leaving an adjusted value for Duplan of $27,190,000,] are explained in the prior two tables. [These adjustments to the capitalized earnings figures accounted for the value of special tax deductions available to the bankrupt company, the value of Duplan's accounts receivable, and the value of a lawsuit that Duplan had brought.]

The valuation of the ongoing business depend[s] on the income forecasts. [O]ur conclusion as to the reorganized company's consolidated earnings potential does not differ significantly from that of Bear Stearns. We accept Bear Stearns' conclusion as to annual after-tax earnings of about $2.9 million.

---

[47] [Jerome] Frank, Epithetical Jurisprudence and the Work of the Securities and Exchange Commission, 18 N.Y.U.L.Q. Rev. 317, 342, n.68 (1941).

The capital value of Duplan's common stock is expressed as a times-earnings multiple of income. A multiple of five, for example, means a 20% annual return of yield on the investment. The expected yield differs according to the kind and quality of the investment, since it reflects the risks and uncertainties as to what the actual earnings will be.

The times-earnings multiplier is linked to actual market values by looking to the relationship between market price and earnings of comparable investments, as Bear Stearns did. Here again, the reorganization valuation process conforms to standard methods of investment decision making. Prices actually being paid for equivalent commodities are the best evidence of the yield that should be employed in determining current capital values of projected income.

\* \* \*

Bear Stearns concluded that the four-year average of management's *projected* after-tax earnings of $2,890,000, would be a reasonable estimate of reorganized company's earning power. The forecast for 1980 allows for an anticipated recession, 1981 is treated as a normal year, and 1982 and 1983 reflect Wundies' expectations of entry into new products. Bear Stearns was impressed by the market positions of both divisions and by the business strategy and merchandising concepts of the present operating management of both companies.

\* \* \*

For each of the years 1974–1978, Bear Stearns divided the average of the annual high and low market prices of the common shares by the annual earnings per share for each of the 15 companies. For 1979, market quotations through August 31, 1979, and the latest available twelve months earnings were used. A spot ratio was also computed for the September 10, 1979, market price. The result, as tabulated in the Bear Stearns' report, (excluding six deficits and four very high ratios representing nominal earnings) produced 80 annual ratios, three of which exceeded ten and two of which were less than three. The average ratios of all companies for each year ranged from 5.1 to 6.3.

Applying a multiplier of five to the estimate of annual foreseeable earnings of $2,890,000, Bear Stearns determined that the continuing operations of Duplan had a value of $14,450,000.

\* \* \*

In light of the foregoing, we are satisfied that Bear Stearns' valuation of the reorganized company gave adequate weight to all relevant factors.

\* \* \*

## Appendix B
### Description of Continuing Operations
### I. Wundies Inc.

* * *

Current and Projected Operations [edited table]
WUNDIES AND KICKAWAY
SALES AND INCOME [edited]
(000 omitted)

#### Current Operations

| Fiscal Year | Net Sales | Gross Profit | Selling General and Administrative Expenses | Interest Income & Expenses Net | State Income Tax | Income Before Federal Taxes |
|---|---|---|---|---|---|---|
| 1976 | $14,186 | $2,905 | $1,663 | $6 | $(79) | $1,169 |
| 1977 | 15,142 | 3,019 | 1,767 | 33 | (77) | 1,208 |
| 1978 | 18,272 | 4,178 | 2,362 | 84 | (104) | 1,796 |
| 1979 | 21,014 | 4,707 | 2,211 | 105 | (101) | 2,500 |

#### Projected Operations

| 1980 | $24,000 | $4,926 | $2,331 | | $(106) | $2,435 |
|---|---|---|---|---|---|---|
| 1981 | 27,000 | 5,541 | 2,594 | | (180) | 2,767 |
| 1982 | 31,000 | 6,373 | 2,859 | | (215) | 3,299 |
| 1983 | 35,000 | 7,193 | 3,158 | | (250) | 3,785 |

**In re The Duplan Corporation, 9 Bankr. 921 (Bankr. S.D.N.Y. 1980)**

Duffy, District Judge

Expert witnesses for the noteholders had different views [than the SEC] on the choice of the multiple and their approach to going concern valuation. Obviously, the choice of [a] multiplier is inextricably tied to the choice of an earnings figure when valuing a reorganized company. Essentially, the noteholders would have no objection to the use of a multiple of five provided it is applied to an historical earnings figure. The thrust of the noteholders' objections is that the Bear Stearns' analysis [adopted by the SEC] overvalues Duplan's continuing operations. The noteholders argue that the calculation of the price earnings ratio of five was based on a study of present ratios of other companies. These ratios reflect an expectation by the marketplace of future earnings. By applying this multiplier to a projected average future earnings, *the same expectations regarding Duplan's future have been considered twice*. Thus, the noteholders suggest either lowering the ratio used, applying the ratio of five to historical instead of prospective earnings or applying the ratio of five to discounted earnings projections.

The noteholders' reliance on historical earnings is misguided in the context of these proceedings. To value an ongoing business for Chapter X purposes, it is well settled that prospective earnings are capitalized. Certainly past earnings provide a useful reference point from which to calculate present value and develop projections. To rely on the past exclusively, however, would be misleading. If Duplan is to be transformed into a viable company, "freed from the heavy hand of past errors" its valuation must be based on its future earnings capacity as a reorganized entity. Consolidated Rock Products Co. v. DuBois, 312 U.S. at 526. Therefore, the value of Duplan's new securities must be based on prospective income .... Forecasts are a necessary part of the valuation process. Disagreement is therefore inevitable. Although mathematical certainty is not required in order for valuation to be fair, an informed judgment is. I am satisfied that the Trustee's projections rely on a reasonable assessment of the reorganized company's position in the marketplace.

[The Court concluded the plan was fair and equitable.]

## ¶322: Questions on *Duplan*

1. Why do the noteholders claim an overvaluation? That is, why substantively do they say Duplan was overvalued and why tactically do they say so?
2. Does the SEC in *Duplan* look to past earnings as a guide to future earnings?
3. Does the court find a capitalization rate and then apply it to its earnings base in the same way that the SEC advises the court to do in *Atlas Pipeline*?
4. Why do the SEC and the court use the price/earnings ratio, instead of a capitalization rate?
5. Does use of the P/E ratios ever tell us anything about Duplan's proper capitalization rate? Consider the following:

   "[S]ince the market is engaged in capitalizing future (not past or even solely current) earnings, the capitalization rate cannot be observed directly or determined precisely. Thus the ratio of current earnings to the present price of a company's shares represents the market capitalization rate only if current earnings are expected to continue unchanged into the future. If earnings are expected to grow as time goes by, then the company's capitalization rate is necessarily greater than the current earnings-price ratio. In effect, the greater the anticipated rate of growth the higher also is the capitalization rate that equates future earnings with the present market price of the company's shares"—Victor Brudney & Marvin Chirelstein, Corporate Finance 72 (3d ed. 1987).

6. The market is capitalizing a firm's expected future earnings, according to conventional theory. So when one observes a firm with a stock price of $100 and current earnings of $10, yielding a P/E ratio of 10, one has learned *nothing at all* about the market's capitalization rate. One has to know what the consensus estimate of that firm's prospective, *future* earnings is in order to find the rate at which the

market is capitalizing the firm in question. The market might expect the current $10 earnings to continue into the future, meaning it is using a 10% capitalization rate. Or it might expect earning to double to $20 next year and then stay at that higher level, indicating a capitalization rate of the expected earnings of 20%.

7. A separate criticism of the use of clones' P/E's is that the ratios are based on *reported* earnings. Reported earnings are subject to accounting manipulation and error. Take another look at the use of depreciation in *Atlas Pipeline,* if this isn't apparent. Valuers on Wall Street in 1980, when *Duplan* was decided, would probably prefer to use the clone's cash flow before making any comparisons. So, for example, an investment analyst might look at the clones' cash flow, which would more likely be captured in the clones' earnings *before* interest, taxes, depreciation, amortization, and unusual charges. Thus, the use of P/E's in 1980 probably didn't correspond to investment analysts' state of the art. Put this criticism aside and try to see what made the use of P/E's attractive to the SEC and the court, and whether the ratios were used accurately.

8. If P/E ratios do not capture the capitalization of future earnings, does that mean that the methodology in *Duplan* is of necessity wrong? If you found truly comparable clones of Duplan, is it possible to use the P/E ratio to value Duplan without ever making a determination of what the proper capitalization rate ought to be?

9. The rub lies in the "if"? That is, in determining the degree of cloneness for the comparable companies, do we have to do everything that the *Atlas Pipeline* authorities did, and did imperfectly? Don't we have to see whether the opportunities for the bankrupt are comparable to the clones' opportunities? Do we have to judge how risky the projections are? Would the judge not then be doing just what was done in *Atlas Pipeline*? Could use of P/E's then just be a starting point, not an ending point?

10. Or could we use P/E ratios as a reality check? That is, we use P/E's and come to a valuation based on comparable other companies in the industry. Then we adjust for the weaknesses of the bankrupt. Or, alternatively, we start from scratch and conclude that the value is "X." If X is twice that of the value arrived by P/E ratios, and the other elements indicate the bankrupt is weaker than other firms in the industry, then the start-from-scratch valuation was way off.

11. Another point about the use of the price/earnings ratio: The SEC used the P/E ratio of the comparable companies during the base period of 1974–1978. Consider the New York Times description of P/E ratios on February 1, 1986:

    If the 1974–1978 numbers were like the February 2, 1986 numbers, a fact that could be verified, does the historical method lead to a gross misvaluation of Duplan?

12. The SEC used the market's valuation of clone companies to come up with a P/E for Duplan. One wonders whether bankruptcy administration could use the market

to value the firm more directly and more explicitly than by observing the P/E ratio of comparable firms.

The trustee sold several money-losing divisions. The buyer of each division put a value on it before paying for it. Presumably others could have out-bid the buyer and presumably if none did, then no one with money thought the division was worth more than what was paid. Because each buyer was paying out its own money, it had some incentive not to bid too much.

During the course of valuing the remaining parts of Duplan, the SEC says: "Prices actually being paid for equivalent commodities are the best evidence of the yield that should be employed in determining current capital values of projected income."

Is there a more direct way to use market values? Could Duplan in its entirety have been put out for bids? Was Duplan really being sold to its creditors, with the court as both auctioneer and constructive bidder for the creditors? If so, why couldn't others bid? Could this scenario help us solve bankruptcy reorganization problems, which are already—only a few weeks into the course—tending toward intractability?

13. Will mock bids—bids when no real sale is intended—be spurious? Must Duplan actually be sold to the highest bidder for a market-based solution to be even remotely functional?

---

## ¶323: Using price/earnings multiples in *Duplan*

The SEC likened Duplan to similarly-situated textile companies. To value Duplan directly, it would have had to project Duplan's earnings (or cash flow), and then would have had to have found a capitalization rate that reflected the risks inherent in those projected earnings. The court might have tried to surmise Duplan's earnings by analogizing them to the earnings of clone companies. Did the court have to project Duplan's earnings once it found true clones? (We are about to enter a circle, do you see where and how?)

$$(1) \quad \frac{\text{Duplan's constructed value}}{\text{Duplan's future earnings}} = \frac{\text{Clones' value}}{\text{Clones' future earnings}}$$

If these numbers (other than Duplan's constructed value, which is the number sought in the appraisal) could have been found, then the court would have found a capitalization rate for Duplan. Using the capitalization rate for the clones, the court could have capitalized its estimate of Duplan's future earnings. To be specific, the capitalization rate for the clones is nothing more than the reciprocal of their *current* price to their *future* earnings. For example, if price were $100 and projected *future* earnings were $20, the P/E ratio (of price to *future* earnings) would be 5 and the capitalization rate would be 20%. I.e., investors in the clones insist that to put up with the risks of realizing (and not realizing) the expected $20 per year earnings, they would invest as much as, but no more than, $100: 20% of X = $20. X = $100.

The problem that the SEC faced was that it could not obtain the clones' future earnings. It tried to guess at Duplan's future earnings and it got some expert testimony from the conflicting parties. The experts contradicted one another.

Could the use of *current* P/E's, if correctly done, offer a way out of the dilemma? Is the following statement correct? (Indeed is it not tautological?): If we are dealing with true clones, the ratio of Duplan's current earnings to the clones' current earnings will be the same as the ratio of Duplan's projected future earnings to the clones' future earnings. If they are both moving in tandem won't current ratios be the same as future ratios?

$$(2) \quad \frac{\text{Duplan's current earnings}}{\text{Clones' current earnings}} = \frac{\text{Duplan's future earnings}}{\text{Clones' future earnings}}$$

Is the following statement correct? The ratio of Duplan's price to the clones' price is the same as the ratio of Duplan's future earnings to the clones' future earnings. For example, if the clones future earnings are expected to be $20, Duplan's future earnings $10, and the clones' stock price is $100, then isn't Duplan's stock value $50?

$$(3) \quad \frac{\text{Duplan's value}}{\text{Clones' value}} = \frac{\text{Duplan's future earnings}}{\text{Clones' future earnings}}$$

This is only a reorganization of the first ratio, equation (1). But once again the real-world problem is the difficulty of observing *future* earnings. Especially for an entire industry.

But now can we see a way out of the dilemma? Why can't we just drop the right hand ratio in each of the last two equations? If we are dealing with true clones, why isn't this true?

$$(4) \quad \frac{\text{Duplan's value}}{\text{Clones' value}} = \frac{\text{Duplan's current earnings}}{\text{Clones' current earnings}}$$

Now we have three terms that are easily observable. We have derived this from equation (1), which can be seen as a variant of capitalizing future earnings. We could also have gotten to (4) intuitively: if we've got true clones, then Duplan's and the clones' earnings should move in tandem with their stock prices. Straightforward algebra would tell us that equation (4) is the same thing as the clones' current P/E times Duplan's current earnings. I.e.,

(5) Duplan's value = $\dfrac{\text{Duplan's current earnings}}{\text{Clones' current earnings} \times \text{Clones' value}}$

Or, since the last term on the right hand side when combined with the denominator of the fraction is the clones' P/E:

(6) Duplan's value = Duplan's current earnings × Clones' P/E

We have finessed ourselves out of having to determine future earnings and a capitalization rate. Or more accurately, we make that estimate only by determining that the clone companies are indeed clones. If we found perfect clones of exactly the same size, with exactly the same number of shares outstanding, as Duplan, we would not have to do anything at all with ratios. Their value would be precisely equal to Duplan's value. The ratios then would only be needed to adjust for different size companies or different numbers of shares outstanding.

Caveats are in order. The process is only as good as the estimation of how good the comparative companies are as clones. If they are a little off, the ratios will be a little off and the valuation result will be wrong. If they are way off, the ratios will be way off and the valuation result will be very wrong. Seemingly small things could throw the ratio off. For example, more debt in the "clones" than in Duplan will throw the ratio off.[48] Either the clones will have to have the same amount of debt as Duplan or adjustments are necessary; the "clones" aren't really clones if they have more (or less) debt than Duplan. If the "clones" have better future business opportunities, then they're not "clones." If the "clones" lack tax advantages that Duplan will have after chapter 11, then they've not clones. If managerial uncertainty is high at Duplan, but low in the "clones," then they're not clones.

Is the inability to be precise in determining whether the comparative companies are really clones irreparably debilitating? Perhaps not, for reasons similar to those offered by Gardner, see ¶316, in defending his approach. Incrementalism may well reduce the chance of gross error. That is, one could use the P/E approach to get a value that puts the court in the ballpark. Then that number could be adjusted to account for factors that the court concludes establish differences between the company to be valued and the quasi-clones.

But what did the SEC do in *Duplan*? Did its use of P/E's correspond to this heavily-caveated justification for using price-earnings ratios? Read the next paragraph.

---

[48] This is a problem because the usual form of P/E ratio, such as those used in newspaper stock tables, uses earnings after payment of interest. If it's not obvious right now why different debt levels can seriously throw the formulas off, don't worry. We'll discuss this general problem later in the course, in connection with the Modigliani-Miller hypotheses.

## ¶324: *Duplan* problem

1. Could one accuse the *Duplan* trustee, the SEC, and the confirming court of a double count, similar to the charge some might level against the SEC's *Atlas Pipeline* opinion? The noteholders are arguing that inflation and rising prices are counted twice, once in the comparable companies P/E and then again in the projected earnings of Duplan. The double count thereby yields too high a paper value for Duplan.

2. Consider the following problem. XYZ reorganizes in 1993. Its 1993 earnings are running at $910,000. Inflation has come back and is expected to run in the 1990s at 10% per year. Nominal (i.e., inflated) revenues, expenses, and earnings are expected to be:

|  | 1994 | 1995 | 1996 | 1997 | 1998 |
|---|---|---|---|---|---|
| Sales | $20M | $22M | $24.2M | $26.6M | $29.2M |
| Expenses | 18M | 19.8M | 20.2M | 24M | 26.2M |
| Earnings | 2M | 2.2M | 2.4M | 2.6M | 3M |

Average 5 years earning projection: $2.44 million

Clone companies have a P/E of 10. (E.g., one nearly identical clone, ABC, Inc., has 1993 annual earnings per share running at $18 and a stock price of $180 on the XYZ valuation date. It has 100,000 outstanding shares.)

What is the value of XYZ, using the valuation methodology adopted by the SEC and the court in *Duplan*? By the way, what would the *Duplan* valuation authorities say should be the value of ABC? Sensible?

(Would it make any difference if the increases in earnings were expected to be real increases?)

3. Would a look at the historical earnings for the calculation be any better? For example,

|  | 1990 | 1991 | 1992 | 1993 | 1994 |
|---|---|---|---|---|---|
| Sales | $13.7M | $15.2M | $16.6M | $18.2M | $20M |
| Expenses | 12.4M | 13.7M | 14.9M | 16.1M | 18M |
| Earnings | 1.4M | 1.5M | 1.7M | 1.8M | 2M |

Average 5 years historical earnings: $1.7 million

Would this yield a more accurate valuation than the SEC's valuation?

4. Again, why do the noteholders object to the trustee's valuation? After all doesn't the trustee's plan contemplate that they, unlike every other major creditor, be paid in full? See Table III, Distribution Pursuant to Trustee's Plan, p. 84.

5. Bear Stearns calculated 80 ratios of price to earnings for about 15 companies over a 5-year historical period. It didn't average the earnings for 5 years and then divide those earnings into the most recent stock price. Instead it averaged the high and low for the year and divided by the earnings for that year. It then averaged these 80 calculations of the "clones'" P/E to find a usable P/E. Why did Bear Stearns make 80 separate calculations? See p. 86.

CHAPTER 4

# PRIORITY

A. The concepts: absolute priority
B. The statute today
C. The reality of delay in chapter 11
D. The lawyers
E. The managers
F. The costs of delay
G. A note on purposes

...........................................................................................................................

## A. The concepts: absolute priority

### ¶401: Priorities in reorganization

The ordering of liabilities in reorganization will now command our attention. First we must master the statutory intricacies. Upon doing so, we shall again see that the ordering of liabilities in reorganization importantly depends on the value assigned the firm in reorganization. With that value in mind, lawyers can advise clients on what to expect in reorganization, thereby facilitating a quick settlement in reorganization. However, if value is unpredictable (because courts will not use objective measures or because objective measures, like the market, are highly mutable during the two or three years of a chapter 11 proceeding), then settlements cannot be easily reached. From a public policy perspective, a serious question worth addressing is whether a framework can be designed to achieve quick corporate reorganization settlements.

From a more practical perspective, some financiers will seek priority in position should a reorganization come to pass. Other financiers will accept lower priority as long as they are appropriately compensated for the added risk. Four main methods to control priority are worth our attention: contractual subordination, security, the negative pledge clause, and the holding company.

The mechanisms of contract formation, acquisition of a secured position, and incorporation of separate subsidiaries, are all subjects for other courses in the law school. What will concern us is the treatment in bankruptcy of properly-formed subordination agreements, security interests, negative pledge agreements and holding companies. Their treatment is at the core of the legal framework for corporate reorganization.

Related to these four institutions that would order priorities in reorganization are the doctrines concerning equitable subordination, substantive consolidation of holding companies, and the treatment of illegal securities issuances in bankruptcy. The rules for these doctrines depend not so much on contract and the reorganization rules governing contract, as on the actions of the debtor or its creditors at, or after, the time of contract.

Lastly, but of vital concern to financiers in determining the economic value of whatever priority they may have, is the treatment of interest accruing during the firm's reorganization, which characteristically takes two or three years. The results in the Bankruptcy Code are neither intuitively obvious as consistent (like creditors are not always treated alike) nor clearly easy to predict.

## ¶402: The setting of reorganization

Although we will be primarily concerned in next few chapters with priority, we should know the typical sequence in a chapter 11 reorganization.

The debtor files its petition with the bankruptcy court and the automatic stay (§ 362) enjoins all attempts to collect from the debtor. No creditor can sue, seize collateral, continue a lawsuit, levy on a judgment, or even demand repayment.

For large companies, a trustee usually is nowadays *not* appointed to take possession of the bankrupt company and its assets. The company's ongoing management takes on the duties of the trustee. The bankrupt entity is called a debtor-in-possession (DIP). Occasionally but rarely, creditors seek to oust management and appoint a trustee under § 1104 ("for cause, including fraud, dishonesty, incompetence, or gross mismanagement of the ... debtor by current management ... or if such appointment is in the interests of creditors").

Many bankrupt companies need financing for ongoing operations. The *new* post-petition lender usually gets a super-priority above pre-bankruptcy lenders.

Meanwhile, the pre-bankruptcy lenders are unhappy with the bankruptcy stay. Secured creditors often ask the court to lift the stay, so they can foreclose. (Aggressive secured creditors get the debtor to waive the automatic stay in the basic loan documents. Generally courts will not enforce the waiver, and secured creditors don't think that the waiver allows them room for unilateral action without a court lifting the stay. But secured creditors sometimes find having a waiver useful, because it helps persuade the court to lift the stay.) The statute requires that the debtor and court provide the secured creditors with adequate protection of their security interests, which usually is done via periodic cash payments to compensate the secured creditor for the deteriorating value of its collateral. Sometimes the secured property produces cash, which could be subject to a creditor's lien. The debtor would like to use this cash and usually asks the court to find some other adequate protection for the secured creditor so that the debtor can use the cash to revive itself.

While the stay, DIP financing and fights over the disposition of cash collateral are going on, a creditors' committee is appointed, usually of the seven largest creditors of the debtor. Negotiations for a plan of reorganization begin. The debtor has the statutory right to be the only one to propose a plan for the first four months. Typically bankruptcy judges extend this period of exclusivity, often for years.[1] This agenda control gives the debtor leverage in getting its favored result.

Some operations are closed, some sold, some continued. The people running the debtor-in-possession—often its pre-bankruptcy management[2]—can make all "ordinary course" decisions for the business. But the court must approve out-of-the-ordinary-course decisions.

Eventually a plan is proposed and confirmed by the court. *Los Angeles Lumber* helps us with general ideas about the range of priority mutation that could be permitted and helps us see the framework for priority that dominated bankruptcy reorganization for forty years. Some of that framework, but not all of it, survived the last major overhaul of the bankruptcy system, in the Bankruptcy Act of 1978.

In reviewing the decision, one should consider the extent to which a court should oversee the bargain of the parties. What standard of priority should the court use? Should it allow the parties to deviate from that standard?

## ¶403: <u>Case v. Los Angeles Lumber Prods. Co., 308 U.S. 106 (1939)</u>

MR. JUSTICE DOUGLAS delivered the opinion of the Court. These cases present the question of the conditions under which stockholders may participate in a plan of reorganization under ... the Bankruptcy Act where the debtor corporation is insolvent ....

---

[1] The 1994 bankruptcy amendments sought to keep short incumbent management's monopoly over proposing a plan. It's too early to see whether the amendments will succeed.

[2] There is a growing literature on managerial turnover before the bankruptcy, at the time of the petition, and at the time—two years later—of plan confirmation. By the time the judge confirms a plan of reorganization, managerial turnover is more likely than not.

... [The plan] provides for the formation of a new corporation, which will acquire the assets of Los Angeles Shipbuilding and Drydock Corporation, and which will have a capital structure of 1,000,000 shares ....

... 641,375 shares of the preferred are to be issued to the bondholders, 250 shares to be exchanged for each $1000 bond. The [old] Class A stockholders will receive the 188,625 shares of common stock, without the payment of any subscription or assessment ....

The plan was assented to by approximately 92.81% of the face amount of the bonds, 99.75% of the Class A stock, and 90% of the Class B stock. Petitioners own $18,500 face amount of the bonds. They did not consent ... [a]nd throughout the present ... proceedings they appropriately objected that the plan was not fair and equitable to bondholders.

The District Court found that the debtor was insolvent both in the equity sense and in the bankruptcy sense[;][3] the total value of all assets of Los Angeles Shipbuilding and Drydock Corporation was $830,000 .... Yet in spite of this finding, the court ... confirmed the plan ... despite ... that the old stockholders, who have no equity in the assets of the enterprise, are given 23% of the assets and voting power in the new company without making any fresh contribution .... The court, however, justified inclusion of the stockholders in the plan (1) because it apparently felt that the relative priorities of the bondholders and stockholders were maintained by virtue of the preferences accorded the stock which the bondholders were to receive and the fact that the stock going to the bondholders carried 77% of the voting power of all the stock presently to be issued under the plan; and (2) because it was able to find that they had furnished the bondholders certain "compensating advantages" or "consideration." This so-called consideration was stated by the District Court in substance as follows:

>  1. [**Managerial expertise**.] It will be an asset of value to the new company to retain the old stockholders in the business because of "their familiarity with the operation" of the business and their "financial standing and influence in the community"; and because they can provide a "continuity of management."
>  2. [**Liquidation value**.] If the bondholders were able to foreclose now and liquidate the debtor's assets, they would receive "substantially less than the present appraised value" of the assets.
>  3. [**Avoid litigation**.] By reason of the so-called voluntary reorganization in 1930, the bondholders cannot foreclose until 1944, the old stockholders having the right to manage and control the debtor until that time. At least the bondholders cannot now foreclose without "long and protracted litigation" which would be "expensive and of great injury" to the debtor. Hence, the virtual abrogation of the agreement deferring foreclosure until 1944 was "the principal valuable consideration" passing to the bondholders from the old stockholders.

---

[3] [I.e., the debtor was unable to meet its debts as they came due and the debtor's liabilities were more than its assets.—Roe.]

\* \* \*

[We conclude that] as a matter of law the plan was not fair and equitable.

[W]here a plan is not fair and equitable as a matter of law it cannot be approved by the court even though the percentage of the various classes of security holders required by [the Bankruptcy Act] for confirmation of the plan has consented .... Congress has required both that the required percentages of each class of security holders approve the plan and that the plan be found to be "fair and equitable."[4] The former is not a substitute for the latter. The court is not merely a ministerial register of the vote of the several classes of security holders. All those interested in the estate are entitled to the court's protection. Accordingly the fact that the vast majority of the security holders have approved the plan is not the test of whether the plan is a fair and equitable one .... The contrary conclusion in such cases would make the judicial determination on the issue of fairness a mere formality ....

Hence, in this case the fact that 92.81% in amount of the bonds ... have approved the plan is as immaterial on the basic issue of its fairness as is the fact that petitioners own only $18,500 face amount of a large bond issue.

\* \* \*

We come then to the legal question of whether the plan here in issue is fair and equitable within the meaning of that phrase as used in [the Act].

We do not believe it is .... [T]here are assets not in excess of $900,000, while the claims of the bondholders for principal and interest are approximately $3,800,000. Hence even if all of the assets were turned over to the bondholders they would realize less than 25 percent on their claims. Yet in spite of this fact they will be required under the plan to surrender to the stockholders 23 percent of the value of the enterprise.

True, the relative priorities of the bondholders and the old Class A stockholders are maintained by virtue of the priorities accorded the preferred stock which the bondholders are to receive. But this is not compliance with the principle expressed in Kansas City Terminal Ry. Co. v. Central Union Trust Co., that "to the extent of their debts creditors are entitled to priority over stockholders against all the property of an insolvent corporation," for there are not sufficient assets to pay the bondholders the amount of their claims. Nor does this plan recognize the "equitable right" of the bondholders "to be preferred to stockholders against the full value of all property belonging to the debtor corporation," within the meaning of the rule announced in that case, since the full value of that property is not first applied to claims of the bondholders before the stockholders are allowed to participate. Rather it is partially diverted for the benefit of the stockholders even though the bondholders would obtain less than 25% payment if they received it all. Under that theory all classes of security holders could be perpetuated in the new company even though the assets were insufficient to pay—

---

[4] It provides in part: "After hearing such objections as may be made to the plan, the judge shall confirm the plan if satisfied that (1) it is fair and equitable and does not discriminate unfairly in favor of any class of creditors or stockholders, and is feasible; ... (3) it has been accepted as required by the provisions of subdivision (e), clause (1) of this section; ..."

in new bonds or stock—the amount owing senior creditors. Such a result is not tenable.

It is, of course, clear that there are circumstances under which stockholders may participate in a plan of reorganization of an insolvent debtor[.] Where ... the old stockholders make a fresh contribution and receive in return a participation reasonably equivalent to their contribution, no objection can be made ....

* * *

... [T]o accord "the creditor his full right of priority against the corporate assets" where the debtor is insolvent, the stockholder's participation must be based on a contribution in money or in money's worth, reasonably equivalent [in value to the stock received].

The alleged consideration furnished by the stockholders in this case falls far short of meeting those requirements.

### [Debtor's managerial know-how does not support award of stock]

1. The findings below that participation by the old Class A stockholders will be beneficial to the bondholders because those stockholders have "financial standing and influence in the community" and can provide a "continuity of management" constitute no legal justification for issuance of new stock to them. [I]f [these were] recognized as adequate consideration for issuance of stock to valueless junior interests, [they] would serve as easy evasions of the principle of full or absolute priority .... Such items, on facts present here, are not adequate consideration for issuance of the stock in question. On the facts of this case they cannot possibly be translated into money's worth reasonably equivalent to the participation accorded the old stockholders. They have no place in the asset column of the balance sheet of the new company. They reflect merely vague hopes or possibilities ....[5]

### [Bondholders entitled to more than liquidation value of assets]

2. The District Court's further finding that if the bondholders were to foreclose now they would receive "substantially less than the present appraised value" of the assets of the debtor corporation is no support for inclusion of the old stockholders in the plan. The fact that bondholders might fare worse as a result of a foreclosure and liquidation than they would by taking a debtor's plan ... can have no relevant bearing on whether a proposed plan is "fair and equitable" under [the Act] .... To hold that in a [bankruptcy] reorganization creditors of a hopelessly insolvent debtor may be forced to share the already insufficient assets with stockholders because apart from rehabilitation under that section they would suffer a worse fate, would disregard the standards

---

[5] This conclusion is reemphasized here by the fact that not all of the Class A stockholders who receive new stock are part of the management of the debtor.

of "fair and equitable"; and would result in impairment of the Act to the extent that it restored some of the conditions which the Congress sought to ameliorate by that remedial legislation.

\* \* \*

**[Compromise of legitimate legal disputes allowable]**

4. The holding of the District Court that the value to the bondholders of maintaining the debtor as a going concern and of avoiding litigation with the old stockholders justifies the inclusion of the latter in the plan is likewise erroneous .... Of course, this is not to intimate that compromise of claims is not allowable under [the Act] .... Thus, ambiguities in the wording of two indentures may make plausible the claim of one class of creditors to an exclusive or prior right to certain assets as against the other class in spite of the fact that the latter's claim flows from a first mortgage. Close questions of interpretations of after-acquired property clauses in mortgages, preferences in stock certificates, divisional mortgages and the like will give rise to honest doubts as to which security holders have first claim to certain assets. Settlement of such conflicting claims to the res in the possession of the court is a normal part of the process of reorganization. In sanctioning such settlements the court is not bowing to nuisance claims; it is administering the proceedings in an economical and practical manner. But that is not the situation here ....

\* \* \*

We therefore hold that the plan is not fair and equitable and that the judgment below must be and is

Reversed.

---

## ¶404: Notes on *Los Angeles Lumber*

1. *Los Angeles Lumber* is at the heart of modern bankruptcy doctrine. Prior to the decision, debate was fierce as to whether absolute priority, sometimes called strict priority, ought to govern in reorganization proceedings. First, hadn't all of claimants made a bad investment? Shouldn't they all share in the common disaster?

   Second, is it clear that the face value of the claims in bankruptcy should be the value distributed in bankruptcy? For example, if the creditor had obtained bad investment features when it lent to the debtor, such as a below-market interest rate, should the bad deal be reflected in the creditors' compensation if the firm is continued? If the firm is continued, shouldn't the bad deal be continued? Why shouldn't the creditors receive just their expected going concern values? (And these going concern values, as the Gardner reading made clear, would often be below the face amount of their debt.)

Third, didn't the creditor bargain for liquidation value? Its nonbankruptcy remedy was to seize security (or levy on a judgment). If there's an excess of going concern value, is it clear who's entitled to it, the creditors or the stockholders?

Fourth, and most importantly, if the creditor class *agreed* in the reorganization proceeding to give up their strict priority, why should a court not accede to the class' will?

And, fifth, does strict priority follow directly from the language of the statutory requirement (that the plan be fair and equitable, see Los Angeles Lumber, 308 U.S. at 114, at p. 99)? Isn't the standard quite open-ended?

Several elements of the absolute priority rule are inter-connected: (i) creditors have "absolute" priority over stockholders, i.e., they are to be paid in full before stockholders receive anything, (ii) creditor consent to deviation from that priority via a creditor vote is not dispositive, (iii) when there are intermediate creditors, creditors cannot skip over an intermediate class to consent to a lower class' participation.

2. *One* of the considerations advanced in favor of giving the stockholders an interest in the reorganized company was that the stockholder/managers had business contacts vital to the shipyard's success. The Supreme Court said this consideration was illegitimate.

3. Bank, due $2000, forecloses on Shipyard Company. Bank concludes that the company's current management is not incompetent, just unlucky. Bank wants current managers to run the company. Without current management, the company is worth $1000. With current management, if properly motivated, the company is worth $2000. The Bank forecloses, obtaining all of the company in Douglas-type, absolute priority reorganization. After the reorganization, which takes place overnight, the Bank then hires the prior management. To motivate the managers properly, the Bank first considers giving them a straight salary, then salary with a bonus, then salary with stock options. Finally, it decides to give them 25% of the stock of the Shipyard Company. Any legal problems?

4. What if the Bank negotiated the deal with management while the firm was in reorganization? The reorganization takes two years, and Bank wants managers to be motivated by stock during the reorganization. It concludes that if managers know that the Bank's plan gives them 25% of the stock, then the managers will be properly motivated while waiting for the court's approval. What result under *Los Angeles Lumber*?

5. Recall the fair and equitable standard, which is the statutory basis for the doctrinal result. Would it be relevant in determining whether the result was fair and equitable to note, as the lower court had, that the creditors took the bonds under a bond indenture that allowed a majority vote to compromise the claim of the bonds and that the bondholders had given an approving vote prior to the reorganization of Los Angeles Lumber? See In re Los Angeles Lumber Prods., 24 F. Supp. 501, 504

(S.D. Cal. 1938), rev'd sub. nom. Case v. Los Angeles Lumber Prods. Co., 308 U.S. 106 (1939).

6. Presumably a strong basis for strict priority is that priority is what the parties bargained for. Is that strong basis vitiated if the parties *also* bargained to allow a majority vote of the bondholders to recapitalize the bonds and that majority vote is obtained?

7. Is the stockholders' hindrance value a persuasive reason to prohibit the creditors from giving the stockholders something? 308 U.S. at 129. A partnership agrees to take most actions by a 2/3 vote. A customer of the partnership defaults in payment for $1000 of goods sold and delivered. The partnership votes to accept $900, because the litigation process is slow, uncertain and expensive. Could similar considerations have motivated the bondholders in *Los Angeles Lumber*?

   Douglas says that mere nuisance value cannot support the settlement. If the stockholders have a colorable legal claim can they dispute with the bondholders, then settle?

8. *Los Angeles Lumber* was decided toward the end of the depression; markets were distrusted, administrators trusted. At the heart of the decision was a faith in the valuation process. Courts could quickly and accurately value the firm. Claims could then be compensated. That New Deal faith in the valuation process seems to have been misplaced, and by 1978, Congress sought to *avoid* the valuation hearing in chapter 11. See infra Bankruptcy Code § 1129. When you go through the following priority problems, ask yourself how much of *Los Angeles Lumber Products* survives the new Bankruptcy Code.

9. Does a nonwaivable rule give the bondholders a negotiating advantage? I.e., by being available to negotiate, they might give up something in the negotiation. Lack of availability can sometimes be advantageous. The Court says that the bondholders are "scattered and unorganized." 308 U.S. at 129. Would appointment of a bargaining agent be better than the *Los Angeles Lumber* solution? Would that advantage redress perceived disadvantages? Bondholders today are not scattered. The bonds are usually in institutional hands, often in concentrated blocks. See Board of Governors of the Federal Reserve System, Flow of Funds Accounts First Quarter 1986, at 34 (1986) (lines 8 and 9) (bond market is 90% institutional). (Actually, even in the Thirties the bond market was substantially an institutional one, although less so.)

10. Why was it so important to bind the dissenting bondholders? After all, 92.81% of the bondholders agreed to the plan. Why couldn't they recapitalize the company and leave the "trivial" dissenters alone? No need to figure this out now; we'll see the answer in Chapter 12, especially ¶1206 and ¶1207, on holding out and "buoying" up.

11. Justice Douglas said prior Supreme Court decisions determined the result in *Los Angeles Lumber:*

[In prior decisions,] this Court reaffirmed the "familiar rule" that "the stockholder's interest in the property is subordinate to the rights of creditors; first of secured and then of unsecured creditors." And [we] went on to say that "any arrangement of the parties by which the subordinate rights and interests of stockholders are attempted to be secured at the expense of the prior rights of either class of creditors comes within judicial denunciation" .... This doctrine is the "fixed principle" according to which Northern Pacific Ry. Co. v. Boyd, [228 U.S. 482 (1913),] decided that the character of reorganization plans was to be evaluated.

*Los Angeles Lumber* at 116. *Boyd*, however, involved different facts. A common pattern for railroad reorganizations at the end of the 19th century involved senior secured bondholders represented by, say, J.P. Morgan, who had directors on the railway's board. In between the secured bondholder layer and the stockholder layer were unsecured creditors, often trade creditors who were poorly informed about the railroad's prospects. The fear was that the railroad was worth enough to pay not only the bondholders back but that it could also have paid something to the unsecured creditors. But the insider bondholders and insider stockholders cut a deal that cut out the unsecured layer. Even though the firm was worth enough to get down to the unsecured layer, the insiders said it wasn't, and gave the stockholders something nevertheless, something that was said to compensate them for their management skills or to avoid litigation. In *Boyd*, the Court justified a rule of absolute priority that precluded skipping layers in the capital structure, in order to force the stockholders to reveal any optimistic information they had. Faced with an anti-skipping rule, the stockholders could get something in the reorganization only by convincing the judge that the firm was worth enough to get down to their layer. Randal C. Picker, Designing Verifiability: Boyd's Implications for Modern Bankruptcy Law (U. Chi. Law School Working Paper 1997). This "layer-skipping" scenario was not in play in *Los Angeles Lumber,* which involved the complaints of dissenters to a bond issue's vote.

## B. The statute today

### ¶405: Background to the 1978 Act: Report of the Commission on the Bankruptcy Laws of the United States, House Doc. 93-137, 93d Cong., 1st Sess 255 et seq. (1973)

The incorporation of the absolute priority rule into Chapter X's requirement of "fair and equitable" was not by accident. Mr. Justice Douglas, who wrote for a unanimous Court in *Case* [v. *Los Angeles Lumber*] and *Consolidated Rock* [infra], had, more than any other person, shaped the conclusions and recommendations of the Securities and Exchange Commission's Report on Protective Committees as to corporate reorganizations.[6] The Report concluded that an independent trustee and the absolute

---

[6] [See Joseph Kennedy's similar views of these committees, supra at p. 79.—Roe.]

priority rule were necessary to insure that "the great power exercised outside the proceedings by the inside few will be exercised within the proceedings for the benefit of the investor."

The target of the Report was the ability of a few insiders, whether representatives of management or major creditors, to use the reorganization process to gain an unfair advantage. The Report rejected the "relative priority" doctrine, which required only that "relative priorities of the old securities, senior to the most junior securities which continue to have an interest in the property, must not be inequitably disturbed." The Report also rejected the use of the "composition result" (best interests) test which "was always to give old shareholder [stock valued at the] difference between liquidation and full going concern value of the assets." ... [It] was believed that creditors, because of management's position of dominance, were not able to bargain effectively without a clear standard of fairness and judicial control.

## ¶406: Statement By The Hon. Dennis DeConcini, Chairman of the Subcommittee on Improvements in Judicial Machinery ..., Upon Introducing the Senate Amendment to the House Amendment to H.R. 8200, 124 Congressional Record S 17406 (Oct. 6, 1978)

The record of [our] hearings ... is replete with evidence of the failure of the reorganization provisions of the existing Bankruptcy Act to meet the needs of insolvent corporations in today's business environment. Chapter X was designed to impose rigid and formalized procedures upon the reorganization of corporations and, although designed to protect public creditors, has often worked to the detriment of such creditors. As the House report has noted:

> The negative results under chapter X have resulted from the stilted procedures, under which [a] management is always ousted and replaced by an independent trustee, [b] the courts and the Securities and Exchange Commission examine the plan of reorganization in great detail, no matter how long that takes, and [c] the court values the business, a time consuming and inherently uncertain procedure.

\* \* \*

The primary problem posed by chapter X is delay. The modern corporation is a complex and multifaceted entity .... Over and over again, it is demonstrated that corporations which must avail themselves of the provisions of the Bankruptcy Act suffer appreciable deterioration if they are caught in a chapter X proceeding for any substantial period of time.

\* \* \*

One cannot overemphasize the advantages of speed and simplicity to both creditors and debtors. Chapter XI [which was another reorganization mechanism under the old, pre-1978 Act, intended for use by small, non-public firms] allows a debtor to negotiate a plan outside of court and, having reached a settlement with a majority in number and amount of each class of creditors, permits the debtor to bind all unsecured creditors to the terms of the arrangement ....

... [T]he practical experience of those involved in business rehabilitation cases, practitioners, debtors, and bankruptcy judges, has been that the more simple and expeditious procedures of chapter XI are appropriate in the great majority of cases .... Second, chapter X has been far from a success. Of the 991 chapter X cases filed during the period of January 1, 1967, through December 31, 1977, only 664 have been terminated. Of those cases recorded as "terminated," only 140 resulted in consummated plans. This 21 percent success rate suggests one of the reasons for the unpopularity of chapter X.

## ¶407: Absolute priority under the half-century old Bankruptcy Act of 1938

While *Los Angeles Lumber* enshrined absolute priority in doctrine, the actual results deviated from an economic concept of absolute priority. First, the securities of the reorganized firm usually traded below the value of the claim. A creditor due $1 million did in fact get securities with a face value of $1 million, but the terms of the new securities and the weakness of the reorganized company led the marketplace to value those securities to be below $1 million.

Some argued that for priority to be absolute, the trading value, or the cash value of the compensation, should equal the amount of the claim. Jerome Frank, *Epithetical Jurisprudence and the Work of the Securities and Exchange Commission in the Administration of Chapter X of the Bankruptcy Act*, 18 N.Y.U.L.Q. Rev. 317, 340 (1941); Henry J. Friendly, *Some Comments on the Corporate Reorganizations Act,* 48 Harv. L. Rev. 39, 77–78 (1934). The new securities' interest rate was often too low in relation to the market's perception of the firm's risk. This was formally reconciled with absolute priority doctrine in two ways. One, the face value was equal to the amount of the claim. That, in a bankruptcy system that turned a blind eye toward some elements of present value, was enough. Two, the market for securities was a bad one. In time, the market value would approach the reorganization value.

## ¶408: The 1978 Bankruptcy Code changes

Because by 1978, the absolute priority rule, as established by Douglas, and the time-consuming valuation hearing, as reflected in *Atlas Pipeline* and *Duplan*, were thought to be less than perfect, Congress sought a way to reorganize in bankruptcy without a mandated valuation hearing.

Congress set up a Bankruptcy Commission, which reported back to Congress in Report of the Commission on the Bankruptcy Laws of the United States, House Doc. 93-137, 93d Cong., 1st Sess 257 (1973):

> The heart of the application of the absolute priority rule is the valuation of the business. The participation of junior creditors and equity security holders depends upon the finding of a value in the business over and above that of the claims of the senior interests.
>
> * * *
>
> ... Since valuation, which is at the heart of the absolute priority rule, is at best an educated guess, the courts and the parties (including the Securities and Exchange Commission) have considerable freedom to overcome the strait jacket of the absolute priority rule. [By] a slight change of the capitalization rate, an insolvent company in which equity security holders are denied participation becomes a solvent company in which equity security holders are entitled to an interest. [The choice of a capitalization rate might just] rationalize a predetermined result[.] There is ample inducement for the trial court to choose a valuation which will eliminate controversy.
>
> ... Courts, writhing under conflicting and plentiful testimony on valuation, may be impelled, therefore, to circumvent the spirit of the *Los Angeles Lumber* case by making generous estimates of the valuation of assets .... [V]aluation is so inexact a process and so much a matter of discretion ....

Reorganization in the 1938 Bankruptcy Act came in two basic varieties, chapter X and chapter XI. Chapter X, which we have observed, was for public companies. Chapter XI was originally for smaller, closely-held companies and had standards for reorganization different from those in chapter X. A majority of the creditors could force dissenting creditors to accept a plan, even if the plan violated absolute priority, although it could not violate absolute priority so much that the dissenting creditors would receive less than their liquidation value. The standard arose from the belief that chapter XI was structurally an alternative to the usual liquidation of the small failing business. As long as the creditors got liquidation value, they should have had little reason to complain. Toward the end of the life of the Bankruptcy Act of 1938, some public companies sought to use the old chapter XI's more flexible consent standards. This standard was to be the one Congress adopted for chapter 11 in 1978.

The legislative history to the Bankruptcy Code says (in H.R. Report No. 595, 95th Cong., 1st Sess. (1977)):

> The consolidated chapter is chapter 11 of proposed title 11. It adopts much of the flexibility of chapter XI of current law, and incorporates the essence of the public protection features of current chapter X. The areas of greatest importance are the financial standard for confirmation; the court hearing on the plan and the report on the plan to creditors and stockholders; the right to propose a plan; and the appointment of a trustee.

## II. THE FINANCIAL STANDARD

> The premise of the bill's financial standard for confirmation is the same as the premise of the securities law: parties should be given adequate disclosure or

relevant information, and they should make their own decision on the acceptability of the proposed plan .... The parties are left to their own to negotiate a fair settlement. The question of whether creditors are entitled to the going-concern or liquidation value of the business is impossible to answer. It is unrealistic to assume that the bill could or even should attempt to answer that question. Instead, negotiation among the parties after full disclosure will govern how the value of the reorganizing company will be distributed among the creditors and stockholders. The bill only sets the outer limits on the outcome: it must be somewhere between the going-concern value and the liquidation value.

Only when the parties are unable to agree on a proper distribution of the value of the company does the bill establish a financial standard. If the debtor is unable to obtain the consents of all classes of creditors and stockholders, then the court may confirm the plan anyway on request of the plan's proponent, if the plan treats the nonconsenting classes fairly .... [T]he bill permits senior classes to take less than full payment, in order to expedite or insure the success of the reorganization.

## ¶409: Priority today: understanding § 1129(a)(8)

The best way to see how the Bankruptcy Code's priority provisions function is to work through problems. The statutory sections needed are in ¶410. The critical sections are § 1129(a)(8), § 1126(c), § 1124, and § 1129(b). (Section 1129(a)(7), which also is important, comes up in ¶415; leave it aside for now, or at least leave it aside until you get to paragraph E.)

A. XYZ Corp. has a capital structure of (a) $1 million of secured debt due in 10 years, (b) $1.2 million in unsecured debentures due in a few months, and (c) common stock. XYZ Corp. defaults on an interest payment to the unsecured debentureholders. They elect, through their trustee, to accelerate their debt. (How can they do this? See infra ¶603, the prospectus of Drum Financial Corporation under "Description of Debentures—Events of Default and Notice Thereof" at p. 185.) The debentureholders sue and obtain a judgment. XYZ Corp., not having any cash, cannot and does not pay. Under a cross-default provision in the secured creditor's indenture, the secured debt's maturity is accelerated; the secured creditor demands payment. (What is a cross-default provision? See id.) XYZ Corp., still without cash, refuses. The debentureholders begin attachment proceedings on XYZ Corp.'s unsecured property. The secured creditor begins proceedings to arrange for a sheriff's sale of the property (about one-half of the property of XYZ Corp.) on which it has a lien; the proceeds of such a sale to be used to satisfy their claim.

XYZ Corp. files a bankruptcy petition. The debentureholders' and secured creditor's proceedings stop. (Why? Does any section of the Bankruptcy Code require this?)

The following plan is proposed:

# Ch. 4 PRIORITY 109

1. The secured creditor will have her maturity reinstated and interest payments will be paid when due under the old indenture. Her lien on XYZ Corp.'s property will continue. One interest payment was missed during the reorganization proceedings. She will be paid the missed interest payment with an added premium for the delay.
2. The unsecured creditors will receive 6 annual installments of $300,000 each.
3. The common stockholders will remain as such. (XYZ Corp. is, or would be, valued at $2 million, if that is important to know.)

B. The secured creditor objects to the plan. The others accept the plan. Can the court confirm the plan over the secured creditor's objection? Are all of the standards of § 1129(a) met? Does § 1124 have any bearing on whether § 1129(a)(8) is satisfied?

C. Same facts and plan as A, but this time one debentureholder (out of the 100 debentureholders in all, holding 25% of the principal amount of the voting outstanding debentures) objects. (The secured creditor and the other 99 debentureholders accept the plan.) Is § 1129(a)(8) satisfied? See § 1126.

D. Same facts and plan as A, but this time all the debentureholders object. (The secured creditor accepts the plan.) Can the plan be confirmed? Does the plan comply with § 1129(a)(8)? Does § 1129(b) provide an alternative if the plan fails under § 1129(a)(8)? Is it an alternative to noncompliance with every requirement of § 1129(a), or just noncompliance with (a)(8)?

What did the balance sheet of XYZ Corp. look like? What would it look like if the plan is confirmed?

How does one calculate the present value of the six annual payments of $300,000 per year to the debentureholders? How is the present value of the payment promised important? If a 10% discount rate was used in calculating the enterprise's $2 million valuation, should the same rate be used in discounting the six payments offered to debentureholders? Why? Why not?

Is the value of the secured creditor's claim $1 million? Could it ever be more? Less? Does the answer depend upon the contractual rate of interest?

Even if the plan could be crammed down on the debentureholders, could the judge confirm it? Is § 1129(a)(11) relevant? What would you argue if you represented the debentureholders? If you represented the trustee?

E. What minimum amount must be given every claimant? What does § 1129(a)(7) say? Can the secured creditor in B. invoke § 1129(a)(7)? See ¶415.

## ¶410: Reorganization statutory provisions for ¶409

A sensible way to read the statute is to start with § 1129(a)(8) and then look at the other sections to see how they give content to the key terms that § 1129(a)(8) uses—acceptance and nonimpairment—and how the other sections act as alternatives to (a)(8).

**§ 1129. Confirmation of plan**

(a) The court shall confirm a plan only if all of the following requirements are met:

\* \* \*

(3) The plan has been proposed in good faith and not by any means forbidden by law.

\* \* \*

(8) With respect to each class of claims or interests—

(A) such class has accepted the plan; or

(B) such class is not impaired under the plan.[7]

(10) If a class of claims is impaired under the plan, at least one class of claims that is impaired under the plan has accepted the plan, determined without including any acceptance of the plan by any insider.

(11) Confirmation of the plan is not likely to be followed by the liquidation, or the need for further financial reorganization, of the debtor or any successor to the debtor under the plan, unless such liquidation or reorganization is proposed in the plan.

(b) (1) ... if all of the applicable requirements of subsection (a) of this section other than paragraph (8) are met with respect to a plan, the court, on request of the proponent of the plan, shall confirm the plan notwithstanding the requirements of such paragraph if the plan does not discriminate unfairly,[8] and is fair and equitable,[9] with respect to each class of claims or interests that is impaired under, and has not accepted, the plan.

(2) For the purpose of this subsection, the condition that a plan be fair and equitable with respect to a class includes the following requirements:

\* \* \*

(B) With respect to a class of unsecured claims—

(i) the plan provides that each holder of a claim of such class receive or retain on account of such claim property of a value, as of the effective date of the plan, equal to the allowed amount of such claim; or

(ii) the holder of any claim or interest that is junior to the claims of such class will not receive or retain under the plan on account of such junior claim or interest any property.

---

[7] [Acceptance is defined in § 1126. A definition of impairment is in § 1124. An alternative to compliance with § 1129(a)(8) is in § 1129(b).]

[8] [Unfair discrimination is exemplified, although not defined, in the legislative history to the Code, reproduced in ¶412.]

[9] [Fair and equitable is defined in § 1129(b)(2).]

## § 1124. Impairment of claims or interests

[Unless a holder of a claim or interest agrees to less favorable treatment] a class of claims or interests is impaired under a plan unless, with respect to each claim or interest of such class, the plan [either]—

(1) leaves unaltered the legal, equitable, and contractual rights to which such claim or interest entitles the holder of such claim or interest; [or]

(2) notwithstanding any contractual provision or applicable law that entitles the holder of such claim or interest to demand or receive accelerated payment of such claim or interest after the occurrence of a default—

(A) cures any such default that occurred before or after the commencement of the case under this title, other than a default of a kind specified in section 365(b)(2) of this title; [and][10]

(B) reinstates the maturity of such claim or interest as such maturity existed before such default; [and]

(C) compensates the holder of such claim or interest for any damages incurred as a result of any reasonable reliance by such holder on such contractual provision or such applicable law; and

(D) does not *otherwise* alter the legal, equitable, or contractual rights to which such claim or interest entitles the holder of such claim or interest[.]

## § 1126. Acceptance of plan

(c) A class of claims has accepted a plan if such plan has been accepted by creditors ... that hold at least two-thirds in amount and more than one-half in number of the allowed claims of such class held by creditors ....

\* \* \*

(f) Notwithstanding any other provision of this section, a class that is not impaired under a plan, and each holder of a claim or interest of such class, are conclusively presumed to have accepted the plan, and solicitation of acceptances with respect to such class from the holders of claims or interests of such class is not required.

(g) Notwithstanding any other provision of this section, a class is deemed not to have accepted a plan if such plan provides that the claims or interests of such class do not entitle the holders of such claims or interests to receive or retain any property under the plan on account of such claims or interests.

---

[10] [Section 365(b)(2) lists these items:

[(A) the insolvency or financial condition of the debtor at any time before the closing of the case;

[(B) the commencement of a case under this title; or

[(C) the appointment of or taking possession by a trustee in a case under this title or a custodian before such commencement.]

## ¶411: Trade creditors and unfair discrimination

You'll have noticed that § 1129(b) requires that the plan both be fair and equitable (the priority standard) and that the plan not discriminate unfairly. Section 1129(b) must be satisfied if § 1129(a)(8) is not; functionally § 1129(b) is "subsection (c)" of § 1129(a)(8). You should figure out why. If subsection (A) or (B) of (a)(8) has been satisfied, the court need not turn to § 1129(b).

The fair and equitable concept is carefully defined in § 1129(b)(2) and normally would require a valuation hearing, unless the lower ranking claimants and interests are wiped out. "Unfair discrimination" turns out to be a carefully worked out concept—pro rata, equal treatment, after giving effect to side-deals. It's in fact so carefully worked out that it is left undefined in the Bankruptcy Code. The following problems show how it works; but to understand the concept of unfair discrimination one must carefully consult the statute's legislative history, whose relevant portions appear in the next paragraph, ¶412.

A. XYZ Corp. has outstanding $1 million in subordinated debentures with the same subordination provision as described in the Drum Financial Corporation prospectus (¶603) under "Description of Debentures—Subordination of Debentures." It has $1 million of bank debt issued under an indenture designating the bank debt as superior in right of payment to the subordinated debentures. It also has $1 million of trade debt on open account for raw materials shipped to XYZ Corp.'s plant 20 days ago. (Trade debt arises when a supplier sends the debtor supplies and expects payment after delivery. Is the trade debt "senior" to the subordinated debentures? Does it share equally and ratably with the subordinated debentures? With the senior bank debt? With the two combined?)

B. XYZ Corp. goes bankrupt. Its business is valued at $990,000. (That is its going concern value.) What does XYZ Corp.'s balance sheet look like prior to reorganization?

C. The trustee proposes that the bank get property worth $600,000, the trade creditors $330,000, the subordinated debentureholders $60,000. The stockholders are wiped out. The seniors and subordinated consent under § 1126 and § 1129(a)(8)(A). The trade creditors reject the plan.

   i. Can the plan be confirmed under § 1129(a)(8)(A)?
   ii. Can the plan be confirmed as fair and equitable? Under § 1129(b)(2)(B)(i)? Under (b)(2)(B)(ii)?
   iii. Does the plan discriminate unfairly against the trade creditors? See the legislative history in the next section (¶412) of these materials. The best way to de-code the legislative history would be to use paragraph F to tabulate the five "plans" outlined in the legislative history.

# Ch. 4 PRIORITY 113

D. Same facts as A. XYZ Corp.'s value is $990,000. The trustee proposes that the bank debt get $675,000 and the trade debt get $315,000. Can the plan be confirmed over either the bank's or the trade creditors' objection?

  i. Can the plan be confirmed under § 1129(a)(8)(A)?
  ii. Can the plan be confirmed as fair and equitable? Under § 1129(b)(2)(B)(i)? Under § 1129(b)(2)(B)(ii)?
  iii. Does the plan discriminate unfairly against the trade creditors? Again, see the legislative history in the next section of these materials.
  iv. Return to Plan C. Does it discriminate unfairly against the seniors? Is it fair and equitable to the seniors? Is Plan D fair and equitable to the seniors?

E. Same facts as A. XYZ Corp. is worth $1.8 million. The plan proposes that the bank creditor get $1 million, the trade creditors $750,000, and the subordinated debentures $50,000. Is anyone the victim of unfair discrimination? Who?

F. The legislative history illustrates unfair discrimination. To analyze the XYZ problems here, one ought to first understand what the legislative history means by unfair discrimination. For each of the five plans illustrated in the legislative history (¶412), we could fill in these numbers.

**First Plan**

|  | Amount owed | Compensation under plan | Pro rata compensation | Fair non-discriminatory compensation |
|---|---|---|---|---|
| Trade | ? | ? | ? | ? |
| Senior | ? | ? | ? | ? |
| Subordinated | ? | ? | ? | ? |

**Second Plan**

|  | Amount owed | Compensation under plan | Pro rata compensation | Fair non-discriminatory compensation |
|---|---|---|---|---|
| Trade | ? | ? | ? | ? |
| Senior | ? | ? | ? | ? |
| Subordinated | ? | ? | ? | ? |

### Third Plan

| | Amount owed | Compensation under plan | Pro rata compensation | Fair non-discriminatory compensation |
|---|---|---|---|---|
| Trade | ? | ? | ? | ? |
| Senior | ? | ? | ? | ? |
| Subordinated | ? | ? | ? | ? |

### Fourth Plan

| | Amount owed | Compensation under plan | Pro rata compensation | Fair non-discriminatory compensation |
|---|---|---|---|---|
| Trade | ? | ? | ? | ? |
| Senior | ? | ? | ? | ? |
| Subordinated | ? | ? | ? | ? |

### Fifth Plan

| | Amount owed | Compensation under plan | Pro rata compensation | Fair non-discriminatory compensation |
|---|---|---|---|---|
| Trade | ? | ? | ? | ? |
| Senior | ? | ? | ? | ? |
| Subordinated | ? | ? | ? | ? |

Once you've done the five charts, do you see a pattern?

### ¶412: Unfair discrimination and trade creditors (H.R. Rep. No. 95-595, at 415-18 (1977))

While § 1129(a) does not contemplate a valuation of the debtor's business, such a valuation will almost always be required under § 1129(b) in order to determine the value of the consideration to be distributed under the plan. Once the valuation is performed, it becomes a simple matter to impose the criterion that no claim will be paid more than in full.

\* \* \*

... [W]hen an impaired class [of unsecured claims] that has not accepted the plan is to receive less than full value under the plan ..., the plan may be confirmed ... if the class is not unfairly discriminated against with respect to equal classes and if junior classes will receive nothing under the plan. The second criterion is the easier to understand. It is designed to prevent a senior class from giving up consideration to a junior class unless every intermediate class consents, is paid in full, or is unimpaired. This gives intermediate creditors a great deal of leverage in negotiating with senior or secured creditors who wish to have a plan that gives value to equity.[11] One aspect of this test that is not obvious is that whether one class is senior, equal, or junior to another class is relative and not absolute. Thus from the perspective of trade creditors holding unsecured claims, claims of senior and subordinated debentures may be entitled to share on an equal basis with the trade claims. However, from the perspective of the senior unsecured debt, the subordinated debentures are junior. This point illustrates the lack of precision in the first criterion which demands that a class not be unfairly discriminated against with respect to equal classes. From the perspective of unsecured trade claims, there is no unfair discrimination as long as the total consideration given all other classes of equal rank does not exceed the amount that would result from an exact aliquot distribution. [**The first plan.**] Thus if trade creditors, senior debt, and subordinated debt are each owed $100 and the plan proposes to pay the trade debt $15, the senior debt $30, and the junior debt $0, the plan would not unfairly discriminate against the trade debt nor would any other allocation of consideration under the plan between the senior and junior debt be unfair as to the trade debt as long as the aggregate consideration is less than $30. [**The second plan.**] The senior debt could take $25 and give up $5 to the junior debt and the trade debt would have no cause to complain because as far as it is concerned the junior debt is an equal class.

However, in this latter case the senior debt would have been unfairly discriminated against ...;[12] of course the plan would also fail unless the senior debt was unimpaired, received full value, or accepted the plan, because from its perspective a junior class received property under the plan. [**The third plan.**] Application of the test from the perspective of senior debt is best illustrated by the plan that proposes to pay trade debt $15, senior debt $25, and junior debt $0. Here the senior debt is being unfairly discriminated against with respect to the equal trade debt even though the trade debt receives less than the senior debt. The discrimination arises from the fact that the senior debt is entitled to the rights of the junior debt which in this example entitle the senior debt to share on a 2:1 basis with the trade debt.

---

[11] [Cf. the discussion of *Los Angeles Lumber* and *Boyd* in ¶404(11). *Boyd* justified the "anti-skipping" aspect of absolute priority as a way to force stockholders to reveal positive information about the railroad's value.—Roe.]

[12] [I deleted this phrase from the excerpt: "because the trade debt was being unfairly overcompensated." But isn't it the subordinated, not the trade, that was unfairly overcompensated?—Roe.]

Finally, it is necessary to interpret the first criterion from the perspective of subordinated debt. The junior debt is subrogated to the rights of senior debt once the senior debt is paid in full. Thus, while the **[third]** plan that pays trade debt $15, senior debt $25, and junior debt $0 is not unfairly discriminatory against the junior debt, a **[fourth]** plan that proposes to pay trade debt $55, senior debt $100, and junior debt $1 would be unfairly discriminatory. In order to avoid discriminatory treatment against the junior debt, [**a fifth plan, with**] at least $10 would have to be received by such debt under those facts. The criterion of unfair discrimination is not derived from the fair and equitable rule [now found in § 1129(b)(2)] or from the best interests of creditors test [now in § 1129(a)(7)]. Rather it preserves just treatment of a dissenting class from the class's own perspective.

## ¶413: Dieglom problem

And now one more problem to tie this all together:

Dieglom, Inc. is a diversified manufacturing concern making automobile parts (used principally on large, fuel-inefficient cars), steel, rubber tires (nonradial only), shoes, and domestically-produced inexpensive sweaters.

Its balance sheet as of December 31, 1999, and results of operations for the twelve-month period ending December 31, 1999 were:

## DIEGLOM, INC.
### Balance Sheet
(as of December 31, 1999)

| Assets | | | Liabilities and shareholders' equity | | |
|---|---|---|---|---|---|
| Current Assets | | | Current Liabilities | | |
|   Cash | $10M | |   Bank debt due within one year | $10M | |
|   Accounts receivable | 1M | |   Trade accounts payable | 10M | |
|   Inventory and raw materials | 1M | | | | |
| | | 12M | | | 20M |
| Plant and Equipment[1] | 100M | | Long-term Debt | | |
|   Less depreciation | (52M) | |   7% senior debentures (issued 1989), due 2001 | | 20M |
| | | 48M |   3½% mortgage bonds due 2009 (issued 1969) mortgaging principal plants | | 20M |
| | | |   14% subordinated debentures due 2001 (issued 1981) | | 30M |
| | | | Total long-term debt | 70M | |
| | | | Total liabilities | | 90M |
| | | | Accumulated shareholders' deficit | (30M) | |
| Total assets | | 60M | Total liabilities and shareholders' equity | | 60M |

1. Most plant equipment was acquired in 1988 for $100 million, with a then-expected life of 20 years. Changes in the nature of the markets in which Dieglom operates make it uncertain what the continuing value of the plant or associated equipment is. Management estimates a scrap value of $5 million and a replacement value of $10 million.

## DIEGLOM, INC.
### Results of Operations
(for the year ending December 31, 1999)

| | |
|---|---|
| Gross sales | $100M |
|   Less cost of goods sold | (90M) |
| Net sales | 10M |
|   Less depreciation | (5M) |
| Income before interest expense | 5M |
|   Less interest expense | (8M) |
| Net Loss | (3M) |

Income statements for the previous five years have had results similar to the above. Assets have been sold to meet interest payments.

1. For purposes of reorganization valuation in 2000, is the value of Dieglom its assets' book value of $60 million? What factors should make it worth more? Or less?
2. Assume for the remainder of this problem that the reorganization value of Dieglom is $50 million, a number arrived at by discounting its expected cash flow to present value. Assume the scrap value of the mortgaged properties is $5 million, but that their replacement value is $10 million. How would value be distributed in a manner consistent solely with § 1129(b)? Cf. § 506. Ignore the possibility of consented-to-deviations from § 1129(b) or of nonimpairment.

### § 506. Determination of secured status

(a) An allowed claim of a creditor secured by a lien on property in which the estate has an interest ... is a secured claim to the extent of the value of such creditor's interest in the estate's interest in such property, or to the extent of the amount subject to setoff, as the case may be, and is an unsecured claim to the extent that the value of such creditor's interest or the amount so subject to setoff is less than the amount of such allowed claim. *Such value shall be determined in light of the purpose of the valuation and of the proposed disposition or use of such property,* and in conjunction with any hearing on such disposition or use or on a plan affecting such creditor's interest.

In Associates Commercial Corp. v. Rash, 117 S.Ct. 1879 (1997), the debtor retained the collateral and the question presented was whether the value of the collateral would "be determined by (1) what the secured creditor could obtain through foreclosure sale of the property ...; [or] (2) what the debtor would have to pay for comparable property ... [or] (3) the midpoint between these two measurements[.]" The secured creditor said that the debtor would have to pay $41,000 to replace the collateral, a truck. But the debtor said that the secured creditor would only realize $32,000 if it repossessed the truck and sold it. The lower court fixed the value at $32,000, as did the Fifth Circuit, because said the Fifth Circuit, under state law, the secured creditor could only obtain $32,000 of value from the collateral. For a bankruptcy court to allow more than the state rights would be incorrect unless such a result was "clearly compelled" by the Bankruptcy Code.

What does § 506(a) compel?

The first sentence in § 506 speaks of the secured party's interest, which, since the secured party's interest is determined under state law, militates for a state-determined value, i.e., liquidation value. Although this has usually been interpreted by courts and commentators as meaning the state-law value to the secured equals the security's liquidation value, to so conclude is to move too fast. Even here there'd be an indeterminacy, because if the property is worth more to the company than it is to the secured creditor, the two have incentives to make a deal somewhere in between.

The second sentence of § 506 says that the value of the security "shall be determined in light of the purpose of the valuation and of the proposed disposition or use of such property." This sentence would seem to demand a going concern, replacement value attributed to the secured party's claim. The Supreme Court said that the second sentence dominates the first one, making the secured claim the replacement value of the secured property.

3. How do we know which creditor is subordinated and to whom they're subordinated? Would the company have had an incentive in 1981 to designate the subordinated as subordinated to the mortgage bondholders? Could the bondholders have previously constrained the company, by, say, getting the company's promise that all future debt be subordinated?

   Will the company have had an incentive when negotiating loan terms with the bank creditor to designate that loan as senior to the subordinated debentures? Could the company have been constrained in the subordination agreement not to designate them as senior? How? Why? How can the lawyer be sure what is subordinated to what?

4. Assume for the rest of the problem that the subordinated debentures are subordinate to the senior debentures, that they're subordinate only to the senior debentures, and that no other creditor has agreed to subordinate itself to another creditor. Outline a distribution that could withstand attack under § 1129(b)(2) from any single dissenting class.

   Now that you have a plan satisfying § 1129, check for its realism. Describe the considerations that the various parties would raise while negotiating a plan of reorganization.

   i. Will stockholders accept the plan as is, one giving them nothing?
   ii. If the firm declines in value during a delay, who loses?
   iii. If the firm rises in value during a delay, who profits?
   iv. If the firm's operational value neither rises nor falls during a delay, but the judge overvalues the firm under § 1129(b), who profits?
   v. If the firm's operational value neither rises nor falls during a delay, but the judge undervalues the firm under § 1129(b), who profits?

5. Bankruptcy accelerates the claims to the present. Do any of the creditors want to push any of the claims back to the original maturity, with their original interest rate? Do stockholders or creditors have a financial reason to invoke § 1124(2)? Against whom? How could § 1124(2) make a distributional difference?

6. Bankrupt firms are thought not to operate well in bankruptcy. See Summers and Cutler, ¶425 (Texaco bankruptcy), at p. 132, and ¶424. Who bears the costs of the deterioration if the stockholders (or subordinated creditors) insist on a valuation hearing?

7. Who profits if the firm unexpectedly is worth a lot more than its current $50 million? See the story of the Cotton Belt Railroad, ¶418.
8. Who profits if the judge (mistakenly) values the firm at $65 million?

## ¶414: Reinstatement in Dieglom

Why would the non-mortgagee creditors think about seeking reinstatement of the mortgagee bondholders under § 1124(2)? Why could they possibly prefer that the company pay the bondholders $20 million (on the maturity date in 2009) to the company paying the bondholders $15 million in value when the plan of reorganization is confirmed?

**$20 million in value today versus reinstatement:**

First consider a plan that would have given the bondholders $20 million in value. (That is, for a few moments, ignore the mortgage bondholders' deficiency—they'd not be paid in full—and Dieglom's insolvency.) Also, think about the company paying the bondholders their $20 million under § 1129(b)(2). I.e., it's either $20 million cramdown under § 1129, or $20 million under the bonds' original terms.

Let's say that the proper capitalization rate for this company is 20%. (It's worth $50 million as a whole, and is expected to produce $10 million per year.) And let's say that the interest rate for a stream of income with features similar to that which the bondholders have would be about 10%. So, one would set up a simple spreadsheet for amounts to be paid by reinstating the debt, and their present value:

| Year | 1999 | 2000 | 2001 | 2002 | 2003 | 2004 | 2005 | 2006 | 2007 | 2008 | 2009 |
|---|---|---|---|---|---|---|---|---|---|---|---|
| Payment | 700K | 700K | 700K | 700K | 700K | 700K | 700K | 700K | 700K | 700K | 700K+20M |
| PV | | 636K | 579K | 526K | 478K | 435K | 395K | 359K | 327K | 297K | 270K | 245K+7.0M |

The present value of this $20 million, 11-year promise, at 3½% per year interest is about $11,500,000, which comes from discounting each $700,000 payment to present value (at a 10% discount rate), discounting the final $20 million repayment in year 11 to present value (also at a 10% discount rate), and then adding up the present values. Since $11.5 million is less than $20 million, the other impaired creditors prefer reinstatement, because reinstatement gives them all an extra $8,500,000 to divide up among themselves.

Think about what the company would have to promise the bondholders under § 1129(b) if the company sought *under § 1129(b)* to force the bondholders to wait until 2009 to be paid off. (For this problem, it doesn't matter much whether the creditor is "crammed" down under § 1129(b)(2)(A) for its secured claim, or under § 1129(b)(2)(B) for its deficiency claim; under (A) the plan must promise deferred cash payments with a present value equal to the allowed amount of the claim (or financial equivalents) and under (B) the property given for the unsecured would have to have a value equal to the allowed amount of the claim. Ignore the alternative of wiping out lower ranking claimants and interests, which will sometimes be available, sometimes not be available. I.e., imagine that to buy the stockholders' assent, the plan would give them a few shares of the reorganized company.)

For the property given to the bondholders to have a value equal to the allowed amount of the claim, the present value of the promise to pay $20 million in 2009 will have to have an interest rate equal to the market interest rate for such a debt, and that rate we've assumed to be 10%. (The judge must conclude that the property promised has a value of $20 million and a judge's conclusion, although the law, is not necessarily the market: It's possible that the judge will accept an interest rate below the market rate as satisfactory.) So now: If the nonbondholder creditors seek to repay the bondholders in 2009 *using § 1129(b)*.

| Year | 1999 | 2000 | 2001 | 2002 | 2003 | 2004 | 2005 | 2006 | 2007 | 2008 | 2009 |
|---|---|---|---|---|---|---|---|---|---|---|---|
| 1124(2) | 700K | 700K | 700K | 700K | 700K | 700K | 700K | 700K | 700K | 700K | 20M |
| 1129(b) | 2M | 2M | 2M | 2M | 2M | 2M | 2M | 2M | 2M | 2M | 20M |

To prefer using § 1124(2) over § 1129(b) against the bondholders, the nonbondholder creditors only have to know that $2 million is more than $700,000. By using § 1124(2), the other creditors gain $1,300,000 each year to divide up among themselves (or even to throw a little to the shareholders to buy their quick assent to the plan, or to gain their help in proposing the plan).

### $15 million in value today versus reinstatement:

Seeing why the nonbondholder creditors might prefer to promise $20 million in 2009, on the original terms, over $15 million today is only a little harder. The present value of reinstatement of the 2009 maturity date is $11.5 million, because the interest rate is so low, only 3½%:

| Year | 1999 | 2000 | 2001 | 2002 | 2003 | 2004 | 2005 | 2006 | 2007 | 2008 | 2009 |
|---|---|---|---|---|---|---|---|---|---|---|---|
| PV | 636K | 579K | 526K | 478K | 435K | 395K | 359K | 327K | 297K | 270K | 245K+7.0M |

Therefore any plan that compensates the bondholders with $15 million in true value (either cash today, or cash tomorrow with a proper rate of interest) would give the bondholders *more* than the $11.5 million that reinstatement would give them. The other creditors, preferring to give the bondholders as little in true value as is possible, therefore prefer to reinstate them at their 3½% interest rate and original maturity date.

¶415: **Section 1129(a)(7)—The best interests test**

§ 1129. Confirmation of plan

(a) The court shall confirm a plan only if all of the following requirements are met:

* * *

(7) With respect to each impaired class of claims or interests—

(A) each holder of a claim or interest of such class—

(i) has accepted the plan; or

(ii) will receive or retain under the plan on account of such claim or interest property of a value, as of the effective date of the plan, that is not less than the amount that such holder would so receive or retain if the debtor were liquidated under chapter 7 of this title on such date;

1. William Douglas' individualized-consent framework for reorganization in *Los Angeles Lumber* lives on in weakened form in § 1129(a)(7), which allows each impaired claimant to complain and not be bound by the consent of a holder's class. The holder can complain if the class has voted to give away so much that the holder would have received more in a liquidation. In effect, the class can negotiate to give away the "going concern" value of its claim, but can give away no more than the difference between the going concern value and the liquidation value. This test has come to be known as the "best interests" test, i.e., the plan would be seen as in the best interests of the creditors, because it got them at least what they would have gotten if the firm had been liquidated.

2. Review the problems in ¶¶409 and 413 to see how § 1129(a)(7) could affect the judge's authority to confirm those plans.

3. Section 1129(a)(7) seems easy for plan proponents to meet. If the judge concludes that the firm's liquidation value is a pittance, and its going concern value much higher, then the § 1129(a)(7) hearing could be finished quickly.

4. But potential interpretive ambiguities lurk in § 1129(a)(7). In an efficient market a firm's securities will trade at a price representing, in the aggregate, the present value of the firm. Whether or not the market for a bankrupt firm's securities is efficient is an open question. See Edward Altman, *Bankrupt Firms' Equity Securities As an Investment Alternative*, Fin. Analysts' J., July–Aug. 1969, at 129 (excerpted at ¶519).

5. Assume for the moment that the bankrupt public firm's securities trade in an efficient market. Would a sale of securities representing the entire ownership of the bankrupt firm be a liquidation? Or, assume going concern values are fully captured in a quick, overnight sale of the firm to a third party. Would such a sale be a liquidation?

6.  If so, could § 1129(a)(7) override the bargain framework of class consent in § 1129(a)(8)(A)? Would Douglas' framework rise up to dominate all of bankruptcy once again?

7.  Return to the Dieglom problem in ¶413. The lower ranking claimants and interests plan to seek reinstatement of the mortgage bonds under § 1124(2). They calculate that the present value of a 10-year promise to repay $20 million at 3½% interest annually has a present value of $11.3 million. Can the mortgage bondholders invoke § 1129(b)(2)(A) to upset the plan?

    The mortgage bondholders calculate that the liquidation value under § 506 of their security is $14 million. Can they invoke § 1129(a)(7) to upset the plan?

    Consider this alternative plan: The plan proponents would like to cut down the company's post-reorganization debt. They ask the bondholders to accept stock in place of their reinstated bonds. Indeed, they offer $13 million in value (in cash, stock, and other securities) to the bondholders, most of whom prefer the revised offer to reinstatement (because $13 million is more than $11 million). Two-thirds of the bondholders (by dollar amount) and more than one-half in number vote to accept the $13 million plan. Can a dissenting bondholder upset the plan under § 1129(a)(8)(A)-(B)?

    Under § 1129(b)(2)(A)?

    Under § 1129(a)(7)?

---

## ¶416: Fairness

One might argue that no rule of distribution is fairer than any other. As long as the rule of distribution is clear and known, then contract can allocate the risks and rewards of lending. If a legal rule creates the risk that a creditor will not be paid in full, then, foreseeing that risk, creditors will insist on being compensated for this risk when they make the loan. If stockholders will take some part of an insolvent firm, then creditors will react by (a) raising their interest rate slightly, and/or (b) declining to lend to a few borderline firms. Eventually markets will adjust: a little less capital will go into debt markets and a little more into equity markets, but on average investors will get their expected returns. They will not be "unfairly" surprised. The result may be (mildly) inefficient, but it would not be unfair.

To see this another way, law not only protects creditors' expectations, but defines them. Once law defines those expectations, creditors react and will no longer be "surprised" by bankruptcy results that do not fully compensate them.

The critical policy issue might thus ultimately be neither fairness nor expectations. One might have to examine whether one set of rules is clearer and easier to understand (more knowable) than another. For example, a defect of an investment value rule (i.e., one that reduced the compensation to senior bondholders because they, like the stockholders had made a bad investment and their retrospectively poor interest rate could justify compensating them less than the absolute priority, face value of their claim) is that it requires a court to make judgments as to the probability distribution, a requirement that does not lend itself to clarity, certainty, or predictability.

Absolute priority has a great clarity for distribution *once firm value is known.* But, given the rejection of the market as an arbiter, the distributions made under an absolute priority standard are themselves uncertain, because chapter 11's assigned value of the firm is itself uncertain.

A separate examination of the rule of the distribution would have to be made as to expectations. Passage of a law does not make it necessarily widely-known. If creditors assume they have priority, irrespective of the current state of the Bankruptcy Code, they will not seek compensation for bearing risks that they just do not know they are assuming. Such problems, if they exist, would argue for molding the Code to measured expectations. One would expect though that institutional creditors and other players who repeatedly deal with chapter 11 would know, in gross, what to expect.

A seemingly separate examination of the external costs of the rule might seem necessary. Does one set of rules encourage deadlock and delay in reorganization? For example, would absolute priority with a market value encourage stockholders to delay so as to await a favorable turn in the market? Or could the bankruptcy apparatus force a sale fast? And does one set of rules facilitate efficient investment in businesses that risk bankruptcy better than other rules? The external costs are likely to depend primarily on the relative clarity of the rules and the speed with which they could be implemented. Moreover, does one set of rules best facilitate efficient investment before bankruptcy?

The Bankruptcy Code would seem to fall short of the ideal. Not even the question of claim value is answered definitively. Section 1129(b) would give face value according to absolute priority. But § 1124(2), although it does not change the formal value of the claim under § 502, would effectively give investment value. Furthermore, given the flexibility and unpredictability of firm value, the worth of a potential distribution under § 1129(b) is derivatively also uncertain. Whether another rule of reorganization would better approach the ideal is a separate question.

## ¶417: **Other creditors with priority**

Section 507(a) gives a priority, above that of general unsecured creditors, to several claimants. The priorities go to:

1. Administrative expenses, which includes not just the costs of paying the attorneys, accountants, trustees, and professionals who administer the bankrupt firm and preserve it, but also to trade creditors who ship merchandise or provide services to the bankrupt during the bankruptcy proceeding.[13]

---

[13] Administrative expenses include the secured creditor's claim for adequate protection. See § 507(b).

2. "Gap" creditors, who are trade creditors whose claim arose during the moments after a bankruptcy petition was filed, but before the court granted an "order of relief."
3. Back wages to the debtor's employees, limited in amount and time.
4. Monies due to employee benefit plans, again limited in amount and time.
5. Special provision for grain facilities.
6. Return of deposits to those who paid the debtor for goods or services that weren't delivered, but limited in amount.
7. [Some] taxes.

After these claims are paid, general unsecured creditors are paid.

## C. The reality of delay in chapter 11

### ¶418: Value rising: The Cotton Belt Railroad: Walter Blum & Stanley Kaplan, Corporate Readjustments and Reorganizations 485–86 (1976)

1. A dramatic success for the stalling strategy is found in the proceedings to reorganize the St. Louis, Southwestern Railway under § 77.

    "The story of Lazarus has been re-enacted in the case of St. Louis Southwestern shares. By June, 1947, the preferred and common had twice been pronounced dead and valueless by the highest authority of the land—the United States Supreme Court. Yet a month after the latter of these coroner's verdicts the corpse not only opened his eyes and stirred; it rose up completely cured of every vestige of financial ill. The bankruptcy ended; all matured debts and interest were paid; the stockholders took over again as if nothing had happened. In the following year the common stock received its first dividend in the company's fifty-seven-year history. During the bankruptcy the stock had been suspended from New York Stock Exchange dealings as presumably worthless, and it had actually sold for next to nothing in the 'over-the-counter' market. Now it was restored to exchange trading, and in addition its price rose to 139—which made it one of the highest-priced railroad issues in the market.

    "How did these reversals come about? Before 1929 the Cotton Belt had been one of the weaker roads with an irregular record. In the eleven years from 1930 to 1940 it reported continuous deficits. After allowing for preferred dividends (which are non-cumulative) the computed losses aggregated $130 per share of common stock. In 1935 trustees in bankruptcy were appointed. By 1941 the I.C.C. had approved a reorganization plan which scaled down the debt drastically and completely wiped out both the preferred and the common stocks. This plan was approved by the United States District Court, and it was upheld by the next higher court on appeal. The stockholders then went to the United States Supreme Court, which declined to review the case. The stockholders tried their last resort—a request to the Supreme Court for a rehearing. This too was denied, in June, 1947. By every legal precedent the case was now finished and the stock issues were extinct.

    "But, while all this legal maneuvering was taking its tedious course, the financial position of the Cotton Belt was being revolutionized by the impact of the war and post-war traffic. In the 7-year period 1941–47 the road made phenomenal earnings, which were equivalent to over $200 a share on the common—an annual average of $34 per share. It had now become one of the most economically operated carriers in the country, as measured by the ratio of net to gross.

"Thus the Cotton Belt stockholders lost every legal battle but won their war. There was now enough cash to restore the company to a completely solvent condition. Instead of carrying out the reorganization plan, which the Supreme Court had just upheld and which wiped out both stock issues, the lower court was readily persuaded to dismiss the bankruptcy proceedings altogether. Just as in an old-fashioned melodrama, the hero rode up with the mortgage money in the nick of time and the homestead was saved."

From Benjamin Graham, The Intelligent Investor, pp. 195–196 (1949).

2. Obviously, not all enterprises manage to improve their situations during the time consumed by legal maneuvering.

## D. The lawyers

### ¶419: Value uncertain: Practical lawyers, modern delay, and the advantages of the valuation hearing for shareholders

Strategic use (or the passive benefits) of a slow valuation process are not historical anomalies of the 1930s Depression-era reorganizations, such as the reorganization of the Cotton Belt Railroad, described in the prior section.

Consider the following report from attorneys who represented the stockholders' committee in the reorganization in chapter 11 of Saxon Industries. In 1981 Saxon was a Fortune 500 company. The chapter 11 audit showed that its net worth was a negative $200 million. Creditors were owed $320 million.

> Creditors "argued that the concern's ... stockholders had no further interest in the company. Because liabilities appeared to so greatly exceed assets, it did not seem likely that [even] the unsecured creditors would get paid in full under any reorganization plan .... Saxon's stockholders [might have] seemed doomed to getting nothing for their stock.
>
> "[But] under the reorganization plan ultimately confirmed by the bankruptcy court, however, the Saxon shareholders weren't wiped out. They received convertible stock with a total value of $9 million [or almost 10% of the company's book value as shown in the bankruptcy audit].
>
> "How did the shareholders do so well? Mainly because [they] formed a committee, utilized their rightful leverage under the bankruptcy laws, and negotiated with Saxon's creditors and the company itself.
>
> "Today, in almost every instance in which a public company seeks protection under Chapter 11, the shareholders are faced with the same argument that Saxon's [shareholders] encountered—that the debtor is insolvent and, therefore, their equity no longer exists. In effect, the creditors claim they own the company.

"As the Saxon shareholders—and creditors—found out, however, just saying that a company is insolvent doesn't make it so under the bankruptcy laws. In order for shareholders to have their interest eliminated, the bankruptcy court must go through a complicated fact-finding trial [under § 1129(b)(2)] to determine whether the company is insolvent. The court must take extensive testimony on the actual value of the company's assets, listen to experts from opposing sides, and come to some supportable conclusion itself.

"Such trials are very time-consuming. When they are undertaken, confirmation of a plan of reorganization for a company operating under Chapter 11 is delayed ....

"It's not in [the unsecured creditors'] best interest ... to engage in a lengthy battle, especially if the outcome is uncertain. And it usually is very difficult to know in advance whether a court will decide that a bankrupt company is solvent or insolvent under the bankruptcy laws. The unsecured creditors' experts will testify that the corporation is insolvent and that the shareholders' interests should be eliminated. The shareholders' experts will testify that the corporation is clearly solvent and the shareholders should maintain their stock ownership, or have it diluted minimally.

"Creditors, though, will be willing to negotiate only if there are some shareholders with whom they can negotiate. [S]hareholders must ... form a committee [to] negotiate to protect their interests."

Barry Radick & Stephen Blauner, *Shareholders, Unite!—What To Do When a Firm Goes Bankrupt*, Barron's, Apr. 14, 1986, at 22–24.

Lynn LoPucki and William Whitford examined many chapter 11 reorganizations of the 1980s and found substantial deviation from absolute priority, benefiting stockholders. When the court appointed an equity holders' committee, equity was nearly certain to get something, averaging about 7 or 8%, in the § 1129(a)(8) settlement. Lynn LoPucki & William Whitford, *Preemptive Cram Down*, 65 Am. Bankr. L.J. 625, 626 (1991).

Although hold-up value, uncertainty, and creditors' desire to keep shareholder-managers on board helped equity, LoPucki and Whitford believe many firms would quickly have been found insolvent, if an early solvency hearing apart from the late-stage cram-down under § 1129 were readily available under the Code. Why then wasn't cram-down used against the shareholders? They speculate "that the difficulty of cram-down was in large part a convenient myth that served the interests of the relatively small group of lawyers who repeatedly play important roles in major reorganization cases. Because these lawyers appeared against each other so often, they had an interest in preserving their reputations as reasonable and responsible negotiators." Id. at 630–31.

## ¶420: Rule 11

The Federal Rules of Civil Procedure provide:

> The signature of an attorney or party constitutes a certificate by him that he has read the pleading, motion, or other paper; that to the best of his knowledge, information, and belief formed after reasonable inquiry it is well grounded in fact and is warranted by existing law ... and that it is not interposed for any improper purpose, such as to harass or to cause unnecessary delay or needless increase in the cost of litigation .... If a pleading, motion, or other paper is signed in violation of this rule, the court, upon motion or upon its own initiative, shall impose upon the person who signed it, a represented party, or both, an appropriate sanction ....

This rule might worry bankruptcy lawyers for the stockholders of an apparently insolvent firm. But if valuation in bankruptcy is elastic, need an attorney's conscience or sense of professional responsibility be troubled when he or she asserts that the stockholders have an interest in the firm pursuant to § 1129(b)(2)?

Rule 11 sanctions have only infrequently been asserted in private commercial cases; they have usually been invoked in civil rights cases and occasionally in federal income taxation suits. Note, *Plausible Pleadings: Developing Standards for Rule 11 Sanctions*, 100 Harv. L. Rev. 630 (1987) (citing S. Kassin, An Empirical Study of Rule 11 Sanctions (Federal Judicial Center 1985)). Bankruptcy courts have their own rules; Bankruptcy Rule 9011 is substantively similar to Rule 11.

## ¶421: Standards of professional responsibility

### RULE 3.1 of The American Bar Association's Model Rules of Professional Responsibility: Meritorious Claims and Contentions

> A lawyer shall not bring or defend a proceeding, or assert or controvert an issue therein, unless there is a basis for doing so that is not frivolous, which includes a good faith argument for an extension, modification or reversal of existing law ....

### Comment

> The advocate has a duty to use legal procedure for the fullest benefit of the client's cause, but also a duty not to abuse legal procedure. The law, both procedural and substantive, establishes the limits within which an advocate may proceed. However, the law is not always clear and never is static. Accordingly, in determining the proper scope of advocacy, account must be taken of the law's ambiguities and potential for change.
>
> The filing of an action or defense or similar action taken for a client is not frivolous merely because the facts have not first been fully substantiated .... Such action is

not frivolous even though the lawyer believes that the client's position ultimately will not prevail. The action is frivolous, however, if the client desires to have the action taken primarily for the purpose of harassing or maliciously injuring a person or if the lawyer is unable either to make a good faith argument on the merits of the action taken or to support the action taken by a good faith argument for an extension, modification or reversal of existing law.

### RULE 3.2 Expediting Litigation

A lawyer shall make reasonable efforts to expedite litigation consistent with the interest of the client.

### Comment

Dilatory practices bring the administration of justice into disrepute. Delay should not be indulged merely for the convenience of the advocate or for the purpose of frustrating an opposing party's attempt to obtain rightful redress or repose. It is not a justification that similar conduct is often tolerated by the bench and bar. The question is whether a competent lawyer acting in good faith would regard the course of action as having some substantial purpose other than delay. *Realizing financial or other benefit from otherwise improper delay in litigation is not a legitimate interest of the client.*

### ¶422: Psychology

Could the psychology of practicing law contribute to the deadlocks and costs of corporate reorganization? What do the following readings tell us?

> "In cases of civil liability, attorneys frequently fail to negotiate a settlement until well after they have spent enormous amounts of their client's resources. If a case is going to settle, economic rationality would dictate that the parties resolve the dispute before incurring the burdensome costs of pretrial posturing. Why is it that attorneys only rarely achieve this efficient outcome? Several cognitive biases in perception of their cases may prevent attorneys from achieving an early settlement .... Prospect Theory, a psychological theory of the perception of chance events, predicts that all defendants will systematically undervalue the expected utility of the case against them. This undervaluing can lead defendants to reject otherwise acceptable settlement offers and gamble on the outcome at trial ....
>
> "Part of an attorney's job is [to] generate arguments which advance his position. The process of generating such arguments may lead the attorney to believe more strongly in his case. In research on story-generation, cognitive psychologists have found that when a person generates reasons and stories to support a position, they come to believe in that position .... [E]ven if the parties do not feel an enormous need to litigate the case because of some hatred for the other party or desire to

have one's day in court, cognitive biases impede the negotiation and settlement process."

Jeffrey Rachlinski, Prospect Theory and Civil Negotiation, Stanford Center on Conflict and Negotiation, Working Paper No. 17, Oct. 1990.

Consider the possibility that uncertain standards in chapter 11 (and uncertain valuation) could lead each party to differ on their notion of what settlement would be "fair":

> "A major unsolved riddle facing the social sciences is the cause of impasse in negotiations. The consequences of impasse are evident in the amount of private and public resources spent on civil litigation, the costs of labor unrest, the psychic and pecuniary wounds of domestic strife, and in clashes among religious, ethnic and regional groups. Impasses in these settings are not only pernicious, but somewhat paradoxical since negotiations typically unfold over long periods of time, offering ample opportunities for interaction between the parties.
>
> "Economists ... typically attribute delays in settlement to incomplete information. Bargainers possess private information about factors such as their alternatives to negotiated agreements and costs to delay, causing them to be mutually uncertain about the other side's reservation value. Uncertainty produces impasse because bargainers use costly delays to signal to the other party information about their own reservation value ....
>
> "[A] different and relatively simple psychological mechanism [can also] cause ... bargaining impasse. This is the tendency for parties to arrive at judgments that reflect a self-serving bias—to conflate what is fair with what benefits oneself. Such self-serving assessments of fairness can impede negotiations and promote impasse in at least three ways. First, if negotiators estimate the value of the alternatives to negotiated settlements in self-serving ways, this could rule out any chance of settlement by eliminating the contract zone (the set of agreements that both sides prefer to their reservation values). Second, if disputants believe that their notion of fairness is impartial and shared by both sides, then they will interpret the other party's aggressive bargaining not as an attempt to get what they perceive of as fair, but as a cynical and exploitative attempt to gain an unfair strategic advantage. Research in psychology and economics has shown that bargainers care not only about what the other party offers, but also about the other party's motives. Third, negotiators are strongly averse to settling even slightly below the point they view as fair .... If disputants are willing to make economic sacrifices to avoid a settlement perceived as unfair and their ideas of fairness are biased in directions that favor themselves, then bargainers who are 'only trying to get what is fair' may not be able to settle their dispute.
>
> "... [This] self-serving bias, and the impasses it causes, occurs even when disputants possess identical information .... The bias is also present when bargainers have incentives to evaluate the situation impartially, which implies that the bias does not appear to be deliberate or strategic."

Linda Babcock and George Loewenstein, *Explaining Bargaining Impasse: The Role of Self-Serving Biases*, 11 J. Econ. Perspectives 109, 109–10 (1997).

### E. The managers

#### ¶423: The role of managers in chapter 11

*Los Angeles Lumber* paints a picture of managers as allied with shareholders of the bankrupt. The Cotton Belt Railroad reading is implicitly similar. Because the Code gives managers the power to present the first plan, due to the four-month exclusivity period, regularly extended, during which only the debtor can present a plan, an alliance of incumbent managers with shareholders could be powerful.[14]

A modern chapter 11 of a public company is more complex. First, managers of the public company often do not have a lot of their own wealth tied up in the company, nor do they own a substantial fraction of the bankrupt's stock. Second, managerial turnover in chapter 11 is fairly high.[15] Third, the orientation of the new managers can be uncertain. In a few cases the new managers wanted to keep the enterprise going, even when liquidation seemed warranted. Eastern Airlines used its enormous cash reserves up, illustrating how managers (even a manager who was a court-appointed trustee) might prefer to take a chance to be a hero who saves the company. But, fourth, there now is a cadre of professional "turnaround" managers who move from chapter 11 to chapter 11, turn the company around, often with partial liquidations, and then move on. Creditors are often instrumental in bringing these chapter 11 veterans into the reorganizing company.[16]

### F. The costs of delay

#### ¶424: Value declining: cutbacks and bankruptcy costs

Are there bankruptcy costs? Or does the sad state of bankrupt companies just reflect that they are lousy companies, in lousy businesses, often with lousy managements? Does the process of going through chapter 11 cause the bankrupt to suffer damage more than a streamlined process of recapitalization would?

The answers to these questions would help us to know whether bankruptcy reform is important. Although the direct costs of bankruptcy in lawyers', bankers', and

---

[14] Section 1121(b): "only the debtor may file a plan until after 120 days after the date of the order for relief ...."

[15] Stuart Gilson, *Bankruptcy, boards, banks, and blockholders*, 27 J. Fin. Econ. 355 (1987) (over half of the bankrupt's board of directors is gone by the end of a chapter 11).

[16] Lynn M. LoPucki, *Strange Visions in a Strange World*, 91 Mich. L. Rev. 79, 96 (1991).

*The New Yorker, June 24, 1991, at 23*

accountants' fees are large on an absolute scale, they are a small percentage of the bankrupt public firm's assets. They are not grossly out of line with the fees that professionals get in other complex corporate rearrangements. The question then is whether there are large indirect costs, because, say, the bankrupt firm when entangled in chapter 11 operates even more poorly than it would otherwise. This question of how big are bankruptcy costs, central though it may be, has not yet received a satisfactory answer. (See Cutler and Summers, ¶425, next, for some speculation.)

Perhaps the bankrupt must quickly jettison parts of its enterprise that have a disproportionate and negative effect on its remaining operations. A car company goes bankrupt; could it cutback by cutting part of its product? A new car without a transmission is worth less than a complete new car, minus the cost of a new transmission. A consumer products company that cuts back on advertising might disappear. But given the automatic stay and the ability to get debtor-in-possession financing, the chance of this kind of deterioration, illustrated below, seems remote. That kind of bankruptcy cost seems the kind well-addressed by chapter 11. Bankruptcy costs, if there are any, must arise elsewhere.

## ¶425: Some costs of delay: Summers & Cutler,[17] Texaco and Pennzoil Both Lost Big, N.Y. Times, Feb. 14, 1988, at 3, cols. 1–3 (business section)

Economists have long debated the costs of the litigation proceedings and protracted negotiations that surround bankruptcy situations. But as yet, there has been

---

[17] Lawrence Summers [was in 1988 the] Nathaniel Ropes Professor of Political Economy at Harvard University[; in 1999 he was the Secretary of the Treasury]. David Cutler [was] a graduate student in economics at M.I.T.

relatively little hard evidence regarding the magnitude of these costs. The Texaco-Pennzoil case provides an ideal experiment for studying these issues. The stocks of both companies are publicly traded, so that widely agreed-upon estimates of costs may be obtained. In a recent study, we examined the impact of the Texaco-Pennzoil litigation on the market value of the two companies in a way that was carefully controlled for general market movements affecting the value of the companies.

The stock price data deliver a clear verdict about the costs of economic conflict: they are enormous. Over the course of the case, whenever the market received news that Texaco would have to make a large payment to Pennzoil, the combined value of the two companies declined sharply, with Texaco's stock falling by much more than Pennzoil's rose. In the week following the initial $10 billion jury verdict, Texaco's stock market value declined by $1.1 billion, while Pennzoil's rose by only $489 million. Similarly, when the Supreme Court upheld Pennzoil's position in April 1987, Texaco lost $1.3 billion while Pennzoil gained only $518 million.

Over the entire period from November 1985 through Texaco's bankruptcy filing last April, Texaco lost more than $2.2 billion relative to its stock value of $8.5 billion before the case began, while Pennzoil's value rose by only $49.5 million, compared with its initial market value of $2 billion. These figures understate the costs of the conflict since they omit the losses of Texaco's bondholders.

Just as news suggesting that the conflict was likely to continue reducing the combined value of the two companies, recent movements toward a settlement have been associated with dramatic increases in the combined value. The record is somewhat difficult to interpret because some of Texaco's stellar stock market performance may be due to the expectation of a hostile takeover. But the data suggest that the gain in combined value in November and December of last year was more than $2 billion. On the day that Texaco's shareholders committee agreed to a $3 billion settlement with Pennzoil the gain in joint value was more than $1 billion. When Texaco and Pennzoil agreed to the same figure one week later, the gain was a further $500 million. Texaco's shareholders bore the brunt of the earlier losses and were the major beneficiaries of most of the recent increases.

Stock market information suggests that most of what Texaco lost during the conflict was not captured by Pennzoil. Rather, the market suspected that it would be dissipated by the parties ....

Where then did all the money go? A first possibility is that it went to the lawyers and investment bankers involved in the legal struggle between the two companies. Bankruptcy filings reveal that Texaco's legal fees were about $60 million through the end of 1987. Pennzoil reported that its fees for the case will be about $400 million. The two together cannot account for most of the $2 billion loss in joint value during the dispute.

A second possibility is that the market anticipated that Pennzoil would waste part of any settlement it received from Texaco. In this case, it would be rational for investors to reduce their valuation of Texaco by more than they increased their valuation of Pennzoil. However, if this explanation were a large part of the story, we would expect that the combined value of the two companies would now be suffering as Texaco prepares to pay Pennzoil $3 billion. The settlement of the dispute wiped out almost all of the market losses observed during the litigation and bankruptcy periods. This suggests that the market is no longer expecting Pennzoil to waste its payment from Texaco.

A third possibility is that the uncertainty associated with the ongoing conflict interfered with the normal functioning of the two companies. In a business where profits are as slim as they have been in the oil industry in recent years, even small disturbances in a firm's productivity may cut very deeply into its profitability. In its original bankruptcy filing, Texaco described how it had almost been forced to close a refinery because of its inability to get a credit line. It also stressed that financial strain made it impossible for it to undertake otherwise profitable new investments. Finally, it is clear that the conflict diverted management's attention from normal business objectives. We regard this as the most plausible explanation for the puzzling behavior of Texaco and Pennzoil stock prices over the last 27 months.

The lesson of the Texaco-Pennzoil conflict is that large forced wealth transfers from one entity to another also involve large leakages, particularly during ongoing struggles. More is transferred than is received ....

## ¶426: Questions on Summers & Cutler

1. The direct costs of corporate reorganization in lawyers', bankers', and accountants' fees are large in absolute size ($150 million in the Federated bankruptcy alone), but small as a percentage of the firm's value, averaging about 3% for the bankruptcy of public firms. Lawrence A. Weiss, *Bankruptcy resolution: Direct costs and violation of priority of claims*, 27 J. Fin. Econ. 285 (1990). Some recent research suggests that the costs of *purely financial* leverage (i.e., when the firm still has good operations) aren't high. Gregor Andrade and Steven N. Kaplan, *How Costly is Financial (not Economic) Distress?—Evidence from Highly Leveraged Transactions that Became Distressed*, 53 Journal of Finance 1443 (1998); Steven N. Kaplan, *Federated's Acquisition and Bankruptcy: Lessons and Implications*, 72 Wash. U.L.Q. 1103 (1994). See also Frank Easterbrook, *Is corporate bankruptcy efficient?* 27 J. Fin. Econ. 411 (1990).

2. Was Texaco slow to settle because the firm's directors were concerned about personal liability? Once the firm was hit with the $10 billion verdict, the directors feared that a successful suit for negligence liability could bankrupt them personally *even if* they settled the suit for $3 billion; hence, they were gambling at overturning the suit completely. The then-recent decision of the Delaware Supreme Court in *Van Gorkom* might have frightened Texaco's directors: a Delaware court might find them liable for negligence, as it had found the *Van Gorkom* directors.

But when (i) a takeover entrepreneur, Carl Icahn, acquired a block of stock while announcing that he intended to force a settlement, (ii) the bankruptcy judge aggressively pushed for settlement, announcing that he might terminate management's period of exclusivity to file a plan, and (iii) creditors agreed with Pennzoil that a $3 billion settlement was about right, then management settled. See Robert H. Mnookin & Robert B. Wilson, *Rational Bargaining and Market Efficiency: Understanding Pennzoil v. Texaco*, 75 Va. L. Rev. 295 (1989).

---

### ¶427: <u>The common pool problem in general</u>

The creditors' and stockholders' scrambling for position in reorganization (and the resulting deterioration of the firm as managers' time is diverted and relations with suppliers and customers deteriorate) can be analogized to what economists call a "common pool" problem. When there's a common pool, people may overuse the pool, to the detriment of everyone. Each person deciding whether to use the pool could rationally calculate that their own benefits exceed their own costs, because others bear most of the costs. X pollutes the stream, although X lives next to the stream. The full costs of X's pollution are borne by X, Y, and Z. If the convenience to X of polluting exceeds 1/3 of the costs of the pollution (the share of the pollution that X absorbs), then X has an incentive to pollute despite that it's socially wasteful. So do Y and Z.

Libecap and Wiggins describe the common pool problem in oil drilling. Gary Libecap & Steven Wiggins, *Contractual Responses to the Common Pool: Prorationing of Crude Oil Production*, 74 Am. Econ. Rev. 87–88 (1984).

Consider how the oil people tried to solve, or reduce, their common pool problem. Could their efforts help us with corporate reorganization? Does "unitizing" the oil field have an analogue in corporate bankruptcy?

> "Typically, oil reservoirs are compressed between an upper layer of natural gas and a lower layer of water. The two layers, as well as gas dissolved in the oil, drive the oil to the surface when the surrounding formation is punctured by a well. Oil migrates to the well, draining neighboring areas .... As a firm drills additional wells oil migrates more rapidly into the created low pressure zone, raising the firm's share of field output. [But i]ncreases in the rate of production reduce ultimate [aggregate] oil recovery. With high withdrawal rates, the ratio of natural gas and water to oil produced increases, leading to a greater loss in subsurface pressure. Pockets of oil became trapped[] and [un]retrievable ....
>
> "[U]nrestrained oil production in the 1920s and early 1930s [show] extraordinary waste. The Federal Oil Conservation Board estimated recovery rates of only 20–25 percent with competitive extraction, while 85–90 percent was possible with controlled withdrawal.
>
> "[The oil producers tried t]hree contractual solutions ... to the common pool problems: lease consolidation, unitization of production under a single firm, and prorationing of field output among oil firms. In general, [they failed to reach]

agreements for consolidation or unitization ..., and prorationing emerged as the dominant solution. [We analyzed] prorationing contracts ... [in] Oklahoma and Texas from 1926–35, a period when private and state controls were first implemented. [We examined t]he five largest fields discovered during that period[.] ... [Only for the Yates field was] consensus for prorationing ... reached early [and maintained], and dissipation margins were sequentially closed as they appeared. [In other fields] there were partial agreements [with each firm's share] of the ... field ... based on [its] number of wells; hence, [firms had an incentive to drill more wells and] dissipation occurred as firms drilled additional wells, and agreements broke down after short periods. On East Texas, field output limits were only effective during military occupation of the field in 1931 and under [the Federal government's] controls [under the National Industrial Recovery Act] in 1933. Where private contracting failed, firms lobbied for state enforcement ....

"[Some] studies of [government action criticized the government's rules for failing to achieve] production efficiency. [But we believe] that [the government's] prorationing quotas were chosen to bring all firms into broad agreement, rather than to achieve minimum physical production cost. To achieve consensus for control of the most costly sources of rent depletion, concessions permitting less extensive dissipation along other margins were made .... While the costs of the regulatory arrangement were high, our examination explains these rules as optimizing responses to achieve at least some control of rent dissipation."

### ¶428: Bankruptcy as a common pool problem: Thomas H. Jackson, The Logic and Limits of Bankruptcy Law 10-19 (1986)[18]

\* \* \*

The basic problem that bankruptcy law is designed to handle, both as a normative matter and as a positive matter, is that the system of individual creditor remedies may be bad for the creditors *as a group* when there are not enough assets to go around. Because creditors have conflicting rights, there is a tendency in their debt-collection efforts to make a bad situation worse. Bankruptcy law responds to this problem .... [One way to characterize the problem] is as a species of what is called a *common pool* problem ....[19]

This role of bankruptcy law is largely unquestioned. But because this role carries limits on what *else* bankruptcy law can do, it is worth considering the basics of the problem so that we understand its essential features before examining whether and why credit may present that problem. The vehicle will be a typical, albeit simple,

---

[18] Reprinted by permission of the publisher from THE LOGIC AND LIMITS OF BANKRUPTCY LAW by Thomas H. Jackson, Cambridge, Mass.: Harvard University Press, Copyright 1986 by the President and Fellows of Harvard College.

[19] See Hardin, "The Tragedy of the Commons," 162 Science 1243 (1968): Libecap & Wiggins, "Contractual Responses to the Common Pool: Prorationing of Crude Oil Production," 74 Am. Econ. Rev. 87 (1984) ....

common pool example. Imagine that you own a lake. There are fish in the lake. You are the only one who has the right to fish in that lake, and no one constrains your decision as to how much fishing to do. You have it in your power to catch all the fish this year and sell them for, say, $100,000. If you did that, however, there would be no fish in the lake next year. It might be better for you—you might maximize your total return from fishing—if you caught and sold some fish this year but left other fish in the lake so that they could multiply and you would have fish in subsequent years. Assume that, by taking this approach, you could earn (adjusting for inflation) $50,000 each year. Having this outcome is like having a perpetual annuity paying $50,000 a year. It has a present value of perhaps $500,000. Since (obviously, I hope) when all other things are equal, $500,000 is better than $100,000, you as sole owner, would limit your fishing this year unless some other factor influenced you.

But what if you are not the only one who can fish in this lake? What if a hundred people can do so? The optimal solution has not changed: it would be preferable to leave some fish in the lake to multiply because doing so has a present value of $500,000. But in this case, unlike that where you have to control only yourself, an obstacle exists in achieving that result. If there are a hundred fishermen, you cannot be sure, by limiting your fishing, that there will be any more fish next year, unless you can also control the others. You may, then, have an incentive to catch as many fish as you can today because maximizing your take this year (catching, on average, $1,000 worth of fish) is better for you than holding off (catching, say only $500 worth of fish this year) while others scramble and deplete the stock entirely.[20] If you hold off, your aggregate return is only $500, since nothing will be left for next year or the year after. But that sort of reasoning by each of the hundred fishermen will mean that the stock of fish will be gone by the end of the first season. The fishermen will split $100,000 this year, but there will be no fish—and no money—in future years. Self-interest results in their splitting $100,000, not $500,000.

What is required is some rule that will make all hundred fishermen act as a sole owner would. That is where bankruptcy law enters the picture in a world not of fish but of credit. The grab rules of nonbankruptcy law and their allocation of assets on the basis of first-come, first-served create an incentive on the part of the individual creditors, when they sense that a debtor may have more liabilities than assets, to get in line today (by, for example, getting a sheriff to execute on the debtor's equipment), because if they do not, they run the risk of getting nothing. This decision by numerous individual creditors, however, may be the wrong decision for the creditors as a group. Even though the debtor is insolvent, they might be better off if they held the assets together. Bankruptcy provides a way to make these diverse individuals act as one, by imposing a *collective* and *compulsory* proceeding on them. Unlike a typical common pool solution, however, the compulsory solution of bankruptcy law does not apply in

---

[20] Note that this [example] assumes that you are selfish, not altruistic. Where there are a hundred fishermen, it only takes one selfish one to upset the altruism of the others. Thus, the assumption seems quite reasonable.

all places at all times. Instead, it runs parallel with a system of individual debt-collection rules and is available to supplant them when and if needed.

... Exactly how does bankruptcy law make creditors as a group better off? To find the answer to that question, consider a simple hypothetical example involving credit, not fish. Debtor has a small printing business. Potential creditors estimate that there is a 20 percent chance that Debtor (who is virtuous and will not misbehave) will become insolvent through bad luck, general economic downturn, or whatever. (By insolvency, I mean a condition whereby Debtor will not have enough assets to satisfy his creditors.) At the point of insolvency—I shall make this very simple—the business is expected to be worth $50,000 if sold piecemeal. Creditors also know that each of them will have to spend $1,000 in pursuit of their individual collection efforts should Debtor become insolvent and fail to repay them. Under these circumstances Debtor borrows $25,000 from each of four creditors, Creditors 1 through 4. Because these creditors know that there is this 20 percent chance, they can account for it—and the associated collection costs—in the interest rate they charge Debtor. Assume that each party can watch out for its own interest, and let us see whether, as in the example of fishing, there are reasons to think that these people would favor a set of restrictions on their own behavior (apart from paternalism or other similar considerations).

Given that these creditors can watch out for their own interests, the question to be addressed is how these creditors should go about protecting themselves. If the creditors have to protect themselves by means of a costly and inefficient system, Debtor is going to have to pay more to obtain credit.[21] Thus, when we consider them all together—Creditors 1 through 4 and Debtor—the relevant question is: would the availability of a bankruptcy system reduce the costs of credit?

\* \* \*

... [First] the case for bankruptcy's advantages. The common pool example of fish in a lake suggests that one of the advantages to a collective system is a larger aggregate pie. Does that advantage exist in the case of credit? When dealing with businesses, the answer, at least some of the time, would seem to be "yes." The use of individual creditor remedies may lead to a piecemeal dismantling of a debtor's business by the untimely removal of necessary operating assets. To the extent that a non-piecemeal collective process (whether in the form of a liquidation or reorganization) is likely to increase the aggregate value of the pool of assets, its substitution for individual remedies would be advantageous to the creditors as a group. This is derived from a commonplace notion: that a collection of assets is sometimes more valuable together

---

[21] The extent to which this adjustment will result in the costs being fully transferred back to the debtor depends on the elasticities of supply of and demand for credit. See Meckling, "Financial Markets, Default, and Bankruptcy: The Role of the State," 41 Law & Contemp. Probs. 13 (Autumn 1977); Weston, "Some Economic Fundamentals for an Analysis of Bankruptcy," 41 Law & Contemp. Probs. 47 (Autumn 1977).

than the same assets would be if spread to the winds. It is often referred to as the surplus of a going-concern value over a liquidation value.

Thus, the most obvious reason for a collective system of creditor collection is to make sure that creditors, in pursuing their individual remedies, do not actually decrease the aggregate value of the assets that will be used to repay them. In our example this situation would occur when a printing press, for example, could be sold to a third party for $20,000, leaving $30,000 of other assets, but the business as a unit could generate sufficient cash so as to have a value of more than $50,000.[22] As such it is directly analogous to the case of the fish in the lake. Even in the case in which the assets should be sold and the business dismembered, the aggregate value of the assets may be increased by keeping groups of those assets together (the printing press with its custom dies, for example) to be sold as discrete unit.

This advantage, however, is not the only one to be derived from a collective system for creditors. Consider what the creditors would get if there were no bankruptcy system (putting aside the ultimate collection costs). Without a collective system all of the creditors in our example know that in the case of Debtor's insolvency the first two creditors to get to (and through) the courthouse (or to Debtor, to persuade Debtor to pay voluntarily), will get $25,000 [each], leaving nothing for the third and fourth .... A collective system, however, would ensure that they would each get $12,500.

\* \* \*

One other possible advantage of a collective proceeding should also be noted: there may be costs to the individualized approach to collecting (in addition to the $1,000 collection costs). For example, since each creditor [would] know [that, absent bankruptcy] that it must "beat out" the others if it wants to be paid in full, it will spend time monitoring Debtor and the other creditors to make sure that it will be not worse than second in the race (and therefore still be paid in full). Although some of these activities may be beneficial, many may not be; they will simply be costs of racing against other creditors .... Each creditor has to spend this money just to stay in the race because if it does not, it is a virtual certainty that the others will beat it to the payment punch ....

\* \* \*

... The single most fruitful way to think about bankruptcy is to see it as ameliorating a common pool problem created by a system of individual creditor remedies. Bankruptcy provides a way to override the creditors' pursuit of their own remedies and to make them work together.[23]

---

[22] The reasons for this result are complex. The assumption is that the printing press is worth only $20,000 in the hands of a third party but more in the hands of Debtor. If this is so, however, one might think that the third party could then turn and sell the press to Debtor for more than $20,000 (making its value in the hands of the third party more than $20,000) .... Suffice it to say, for our purposes, that informational and transactional barriers are often sufficient to permit this discrepancy to exist.

[23] As such, it reflects the kind of contract that creditors would agree to if they were able to negotiate with each other before extending credit ....

This approach immediately suggests several features of bankruptcy law. First, such a law must usurp individual creditor remedies in order to make the claimants act in an altruistic and cooperative way. Thus, the proceeding is inherently *collective*. Moreover, this system works only if all the creditors are bound to it. To allow a debtor to contract with a creditor to avoid participating in the bankruptcy proceeding would destroy the advantages of a collective system. So the proceeding must be compulsory as well. But unlike common pool solutions in oil and gas or fishing, it is not the exclusive system for dividing up assets. It, instead, supplants an existing system of individual creditor remedies, and as we shall see, it is this feature that makes crucial an awareness of its limitations.

* * *

## ¶429: Miscellaneous Code provisions

### § 502. Allowance of claims or interests

(a) A claim or interest ... is deemed allowed, unless a party in interest ... objects.

(b) ... [T]he court, after notice and a hearing, shall determine the amount of such claim in lawful currency of the United States as of the date of the filing of the petition ... except to the extent that:

(2) such claim is for unmatured interest;

...........................................................................................................

The legislative history of § 502 states: "Section 502(b) thus contains two principles of present law. First, interest stops accruing at the date of the filing of the petition, because any claim for unmatured interest is disallowed under this paragraph. Second, bankruptcy operates as the acceleration of the principal amount of all claims against the debtor."

...........................................................................................................

### § 1125. Postpetition disclosure and solicitation

(a) In this section—

(1) "adequate information" means information of a kind, and in sufficient detail, as far as is reasonably practicable in light of the nature and history of the debtor and the condition of debtor's books and records, that would enable a hypothetical reasonable investor typical of holders of claims or interests of the relevant class to make an informed judgment about the plan, but adequate information need not include such information about any other possible or proposed plan; and ...

(b) An acceptance or rejection of a plan may not be solicited after the commencement of the case [unless] there is transmitted to such holder the plan or a summary of the plan, and a written disclosure statement approved, after notice and a hearing, by the court as containing adequate information. The court may approve a disclosure statement without a valuation of the debtor or an appraisal of the debtor's assets.

\* \* \*

(d) Whether a disclosure statement [under (b)] contains adequate information is not governed by any otherwise applicable nonbankruptcy [securities] law, rule, or regulation ...

(e) A person that solicits acceptance or rejection of a plan, in good faith and in compliance with the applicable provisions of this title ... is not liable, on account of such solicitation ... for violation of any applicable [securities] law, rule, or regulation governing solicitation of acceptance or rejection of a plan ....

## G. A note on purposes

### ¶430: Fresh starts

The purposes of bankruptcy, one might think, should be easy to find and state. Individual bankruptcies seem suffused with the purpose of offering people a "fresh start." On moral grounds, people should not be burdened by crushing debt for their entire lives. And on efficiency grounds, once debt is crushing, the individual's incentives to work off that debt can dissipate. Bankruptcy relief can thus be both fair and efficient.

But one cannot readily apply this principal to corporate reorganization in chapter 11. Bankruptcy can wipe out shareholders' interests without crushing the individual shareholder, who typically has a diversified portfolio that cannot be wiped out by the failure of an individual firm. Creditors are similarly diversified and thus not in need of a fresh start. (Bankruptcy relief—or, more aptly, recapitalization—may align incentives inside the firm better than they were aligned in the fraying "bundle of sticks" firm when that firm is insolvent.)

It's easy to see how a fresh start mentality might have historically suffused business bankruptcy. Individuals get the benefit of the fresh start. Individuals in business might similarly get its benefit. When individuals (or families, or small tight partnerships) were the principal business owners, the fresh start policy could suffuse business bankruptcies. From there, the principal might spread to corporate reorganizations in chapter 11 of public firms with diversified shareholders, although were corporate reorganizations the first bankruptcies to occur when constructing a bankruptcy system, the fresh start principal might not have been primary, or even operative.

The purposes of business bankruptcy can be seen as falling into two large bins. One bin looks at creditor wealth maximization, and can be seen as analogous to the shareholder wealth maximization norm from corporate law, modulated to recognize that in bankruptcy it's usually the creditors who become the residual claimants. In another large bin are the other social interests, the most obvious of which are the interests of the bankrupt firm's employees and the surrounding community.

People beginning from premises in the first bin will tend to favor market-based solutions to chapter 11. People beginning from premises in the second bin will tend to see slow reorganization and props to the decaying firm as justified. Because chapter 11 tends to work more slowly than it seems that it has to, and seems to work more slowly than other similar corporate transactions, the real world of bankruptcy seems to begin with premises, implicitly or explicitly, from the social interests bin.

While these two camps might seem to be at war[24]—creditor wealth maximization contrasting with caring about employees—the market-bin supporters could assert that market solutions are best for employees and communities as a whole.

That is, in the abstract, a utilitarian seeks the greatest good for the greatest number. Creditor wealth maximization in chapter 11 is not a goal in itself, but serves as a rough proxy for the utilitarian norm. A bankruptcy system that pays creditors back, best facilitates the fluidity of capital, a fluidity market-based theorists usually think improves overall employment. The practical problem though is two-fold here: First, when jobs are lost, the visible lost job is politically painful to eliminate even if the abstraction says that unidentified jobs are preserved or created elsewhere in the economy. Second, a utilitarian has trouble comparing the pain felt by the job loser to the gains felt elsewhere in the system. Sometimes, after all, the local pain may exceed the diffuse gains; the free-market norms then depend on the value of generality and the high costs of finding when the local pain is so great that it deserves primacy.

## ¶431: Priority and pre-bankruptcy investments

Priority could also serve two efficiency purposes. One is obvious: By clearly organizing which creditor comes first, the parties might end up expending fewer resources jockeying for position in bankruptcy. A second is more subtle, but perhaps more important. Priority might facilitate the movement of capital and the financing of factories. A system without priority (or a system that enforced priority poorly) might feed back and deter otherwise worthwhile projects if creditors are uncertain where on line they'll end up if the firm goes bankrupt.

An example can illustrate this. A firm has a project that will be worth 200 (based on a .5 chance of being worth 300 and a .5 chance of being worth 100). The firm has 100 in value but needs 100 more to get the project rolling. (The necessary profits and interest are assumed but not denominated in these examples.)

Time (0)

| 100+Unfinanced Project | Common stock |
|---|---|

---

[24] E.g., Donald R. Korobkin, *The Role of Normative Theory in Bankruptcy Debates*, 82 Iowa L. Rev. 75, 103, 105 (1996).

# Ch. 4  PRIORITY  143

The financier considers financing the project. If it finances the project with a 5-year loan of 100, the firm will be worth 200. This project is overall socially worthwhile.

Time (1)

| 200 | 100 debt |
|---|---|
| [.5x300]+ [.5x100] | Common stock |

The financier is happy to finance this project as long it's sure that the firm will stick to this project. But the financier fears that the debtor will borrow again and might dissipate much of the firm's value if the debtor borrows and adopts another project.

That is, the lender fears this scenario: It will lend in year 1 and the loan will be due year 5. It fears that in year 2 a new lender will lend, with the new lender's loan due in year 4. It fears that the debtor will dissipate value in a gamble in year 3. In year 4, the borrower will repay the new lender. Then in year 5, the original lender will seek repayment when its loan comes due, but it will get nothing, because the firm will then be worth nothing, having lost its year 3 gamble and having repaid the second lender in year 4.

| Time | 0 | 1 | 2 | 3 | 4 | 5 |
|---|---|---|---|---|---|---|
| Firm value | 100 | 200 | 290 | 100 | 0 | 0 |
| 1st Lender | 0 | 100 | 100 | 100 | 100 | 100 |
| 2nd Lender | 0 | 0 | 100 | 100 | 0 | 0 |

The lender, fearing this outcome (if it's a reasonably plausible result) will not lend, or at least won't lend on the original terms. (You can see why: to the extent this scenario is a real fear, the first lender gets nothing. If this scenario has only a, say, .5 chance of occurring, the first lender will be lending 100, but will have a .5 chance of getting nothing back. That would deter the loan on its original terms.)

Although this is the "nightmare" scenario for the first lender (with the second lender collecting first), more realistically, there'll be a bankruptcy in time period 3. In the bankruptcy the first and second lenders will collect pro rata, getting 50 each. While not the nightmare of the first scenario, it still gives the first lender an expected loan value of 75, on a loan of 100. Hence it won't lend in year 0.

This scenario tells us what the first lender fears. But it doesn't tell us whether these fears are realistic. After all, the second lender *also* loses if the year 3 gamble doesn't pay off. On the numbers we have so far, the *second* lender won't lend (unless otherwise compensated), and, accordingly the first lender would have nothing to worry about.

But the second lender could readily have reason to lend if its upside from changing the firm's profile is high enough. Thus, if the debtor only used the first loan for the first project, it would get either 100 or 300. But, let's suppose that after the first lender lends, the debtor could with another 100 change to a project that's worth either 100 or 480. Firm value would be increased by only 90 and resources of 100 would be used for the change, but the project is rational for both the *second* lender and the stockholder, because they're gambling with the first creditor's money.

Here's how: If the second creditor's deal is a loan of 100 plus a 20% equity kicker, then the second lender would get either 50 or 156. (The 156 comes from 480, minus 100 to the first lender, minus the 100 to the second lender, leaving 280 for equity, of which the second lender gets 20% via the equity kicker, or 56.) That's a good deal for the second lender. The stockholders would get either 0 or 224, for an expected value of 112, which beats the first project's value to the stockholders of 100.

Time (2)

| | |
|---|---|
| 290 [.5x480]+ [.5x100] | 100 Original debt |
| | 100 New debt (with 20% equity kicker) |
| | Common stock |

Fearing this result and the switch in projects, the first lender seeks promises from the debtor that the debtor won't switch projects, or the first lender seeks a better deal. Quite plausibly the first lender, fearing the project switch, won't lend.

The stockholder/entrepreneur though has a good project, the first project. How can they finance it? Sometimes a promise not to switch will be enough. But when it's not enough, they might *want* to offer the first creditor priority. Why? Well, simply examining the five year flow-chart tells us why: If the first lender has priority, it will have a loan worth 100 *even if* the debtor borrows 100 and switches projects. The first lender can sleep at night without nightmares because even if the debtor borrows and switches, the first lender will be paid back in full.

The first lender's fear is, in the finance jargon, of "asset substitution." (Assets need not be physically substituted for the first lender to be afraid; the same assets, deployed in a riskier way could generate the fear.)

And now comes the bigger social policy issue: once the first lender gets priority, it's no longer sensible for the debtor and the second lender to switch projects. On the numbers we're using, they'll lose money.

Figure out why they'll lose money. When you do, you'll see how priority facilitates good projects and deters bad ones (on these numbers). If the first lender has priority, the second lender won't lend (or the debtor won't borrow again and switch projects). Bankruptcy, by enforcing priority, can make a difference here.

Keep in mind though that priority cannot prevent every configuration of asset substitution that the first lender would fear (imagine if the payoff from the second project were 680 or 100, with equal probabilities); priority just helps it control one configuration of asset substitution.

# CHAPTER 5

# ALTERNATIVES TO CHAPTER 11: SELLING

A. Selling?
B. The judiciary and valuation

······································································································

## A. Selling?

### ¶501: Sale of the firm to provide a value?

Could the firm in its entirety be put up for bids? Why would that not solve the valuation problem? That is, instead of allowing the firm to be dismantled piecemeal outside of bankruptcy, and instead of having a bankruptcy-based two-year renegotiation, the court would solicit bids for the entire bankrupt, to be sold as a whole. Would that help solve the "common pool" problem? If mock bids provide no realistic number (and would be subject to manipulation), why not sell the firm as a going concern?

The sale would not only provide a number for firm value, but would provide cold cash (or securities of some sort). Could such a sale be accomplished other than by an imposed rule? Does the Bankruptcy Code sanction or obstruct a judge seeking such a sale? Would the parties to a bankruptcy ever agree to such a valuation sale during the bankruptcy? Consider the following readings.

### ¶502: Conversion to chapter 7?

If senior creditors are dissatisfied with the plan proposed, can they do more than reject the plan and battle against cram-down under § 1129(b)? Could they seek that the proceeding be converted to chapter 7, and the firm liquidated, presumably by the trustee selling the firm in its entirety if the firm were worth more kept together than sold off piecemeal? Consider § 1112.

### § 1112. Conversion or dismissal

(b) ... [O]n request of a party in interest ... , and after notice and a hearing, the court may convert [a chapter 11 proceeding to] chapter 7 ... for cause, including—

    (1) continuing loss to or diminution of the estate and absence of a reasonable likelihood of rehabilitation;

    (2) inability to effectuate a plan;

    (3) unreasonable delay by the debtor that is prejudicial to creditors;

    (4) failure to propose a plan under section 1121 ... within any time fixed by the court;[1] [or]

    (5) ....

1. The creditor may find each of these standards difficult to meet. The estate may not be diminishing in size, but just not growing "fast" enough to provide financiers a normal rate of return. Low operating profit doesn't seem to satisfy (b)(1). That is, slowness in formulating a plan may mean that the bankrupt fails to maximize its value, but doesn't necessarily create a continuing loss. And even if the estate were diminishing, "a reasonable likelihood of rehabilitation" might still be present, although one at a value lower than the maximum attainable. Subsection (b)(1) requires both loss and no realistic chance of rehabilitation.

2. How could the creditor show "inability to effectuate a plan," the standard under (b)(2)? Could creditors warrant that they will oppose the debtor's plan and insist upon cram-down under § 1129(b)? Presumably some creditors fear that they will lose under § 1129(b) if the firm is overvalued, and in any case do not want to pursue the valuation hearing simply to show that no plan can work. Presumably to show "inability" under subsection (2), a creditor would have to show that all the parties tried (for a year? for two years?) and failed. If the creditor seeking conversion has to wait that long, then conversion to prevent delay isn't valuable at the beginning of a chapter 11 proceeding.

3. This subsection seems the most plausible for creditors. But what amount of delay is "unreasonable" depends on the eye of the beholder. In a chapter 11 system that regularly takes two or three years, delay of a couple of years seems reasonable. (Only when compared to a baseline of other complex corporate transactions that take a few months, it may seem unreasonable. And, since bankruptcy litigation actually moves *faster* than other complex litigation—but *not* as fast as other complex transactions—showing unreasonable delay would be hard.)

---

[1] [Section 1121(b) allows the debtor an exclusive period of 120 days to propose a plan after the filing of the chapter 11 petition. Typically the bankruptcy judge extends this period of exclusivity, often for years.—Roe.]

4. The complexity of the plan usually induces the bankruptcy court to extend the debtor's period of exclusivity for proposing a plan.

Thus while § 1112 might provide a wedge for senior creditors, it has not yet worked out that way. Moreover, conversion from chapter 11 to chapter 7 is usually seen as drastic, as a sign of failure.

Could creditors instead seek to sell the enterprise inside chapter 11?

## ¶503: Sales under § 363

Section 363 authorizes the trustee to sell the bankrupt's property. Could it be used to sidestep the reorganization negotiations under § 1129? Could the judge allow the trustee to sell all of the company's assets and operations, shorn of liabilities? Could the judge then take the cash from the sale, hold it, and then distribute it to the claimants when priority litigation is resolved and a § 1129 plan is confirmed?

Who would oppose such a sale? Who would favor such a sale?

Section 363(c) says that the trustee (or debtor-in-possession) "may enter into transactions, including the sale or lease of property of the estate, in the ordinary course of business, without notice or a hearing ...." A sale of the entire company is not a sale in the ordinary course of business, so § 363(c) is unavailable. But § 363(b)(1) says: "The trustee, after notice and a hearing, may use, sell, or lease, other than in the ordinary course of business, property of the estate."

In lieu of a trustee, the court usually appoints the bankrupt as debtor-in-possession, allowing pre-bankruptcy management to continue running the company. It's the trustee (or debtor-in-possession) that must move the court to make the sale. Creditors cannot move under § 363 by themselves. Would the bankrupt's managers be highly motivated to sell the entire company? Think of the incentives of managers of firms targeted for hostile takeovers. And think of the incentives of managers, if they're allied with equity-holders (because they are themselves substantial stockholders), if the firm's value becomes fixed and certain, by a bid for, say, $47 million, no more and no less.

If creditors dislike the debtor-in-possession's decision to forego a § 363 sale, they can move that the court replace the management of the debtor-in-possession with a trustee friendly to the creditors and amenable to a sale. But although the judge can appoint a trustee to displace the bankrupt's managers, trustee appointment is rare. Under § 1104, the standard for trustee appointment is "for cause, including fraud, dishonesty, incompetence, or gross mismanagement of the ... debtor by current management ... or if such appointment is in the interests of creditors." Or, the creditors could negotiate a plan of reorganization under § 1129(a)(8), with the plan contemplating a sale. But, since creditors presumably want a sale in order to *avoid* negotiating, cramming down, and valuing under § 1129, the last alternative isn't much of a benefit.

Do these conditions make it easy for creditors to seek a sale of the bankrupt enterprise in its entirety? Are managers of the debtor-in-possession more likely to accede to a sale than managers of a nonbankrupt target firm would accede to a hostile tender offer? Even if the debtor-in-possession managers do consent, could equity holders argue that such a sale effectively displaces the bargaining framework of § 1129, in derogation of congressional intent?

The next two decisions shed light on these questions. In the first case, creditors sought the sale of the bankrupt's principal asset, stock in an electronics firm. The company and its managers agreed, but equity holders objected and appealed when the bankruptcy court ordered the sale.

## ¶504: Statutory provisions

### § 363. Use, sale, or lease of property

(b)(1) The trustee, after notice and a hearing, may use, sell, or lease, other than in the ordinary course of business, property of the estate.

\* \* \*

(c)(1) ... [U]nless the court orders otherwise, the trustee may enter into transactions, including the sale or lease of property of the estate, in the ordinary course of business, without notice or a hearing, and may use property of the estate in the ordinary course of business without notice or a hearing.

## ¶505: In re The Lionel Corp., 722 F.2d 1063 (2d Cir. 1983)

PRIOR HISTORY: Appeal from ... an order ... approving a sale of property of the debtor's estate pursuant to 11 U.S.C. § 363(b).
Reversed and remanded. Judge Winter dissents in a separate opinion.
Before: MANSFIELD, CARDAMONE and WINTER, Circuit Judges.
CARDAMONE, Circuit Judge:

This expedited appeal is from an order ... authoriz[ing] the sale by Lionel Corporation, a Chapter 11 debtor in possession, of its 82% common stock holding in Dale Electronics, Inc. to Peabody International Corporation for $50 million.

I — FACTS

On February 19, 1982 the Lionel Corporation—toy train manufacturer of childhood ... filed ... for reorganization under Chapter 11 of the Bankruptcy Code. Resort to Chapter 11 was precipitated by losses totaling $22.5 million that Lionel incurred in its toy retailing operation during the two year period ending December 1982.

There are 7.1 million shares of common stock of Lionel held by 10,000 investors. Its consolidated assets and liabilities [showed] ... a negative net worth of nearly $23 million ....

Lionel [is a debtor-in-possession pursuant to § 1107 and is authorized] to operate its businesses and manage its properties pursuant to [§] 1108[.][2] ...

Lionel's most important asset and the subject of this proceeding is its ownership of 82% of the common stock of Dale, a corporation engaged in the manufacture of electronic components .... Public investors own the remaining 18 percent of Dale's common stock, which is listed on the American Stock Exchange. Its balance sheet reflects ... [a] shareholders' equity of approximately $28.0 million. Lionel's stock investment in Dale ... is Lionel's most valuable single asset. Unlike Lionel's toy retailing operation, Dale is profitable ....

On June 14, 1983 Lionel filed an application under section 363(b) seeking bankruptcy court authorization to sell its 82% interest in Dale to Acme-Cleveland Corporation for $43 million in cash. Four days later the debtor filed a plan of reorganization conditioned upon a sale of Dale with the proceeds to be distributed to creditors. Certain issues of the reorganization remain unresolved, and negotiations are continuing; however, a solicitation of votes on the plan has not yet begun. On September 7, 1983, following the Securities and Exchange Commission's July 15 filing of objections to the sale, Bankruptcy Judge Ryan held a hearing on Lionel's application. At the hearing, Peabody emerged as the successful of three bidders with an offer of $50 million for Lionel's interest in Dale.

The Chief Executive Officer of Lionel and a Vice-President of Salomon Brothers were the only witnesses produced and both testified in support of the application. Their testimony established that while the price paid for the stock was "fair," Dale is not an asset "that is wasting away in any sense." Lionel's Chief Executive Officer stated that there was no reason why the sale of Dale stock could not be accomplished as part of the reorganization plan, and that the sole reason for Lionel's application to sell was the Creditors' Committee's insistence upon it. The creditors wanted to turn this asset of Lionel into a "pot of cash," to provide the bulk of the $70 million required to repay creditors under the proposed plan of reorganization.

In confirming the sale, Judge Ryan made no formal findings of fact. He simply noted that cause to sell was sufficiently shown by the Creditors' Committee's insistence upon it. Judge Ryan further found cause—presumably from long experience—based upon his own opinion that a present failure to confirm would set the entire reorganization process back a year or longer while the parties attempted to restructure it.

---

[2] [That section provides: **§ 1108. Authorization to operate business**

[Unless the court, on request of a party in interest and after notice and a hearing, orders otherwise, the trustee may operate the debtor's business.]

The Committee of Equity Security Holders, statutory representatives of the 10,000 public shareholders of Lionel, appealed this order claiming that *the sale, prior to approval of a reorganization plan, deprives the equity holders* of the Bankruptcy Code's safeguards of disclosure, solicitation *and acceptance [under § 1129(a)(8)]* and divests the debtor of a dominant and profitable asset which could serve as a cornerstone for a sound plan. The SEC also appeared and objected to the sale in the bankruptcy court and supports the Equity Committee's appeal, claiming that approval of the sale side-steps the Code's requirement for informed suffrage which is at the heart of Chapter 11.

The Creditors' Committee favors the sale because it believes it is in the best interests of Lionel and because the sale is expressly authorized by § 363(b) of the Code. Lionel tells us that its ownership of Dale, a non-operating asset, is held for investment purposes only and that its sale will provide the estate with the large block of the cash needed to fund its plan of reorganization.

From the oral arguments and briefs we gather that the Equity Committee believes that Chapter 11 has cleared the reorganization field of major pre-plan sales ...[,] relegating § 363(b) to be used only in emergencies. The Creditors' Committee counters that a bankruptcy judge should have absolute freedom under § 363(b) to do as he thinks best. Neither of these arguments is wholly persuasive. Here, as in so many similar cases, we must avoid the extremes, for the policies underlying the Bankruptcy Reform Act of 1978 support a middle ground—one which gives the bankruptcy judge considerable discretion yet requires him to articulate sound business justifications for his decisions.

II — DISCUSSION

The issue now before this Court is to what extent Chapter 11 permits a bankruptcy judge to authorize the sale of an important asset of the bankrupt's estate, out of the ordinary course of business and prior to acceptance and outside of any plan of reorganization. Section 363(b), the focal point of our analysis, provides that "[t]he trustee, after notice and a hearing, may use, sell, or lease, other than in the ordinary course of business, property of the estate."

On its face, section 363(b) appears to permit disposition of any property of the estate of a corporate debtor without resort to the statutory safeguards embodied in Chapter 11 .... Yet, analysis of the statute's history and over seven decades of case law convinces us that such a literal reading of section 363(b) would unnecessarily violate the congressional scheme for corporate reorganizations.

[The court then examined the sales standard under prior bankruptcy statutes and found it permitted sales of perishable or wasting assets, but usually not otherwise.]

The Third Circuit took an even stricter view in In re Solar Mfg. Corp., 176 F.2d 493 (3d Cir. 1949). Acknowledging that a sale of corporate assets could occur outside and prior to a plan, ... the court concluded that pre-confirmation sales should be "confined to emergencies where there is imminent danger that the assets of the ailing business will be lost if prompt action is not taken." ...

... In re Sire Plan, Inc., 332 F.2d 497 (2d Cir. 1964), corporate owners of a seven-story skeletal building then under construction filed for reorganization .... [We noted] that the evidence demonstrated that in its exposed state a "partially constructed building is a 'wasting asset' [that] can only deteriorate in value the longer it remains uncompleted." Id. at 499.

More recently, other circuits have upheld sales prior to plan approval under the Bankruptcy Act where the bankruptcy court outlined the circumstances in its findings of fact indicating why the sale was in the best interest of the estate. E.g., In re Equity Funding Corporation of America, 492 F.2d 793, 794 (9th Cir.), cert. denied, 419 U.S. 964 (1974) (finding of fact that because market value of asset was likely to deteriorate substantially in the near future, sale was in the estate's best interests); .... In essence, these cases evidence the continuing vitality under the old law of an "emergency" or "perishability" standard. As we shall see, the new Bankruptcy Code no longer requires such strict limitations on a bankruptcy judge's authority to order disposition of the estate's property; nevertheless, it does not go so far as to eliminate all constraints on that judge's discretion.

C. The Bankruptcy Reform Act of 1978

Section 363(b) of the Code seems on its face to confer upon the bankruptcy judge virtually unfettered discretion to authorize the use, sale or lease, other than in the ordinary course of business, of property of the estate. Of course, the statute requires that notice be given and a hearing conducted, but [no] reference is made to an "emergency" or "perishability" requirement nor is there an indication that a debtor in possession or trustee contemplating sale must show "cause." Thus, the language of § 363(b) clearly is different from the terms of its statutory predecessors. And, while Congress never expressly stated why it abandoned the [prior] "upon cause shown" terminology ..., arguably that omission permits easier access to § 363(b). Various policy considerations lend some support to this view.

First and foremost is the notion that a bankruptcy judge must not be shackled with unnecessarily rigid rules when exercising the undoubtedly broad administrative power granted him under the Code .... To further the purposes of Chapter 11 reorganization, a bankruptcy judge must have substantial freedom to tailor his orders to meet differing circumstances. This is exactly the result a liberal reading of § 363(b) will achieve.

Support for this policy is found in the rationale underlying a number of earlier cases that had applied [the old "upon cause shown" standard. Emergency or perishability standards have not always been in play; sometimes] a good business opportunity was ... available, so long as the parties could act quickly. In such cases therefore the bankruptcy machinery should not straitjacket the bankruptcy judge so as to prevent him from doing what is best for the estate.

Just as we reject the requirement that only an emergency permits the use of § 363(b), we also reject the view that § 363(b) grants the bankruptcy judge carte blanche. Several reasons lead us to this conclusion: the statute requires notice and a hearing, and these procedural safeguards would be meaningless absent a further requirement that reasons be given for whatever determination is made; similarly, appellate review would effectively be precluded by an irreversible order; and, finally, such construction of § 363(b) swallows up Chapter 11's safeguards. In fact, the legislative history surrounding the enactment of Chapter 11 makes evident Congress' concern with rights of equity interests as well as those of creditors.[3]

Chapter 5 of the House bill dealing with reorganizations states that the purpose of a business reorganization is to restructure a business' finances to enable it to operate productively, provide jobs for its employees, pay its creditors and produce a return for its stockholders. The automatic stay upon filing a petition prevents creditors from acting unilaterally or pressuring the debtor. The plan of reorganization determines how much and in what form creditors will be paid, whether stockholders will continue to retain any interests, and in what form the business will continue. Requiring acceptance by a percentage of creditors and stockholders [under § 1126] for confirmation [under § 1129] forces negotiation among the debtor, its creditors and its stockholders. [House Report] at 221 ....

The Senate hearings similarly reflect a concern as to how losses are to be apportioned between creditors and stockholders in the reorganization of a public company. [Senate Report] at 9. Noting that "the most vulnerable today are public investors," the Senate Judiciary Committee Report states that the bill is designed to counteract "the natural tendency of a debtor in distress to pacify large creditors with whom the debtor would expect to do business, at the expense of small and scattered public investors." S. Rep. No. 95-989 at 10. The Committee believed that investor protection is most critical when the public company is in such financial distress as to cause it to seek aid under the bankruptcy laws. Id. The need for this protection was plain. Reorganization under the 1938 Act was often unfair to public investors who lacked bargaining power, and these conditions continued. Echoing the conclusion of the House Committee, the Senate Committee believed that the bill would promote fairer and more equitable reorganizations granting to public investors the last chance to conserve values that corporate insolvency has jeopardized. Id. at 10-11.

---

[3] The Commission on the Bankruptcy Laws of the United States submitted a draft provision that would have permitted resort to section 363(b) in the absence of an emergency, even in the case of "all or substantially all the property of the estate." See Report of the Commission on the Bankruptcy Laws of the United States, H.R. Doc. No. 93-137, 93rd Cong., 1st Sess. (1973) at 239 (proposed § 7-205 and accompanying explanatory note). Congress eventually deleted this provision without explanation, an action which we hardly consider dispositive of the issue before us here.

## III — CONCLUSION

The history surrounding the enactment in 1978 of current Chapter 11 and the logic underlying it buttress our conclusion that there must be some articulated business justification, other than appeasement of major creditors, for using, selling or leasing property out of the ordinary course of business before the bankruptcy judge may order such disposition under section 363(b).

The case law under section 363's statutory predecessors used terms like "perishable," "deteriorating," and "emergency" as guides in deciding whether a debtor's property could be sold outside the ordinary course of business. The use of such words persisted long after their omission from newer statutes and rules. The administrative power to sell or lease property in a reorganization continued to be the exception, not the rule .... In enacting the 1978 Code Congress was aware of existing case law and clearly indicated as one of its purposes that equity interests have a greater voice in reorganization plans—hence, the safeguards of disclosure, voting, acceptance and confirmation in present Chapter 11.

Resolving the apparent conflict between Chapter 11 and § 363(b) does not require an all or nothing approach. Every sale under § 363(b) does not automatically short-circuit or side-step Chapter 11; nor are these two statutory provisions to be read as mutually exclusive. Instead, if a bankruptcy judge is to administer a business reorganization successfully under the Code, then—like the related yet independent tasks performed in modern production techniques to ensure good results—some play for the operation of both § 363(b) and Chapter 11 must be allowed for.

The rule we adopt requires that a judge determining a § 363(b) application expressly find from the evidence presented before him at the hearing a good business reason to grant such an application. In this case the only reason advanced for granting the request to sell Lionel's 82 percent stock interest in Dale was the Creditors' Committee's insistence on it. Such is insufficient as a matter of fact because it is not a sound business reason and insufficient as a matter of law because it ignores the equity interests required to be weighed and considered under Chapter 11. The court also expressed its concern that a present failure to approve the sale would result in a long delay .... [I]t is easy to sympathize with the desire of a bankruptcy court to expedite bankruptcy reorganization proceedings for they are frequently protracted[, but this is not a basis for abandoning proper standards]. Thus, the approval of the sale of Lionel's 82 percent interest in Dale was an abuse of the trial court's discretion.

In fashioning its findings, a bankruptcy judge must not blindly follow the hue and cry of the most vocal special interest groups; rather, he should consider all salient factors pertaining to the proceeding and, accordingly, act to further the diverse interests of the debtor, creditors and equity holders, alike. He might, for example, look to such relevant factors as the proportionate value of the asset to the estate as a whole, the amount of elapsed time since the filing, the likelihood that a plan of reorganization will be proposed and confirmed in the near future, the effect of the proposed disposition on future plans of reorganization, the proceeds to be obtained from the disposition vis-a-vis any appraisals of the property, which of the alternatives of use, sale or lease the proposal envisions and, most importantly perhaps, whether the asset is increasing or decreasing in value. This list is not intended to be exclusive, but merely to provide guidance to the bankruptcy judge.

Finally, we must consider whether appellants opposing the sale produced evidence before the bankruptcy court that such sale was not justified. While a debtor applying under § 363(b) carries the burden of demonstrating that a use, sale or lease out of the ordinary course of business will aid the debtor's reorganization, an objectant, such as the Equity Committee here, is required to produce some evidence respecting its objections. Appellants made three objections below: First, the sale was premature because Dale is not a wasting asset and there is no emergency; second, there was no justifiable cause present since Dale, if anything, is improving; and third, the price was inadequate. No proof was required as to the first objection because it was stipulated as conceded. The second and third objections are interrelated. Following Judge Ryan's suggestion that objections could as a practical matter be developed on cross-examination, Equity's counsel elicited testimony from the financial expert produced by Lionel that Dale is less subject than other companies to wide market fluctuations. The same witness also conceded that he knew of no reason why those interested in Dale's stock at the September 7, 1983 hearing would not be just as interested six months from then.[4] The only other witness who testified was the Chief Executive Officer of Lionel, who stated that it was only at the insistence of the Creditors' Committee that Dale stock was being sold and that Lionel "would very much like to retain its interest in Dale." These uncontroverted statements of the two witnesses elicited by the Equity Committee on cross-examination were sufficient proof to support its objections to the present sale of Dale because this evidence demonstrated that there was no good business reason for the present sale. Hence, appellants satisfied their burden.

Accordingly, the order appealed from is reversed and the matter remanded to the district court with directions to remand to the bankruptcy court for further proceedings consistent with this opinion.

WINTER, Circuit Judge, dissenting:

\* \* \*

The following facts are undisputed ...: (i) Lionel sought a buyer for the Dale stock willing to condition its purchase upon confirmation of a reorganization plan. It was unsuccessful since, in the words of the bankruptcy judge, "the confirmation of any plan is usually somewhat iffy," and few purchasers are willing to commit upwards of $50 million for an extended period without a contract binding on the other party;

---

[4] As noted, the bidding for Dale started with a $43 million offer from Acme-Cleveland and has since jumped to $50 million. There is no indication that this trend will reverse itself.

(ii) every feasible reorganization plan contemplates the sale of the Dale stock for cash; (iii) a reorganization plan may be approved fairly soon if the Dale stock is sold now. If the sale is prohibited, renewed negotiations between the creditors and the equity holders will be necessary, and the submission of a plan, if any, will be put off well into the future; and (iv) the Dale stock can be sold now at or near the same price as it can be sold later.

The effect of the present decision is thus to leave the debtor in possession powerless as a legal matter to sell the Dale stock outside a reorganization plan .... This, of course, pleases the equity holders who, having introduced no evidence demonstrating a disadvantage to the bankrupt estate from the sale of the Dale stock, are now given a veto over it to be used as leverage in negotiating a better deal for themselves in a reorganization.

The likely result[] of today's decision [is that] notwithstanding the majority decision, the Dale stock will be sold under Section 363(b) for exactly the same reasons offered in support of the present proposed sale. However, the ultimate reorganization plan will be more favorable to the equity holders, and they will not veto the sale.

It seems reasonably obvious that [this] result ... is contrary to the purpose of the reorganization provisions in causing delay and further economic risk [and] also suffers from the legal infirmity which led the majority to reject the proposed sale, the only difference between the two sales being the agreement of the equity holders.

The equity holders offered no evidence whatsoever that the sale of Dale now will harm Lionel .... The courts below were quite right in not treating their arguments seriously ....[5]

The equity holders argue that Chapter 11's provisions for disclosure, hearing and a vote before confirmation of a reorganization plan stringently limit the authority of trustees under 11 U.S.C. § 363(b). However, a reorganization plan affects the rights of the parties as well as the disposition of assets, and there is no inconsistency in allowing the disposition of property outside the confirmation proceedings. Arguably, *some transactions proposed under Section 363(b) would, if carried out, eliminate a number of options available for reorganization plans and thereby pre-ordain a particular kind of plan or preclude a reorganization entirely. In such a case, a colorable claim can be made for a limitation on a trustee's power under Section 363(b)* narrowly tailored to prevent such a result in order to effectuate the core purposes of Chapter 11. However, it is not disputed that in the present case the final reorganization plan will include a sale of Dale stock. A sale now thus does not preclude any feasible reorganization plan.

---

[5] ... [T]he problem of statutory interpretation is entirely straightforward and not deserving of a lengthy exegesis into legal history. The language of Section 363(b) is about as plain as it could be and surely does not permit a judicial grafting of stringent conditions on the power of trustees. As for its legislative history, the words "upon cause shown" were dropped by the Congress from the predecessor to Section 363(b) in 1978, a signal clearly dictating that Congress meant what it said.

¶506: **Questions on *Lionel***

1. Lionel managers managed the toy company, which held stock in Dale, the electronics company, for investment. Does the operational structure explain why managers consented to sell Dale? Would managers usually agree to such sales of an entire bankrupt company? Would Lionel's managers have as readily agreed to a sale of the toy company? What statutory hurdles would creditors have to overcome if they could not get the bankrupt's managers to agree to the sale? Wouldn't they need to get their own trustee appointed, or get the reorganization moved to chapter 7 for liquidation?

2. The court says that showing perishability suffices to justify a sale, but isn't a sine qua non for sale under § 363. But the judge does not have carte blanche to sell. Under the wasting asset doctrine of the *Lionel* opinion, could creditors, with a nod to the Summers and Cutler reading, supra at p. 132, and related economic data, argue that every bankrupt firm is a wasting asset, and that a quick sale reduces the waste? As such, they'd argue, sales under § 363 are always warranted.

3. Such an argument would be harder to make if the sale would destroy significant private value of the estate. If markets for entire companies are weak and mergers difficult to engineer, then judges might believe that the sale produces inadequate value for the estate, and accordingly even if the asset were "wasting" a sale wouldn't eliminate the waste. Such a view became harder to hold after the merger wave of the 1980s.

4. Lionel had already filed a proposed plan of reorganization, although the plan had not yet been consented to, and open issues remained. The equity holders argued that the sale should proceed under the plan of reorganization, not under a § 363 motion. Obviously, compliance with § 1129(a)(8) (including *shareholder* consent or a valuation hearing under § 1129(b)) was a prerequisite to selling Dale under the plan route, but not under the § 363 route.

5. Is the court's interpretation of § 363 that a sale would scuttle § 1129(a)(8)'s scheme of acceptance and therefore cannot proceed unless proponents of the sale offer a business justification, with creditor preference not an allowable justification? Most subsequent decisions have followed *Lionel*, with some courts imposing a higher burden under § 363. Lee R. Bogdanoff, *The Purchase and Sale of Assets in Reorganization Cases*, 47 Bus. Law. 1367, 1391–92 esp. n.90 (1992). (Note that even a sale with a business justification would scuttle bargaining, disclosure, and acceptance under § 1129; presumably though we'd have a "justified" scuttling.)

6. The court privileges negotiation under § 1129, using the statute's preference for negotiation to inform the court how to interpret § 363. But did Congress prefer negotiation for its own sake? See the legislative history in ¶406, at p. 105. Or did Congress prefer negotiated solutions, not for their own sake, but as superior to an *Atlas Pipeline*-type valuation hearing? If a sale would moot a valuation hearing

under § 1129(b), does the legislative history necessarily condemn it as loudly as the *Lionel* court believes? Might it in fact be stretched to *favor* the sale?

Note that the Bankruptcy Code was enacted in 1978. By the mid-1980s American businesses were going through a huge merger wave.

7. After the court struck down the proposed sale, the company went to market again. Eventually it sold Dale for $78,000,000. The equity holders consented when they were included in the proposed plan of reorganization, as Judge Winter, the dissenter, anticipated.

## ¶507: Side deals under § 363

What if the creditors trying to effectuate the § 363 sale made side deals with creditors and stockholders, gaining the acquiescence of potential opponents? What if they planned to "earmark" for some creditors or stockholders some of the consideration to be received in the sale and thereby "buy" those creditors or stockholders' acquiescence to a § 363 sale? Would that enhance the chance of the deal going through under § 363?

## In re Braniff Airways, Inc., 700 F.2d 935 (5th Cir. 1983)

On May 13, 1982, Braniff ... filed [a] petition[ ] for reorganization under Chapter 11 ... [and] continued in the management and operation of [its] businesses and properties as debtors-in-possession pursuant to §§ 1107 and 1108 of the Code. No trustee or examiner was appointed.

\* \* \*

On December 23, 1982, Braniff [sought] ... [court] approval of a proposed agreement between Braniff and PSA. On December 30, 1982, Braniff filed with the Bankruptcy Court a "Memorandum of Understanding" as a basis for a proposed settlement and compromise of all claims, counterclaims, and potential litigations by and among Braniff, certain unsecured creditors, and certain secured creditors.

Between December 30, 1982, and January 3, 1983, various notices of hearings on the proposed agreements were mailed or published. These documents gave notice of a hearing to be held on January 14, 1983, to consider the matters set forth in the PSA Agreement and the Memorandum of Understanding. As stated in these notices, a hearing commenced ....

\* \* \*

The Bankruptcy Court [and district court] approved ... the PSA [transaction].

... [W]as the district court's approval of the PSA transaction authorized under Section 363(b) of the Bankruptcy Code, 11 U.S.C. § 363(b)? ...

I.

The courts below approved the PSA transaction pursuant to Section 363(b) of the Bankruptcy Code, which provides:

> The trustee, after notice and a hearing, may use, sell, or lease, other than in the ordinary course of business, property of the estate. 11 U.S.C. § 363(b).

The appellants [the unsecured ticketholders committee, Continental Airlines, and the U.S. Pension Benefit Guaranty Corporation] contend that § 363(b) is not applicable to sales or other dispositions of all the assets of a debtor, and that such a transaction must be effected pursuant to the voting, disclosure and confirmation requirements of the Code. Braniff responds that cases decided before and after promulgation of the Code authorize a § 363(b) sale of all of a debtor's assets.

We need not express an opinion on this controversy because we are convinced that the PSA transaction is much more than the "use, sale or lease" of Braniff's property authorized by § 363(b). Reduced to its barest bones, the PSA transaction would provide for Braniff's transfer of cash, airplanes and equipment, terminal leases and landing slots to PSA in return for travel scrip, unsecured notes, and a profit participation in PSA's proposed operation. The PSA transaction would also require significant restructuring of the rights of Braniff creditors. Appellants raise a blizzard of objections to each of these elements of the deal. It is not necessary, however, to decide whether each individual component of the PSA transaction is or is not authorized by § 363 because the entire transaction was treated by both courts below as an integrated whole. Since certain portions of the transaction are clearly outside the scope of § 363, the district court was without power under that section to approve it. Its order must be reversed.

[One] example[] will illustrate our rationale. The PSA Agreement provided that Braniff would pay $2.5 million to PSA in exchange for $7.5 million of scrip entitling the holder to travel on PSA. It further required that the scrip be used only in a future Braniff reorganization and that it be issued only to former Braniff employees or shareholders or, in a limited amount to unsecured creditors. This provision not only changed the composition of Braniff's assets, the contemplated result under § 363(b), it also had the practical effect of dictating some of the terms of any future reorganization plan. The reorganization plan would have to allocate the scrip according to the terms of the PSA agreement or forfeit a valuable asset. The debtor and the Bankruptcy Court should not be able to short circuit the requirements of Chapter 11 for confirmation of a reorganization plan by establishing the terms of the plan sub rosa in connection with the sale of assets.

\* \* \*

For these reasons, we hold that the district court was not authorized by § 363(b) to approve the PSA transaction and that its order is reversed. In any future attempts to specify the terms whereby a reorganization plan is to be adopted, the parties and the district court must scale the hurdles erected in Chapter 11. See, e.g. 11 U.S.C. § 1125 (disclosure requirements); id. § 1126 (voting); id. § 1129(a)(7) (best interest of creditors test); id. § 1129(b)(2)(B) (absolute priority rule). Were this transaction approved, and considering the properties proposed to be transferred, little would remain save fixed based equipment and little prospect or occasion for further reorganization. These considerations reinforce our view that this is in fact a reorganization.

## ¶508: Selling under § 363?

1. Do *Lionel* and *Braniff* decide the pure case: a sale of all of the firm, for cash under § 363, because the firm is operating poorly in chapter 11?
2. In the next few paragraphs consider variations on the sale theme:

    (i) If rapid mergers for bankrupts become economically plausible, what would that do to the statutory scheme that divides the § 1129(a)(7)'s standard (of individual acceptance) from that in (a)(8) and (b)(2) (of class acceptance or cramdown)? (See ¶410). Could it make the subsidiary, otherwise easy-to-meet liquidation standard in § 1129(a)(7) more restrictive than § 1129(a)(8)?

    (ii) Consider whether the "equivalent" of a sale of a bankrupt could be had this way: The creditors who want a sale find a buyer who simultaneously offers to buy a voting majority of each class of claims and interests, intending to vote all of them in favor of a plan that contemplates a sale of the company. If the buyer owns several layers of the bankrupt, is it so conflicted that it can't vote. See § 1126(e).

    (iii) Consider the doctrinal reasons courts offer for their rejecting sales and market valuations. Consider their theoretical and empirical persuasiveness. Compare ¶¶516–520.

    (iv) Consider whether sales that would "enforce" absolute priority are "fairer" than bargaining under § 1129. If "deviations" from absolute priority are foreseeable, are they therefore fair? Is fairness the primary rationale for priority? Or is it to facilitate pre-bankruptcy ordering of creditors and financing of factories?

3. Despite that the statute does not facilitate a sale, especially if management opposes one, its economic and transactional fit is often so good, that the pressure to sell overcomes resistence.

## ¶509: The best interests test

The "best interests" test, a term of art used in the old chapter XI, required that in a reorganization creditors get at least what they would have in a liquidation. In that sense, the test is really a minimal interests test, but the phrase "best interests" has stuck. The "best interests" test continues in chapter 11 in § 1129(a)(7), which, by giving a right to each individual creditor to scuttle a plan, corresponds to William Douglas's *Los Angeles Lumber* individual-veto framework.

Consider:

After six months in chapter 11, a buyer for Dieglom appears. Dieglom has deteriorated in value a bit because of 6 months of haggling between creditors and stockholders, and managers' inattention as they tried to get a plan of reorganization done. A buyer is willing to pay **$47** million for the entire company. The buyer will pay $40 million in cash and $7 million in stock of the buyer's company. Creditors propose that the company in its entirety be sold under § 363. Managers of the debtor-in-possession, in an unusual result, agree, and propose the § 363 sale.

You represent the stockholders. At first stockholders don't like a sale. Why?

They're brought on board by creditors' agreeing to give the old stockholders a sliver of the reorganized company. The deal is that the seniors, subordinated, and trade classes will each give up about $.5 to $1 million to stockholders, depending on how vulnerable they are to misvaluation or losses from a further decline in Dieglom's value. All classes will consent to the give-up. The creditors take quick straw votes. The straw votes would, if done formally, satisfy § 1126 (2/3 in amount, at least 1/2 in number).

The Dieglom mortgagee bondholders at first dislike a sale. They feel that they've already given up too much when § 1124(2) is used against them. They've been asked to take their reinstatement value ($12 million of cash and stock), which they dislike but could be made to take under § 1124(2), because they have little choice. Eventually 2/3 sign on.

But dissenting mortgagee bondholders bring a Braniff type hearing under § 363.

You represent the stockholders and attend the hearing. (Stockholders, having been promised about one-half million dollars from each creditor group, now favor the sale under § 363.) You try to distinguish your sale from Braniff's.

Predict the result. Is the sale a § 363 sale with too many terms of the plan of reorganization under § 1129 already determined? What is the business justification for the sale?

\* \* \*

But then something odd happens. In the midst of oral argument, the associate working for the dissenting mortgagee bondholders whispers to the partner making the oral argument against the § 363 sale.

The dissenting bondholders' attorneys withdraw opposition to the motion for a § 363 sale and leave the court room. The judge asks whether any party in interest opposes the sale and, hearing no opposition, approves the sale.

The associate for the dissenting mortgagee bondholders has left behind a copy of the Bankruptcy Code, opened to § 1129(a)(7), which is covered with doodles and notes.

What's going on? What will happen in a month if the sale goes forward, when the judge is asked to confirm the plan of reorganization under § 1129?

## ¶510: Alternatives: Some kind of sale?

If a primary task in reorganization is valuation, then it should be asked why the judge or the bargain among parties is the best mechanism for achieving that valuation. In a capitalist economy such as the United States the valuation task outside of bankruptcy is specialized and usually assigned to financial professionals. Would it be possible to import the specialized expertise of valuation professionals into the reorganization mechanism? If importation were functionally possible, would it be desirable?

Testimony from financial experts seems a dead-end. As seen in the *Hartford Railroad* case, valuation is itself contestable and the opinions of responsible professionals differ. The judge is then left to assess the credibility of the witness, or to learn valuation techniques herself. But that learning is the very process that we want to avoid.

The court could appoint a valuation expert, not beholden to any party. This might be an improvement but would also have problems. Value is ultimately determined by willingness to pay with one's own (or one's employer's) money. A court-appointed expert can provide neither this nor the competition of multiple bidders, the latter being a common method of selling (and thereby valuing) firms.

Thus the alternative to testimony would be some kind of sale. Either the enterprise would be sold off in its entirety or, for public firms, a slice of common stock sold from which enterprise value could be extrapolated.

Such efforts would seem to have a weak constituency. The benefits are diffuse. While bankrupt companies might operate better, and those gains would accrue to their employees, managers, and indirectly to their creditors, the gains, since they are spread among too many groups, would not readily produce a motivated champion for valuation by sale.

Furthermore, many would believe that the market for bankrupts is too weak or inaccurate to justify its use. During the formation of modern reorganization policy the SEC said: "[A] forced sale of the debtor's property, ... if any cash buyers at all could be found, would [occur] only at ruinously low prices." 7 SEC, Report on the Study of Protective and Reorganization Committees § IIB (1940). Although the question of whether the alternatives to the imperfect market are better ought then to be addressed, the current mechanism (where valuation is a backdrop to negotiation among the financial parties) suppresses the visibility of (but hardly eliminates the reality of) the valuation issue.

Is accuracy the only goal in reorganization? How about speed and low cost? If firms operate poorly in bankruptcy, as Summers and Cutler suggest, could one justify a quick sale, *even if* one believed the sale value would be inaccurate?

Or would judicial sanctification of any *non-judicial* process that seemed less than fully accurate seem illegitimate? Is there a constituency for believing that the judicial-political process must try to "save" the bankrupt firms, to do everything humanly possible?

---

### ¶511: Some kind of sale?: J. Bonbright, The Valuation of Property, ch. xii (1937)

The Stock-and-Bond Method of Enterprise Appraisal

\* \* \*

[In the] stock-and-bond method ... the value of an entire business is derived by a summation of the separate market prices of the outstanding securities and of other proprietary and creditor claims against the corporation. The appraiser determine[s] value by prospective earnings [but] relies upon the investors and speculators who compose "the stock market" to do the forecasting.

\* \* \*

[Where the securities have a readily ascertainable market value], the charm of this method of appraisal lies in its simplicity of application and in its relative freedom from the influence of the appraiser's personal bias. Assume, for example, the problem of valuing a corporate enterprise with no ownership interests outstanding save $100,000 of bonds quoted at $90 on the market place, and 1,000 shares of common stock quoted at $50 per share. A moment's calculation yields an enterprise value of $140,000–$90,000 for the bondholders' interest plus $50,000 for the stockholders' equity.

\* \* \*

[But the firm's debts are not] with only those outstanding legal interests in the property represented by shares of stock and by bonds. [O]ther proprietary and creditor claims should not be ignored. Current liabilities, for however short a term, represent interests in the property no less than funded debt, and they can [not] be omitted[.] The value of option warrants, if any are outstanding, must be considered no less than the value of already issued stock. Contingent liabilities, such as guarantees of the bonds of other companies by the company in question, must not be ignored, since they represent a claim against the whole enterprise which tends to detract from the value of the company's own securities.

The second defect of the stock-and-bond method lies in the practical necessity of taking the quoted stock-market prices of the outstanding shares as a measure of the relevant values of these shares. This necessity may lead to error for either of two reasons. In the first place, buyers and sellers of securities are not always intelligent in their evaluation of investment merits. They hardly deserve to be called the persons "in the best position to know." In the second place, security prices are often influenced by speculative and manipulative motives that have little or no bearing on the value of the entire corporate enterprise.

The third defect lies in the assumption that the value of an entire enterprise can be inferred by a summation of the separate values of small amounts of security interests in the enterprise. The lots of stock from which market quotations are generally derived are small lots representing only a minority interest. They do not carry control, and hence their quoted prices are usually determined without reference to the power and perquisites that would be enjoyed by a sole owner of the business. Sometimes, to be sure, the efforts of rival factions to secure control of a corporation will send the quoted market prices of voting stocks to highly inflated levels, quite unjustified by the investment merits of the shares.

## ¶512: Buying up claims?

Bonbright's stock and bond method suggests another reorganization approach. If sales of the firm are disfavored under § 363, why can't a third party simply buy up the claims? That is, a third-party bidder might make simultaneous offers for the various credit and stock claims of the debtor. If successful, the bidder owns the claims, votes them under § 1129(a)(8), and, hence owns the company.

Consider an offeror who plans to buy up two-thirds majorities of each class, who then plans to propose a plan that will sell the firm to the highest bidder.

Or, what if the offeror tenders for 2/3 of each class of debt, with its obligation to "close" and actually buy up the debt contingent on each class of creditors and interests approving a plan of reorganization that contemplates a third-party sale?

Such efforts have run into problems. See generally In re Allegheny Int'l, 118 Bankr. 282 (Bankr. W.D. Pa. 1990), amended on reconsideration, 1990 Bkrtcy LEXIS 1759 (1990). See generally Chaim J. Fortgang & Thomas Mayer, *Trading Claims and Taking Control of Corporations in Chapter 11*, 12 Cardozo L. Rev. 1 (1990).

Under § 1126(c)-(e), class acceptance does not include acceptance by "any entity whose acceptance or rejection of such plan was not in good faith, or was not solicited ... in good faith[.]"

### § 1126. Acceptance of plan

(c) A class of claims has accepted a plan if such plan has been accepted by creditors, *other than any entity designated under subsection (e) of this section,* that hold at least two-thirds in amount and more than one-half in number ....

(d) [Similar standard for interests.]

(e) On request of a party in interest, ... the court may designate any entity whose acceptance or rejection of such plan was not in good faith ....

Will the buyer of the claims vote all classes based on maximizing the value of that class of claims? Won't the buyer of the claims be interested in its total take in the reorganization, and be prepared to take less on one level if it gets more on another? Isn't this the kind of conflict that Chairman Kennedy identified as a problem in reorganizations during the 1930s?

What if the bidder proposes a plan and, to help get the plan accepted, makes a tender offer for one class of claims? It intends to buy up those claims that accept the tender offer and vote the tendered claims in favor of the plan. Can it make the tender offer at a slight premium above the plan amount? See § 1123(a)(4): "[A] plan shall ... provide the same treatment for each claim or interest of a particular class, unless the holder ... agrees to a less favorable treatment ...." Would the plan also unfairly discriminate under § 1129(b)(1)? In re Allegheny Int'l, 118 Bankr. 282, 295–96 (Bankr. W.D. Pa. 1990). Is the tender offer a payment to creditors to buy their votes? Is that bad faith, which warrants exclusion of the purchased vote from the tally? Is the bidder-proponent thereby acting in bad faith, making the plan unconfirmable under § 1129(a)(3) ("The plan has been proposed in good faith and not by any means forbidden by law.")? See generally *Allegheny*.

### ¶513: Selling: James White, Bankruptcy and Creditors' Rights 288 (1985)[6] (summarizing Roe, Bankruptcy and Debt, 83 Colum. L. Rev. (1983))

Professor Mark Roe, with the inadequacies of workouts and court-imposed reorganizations in mind, has recently advanced a third possibility: use of the market. (Roe, Bankruptcy and Debt: A New Model for Corporate Reorganization, 83 Colum. L. Rev. 527 (1983).) Roe criticizes the current process as "cumbersome, costly, and complex," and proposes an alternative: simplified, all-common stock structures, with a reorganization value determined by selling a slice (e.g., 10%) of stock on the open market.

The disparate interests of different groups can deadlock the negotiating process, resulting in an unwise post-bankruptcy capital structure when all common-equity stock would be the best selection for everyone. "The deadlock problem can thus be seen as a set of overlapping externalities. Each of the critical actors of reorganization can, by making a decision (to delay, to litigate, to reject a plan of reorganization), cause the firm and those with a claim on, or interest in, the firm to bear costs of delay. The decision maker bears only some of the costs that the decision triggers. This is, in the jargon of game theory, a basic form of prisoner's dilemma: the aggregation of individualistic, 'rational' decisions leads to an inferior collective result" (Roe, supra at 544).

Furthermore, courts are likely to misvalue the corporation because they are generally not experts in the field, and may sympathize overmuch with junior creditors.

---

[6] Reprinted with permission of the West Group.

Roe contends that the market could more accurately and more quickly determine the value of a corporation; courts tend to have less information and less skill in this type of evaluation. Roe's contention depends on the "efficient market capital" theory, which holds that the market is the most accurate appraiser of value. This hypothesis is relatively new, and current bankruptcy practices are based on earlier theories; Roe urges bankruptcy institutions to consider the impact of the efficient market capital theory.

The precedents and the Code do not necessarily support a standardized all common stock rule. Roe suggests either amending the Code, or implementing the practice on a case by case basis, and notes that other courts have standardized substantive aspects in areas where the judiciary has the authority to determine whether a practice is reasonable. While recognizing that a market approach may still require some judicial administration, Roe nevertheless argues that the all-common-equity stock solution means a healthier company, and meets the best interests of the parties overall. "Whatever the relative accuracy of the mechanisms, a market based valuation and recapitalization via the slice-of-common-stock sale begins with the potential to be quicker and cheaper than the alternatives, without undermining the legitimacy or predictability of the process" (Roe, supra at 601). See also Brudney, The Bankruptcy Commission's Proposed "Modifications" of the Absolute Priority Rule, 48 Bankr. L. J. 305 (1974); Blum, The Law and Language of Corporate Reorganization, 17 U. Chi. L. Rev. 565 (1950); Heymann, The Problem of Coordination: Bargaining and Rules, 86 Harv. L. Rev. 797 (1973).

## ¶514: A chapter 11 mismatch?

Chapter 11 entails a renegotiation, which usually takes two years, among creditors, managers, and stockholders. Could the renegotiation be seen as best fitting with closely-held firms, where the owner and manager are the same? If the manager is a good one, but just unlucky, the creditors will want to keep the manager. Absolute priority would wipe out the manager as stockholder. But to motivate the manager properly, the new owners will want to give the old owner-manager some equity interest, perhaps in stock options or stock ownership. A negotiation is necessary. And chapter 11 can be seen as a good setting for that renegotiation.

For *public* companies, however, stock is widely dispersed, often in the hands of institutional investors. Individuals owning stock in the public company are usually diversified, as are institutions. They are in a good position to accept the risks of being wiped out by a harsh application of the absolute priority rule. Because they are typically less involved with the firm, there is less reason for the kind of renegotiation that an owner-managed firm entails.

## B. The judiciary and valuation

### ¶515: In re Equity Funding Corp. of America, 391 F. Supp. 768 (1975)

\* \* \*

Counsel for certain Class 8 Creditors also contend that the valuation opinions are inadmissible because the experts failed to consider market prices and price earnings ratios in rendering their opinions on reorganization value. The court disagrees.

\* \* \*

... [E]xisting market prices, conditions, and comparable sales need not be significant factors in determining reorganization value. In reorganization proceedings, it is assumed that the commercial value of property arises from the expectation of income from it. Consolidated Rock Products Co. v. Du Bois, 312 U.S. at 526. Thus, the basic question is "how much the enterprise in all probability can earn," Group of Institutional Investors v. Chicago, Milwaukee, St. Paul and Pacific R. Co., 318 U.S. 523, 540 (1943), and the proper method of valuation is "to value the whole enterprise by a capitalization of prospective earnings." Consolidated Rock at 525. In effect, this approach frees reorganizations from prices which are pegged by forced sales or by the temporary conditions of the market place. Instead, reorganization value is intended to approach the value that would prevail in a perfect market adequately stocked with willing and informed buyers and sellers. Therefore, the Court concludes that the experts considered market factors and that the weight they gave these factors adequately accords with the concept of reorganization value.

### In re Equity Funding Corp. of America, 416 F. Supp. 132 (C.D. Cal. 1975)

Reorganization value represents the best estimate of value the marketplace would put on a company comparable to New Company. However, because of uncertainties associated with a company emerging from Chapter X proceedings, possible initial selling pressure, and perhaps other factors, individual shares of stock of New Company may trade in the near future at less than reorganization value.

### ¶516: In re New York, New Haven and Hartford RR. Co., 632 F.2d 955 (1980) (Mulligan)

Under the compromise Plan the Debtor will be reorganized to carry on business as a[n] ... investment company .... It will be known as the New Haven Corporation and will be organized under the laws of Connecticut. Since it is recognized that the reorganized corporation will enjoy substantial tax advantages and has growth potential, the merits of reorganization over a straight liquidation are uncontested. The certificate of incorporation will authorize one class of 20,000,000 shares of new common stock having a par value of $1 per share.

It is uncontroverted that the Mortgage Bonds, which were initially issued when the New Haven emerged from a bankruptcy proceeding in 1947, are system mortgages secured by all the New Haven's assets and are in all respects senior to the Income bonds secured by the same collateral. The Mortgage Bondholders therefore must receive full compensation for their claim before the Income Bondholders receive anything. The claim of the Income Bondholders depends upon the extent to which the New Haven's assets exceed the claim of the Mortgage Bondholders. Thus, one of the more hotly contested issues during the proceedings before Judge Zampano was the valuation of the debtors' assets. The Mortgage Bondholders urged that the net asset valuation of the Debtor was approximately $75 million; the Income Bondholders placed the valuation in the range of between about $175 million and $246 million and the New Haven Trustee computed the range between $120 and $150 million. Judge Zampano in his February 14th Opinion determined the value to be $149.5 million. If the Mortgage Bondholders were to prevail on the valuation issue, then the appellant would receive no part of the Debtor's assets .... This is so because the Mortgage Bondholders' uncontested claim to principal and interest up through December 2, 1968, amounts to about $101 million.

The sole tangible assets of the Debtor consist of cash and Penn Central securities ....

In valuing the securities held by the Debtor, Judge Zampano attempted to determine their "intrinsic" value, instead of looking to what they were trading for on the market. Calculating the intrinsic value requires an estimate of how much the enterprise, the reorganized company, could earn. This, of course, involves a prediction which cannot be made with any degree of certainty. Penn Central owns certain ongoing non-railroad businesses so that valuation based on intrinsic value requires an estimation of the evaluations of these subsidiary companies. Penn Central's active acquisition program is continuing apace. Moreover, Penn Central is liquidating its assets consisting of real estate, rail lines, coal lands and certain investments .... Another unpredictable is the amount to be received by Penn Central for the transfer of its rail assets to Conrail on April 1, 1976. That issue is in litigation, ... and while guidelines have been established, until a determination is made, predictions of how the award will affect Penn Central's ability to redeem its debt-type securities and what "spillover" would remain to increase the value of the Common Stock are, of course, highly conjectural.

On the other hand, use of market value, which was the approach urged by the Mortgage Bondholders, is a straightforward and usually reliable method of ascertaining the worth of securities. We have recently held that "in a free and actively traded market absent compelling reasons to believe otherwise, the market price [of stock] is held to take account of asset value as well as the other economic, political, and financial factors that determine 'value.'" Seaboard World Airlines, Inc. v. Tiger International, Inc., 600 F.2d 355, 361–62 (2d Cir. 1979). In E.I. Dupont de Nemours Co. v. Collins, 432 U.S. 46 (1977), the Supreme Court sustained the SEC's method of valuing a closed-end investment company by the market price of the underlying securities which it owned. Other courts have also accepted the market value as the preferred method of valuing securities ....

While Judge Zampano recognized the force of these precedents, he concluded that the stigma of the Penn Central bankruptcy and the inability of investors to absorb and digest available information concerning the Asset Disposition Program, the Valuation case, and the complex capital structure of the Penn Central caused the market to underrate the securities. Yet the stigma of bankruptcy surely lessens as time goes by; the Penn Central securities have now been actively traded for almost two years and the price has remained fairly stable. And it is not unreasonable to assume that today's sophisticated investor is capable of analyzing with some success the future prospects of the Penn Central.

We need not, however, authoritatively determine whether the intrinsic value selected by Judge Zampano, or market value, or some value in between is the proper valuation for the securities held by the Debtor. The point is that the market value approach advocated by the Mortgage Bondholders is a plausible methodology and one which we cannot say would not prevail if the valuation issues were appealed. Applying this method to the Debtor's assets would result in a valuation well below $101 million[7] and would leave the Income Bondholders with no equity. Thus, if the Compromise Plan were not adopted, it is within the range of litigation possibilities that appellant Barry will receive nothing, which is certainly less than what he stands to receive under the Compromise Plan.

We conclude that after 19 years of litigation and tribulation it was due and fitting that settlement be reached. We are fully persuaded that the Plan is equitable and fair and that it strikes a reasonable balance between the conflicting claimants. The underlying legal issues here were complicated and the settlement avoided the litigation which would unquestionably have occurred had there been no compromise. We find no abuse of discretion by Judge Zampano in approving the Compromise Plan and affirm his order of April 10, 1980.

## ¶517: James Lorie, Peter Dodd & Mary Hamilton, The Stock Market: Theories and Evidence (2d ed. 1985)

The efficient market hypothesis

INTRODUCTION

\* \* \*

... This led to the theory of efficient markets. An efficient market has been defined in many ways but perhaps the simplest, yet most general, statement of the

---

[7] As of December 31, 1979, the market value of the Penn Central securities held by the New Haven Estate aggregated $56,344,969. Report of the Trustee dated February 12, 1980.

proposition is offered by Fama: "Market efficiency requires that in setting the prices of securities ... the market correctly uses all available information."[8]

Another useful definition is from Jensen:

> A market is efficient with respect to a given information set if it is impossible to make profits by trading on the basis of that information set. By economic profits is meant the risk-adjusted returns net of all costs.[9]

\* \* \*

## CONCLUSIONS

... The quest for an explanation led to the theory of efficient markets, which has implications far beyond the mere statistical independence of successive changes in stock prices. An efficient market is one in which many buyers and sellers react through a sensitive and efficient mechanism to cause market prices to reflect fully and virtually instantaneously what is knowable about the future of companies whose securities are being traded ....

The importance of market efficiency must not be understated. The efficiency of the capital market is one powerful reason investors are so willing to invest in that market: they are protected by this efficiency and can be confident when buying or selling shares that they are not at a disadvantage, since the price they trade at incorporates all that is publicly knowable about those stocks.

It must be noted that the results discussed in this chapter apply on the average, and individuals with superior skill in generating and processing investment information can earn substantial economic rents. In light of the accumulated evidence, individual investors should be skeptical about others' proclaimed abilities at selecting stocks and humble about their own. However, the search for superior investment performance is continual, and for those with the necessary skills, the rewards are great.

### ¶518: Efficient markets for a bankrupt's securities?

1. Is the judge likely to "beat the market"?
2. If the judge has nonpublic information, should it be made public?
3. In the end the question is empirical, isn't it? If a bankrupt firm's securities are undervalued because of stigma, selling pressure, or misunderstanding (see *Equity Funding* decisions, supra, ¶515), then they'll sell low at and around the time of bankruptcy. In later months (or years?), as the stigma wears off, as the selling

---

[8] Eugene F. Fama, "Reply," Journal of Finance 31 (March 1976), pp. 143–44.

[9] Michael C. Jensen, "Some Anomalous Evidence Regarding Market Efficiency."

pressure abates, and as misunderstood companies become understood, what should happen to the previously bankrupt company's stock price?

## ¶519: Edward Altman, Bankrupt Firms' Equity Securities as an Investment Alternative, Fin. Analysts J., July–Aug. 1969, at 129[10]

The purpose of this paper is to examine the common stockholders' experience of bankrupt companies and to investigate rigorously the expected return to investors who consider the purchase of these same bankrupt equities after the firm has legally petitioned the courts to reorganize under the guidelines of the National Bankruptcy Act. The first section of this paper will suggest a relatively simple but comprehensive model for measuring stockholder performance. Section II specifies the model more explicitly and examines the post-bankruptcy experience of approximately 70 corporations. Empirical results will include stockholder experience of individuals who purchased these companies at three different times: one month prior to bankruptcy declaration, one month after, and finally one year after. The results will be tested statistically to answer the questions implied above. The final section explores the implications of the results.

II. Empirical Test Methodology

The initial step in the empirical examination of bankrupt firms' shareholder experience is to compile an extensive list of those corporations that have petitioned the courts to reorganize under the rules of the National Bankruptcy Act between 1941 and 1965. After a corporation is granted permission to reorganize, it is incumbent upon the court appointed trustees(s) to work out a fair and feasible plan, sanctioned by the courts whose purpose is to rehabilitate an enterprise which otherwise would have had to be liquidated. In almost every case the reorganization plan provides for a restructuring of the firm's capital accounts. If it is assessed that the firm is insolvent, meaning that the old shareholders no longer possess an equity in the firm, then the equity segment of security holders is eliminated from participation in the reorganized entity. On the other hand, if some participation is allowed to the old shareholders, their interests are usually compensated with new common stock or a retention of part or all of their old securities. Regardless of the accepted reorganization format, a basis for assessing the post-bankruptcy experience of the old shareholders and any new investors is provided.

[We] record[ed] market values of the old securities from just prior to the bankruptcy petition date to the reorganization consummation date. Market value data are also compiled for the common stock one month and one year after the declaration

---

[10] Copyright, 1969, *Financial Analysts Journal*. Reproduced and republished with permission from the Association for Investment Management and Research. All rights reserved.

date. If a continued equity interest is provided for, the market values of the new (or old) securities are traced for a period up to ten years after bankruptcy. A surprisingly large number (about 50%) of bankrupt firms that attempted reorganization and were listed in the previous cited sources were found to possess quoted publicly traded equity securities thus enabling usage of market value variables in this study. Total equity loss is recorded in the event of no available market data or the cessation of an equity interest.

III. Implications

The paper has attempted to rigorously measure returns to equity holders of financial bankrupt corporations. *The findings showed insignificant differences of returns between these bankrupt equities (purchased after the declaration date) and the average return on common stocks listed on the New York Stock Exchange* ....[11]

## ¶520: Walter Blum, The Law and Language of Corporate Reorganization, 17 U. Chi. L. Rev. 505, 571–80 (1950)

Reorganization value is the substitute for market value in reorganization .... Basically it purports to determine what classes of claimants are entitled to be satisfied in whole or part out of the assets of the distressed company.

\* \* \*

The difference between market value and reorganization value is a touchstone for analyzing the reorganization system. Market value is a real value in that it not only is expressible in dollar terms but is realizable in dollars. Property can always be exchanged for cash at market price because that price is made by those who are ready and willing to back up their own estimates of value with money. For the same reason market value can always be ascertained objectively noting the highest bid. In marked contrast, reorganization value has the opposite characteristics. It is a fictional value which cannot command real money dollar for dollar. It is set by the estimates of persons who are not standing back of them with a willingness to invest their own funds. Accordingly it can never be objectively ascertained or verified but always remains in the realm of opinion or belief.

\* \* \*

Though reorganization value is in a world apart from market value the two realms are never completely isolated from each other. Securities of the reorganized company will be independently priced by the market regardless of how they were val-

---

[11] [Results for a later period showed stock doing well post-bankruptcy. Allan Eberhart, Edward Altman & Reena Aggarwal, *The Equity Performance of Firms Emerging from Bankruptcy*, 54 J. Fin. 1855 (1999).—Roe.]

ued for purposes of the reorganization. In the period immediately following reorganization [under the Bankruptcy Act in force until 1978], and for some indefinite time thereafter, it is to be expected that in the aggregate the new securities will sell below the values assigned them in the reorganization. That is, the total of market prices will fall substantially short of the total of their par or stated or face values. These nominal values at the outset will be discounted [bankruptcy doctrine presumes] because of the very factors which produced the "low" prices that led to discarding market value of the business as the standard for determining the rights of the parties upon default. In time the security prices should, on the whole, approximate nominal values if the guesses and assumption behind the calculation of reorganization value turn out to be fairly close to reality. The new securities, in other words, should approach becoming wholly sound to the extent the figure chosen for reorganization value happens to be a sound estimate.

\* \* \*

These collateral observations concerning reorganization value should not obscure the main point about the concept. Not only is it different from valuation by the market, but it can be understood fully only when contrasted with market value. A sharp reminder of the contrast is supplied by the case of a distressed holding company which owns nothing but relatively small blocks of publicly traded securities of enterprises not undergoing reorganization. The market value of the company's assets can be ascertained immediately and accurately by referring to present quotations, and the market value of the company itself obviously is the sum of those values. To assign a higher amount as reorganization value is to assume that the company's officers will manage its assets more profitably than investors believe these or similar assets will or can be managed. The evident brashness of that assumption is a deterrent to departing from market values in such a situation. In the more usual reorganization the market values of the debtor's assets, treated either individually or as a going business, are not so easily or surely or definitely determinable. To use a reorganization value greater than the best gauged market value is not as jarring in these circumstances. But doing so nevertheless assumes that the debtor's officers will perform better, or that general economic conditions will be better, than is believed likely by those who make the market.

\* \* \*

1. What is the relevance of Altman's study? If bankrupts' stocks on average have the same return as a portfolio of New York Stock Exchange stocks, how bad can the market for bankrupt companies (or their stocks) be?
2. Does the *New Haven Railroad* appellate decision reflect a change in doctrine (however slight)?

## ¶521: Overvaluation and undervaluation in reorganization

"The other reason for urging a relatively conservative approach to valuation ... is more basic. Creditors cannot protect themselves against an overvaluation. But the shareholders, once disputes over creditors' claims have been settled, have a means of protecting their interests from an undervaluation of the firm. This they can do by turning to the market for either debt or equity funds to pay off creditors. And if worse comes to worse they can even appeal to the market to buy out both the creditors and their own position."

Walter Blum, *Some Marginal Notes on TMT Ferry Reorganization: The New Math?*, 1968 Sup. Ct. Rev. 77, 85.

The problem of course is that many reorganization actors believe that the market value of firms in reorganization is unduly low.

## Chapter 6

# JUNK BONDS

A. Characteristics of bond indentures
B. The junk bond
C. Financial markets and junk bonds
D. Negative pledge clauses
E. Secured credit and finance theory
F. Morality, markets, and practicing law with bond indentures
G. Low priority

........................................................................................................................

**Introduction: Priority among financial claimants**

Priority is determined not only by the statute but by contract. The creditors can order themselves, making deals at the time that they lend as to who would come first and who would come second and, generally speaking, the Bankruptcy Code will enforce these deals. These deals could depend on which creditor takes security. The creditor who gets a mortgage on the debtor's real property or a security interest on the debtor's equipment and inventory under the Uniform Commercial Code would be paid out of that asset and, usually, become a general unsecured creditor of the company for any deficiency. Or the creditors could in these deals just say who would come first and who would come last. The creditor who comes last presumably is paid up front to do so, getting a higher promised interest rate and, hence, more compensation if the firm doesn't run into trouble. Such creditors who agree to stand aside until another creditor gets paid are said to "subordinate" themselves to the creditor who will come first. That creditor who comes first is said to be "senior" to the "subordinated" creditor. The most famous of these creditors who agree to take a place near the end of the priority line are junk bondholders.

In this chapter we analyze the principal means of contractual ordering of priority, looking at what limits creditors put on how far back on line they can be placed, mostly via financial covenants.

"What's a debenture?"

Drawing by Stevenson; © 1967
The New Yorker Magazine, Inc.

## A. Characteristics of bond indentures

### ¶601: Background to the bond indenture

The bond indenture is the bondholders' loan agreement. It's core establishes the interest rate, maturity date, and amount loaned. It can provide for security for the creditor bondholders. It can control the level of debt claims that will be superior to or inferior than the subject bondholders, set up the mechanisms by which the debt will be assumed in the event of a merger, constrain the amount of dividends that the firm can pay, require sinking funds, and restrict the type of investments the firm can make.

Bonds, in the classic notion, are long-term corporate debt obligations, issued under an indenture, under which a trustee takes title to, or a lien on, property of the corporation. Debentures are also issued under an indenture, but the trustee takes no security. The trustee's job is to ascertain corporate compliance with various financial covenants (usually via certificates from the company), to collect and disburse the money to the debentureholders, and to bring legal action against the corporation for the debentureholders. In common usage, no distinction is made and debentures are often also called bonds. Corporate notes are debt obligations not issued under an indenture.

The bond indenture (a term used for both secured bonds and unsecured debentures), seeks to govern conflict between the creditors and the stockholders.

In this chapter, after we read background material, we'll focus on the interplay among three key priority elements: seniority and subordination, negative pledge clauses, and security interests. First, some background:

"[T]here are four major sources of conflict which arise between bondholders and stockholders:

"Dividend payment. If a firm issues bonds and the bonds are priced assuming the firm will maintain its [current] dividend policy, the value of the bonds is reduced by [the firm's] raising the dividend rate and financing the increase by reducing investment. At the limit, if the firm sells all its assets and pays a liquidating dividend to the stockholders, the bondholders are left with worthless claims.

"Claim dilution. If the firm sells bonds, and the bonds are priced assuming that no additional debt will be issued, the value of the bondholders' claims is reduced by issuing additional debt of the same or higher priority.

"Asset substitution. If a firm sells bonds for the stated purposed of engaging in low variance projects and the bonds are valued at prices commensurate with that low risk, the value of the stockholders' equity rises and the value of the bondholders' claim is reduced by substituting projects which increase the firm's variance rate [i.e., high risk projects].

"Underinvestment. [A] substantial portion of the value of the firm is composed of intangible assets in the form of future investment opportunities. A firm with outstanding bonds can have incentives to reject projects which have a positive net present value if the benefit from accepting the project accrues to the bondholders."

[To reduce these conflicts, bondholders and stockholders use covenants to specify what risks can be taken. But some of these specific conflicts cannot be anticipated. In fear of the general risk of these conflicts, the bondholders will insist on some risk premium in their interest rate.]

"Covenants which directly restrict the shareholders' choice of production/investment policy ... impose restrictions on the firm's holdings of financial investments, on the disposition of assets, and on the firm's merge activity. [Although specific limits on investments are rare,] covenants which restrict dividend and financing policy also [have the effect of] restrict[ing] investment policy.

"Bond covenants which directly restrict the payment of dividends [usually do] not take the form of a constant dollar limitation. Instead, the maximum allowable dividend is a function of both accounting earnings and the proceeds from the sale of new equity ....

"Financing policy covenants ... restrict not only the issuance of senior debt, [but also] the issuance of debt of any priority, [and the granting of security]. In addition, the firm's right to incur other fixed obligations such as leases is restricted ....

"[Other] covenants ... include the [promise to provide] audited financial statements, the specification of accounting techniques, the required purchase of insurance, and the periodic provision of a statement, signed by the firm's officers, indicating compliance with the covenants."

Clifford Smith & Jerold Warner, *On Financial Contracting: An Analysis of Bond Covenants*, 7 J. Fin. Econ. 117 (1979).

## ¶602: Dewing, The Financial Policy of Corporations (5th ed. 1953)[1]

[The contents of the bond indenture can be summarized:]

This rather elaborate document has, ordinarily, six important sets of provisions, some of which are mere recapitulations or elaborations of statements made in the primary contract, the bond [formerly a simple piece of paper stating that the company owes, and will pay the specified sum of money and the specified interest, on the specified due dates, and now more typically a computer entry—Roe], and some provisions only indirectly referred to in the bond. There is, first, the set of provisions summarizing the amounts [due and the] future date of payment, the interest rate and the time of interest payment—provisions which acknowledge that the bondholder is a creditor of the corporation entitled to the payment of his loan with interest. Furthermore, if the payment of the debt may be anticipated by the corporation [i.e., paid by the debtor in advance of maturity—Roe], the fact will be clearly stated, together with the specific mechanism of prepayment which shall insure fairness to all the scattered bondholders. The second set of provisions describes the character and the extent of property against which the bondholder may levy in order to satisfy his debt. If there is no such property, the agreement will categorically state that fact. Thirdly, there is a set of provisions which represents the special covenants accepted by the corporation which insure the preservation of the value of the corporate property, during the long period while the debt shall endure. The corporation will pay its taxes, make the necessary repairs, set aside adequate reserves for depreciation, replace worn-out or obsolete equipment, protect its franchises or patent rights; it will not give a prior lien to the property reserved for the bondholders. The corporation agrees not to permit the wastage or destruction of the property covered by the agreement. Fourthly, there is a set of provisions which defines with a high degree of precision the exact course the bondholders, acting individually or together, must pursue in order to levy on the corporation, as general creditors, or to levy on the specific property, if any, set aside for the security of the bonds issued under the indenture. Again, fifthly, there are provisions describing the duties and the obligations of the trustee. These clauses define with precision what he can and what he cannot do, on behalf both of the corporation and of the individual and collective bondholders. Finally—as a matter of tradition because the trustee could not legally do otherwise—there is a covenant on the part of the bondholders, acting through the trustee, that when the corporation has paid back the original loans—the face of the bonds—and has met the successive payments of interest, the lien or claims of bondholders will cease and the corporation will no longer be bound by any of the promises of the bonds or the supplementary agreement.

..................................................................................................

---

[1] As reproduced in Victor Brudney and Marvin Chirelstein, Corporate Finance (3d ed. 1987).

Victor Brudney & Marvin Chirelstein, Corporate Finance: Cases and Materials 166 note e, 171 (3d ed. 1987):

The impetus for the early long-term corporate debt securities, the mortgage bonds issued by railroads in the 19th century, came from entrepreneurs who were forced to sell mortgage notes to many persons, since no one person was willing or able to furnish all of the funds to be raised. The problem was to give the numerous and widely dispersed purchasers of these mortgage notes, or bonds, the security of a mortgage on the railroad's assets without conveying individual fractional interests in the collateral to each bond purchaser. At the same time, the bonds were to be marketable and to carry along the lien on the mortgaged property. The solution was to convey the mortgaged assets, under a trust indenture, to someone as trustee, for the equal and ratable benefit of each of the bondholders.

* * *

The mortgage bond is an obligation secured by specified property which either is made subject to the obligee's lien by the mortgage (although technically title continues to be held by the obligor) or, in some states, is technically transferred to the obligee to be held solely as security for the repayment of the debt. In theory, the mortgagee of a corporate mortgage, like the mortgagee of a simple home mortgage, applies the security in payment of the defaulted debt by foreclosure on the mortgaged property in a proceeding which results in a sale. [If the debtor defaults, the property is usually sold under state law and t]he mortgagee may purchase the property at the sale which ideally is an auction at which competitive bidding is designed at least formally, to assure a fair price. Whether the property is sold to the obligee or otherwise, its proceeds are applied in payment of the obligation. The inadequacy of the foreclosure procedure to protect the corporate bondholders has been the subject of considerable literature and has resulted in the development of bankruptcy reorganization procedure under federal legislation.

To the extent that the property subject to a corporate mortgage is an integral part of a going concern, it generally has a higher monetary value if it continues to be a part of the going concern than if it is sold for cash, piecemeal or *in toto*. Hence, even when mortgage foreclosure was technically an available remedy of the bondholders, it functioned to enable them to acquire new participations in the continuing enterprise (i.e., the securities of a newly formed corporation, in exchange for which the insolvent's assets were "sold"), rather than to force the sale of the liened property to third persons for cash. When reorganizations thus were consummated through the process of mortgage foreclosure—principally in the case of railroads—the value of the property subject to the mortgage was theoretically available to pay the debt it secured to the extent thereof. If the pledged property was "worth" more than the amount of the debt, the surplus was available to second or even more junior mortgagees or to general creditors. On the other hand, if the property was not "worth" enough to pay the debt, the unpaid balance became an unsecured claim against the borrower, and the mortgage bondholders shared with other general creditors in the borrower's unsecured assets. The principle of allocating the full "value" of the mortgaged property to satisfy the mortgage bondholder before any other creditor could receive any part of the proceeds was imported into the statutory procedure for bankruptcy reorganization ....

## B. The junk bond

### ¶603: Drum Financial prospectus

Prospectus

$20,000,000

### DRUM FINANCIAL CORPORATION

**12⅞% Senior Subordinated Debentures due September 15, 1999**
Interest payable March 15 and September 15

Redeemable at the option of the Company, as a whole at any time or in part from time to time at 112.875% of principal amount prior to September 15, 1984 and thereafter at prices declining to 100% of principal amount on and after September 15, 1989 together in each case with accrued interest, except that no such redemption may be made prior to September 15, 1984, directly or indirectly, using borrowed funds having an interest cost of less than 12⅞% per annum.

\* \* \*

The Debentures will be subordinated to all Senior Indebtedness (as defined) of the Company. As of June 30, 1979, after giving effect to the sale of the Debentures and the application of the estimated net proceeds therefrom, the Company's Senior Indebtedness would have been $480,713. See "Use of Proceeds." The Debentures will rank senior to the Company's 5½% Convertible Subordinated Debentures due May 1, 1988. For a discussion of restrictions in the indenture upon the creation of Senior Funded Debt and debt ranking pari passu with the Debentures, see "Description of Debentures—Certain Covenants."

**DREXEL BURNHAM LAMBERT INCORPORATED**

**THE ROBINSON-HUMPHREY COMPANY, INC.**

September 26, 1979

## SELECTED FINANCIAL INFORMATION
(Dollars in thousands)
**Consolidated Operating Summary**
[edited]

|  | Year Ended December 31 | | | | | Six months Ended June 30 | |
|---|---|---|---|---|---|---|---|
|  | 1974 | 1975 | 1976 | 1977 | 1978 | 1978 | 1979 |
|  |  |  |  |  |  | (Unaudited) | |
| Income (loss) from continuing operations before realized investment gains (losses) and extraordinary items | (6,237) | (7,939) | 737 | 3,615 | 5,487 | 2,137 | 3,254 |
| Realized investment gains (losses) less federal income taxes | 647 | 140 | 50 | 2,044 | (121) | (48) | (499) |
| Loss related to discontinued operations | (1,302) | (15,496) | (1,855) | (6,671) | (53) | (25) | — |
| Extraordinary items | 398 | — | 8,446 | 3,543 | 3,130 | 1,404 | 1,180 |
| Net income (loss) | (6,494) | (23,295) | 7,378 | (1,557) | 8,443 | 3,468 | 3,935 |

**Summary of Consolidated Balance Sheet**
(Unaudited)
[edited]

|  | June 30, 1979 Actual |
|---|---|
| Total assets | $141,538 |
| Stockholders' Equity | 22,088 |

## THE COMPANY

Drum Financial Corporation (formerly Fidelity Corporation) is an insurance holding company engaged through its subsidiaries in the sale, underwriting and servicing primarily of property and casualty insurance as well as of credit life insurance, both group and individual. In 1978, approximately 70% of the Company's net insurance premiums written arose from consumer credit transactions originated by banks, finance companies, credit unions and retail merchants .... For a description of estimated recent losses resulting from Hurricanes David and Frederic, see "Business—Property and Casualty Insurance—Mobile home insurance."

During the late 1960s and early 1970s the Company was engaged in an expansion and diversification program which included the acquisition of several businesses, primarily in the insurance and financial service fields and the marketing of insurance lines not previously included among the Company's principal insurance products. This program ... resulted in substantial losses for the Company, most of which were realized between 1973 and 1975. Of significance were the following: (i) a $23.5 million loss in 1973 on the Company's investment in Equity Funding Corporation of America, (ii) [substantial losses in the firm's other insurance businesses]. In view of these adverse developments, changes in senior management of the holding company were initiated in late 1975. Since that time the Company has emphasized, and plans to continue to emphasize, those insurance product lines which have historically been profitable.

* * *

## DESCRIPTION OF DEBENTURES

### General

The Debentures are to be issued under an Indenture (the "Indenture") to be dated as of September 15, 1979, between the Company and The Omaha National Bank, as Trustee (the "Trustee"). The Debentures will bear interest from September 15, 1979 at the rate shown on the cover page of this Prospectus payable on March 15, 1980. (Section 2.02)

* * *

### Sinking Fund

The Debentures will be entitled to a sinking fund, which provides for the mandatory redemption by the Company on or before September 15, in each year, beginning with the year 1989 and ending with the year 1998, of $1,500,000 principal amount of Debentures, at a redemption price equal to the principal amount thereof together with interest accrued to the redemption date. The Company may, at its option, receive credit against sinking fund requirements for the principal amount of Debentures acquired by the Company and surrendered for cancellation.

### Certain Definitions

The following summarizes certain definitions to be used in the Indenture.

"Consolidated Net Income" shall mean net income of the Company and its Subsidiaries determined in accordance with generally accepted accounting principles.

"Consolidated Net Worth" shall mean the excess of the Company's and its Subsidiaries assets over their liabilities.

"Consolidated Senior Funded Debt" shall mean the aggregate Senior Funded Debt of the Company and its Subsidiaries ....

"Funded Debt" ... shall mean any Indebtedness with a stated maturity more than one year from the date of determination ....

"Indebtedness" shall mean any indebtedness for borrowed money or evidenced by bonds, notes, debentures or similar instruments, or the deferred and unpaid balance of the purchase price of any property which would appear as a liability upon a balance sheet prepared in accordance with generally accepted accounting principles and shall also include capitalized lease obligations and equity convertible into debt.

"Insurance Subsidiaries" shall mean any Subsidiary [now owned or subsequently] acquired or organized that engages, directly or indirectly, in the insurance business and any successor to any of the foregoing.

"Pari Passu Funded Debt" shall mean the Debentures and all other unsecured Funded Debt of the Company that both (i) ranks, as to payment of principal, premium, if any, and interest, pari passu with the Debentures and (ii) is subordinated to Indebtedness that is Senior Indebtedness under the Indenture. Unsecured Funded Debt that ranks pari passu with the Debentures would share ratably with the Debentures should there be funds insufficient to discharge both the Company's obligations on such unsecured Funded Debt and the Debentures.

* * *

"Senior Funded Debt" shall mean all Funded Debt other than Pari Passu Funded Debt and Subordinated Funded Debt.

"Subordinated Funded Debt" shall mean (i) the Company's unsecured Funded Debt if designated by the Company to be subordinate in right of payment to the Debentures and (ii) the Company's 5½% Convertible Subordinated Debentures due May 1, 1988.

"Subsidiary" shall mean any corporation of which at least a majority in voting power of the outstanding stock shall be owned by the Company directly or through Subsidiaries.

**Certain Covenants**

Limitation on Senior and Pari Passu Funded Debt. The company will not, and will not permit any Subsidiary to, incur any Senior ... Funded Debt ... unless after giving effect thereto, the aggregate Consolidated Senior Funded Debt and Pari Passu Funded Debt of the Company and its Subsidiaries shall be less than the sum of Consolidated Net Worth and Subordinated Funded Debt ....

At June 30, 1979, after giving effect to the sale of the Debentures and the use of a portion of the net proceeds to retire bank debt, an additional $7,939,957 aggregate principal amount of Senior and Pari Passu Funded Debt could have been incurred.

Limitation on Dividends, Stock Purchases and Restricted Investments. The Company will not (i) pay dividends or make distributions on its capital stock (other than in shares or stock rights), (ii) purchase or redeem, or permit a Subsidiary to purchase or redeem, capital stock of the Company ... if the sum of ... the amount[s] expended for any such purpose ... would exceed the sum of (1) 50% of Consolidated Net Income accrued subsequent to December 31, 1978; (2) the net proceeds received by the Company after December 31, 1978 from the sale of its capital stock, other than to a Subsidiary, for cash or upon certain conversions of Indebtedness (other than the 5½% Convertible Subordinated Debentures) and (3) $2,000,000 ....

Limitations on Dispositions of Insurance Subsidiaries. The Company will not, and will not permit any Subsidiary to, dispose (except to the Company) of any capital stock of any Subsidiary that was, or is the successor to, an Insurance Subsidiary on the date of the Indenture, or of any options therefor, except for sales for fair value of 100% of the capital stock of such an Insurance Subsidiary. (Section 6.08)

Limitation on Investments....

Limitation on Guarantees and Other Contingent Liabilities....

Limitation on Mergers and Dispositions of Assets....

**Subordination of Debentures**

The payment of the principal of and premium, if any, and interest on the Debentures is subordinated in right of payment, as set forth in the Indenture, to the prior payment in full of all Senior Indebtedness of the Company, as defined in the Indenture, whether outstanding on the date of the Indenture or thereafter created, incurred, assumed or guaranteed. Upon (i) the maturity of Senior Indebtedness by lapse of time, acceleration or otherwise or (ii) any distribution of the assets of the Company upon any dissolution, winding up, liquidation or reorganization of the Company, the holders of Senior Indebtedness will be entitled to receive payment in full before the holders of Debentures are entitled to receive any payment. If in any of the situations referred to in clause (ii) above a payment is made to the Trustee or to holders of Debentures before all Senior Indebtedness has been paid in full or provision has been made for such payment, the payment to the Trustee or holders of Debentures must be paid over the holders of the Senior Indebtedness.

Senior Indebtedness is defined as the principal of and premium, if any, and interest on indebtedness (other than the Debentures and the Company's 5½% Convertible Subordinated Debentures), whether outstanding on the date of the Indenture or thereafter created, (i) incurred or guaranteed by the Company for money borrowed from lending or financing institutions, (ii) evidenced by notes, bonds or debentures of the Company issued under the provisions of an indenture or similar instrument, or (iii) incurred, assumed or guaranteed in connection with the acquisition by the Company or a subsidiary of a business; provided the terms of the instrument creating or evidencing such future indebtedness provide that such indebtedness is superior in right of payment to the Debentures. (Article 4.)

By reason of such subordination, in the event of insolvency holders of the Debentures may recover less than the general creditors of the Company.

### Priority of Debentures

Under the indenture relating to the Company's 5½% Convertible Subordinated Debentures due 1988, the Debentures will be "Senior Debt" (as defined therein). As a result, the Company's obligations with regard to those debentures will be subordinate to the Company's obligations with regard to the Debentures.

### Events of Default and Notice Thereof

The term "Event of Default" when used in the Indenture shall mean any one of the following: failure to pay interest for thirty days, or principal (including premium, if any) or any sinking fund or other redemption installment when due; failure to perform any other covenant for sixty days after notice; acceleration of other indebtedness of the Company under the terms of the indenture or instrument evidencing such indebtedness unless rescinded or annulled within ten days after notice; final judgment for the payment of more than $100,000 rendered against the Company and not discharged within sixty days after the judgment becomes final; and certain events of bankruptcy, insolvency or reorganization. (Section 7.01.)

The Indenture provides that the Trustee shall, within ninety days after the occurrence of a default, give to the Debentureholders notice of all uncured defaults known to it (the term "default" to include the events specified above without grace or notice) .... (Section 10.03.)

In case an Event of Default shall occur and be continuing, the Trustee or the holders of at least 25% in aggregate principal amount of the Debentures then outstanding, by notice in writing to the Company (and to the Trustee if given by Debentureholders), may declare the principal of all the Debentures to be due and payable immediately. Such declaration may be annulled and past defaults (except, unless theretofore cured, a default in payment of principal of and interest or premium, if any, on the Debentures or failure to make any sinking fund payment) may be waived by the holders of a majority in principal amount of the Debentures, upon the conditions provided in the Indenture. (Section 7.02.)

The Indenture includes a covenant that the Company will file annually with the Trustee a statement regarding compliance by the Company with the terms thereof and specifying any defaults of which the signers may have knowledge. (Section 6.12.)

The Company will furnish to the holders of the Debentures annual reports containing financial statements certified by independent public accountants.

### Modification of the Indenture

Under the Indenture, the rights and obligations of the Company and the rights of the holders of the Debentures may be modified by the Company and the Trustee only with the consent of the holders of 66⅔% in principal amount of the Debentures then outstanding; provided, however, that, among other things [no (i)] change in the time of payment of principal of, or any installment of interest on, any Debenture, or (ii) reduction in the principal amount thereof or the rate of interest thereon or any premium payable upon the redemption thereof, or (iii) reduction in the aggregate principal amount of Debentures required to be redeemed pursuant to the sinking fund, or (iv) impairment in the right to institute suit for the enforcement of any such payment, or (v) reduction in the percentage required for modification of the Indenture or the consent for any waiver provided for in the Indenture, may be made without the consent of the holder of each outstanding Debenture affected thereby. (Section 14.02.)

**The Trustee**

The Omaha National Bank will be the Trustee under the Indenture.

The Indenture contains certain limitations on the right of the Trustee, should it become a creditor of the Company, to obtain payment of claims in certain cases, or to realize on certain property received in respect of any such claim as security or otherwise. (Section 10.08.) The Trustee will be permitted to engage in certain other transactions; however, if it acquires any conflicting interest (as described in the Indenture) it must eliminate such conflict or resign. (Section 10.05.)

Subject to certain limitations, the holders of a majority in principal amount of all outstanding Debentures will have the right to direct the time, method and place of conducting any proceeding for exercising any remedy available to the Trustee. (Section 7.06.) The Indenture provides that in case an Event of Default has occurred and is continuing the Trustee must exercise such of the rights and powers vested in it by the Indenture, and use the same degree of care and skill in their exercise, as a prudent man would exercise or use under the circumstances in the conduct of his own affairs. (Section 10.01.) Subject to the foregoing, the Trustee will be under no obligation to exercise any of its rights or powers under the Indenture at the request or direction of any of the holders of Debentures, unless they shall have offered to the Trustee reasonable security or indemnity against the costs, expenses and liabilities which might be incurred by it in compliance with such request or direction. (Section 10.01.) Except for the right to collect principal, premium if any, and interest on the Debentures when due, no holder of any Debentures has the right to institute any action, suit or proceeding at law or in equity for the enforcement of any remedy under the Indenture, unless the holders of 25% in principal amount of Debentures shall have submitted written requests to the Trustee to take action and shall have afforded the Trustee satisfactory security and indemnity against costs, expenses and liabilities, and the Trustee shall not have taken such action for 60 days thereafter. (Section 7.07.)

---

## ¶604: Questions on the Drum Financial Indenture

1. Do the creditors rely on state dividend statutes to protect them from the debtor paying out high dividends, which would make the debentures riskier than if the dividends were not paid out?

2. Can Drum Financial incur an unlimited amount of senior debt? That is, the compensation of the debentureholders is capped (see the cover page of the prospectus) at 12⅞%. Does the definition of "Senior Indebtedness" similarly cap the risk to which the debentureholders can be subjected? Compare "Subordination of Debentures" with "Certain Covenants."
3. Consider Drum Financial with the following balance sheet:

| Assets | Liabilities and Shareholders' Equity | |
|---|---|---|
| $100M | Senior | $30M (A) |
| | The Debentures | $20M (B) |
| | Further Subordinated | $10M (C) |
| | Common Stock | $40M (D) |

The $10 million of "Further Subordinated" debt is debt that is subordinated to the debentures. The creditors are organized in three layers of priority. Could another $20 million of senior debt be issued under the debentures' indenture? Could any senior debt be issued?

4. Can future creditors come before the subordinated debentures without being designated as "Senior Indebtedness"? If a creditor obtains a mortgage but Drum doesn't designate it to be senior, is it "Senior Indebtedness" under "Subordination of Debentures"? Is it "Senior Funded Debt"? What is the effect of "Certain Covenants"?
5. If Drum Financial merely issues a lot of long-term debt, without designating the debt as senior, must it comply with any covenants? Were the debenture buyers unconcerned with claims' dilution? See the definition of "Senior Funded Debt" and the "Limitation on Senior ... Funded Debt."

## ¶605: American Bar Foundation, Corporate Debt Financing Project, Commentaries on Model Debenture Indenture Provisions (1971)

[The American Bar Foundation drafted a model sample indenture, with typical terms, and provided a commentary on these typical terms. The following is from the Foundation's chapter on subordination provisions.]

### I. Introduction

Although present day subordination provisions contained in indentures are a complex of legal refinements, the underlying concept of subordination can be stated quite simply: it is the agreement by the holder of certain debt (the "subordinated debt") that the holder of certain other specified indebtedness of the same debtor (the "senior debt") will receive prior payment in full of that Senior Debt. Put another way—to illustrate the operation of subordinations—in the circumstances specified in the subordination provisions, payments or distributions on the subordinated debt are turned over to the holders of senior debt for application thereon until the senior debt is paid in full. In should be emphasized that, so far as the debtor is concerned, subordinated debt is just as truly debt as is the senior debt, and, in the event of the bankruptcy of the debtor, both subordinated debt and senior debt are proved on a parity with each other. It is by virtue of the subordination provisions that the holders of the subordinated debt are not entitled to retain payments or distributions thereon and, as a practical matter, are placed in a junior position with respect to the holders of the senior debt.

Part II sets forth an example of an entire Article Fourteen containing the subordination provisions, sometimes referred to as the "subordination agreement," which would appear in an indenture. This Article provides for a common type of subordination (sometimes referred to as the "inchoate" type of subordination) normally utilized in connection with debentures to be publicly issued or privately placed with institutional investors. This type of subordination (as distinguished from other less common types) is so drafted that payments may be made on the subordinated debt until a specified event, such as bankruptcy, insolvency or liquidation of the debtor, or other voluntary or involuntary distribution of its assets (or, in some cases, default in payment of senior debt) triggers the subordination.

* * *

## II. Covenant to Subordinate

A sample of a complete Article Fourteen on subordination of one type is set forth in Section A ....

### A. Sample Provisions

### § 14-1. Agreement to Subordinate

The Company covenants and agrees, and each Holder of Debentures, or any coupon, by his acceptance thereof, likewise covenants and agrees, that the indebtedness represented by the debentures and the payment of the principal of (and premium, if any) and interest on each and all of the Debentures is hereby expressly subordinated, to the extent and in the manner hereinafter set forth, in right of payment to the prior payment in full of all Senior Debt.

The term "Senior Debt" means indebtedness of the Company, whether outstanding on the date of execution of this Indenture or thereafter created, for money borrowed from banks, insurance companies and other financial institutions, unless in the instrument creating or evidencing such indebtedness it is provided that such indebtedness is not senior in right of payment to the Debentures.

## § 14.2. Distribution of Assets, etc.

Upon any distribution of assets of the Company upon any dissolution, winding up, liquidation or reorganization of the Company, whether in bankruptcy, insolvency, reorganization or receivership proceedings or upon an assignment for the benefit of creditors or any other marshalling of the assets and liabilities of the Company or otherwise,

> (a) the holder of all Senior Debt shall first be entitled to receive payment in full of the principal thereof (and premium, if any) and interest due thereon, or provision shall be made for such payment in cash, before the Holders of the Debentures or coupons are entitled to receive any payment on account of the principal of (or premium, if any) or interest on the indebtedness evidenced by the Debentures;
>
> (b) any payment by, or distribution of assets of, the Company of any kind or character, whether in cash, property or securities, to which the Holders of the Debentures or coupons or the Trustee would be entitled except for the provisions of this Article shall be paid or delivered by the person making such payment or distribution, whether a trustee in bankruptcy, a receiver or liquidating trustee or otherwise, directly to the holders of Senior Debt or their representative or representatives or to the trustee or trustees under any indenture under which any instruments evidencing any of such Senior Debt may have been issued, ratably according to the aggregate amounts remaining unpaid on account of the Senior Debt held or represented by each, to the extent necessary to make payment in full of all Senior Debt remaining unpaid after giving effect to any concurrent payment or distribution (or provision therefor) to the holders of such Senior Debt; and
>
> (c) in the event that, notwithstanding the foregoing, any payment by, or distribution of assets of, the Company of any kind or character, whether in cash, property or securities shall be received by the Trustee or the Holders of the Debentures or coupons before all Senior Debt is paid in full, such payment or distribution shall be paid over to the holders of such Senior Debt or their representative or representatives or to the trustee or trustees under any indenture under which any instruments evidencing any of such Senior Debt may have been issued, ratably as aforesaid, for application to the payment of all Senior Debt remaining unpaid until all such Senior Debt shall have been paid in full, after giving effect to any concurrent payment or distribution (or provision therefor) to the holders of such Senior Debt.

## § 14-4. Obligation of Company Unconditional

Nothing contained in this Article or elsewhere in this Indenture or in the Debentures is intended to or shall impair, as between the Company, its creditors other than the holders of Senior Debt, and the Holders of the Debentures and coupons, the obligation of the Company, which is absolute and unconditional, to pay to the Holders of the Debentures and coupons the principal of (and premium, if any) and interest on the Debentures as and when the same shall become due and payable in accordance with their terms, or affect the relative rights of the Holders of the Debentures or coupons and creditors of the Company other than the holders of Senior Debt ....

\* \* \*

[Discussion of Model Indenture Provisions]

**C. Senior Debt**

[Debtor and creditors—the underwriter on behalf of the creditors if the subordinated debt is publicly issued—will carefully] negotiat[e] the definition of "Senior Debt," i.e., the indebtedness which is to be entitled to the benefits of the subordination. A review of currently outstanding indentures will reveal wide variations among such definitions .... All other things being equal, the greater the senior debt, the less attractive the subordinated debentures.

\* \* \*

It should go without saying that a careful analysis of what is or is not included in the definition of "Senior Debt" is of paramount importance to any potential lender, senior or junior. The exact wording of the definition will determine the type and amount of senior debt which will be entitled to the benefits of the subordination.

\* \* \*

---

**C. Financial markets and junk bonds**

**¶606: Jan Loeys[2], Low-Grade Bonds: A Growing Source of Corporate Funding, Fed. Res. Bank of Phil., Bus. Rev., Nov./Dec. 1986 (background)**

In recent years, a growing part of corporate borrowing has taken the form of "low-grade bonds." Called "junk bonds" by some, and "high-yield bonds" by others, these bonds are rated as speculative by the major rating agencies, and they are therefore considered more risky than high- or investment-grade bonds. Lately, low-grade bonds have received a lot of public attention because of their use in corporate takeovers. But in fact, most low-grade bond issues are not used for this purpose. Corporations that now issue low-grade bonds are firms that, because of their lack of size, track record, and name recognition, used to borrow mostly via bank loans or privately placed bonds. Recently, investors have become more willing to lend directly to smaller and less creditworthy corporations by buying these low-grade bonds. There are several reasons for the new popularity of these bonds. But before discussing those

---

[2] Jan Loeys is a Senior Economist in the Macroeconomics Section of the Research Department at the Federal Reserve Bank of Philadelphia.

reasons, it is useful to examine in more depth exactly what low-grade bonds are and how their market first developed.

## WHAT ARE LOW-GRADE BONDS?

Low-grade bonds represent corporate bonds that are rated below investment grade by the major rating agencies, Standard & Poor's and Moody's. These ratings, which firms usually request before issuing bonds to the public, reflect each agency's estimate of the firm's capacity to honor its debt (that is, to pay interest and repay principal when due). The highest rating is AAA (for firms with an "extremely strong" capacity to pay interest and repay principal), and then AA ("very strong"), A ("strong"), and BBB ("adequate"). Bonds rated BB, B, CCC, or CC are regarded as "speculative" with respect to the issuer's capacity to meet the terms of the obligation. Firms generally strive to maintain at least a BBB rating because many institutions or investment funds cannot, because of regulation, or will not, because of firm policy, invest in lower grade bonds. This explains why bonds rated below BBB are also known as "below-investment" grade bonds.

\* \* \*

## THE MARKET FOR LOW-GRADE BONDS

Low-grade bonds have received widespread attention from the press in recent years, largely because of their association with ... corporate takeover[s]. But low-grade bonds have been around for a long time. In fact, during the 1920s and 1930s, about 17 percent of domestic corporate bond offerings (that is, new issues) were low grade. Furthermore, as the Depression of the 1930s wore on, many bonds that were originally issued with a high-grade rating were downgraded to below-investment grade. These so-called "fallen angels" were bonds of companies that had fallen on hard times. By 1940, as a result of both these downgradings and the earlier heavy volume of new low-grade offerings, low-grade bonds made up more than 40 percent of all bonds outstanding.

\* \* \*

In 1977, Drexel Burnham Lambert, an investment bank that was already making a secondary market in fallen angels, started an effort to revitalize the market for original-issue low-grade bonds by underwriting new issues and subsequently making a secondary market in them .... By the end of 1985, the total stock of low-grade bonds outstanding reached about $75 billion (or 14 percent of the total), less than a third of which consisted of fallen angels. To compensate investors for th[e default] risk they bear by holding low-grade debt ... rather than (presumably) default-free Treasury securities, firms promise to pay higher yields on their debt than the Treasury does. This difference between yields is call a "risk premium." ...

* * *

The recent revival of the low-grade bond market raises the question of why this product has become successful again. One popular misconception is that these bonds are used solely to finance corporate takeovers. But ... the market had taken off well before the first major use of low-grade bonds in corporate takeover attempts in 1983. And even in 1985—a year of unprecedented merger activity—low-grade bonds issued for takeover purposes made up only about 38 percent of total low-grade bond issuance .... Rather than reflecting a rise in one particular use for low-grade bonds, the reemergence of the market paralleled more fundamental changes in financial markets that made low-grade bonds relatively more attractive compared with other forms of financing.

## WHY DID THE MARKET GROW?

The main alternative to issuing public debt securities directly in the open market is to obtain a loan from a specialized financial intermediary that issues securities (or deposits) of its own in the market. These alternative instruments usually are commercial bank loans—for short- and medium-term credit—or privately placed bonds for longer-term credit ....

Before the reemergence of original-issue low-grade bonds, only large, well-known firms with established track records found it economical to raise money by issuing their own debt securities in the public capital markets. For smaller, relatively new or unknown firms, the expense was usually prohibitive. Because of the risk of underwriting low-grade bonds, investment bankers would demand hefty underwriting fees. Also, less creditworthy issuers would have had to pay a very high premium on their debt because investors perceived them as particularly risky investments.

Such borrowers thus found it more economical simply to obtain a loan from a bank or to place a private bond issue with a life insurance company ....

The reemergence of a market for public original issue low-grade bonds suggests that this situation is changing .... As with many financial innovations, it is impossible to identify all the factors responsible for this development. But it is possible to suggest several important ones that may have made a contribution to the reemergence of original-issue low-grade bonds, and three seem particularly noteworthy—a greater demand by investors for marketable assets; lower information costs; and changes in investors' risk perceptions.

**Marketability vs. Covenant Restrictions.** ... [B]uyers of privately placed bonds have become more willing to trade some of the safety they found in the contractual restrictions they placed on borrowers in return for the marketability and higher yields of publicly issued low-grade bonds. Private placements are bilateral, customized loan agreements with complex contractual restrictions on borrowers' actions. However, the

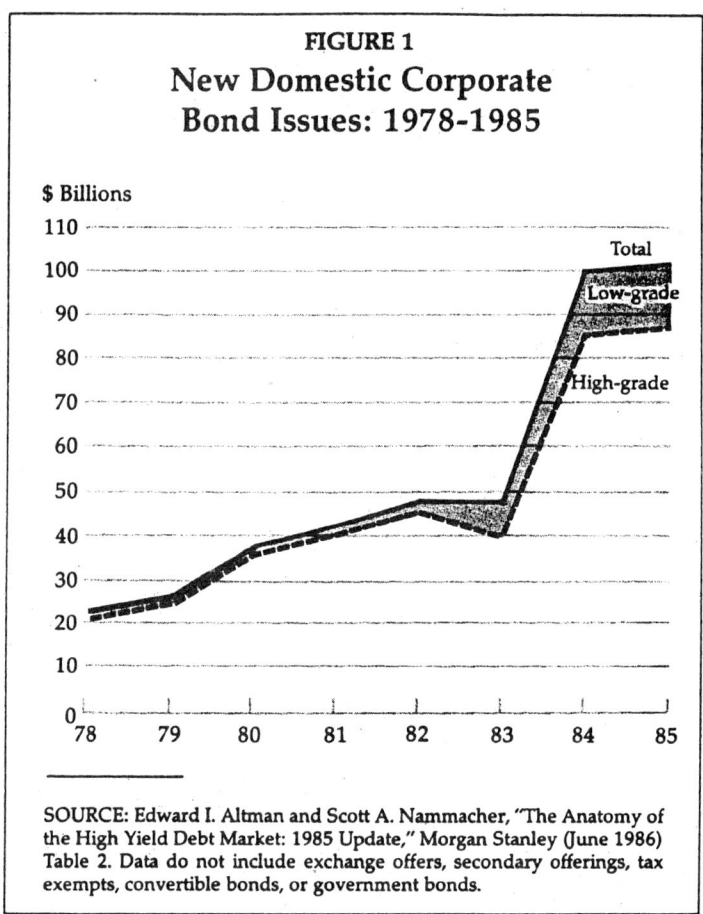

SOURCE: Edward I. Altman and Scott A. Nammacher, "The Anatomy of the High Yield Debt Market: 1985 Update," Morgan Stanley (June 1986) Table 2. Data do not include exchange offers, secondary offerings, tax exempts, convertible bonds, or government bonds.

lack of standardization of these covenants and the frequent need for renegotiation when borrowers want to transgress the covenant restrictions make it very costly to have a lot of lenders per issue, or to change the identity of the lenders. As a result, there is not much of a secondary market for private placements. That is, they are not marketable.

Low-grade bonds, in contrast, are public securities and are issued with relatively simple, standardized contracts without cumbersome restrictions on borrowers' actions, in order to facilitate their trading in a secondary market. And in exchange for the added freedom from covenant restrictions, borrowers pay a higher yield on low-grade bonds than on private placements ....

\* \* \*

**Information Costs.** A second factor contributing to the growth of the low-grade bond market is that, in recent years, it has become much easier for individual and institutional investors to obtain and maintain information about the condition of corporate borrowers. Thus lenders are now more likely to find it cost-effective to lend directly to smaller and less well-known corporations, rather than indirectly through financial intermediaries such as commercial banks.

Indeed, recent technological improvements in such areas as data manipulation and telecommunications have reduced greatly the costs of obtaining and processing information about the conditions—whether international or domestic, industry-wide or firm-specific—that affect the value of a borrowing firm. Any analyst now has computerized access to a wealth of economic and financial information at a relatively low cost. New information reaches investors across the world in a matter of minutes. Given the reduction in information costs, the cheapest method of lending to certain smaller and less creditworthy borrowers may no longer require a specialized intermediary as the sole lender to these borrowers, especially after recognizing the other expenses of using the intermediary.[3] ...

**Risk Perceptions.** A third explanation of the growth in low-grade bond offerings is more on the psychological side. Investors [may not have become any] better informed about the risks they take on, but they may have also become more willing to invest in risky securities. After the 1930s, the market for newly issued low-grade bonds shrank as most investors—with the losses incurred during the Depression still vividly in mind—turned to high-grade securities and left it to financial intermediaries to manage the risk of lending to less creditworthy borrowers. But as time passed and the memory of the 1930s faded ... .

## SUMMARY

Low-grade bonds are bonds that are rated "speculative" by the major rating agencies and that are therefore considered very risky investments. These bonds are either corporate bonds that have been downgraded, or, more recently, bonds that are issued originally with a rating below investment grade. Original-issue low-grade bonds are issued mostly by corporations that previously borrowed in the form of commercial loans or privately placed bonds.

Several factors seem to have contributed to the growth in low-grade bond offerings. For one, increased volatility in their sources of funds and a worsening of interest rate and credit risk have forced life insurance companies, which are the major buyers of private placements, to shift their investment focus towards assets that are somewhat more marketable and liquid, such as low-grade bonds. Also, improvements in computer technology have lowered the information and monitoring costs of investing in securities and have thus allowed smaller and less known corporations to borrow directly from private and institutional investors. Third, it may be that the favorable post-

---

[3] These added costs of using a financial intermediary instead of lending directly to a firm by buying its debt securities involve, for example, taxes, administration costs, and the costs of monitoring the condition and behavior of the intermediary.

World War II default experience on low-grade bonds has made investors more receptive towards investing directly in riskier securities, including low-grade bonds.

The growth in low-grade bond offerings thus represents mostly a rechanneling of corporate borrowing, away from individually negotiated loans, towards public securities. As such, it exemplifies a continuing effort by financial market participants to search out the most cost-effective way to channel funds from lenders to borrowers.

## D. Negative pledge clauses

### ¶607: <u>The negative pledge clause</u>

1. You represent a creditor. The creditor has refused to take a subordinated position. You have advised the creditor that if it lends, it will effectively be subordinated (i.e., will come second in a distribution in bankruptcy) if the company has granted security interests under Article 9 of the U.C.C. or realty mortgages. You check with the county clerk's office and find no filings.

2. Have you adequately protected the client's position? Will the client necessarily share ratably with all creditors at the time of a bankruptcy even if there are no security arrangements now?

3. In 1979 Chrysler neared bankruptcy and the government sought to support it. The act that enabled the U.S. government to guarantee repayment of new loans to Chrysler in 1979 and 1980 also required the responsible governmental board to be reasonably assured of repayment. To implement that requirement, the government board sought a security interest in Chrysler's manufacturing facilities, which were subject to negative pledge clauses in Chrysler's preexisting loan agreements.

4. What is a negative pledge clause? See the Chrysler Consent Solicitation.

5. Would the preexisting creditors have been able to enforce the negative pledge clauses in a Chrysler bankruptcy? What if Chrysler ignored the clauses and mortgaged its Principal Automotive Plants despite the contractual bar? That is, what if Chrysler decided that with its back to the wall, it had to do something. A bank—or a government—came along and offered new debt, but only if it could obtain security. Chrysler gave the security. (As the consent solicitation says at p. 199: "Should Chrysler's efforts to obtain Consents be unsuccessful, Chrysler would seek alternative means to remove the need for the Consents in order to satisfy the conditions ... for federal loan guarantees.") Then, unlike the historical result, no import quotas stifled competition from Honda and Toyota, the economy didn't pull out of the 1981 recession so quickly, and the K-car did not obtain sufficient consumer acceptance. Chrysler then went bankrupt.

   In this hypothetical bankruptcy the last creditor—the big bank or the government—seeks priority based upon its security. The debentureholders argue that their contract and its negative pledge clause protect them. They, the debentureholders, must be brought along equally and ratably by giving effect to, by enforcing, the negative pledge clause.

The big creditor says its security interest and mortgage are valid; it has priority, notwithstanding the negative pledge clause.

6. Who wins? Consider *Kelly* and the U.C.C. provisions in the following paragraphs. But first make sure you understand how a negative pledge clause works by reading the Chrysler negative pledge, which follows next. Why did Chrysler seek to amend the clause? Who made them seek the amendment?

## ¶608: Chrysler solicitation of consents

### CHRYSLER CORPORATION

February 23, 1980

To the Holders of Chrysler's
   8⅞% Sinking Fund Debentures Due 1995
   8  % Sinking Fund Debentures Due 1998

Dear Debentureholders:

The United States Congress has passed, and the President has signed, the Chrysler Corporation Loan Guaranty Act of 1979. Under that Act, Chrysler may receive commitments for federal guarantees of up to $1.5 billion of loans. To obtain these commitments, which are essential to Chrysler, Chrysler must satisfy certain conditions under the Act.

As part of Chrysler's efforts to satisfy these conditions, Chrysler requests your Consents to Supplemental Indentures [to] amend the Indentures under which your Debentures were issued. Your Consents must be received by March 31, 1980, unless that date is extended by Chrysler.

The Supplemental Indentures become effective only after the Loan Guarantee Board has issued the first federal commitment for guaranteed loans. Before that commitment may be issued, Chrysler must have a ... financing plan that includes at least $1.43 billion of assistance not guaranteed by the government and employee concessions of $587.5 million. Also, the Loan Guarantee Board must determine that Chrysler's financing plan is adequate and that its operating plan is realistic ....

    The attached Explanatory Statement contains information concerning Chrysler, the consents and Indentures. You should read it carefully.

* * *

Your Consents are extremely important to our efforts. I urge you to send in your Consents as soon as possible.

Very truly yours,<br><br>/s/ LEE IACCOCA<br>Chairman of the Board

## CHRYSLER CORPORATION

Solicitation of the Holders of
8⅞% Sinking Fund Debentures Due 1995
8% Sinking Fund Debentures Due 1998

### EXPLANATORY STATEMENT

**You are urged to read carefully this Explanatory Statement, including the attached financial statements of Chrysler, the notes thereto, and the report of the certified public accountants of Chrysler relating thereto, Management's Discussion and Analysis of the Consolidated Statements of Operations, and the Attached Exhibits. The Explanatory Statement contains important information with respect to the business, management and financial condition of Chrysler which should be considered in reaching a decision as to whether to execute the Consents sought by Chrysler.**

**Your Consent must be received by March 31, 1980 ....**

## CERTAIN MATTERS RELATING TO THE SOLICITATION

### Introduction

This Explanatory Statement is furnished by Chrysler Corporation ... in connection with Chrysler's solicitation of Consents ("Consents") to Supplemental Indentures (the "Supplemental Debentures") to amend certain covenants in the indentures pursuant to which the 8⅞% Debentures and the 8% Debentures were issued.

### Background

Chrysler is faced with pressing financial problems which have significantly weakened its financial condition. Chrysler had a loss of approximately $1.1 billion for 1979 and a loss of approximately $205 million for 1978 .... Chrysler's loss for the fourth quarter of 1979 was approximately $376 million and Chrysler estimates that losses are continuing at approximately that rate in the first quarter of 1980. Chrysler's working capital[4] has decreased from approximately $1.1 billion at December 31,

---

[4] [Working capital is the difference between short-term assets (inventory, raw materials, accounts receivable) and short-term liabilities (short-term loans, accounts payable, trade credit). The working capital of most firms is positive.—Roe.]

1978, to a negative position of approximately $111 million at December 31, 1979. Chrysler is in default under the agreements covering most of its institutional indebtedness and could not pay its institutional indebtedness if the lenders accelerated their loans. In that event, Chrysler also could not pay its indebtedness in respect of the Debentures ....

Chrysler's ability to continue operations is dependent at this time on its ability to obtain interim financing and cash flow from operations sufficient to permit it to meet its cash requirements until it can fulfill the conditions for a United States guaranteed loan .... If Chrysler cannot obtain sufficient interim financing or fails to meet the conditions for guaranteed loans, Chrysler would probably have to seek relief under the federal Bankruptcy Code, either seeking to reorganize Chrysler or, if reorganization is not possible, to liquidate Chrysler's assets. Even if Chrysler meets the conditions for guaranteed loans, its longer term viability is not assured.

**Reasons for Solicitation**

The Loan Guarantee Act generally requires that Chrysler grant [to the government as a guarantor of the loans to Chrysler] security in connection with the guaranteed loans ....

[But] Sections 1004 and 1005 of each of [Chrysler's preexisting] Indentures limit the ability of Chrysler to borrow money secured by liens on, or through the use of sale and leaseback transactions affecting, its Principal Domestic Automotive Plants ... unless the Debentures are equally and ratably secured. However, under the Loan Guarantee Act it may not be possible to secure the Debentures equally and ratably with the federally guaranteed loans [because the government loan board must find that the government loans will in all likelihood be repaid and, unless Chrysler gives nearly all of its assets as security, it may not be possible for the government board to make a finding that repayment is likely]. In addition, as is often the case in workouts or companies with financial problems, any extensions of credit ... [including those] required under the Loan Guarantee Act, will probably be made available only if secured ahead of the Debentures. Chrysler is seeking the Consents to authorize the Trustee to enter into the Supplemental Indentures which will amend each of the Indentures to permit Chrysler without equally and ratably securing the Debentures, to use Principal Domestic Automotive Plants to secure the federally guaranteed loans and nonfederally guaranteed assistance.

Chrysler is not seeking any other concessions from the holders of the Debentures. It is not asking the Debentureholders ... to waive or defer interest or sinking fund payments ....

**Supplemental Indentures**

\* \* \*

The Supplemental Indentures would permit Chrysler's Principal Domestic Automotive Plants to be mortgaged or otherwise used as security, without the Debentures being equally and ratably secured, for ... federally guaranteed loans ....

Should Chrysler's efforts to obtain Consents be unsuccessful, Chrysler would seek alternative means to remove the need for the Consents in order to satisfy the conditions for obtaining the first commitment for federal loan guarantees. However, Chrysler has no way of knowing whether or not these efforts would be successful. Failure to obtain the commitment for loan guarantees would probably result in Chrysler seeking relief under the Bankruptcy Code.

CHRYSLER CORPORATION
and

_____

Trustee


SUPPLEMENTAL INDENTURE
Dated as of          , 1980

to Indenture between

CHRYSLER CORPORATION

and

BANK


Dated as of     , 19

_____


__% Sinking Fund Debentures due___

THIS SUPPLEMENTAL INDENTURE, dated as of _____, 1980, between CHRYSLER CORPORATION, a Delaware corporation (the "Company"), and _____ Bank, a New York banking corporation (herein together with its predecessor and any future successor or successor, sometimes referred to as the "Trustee"), as successor to _____ Bank.

WITNESSETH

(Here insert appropriate recitals.)

NOW, THEREFORE, THIS SUPPLEMENTAL INDENTURE WITNESSETH:

That in order to enable the Company to meet certain of the conditions required under the Loan Guarantee Act to obtain the loan guarantees of the United States contemplated thereby, the parties hereby agree as follows:

\* \* \*

Section 1004 of the Indenture is hereby amended to read as follows:[5]

SECTION 1004. <u>Limitation on Liens.</u> The Company will not itself, and will not permit any Subsidiary to, incur, issue, assume, guarantee or suffer to exist any notes, bonds, debentures or other similar evidences of indebtedness for money borrowed, secured by a Mortgage on any Principal Domestic Automotive Plant, or on any shares of stock of or indebtedness of any Subsidiary which owns or leases a Principal Domestic Automotive Plant, without effectively providing that the Debentures ... shall be secured equally and ratably with (or prior to) such secured indebtedness, so long as such secured indebtedness shall be so secured, unless, after giving effect thereto, the aggregate amount of all such secured indebtedness plus all Attributable Debt of the Company and its Subsidiaries in respect of sale and leaseback transactions ... would not exceed 5% of [Chrysler's] Consolidated Net Worth: <u>provided, however,</u> that this Section shall not apply to indebtedness secured by:

[List of exceptions]

*and, provided, further, that, ... this Section shall not apply to indebtedness secured by Mortgages if such indebtedness ... has been guaranteed by the United States under the Loan Guarantee Act.*

## ¶609: <u>Questions about Chrysler's negative pledge</u>

1. Why did Chrysler have negative pledge clauses in its preexisting loan agreements and bond indentures? What were the previous creditors concerned about?

---

[5] *[Italicized]* material at the end of Section 1004 indicates changes from Section 1004 of the indenture.

2. What problem did these negative pledge clauses present to Chrysler's new prospective creditor in 1980?

3. How are sales and leaseback transactions treated under the negative pledge clause? Why are they treated that way?

4. Two related side-issues, which we'll examine carefully later. (See Chapter 11 for an inquiry into renegotiating bond indenture terms.) First, note that in its consent solicitation Chrysler said it was not seeking that the debentureholders "waive or defer interest ... payments." Nor did Chrysler ask the debentureholders to "writedown" their loans, accepting a promise to repay, say, $500, on each $1000 bond. Other creditors made chapter 11-type concessions; the debentureholders did not. Second, the conventional wisdom as to renegotiation of public debentures is that renegotiation is difficult or impossible:

> In a private borrowing from an institutional lender, the debtor may be less concerned with the scope of restrictions on additional debt in the loan agreement than in the case of a public borrowing from scattered debenture holders. In the former case, not only is obtaining the lender's waiver, or consent to alteration, mechanically feasible, but the creditor is likely to be responsive to changes which it perceives will enhance the borrower's economic well being. In the latter case, the mechanics of consent to change are more cumbersome, and the scattered debenture holders are less likely to be able or willing to make the judgment that concessions are advantageous to themselves as well as to the debtor.

Victor Brudney & Marvin Chirelstein, Corporate Finance 175 note h (3d ed. 1987). Was Chrysler's refinancing a special case? Chrysler did, after all, seek and obtain consents that renegotiated the terms of the bond indenture, namely by amending its negative pledge clauses. The institutional structure of debt-holding, with the debt disproportionately in a handful of junk bond funds, challenges the continuing accuracy of the conventional wisdom. A debtor can find and talk with its bondholders.

5. What if Chrysler ignored the negative pledge clause and mortgaged its principal automotive plants anyway, without having obtained sufficient consents to modify the indenture? The new creditor would have taken a mortgage and security interest in Chrysler's principal automotive assets. In the subsequent bankruptcy, the bondholders and lenders with negative pledge clauses argue that they should share ratably with the secured creditor. What would the result have been? See *Kelly* and the U.C.C., next.

Similarly, what if Drum Financial issued too much debt under "Certain Covenants" and then went bankrupt. How would the violation of the covenants affect the bankruptcy distribution? See Chrysler, supra, and *Kelly*, next.

## ¶610: Kelly v. Central Hanover Bank & Trust Co., 11 F. Supp. 497, rev'd 85 F.2d 61 (2d Cir. 1936)

OPINION: MACK, Circuit Judge.

These class suits were brought by a debenture holder of the Insull Utility Investments, Inc. (hereinafter referred to as I.U.I.), after the latter's adjudication in bankruptcy .... Plaintiff asks, on behalf of ... all ... debenture holders ... that stock pledged to defendants by I.U.I. as collateral to certain loans made by each of them in 1931, be returned or that the debenture holders share equally and ratably with those defendants in such securities.

\* \* \*

I.U.I. was incorporated in December, 1928 .... In January, 1929, $6,000,000, 20-year 6 per cent debentures (series A) were issued .... Then followed a period of short-term borrowing, largely from the Continental Illinois Bank & Trust Company of Chicago ....

\* \* \*

As the company was already largely indebted to the Chicago banks, the officers of the company turned their attention to the New York banks .... Negotiations with each of the defendant [New York] banks resulted in loans by them to I.U.I. totaling $17,000,000, made between March 14, 1931, and August 12, 1931 .... Each of the loans was secured by pledges of stock of Insull group companies, held in the I.U.I. portfolio ....

\* \* \*

Plaintiff[s, who are previous, unsecured creditors,] base the[ir] suits against each defendant on the charge that the defendant therein made and renewed the loan and received and held the original and the subsequent collateral as security therefor, with knowledge or charged with notice that each of the transactions was in violation of ... [a] restrictive covenant[ ] (hereinafter called the "negative pledge clause"[6]) ... contained in the I.U.I. debentures ....

*Immediately following the covenant[], there is, in each debenture of each series, [an acceleration] clause ....*

Each defendant denies that it had actual knowledge or is chargeable with notice of the existence and/or text of the restrictive covenants. While contending that under a

---

[6] The negative pledge clause reads: "The Company hereby covenants and agrees with the holder hereof that ... it will not mortgage or pledge any of its property unless the instrument creating such mortgage or pledge shall provide that this debenture shall be secured thereby equally and ratably with all other obligations issued or to be issued thereunder, except that the company without so securing this debenture (a) may at any time mortgage or pledge any of its property for the purpose of securing loans to the Company contracted in the usual course of business for periods not exceeding one year, and (b) ...."

proper interpretation of the covenants, neither the loan nor the pledge transactions constituted a breach thereof, it alleges that, in any event, it had no actual knowledge and is not chargeable with notice of any such breach. Each defendant further contends that *even if any of the transactions had constituted a breach of [the negative pledge] covenant[ ] and if such transaction had been made with actual knowledge that it did involve such a breach, defendant nevertheless would not be liable because it did not induce and is not charged with having induced I.U.I. to violate the covenant.*[7]

[The court held that as drafted the negative pledge clause did not apply to the subject transaction. Although perhaps ambiguous, the clause did not bar the firm from pledging assets to secure short-term borrowings. But even if it did bar them, the beneficiaries of the clause could not seek remedy by following the assets into the hands of the pledgee. The debentureholders had no equitable servitude in the asset; they held—if the clause were applicable at all—only a claim against the bankrupt for breach of a covenant.]

\* \* \*

By the negative pledge clause, I.U.I. agrees not to mortgage or pledge any of its assets "unless the instrument creating the mortgage or pledge" provides for equal and ratable security to the debenture holders with "obligations issued or to be issued thereunder." These words appear clearly to refer to the creation [not of a short-term loan but] of a funded [long-term financial] debt secured by a mortgage or trust instrument, ....

\* \* \*

[The plaintiffs argue]: (1) That the issuance of the debentures created an equitable lien for the benefit of the debenture holders on all of the assets of I.U.I., whether held by the company at that time or thereafter acquired; (2) that the covenants created "something in the nature of an equitable servitude" on all such assets of I.U.I.; (3) that defendants are constructive trustees of the pledged collateral for the benefit of the debenture holders, either because they participated in a breach of trust or knowingly and

---

[7] Knowledge is sought to be imputed and notice charged to defendants in many ways .... It was also established at the trial that annual statements of I.U.I., revealing the existence, though not the terms of the debentures, were in the credit files of each of the banks prior to the loans, and were consulted by most of the loaning officers. Plaintiff and cross-plaintiff urge that, due to the prevalence of restrictive covenants in debenture issues, knowledge that there are outstanding debentures puts defendants on inquiry as to whether there are restrictive covenants therein, and, if so, what the terms thereof are ....

Only one of the witnesses called by plaintiff and cross-plaintiff, was asked on direct examination whether he knew of the existence of the restrictive covenants at the time that a defendant for which he had acted made its loan; his answer was in the negative. Most of the other bankers were asked, on cross-examination, whether they had such knowledge at the time of the respective loans and renewals made by them, and all of them, except McGee of the Bankers Trust, asserted that they had no such knowledge. McGee testified that he had no such knowledge at the time of the original advance made by Bankers Trust, but that he learned about the covenants prior to the date of renewal.

unjustifiably interfered with the debenture holders' contract rights; (4) that the debenture holders had a right, enforceable in equity, to continued performance of their contract by I.U.I., and consequently now have an equitable right of reparation against those who knowingly invaded that right, even though they did not induce the breach of contract.

... The claim of an equitable lien on all of the assets of I.U.I then held and subsequently acquired, created by the issuance of the debentures, is without foundation. This claim, as well as that of "something in the nature of an equitable servitude" is rested on the negative pledge clause, for that covenant alone purports to restrict the use of property .... [N]o equitable lien can be created out of that prohibition ....

*[T]he I.U.I debenture covenants created only personal rights against the company, not a present security interest in its assets.* Furthermore, the company at all times, whether before or after breach of the covenant, had the right while solvent to sell all of the stock in its portfolio to a purchaser with knowledge of the restrictive covenants and of their violation. That right, although not contradictory to the restrictive covenants, is inconsistent with a right to an equitable lien on the assets. It therefore compels the rejection of the equitable lien theory.

\* \* \*

... The contention that the covenants created "something in the nature of an equitable servitude" is also, in my judgment, unfounded, even as applied to the negative pledge covenant ....

\* \* \*

Plaintiff and cross-plaintiff also seek to charge defendants as constructive trustees on the theory that receipt of property with knowledge that the transfer is in violation of a contractual obligation creates a liability in equity in favor of the obligee. But the cases do not support this broad proposition. [One cited case] is not in point. All that it holds is that where A, by fraudulent means, *induces* B to break his contract with C, as a result of which A obtains property which would otherwise have gone to C, A holds that property in constructive trust for C. No such case is before me; defendants are charged neither with actual fraud nor with inducing a breach of contract.

\* \* \*

... The premise of this [final] proposition, as hereinabove stated, is that the debenture holders had a right to enjoin both the making and the renewal of each loan and the pledging and the retention of the collateral, because such act would involve breaches of both clauses; the conclusion sought to be drawn therefrom, is that the debenture holders, after such a breach of either covenant, acquired something in the nature of an equitable lien on the wrongfully pledged certificates of stock, enforceable against the defendants, on the assumption that they had knowledge of or are chargeable with notice of the debenture holders' rights.

The fundamental question to be considered in this connection is whether the acceleration provision in the debentures gave the holders thereof such an adequate remedy at law for breach of the covenants as to preclude equitable jurisdiction. Although in a few cases there are statements to the contrary, the general rule is that *an injunction against breach of a negative covenant will not issue unless the remedy therefor at law is inadequate.*

* * *

At the time of the original loans by these defendant banks, I.U.I. was abundantly solvent; therefore, if a debenture holder had known of any violation, he could have recovered at law the full amount of the debentures, certainly a perfectly adequate remedy ....

* * *

The conclusion that the debenture holders would have had no right to enjoin the consummation of the loans made by defendant banks is decisive of the present suits against them. If the making of the loans gave the debenture holders no legal or equitable rights against the banks, the subsequent insolvency of I.U.I. did not create such rights. It would be a novel doctrine that a breach of contract, causing no irreparable injury at the time, is yet cognizable in equity because the subsequent insolvency of the promisor robs the promisee of the practical value of his remedy at law. Since there is no legal liability of defendant banks because none of them *induced* I.U.I.'s alleged breach of covenant and no equitable jurisdiction because the legal remedy against I.U.I. was adequate, the bills and cross-bills brought against them must be dismissed.

---

The district court decision was reversed and remanded in a one paragraph opinion, directing the lower court to "pass upon the questions presented, (a) whether the loans were made in the ordinary course of business, and (b) whether the banks had knowledge of the restrictive covenants in the debentures." Kelly v. Central Hanover Bank & Trust Co., 85 F.2d 61, 63 (2d Cir. 1936). The appellate opinion is cryptic, with instruction (a) probably directed toward interpretation of the actual clause, and instruction (b) directed toward other doctrines, such as fraudulent conveyance or equitable subordination, matters to be discussed in Chapters 8 and 16, or fraudulent inducement.

1. If a potential new lender typically has copies of the old credit agreements or can get copies, should knowledge be imputed to the new lender?
2. The negative pledge clause by its terms had an exception allowing short-term borrowings in the ordinary course of business, implying that short-term secured loans not in the ordinary course of business would be covered by the negative pledge clause. The appellate court's first question seems directed toward the lower court's view of the applicability of the clause to the loans actually made.

3. Does the Uniform Commercial Code speak to the issues dealt with in *Kelly*? See the next paragraph.

## ¶611: The UCC, *Kelly* and the negative pledge clause

1. Is the negative pledge clause a secret lien, not publicly recorded, and accordingly unenforceable against third parties?
2. Consider the following sections of the Uniform Commercial Code:

> **§ 9-102. Policy and Subject Matter of Article.**
>
> (1) Except as otherwise provided ... this Article applies
> > (a) to any transaction (regardless of its form) which is intended to create a security interest in personal property or fixtures including goods, documents, instruments, general intangibles, chattel paper or accounts; and also
> > (b) to any sale of accounts or chattel paper.

The official comment says that "[t]he main purpose of this Section is to bring all consensual security interests in personal property and fixtures under this Article[.]" In general Article 9 is a filing and notice statute: one acquires security interests usually by public filing and, generally, without a public filing one cannot defeat a subsequent creditor who publicly files notice of its own security interest. Moreover:

> **§ 9-401. Alienability of Debtor's Rights.**
>
> (b) **[Agreement does not prevent transfer.]** An agreement between the debtor and a secured party which prohibits a transfer of the debtor's rights in collateral or makes the transfer a default does not prevent the transfer from taking effect.

Comment 5 to UCC § 9-401 states:

> 5. **Negative Pledge Covenant.** Subsection (b) is an exception to the general rule in subsection (a). It makes clear that in secured transactions under this Article the debtor has rights in collateral (whether legal title or equitable) which it can transfer and which its creditors can reach. It is best explained with an example.
>
> **Example 2:** A debtor, D, grants to SP a security interest to secure a debt in excess of the value of the collateral. D agrees with SP that it will not create a subsequent security interest in the collateral and that any security interest purportedly granted in violation of the agreement will be void. Subsequently, in violation of its agreement with SP, D purports to grant a security interest in the same collateral to another secured party.
>
> Subsection (b) validates D's creation of the subsequent (prohibited) security interest, which might even achieve priority over the earlier security interest. ...

[S]ubsection (b) does not provide that the agreement restricting assignment is "ineffective." Consequently, the debtor's breach may create a default.

**§ 9-322. Priorities Among Conflicting Security Interests in ... [the] Same Collateral.**

(1) Conflicting perfected security interests ... rank according to priority in time of filing or perfection ... .

...........................................................................................................................

3. Debtor borrows $1000 from creditor X, and offers X security worth $5000. X fails to file a notice of the security agreement. Later, Y gets a security agreement in the same property and files its security agreement. In bankruptcy, who wins?

4. Same debtor borrows $1000 from creditor X, and gives X a security agreement (this time properly filed) on security worth $5000. Debtor would like to give the remaining $4000 as security to creditor Y. Can debtor do so under § 9-311? Would the debtor be any less able to give security to Y if the secured interest of X were never recorded? If X had never taken any security interest in the $5000 of collateral, could the debtor give a security interest in all of it to Y?

   If X had never taken any security interest in the $5000 of collateral, but Debtor promised never to give a security interest to anyone, could Debtor still give a security interest in all of it to Y?

5. "Despite the reversal by the Second Circuit ... in *Kelly*, most lawyers have assumed that negative pledge clauses and other covenants in transactions involving personal property are not enforceable against third parties. 9-311 seems to say that the debtor can transfer rights in the property despite a provision in the security agreement to the contrary. The effectiveness of negative pledge clauses and other covenants would seem to be very limited because Article 9 purports to be the exclusive means by which a creditor can create a consensual property interest to ensure repayment of his debt. Comment 5 to 9-203 says explicitly that the concept of the equitable mortgage has been abandoned. Given the role of ostensible ownership in Article 9, isn't this conclusion the one most consistent with the structure of Article 9?" Douglas Baird & Thomas Jackson, Security Interests in Personal Property 929-30 (1984).

6. Is there any value to a creditor of a negative pledge clause, even if unenforceable against a pledge once a pledge is made?

   First, note once again that there are other noncontractual doctrines that might be available to the lender with a negative pledge clause. Equitable subordination (Chapter 8), fraudulent conveyance law (Chapter 16), and preference law (Chapter 7, sub-part C) might be useful to the creditor. (Tort doctrine might give the early lender a cause of action against the later, knowing lender for inducing a breach of contract, but perhaps the suit would fail if the debtor had *already* decided to breach *before* speaking with the later lender; hence, the later lender wouldn't have *induced* the breach.)

But is the contract itself, the negative pledge clause itself, directly valuable to the creditor in keeping the property free from security interests?

7. Time (1): Debtor borrows and uses a negative pledge clause at Time 1.

| 10M in assets | 10M unsecured debt with NPC |
|---|---|

Time (2): Later, at Time 2, the debtor borrows from another creditor, and gives the new creditor security in all of the debtor's assets.

| 20M in assets | 10M secured debt (all assets) |
|---|---|
| | 10M unsecured with NPC |

In the next year, the company suffers serious reverses, declines in value and files for bankruptcy.

Time (3): Bankruptcy after decline in value of firm and assets

| 10M assets | 10M secured debt (seeking all assets) |
|---|---|
| | 10M unsecured with NPC |

The NPC creditors seek an equitable lien. What result? The NPC creditors seek equitable subordination? What are the arguments in favor? And the arguments against? What should the NPC creditor have done at Time 2?

## E. Secured credit and finance theory

The following readings explain the basics of security interests and the theory of what security interests do. Basically, a creditor seeks assurance that if the debtor cannot pay the loan back, the creditor can seize property of the debtor. The fundamental legal problems are of priority and notice: What happens if two creditors have security interests in the property? Who collects first?

The property to be secured could be realty or not. Realty interests are generally governed by state realty mortgage statutes. They set up a local realty filing system, with mortgage priority accorded to the first filer in the realty records. Non-realty interests (in machinery, inventory, raw materials, patents, etc.) are governed by Article 9 of the Uniform Commercial Code. The UCC sets up a filing and notice system, not all that different from the mortgage system. The UCC's mechanics are detailed in the next reading, after the basic UCC Form 1.

Uniform Commercial Code — FINANCING STATEMENT — Form UCC-1

IMPORTANT — Read instructions on back before filling out form

| This FINANCING STATEMENT is presented to a Filing Officer for filing pursuant to the Uniform Commercial Code. || No. Of Additional Sheets Presented: | 3. ☐ The Debtor is a transmitting utility |
|---|---|---|---|
| 1. Debtor(s) (last Name First) and Address(es): | 2. Secured Party(ies) Name(s) and Address(es) || 4. For Filing Officer: Date, Time, No. Filing Office |
| 5. This Financing Statement covers the following types (or items) of Property ||| 6. Assignee(s) of Secured Party and Address(es) |
| 8. Describe Real Estate Here: ☐ This statement is to be indexed in the Read Estate Records: || 9. Name of a Record Owner | 7. ☐ The described crops are growing or to be grown on:* ☐ The described goods are or are to be affixed to:* ☐ The lumber to be cut or minerals or the like (Including oil and gas) is on:* *(Describe Real Estate Below) |
| No & Street Block | Town or City Lot | County | Section |

10. This statement is filed without the debtor's signature to perfect a security interest in collateral (check appropriate box)
  ☐ Under a security agreement signed by debtor authorizing secured party to file this statement, or
  ☐ which is proceeds of the original collateral described above in which a security interest was perfected, or
  ☐ Acquired after a change of name, identity or corporate structure of the debtor, or
  ☐ as to which the filing has lapsed, or already subject to a security interest in another jurisdiction:
  ☐ When the collateral was brought into the state, or
  ☐ when the debtor's location was changed to this state.

By _____    By _____
    Signature(s) of Debtor(s)                Signature(s) of Secured Party(ies)

(1) Filing Officer Copy-Numerical

(5/82)    STANDARD FORM - FORM UCC-1 — Approved by Secretary of State of New York

¶612: __Secured Transactions: Donald W. Baker, A Lawyer's Guide to Secured Transactions 18-24, 67-69, 89-90 (1983)__[8]

§ 1-3. An Overview of Secured Transactions Under Article 9

\* \* \*

**B. Significance of a Security Interest; Unsecured Creditors and the Process of Obtaining a Judicial Lien**

Assume that Debtor Corporation purchases business equipment from Supply Company on "open account," that is, "on its signature" alone, that is, on unsecured credit. When Debtor fails to repay Supply Company at the appropriate time, may Supply Company simply repossess the equipment? No; as an *unsecured* creditor, Supply Company cannot retake the equipment until it has first gone through the sometimes lengthy, expensive process of obtaining a "judicial lien." In many states this process, sometimes called the "collection process," requires that the unsecured creditor file suit on the debt, obtain a judgment, and—if the defendant debtor does not voluntarily pay the judgment—obtain from the court a writ of execution ordering the sheriff to seize whatever property of the debtor is available. After seizing the property—called levying—the sheriff sells it at a public sale, whereupon the proceeds are paid to the creditor to satisfy the debt. By contrast, had Supply Company taken a valid Article 9 security interest, it would generally be entitled to repossess and sell the collateral itself, without resort to judicial proceedings.

A second major advantage to having a security interest arises when a third party, such as a competing creditor, lays claim to the property covered by the security interest. When the rules of Article 9 give the secured creditor priority, he has sole claim to the collateral, meaning he can use it to fully satisfy his loan before the competing party has any rights. This advantage is apparent, for instance, when the debtor has gone into bankruptcy. Assume the bankrupt's sole asset is a machine having a resale value of $10,000, against which X, who took an Article 9 security interest, loaned $9,000. The bankrupt debtor has two unsecured creditors, Y and Z, each of whom he owes $10,000. If X satisfies the appropriate requirements of Article 9 (and the Bankruptcy Act), he will be entitled to $9,000, leaving Y and Z to share in the remaining $1,000. On the other hand, if X were an unsecured creditor, he would share pro rata with Y and Z, in this case receiving less ($3,103) than the latter two parties ($3,448 each).

---

[8] Copyright 1983 by The American Law Institute. Reprinted with the permission of The American Law Institute-American Bar Association Committee on Continuing Professional Education.

## C. Basic Concepts and Terminology of Article 9

The parties to a secured transaction are the "debtor" and the "secured party." The "debtor" is the person who owes performance of the obligation secured—usually payment of a debt. The "secured party" (also commonly referred to in the literature as the secured creditor) is the party in whose favor the security interest exists. A "security interest" is an interest in personal property or fixtures that secures payment or performance of an obligation. The "collateral" is the property covered by the security interest. The debtor usually grants the security interest to the secured party in a written contract called a "security agreement."

A security interest is not enforceable by the secured party against anyone—either the debtor or third parties—unless and until it "attaches," which generally requires that the debtor ha[s] executed a written security agreement, that the secured party ha[s] given value, and that the debtor ha[s] acquired rights in the collateral. Upon execution of the security agreement and satisfaction of the other requirements for attachment, the security interest becomes enforceable against the debtor, meaning that should the debtor "default"—as by failure to pay the debt owed the secured party at the appropriate time and in the appropriate manner—the secured party can ... repossess the collateral and either retain it or sell it to satisfy the debt.

In many instances the secured party will be in conflict with a third party asserting a claim to the collateral, rather than with the debtor. The third party may be an unsecured creditor of the debtor with a judicial lien on the collateral, a buyer who has purchased the collateral from the debtor, another Article 9 creditor with a security interest in the collateral, or a bankruptcy trustee representing the debtor's unsecured creditors. When the debtor has sold the original collateral covered by the security interest, the conflict with the third party may concern the cash or other items received by the debtor upon the sale—called proceeds—rather than the original collateral. In conflicts of the foregoing types, the Article 9 "rules of priority" dictate whether the secured party or the third party prevails. These rules, which vary depending on the type of third party, the type of secured transaction, and the type of collateral involved, generally provide (with important exceptions) that the secured party has priority only if he "perfects" his security interest before the third party's interest arises or (in the case of a competing secured creditor) is perfected .... [P]erfection usually entails either taking possession of the collateral or filing a public notice of the security interest—called a financing statement—in the appropriate state office (the latter method being the most common).

Various Article 9 rules, including the priority rules, hinge on the type of secured transaction involved. For instance, a "possessory" security interest (often called a "pledge") involves the secured party's taking possession of the collateral, whereas under a "nonpossessory" arrangement possession is in the debtor. Another important distinction is that drawn between a "purchase money" security interest and a "non-purchase-money" one. In the "purchase-money" situation the credit advanced by the secured party enables the debtor to purchase the item covered by the security interest. The purchase money creditor may be either the seller himself, who sells the item (for example, an automobile) on credit to the debtor, or some other party, like a bank, that advances funds to the debtor to be paid to the seller. The security interest is a "non-purchase-money" one if the loan is not made to enable the debtor to purchase the collateral, for example, a finance company's advancing funds against an automobile already owned by the debtor.

## § 1-4. Applicability of Article 9

The first question one must always ask is whether the problem at hand is governed by Article 9. The answer will usually be found in the rules set forth in Sections 9-102, 1-201(37), and 9-104, as discussed infra.

### A. Basic Aspects of Coverage

The basic scope provision of Article 9 is found in Section 9-102, several aspects of which deserve close attention. Section 9-102(1)(a) provides that, except for certain types of transactions explicitly excluded from its scope, Article 9 applies "to any transaction (regardless of its form) which is intended to create a security interest in personal property or fixtures." This language makes it clear that the determinative factor is the intent of the parties to create a security interest, rather than the particular form in which they cast their transaction. Taken together with the broad definition of "security interest" in Section 1-201(37), it also indicates that Article 9 is sufficiently flexible to encompass not only traditional forms of secured transactions (including the various pre-Code devices) but also new arrangements that may be invented by innovative lawyers and business[-people] in the future.

Sections 9-102(1) and 1-201(37) also indicate that Article 9 applies only to security interests in personal property, as opposed to realty, with one exception: security interest in fixtures, which lie somewhere between the two categories, are covered.

As indicated by the statement in Section 9-102(2) that "[t]his Article applies to security interests created by contract," Article 9 governs encumbrances voluntarily created by the debtor but generally not those imposed by law, such as statutory liens.

Section 9-102(3) indicates that even though certain types of secured transactions are themselves excluded from Article 9, subsequent security transfers relating to them may be covered. Assume, for instance, that A, the owner of Blackacre, gives a note and real estate mortgage to B as security for a loan from B. This transaction, involving a security interest in real estate, is outside the scope of Article 9. If B then pledges A's note to C as security for a loan from C to B, however, this pledge, involving the creation of a security interest in an instrument, is governed by Article 9.

The major advantage in having an Article 9 security interest has previously been discussed, namely that the secured party who has previously perfected his interest will usually prevail against an adverse party, such as a competing creditor or judicial lienor, who lays claim to the collateral ....

\* \* \*

## § 2-1. INTRODUCTION: SIGNIFICANCE OF ATTACHMENT

In order for a secured party to enjoy the maximum protection afforded by Article 9, he must satisfy two overlapping sets of requirements: (1) the requirements for "attachment" (essentially the Code term for creation) of the security interest and (2) the requirements for "perfection." The subject of attachment is taken up in this chapter; perfection is discussed in the next.

A determination of whether, and when, the requirements for attachment have been satisfied is important in two distinct respects: First, attachment is a condition precedent to enforcement of the secured party's Article 9 rights against the debtor upon default. Second, attachment is a prerequisite to perfection of the security interest, and in most cases the secured party must perfect in order to prevail over third-party claims to the collateral under the Article 9 priority rules.

The ... attachment ... requirements are (1) that the debtor [has] executed a written security agreement (unless the secured party has taken possession of the collateral), (2) that the secured party [has] given "value," and (3) that the debtor [has] acquired "rights" in the collateral .... [T]he three events may take place in any order and ... the time of attachment will be the time when the last of the three, whichever that may be, occurs.

## § 2-2. THE SECURITY AGREEMENT

One of the prerequisites for attachment is that the debtor have executed a security agreement[, which] ... must: (1) be in writing (unless the secured party has possession of the collateral) and contain language indicative of an intent to create a security interest, (2) be signed by the debtor, and (3) adequately describe the collateral .... The secured party's failure to meet these requirements can have dire consequences, the most common one being lack of perfection (because of the absence of attachment) resulting in subordination of the security interest to the claim of a third party.

\* \* \*

## § 3-1. INTRODUCTION; TIMING OF PERFECTION

Section 9-303(1) states that a security interest is perfected "when it has attached and when all of the applicable steps required for perfection have been taken." In most cases, whether, and when, the security interest has been perfected determines whether the secured party has first claim on the collateral covered by the security interest as against the competing claim of a third party such as a lienor, a buyer from the debtor, another secured party or the debtor's bankruptcy trustee. Although perfection does not always guarantee priority over such parties, it is usually a prerequisite thereto.

Article 9 provides for three basic methods of perfection: (1) the filing of a financing statement—the most frequent method; (2) the secured party's taking possession of the collateral—often referred to as the "pledge"; and (3) in a limited number of situations, attachment alone without the necessity of either filing or taking possession ....

## ¶613: The avoiding power

The Bankruptcy Code respects state-created security interests. In § 506, the Code divides a secured loan into a secured portion to the extent of the security, and an unsecured portion for the remainder. In § 1129(b)(2), the Code says that the requirement that a plan be fair and equitable (and hence confirmable even if the affected creditor dissents and is impaired) includes the following.

### § 1129. Confirmation of plan

\* \* \*

(b) (2) For the purpose of this subsection, the condition that a plan be fair and equitable with respect to a class includes the following requirements:

(A) With respect to a class of secured claims, the plan provides—

(i) (I) that the holders of such claims retain the liens securing such claims, whether the property subject to such liens is retained by the debtor or transferred to another entity, to the extent of the allowed amount of such claims; and

(II) that such holder of a claim of such class receive on account of such claim deferred cash payments totaling at least the allowed amount of such claim, of a value, as of the effective date of the plan, of at least the value of such holder's interest in the estate's interest in such property;

(ii) for the sale ... of any property that is subject to the liens securing such claims, free and clear of such liens, with such liens to attach to the proceeds of such sale ... ; or

(iii) for the realization by such holders of the indubitable equivalent of such claims.

Some statutory liens (such as mechanics' liens for work done on construction projects or tax liens) are respected under § 545 if they would be valid under state law against a bona fide purchaser of the underlying property.

Three sections of the Bankruptcy Code can directly upset an otherwise valid security interest. A security interest given to a prior creditor on the eve of bankruptcy may be a "preference," one that the bankruptcy trustee can recover. See § 547 and chapter 7. It could also be a fraudulent conveyance, see § 548 and chapter 7. It could also be avoided under what's known as the strong-arm power.

### § 544. Trustee as lien creditor ...

(a) The trustee shall have, as of the commencement of the case ... the rights and powers of, or may avoid any transfer of property of the debtor or any obligation incurred by the debtor that is voidable by—

(1) a creditor that extends credit to the debtor at the time of the commencement of the case, and that obtains, at such time and with respect to such credit, a judicial lien on all property on which a creditor on a simple contract could have obtained such a judicial lien, *whether or not such a creditor exists;*

(2) a creditor that extends credit to the debtor at the time of the commencement of the case, and obtains, at such time and with respect to such credit, an execution against the debtor that is returned unsatisfied at such time, *whether or not such a creditor exists; ....*

The effect of the strong-arm power is as follows. A creditor lends money to the firm and takes a security interest in the firm's inventory, but neglects to perfect the security interest, by, say, neglecting to file the financing statement. During the bankruptcy, the trustee can set aside the security interest (even if no real creditor could do so), because the trustee takes on the power of a hypothetically ideal creditor, whether or not such an ideal creditor exists.

---

### ¶614: Secured interests and finance theory

The explanation why public firms use security is not abundantly clear. The intuitive notion explaining security is that the secured party takes less risk by obtaining security. Taking less risk, it requires a lower interest rate. Or stated more practically, whether or not the creditor takes a security interest depends on its negotiating power.

But analysis shows weaknesses in this explanation. The risk sought to be avoided by the secured party is not eliminated. It is shifted to other shoulders. If the secured party takes less risk, someone else takes more. If for example the potentially secured party will give 2% off of its interest rate if it takes the security, and the risk it avoids is placed on the shoulders of, say, creditor A, why doesn't creditor A insist on a 2% interest premium? If the gains are offset by the costs, why does the public corporation bother?

Perhaps there's room for a mutually worthwhile deal. The secured party takes less risk and gives up 2%, while creditor A takes more risk but only asks for a 1% premium, perhaps because it can institutionally handle that risk better. But even if such a deal were obtainable, why should the parties use security interests and mortgages to reflect the shifting of risk? A contractual seniority/subordination agreement is cheaper to negotiate; after all, it's just a few clauses in the loan agreements. Neither cumbersome security interests nor mortgages nor the resultant policing of the security are necessary.

In fact, many (but not all) public firms never use security, perhaps because of these considerations. They do use negative pledge clauses or debt limitation covenants, so that once a credit commitment is made, the creditor knows it will not be made inferior to new creditors (or at least knows the range of inferiority it will face). Morey McDaniel, *Are Negative Pledge Clauses in Public Debt Issues Obsolete?*, 38 Bus. Law. 867 (1983). Some public firms may prefer to use unsecured loans because the unsecured lender investigates the firm before lending, thereby sending a signal to distant public stockholders that managers are doing a good enough job, a signal that is stronger coming from the unsecured lenders than it would be if it came from a low-risk secured lender. See Barry E. Adler, *An Equity-Agency Solution to the Bankruptcy-Priority Puzzle*, 22 J. Legal Stud. 73 (1993).

Why then is security used ever? The efficiency explanations rely on other monitoring, screening, and priority explanations. First, the secured creditor can monitor the security offered and thereby sometimes stop the debtor from substituting riskier projects than it anticipated at the time it lent to the debtor. Second, the creditor may cut down on its own information gathering: it understands one part of the debtor's business and lends on the assets in the business it understands; or, similarly, the creditor can assess with confidence the value of the physical asset, but has less confidence in its estimate of the cash flows that the debtor can generate from that asset. Third, the first creditor is worried about the debtor borrowing and dissipating the proceeds of future loans, leaving the first creditor with a diluted claim that it must share with other creditors; grabbing priority and a key asset reduces the debtor's and the new lender's incentives to borrow and take on risky projects in which the proceeds of the loan could be dissipated.

Another explanation is that, like the explanation given by some analysts for all property, security is theft. The secured party takes less risk. That risk is shifted to the shoulders of others in an equal and offsetting transfer. But those others are unable (because they are uninformed or do not bargain with the firm) to insist on compensation (via a higher interest rate) for the increase in risk. Who are these hapless victims? Tort claimants, consumer claimants, labor claimants, (some, usually smaller) trade creditors, and financial claimants with a gap in their loan agreement.

This explanation tells a story consistent with the observation that public firms tend not to use security. Why? Substantial tort and labor claimants in bankruptcy have until recently been unusual. Trade creditors are more substantial, but still not overwhelming in the public firm bankruptcy. These claimants (particularly trade creditors) are more substantial in the small firm bankruptcy.

If analysis indicates that security is theft, why not prohibit it? The answer is that the theft analysis is incomplete. Efficiency explanations for security, usually outside of the public firm context, have been given: the security device helps creditors monitor debtor misbehavior (i.e., reduce the chances that the debtor steals from the creditor in question), the security helps make sure that the debtor stays in the same business (or gets the creditor's consent before selling the machinery that is subject to the security), or the security helps screen bad credit risks from good credit risks at the time the loan is negotiated.

These results (or the indeterminacy of whether efficiency or theft considerations predominate) lead economically-informed policy-thinkers to suggest a super-priority for the uninformed (tort claimants, consumer claimants, and maybe some trade creditors). But then one would leave room for security to sort the results out for those creditors that really bargain (i.e., financial institutions and some large trade creditors).

The basic weakness in the intuitive explanation for security was first analyzed in Alan Schwartz, *Security Interests and Bankruptcy Priorities: A Review of Current Theories*, 10 J. Legal Stud. 1 (1981). Additions to this analysis can be found in Thomas Jackson & Anthony Kronman, *Secured Financing and Priorities Among Creditors,* 88 Yale L.J. 1143 (1979); Saul Levmore, *Monitors and Freeriders in Commercial and Corporate Settings,* 92 Yale L.J. 49 (1982); Alan Schwartz, *The Continuing Puzzle of Secured Debt,* 37 Vand. L. Rev. 1051 (1984); Homer Kripke, *Law and Economics: Measuring the Economic Efficiency of Commercial Law in a Vacuum of Fact*, 133 U. Pa. L. Rev. 929 (1985); Robert Scott, *A Relational Theory of Secured Financing*, 86 Colum. L. Rev. 901 (1986); Frank Buckley, *The Bankruptcy Priority Puzzle,* 72 Va. L. Rev. 1392 (1986); Lucian Bebchuk & Jesse M. Fried, *The Uneasy Case for the Priority of Secured Claims in Bankruptcy,* 105 Yale. L.J. 857 (1996).

---

## ¶615: A note on marshalling

The marshalling doctrine is classically invoked by junior lienors against a senior lienor having two or more funds from a common debtor from which the senior lienor could be satisfied. When successfully invoked, the senior lienor must satisfy itself first from the fund against which it alone can claim, thereby freeing up more assets for the junior lienor to levy against. Unsecured creditors usually lose when it is invoked, since more collateral is taken by secured creditors than might be if the assets are not marshalled.

The doctrine can trap the unwary senior lienor. What if the debtor asks the senior lienor to release one pool of collateral to help the debtor operate better? The debtor notes that since the senior lienor has another pool of collateral against which it can claim, the senior lienor will be no worse off, and the improved operations would allow the debtor to pay the senior a small premium. Held: if the senior lienholder has notice of the junior's lien in the remaining collateral, then the release of the fund to which the senior alone has access acts to *reduce* the amount of the second fund to which the senior can claim. Continental Supply Co. v. Marshall, 152 F.2d 300, cert. denied, 327 U.S. 803 (1946).

The doctrine has been invoked—not always successfully—by unsecured creditors trying to force a senior creditor to levy against the assets of a guarantor (that has guaranteed the senior's loan but not the unsecured creditors' loan) before the senior levies on the assets of the common debtor. Since the classical form of the doctrine requires that there be a common debtor, the doctrine is not precisely applicable; veil-piercing alter ego doctrines might link the guarantor with the corporate debtor.

The doctrinal tangle can be complicated. The guarantor usually is subrogated to the guaranteed's claim. (Subrogation allows the guarantor to step into the guaranteed creditors' shoes. The guarantor, once subrogated, can assert the guaranteed secured creditor's security interest.) Thus the guarantor would become a secured creditor claiming against the very pool of collateral that the unsecured creditors would like to obtain for themselves. When inequitable or fraudulent action was taken by the guarantor, the subrogation rights of the guarantor have been subordinated to the unsecured claims.

See generally Benjamin Weintraub & Alan Resnick, *Subordination of the Guarantor's Subrogation Rights—The Marshalling Doctrine Revisited*, 18 U.C.C. L. J. 364 (1986); Comment, *The Proper Application of Marshaling on Behalf of Unsecured Creditors*, 1983 Brigham Young U.L. Rev. 639.

## F. Morality, markets, and practicing law with bond indentures

### ¶616: Harry M. Markowitz,[9] Markets and Morality: Or Arbitragers Get No Respect, Wall St. J., May 14, 1991

Usually the only thing I lecture on lately is portfolio theory [for which Markowitz won a Nobel Prize—Roe], but this time ... I have decided, instead, to discuss questions of right and wrong, especially as applied to participants in financial markets ....

There are many obvious ways in which a society's rules of right and wrong influence its quality of life. Where littering is not frowned upon, all live in a world of litter. Where "excuse me" and "thank you" are passe, all live in a rude world.

The consequences of rules of right and wrong are sometimes subtler. [Russia may be hobbled in converting to a capitalist economy, due to the] Russian people's attitude toward profit .... [In their minds,] the [recent] source of the Soviet ill was the greedy, evil people who seek to benefit from the misfortunes of others by moving goods from where they are to where they are needed, not out of altruism but out of avarice.

My own views are much closer to the gospel according to Adam Smith. The invisible hand is clumsy, heartless and unfair, but it is ever so much more deft and im-

---

[9] Mr. Markowitz ... shared the 1990 Nobel Prize in economics ....

partial than a central planning committee. Consequently, I am troubled by the indiscriminate way many Americans use "greed" as an explanation of economic events.

The blanket condemnation of the "greedies" of the 1980s fails to distinguish between the complaint that too many people sought to maximize their own well being, as Adam Smith would have us all do, legally, and the complaint that too much leverage was used in the 1980s. If the latter is the true complaint, the blanket condemnation of "the greedies" fails to ask whether the reason for excess leverage was the fact that slick salesmen disguised the true risks of the junk bonds they sold. Or was it that unwise laws structured institutions so that they were induced, and sometimes compelled, to take high risks?

* * *

[S]ince I have emphasized the efficacy of markets as compared to bureaucrats, you may think I think that markets can run themselves. This is not the case. Laws and law enforcement are needed to assure me that the meal I buy is not poisoned and the airplane I fly on is well maintained; ... that if I deposit money with a bank or pay a premium to an insurance company the banker or insurer will not go to Las Vegas to gamble with my money.

[This] said, let's return to the alleged greedies of the 1980s. I would like to organize my remarks around two product areas of major importance in the 1980s. One is mortgage bond products as pioneered at Salomon Brothers; the other is junk bonds—that is, high-yield, high-risk bonds, whose market was dominated by Mr. Milken at Drexel.

"Liar's Poker" is the story of Salomon Brothers as told by Michael Lewis, who entered the firm early in 1985 as a young trainee and left it three years later when he decided making that much money wasn't that important. When he speaks generally, he speaks of the greed that permeated and dominated Salomon Brothers. When he describes specific individuals and actions we find that some are mean and some kind, some are stingy and others generous, some you can trust and some you cannot. The individuals seem no more nor less than human.

Mr. Lewis considers his to be a tale of greed. I view the same events and find in them the triumph of two great ideas: Adam Smith's invisible hand at its clumsy but beneficent best; and option-pricing theory as applied and enhanced by the "rocket scientists" whom Salomon Brothers had gathered.

... By February 1979, Lewis Ranieri, who had started in the mail room, was officially placed in charge of mortgage operations. ...

In the following years the market grew. It also changed character. Mr. Lewis quotes Samuel Sachs, longtime mortgage bond salesman, as saying: "They wheeled in the rocket scientists, who started to carve up mortgages into itty-bitty pieces. The market became more than the five things that Ranieri could hold in his brain at any one time."

Mr. Lewis contrasts the refinement of analysis that lay behind some mortgage products with the crudeness of some of the traders who bought and sold these products. My own view is that the fact that the invisible hand could work its magic through mere humans is an essential part of Adam Smith's insight. Not many thousands of years ago, men like this would have clubbed each other over hunting rights. A few hundreds of years ago they would have hacked each other with axes and swords. Now they yelled at trainees while they brought together the supply and demand of home mortgages on a world wide scale.

At first, Salomon Brothers had a great advantage over other investment banks in the mortgage product area. This advantage was temporary ... [because competition would eventually erode it no matter what Salomon did, because Salomon had] no monopoly over bright young people .... In short, I take the story of mortgage products at Salomon as an example of Adam Smith's thesis that individuals seeking their own self-interest through the marketplace will promote the common good, even if some of them are crude.

Now let us turn to the junk bond market under Michael Milken at Drexel .... In the 1980s Michael Milken engaged in illegal and near-illegal behavior as a regular part of doing business. Part of this behavior had as its purpose the suppression of competition in the junk bond business.

For example, in 1985 the board of Wickes decided to do a debt underwriting through Salomon Brothers, which had been trying to break into the junk-bond business. After Mr. Milken learned of the forthcoming underwriting, Saul Steinberg, a close Milken associate, accumulated 10.4% of Wickes's stock, and duly reported this to the SEC. Then Mr. Milken had a Saturday breakfast meeting with Sandy Sigoloff, president of Wickes. According to a Wickes director, "Mike told Sandy what Saul held, what Drexel held, and how, when you combined that with whatever other pockets Mike might have placed stock in, it meant they would have control of the company." In the next few days Drexel became co-manager and then sole manager of the Wickes underwriting.

... [I]f Mr. Steinberg, Drexel and perhaps "other pockets" did plan to act in concert, they were in violation of securities laws by not filing with the SEC as a group. Ms. Bruck also provides other examples of "the brass knuckles, threatening, market manipulating Cosa Nostra of the securities world."

\* \* \*

Returning to Michael Milken and the junk market, as we noted already Mr. Milken engaged in illegal activities, in part to maintain a near monopoly in junk bonds. One use of this monopoly was to obtain high fees for junk-bond underwriting ....

But the chief complaint about junk bonds was not that Drexel charged too much for them but that they were used for destructive purposes, that they weakened the American economy ....

Only a small minority of companies command investment-grade ratings from the bond-rating services. The junk-bond market provides a major source of capital for the rest. Clearly this market serves a useful purpose in bringing together supply and demand for such higher-risk and therefore higher-yield securities.

The chief complaint about junk bonds is that they were used to finance highly leveraged deals[, in many] management buy outs or hostile takeovers ....

\* \* \*

In general in such situations, either the market has set an irrationally low value on the company or, as corporate raiders often contend, the market reflects the poor way entrenched management uses resources. This point is well taken. Such raids, and the threats of such raids, tend to put a boundary on how inefficient management can become in corporations where no individual or small group considers itself the company's owner ....

\* \* \*

[But o]ld bondholders lost as the firm became more risky, since the quality and therefore the price of their old bonds fell. Perhaps better bond covenants could [have] protect[ed] bondholders against such increases in firm risk at their expense. The people who were laid off [also] lost. But it is hard to see how to protect them without passing laws that generally restrict firms' abilities to lay off workers. In the long run it would lead to a rigid and less productive economy—therefore a much smaller pie for all to share.

What about the investors in the junk bonds? Were they winners or losers? Here we must distinguish between those who chose to invest in junk bonds and those who had their funds put at risk in these bonds without their knowledge or consent. If people invest in a high-yield investment fund, they have little or no cause to complain if they lose. But Mr. Milken's vast sources of funds were not such investment trusts; they were pension plans, S&Ls and certain kinds of insurers.

The S&L structure encouraged gambling by S&L managements with S&L funds. The risks they took were in real estate and junk bonds. The game was structured so that if bets were won on average, then the S&L and its management gained; if they lost, then the U.S. taxpayer lost.

\* \* \*

This situation raises regulatory and moral questions. On the regulatory side, we should try to eliminate situations where one party makes the decisions and reaps the gains while someone else pays the costs or suffers the losses. The individual needs protection against such financial risk, as he needs protection against bad food and unsafe planes.

The moral question is this: Suppose you can legally gain the reward and stick other people with the risk. It is easy enough for me to tell you not to do it. But will it change you action? Perhaps you should weigh this in your decision: Someday people you put at risk without comparable reward may seek retribution. Even if what you did to them was legal, some regulator or prosecutor may look at everything else you did to see if anything can be used to embarrass or punish you. Is it worth it?

**Summary**

Crimes were committed in the financial industries during the 1980s. But I know of no study that shows that, per person with comparable opportunity, the financial industries of the 1980s had more lawbreakers than other industries or other times. It is also true that members of the financial communities have been the victims of overzealous prosecutors. It is this that makes me feel that the blanket condemnation of the greedies of the 1980s is not just silly, but destructive.

The chief complaint about Wall Street in the 1980s was not about lawbreaking, but about highly leveraged hostile takeovers. I now hold the hypothesis that excesses in this area were primarily due to the availability of large pools of money whose ultimate owners or guarantors could be stuck with risk with little or none of the reward, without their knowledge or consent. Without these pools the junk bond would mostly be a vehicle for bringing together those who need funds, but do not have an investment-grade rating, with those who seek higher return, understanding that it comes with higher risk.

## ¶617: Data on the growth of the junk bond market

Markowitz wrote the prior article in 1991, when the junk bond market had been softening. Later in the 1990's it picked up steam. Possibly the institutional savings and loan arrangements he described perniciously accelerated junk bond sales in the 1980s. But the fact that the junk bond market continued to grow after the savings & loan institutional difficulties were resolved suggests there were underlying economic reasons for the persistent growth of the junk bond market.

Drexel, as he noted, had a near monopoly in the junk market at the time of its demise at the end of the 1980s. Arguably the softness in the junk bond market from 1989 to 1992 reflects the soft economy *and* the time needed for other investment banks to learn Drexel's expertise (sometimes by hiring and integrating Drexel's senior managers into their operations).

**Default Rates and Losses (1978–1997)**

| Year | Outstanding ($MMs) | Par value of defaulted debt ($MMs) | Default Rate % |
|---|---|---|---|
| 1997 | $335,400 | $4,200 | 1.25% |
| 1996 | $271,000 | $3,336 | 1.23% |
| 1995 | $240,000 | $4,551 | 1.90% |
| 1994 | $235,000 | $3,418 | 1.45% |
| 1993 | $206,907 | $2,287 | 1.11% |
| 1992 | $163,000 | $5,545 | 3.40% |
| 1991 | $183,600 | $18,862 | 10.27% |
| 1990 | $181,000 | $18,354 | 10.14% |
| 1989 | $189,258 | $8,110 | 4.29% |
| 1988 | $148,187 | $3,944 | 2.66% |
| 1987 | $129,557 | $7,486 | 5.78% |
| 1986 | $90,243 | $3,156 | 3.50% |
| 1985 | $58,088 | $992 | 1.71% |
| 1984 | $40,939 | $344 | 0.84% |
| 1983 | $27,492 | $301 | 1.09% |
| 1982 | $18,109 | $577 | 3.19% |
| 1981 | $17,115 | $27 | 0.16% |
| 1980 | $14,935 | $224 | 1.50% |
| 1979 | $10,356 | $20 | 0.19% |
| 1978 | $8,946 | $119 | 1.33% |
| **Arithmetic Average 1978–1997**: | | | 2.85% |
| **Weighted Average 1978–1997**: | | | 3.34% |

Source: Edward I. Altman, The Anatomy of the High Yield Bond Market: After Two Decades of Activity-Implications for Europe 5 (NYU Center for Law and Business Working Paper #CLB-98-021).

## G. Low priority

**¶618: Agency costs and monitoring: Mitchell Berlin,[10] Bank Loans and Marketable Securities: How Do Financial Contracts Control Borrowing Firms?, Fed. Res. Bank of Phil., Bus. Rev., July–Aug. 1987, at 9**

### INTRODUCTION

[In financial markets], the same basic [problems are] being solved over and over again by savers, borrowers, and the financial specialists who serve them. Market participants are seeking the most efficient way to transfer the savings of households to firms who need funds. This happens whenever a saver decides whether to deposit her funds in a bank or to call her broker to purchase securities for her portfolio. The same is true when a firm chooses whether to take out a bank loan or to sell securities to the public.

... [S]ome firms that used to rely primarily on commercial loans have begun to sell securities directly to the public. The growth of the markets for commercial paper, medium-term notes, and low-grade bonds has raised questions about the preeminent role of commercial banks as intermediaries between savers and businesses ....

... What functions do intermediaries perform that individual security holders can't perform themselves? Why do some firms seek bank loans while others sell bonds to the public? Why do many firms secure finance through a mixture of bank loans and marketed securities? How do these different types of financial contracts control the behavior of firms?

... [T]he answers to these questions begin with a simple observation: it is too costly for investors who are not intimately involved in the day-to-day running of the firm, firm outsiders, to stay informed about developments inside the firm. In sum, they are unable to influence the firm to prevent mismanagement. Banks arise to fill this gap; they play the part of delegated monitors to keep a check on the behavior of firm insiders, the managers who run the firm on a day-to-day basis.

### BANKS AND OTHER FINANCIAL INTERMEDIARIES

**Depository Intermediaries Reduce Transactions Costs.** Depository intermediaries like savings and loans, mutual funds, and banks link ultimate borrowers, especially firms, and ultimate savers, the households of the economy. While borrowers and savers might seek each other out and strike deals without going through intermediaries, traditional banking theory says that this will be a groping and inefficient process.

---

[10] Mitchell Berlin is an Economist in the Banking Section of the Research Department of the Federal Reserve Bank of Philadelphia.

... First, [a saver] would have to locate a firm that needs money and determine whether this firm is creditworthy. Then, she and the firm would have to bargain over how much money she will invest, for how long, and at what rate of return. She would probably prefer to buy securities with small denominations that pay off quickly so that her money isn't all tied up. The firm, on the other hand, would most likely rather sell just a few large securities, and it may need money for a project that will not pay off until sometime far in the future. Suppose the firm and the saver overcome all of these problems and actually strike a deal. Then she still has to keep a close watch on the firm until she is paid back.

... [I]ntermediaries ... [bring together] borrowers and savers. They buy large securities [from firms], while offering savers small accounts, a function called "size transformation." They hold securities that are hard to sell while offering savers immediate access to their savings—known as "liquidity transformation." By holding a large portfolio of the securities of many firms, they allow even small savers to diversify. Finally, they monitor the firms in their portfolio. Monitoring includes not only keeping track of each firm's financial condition, but also supervising firms and enforcing loan contracts.

**But Not All Intermediaries Act Like Banks.** Like banks, other intermediaries such as mutual funds and money market mutual funds overcome many transactions costs. They assemble diversified portfolios of securities and sell different size shares that are readily transformed into cash.

\* \* \*

## THE TROUBLES WITH SECURITIES MARKETS

**Insiders, Outsiders, and "Agency Problems."** "Agency problems" don't just arise in securities markets, they crop up any time people expect somebody else to do something for them. When someone hires a lawyer to represent him in court or pays a mechanic to fix his carburetor, the lawyer and the mechanic are both agents. They are supposed to act on someone else's behalf. Problems may arise, though, because the agents have their own interests to think about. The lawyer may do a shoddy job because he wants to concentrate on a more important case. And the mechanic's bill may include a charge for repairs to a fuel pump that was working perfectly when the car was brought in. In other words, agents may well pursue their own interests whenever they can get away with it, even at the expense of their delegated responsibilities.

\* \* \*

Insiders have more information than bondholders about the firm's current revenues and about the future of long-term investments. Therefore, they can better assess whether the bondholders will be repaid in full or not. Managers are also in a much better position than stockholders and bondholders to know if the firm is being run efficiently, that is, if costs are being kept down to a minimum and if people in the organization are exerting all their effort. In addition, many complex and uncontrollable factors affect firm performance besides management decisions. When a firm performs badly, outsiders often can't tell what is at fault: bad management or bad luck.

\* \* \*

In fact, even though each investor may be acting rationally when he chooses not to monitor, too little monitoring [is] often [the] result. This is possible because monitoring is an example of what economists call a public good. When an investor supervises the firm, all other investors benefit whether they monitor or not. But each investor will ignore the benefits he provides for others when he decides whether monitoring is worth the time and trouble. Thus, every investor may decide that his personal gains from monitoring are too small, even when the total gains to all investors are quite large. Everyone would be better off if someone chose to monitor, yet no one may be willing to do so. In this sense, too little monitoring occurs in securities markets.

**Contracts Inside and Outside the Firm Are Alternatives to Monitoring.** [Incentive compensation for managers and monitoring by boards of directors both help to align managers with shareholders.]

Many common features of bond contracts ... reduce firm insiders' ability to misrepresent the firm's current and prospective performance. Unlike shares of stock, bonds require the firm to pay a fixed return to investors .... And if a firm misses a payment, bondholders can place the firm in default. In addition, bonds contain covenants that require the firm to satisfy a number of conditions or face default. Some covenants require the firm to meet minimum values for certain financial ratios—such as the ratio of working capital to total assets or the equity-debt ratio—to prove that its financial condition is healthy. If the firm cannot meet these ratios, it is often an early signal that the firm may not be able to make payments to bondholders.

The threat of default ensures that firm management will make every effort to repay bondholders whenever possible, which reduces bondholders' need to monitor the firm's revenues. And covenant restrictions give bondholders the legal right to intervene to protect their investment when the firm appears to be in trouble ....

\* \* \*

## BANKS ACT AS DELEGATED MONITORS

**Bank Loans Are a More Flexible Substitute for Securities.** ... By borrowing from a bank, the firm replaces many small lenders with a single lender. Since the bank makes large investments in firms, it will be more willing to monitor and renegotiate contracts than would a group of individual investors.

When a firm cannot make interest payments on time or when its balance sheet indicates trouble, a banker's first response is to take a closer look at the firm's condition. If he finds that the firm's longer term prospects are good, the banker may offer to reschedule interest payments or waive temporarily some covenant. To make sure that good money is not being thrown after bad, however, the banker must stand ready to respond quickly to further declines in the firm's health. It is the bank's willingness to monitor that allows it to be flexible without taking on excessive risks.

By monitoring the banker is also better able to determine whether the firm's managers are acting efficiently. While it is clearly impossible (and undesirable) for the banker to become involved routinely in detailed management decisions, the bank's watchful eye can reduce the occurrence of serious managerial abuses. In this sense, one can think of the bank as setting a minimum standard of managerial effort.

**But Bank Loans Don't Replace All Securities.** Although bank loans offer some real advantages over marketable securities, there are good reasons why we see a mix of both loans and securities in financial markets. The first is that a little monitoring may go a long way, because monitoring is a public good. While it is true that a bank must have a substantial stake in a firm or else it will act much like other small security holders—it doesn't follow that the bank needs to hold all of the firm's debt. As long as the bank is closely monitoring the firm, the firm's other investors also benefit, even if they remain passive.

Since bank supervision ensures that managers exert at least some minimum amount of effort, the firm's other investors know that the average level of effort is higher than it would be without monitoring. Indeed, bank supervision also benefits the firm, because investors will be willing to pay a higher price for the firm's securities if they know that managers are being watched. When a firm takes out a bank loan, in effect, it hires the bank to certify that the firm is behaving efficiently ....

\* \* \*

The second reason why bank loans do not replace securities is that a bank, after all, is a firm much like any other firm. When savers lend to firms indirectly through a bank, they have not found a magic wand that makes agency problems disappear. The bank itself is an agent of its depositors, delegated to monitor on their behalf ....

\* \* \*

## SUMMARY AND OUTLOOK

Recent economic theory has provided new insights into the particular role banks play in credit markets and the essential differences between bank loans and marketed securities. When a firm requires outside finance, lenders either must monitor the firm's affairs or provide incentives for firm insiders to run the firm efficiently. Marketed securities do provide such incentives, but security holders will seldom be willing to bear the costs of monitoring the firm. By depositing their funds in a bank, savers hire an agent to make loans and monitor the investments on their behalf.

\* \* \*

Many observers have claimed that technological improvements have lowered the costs to individual security holders of obtaining and processing information about firms. In particular, the largest firms are watched closely by many markets specialists, and individual investors may have found that the cost of purchasing and interpreting this information in a timely fashion is decreasing. In fact, the larger firms have reduced their reliance on bank loans .... Should information costs continue to fall, the theory predicts that more firms will rely primarily on marketed securities.

... [F]irms in unsettled markets and firms entering new markets should continue to rely primarily on bank loans, because bond contracts are too inflexible. Finally, since bank monitoring benefits all security holders, even firms that sell securities will continue to borrow through a mixture of bank loans and direct securities.

## ¶619: Bases for subordination

Why would the firm want to pay new creditors to take the risks of subordination?

One easy case is when previous creditors have insisted on the subordination of future creditors. They may insist upon future creditors' subordination via a covenant, like that in the Drum Financial indenture, in which the firm promises not to issue new debt at the same level, unless certain financial ratios are met. Or the previous creditors may simply insist that no new debt come in at the same level. One substantial reason why both the firm and the previous creditors would find it worthwhile to limit the firm's future ability to borrow is that the previous creditor may have feared that the firm would have future risky projects that might be substituted, subjecting the previous creditor to added risk. This possibility of asset substitution is outlined at the end of Chapter 4; the risk of asset substitution is mitigated (but not eliminated) by the firm promising the previous creditor priority.

But this does not help explain why the firm would find it valuable to pay for subordination when it doesn't *already* have senior, priority debt in its capital structure. True, it may wish to keep a reserve for a rainy day, a financial insurance policy. And institutional considerations may make marketing subordinated "junk" bonds relatively cheap at times: some institutions might not be allowed to buy equity; the low-grade bonds could be near-equity for the regulated (or may allow insured institutions to take on pernicious risk at deposit-holders or government-guarantors expense). Similarly, the tax advantages of debt (via the deductibility of interest payments) may make the junk bonds "really" equity disguised as debt.

If the firm doesn't have the super-high-risk asset substitution potential that drives the first scenario from Chapter 4 (in which the first creditor insists on priority), then this cost to the creditor (i.e., the risk of substitution) of foregoing priority is absent. Or, as long as the lender expects that the firm will have lots of good projects with a value to the stockholders that'll be higher to stockholders than the value to stockholders of substituting a high-risk project, then the lender won't fear substitution and dissipation of the second loan, so it won't need to pay for priority.

In this setting of lots of good projects, the cost to the first creditor and to the firm of foregoing priority is absent. But where's the gain to voluntary subordination? Or, seen from the firm's perspective, why would the stockholders pay the first creditor to agree to come last?

Another financial scenario is available to help us, one parallel to the "asset substitution" or "over-investment" explanation for priority of the first lender. This new scenario also looks at the debtor firm's operations and opportunities.

Imagine a firm that has a set of risky opportunities. Its first opportunity has a payoff of 0 or 400 (with equal likelihood). Its second opportunity will have a payoff, if the opportunity emerges, of 100 or 150, each with equal likelihood and with the downside (100) correlating with first project's downside (of 0). The second project will cost 100 to put onstream. The firm must put the first project on stream first though, then, when it gets the first going, it might be able to take on the second project.

The bottom line: if the firm finances the first project with regular debt, it will find that it cannot borrow to finance the second project when and if the second one becomes available. The *second* lender will refuse to lend unless *it* can get priority. Let's see why.

Time (1)

| 0 or 400 | 100 Junk bonds [with a 0 or 200 payoff] |
| [200] | 100 Common stock |

The junk bondholders lend 100, but are promised repayment of 200. Half the time the firm fails, leaving the junk bondholders nothing. Half the time the firm succeeds, paying the bondholders 200. (The extra 100 above the 100 lent can be thought of as the very high promised interest rate; setting this out as a high interest rate would, however, complicate the exposition, so we think of the bondholders as promised a total of 200 if the project succeeds.)

After the first project is rolling, the next project does become available. It will increase the failure result of the firm to 100, and raise the successful result to 550. Hence, its present value is operationally 125 (i.e., [.5x100]+[.5x150]). Because the project is worth 125 but will cost only 100 to finance, it's a good project.

Time (2)

| 325 | 100 new priority debt [100 or 100] |
| [100 or 550] | 100 [0 or 200] subordinated junk bonds |
| | 125 Common stock |

But if the firm had used non-subordinated, ordinary debt, could the firm borrow to finance the second project?

No. *If* the firm's previous debt were *general* unsecured *non*-subordinated debt, then the new lender would calculate its chances of pay-back this way: "If the two projects fail, the firm will be worth 100. I will *share* that 100 with the previous creditors, so I will get 50. If the projects succeed, I'll get paid my 100 back. The present value of my loan of 100 is only 75, from [.5x50]+[.5x100]. Therefore I won't lend, the firm cannot take on the second project, and the stockholder won't make that extra profit."

Time (3) **No priority for second lender**
(Firm did not pay first lender for subordination)

**First project alone:**

|  | Value | Expected value to creditor 1 | (No second creditor yet) | Expected value to stockholder |
|---|---|---|---|---|
| Fail | 0 | .5x0 |  | 0 |
| Success | 400 | .5x200 |  | .5x200, or 100 |
| Total | 200 | 100 |  | 100 |

**Second project:**
**Second lender's "spreadsheet" if it can't take priority:**

|  | Value | Expected value to creditor 1 | Expected value to creditor 2 | Expected value to stockholder |
|---|---|---|---|---|
| Fail | 100 | .5x50, or 25 | .5x50, or 25 | 0 |
| Success | 550 | .5x200, or 100 | .5x100, or 50 | .5x250, or 125 |
| Total |  | 125 | 75 | 125 |

The second lender, anticipating this result, won't lend. (The firm asks it to lend 100, but the lender would be getting an expected return of only 75.)

The second project is worth 125 but the lender gets only 75. Where would this 50 go to if the project failed after the second lender financed it without getting priority? It would go to the first lender when the projects fail, because if the first lender isn't subordinated, if it's a general creditor, it'd get 50 even if the firm fails, even though it originally lent expecting to get nothing if the project failed. But they'd still get their 200 when there's success.

The stockholder though would like the second project to go forward (because 125>100) if it can capture some, or all, of the profit. But the stockholder can't, or won't, finance the project herself. (The stockholder's reason for not financing the project herself precisely parallels the potential second lender's reason: too much value would shift to the first lender. If the equity holders invested 100, the value of the firm's operations will go up by 125, but the equity holders will only get 75 of the increase, because the first creditor would get .5x100 beyond what they first anticipated if the firm fails in both projects. *The first creditor would* get the 100 in the down-side, not the stockholder. If you don't see this yet, you'll get another chance when we look at the Chrysler reorganization and the problems of workouts in Chapter 12.)

True, the *stockholder* could make the project happen by promising the second lender a payoff of 150 if the projects succeed. They *can* make the second project happen by giving the new lender *all* of *their* expected extra profit of 50 if the project succeeds. But then there'd be nothing in it for the stockholders; they're indifferent. (If the project had a value of just a little less, they'd be opposed.) They want the second project to go ahead, but they want its profit.

But now we can work through how the firm *can* take the second project if it had set up the first loan correctly. By subordinating the first loan *in advance*, the stockholder keeps the flexibility to strike a deal with the second lender. The second lender lends its 100 *and takes priority.* If the project fails, it gets 100; if the project succeeds, it gets 100. As for the subordinated bondholders, they get 200 if the project succeeds, just as they were originally promised, and nothing if both projects fail (just as they originally expected). Stockholders get nothing if the projects fail, and 250 if the projects succeed; they thereby get 50 more when there's success (25 more in expected value) than they'd get from just the first project alone. The stockholders' paying the first creditor for future subordination allows the stockholders to finance the second project profitably.

Time (4)            **With subordination of first lender**

**First project alone:**

|  | Value | Expected value to creditor 1 | (No second creditor yet) | Expected value to stockholder |
|---|---|---|---|---|
| Fail | 0 | .5x0 |  | 0 |
| Success | 400 | .5x200 |  | .5x200, or 100 |
| Total | 200 | 100 |  | 100 |

**Second project:**

|  | Value | Expected value to creditor 1 | Expected value to creditor 2, with priority over creditor 1 | Expected value to stockholder |
|---|---|---|---|---|
| Fail | 100 | .5x0, or 0 | .5x100, or 50 | .5x0, or 0 |
| Success | 550 | .5x200, or 100 | .5x100, or 50 | .5x250, or 125 |
| Total | 325 | 100 | 100 | 125 |

Thus, by paying to subordinate the first creditor, the stockholder can get financing for the second project, but wouldn't be able to get financing otherwise.

## ¶620: Drafting a bond indenture

How should one begin the task of drafting a bond indenture? Consider the following advice from a prominent lawyer about drafting a similar deposit agreement (for bondholders participating in a workout). The excerpt comes from Paul Cravath, The Reorganization of Corporations, *in* Some Legal Phases of Corporate Financing, Reorganization and Regulation 153, 164–65 (1917):

> "I will not attempt to indicate in any detail what should be the provisions of a [bond indenture], whether it be for bonds or unsecured obligations ..., but I will tell how you may simplify your task in preparing such an agreement if you pursue the course most lawyers do. Do not attempt to evolve the agreement out of your own consciousness, for it would take you days to work out clauses covering half of the contingencies for which provision should be made. If you have not a model for such an agreement in your own office, go to some friend, a lawyer or banker or broker, and get from him a copy of the deposit agreement used in some previous transaction of such magnitude and dignity that the agreement must have been the workmanship of some experienced and competent counsel. You can, without much difficulty, find a model which, with some change, will fit almost any situation. It is then a comparatively simple task to eliminate the provisions which are inapplicable to your situation and to add the provisions required by its special circumstances.
>
> "I do not intend to give you the impression that the greatest care is not required in the preparation of such an agreement, for few instruments call for greater care or more painstaking attention to detail ....
>
> "There will be no opportunity to correct mistakes, because there will be as many parties to the agreement ...—and the agreement cannot be changed without the[ir] consent ...."

# Chapter 7

# RERANKING IN THE HOLDING COMPANY: SUBSTANTIVE CONSOLIDATION, FRAUDULENT CONVEYANCES, AND PREFERENCES

**A. Substantive consolidation of the holding company**
**B. Fraudulent conveyances and the holding company**
**C. Preferences and the holding company**
**D. Intercorporate payments in the holding company**

---

Businesses sometimes organize themselves as conglomerate holding companies. One company, the headquarters company, owns several separate corporations, each in their own business. This might facilitate organizational decentralization. It might be the legacy of a history of corporate acquisitions.

The bankruptcy problem arises when assets are transferred among the related companies and then one or more of them goes bankrupt. The assets might be transferred from a subsidiary up to a parent company. That transfer might be a fraudulent conveyance, an illegal dividend, or a breach of the subsidiary directors' corporate fiduciary obligations. The assets might be transferred down from the parent company to the subsidiary; in the subsequent bankruptcy, the creditors of the subsidiary would get first crack at these transferred assets, unless a bankruptcy doctrine, such as fraudulent conveyance doctrine, brings the assets back up to the parent company.

Creditors often use contract to restrict the transfer of assets among related businesses. A creditor of one subsidiary prefers that enough assets be available for that creditor if the subsidiary goes bankrupt. Some bankruptcy doctrines substantively consolidate all of a conglomerate's debts and liabilities into a single company. In this chapter we examine these doctrines.

---

## A. Substantive consolidation of the holding company

### ¶701: Holding companies

If debt is lodged in a subsidiary of a company, who gets first crack at the subsidiary's value in a reorganization? Who gets first crack at the parent company's value?

Normally the subsidiary's creditors would get the subsidiary's assets. If the subsidiary is solvent, assets will be left over for the subsidiary's stockholder, which is the parent company. The bankruptcy plan could distribute those assets as a liquidating dividend of the subsidiary. If the subsidiary were not liquidated, the subsidiary's common stock, which is an asset of the parent company, would be worth something, i.e., the net worth of the subsidiary. If the parent company were also in bankruptcy, that stock would provide value to the parent company's creditors. Only when the parent company's creditors were paid off in full would there be a bankruptcy distribution to the parent company's stockholders.

It's possible to imagine that although the subsidiary's value becomes insufficient to pay off the subsidiary's creditors in full, these creditors could not claim against the parent company, even if the parent company were solvent and able to pay off all of *its* creditors. True, the subsidiary's creditors, when they lent to the subsidiary, could have gotten a guarantee from the parent company. But if they didn't, they would lack a contractual claim against the parent in bankruptcy. Sometimes the subsidiary's creditors could invoke protective doctrines, like veil-piercing, illegal payment of dividends, or fraudulent conveyance law. When they can't, they collect against the subsidiary only and, due to corporate limited liability, the subsidiary's creditors can't claim against the subsidiary's corporate owner; thus, the creditors and stockholders of the parent get the assets in the parent company.

Veil-piercing, a corporate doctrine, allows a creditor to claim directly against the owners of a corporation. It's often employed if the owner misrepresented the corporate status of the business (and hence veil-piercing might often be viewed as a direct claim in tort and not a corporate doctrine) or if the corporate formalities have not been observed. Dividend statutes restrict the dividends that a corporation can pay; the statutes provide remedies that allow the wronged creditors to force the corporation to recover illegal dividends. Fraudulent conveyance law allows the trustee in bankruptcy to recover assets transferred when the corporation was insolvent (if transferred for insufficient consideration) and assets transferred with the intent to delay or defraud the bankrupt company's creditors.

Bigger problems arise when money and assets move back and forth between the parent and subsidiary. What if the parent and subsidiary operate together, and not in separate businesses? Could the subsidiary and parent company be collapsed in bankruptcy into a single entity? This result—substantive consolidation—would disrespect the separate corporate entities, cancel all inter-corporate contracts and claims (including state law fiduciary duty, veil-piercing, and fraudulent conveyance claims that one related corporation might have against another). Related companies often go bankrupt together and often are administered together; they are less frequently substantively consolidated. What are the justifications for substantively consolidating parent and subsidiary, bringing all of their assets and claims together as if they had been a single firm? The next two cases deal with those facts.

## ¶702: <u>Consolidated Rock Prods. Co. v. DuBois, 312 U.S. 510 (1941)</u>

SYLLABUS: ... Held: ...

3. Assuming that, because of the extension provision, the operating contract is still executory, the trustees of the subsidiaries are entitled ... to prove their claims at present worth.

4. Equity will not permit a holding company, which has dominated and controlled its subsidiaries, to escape or reduce its liability to them by reliance upon self-serving contracts which it has imposed on them.

5. A holding company in a dominating and controlling position has fiduciary duties to security holders of its system which will be strictly enforced.

6. A holding company owing money to its subsidiaries under an agreement between them can not defeat or postpone an accounting in the interest of their bondholders by resort to a declaration in the agreement that it was made for the benefit of the parties to it, not "for the benefit of any third person."

7. The bankruptcy court, having exclusive jurisdiction over the holding company and the subsidiaries, has plenary power to adjudicate all the issues pertaining to such intercompany claims.

8. In view of the unified operation of all the properties by the parent company, the commingling of assets, and the treatment of the subsidiaries as mere departments of its business, that company is in no position to assert that its assets are insulated from the claims of the subsidiaries' bondholders.

9. The value of the assets of the holding company must be determined, to furnish criteria for appropriate allocation of the new securities between bondholders and stockholders in case any equity remains after bondholders have been made whole.

10. To determine the fairness of the plan as between the bondholders of the subsidiaries there must be at least an approximate ascertainment of the value of their respective assets, notwithstanding the difficulties occasioned by the lack of earnings records and by the commingling of properties.

* * *

MR. JUSTICE DOUGLAS delivered the opinion of the Court.

This case involves questions as to the fairness ... of a plan of reorganization for a parent corporation (Consolidated Rock Products Co.) and its two wholly owned subsidiaries—Union Rock Co. and Consumers Rock and Gravel Co., Inc. The District Court confirmed the plan; the Circuit Court of Appeals reversed. We granted the petitions for certiorari ....

The stock of Union and Consumers is held by Consolidated. Union has outstanding in the hands of the public ... a total mortgage indebtedness of $2,280,555. Consumers has outstanding in the hands of the public ... a total mortgage indebtedness of $1,358,715. Consolidated has outstanding ... preferred stock and ... common stock.

The plan of reorganization calls for the formation of a new corporation to which will be transferred all of the assets of Consolidated, Union, and Consumers free of all claims. The securities of the new corporation are to be distributed as follows:

> Union and Consumers bonds held by the public will be exchanged for ... bonds and preferred stock of the new company .... Union bondholders for their claims of $2,280,555 will receive ... bonds and preferred stock in the face amount of $1,877,000; Consumers bondholders for their claims of $1,358,715 will receive income bonds and preferred stock in the face amount of $1,137,000. Each share of new preferred stock will have a warrant for the purchase of [some new common stock].
>
> *Preferred stockholders of Consolidated will receive one share of new common stock ($2 par value) for each share of old preferred or an aggregate of 285,947 shares of new common.*
>
> *A warrant to purchase one share of new common for $1 within three months of issuance will be given to the common stockholders of Consolidated for each five shares of old common.*
>
> * * *
>
> *The bonds of Union and Consumers held by Consolidated, the stock of those companies held by Consolidated, and the intercompany claims (discussed hereafter) will be canceled.*

... The average of the valuations (apparently based on physical factors) given by three witnesses at the hearing before the master were $2,202,733 for Union as against a mortgage indebtedness of $2,280,555; $1,151,033 for Consumers as against a mortgage indebtedness of $1,358,715. Relying on similar testimony, Consolidated argues that the value of its property, to be contributed to the new company, is over $1,359,000, or exclusive of an alleged good will of $500,000, $859,784 .... [But] the earnings record of the enterprise casts grave doubts on the soundness of the estimated values .... [E]xcept for the year 1929, Consolidated had no net operating profit, after bond interest and amortization, depreciation and depletion, in any year down to September 30, 1937. Yet on this record the District Court found that the present fair value of all the assets of the several companies, exclusive of good will and going concern value, was in excess of the total bonded indebtedness, plus accrued and unpaid interest. And it also found that such value, including goodwill and going concern value, was insufficient to pay the bonded indebtedness plus accrued and unpaid interest and the liquidation preferences and accrued dividends on Consolidated preferred stock. It further found that the present fair value of the assets admittedly subject to the trust indentures of Union and Consumers was insufficient to pay the face amount, plus accrued and unpaid interest of the respective bond issues. In spite of that finding, the District Court also found that "it would be physically impossible to determine and segregate with any degree of accuracy or fairness properties which originally belonged to the companies separately"; that as a result of unified operation properties of every character "have been commingled and are now in the main held by Consolidated without any way of ascertaining what part, if any thereof, belongs to each or any of the companies separately"; and that, as a consequence, an appraisal "would be of such an indefinite and unsatisfactory nature as to produce further confusion."

The unified operation which resulted in that commingling of assets was pursuant to an operating agreement which Consolidated caused its wholly owned subsidiaries to execute in 1929. Under that agreement the subsidiaries ceased all operating functions and the entire management, operation and financing of the business and properties of the subsidiaries were undertaken by Consolidated. The corporate existence of the subsidiaries, however, was maintained and certain separate accounts were kept. Under this agreement Consolidated undertook, inter alia, to pay the subsidiaries the amounts necessary for the interest and sinking fund provisions of the indentures and to credit their current accounts with items of depreciation, depletion, amortization and obsolescence. Upon termination of the agreement the properties were to be returned and a final settlement of accounts made, Consolidated meanwhile to retain all net revenues after its obligations thereunder to the subsidiaries had been met. It was specifically provided that the agreement was made for the benefit of the parties, not "for the benefit of any third person." *Consolidated's books as at June 30, 1938, showed a net indebtedness under that agreement to Union and Consumers of somewhat over $5,000,000. That claim was canceled by the plan of reorganization,* no securities being issued to the creditors of the subsidiaries therefor. The District Court made no findings as respects the amount or validity of that intercompany claim; it summarily disposed of it by concluding that any liability under the operating agreement was "*not made for the benefit of any third parties and the bondholders are included in that category.*"

We agree with the Circuit Court of Appeals that it was error to confirm this plan of reorganization.

I.

On this record no determination of the fairness of any plan of reorganization could be made. Absent the requisite valuation data, the court was in no position to exercise the "informed, independent judgment" which appraisal of the fairness of a plan of reorganization entails. Case v. Los Angeles Lumber Products Co., 308 U.S. 106. There are two aspects of that valuation problem.

### [Intercorporate debt as an asset of the subsidiary]

In the first place, there must be a determination of what assets are subject to the payment of the respective claims. This obvious requirement was not met. The status of the Union and Consumers bondholders emphasizes its necessity and importance. According to the District Court the mortgaged assets are insufficient to pay the mortgage debt. There is no finding, however, as to the extent of the deficiency or the amount of unmortgaged assets and their value. It is plain that the bondholders would have, as against Consolidated and its stockholders, prior recourse against any unmortgaged assets of Union and Consumers. The full and absolute priority rule of ... Case v. Los Angeles Lumber Products Co. would preclude participation by the equity interests in any of those assets until the bondholders had been made whole. *Here there are some unmortgaged assets, for there is a claim of Union and Consumers against Consolidated—a claim which according to the books of Consolidated is over $5,000,000 in amount.* If that claim is valid ..., then the entire assets of Consolidated would be drawn down into the estates of the subsidiaries. In that event Union and Consumers might or might not be solvent in the bankruptcy sense. But certainly it would render untenable the present contention of Consolidated and the preferred stockholders that they are contributing all of the assets of the Consolidated to the new company in exchange for which they are entitled to new securities. On that theory of the case they would be making a contribution of only such assets of Consolidated, if any, as remained after any deficiency of the bondholders had been wholly satisfied.

### [State law claims?]

... Consolidated makes some point of the difficulty and expense of determining the extent of its liability under the operating agreement and of the necessity to abide by the technical terms of that agreement in ascertaining that liability. But equity will not permit a holding company, which has dominated and controlled its subsidiaries, to escape or reduce its liability to those subsidiaries by reliance upon self-serving contracts which it has imposed on them. A holding company, as well as others in dominating or controlling positions (Pepper v. Litton, 308 U.S. 295), has fiduciary duties to security holders of its system which will be strictly enforced. See Taylor v. Standard Gas & Electric Co., 306 U.S. 307. In this connection Consolidated cannot defeat or postpone the accounting because of the clause in the operating agreement that it was not made for the benefit of any third person. The question here is not a technical one as to who may sue to enforce that liability. It is merely a question as to the amount by which Consolidated is indebted to the subsidiaries and the proof and allowance of that claim. *The subsidiaries need not be sent into state courts to have that liability deter-*

*mined*. The bankruptcy court having exclusive jurisdiction over the holding company and the subsidiaries has plenary power to adjudicate all the issues pertaining to the claim. The intimations of Consolidated that there must be foreclosure proceedings and protracted litigation in state courts involve a misconception of the duties and powers of the bankruptcy court. The fact that Consolidated might have a strategic or nuisance value ... does not detract from or impair the power and duty of the bankruptcy court to require a full accounting as a condition precedent to approval of any plan of reorganization. The fact that the claim might be settled, with the approval of the Court after full disclosure and notice to interested parties, does not justify the concealed compromise effected here through the simple expedient of extinguishing the claim.

### [Substantive consolidation and veil-piercing]

So far as the ability of the bondholders of Union and Consumers to reach the assets of Consolidated on claims of the kind covered by the operation agreement is concerned, *there is another and more direct route* which reaches the same end. There has been *a unified operation* of those several properties by Consolidated pursuant to the operating agreement. That operation not only resulted in extensive commingling of assets. All management functions of the several companies were assumed by Consolidated. The subsidiaries abdicated. Consolidated operated them as mere departments of its own business. *Not even the formalities of separate corporate organizations were observed*, except in minor particulars such as the maintenance of certain separate accounts. In view of these facts, Consolidated is in no position to claim that its assets are insulated from such claims of creditors of the subsidiaries. To the contrary, it is well settled that *where a holding company directly intervenes in the management of its subsidiaries so as to treat them as mere departments of its own enterprise, it is responsible for the obligations of those subsidiaries* incurred or arising during its management .... We are not dealing here with a situation where other creditors of a parent company are competing with creditors of its subsidiaries. If meticulous regard to corporate forms, which Consolidated has long ignored, is now observed, the stockholders of Consolidated may be the direct beneficiaries. Equity will not countenance such a result. A holding company which assumes to treat the properties of its subsidiaries as its own cannot take the benefits of direct management without the burdens.

We have already noted that no adequate finding was made as to the value of the assets of Consolidated. In view of what we have said, it is apparent that a determination of that value must be made so that criteria will be available to determine an appropriate allocation of new securities between bondholders and stockholders in case there is an equity remaining after the bondholders have been made whole.

* * *

Affirmed.

## ¶703: Questions on *Consolidated Rock*

1. As apparently argued by the stockholders and bondholders of Consolidated Rock, what were the balance sheets of Consolidated Rock (the parent company) and each of its subsidiaries? What was each subsidiary and each creditor and stockholder contributing to the reorganization?

   Complete these balance sheets, as the stockholders would have wanted the bankruptcy court to complete them:

   **Consolidated Rock (parent only)**

   | | |
   |---|---|
   | Assets+goodwill | 300,000 preferred shares |
   | C/S of Union | 400,000 common shares |
   | C/S of Consumers | |

   **Union**

   | | |
   |---|---|
   | Plant | $2.3M bondholders |
   | | C/S (owned by Con. Rock) |

   **Consumers**

   | | |
   |---|---|
   | Plant | $1.4M bondholders |
   | | C/S (owned by Con. Rock) |

   Complete these balance sheets as the *bondholders* would have wanted the bankruptcy court to complete them:

   **Union**

   | | |
   |---|---|
   | Plant | $2.3M bondholders |
   | Other asset? | C/S (owned by Con. Rock) |

   So, the bondholders would argue that the balance sheet of Consolidated Rock (parent only) should be completed to look like:

   **Con. Rock (parent only)**

   | | |
   |---|---|
   | $1.4M assets + goodwill | Debts due to? |
   | C/S Consumers | Preferred |
   | C/S Union | Common |

If the entire holding company structure were substantively consolidated, how would the balance sheet look?

**Con. Rock (consolidated)**

| | |
|---|---|
| $1.4M assets + goodwill | Debts due to? |
| Plants? | |
| C/S Consumers? | Preferred |
| C/S Union? | Common |

What distribution if absolute priority is respected, but the holding company is substantively consolidated?

2. In a reorganization consistent with absolute priority, who would get what, if both the holding company is respected and the inter-company debt is enforced? What if the holding company is respected and the inter-company debt canceled?

3. How did the properties become commingled? Did the original arrangement blending together the operations also blend together the subsidiaries' debt?

4. The inter-corporate contract says that it's not for the benefit of third parties, presumably meaning not for the benefit of the subsidiaries' creditors. Does that mean that the court must ignore the contract to the extent it gives the *subsidiaries themselves* a cause of action against the parent company?

5. What is the source of law by which Douglas instructs the lower courts to consider a direct action by the creditors against the parent company? State law? If so, which state and what provision (dividend statute, veil-piercing, fraudulent conveyance)? Or does the authority to consolidate come from the bankruptcy requirement that the plan of reorganization be fair and equitable? Or is it from the "nature" of bankruptcy administration, either as a court of equity or as a practical court trying to get a reorganization completed?

6. Are the considerations offered in *In re Commercial Envelope*, ¶708, at 248, identical to those offered in *Consolidated Rock*? Are they even consistent with those offered in *Consolidated Rock*?

7. If it will cost $500,000 to parse out the value of the separate subsidiaries, does it make sense to do so? Does the *Consolidated Rock* opinion, like that in *Atlas Pipeline,* evince an unstated faith in the valuation process?

8. XYZ owns a hotel/casino. The casino and hotel are separately incorporated. The hotel company has creditors; the casino company has creditors. The hotel and the casino are in the same building. The hotel company owns the building and its nongambling fixtures; the casino owns the gambling fixtures and holds the state's gambling license. At the bankruptcy of XYZ, the creditor of the casino would like the subsidiaries and parent company substantively consolidated.

An economist and a hotel/casino businessperson both testify that it is impossible to economically segment out the earnings of any hotel or casino from any hotel/casino complex. People pay their hotel bill so that they can be at the casino. Casino gambling depends upon the attractiveness of the hotel facilities. The economist says that the hotel/casino is a joint production business.

What distribution in bankruptcy? What do the cases say?

## ¶704: Fraudulent conveyances, veil-piercing, illegal dividends, improper use of control, and substantive consolidation

State law provides several ways a creditor of a subsidiary can recover funds shunted from a subsidiary to a parent.

Fraudulent conveyance. The transfer might be a fraudulent conveyance. Generally speaking, if the transfer was for an inadequate consideration (Uniform Fraudulent Conveyance Act § 4), *and* the firm was rendered insolvent (or was already insolvent), the wronged creditor may attack the recipient of the conveyance, including a recipient such as the parent firm. *Alternatively*, even if the transfer did not render the subsidiary insolvent, but was done with *intent to hinder, delay or defraud* the creditor, the wronged creditor may attack the transfer. U.F.C.A. § 7. Usually a single fraudulent conveyance from the subsidiary to the parent would not in itself justify substantive consolidation of parent and subsidiary.

Veil-piercing and corporate waste. As a matter of corporate law, sometimes creditors can attack the parent directly. If the parent, as controller of the subsidiary, operated the firm in a way that improperly hurt the subsidiary's creditors, the subsidiary's creditor can claim against the controlling person, the parent. Cf. *Deep Rock,* infra. Roughly similarly, the subsidiary could have a direct claim (that the subsidiary's creditors wish the subsidiary to assert) if the subsidiary were so badly run that breach of the duty of care, of the business judgment rule, could be found. Again, does such a breach ordinarily mean that the parent and subsidiary will be substantively consolidated into one firm for bankruptcy purposes? Or does it mean that the subsidiary (or its creditors) will have a claim against the parent to the extent of the mismanagement?

Dividend statutes. State corporate statutes regulate the size of the dividends that a corporation can pay. The dividend limitations are roughly similar to the limitations on fraudulent conveyances. Insolvents cannot properly pay dividends. In many states, dividends can only be paid out of certain capital accounts. The authorities are mixed as to whether a dividend, if properly paid under the dividend statute, can be attacked under more stringent fraudulent conveyance provisions.

## ¶705: Disclosure and consolidation: Regulation S-X

"Part 210 - Form and Content of Financial Statements, Securities Act of 1933, Securities Exchange Act of 1934, Public Utility Holding Company Act of 1935, Investment Company Act of 1940, and Energy Policy and Conservation Act of 1975."

\* \* \*

"§ 210.4-08 General notes to financial statements.

[In connection with the filing and distribution of financial statements in certain securities offerings, tender offers, and annual reports to shareholders, the following information shall be set forth:]

"(e) Restrictions which limit the availability of retained earnings or net income for dividend purposes ....

"(2) Describe the most significant restrictions on the payment of dividends *by ... subsidiaries to the issuer*, indicating briefly their sources, their pertinent provisions, and, where determinable, the amount of retained earnings or net income (i) so restricted or (ii) free of such restrictions."

[Reprinted from BNA, Securities Reg. & L. Report, No. 569, at 50–52 (special supplement).]

Who would restrict? Why?

## ¶706: Richard Posner, The Rights of Creditors of Affiliated Corporations, 43 U. Chi. L. Rev. 449, 507-09 (1976)

\* \* \*

### C. Creditor Protection: The Problems of Information and Supervision

Let us take a closer look at the types of protection that creditors would normally insist upon and that would therefore be found in an efficient corporation or bankruptcy statute. It is convenient to divide the sources of risk faced by the creditor into two types .... The first is the risk of default based on circumstances known or anticipated when the loan is made. The creditor's interest is not necessarily in minimizing this risk; since it is compensated for risk, any measures taken to reduce it will also reduce the interest rate. The creditor's interest lies rather in forming an accurate idea of the risk, for otherwise he cannot determine what interest rate to charge. Assessment of the risk of default requires accurate information about the existing and expected assets and liabilities of the borrowing corporation and of anyone else who may be liable for the corporation's debts, insofar as those assets and liabilities effect the creditor's ability to obtain repayment. Coping with this risk presents the problem of information. Measures that increase the creditor's costs of information are prima facie undesirable. A good example of such a measure would be misrepresentation by the borrower of his solvency.

The second source of risk to the creditor is the possibility that the corporation will take steps to increase the riskiness of the loan after the terms have been set. The problem of coping with this risk is the problem of supervision; the creditor must supervise or regulate the corporation's disposition of its assets to the extent necessary to prevent any deliberate attempts to reduce the assets available to repay the loan. Dividend limitations are an illustration of the supervision type of credit term.

Obtaining information and supervising a corporation's internal affairs are costly undertakings. Economizing on these costs is one objective, social as well as private, of the provisions in a credit instrument. The first question to ask about any existing or proposed creditor's right under corporation or other laws is whether it actually reduces the creditor's information or supervision costs. It is often a difficult question to answer, because of differences in the costs of information and supervision to financial, trade, and nonbusiness creditors, because of the debtor's ability to increase those costs by various acts and omissions, and because of differences in the nature of the collateral put up by different debtors (e.g., land versus inventory).

The analysis, moreover, cannot stop with a consideration of the creditor's costs. The goal is to minimize not just the administrative costs of the credit transaction but its total social costs. Even if a rule abrogating the limited liability of corporate shareholders would lower the costs of credit administration by reducing the risk of defaulting on a loan and thereby decreasing the optimal level of expenditures on supervision and information,[1] it would probably be an uneconomical rule because it would prevent a type of risk shifting (from shareholders to creditors) that is apparently highly efficient, judging by its prevalence. To the extent that—paradoxical as it may seem—risk can often be borne more cheaply by creditors than by shareholders, a rule that prevented the shifting of risk from the latter to the former would impose costs in undesired risk that might be much greater than the savings in reduced costs of credit administration. Similarly, a rule that forbade any payment of dividends to corporate shareholders would reduce supervision costs by increasing the assets available for the payment of creditors' claims, but it would also reduce the attractiveness of owning stock to those investors who do not consider appreciation a perfect substitute for periodic income.[2] It would probably not be an optimal rule considering all the relevant costs and benefits of corporate activity.

---

[1] It is not certain that it would reduce those costs overall, however, since creditors of individuals exposed to unlimited liability for the debts of corporations in which they had invested might, in consequence, have to make a more extensive investigation of such individuals' creditworthiness.

[2] The transaction costs involved in selling stock in order to convert appreciation into cash income may make periodic income preferable to appreciation for some investors. [Some owners prefer that a firm commit a large portion of its expected cash flow to debt repayment, because the commitment increases the chance that managers will produce that cash. If the ownership is all in stock, managers may relax more than if ownership is largely in debt.]

The ultimate objective of the credit process is to minimize the overall social costs of capital through a complex allocation of costs, including the disutility of risk, between borrower and lender. Measures that minimize the risk borne by the creditor will lower interest rates both directly and by reducing the creditor's optimum expenditure on obtaining information and supervising the debtor's business.[3] But beyond a certain point the cost to the investors of the added risk they are made to bear may well exceed the reduction in interest rates. It is of no benefit to a corporation to be able to borrow at six percent on condition that its shareholders personally guarantee repayment of the loan, if the expected earnings of the corporation are insufficient to compensate the shareholders for giving such a guarantee. An efficient corporation law is not one that maximizes creditor protection on the one hand or corporate freedom on the other, but one that mediates between these goals in a fashion that minimizes the costs of raising money for investment.

## ¶707: Questions on complex corporate structures and seniority

What if the parent company in *Consolidated Rock* had its own outstanding indebtedness? If so, then substantive consolidation might harm an "innocent" bystander, the parent's creditor, who expected to get first crack at the parent's assets. Presumably then, substantive consolidation would hurt that creditor and be disfavored. The values of the subsidiaries and parent would have to be sorted out, a sorting Douglas sought to require in *Consolidated Rock*.

But what if it turned out that sorting out the inter-company accounts was especially expensive? For a corporate group more complex than that in *Consolidated Rock*, there could have been multiple transfers up and down from parent to subsidiary, from subsidiary to parent, and from one subsidiary to another subsidiary, of assets, opportunities, guarantees, and managers. For a court to value each transfer would be hard, expensive, and inaccurate. Does Douglas in *Consolidated Rock* contemplate this case? (Indeed, he rejected the lower court's protestations that a sorting would have been too hard.)

In *In re Augie/Restivo Baking Company, Ltd.*, 860 F.2d 515 (2d Cir. 1988), Judge Winter stated:

> Substantive consolidation has no express statutory basis but is a product of judicial gloss. Substantive consolidation usually results in ... pooling the assets of, and claims against, the two entities; satisfying liabilities from the resulting common fund; eliminating inter-company claims; and combining the creditors of the two companies for purposes of voting on reorganization plans. The effect in the present case is ... [to pay one creditor less than another]. Because of the dangers in

---

[3] Capital requirements imposed by the lender on the borrower are to be understood in this light: the more heavily capitalized the borrower is, the less likely he is to dissipate assets necessary to repay the loan by withdrawing capital from the enterprise in the form of dividends or otherwise.

forcing creditors of one debtor to share on a parity with creditors of a less solvent debtor, we have stressed that substantive consolidation "is no mere instrument of procedural convenience ... but a measure affecting substantive rights."

... [Substantive consolidation is based] on two critical factors: (i) whether creditors dealt with the entities as a single economic unit and "did not rely on their separate identity in extending credit" ...; or (ii) whether the affairs of the debtors are so entangled that consolidation will benefit all creditors ....

With regard to the first factor, creditors who make loans on the basis of the financial status of a separate entity expect to be able to look to the assets of their particular borrower for satisfaction of that loan. Such lenders structure their loans according to their expectations regarding that borrower and do not anticipate either having the assets of a more sound company available in the case of insolvency or having the creditors of a less sound debtor compete for the borrower's assets ....

The second factor, entanglement of the debtors' affairs, involves cases in which there has been a commingling of two firms' assets and business functions. Resort to consolidation in such circumstances, however, should not be Pavlovian. Rather, substantive consolidation should be used *only* after it has been determined that *all* creditors will benefit because untangling is either impossible or so costly as to consume the assets. Otherwise ... a series of fraudulent conveyances might be viewed as resulting in a "commingling" that justified substantive consolidation. That consolidation, because it would eliminate all inter-company claims, would prevent creditors of the transferor from recovering assets from the transferee ....

The evidence of commingling of assets and business function in the state case in no way [was hopelessly obscure.] ... [R]ecords exist of all transactions ....

## ¶708: Administrative consolidation: In re Commercial Envelope Mfg. Co., 14 Collier Bankr. Cas. (MB) 191 (Bankr. S.D.N.Y. Aug. 22, 1977)

[Four interrelated corporations, each of which had filed a separate Chapter XI petition, moved for substantive consolidation, asserting that a merger of all their assets and liabilities was the only way to viably formulate a Chapter XI plan. The debtors were interrelated through ownership of their common stock and there were intercorporate guarantees and intercorporate credit arrangements. Two creditors filed objections to consolidation asserting that substantive consolidation would jeopardize their claims.]

[The court determined that since the objectants had failed to establish that the consolidation would have an adverse affect on their claims and because consolidation would benefit all creditors in that the debtors would operate profitably together, consolidation should be allowed.]

BABITT, Bankruptcy Judge: The movants are four related corporations, each of which filed its own separate petition seeking the relief contemplated by Chapter XI of the Bankruptcy Act, on October 20, 1976. [T]hese cases are being jointly administered. [J]oint or procedural administration in the interest of economy of judicial and clerical time [does not] affect ... substantive rights .... The relief sought by the motion now before the court is for a substantive consolidation which *does* deal with the rights of the debtors' creditors. Substantive consolidation, as will be seen, is now part of the warp and woof of the fabric of the bankruptcy process involving related debtors, though to be used sparingly. *It has no statutory or rule basis:* rather it is the product of judicial gloss in the face of *changes in the makeup of companies involved with the country's insolvency laws.*

Although each of the debtors is a separate corporation, all four are related by virtue of common stock ownership, in that the common stock of Commercial Envelope Manufacturing Co., Inc. is owned by Mr. and Mrs. Ira B. Kristel: Commercial Envelope Manufacturing Co., Inc., in turn owns the common stock of Business Envelope Manufacturers, Inc., and Business Envelope Manufacturers, Inc. owns the common stock of the remaining debtors, Business Envelope Manufacturers of Tennessee, Inc. and Business Envelope Manufacturers of California, Inc. All of the directors of these debtors are the same individuals—members of the Kristel family.

The debtors are convinced, and hope to convince the court, that the only way a meaningful Chapter XI plan can be presented to creditors is for that plan to be a single, unitary one affecting all of the debtors and all of their creditors. To achieve this result, the debtors have moved for a multi-faceted order authorizing and directing the consolidation of all four cases into a single one with a concomitant merger of all of the assets and liabilities of the four corporations into the consolidated entity. As a necessary corollary of such relief the debtors ask that all claims filed in each of the individual cases be treated as having been filed in the consolidated case; that all duplicate claims for the same indebtedness filed in more than one case be expunged; that all intercompany claims be eliminated and disallowed; that all cross-corporate guarantees of these debtors be eliminated and disallowed; and finally, that all the consolidated debtors be authorized to file a single set of schedules and a single plan in the consolidated proceeding. In a matter as pregnant with consequence to all concerned as is substantive consolidation and alert to the frequent reminders that the grant is to be given only a proper showing of the criteria the courts have engrafted on the power, the court is to scrutinize the evidence offered. The evidence in support should satisfy the court and should be more than a pro forma exercise. This is particularly so here where a creditor claims he would be prejudiced by the favorable exercise of this court's power to achieve what the debtor seeks.

The facts underlying the relationship between the parties, as gleaned from the pleadings, many be briefly summarized as follows. In 1971, the Industrial Development Board of Anderson County ("Industrial Board"), State of Tennessee, purchased a building to be used by the now debtor, Business Envelope Manufacturers of Tennessee, Inc. To fund the purchase, the Industrial Board issued first mortgage revenue bonds in the aggregate principal amount of $1,350,000 pursuant to an indenture of mortgage and deed of trust dated October 1, 1971. Simultaneously, the Tennessee Company entered into a lease for the property with the Industrial Board which lease was guaranteed by Commercial Envelope Manufacturing Co., Inc. Both the lease and the guarantee were security for the payment of the bonds. When the motion to consolidate was filed the Industrial Board interposed objection insisting that the Tennessee plant and the operation there were profitable and that a consolidation and concomitant merger of assets and liabilities would jeopardize its claim in these proceedings. Subsequently, the Security Bank and Trust Company of Ponca City, Oklahoma ("Bank"), as Indenture Trustee, also filed its objection to the motion to consolidate alleging that consolidation would or could adversely affect the substantive rights of the holders of the first mortgage revenue bonds, since such consolidation would render assets of the debtors Commercial Envelope Manufacturing Co., Inc. and Business Envelope Manufacturers of Tennessee, Inc. subject to claims of creditors of the other debtors, a result which would reduce the amounts available to satisfy the bonded indebtedness.

At the trial, the debtors elicited testimony from an accountant, one Abraham Nowick, a member of the firm of accounts authorized in these proceedings to conduct an audit of the debtors' books and records.

* * *

Nowick testified as to the difficulty of isolating and ascertaining the individual assets and liabilities of each of the debtors. This was due to the arbitrary and inaccurate system of bookkeeping maintained by the companies. No separate accounting was had nor were separate records kept. Financial statements were issued on a consolidated basis. Each debtor had cross-guaranteed obligations of the others. Mr. Nowick went on to describe the astronomical cost of performing such audit as might be necessary to permit one to distinguish between the assets and liabilities of the debtors. However, this witness continued, because of the complexity and length of time over which the intercorporate transactions had taken place, he could give no guarantee that such an audit would be successful. He also testified that it was impossible to determine whether or not the individual operations of each of the debtors were even profitable. He expressed his opinion that physical consolidation into a single location would probably improve the profitability of the entire operation.

* * *

There are numerous cases emanating from this circuit which have dealt with consolidation. Although none of these cases has described conclusively the criteria that must exist before a case for consolidation is established, the cases do describe the common ingredients that seem to be present in all instances where consolidation was permitted. It is the opinion of this court that those elements exist in the present context and that therefore consolidation should proceed.

I turn to the cases. In Soviero v. Franklin National Bank of Long Island, supra, the court authorized consolidation upon the finding of extensive co-mingling of assets and business functions and the existence of a unity of interest and ownership common to all the debtor companies. All the debtors in Soviero had been engaged in the same business, and gratuitous transfers of assets were made from one debtor to another. Guarantees to purchasers had been given in the parent's name.

In Matter of SeaTrade Corporation, 255 F.Supp. 696 (S.D.N.Y. 1966), the debtors, almost entirely owned by one family, operated with frequent disregard of the corporate formalities usually observed in independent corporations. *The court found that it would have been unreasonable in terms of time and cost to attempt to separate the assets and liabilities of this corporation, and even if audit steps were to be taken, there was no assurance that the true situation of the debtors would fairly be reflected.* The court also found that there was *no evidence that particular creditors would be unfairly dealt with on a consolidated basis.* There also existed inter-corporate guarantees and frequent transfers of assets without formal observance of accounting proprieties. Again, that court authorized consolidation of the debtors.

In Chemical Bank, N.Y. Trust v. Kheel, supra, the Court of Appeals for this Circuit, for the first time relying on Soviero, set forth an additional criterion to justify consolidation. That criterion turned on the findings that the inter-relationship of the group of debtors was hopelessly obscured and that the time and expense necessary to even attempt to unscramble them was so substantial that it would threaten the realization of any net assets for all creditors. The court felt that if such findings could be made, an equitable base existed for the invocation of the court's broad equity powers to consolidate even in the absence of a showing that the creditor dealt with the bankrupt and its affiliates as one.

* * *

The essence of the objecting creditor's resistance to consolidation is that it could adversely affect the substantive rights of the holders of the First Mortgage Revenue Bonds, since such consolidation will render assets of [their debtors, which may be in better financial shape than the other companies in the complex] subject to the claims of creditors of the other debtors, thereby reducing the amounts available to satisfy the bonded indebtedness. Support is claimed for this assertion in the decision by the Court of Appeals for this Circuit in In re Flora Mir Candy Corporation, supra. There the court, while upholding consolidation of twelve of the thirteen debtors involved, refused such relief in the face of objection by the creditors of one of the thirteen debtor companies. The court concluded that under the circumstances surrounding the Flora Mir corporate complex, the inequities of consolidation were overwhelming and insurmountable. However, Flora Mir must be limited to its own facts, for it emerges as the "rare case" rather than the common one. An analysis of the facts there is in order.

Debentures had been issued more than six years before the debtor Meadors had been acquired by the parent, Flora Mir. Prior to its association with this parent, Meadors had existed as a separate, independent, corporate entity with its own history and its own creditors. Almost immediately upon its acquisition, it ceased all operations and eventually became defunct. The court, convinced of the "near certainty of unfair treatment," commented on the adverse impact that consolidation would have on Meadors' creditors, observing that

> "Consolidation not only would wipe out Meadors' claim against Flora Mir for the misappropriation of its assets but also would permit the creditors of Flora Mir and the other corporations to share in any recovery ... for transactions antedating Meadors' joining the Flora Mir Group—transactions in which these creditors had not the slightest legitimate interest. We doubt that any showing of accounting difficulties would warrant consolidation under such circumstances, at least if the Meadors creditors were willing to confine themselves to assets that were obviously theirs.
>
> "But here there was no evidence such as in the Chemical Bank case cited, that the inter-relationships of the group are hopelessly obscured and the time and expense necessary even to attempt to unscramble them so substantial as to threaten the realization of the net assets for all the creditors. 369 F.2d 847. To the contrary the accountants in relatively short order had managed to come up with financial statements of each of the debtors. Whatever problems there might be with respect to inter-company accounts among other debtors those with respect to Meadors were few for the reasons stated." Id. at 1063.

The above lengthy excerpt highlights the numerous differences between the plight of the creditors here and those victimized in the "Flora Mir plot," for in Flora Mir, Meadors' creditors "clearly bargained on a different basis than the creditors of the other Flora Mir companies," and "were indeed being ripped off."

\* \* \*

When all is said and done, there is a practicability to authorizing consolidation here. In effect, by this consolidation, all of the assets of all of the debtors are to be treated as common assets, and claims of all creditors against any of the debtors are to be treated as claims against this created common fund. This would eliminate duplicated claims filed against several of the debtors by creditors uncertain as to where the liability should be allocated. There appears to be no feasible alternative to consolidation from a practical standpoint, particularly where, as here, all of the companies are already before the court[.]

This court cannot read Flora Mir as a mandate that consolidation must inevitably be refused where some creditor might be marginally injured. All conflicting interest must be balanced. Here the balance is decidedly in favor of all of the creditors of all of the debtor companies and in favor of achieving that debtor rehabilitation which Chapter XI contemplates and which cannot be achieved unless consolidation is granted. So much is implicit in the words of the Chemical Bank case that consolidation may be had in order

> "to reach a rough approximation of justice to some rather than deny any to all." 369 F.2d at 847.

It is, therefore, the judgment of this court that in order that a meaningful plan might be proposed and accepted and found to be in the best interests of creditors ... consolidation is warranted. The motion is Granted and the objection Overruled.

Submit an Order.

## B. Fraudulent conveyances and the holding company

### ¶709: Holding companies and effective seniority

1. You represent a prospective creditor (creditor A) of company X. Company X has $3000 of assets. Your client expects to loan $1000, lifting the company's assets to $4000. On a pro forma basis (i.e., after giving effect to the contemplated transaction, the loan), the company's balance sheet looks like this:

| Company X | |
|---|---|
| $4000 | $1000 Creditor A |
| | $2000 Creditor B |

Creditor A informs you that it expects to take the general risks of being a creditor of Company X. It will not make the loan on the contemplated terms if B has security. You check; B has no security. It will not make the loan if B is contractually senior to A. You inform A that without A's consent, B cannot be contractually senior. It will not make the loan if future security can be granted to creditors. You draft a negative pledge clause for insertion into the loan agreements (and inform A of the consequences of a violation of the negative pledge clause if there is a subsequent bankruptcy).

2. Have you done enough?
3. One year after A disburses the loan, X declines in value to $2000 and recapitalizes. Operations are sent down into an operating subsidiary. X becomes a holding company. B cancels its note from X and becomes a creditor of the subsidiary.
4. X's balance sheet looks like this:

| Company X | |
|---|---|
| C/S of Subsidiary | $1000 Creditor A |
| | Common stock |

The subsidiary's balance sheet looks like this:

| Subsidiary | |
|---|---|
| $2000 | $2000 Creditor B |
| | Common stock |

Is B effectively senior to A? Assume for the moment that there would be no substantive consolidation in bankruptcy. (In a more realistic transaction, A and B would remain as creditors of the parent and the subsidiary would take on a new creditor, Creditor C.) What kind of financial covenants could A obtain if it fears a holding company? How is debt of a subsidiary treated in the Drum Financial indenture?

5. Is the transfer from X to the subsidiary a fraudulent conveyance? See ¶710.
   (i) Is the conveyance by an insolvent? (U.F.C.A. § 4.) Does it render X insolvent? Is there fair consideration?
   (ii) Is the conveyance made with intent to defraud? (§ 7.)
6. The restructuring is done when X is still worth $4000. Consider two possibilities at that time. First, what if there were no purpose to the transfer other than to obtain a better interest rate from B? Second, what if the purpose was to have operations run in a separate company and "headquarters" operations run in the parent company? Many companies, you are told, do this, including many companies about which there is not even a whisper of insolvency and bankruptcy. Incidental to this, creditor B might offer a better interest rate.

Read and apply each of §§ 4, 7 and then 6 of the Uniform Fraudulent Conveyance Act. See ¶710.

## ¶710: Fraudulent conveyances and finance companies

1. If the intra-holding company dealings can be viewed as a fraudulent conveyance, a benefitted creditor somewhere in the corporate structure could obtain the same benefits as if the complex corporate structure were consolidated. More precisely, creditors whose debtor made the fraudulent conveyance can sue to recover the conveyance.
2. Key provisions that will trigger a fraudulent conveyance are §§ 4 and 7 of the Uniform Fraudulent Conveyance Act:

> § 4. <u>Conveyances by Insolvent</u>. Every conveyance made and every obligation incurred by a person who is or will be thereby rendered insolvent [which is defined as occurring when liabilities exceed assets] is fraudulent as to creditors without regard to his actual intent if the conveyance is made or the obligation is incurred without fair consideration.
>
> \* \* \*
>
> § 7. <u>Conveyance Made With Intent to Defraud</u>. Every conveyance made and every obligation incurred with actual intent, as distinguished from intent presumed in law, to hinder, delay, or defraud either present or future creditors, is fraudulent as to both present and future creditors.

Section 6 of the Uniform Fraudulent Conveyance Act could also apply:

> § 6. <u>Conveyances by a Person About to Incur Debts</u>. Every conveyance made and every obligation incurred without fair consideration when the person making the conveyance or entering into the obligation intends or believes that he will in-

cur debts beyond his ability to pay as they mature, is fraudulent as to both present and future creditors.

Remedies are provided in §§ 9 and 10:

> § 9. Rights of Creditors Whose Claims Have Matured. .... Where a conveyance or obligation is fraudulent as to a creditor, such creditor, when his claim has matured, may, as against any person except a purchaser for fair consideration without knowledge of the fraud at the time of the purchase ...
>
> (a) Have the conveyance set aside or obligation annulled to the extent necessary to satisfy his claim, or
>
> (b) Disregard the conveyance and attach or levy execution upon the property conveyed.
>
> § 10. Rights of Creditors Whose Claims Have Not Matured. Where a conveyance made or obligation incurred is fraudulent as to a creditor whose claim has not matured he may proceed in a court of competent jurisdiction against any person against whom he could have proceeded had his claim matured, and the court may,
>
> (a) Restrain the defendant from disposing of his property,
>
> (b) Appoint a receiver to take charge of the property,
>
> (c) Set aside the conveyance or annul the obligation, or
>
> (d) Make any order which the circumstances of the case may require.

Notice that § 4 requires that the debtor be, or be rendered, insolvent; § 7 does not require insolvency. Notice that §§ 4 and 6 require that the consideration be unfair; § 7 does not.

The transfer might move in another direction. An acquiring company might form an empty "shell" corporation. The acquiring corporation gets financing to buy another corporation, contingent on the acquirer eventually offering the acquired corporation's assets as security for the acquisition loan. The acquiring corporation buys the target, merges it (that is, transfers all of its assets and liabilities) into the "shell" company and then gives the assets to acquisition lender as security.

Does that create a fraudulent conveyance problem? See Chapter 16, The LBO.

3. In the 1960s and 1970s many industrial firms set up finance companies. The finance subsidiary was used to provide credit to purchasers of the industrial company's product. The reasons for using this kind of a financing structure were often those offered by Posner, above. The separate finance company could approach a set of creditors different from those of the industrial company. Creditors that understood how to value and monitor accounts receivable would lend to the finance company, presumably at a cheaper rate than if they lent to the operating company that directly provided its financing services. Also, there might have been operating efficiencies in having a separate division or subsidiary with its own set of personnel who would be or become expert in financing activities.

Since the financing company was new and unexpected, preexisting creditors of the operating company generally had no covenants to deal with the formation of a finance subsidiary. Did they have any reason to? If a creditor lent to an industrial firm and did not want to be subordinate to any other creditor what did it need? An absence of a subordination agreement? An absence of lending to a subsidiary with a limited set of assets? A negative pledge clause to protect against security?

4. International Farm Machinery Company forms a finance subsidiary in the 1960s, when its operations are borderline profitable. Since the receivables of the finance subsidiary are good quality, short-term credits, it can borrow through the finance subsidiary at prime quality rates. Since the creditors of the industrial company, the parent, can no longer obviously get first crack at the receivables, those credits are perceived as being slightly more risky than they had been. They decline in value a fraction of a percent.

Finance economists note that the preexisting debt of industrial firms that formed finance subsidiaries declined in value, although only slightly. E. Han Kim, John McConnell & Paul Greenwood, *Capital Structure Rearrangements and Me-first Rules in an Efficient Capital Market*, 32 J. Fin. 789 (1977). (Presumably firms that expected to return to capital markets repeatedly would have wanted to maintain a reputation for not taking these "expropriations." See Ileen Malitz, *A Re-Examination of the Wealth Expropriation Hypothesis: The Case of Captive Finance Subsidiaries*, 44 J. Fin. 1039 (1989) (stockholders gained more than bondholders lost after the finance subsidiary recapitalizations; accordingly, there must have been some efficiency properties to the recapitalization).)

In the 1970s, the bottom falls out of the farm machinery market. Creditors of the finance subsidiary, although unhappy, expect that in any bankruptcy they will be paid close to in full. The short-term receivables are about 90% collectible.

Creditors of the industrial parent are less happy. They believe that if they collect only out of assets of their beleaguered debtor, they will receive 30 cents on the dollar.

Can creditors that lent to the industrial firm before the finance subsidiary was established attack the subsidiary's formation as a fraudulent conveyance? Did the conveyance render International Farm Machinery Company insolvent? Or did the collapsing farm machinery market of the 1970s? Was the conveyance made with actual intent to hinder, delay or defraud? Prime-grade credits, including companies such as General Electric, formed finance subsidiaries for operating or lending efficiencies.

---

## ¶711: Fraudulent conveyances under the Bankruptcy Code

Section 544(b) of the Bankruptcy Code authorizes the trustee to avoid any transfers by the debtor that an unsecured creditor with an allowable claim could avoid under state fraudulent conveyance law. And just to be sure, the Bankruptcy Code has its own mini-version of the Uniform Fraudulent Conveyance Act, although with a shorter one-year statute of limitations. Section 548 of the Bankruptcy Code states:

(a) (1) The trustee may avoid any transfer of an interest of the debtor in property, or any obligation incurred by the debtor, that was made or incurred on or within one year before the date of the filing of the petition, if the debtor voluntarily or involuntarily—

(A) made such transfer or incurred such obligation with actual intent to hinder, delay, or defraud any entity to which the debtor was or became, on or after the date that such transfer was made or such obligation was incurred, indebted; or

(B) (i) received less than a reasonably equivalent value in exchange for such transfer or obligation; and

(ii) (I) was insolvent on the date that such transfer was made or such obligation was incurred, or became insolvent as a result of such transfer or obligation;

(II) was engaged in business or a transaction, or was about to engage in business or a transaction, for which any property remaining with the debtor was an unreasonably small capital; or

(III) intended to incur, or believed that the debtor would incur, debts that would be beyond the debtor's ability to pay as such debts matured.

* * *

(c) ... a transferee or obligee of such a transfer or obligation that takes for value and in good faith has a lien on or may retain any interest transferred or may enforce any obligation incurred, as the case may be, to the extent that such transferee or obligee gave value to the debtor in exchange for such transfer or obligation.

## ¶712: The origins of fraudulent conveyance law: Garrard Glenn, Fraudulent Conveyances and Preferences 79-87 (1940)

### [The Act of 1571 (13 Eliz. c. 5) as the Basis of Our Law]

Our notion of the fraudulent conveyance traces to a statute of Elizabeth, cited in the above caption, and commonly called the Statute of Fraudulent Conveyances. This ... was largely due to the restatement of the law which was made by Sir Edward Coke ....

The statute ... became part of our inheritance. We find colonial enactments repeating its words with more or less fullness and certainly emphasizing its principle. After the Revolution it was reenacted in some States, and in others the courts considered it as part of the common law in force. Of course there have been divergences in form; but fundamentally, with some variations ..., this legislation has remained pretty true to the original mold. It is, indeed, a remarkable fact that the divergences among the States, whether in legislation or in case law, are traceable, not to discontent with the Statute of Elizabeth, but to the different lines of thought that were charted by the English courts themselves ....

The statute, indeed, needed judicial aid from the outset, for on its face it was singularly inadequate. Thus it did not cover all situations that were possible even in that day, to say nothing of those that later arose when the Chancery again functioned as a court available for the needs of the mercantile public. The Act of Elizabeth aided the creditor in his pursuit of legal assets that were attainable only under the process of equity. But courts of equity took care of this situation. And the courts, both of law and equity, also settled other open questions, viz: as to one who *bona fide* purchases from a guilty grantee, the rights of debtor and grantee as between themselves, and the methods of asserting creditors' rights under the Act.

The result was that at the beginning of this century, the law of fraudulent conveyances was a mosaic of statutes and decisions, which had been developed around the statute of Elizabeth. In such circumstances legislation of a modern type was to be expected. It came, and we propose to examine it, but before we do so, we should ask why this famous statute of Elizabeth was so strangely inadequate, why it was passed at all, and whether we could not have got along without it.

\* \* \*

### [Imprisonment for Debt, and Sanctuary, with Resulting Statutes]

To get the point, we should recall that England had certain sanctuaries into which the King's writ could not enter, with the result that if a debtor should gain the precincts of such a place, his creditors could not take his body in execution. This right, and the abuses of it, were well known in the bankruptcy legislation of Europe, for the Church, in sanctioning the right, was fortified by the custom of the Empire and certain passages of the Old Testament. Hence sanctuary meant, not so much the interior of a church with its altars, as certain precincts which were defined by custom or royal grant; and so the sanctuary of Westminster, for instance, embraced many nests and rookeries. Taking sanctuary was enumerated as an act of bankruptcy in the general bankruptcy laws which England enacted in 1542 and again in 1571 .... [S]anctuary was abolished in 1623 ....

Now, the association of sanctuary with fraudulent conveyance appeared on the face of the medieval legislation above discussed. In these statutes Parliament recited the common practice by which a debtor would transfer his assets to some friend but in trust for the debtor; and, that accomplished, the rascal would take himself to sanctuary and there "live a great time with a high countenance" until his creditors, being unable to reach the property which was held in trust for the debtor, would compromise their claims at a low figure, whereupon the delinquent would resume the ordinary course of life, and doubtless run up more bills. The idea of these statutes, as outlined by Bacon's Reading, was to make the debtor's lands and goods liable to his creditor's execution, despite the previous transfer. Here, then, we have the germ of the idea ... that the judgment creditor may ignore the fraudulent conveyance and levy upon its subject matter.

* * *

### ¶713: <u>The creditor of the subsidiary</u>

Thus far we have been principally analyzing the legal and financial risks to the creditor of a firm that, after the loan is made, reorganizes into a holding company. Now let's consider the creditor of the holding company's subsidiary.

The subsidiary's creditor will be concerned with dividends leaving the subsidiary, and with other transfers to the parent company or other subsidiaries. What will fraudulent conveyance law do for it? How protective is fraudulent conveyance law if there are transfers and the subsidiary thereafter declines in value?

Consider the advice you must give a client in a holding company position analogous to Creditor B in ¶709. Creditor B considers the fraudulent conveyance protections inadequate and would like to control the subsidiary's dividends more tightly. Would the dividend covenant in Drum Financial, ¶603 be of use? How would it help Creditor B?

The subsidiary is in the chemical business. Creditor B understands the subsidiary's business, but doesn't understand all of the holding company/conglomerate's other businesses. It wants most of the subsidiary's earnings retained inside the subsidiary. The creditor and the managers of the subsidiary agree to this. Often that is the end of the legal and financial inquiry.

But this time the managers of the parent company come back and say they'll need to water down the dividend covenant. One of the rationales for this kind of conglomerate organization—sometimes called the M-form or multiform organization in business schools—is this: the holding company is run by superstar strategic business planners. They don't supervise, manufacture or market anything. But they see big picture trends and allocate capital among the holding company operations based on their strategic view of where the economy is going. They need flexibility to pull money out of the chemical subsidiary and put it into the steel subsidiary or go into the computer business.

The parent company's managers say they can't anticipate how much and when they'd change their strategic vision for the subsidiary's business. They don't want to be too tied down. They say they understand that our client, creditor B, has two worries about not having a tight dividend covenant. Creditor B is worried that even if the parent company managers come to honestly believe that the subsidiary's business is going nowhere, their yanking money out of the subsidiary would nevertheless make creditor B's loans riskier. They want to be repaid *before* the parent company yanks money out of the subsidiary, and not take the risks of repayment afterward. (Fraudulent conveyance law would only bite if at the time of the transfer out from the subsidiary, the subsidiary was insolvent, there was actual intent to hinder, or the sub was left with capital too small. That kind of protection isn't good enough for creditor B.) That is, your client understands that if the subsidiary is rendered insolvent it will have fraudulent conveyance protection. But the client is worried that the parent will yank the money out, the subsidiary wouldn't thereby be rendered insolvent, but thereafter the subsidiary's value would decline, leaving the client unpaid.

Moreover, the parent company managers say they understand that creditor B is worried that without constraints, the managers might yank funds out of the subsidiary even if the subsidiary's business is passable if financial problems elsewhere in the organization demand a transfer of cash.

Here's what the parent company strategic managers propose to maintain flexibility and still give creditor B protection. They propose to keep the dividend covenant, but to water it down. B will be still, they say, primarily lending on the credit-worthiness of the subsidiary and its understanding of the subsidiary's chemical business. But don't let the weaker dividend covenant induce you, B, to raise the interest rate, or at least don't let it induce you to raise it too much, they say. Why not too much? Because the parent company will guarantee repayment of the loan. So if the parent yanks too much money out, and the chemical company later collapses, B will have a claim not only on the chemical subsidiary but also against the parent company. Double protection.

There's a business problem with this. The bank, B, says the reason they were willing to lend at this low rate to the chemical subsidiary was that they understood the chemical business and didn't have to get smart about the company's steel business or computer business and this company's position in each. The parent company is now proposing a hybrid, based on the credit-worthiness of both. The principal credit risk is still the chemical subsidiary, but B would be relying at least in part on the strength of the conglomerate's other businesses. This reduces the benefit of lending to a targeted subsidiary.

The trade-off might work or it might not work. This time, so that we can move on to the next appellate decision, it works. All the business-people at the bank, at the subsidiary, and at the parent company will accept the trade-off.

Do other creditors of the subsidiary have special reason to fear mistreatment in the year before the subsidiary's filing for bankruptcy? Consider preference law in § 547 of the Bankruptcy Code, the *Deprizio* decision, which follows in ¶714, and the 1994 amendments to § 550, which follow *Deprizio*.

## C. Preferences and the holding company

### ¶714: Deprizio Construction Co. v. Ingersoll Rand Financial Corp., 874 F.2d 1186 (7th Cir. 1989)

EASTERBROOK, Circuit Judge.

We must decide a question no other appellate court has addressed: whether payments to creditors who dealt at arms' length with a debtor are subject to the year-long preference-recovery period that 11 U.S.C. § 547(b)(4)(B) provides for "inside" creditors, when the payments are "for the benefit of" insiders, § 547(b)(1). The bankruptcy court in this case answered "no," and the district court "yes." We agree with the district court ....

I

In 1980 V.N. Deprizio Construction Co. was awarded contracts to do $13.4 million of work on the extension of Chicago's subway system to O'Hare Airport. By 1982 the company was in financial trouble. Because Mayor Byrne wanted the line open before the primary election for that office in February 1983, the City made the firm extraordinary loans of $2.5 million; the firm in turn donated $3,000 to the Mayor's campaign fund. Neither outlay achieved its purpose. The line wasn't finished on time, and Byrne lost. These and other dealings by Richard N. Deprizio, the firm's president, including suspicions of affiliation with organized crime, led the United States Attorney to open an investigation. In April 1983 Deprizio Co. filed a petition under the Bankruptcy Code of 1978. Other firms finished the subway, which opened in 1984.

As the investigation continued and Deprizio's indictment was imminent, word circulated that he might "sing." So in January 1986 Deprizio was lured to a vacant parking lot, where an assassin's gun and the obligations of a life-time were discharged together. Corporations are not so easily liquidated.

Deprizio Co. had borrowed money from many sources other than the City of Chicago, including [several banks]. Richard Deprizio and his brothers ... , all insiders of the firm, also guaranteed its debts to other lenders. ("Insider," a term to which we return, includes officers of the debtor and the officers' relatives.)

As the district court observed "the record is devoid of detail" concerning these guarantees. Details are potentially important ....

Payments out of the ordinary course in the 90 days before filing a bankruptcy petition may be recovered for the estate under §§ 547 and 550. Creditors then receive shares determined by statutory priorities and contractual entitlements rather than by their ability to sneak in under the wire. Payments to or for the benefit of an insider during a full year, not just 90 days, may be recovered [for the bankrupt] by virtue of

§ 547(b)(4)(B). The Trustee filed adversary proceedings against the lenders ... —none of them insiders—seeking to recover payments made more than 90 days but within the year before the filing. The Trustee reasoned that the payments made to these outside creditors were "for the benefit" of inside co-signers and guarantors, because every dollar paid to the outside creditor reduced the insider's exposure by the same amount.

Without deciding whether any of the payments was preferential within the meaning of § 547 or worked to the benefit of any insider, the bankruptcy judge denied the Trustee's request. Judge Eisen concluded that any transfer to an outside creditor for the benefit of an insider should be treated as two transfers: one being the money, and the other the benefit. A transfer may be recovered under § 550(a) only to the extent it is avoidable under § 547. The monetary transfer to the outsider is not avoidable, Judge Eisen concluded, when made more than 90 days before the filing. Thus it may not be recovered from the outsider, even though the benefit to the insider may be recovered from the insider.

On an interlocutory appeal to the district court, Judge Plunkett reversed. He concluded that payment is only one transfer, although a transfer may create benefits for many persons. If the insider receives a benefit, then the transfer is avoidable under § 547(b)(4)(B) if made within a year of the bankruptcy and does not qualify for the exclusions in § 547(c). (These include payments in the ordinary course of business, payments for equivalent value received, and so on.) Section 550(a), as Judge Plunkett read it, allows the Trustee to recover the transfer from either the recipient or the indirect beneficiary, at the Trustee's option. The district court remanded the case so that the bankruptcy court could determine whether the payments identified by the Trustee occurred, whether an insider received a benefit from any particular payment, and whether any of them was protected by § 547(c) .... [W]e granted leave to appeal.

II

Many bankruptcy and district judges have addressed the question we confront, as have commentators. A majority of judges have concluded that insiders' guarantees do not expose outside lenders to an extended preference-recovery period, frequently because they believe that recovery would be inequitable when ordinarily outside creditors need restore only preferences received within the 90 days before bankruptcy. The commentators are evenly divided.

A

Six sections of the Bankruptcy Code supply the texts. Section 547(b) says:

... [T]he trustee may avoid any transfer of an interest of the debtor in property—
   (1)  to or for the benefit of a creditor;
   (2)  for or on account of an antecedent debt owed by the debtor before such transfer was made;

(3) made while the debtor was insolvent;

(4) made—

(A) on or within 90 days before the date of the filing of the petition; or

(B) between ninety days and one year before the date of the filing of the petition, if such creditor at the time of such transfer was an insider; and

(5) that enables such creditor to receive more than such creditor would receive if—

(A) the case were a case under Chapter 7 of this title;

(B) the transfer had not been made; and

(C) such creditor received payment of such debt to the extent provided by the provisions of this title.

This is § 547(b) as amended in 1984 ....

Section 547(b) uses three terms of art: "creditor," "insider," and "transfer," and the definition of "creditor" brings in a fourth: "claim." Section 101 defines each.

[5] "claim" means—

(A) right to payment, whether or not such right is reduced to judgment, liquidated, unliquidated, fixed, contingent, matured, unmatured, disputed, undisputed, legal, equitable, secured, or unsecured; ...

[10] "creditor" means—

(A) entity that has a claim against the debtor that arose at the time of or before the order for relief concerning the debtor; ...

[31] "insider" includes—

...

(B) if the debtor is a corporation—

(i) director of the debtor;

(ii) officer of the debtor;

(iii) person[4] in control of the debtor;

...

(vi) relative of a general partner, director, officer, or person in control of the debtor;

...

[54] "transfer" means every mode, direct or indirect, absolute or conditional, voluntary or involuntary, of disposing of or parting with property or with an interest in property, including retention of title as a security interest ...

---

[4] [Section 101(41) says "'person' includes individual, partnership, and corporation, but does not include [a] governmental unit ...." Hence a holding company would be a "person."—Roe.]

Finally there is § 550, which specifies who is liable for a transfer avoided under § 547:

> (a) Except as otherwise provided in this section, to the extent that a transfer is avoided under section ... 547, ... the trustee may recover, for the benefit of the estate, the property transferred, or, if the court so orders, the value of such property, from—
>
>> (1) the initial transferee of such transfer or the entity for whose benefit such transfer was made; or
>> (2) any immediate or mediate transferee of such initial transferee.
>
> (b) The trustee may not recover under section (a)(2) of this section from—
>
>> (1) a transferee that takes for value, including satisfaction or securing of a present or antecedent debt, in good faith, and without knowledge of the voidability of the transfer avoided; or
>> (2) any immediate or mediate good faith transferee of such transferee.
>
> (c) The trustee is entitled to only a single satisfaction under subsection (a) of this section.[5]

The Trustee's argument for extended recovery from outside creditors flows directly from these interlocked provisions.

Suppose Firm borrows money from Lender, with payment guaranteed by Firm's officer (Guarantor). Section 101[(31)](B)(ii) renders Guarantor an "insider." Guarantor is not Firm's creditor in the colloquial sense, but under § 101[(10)] of the Code any person with a "claim" against Firm is a "creditor," and anyone with a contingent right to payment holds a "claim" under § 101[(5)](A). A guarantor has a contingent right to payment from the debtor: if Lender collects from Guarantor, Guarantor succeeds to Lender's entitlements and can collect from Firm. So Guarantor is a "creditor" in Firm's bankruptcy. A payment ("transfer") by Firm to Lender is "for the benefit of" Guarantor under § 547(b)(1) because every reduction in the debt to Lender reduces Guarantor's exposure. Because the payment to Lender assists Guarantor, it is avoidable under § 547(b)(4)(B) unless one of the exemptions in § 547(c) applies. Once the transfer is avoided under § 547, the Trustee turns to § 550 for authority to recover.

---

[5] [In 1994, several years after *Deprizio*, Congress amended § 550, by adding:

> If a transfer made between 90 days and one year before the filing of the petition—
>
> (1) is avoided under section 547(b) of this title; and
> (2) was made for the benefit of a creditor that at the time of such transfer was an insider;
>
> the trustee may not recover under subsection (a) from a transferee that is not an insider.

See notes after the case.—Roe.]

Section 547(b)(4) distinguishes according to [whether Guarantor is an "insider"], but § 550 does not.[6] It says that if a transfer is recoverable by the trustee, it may be recovered from either the "initial transferee" (Lender) or the "entity for whose benefit such transfer was made" (Guarantor). So Lender may have to repay transfers received during the year before filing, even though Lender is not an insider.

Judge Plunkett accepted this chain of reasoning. The creditors seek to break it at three links. First, they observe that § 550(a) allows the trustee to recover only "to the extent that a transfer is avoided under" § 547. Viewing each payment as two "transfers"—one to Lender, another to Guarantor—they insist that the only transfer avoidable under § 547 is the one to Guarantor ....

III

Now for the principal question: whether the Trustee may recover from an outside creditor under § 550(a)(1) a transfer more than 90 days before the filing that is avoided under § 547(b) because of a benefit for an inside creditor. The textual argument, which we have already given, is simple. Section 547(b) defines which transfers are "avoidable." No one doubts that a transfer to Lender produces a "benefit" for Guarantor. After § 547 defines which transfers may be avoided, § 550(a) identifies who is responsible for payment: "the initial transferee of such transfer or the entity for whose benefit such transfer was made." This gives the trustee the option to collect from Lender, Guarantor, or both, subject only to the proviso in § 550([d]) that there can be but one satisfaction.

More than language lies behind this approach. The trustee's power to avoid preferences (the "avoiding power") is essential to make the bankruptcy case a collective proceeding for the determination and payment of debts. Any individual creditor has a strong incentive to make off with the assets of a troubled firm, saving itself at potential damage to the value of the enterprise. Many a firm is worth more together than in pieces, and a spate of asset grabbing by creditors could dissipate whatever firm-specific value the assets have. Like fishers in a common pool, creditors logically disregard the fact that their self-protection may diminish aggregate value—for if Creditor A does not lay claim to the assets, Creditor B will, and A will suffer for inaction. All creditors gain from a rule of law that induces each to hold back. The trustee's avoiding powers serve this end in two ways: first, they eliminate the benefit of attaching assets out of the ordinary course in the last 90 days before the filing, so that the rush to dismember a firm is not profitable from a creditor's perspective; second, the avoiding powers assure each creditor that if it refrains from acting, the pickings of anyone less civil will be fetched back into the pool. See Thomas H. Jackson, Avoiding Powers in Bankruptcy, 36 Stan. L. Rev. 725, 727–31, 756–68 (1984).

---

[6] [Section 550 did not so distinguish at the time *Deprizio* was decided. After Congress amended § 550 it did so distinguish. See notes after the case.—Roe.]

How long should this preference-recovery period be? If one outside creditor knows that the firm is in trouble, others will too. Each major lender monitors both the firm and fellow lenders. If it perceives that some other lender is being paid preferentially, a major lender can propel Firm into bankruptcy. Reasonably alert lenders can act with sufficient dispatch to ensure that the perceived preference is recoverable even when the preference period is short. Section 547(b) makes 90 days the rule, time enough (Congress concluded) for careful creditors to protect themselves (and when one does, small unsecured trade creditors get the benefits too).

Insiders pose special problems. Insiders will be the first to recognize that the firm is in a downward spiral. If insiders and outsiders had the same preference-recovery period, insiders who lent money to the firm could use their knowledge to advantage by paying their own loans preferentially, then putting off filing the petition in bankruptcy until the preference period had passed. Outside creditors, aware of this risk, would monitor more closely, or grab assets themselves (fearing that the reciprocity that is important to the pooling scheme has been destroyed), or precipitate bankruptcy at the smallest sign of trouble, hoping to "catch" inside preferences before it is too late. All of these devices could be costly. An alternative device is to make the preference-recovery period for insiders longer than that for outsiders. With a long period for insiders, even the prescient managers who first see the end coming are unlikely to be able to prefer themselves in distribution.

Loans from insiders to their firms are not the only, or even the most important, concern of outside creditors. Insiders frequently guarantee other loans. If the firm folds while these loans are outstanding, the insiders are personally liable. So insiders bent on serving their own interests (few managers hold outside lenders' interests of equal weight with their own!) could do so by inducing the firm to pay the guaranteed loans preferentially. If the preference-recovery period for such payments were identical to the one for outside debts, this would be an attractive device for insiders. While concealing the firm's true financial state, they would pay off (at least pay down) the debts they had guaranteed, while neglecting others. To the extent they could use private information to do this more than 90 days ahead of the filing in bankruptcy, they would come out like bandits. The guaranteed loans would be extinguished, and with them the guarantees. True, it is logically possible to recover from the insider the value of the released guarantee, even if the trustee could not reach the proceeds in the hands of the outside lender. But it is hard to determine the value of a released guarantee, and anyway insiders might think that they would be more successful resisting the claims of the trustee than the hounds of the outside creditors. So an extended recovery period for payments to outside creditors that benefit insiders could contribute to the ability of the bankruptcy process to deter last-minute grabs of assets. The outsiders who must kick into the pool when the trustee uses the avoiding powers retain their contractual entitlements; all the trustee's recovery does is ensure that those entitlements (as modified by any statutory priorities)—rather than the efforts of insiders to protect their own interests, or the cleverness of outsiders in beating the 90-day deadline—determine the ultimate distribution of the debtor's net assets.

A

\* \* \*

The parties agree that there is no helpful legislative history ....

... An extended recovery period is consistent with the structure of the Code and does not subvert any of its functions. A longer period when insiders reap benefits by preferring one outside creditor over another facilitates the operation of bankruptcy as a collective process and ensures that each creditor will receive payment according to the Code's priorities and non-bankruptcy entitlements. Silence in the legislative history therefore does not require or authorize a court to depart from the text and structure of the Code.

B

The creditors do not argue that even if the Code extends the preference period, the extension should not be enforced because [it is] "inequitable." Perhaps our rebuff to "equity" arguments in other bankruptcy cases is responsible ....

Nonetheless, "equity" arguments have captivated a majority of the bankruptcy judges and several of the commentators who have spoken on this subject .... So it is worth pointing out that even if equity arguments were admissible, they would not help the creditors' cause. Rules of law affecting parties to voluntary arrangements do not operate "inequitably" in the business world—at least not once the rule is understood. Prices adjust. If the extended preference period facilitates the operation of bankruptcy as a collective debt-adjustment process, then credit will become available on slightly better terms. If a longer period has the opposite effect, creditors will charge slightly higher rates of interest and monitor debtors more closely. In either case creditors will receive the competitive rate of return in financial markets—the same risk-adjusted rate they would have received with a 90-day preference-recovery period. A rule may injure debtors and creditors by foreclosing efficient business arrangements and increasing the rate of interest low-risk borrowers must pay, ... but inefficiency is not inequity. At all events, in what sense is it "inequitable" to recapture payments to creditors that may have been favored only because payment reduced insiders' exposure (recall that the insiders select which debts to pay first), then distribute these monies according to statutory priorities and contractual entitlements? In what sense is it "inequitable" to require the outside lenders to pursue the inside guarantors for any shortfall, when they bargained for exactly that recourse?

Our creditors press a cousin to "equity" arguments: "policy" arguments. According to the creditors, an extended preference period will force lenders to precipitate bankruptcy filings at the slightest sign of trouble in order to prevent erosion of their positions. The lenders paint a bleak picture of firms driven under when the problems could have been worked out—if only the lenders knew that they would keep what they receive in the "workout." Workouts often involve guarantees, and if these mean longer preference periods, then workouts may become less common (and formal bankruptcy more common) ....

For what it may be worth, we doubt that an extended preference-recovery period will cause a stampede from workouts to bankruptcies. Unless there is a "preference," there is nothing for the trustee to avoid. Most of the tales of woe presented by the creditors do not involve preferences in light of § 547(b)(5), which says that a transfer is a preference only to the extent the creditor got more than it would have received in a liquidation, and § 547(c), which specifies situations that do not create avoidable preferences.

> § 547(c) The trustee may not avoid under this section a transfer—
>
> (1) to the extent that such transfer was—
>
> (A) intended by the debtor and the creditor to or for whose benefit such transfer was made to be a contemporaneous exchange for new value given to the debtor; and
> (B) in fact a substantially contemporaneous exchange;
>
> (2) to the extent that such transfer was—
>
> (A) in payment of a debt incurred by the debtor in the ordinary course of business or financial affairs of the debtor and the transferee;
> (B) made in the ordinary course of business or financial affairs of the debtor and the transferee; and
> (C) made according to ordinary business terms;
>
> (3) that creates a security interest in property acquired by the debtor—
>
> (A) to the extent such security interest secures new value [in the nature of a purchase-money security interest] ...
>
> (4) to or for the benefit of a creditor, to the extent that, after such transfer, such creditor gave new value to or for the benefit of the debtor ...
> (5) that creates a perfected security interest in inventory or a receivable or the proceeds of either, except to the extent that the aggregate of all such transfers to the transferee caused a reduction ... to the prejudice of other creditors holding unsecured claims, of any amount by which the debt secured by such security interest exceeded the value of all security interests for such debt on [one of three defined dates] ...

(6) that is the fixing of a statutory lien that is not avoidable under section 545 of this title; or

(7) [aggregate transfers of less than $600 for an individual debtor].

\* \* \*

Consider some of the transactions the lenders use to illustrate what they view as pernicious consequences of an extended preference-recovery period:

■A fully-secured creditor with an insider's guarantee to boot is paid off nine months before bankruptcy and releases its security interest. The debtor uses the property as security for a new loan. The trustee recovers the payment as a preference, and the creditor has been stripped of its security.

The trustee confronts two obstacles in such a case. First, if the creditor was fully secured, then payment does not produce a benefit for the inside guarantor, whose exposure was zero. The preference-recovery period therefore would be only 90 days. Second, under § 547(b)(5) a transfer is avoidable only to the extent the creditor received more than it would have in a Chapter 7 liquidation. A fully-secured creditor will be paid in full under Chapter 7, so there is no avoidable preference in this case with or without a guarantee by an insider. If, on the other hand, the security covered only 90% of the debt, then only the remaining 10% of the payment is avoidable as a preference.

\* \* \*

■A creditor makes an unsecured loan guaranteed by an insider and requires monthly payments over a number of years. The trustee seeks to recover all of the payments during the year before the filing. To the extent the debtor paid on time, the creditor is protected by ... § 547(c)(2), the "ordinary course rule" ....

■Lender #1 extends credit and takes security. It is so over-secured that Lender #2 is willing to make a second loan and take a junior security interest. This second loan (but not the first) is backed up by an insider's guarantee. Every payment to Lender #1 increases the amount of security available for Lender #2, which produces a benefit to Guarantor by reducing his exposure. Cf. In re Prescott, 805 F.2d 719, 731 (7th Cir. 1986). The trustee seeks to recover all payments to Lender #1 during the year before the filing, even though Lender #1 did not negotiate for an insider's guarantee.

... [Section] 547(c)(2) would prevent recovery ... [if the payments and loan were made in the ordinary course of business].

In light of these exclusions, there is no reason to use ambulatory arguments of "equity" or "policy" to defeat the Trustee's claims in this case. Congress has considered and addressed specifically the situations that most concern lenders. If these exclusions and exemptions are not "enough," creditors should complain to Congress.

IV

To sum up: ... We hold in Part III that the preference-recovery period for outside creditors is one year when the payment produces a benefit for an inside creditor, including a guarantor.

## ¶715: **Preferences**

To hold the bankrupt estate together, the Bankruptcy Code stays all creditors from collecting on their debts from the bankrupt. Before the bankruptcy ensues though, creditors could rush to twist the debtor's arm for repayment and the debtor may prefer to pay a stronger or more diligent creditor. To reduce the incentives for such a race, the Bankruptcy Code allows the bankrupt estate to recover preferential payments, even those paid to innocent creditors. The elements of a preference are in § 547(b). Defenses are in § 547(c). From whom the preference can be recovered is delineated in § 550.

The basic elements of a preference are:

1. Debtor makes a payment
2. Within 90 days of bankruptcy petition
3. On an antecedent debt
4. When the debtor is insolvent
5. That allows the recipient to collect more (i.e., to be preferred)

Several defenses are listed in subsection (c); the key defense is that the trustee cannot recover payments made in the ordinary course of business.

The basics can be seen better by reading the statute and then working through each of these problems:

Example #1: Creditor is secured with good security, paid off one day before bankruptcy in full, after creditor made several collection calls? Is it a preference?

Example #2: Creditor has no security. It lent last year. Worried, it asks for payment. Debtor says "don't have the cash, but please take the security to make you comfortable with your antecedent debt." Creditor takes security. Next day the debtor goes bankrupt. Is the taking of security a preference?

Example #3: Creditor has no security. Creditor also has made no loan. Today creditor makes a loan and takes full security, all the property of the debtor. Tomorrow the company goes bankrupt. Is the taking of security a preference?

Example #4: The following events occur. Is the payment a preference?

| | | |
|---|---|---|
| March 1: | Creditor ships goods to debtor, payable in 30 days. | |
| On April 1: | No payment comes. (Prior shipments were paid on time, and the industry practice is usually on-time payment.) | |
| On April 5: | Creditor's bookkeeper calls debtor, asks for payment. | |
| April 5–10: | No payment. | |

Ch. 7                                    RERANKING                                                271

April 10:       Bookkeeper calls, asks for payment.
April 15:       Debtor writes a check to pay for half of the goods.
April 20:       Check clears.
April 25:       Debtor files for bankruptcy.

Creditor is innocent and knows nothing of insolvency and impending bankruptcy. The creditor has no influence on debtor. The creditor's bookkeeper was just making a credit collection call.

Example #5: Director lends $2000 to her own company, when it has assets of $10,000 and other creditors owed $2000. Later, after the company's value has declined to $2000, director pesters the bookkeeper and gets repaid. Is the repayment a preference in the bankruptcy *six* months later?

* * *

The following two problems are harder and best resolved after fully understanding *Deprizio*.

Example #6: Senior secured is, and has always been, fully secured, and is owed $1000. There's a junior secured due $1000. (The junior secured does not have a subordination arrangement on the debt, but on the security. It can claim out of the security after the senior secured is paid in full, with the senior secured getting first crack at the security.) On February 23rd, when the security is worth $1500, the debtor gets a collection call from the senior's bookkeeper, who says the debtor is late in paying the loan off. The debtor then writes a check for $1000 to the senior. Senior was always fully secured.

Is the payment on February 23rd a preference in the bankruptcy filed on March 1?

(1) Debtor, before payment:

| $1500 security | Senior secured | $1000 |
| $1000 cash | Junior secured | $1000 |
| | Unsecured | $2000 |

(2) Debtor pays senior with cash, then goes bankrupt

Debtor after payment:

| $1500 security | | |
| Preference claim? | Junior secured | $1000 |
| | Unsecured | $2000 |

Example #7: Subsidiary, a chemical company, borrows $1000 from (the former) Chemical Bank, which understands the chemical business. The bank seeks a tight dividend covenant, but the holding company managers, who want to be able to pull cash up from subsidiaries with a bad future and invest that cash in subsidiaries with a good future, resist the tight dividend covenant. The debtor and the bank strike a deal to use a slack (but not trivial) dividend covenant in the loan agreement and for the holding company to guarantee Chemical Bank that the holding company will pay up if the chemical subsidiary doesn't. The chemical subsidiary has $5000 in assets and owes $500 to other creditors.

Later, the chemical subsidiary declines in value. When its operations are worthless and it only has $1000 left in its own bank account, the loan officer seeks repayment. He threatens lawsuit, he calls up the holding company's CFO, and the CFO tells the subsidiary's bookkeeper to pay off the bank. Finally the bookkeeper writes the check out to the bank.

Six months later, the subsidiary files for bankruptcy. The other creditors of the subsidiary are unhappy. Was the $1000 payment to Chemical Bank preferential under § 547(b)?

(1)

| Holding company | |
|---|---|
| Assets<br>C/S of Chemical Subsidiary<br>C/S of Computer Subsidiary | Guarantee to Chemical Bank |

| Chemical Subsidiary | | Computer Subsidiary | |
|---|---|---|---|
| $5,000 | $1000 Chemical Bank<br>500 Creditor A | | |

(2)

| Holding company | |
|---|---|
| Assets<br>C/S of Chemical Subsidiary<br>C/S of Computer Subsidiary | Guarantee to Chemical Bank |

| Chemical Subsidiary | | Computer Subsidiary | |
|---|---|---|---|
| $1000 | $1000 Chemical Bank<br>500 Creditor A | | |

(3) Subsidiary pays the bank the $1000 cash, then files for bankruptcy six months later:

| Holding company | |
|---|---|
| Assets<br>C/S of Chemical Subsidiary<br>C/S of Computer Subsidiary | Guarantee to Chemical Bank |

| Chemical Subsidiary | | Computer Subsidiary | |
|---|---|---|---|
| 0 | $500 Creditor A | | |

¶716: **Questions on** *Deprizio*

1. What is a preference? Is it related to the automatic stay, in that both help to keep the bankrupt estate together, preventing aggressive creditors from dismembering the bankrupt company?
2. How is a preference to an insider treated differently than a preference to an outsider? Why is an insider preference treated differently than an ordinary preference?
3. Were the financial creditors of the Deprizio Corporation insiders? If they weren't, was Richard Deprizio, the principal guarantor, an insider? Must he be a creditor for the insider provisions to be triggered? Did Deprizio hold a *contingent* claim against the company? Did that make him a creditor of the subsidiary? See the Code's definitions of claim and creditor in § 101.
4. If the lender is not an insider, what's the point of making it "pay" for the insider's guarantee by subjecting it to the more severe preference period? Was the statute just badly drafted? What's the policy basis behind the court's reading of the statute?
5. Are there any policy costs to tagging the outside, noninsider creditor with the extended insider preference period? Your client plans to loan to a subsidiary. It believes (as per the Posner reading) that it can assess and monitor the risks of the subsidiary better than it can assess the risks of the entire holding company. But it fears that despite all the protections of the loan agreement (and the limited protections of fraudulent conveyance law and preference law) assets might nevertheless be transferred up from its debtor to the parent company. It fears that thereafter the subsidiary, the expected debtor, will become insolvent. It therefore wants to obtain a guarantee.
6. Is a guarantor always a creditor? Normally a guarantor is subrogated to the loans she pays off. That is, she takes over the loan she has paid, and she can assert the original creditor's claim against the debtor. Is she therefore a creditor, holding a contingent claim against the underlying debtor even before she takes over the loan? Are payments to the creditor payments for the benefit of an insider? Aren't the policy reasons for making loan payments to insiders (if the guarantor is an insider) absent when an insider-guarantor is benefitted?
7. Ordinary course payments are excepted from the bite of § 547(c)(2). As a company slides to bankruptcy, it's not unusual for the firm and its creditors to recapitalize, to have a "work-out" of its debts. The debtor may agree to close one unprofitable factory and use the proceeds to pay off some portion of a major creditor's loan, in return for the major creditor's promise not to accelerate and demand repayment in full. That kind of payment will be out of the ordinary course of business.

How about regular payments of interest under a long-term loan? Do they come under the "ordinary course" exception? Appellate Circuits split, with the Ninth Circuit (for a time) concluding that long-term creditors could not use the ordinary course exception, which the court apparently limited to the debtor's ordinary purchases, which gave rise to a short-term debt that, if paid in a timely manner, would get the ordinary course exception. In re CHG Int'l, Inc. 897 F.2d 1479 (9th Cir. 1990). The Supreme Court took certiorari, read the words of the statute, and concluded that there was no reason why payments on long-term debt were necessarily out-of-the-ordinary, or necessarily ordinary. Facts and circumstances need to be examined. Union Bank v. Herbert Wolas, 502 U.S. 151 (1991).

Judge Scalia concurred in a single paragraph opinion that stated: "It is regrettable that we have a legal culture in which such arguments [from legislative history and policy] have to be addressed (and are indeed credited by a Court of Appeals), with respect to a statute utterly devoid of language that could remotely be thought to distinguish between long-term and short-term debt."

Note that the Supreme Court did not say that the creditor must win. The *Union Bank* decision just stopped the bank from being a sure loser. If the bank loan was not made in the ordinary course or if the actual payment to the bank was not in the ordinary course—i.e., if made during protracted negotiations or with accompanying unusual terms or facts—then the interest payment could be a preference.

8. The Ninth Circuit followed *Deprizio*, In re Sufolla, 2 F.3d 977 (9th Cir. 1993), as did three other circuits. Bankers, the typical beneficiaries of the insiders' guarantees, were unhappy. Proposals, many originating with bankers and their representatives, arose to amend the Bankruptcy Code to overturn *Deprizio*. In 1994 Congress added a new subsection to § 550 (and renumbered the old sections). New § 550(c) reads:

> (c) If a transfer made between 90 days and one year before the filing of the petition—
> (1) is avoided under section 547(b) of this title; and
> (2) was made for the benefit of a creditor that at the time of such transfer was an insider;
> the trustee may not recover under subsection (a) from a transferee that is not an insider.

9. After 1994, who needs advice about the "*Deprizio* problem?" What risks do the other creditors of the subsidiary run when the subsidiary borrows and the lender gets a parent-company (or owner-officer) guarantee? Anticipate the major contracting and strategic problems for deals involving holding company and controlling shareholder guarantees now, after the amendment to § 550.

10. Before Congress amended § 550, what if the guarantor renounced all claims of subrogation in the guarantee agreement? Who would have wanted the guarantor to renounce subrogation?

## ¶717: Priority equalizations across time: Preferences; Lynn LoPucki, Strategies for Creditors in Bankruptcy Proceedings 41 (1985)[7]

### § 2.4 Avoidable preferences in general

Nonbankruptcy collection law encourages creditors to take action against a defaulting debtor. It does this by allowing priority in the distribution of the debtor's assets to unsecured creditors in ... the order in which they ... seize or encumber the debtor's property. Outside bankruptcy the policy for distributing assets among creditors is first come, first served.

Bankruptcy law, on the other hand, honors the maxim that "equality is equity" by favoring a distribution to unsecured creditors pro rata, in proportion to their claims. Asserting its supremacy over nonbankruptcy law, bankruptcy law seeks to impose its policy not only during bankruptcy cases, but also retroactively for a period of 90 days[8] before the filing of the bankruptcy petition. It does this by giving the debtor or the bankruptcy trustee the power to "avoid" transactions which took place during that period and which, if not set aside, would enable the creditors involved to fare better than others who simply waited to share pro rata in the bankruptcy proceeding. Such transactions are "avoidable" as preferences.

Some examples will help to illustrate that preference law is trying to prevent exactly what collection lawyers are trying to accomplish in the period before bankruptcy. In each of these examples it will be assumed that the debtor is insolvent at the time of the transaction[9] and that the debtor's bankruptcy estate is sufficient to pay unsecured creditors only a portion of what is owing:[10]

**Example 1: Payment.** The debtor owes $10,000 to unsecured creditor C. C brings collection pressure and as a result the debtor makes a partial payment of

---

[7] Copyright 1983 by The American Law Institute. Reprinted with the permission of The American Law Institute-American Bar Association Committee on Continuing Professional Education.

[8] The period is one year if the recipient of the preferential transfer is an "insider." See Bankruptcy Code § 547(b)(4)(B).

[9] A transfer can be avoided as a preference only if the debtor was insolvent at the time it was made. See Bankruptcy Code §§ 547(b)(3) and 101[(32)]. There is a presumption of insolvency for purposes of Bankruptcy Code § 547. See Bankruptcy Code § 547(f).

[10] Full payment to an unsecured creditor in the period before bankruptcy would not be an avoidable preference if all unsecured creditors were paid in full in the bankruptcy case. See Bankruptcy Code § 547(b)(5). What is objectionable about the avoidable transfer is that it permits the creditor who received it to recover a greater portion of its debt than other creditors will recover of theirs.

$4,000. Less than 90 days later, the debtor files bankruptcy. The payment is probably an avoidable preference.[11]

**Example 2: Grant of a security interest.** The debtor owes $10,000 to unsecured creditor C. C brings collection pressure and as a result the debtor grants C a mortgage or security interest against some of the debtor's property. C immediately perfects the interest by recording it in the appropriate public records. Less than 90 days after the recording, the debtor files bankruptcy. The grant is an avoidable preference.[12]

**Example 3: Additional collateral.** The debtor, D, owes $10,000 to C. C has a perfected security interest in the inventory of D's business. The inventory has a value of $6,000. D purchases $3,000 of additional inventory, which becomes additional collateral for the $10,000 debt as a result of an after acquired property clause in the security agreement. There is now $9,000 of collateral securing the debt to C. Less than 90 days after D acquired the additional inventory, D files bankruptcy. The addition of collateral to the security for this debt is an avoidable preference.

**Example 4: Execution.** The debtor, D, owes $10,000 to unsecured creditor C. C obtains a judgment against D and levies against D's property. The property is sold at a sheriff's sale and C is paid in full from the proceeds of sale. Less than 90 days after C acquired the execution lien against D's property, D files bankruptcy. The acquisition of the execution lien and the later payment to C [is] an avoidable preference.[13]

Notice that in each of these examples the transaction entered into, if not avoided, would have had the effect of enabling C to collect a greater portion of the debt owing to C than other unsecured creditors would collect of the debts owing to them. It is that improvement in position, as against other creditors, that preference law seeks to prevent.

It is neither illegal nor improper for a debtor to make a preferential transfer or for a creditor to exact one. However, once the bankruptcy proceeding has been filed, the trustee or the debtor in possession can sue to "avoid" the transfer and recover either the property transferred or its value.[14]

---

[11] See Bankruptcy Code § 547(b). However, some transfers which admittedly have a preferential effect are made unavoidable for policy reasons. The payment described here would not be an avoidable preference if the creditor could show that it was "made in the ordinary course of business." Bankruptcy Code § 547(c)(2).

[12] "Transfer" includes the granting of a security interest. See Bankruptcy Code § 101[(54)].

[13] "Transfer" includes involuntary parting with an interest in property. See Bankruptcy Code § 101[(54)].

[14] See Bankruptcy Code § 550(a).

## § 2.5 Implications of the avoidability of preferences

The avoidability of preferences has several implications for unsecured creditors who attempt collection in the period before a bankruptcy has been filed. First, if they extract a preferential payment from a debtor, they should structure the transaction, if possible, in such a way that the payment would not be avoidable in a later bankruptcy. For example, if the creditor has the bargaining leverage to do so, the creditor might insist that the payment be made by a third party ....

Second, most improvements in the position of an unsecured creditor, whether by obtaining payment or security from the debtor, must be regarded as tentative until the preference period has expired. For example, a debtor who wishes to "buy time" from an unsecured creditor can enter into a settlement under the settlement agreement, take advantage of the forbearance thus purchased, then file a chapter 11 proceeding, and, acting as debtor-in-possession, avoid the settlement and recover the payment.

Third, the tentative nature of payments or other benefits extracted from a debtor in financial difficulty must be taken into account in determining whether it will be cost effective to extract them. To illustrate: If a creditor estimates that it will take four months to file suit, obtain a judgment, and obtain a lien by levying on the debtor's property, the collection action can be expected to be futile if the debtor refuses to settle and files bankruptcy within seven months.[15] If an attempt at collection was considered marginal before the avoidability of preferences was taken into account, this additional period of exposure to risk may tip the balance against making the attempt.

Fourth, since many of the debtor's transactions with creditors only become unavoidable 91 days after they are made, other creditors have the opportunity to discover, interpret, and respond to these transactions before they become irreversible. In particular, by observing the pattern of transfers which a debtor makes in the period before bankruptcy, an unsecured creditor may be able to reliably predict the date upon which the debtor will file its voluntary petition and adjust its own strategy accordingly. For example, if the debtor has given a mortgage or security interest to secure a debt owing to a friendly creditor, the debtor probably will not file a bankruptcy proceeding until the preference period on that transfer has expired. On the other hand, if an unfriendly creditor has exacted a substantial preference from a debtor, perhaps by obtaining a judgment lien, there will be a tendency for that debtor to file bankruptcy before the end of the preference period for that transfer.

Possible responses to the discovery of preferential transfers to insiders or others might include the filing of an involuntary bankruptcy petition or a demand to share in the preferential transfers.

---

[15] It will take four months for the collection to be completed .... [I]t will be avoidable in a bankruptcy proceeding filed within three months thereafter, making a total of seven months.

## D. Intercorporate payments in the holding company

### ¶718: Sinclair Oil and intercorporate payments

**Levien v. Sinclair Oil Corp., Court of Chancery of Delaware, New Castle, 261 A.2d 911, December 23, 1969**

[Sinclair owned 97% of a Venezuelan subsidiary, Sinven. A minority stockholder of Sinven, Levien, sued Sinclair, alleging the Sinclair had forced Sinven to distribute heavy dividends. The heavy dividends enabled Sinclair to pursue exploration activities, but denied Sinven the opportunity to explore outside of Venezuela. Between 1960 and 1966 Sinven paid out $108 million of dividends, but earned only $70 million. While the dividends were distributed proportionately to all shareholders, Sinven was thereby denied the opportunity for any new oil investments.

[The court found that Sinclair controlled the subsidiary's Board of Directors. Accordingly, the court held that Sinclair owed a fiduciary duty to Sinven.]

Duffy, Chancellor:

\* \* \*

In times past the Company had interest in oil and gas leases in Texas and in Panama but since 1959, at least, it has operated only in Venezuela. Sinclair, of course, is also in the business of exploring for oil and of producing and marketing crude oil and oil products. It functions as an international oil enterprise in the production, transportation, refining and marketing of petroleum and its products throughout the world.

\* \* \*

Sinclair's majority control of Venezuelan has been implemented by nomination of all members of its Board of Directors .... Those directors were ... officers, directors or employees of other corporations in the Sinclair complex .... [A]t all relevant times the Venezuelan directors were not "independent" of Sinclair. They were not in a position to make judgments as to what was in Venezuelan's best interest, alone, without regard to Sinclair's other operations, and it would be surprising if they were ....

\* \* \*

... [I]n the ordinary case the combination of the [state dividend] statute and deference to business judgment exercised by directors ends the matter. Here, however, we deal with payment of enormous sums to a stockholder fiduciary at a time when the latter had need for large amounts of cash.

\* \* \*

... [P]laintiff [argues that Sinclair took] "opportunities" ... in Alaska, Canada, Paraguay, Algeria, Somalia and other places around the world. He said that these were all opportunities of Venezuelan and could have been taken by it .... [Plaintiff argues]:

"Venezuelan was prevented from expanding, it was prevented from seeking out new sources of revenue, and it was denied the fundamental opportunity of industrial development." Logically, it seems to me, this contention is a companion piece to plaintiff's attack upon the dividends.

* * *

Sinclair voluntarily took on a fiduciary duty. To meet that obligation it could have installed a truly independent board and had it done so the business judgment test might have been dispositive of most of this case. But Sinclair elected not to do that. Looking past form, then, we find Sinclair determining what policies Venezuelan was to follow ....

What, then, did Sinclair cause Venezuelan to do in the years 1960 through 1966? Was the subsidiary in fact denied industrial development and, if so, was that a course of dealing fairly under the circumstances?

The undisputed facts show that from 1960 through 1966 Venezuelan paid out $108,000,000 in dividends ($38,000,000 more than it earned), stockholder equity dropped from $22.99 per share to $12.33, and capital expenditures dropped from a $3,000,000 annual level to a low of $604,000 in 1965. Acreage was surrendered, no more was acquired and the company did not undertake any significant new activity.

This is the picture of a company in partial liquidation.

* * *

It seems to me that these two facets of the case, extraordinary dividends and the absence of any serious efforts to expand or develop industrially when considered together, are significant in showing how Sinclair managed Venezuelan's business. As to the first of these, the overwhelming inferences from the record are, and I so find as facts, that (a) the dividend payments coincided with *Sinclair's* substantial needs for large amounts of cash (Sinclair received 97% of the distributions), and (b) Sinclair's need for cash was the dominant factor in the decision to pay the dividends, particularly in 1963. There is indeed little to show that Venezuelan's corporate needs were weighed in the process. Dividends were first paid only when Sinclair could receive them tax-free, and thereafter the amounts were irregular because they were almost a function of Sinclair's need for cash ....

As to the absence of serious expansion or development efforts, the withdrawal of such enormous amounts of cash obviously had an impact on what the Company could do ....

I find that Venezuelan was not treated fairly because of the extraordinary and large cash withdrawals combined with the absence of any serious effort to add to revenue or to use corporate resources available for that purpose. The result was a drying up of the subsidiary and the only reasonable conclusion is that this was done because it was in the interest of Sinclair to do so. It was not in Venezuelan's.

Sinclair's motion to dismiss the complaint will be denied and an order will be entered in accordance with the rulings made herein.

### Sinclair Oil Corp. v. Levien, 280 A.2d 717 (Del. 1971)

Wolcott, Chief Justice:

This is an appeal by the defendant, Sinclair Oil Corporation (hereafter Sinclair), from an order of the Court of Chancery, 261 A.2d 911 in a derivative action requiring Sinclair to account for damages sustained by its subsidiary, Sinclair Venezuelan Oil Company (hereafter Sinven), organized by Sinclair for the purpose of operating in Venezuela, as a result of dividends paid by Sinven [and] the denial to Sinven of industrial development ....

\* \* \*

Sinclair argues that the transactions between it and Sinven should be tested, not by the test of intrinsic fairness with the accompanying shift of the burden of proof, but by the business judgment rule under which a court will not interfere with the judgment of a board of directors unless there is a showing of gross and palpable overreaching. A board of directors enjoys a presumption of sound business judgment, and its decisions will not be disturbed if they can be attributed to any rational business purpose. A court under such circumstances will not substitute its own notions of what is or is not sound business judgment.

We think, however, that Sinclair's argument in this respect is misconceived. When the situation involves a parent and a subsidiary, with the parent controlling the transaction and fixing the terms, the test of intrinsic fairness, with its resulting shifting of the burden of proof, is applied.

\* \* \*

A parent does indeed owe a fiduciary duty to its subsidiary when there are parent-subsidiary dealings. However, this alone will not evoke the intrinsic fairness standard. This standard will be applied only when the fiduciary duty is accompanied by self-dealing—the situation when a parent is on both sides of a transaction with its subsidiary. Self-dealing occurs when the parent, by virtue of its domination of the subsidiary, causes the subsidiary to act in such a way that the parent receives something from the subsidiary to the exclusion of, and detriment to, the minority stockholder of the subsidiary.

\* \* \*

... [I]t must be determined whether the dividend payments by Sinven were, in essence, self-dealing by Sinclair. The dividends resulted in great sums of money being transferred from Sinven to Sinclair. However, a proportionate share of this money was received by the minority shareholders of Sinven. Sinclair received nothing from Sinven to the exclusion of its minority stockholders. As such, these dividends were not self-dealing. We hold therefore that the Chancellor erred in applying the intrinsic fairness test as to these dividend payments. The business judgment standard should have been applied.

We conclude that the facts demonstrate that the dividend payments complied with the business judgment standard and with 8 Del.C. § 170. The motives for causing the declaration of dividends are immaterial *unless the plaintiff can show that the dividend payments resulted from improper motives and amounted to waste.* The plaintiff contends only that the dividend payments drained Sinven of cash to such an extent that it was prevented from expanding.

*The plaintiff proved no business opportunities which came to Sinven independently and which Sinclair either took to itself or denied to Sinven.* As a matter of fact, with two minor exceptions which resulted in losses, all of Sinven's operations have been conducted in Venezuela, and Sinclair had a policy of exploiting its oil properties located in different countries by subsidiaries located in the particular countries .... [T]he plaintiff could point to no opportunities which came to Sinven. Therefore, Sinclair usurped no business opportunity belonging to Sinven. Since Sinclair received nothing from Sinven to the exclusion of and detriment to Sinven's minority stockholders, there was no self-dealing ....

\* \* \*

## ¶719: Questions on *Sinven*

1. Review Drum Financial's covenant concerning the disposition of insurance subsidiaries in ¶603, at p. 184. Why would the creditors want that covenant?
2. You represent a creditor about to lend to a holding company. Most of the holding company's cash comes from operating subsidiaries. Does the *Sinven* fact situation cause you to raise some issues with the creditor? Does the Delaware court's holding in *Sinven* assure access to the subsidiary's funds when it's in the interest of the parent to give up a business opportunity in the subsidiary so as not to default on a major debt covenant signed by the parent? What covenants might you seek? Cf. Drum Financial Indenture at ¶603 (sale of subsidiary covenant on p. 184).
3. In Tanzer v. Int'l General Indus., 1975 WL 1953, 1 Del. J. Corp. L. 444 (Del. Ch. 1975), the defendant corporation said that it squeezed out the minority shareholders of the subsidiary corporation to facilitate financing of the parent corporation. The issue was whether the corporate purpose needed under Delaware law at that time to justify the squeeze-out was satisfied by facilitating the parent's financing needs.

4. Is there a disclosure issue lurking for lawyers if the creditors are public debenture buyers? If most of the cash to satisfy the debt must come from subsidiaries, must the existence (current or potential) of minority shareholders and consequences of fiduciary duties be disclosed? Cf. Securities rules for disclosure under Regulation S-X, in ¶705, at p. 245.

## CHAPTER 8

# EQUITABLE SUBORDINATION

A. General
B. Equitable subordination of a stockholder's debt claim
C. Subordination of securities law claims

••••••••••••••••••••••••••••••••••••••••••••••••••••••••••••••••••••••••••••••••••••••••••

## A. General

### ¶801: Introduction: Equitable subordination and rescission

In addition to the contract terms that control priority—subordination clauses, security, negative pledge clauses, and use of the holding company—the noncontractual actions of a party to the reorganization may affect the priority of the creditors or stockholders.

If a creditor also controls the debtor-subsidiary as its stockholder, problems arise. The controlling creditor could manipulate the debtor's business to its own advantage as creditor, to the detriment of other creditors. We've already seen one way and one remedy; insiders might prefer to repay themselves as the debtor slides toward bankruptcy. Accordingly, Congress set up a longer, one-year preference period for insiders under § 547. As insiders, the controlling stockholder might give itself beneficial terms when it sells product to (or buys product from) the subsidiary; these sales and purchases could be attacked as fraudulent conveyances. And, as a controlling stockholder it could be liable to other stockholders (preferred and minority common) for mismanagement. Suits against controlling stockholders will usually be judged under the low standard of the business judgment rule, but the controlling stockholder's loan could be the conflict that would deny the stockholder use of the business judgment rule.

In *Taylor v. Standard Gas* (usually referred to as *"Deep Rock"*), we stay with the holding company setting and again examine the treatment of intra-holding company debts due to a controlling stockholder. Does the court in *Deep Rock* simply conclude that the parent company mismanaged Deep Rock and is accordingly liable for that mismanagement? Does the court conclude that *all* debts due to a parent company are, because of the fact of the parent's control, subordinated to all other debts and all other stockholder claims? What is the creditor's conduct that led to the subordination of the creditor's claim in *Deep Rock?*

In *Oppenheimer* and related readings, we shift from the creditor's conduct to the debtor's conduct. We examine treatment of a stockholder's or a contractually subordinated creditor's claim for rescission due to the debtor's fraud in the issuance to it of the stock or debenture. Then, in the next chapter, in *American Lumber* and *W.T. Grant*, we shift back to the creditor's conduct and examine how a creditor's priority can be affected by its aggressive collection of debt or by its efforts to upgrade the seniority or security protecting its loan. Lastly, in *Farah*, we see how a creditor's actions that affect a troubled company outside of bankruptcy can lead to its own liability for the damage and lost earnings that a court finds the lender caused.

## B. Equitable subordination of a stockholder's debt claim

### ¶802: Taylor v. Standard Gas & Electric Co., 306 U.S. 307 (1939)

MR. JUSTICE ROBERTS delivered the opinion of the Court.

The question presented is whether the District Court abused its discretion in approving the compromise of a claim by a parent against a subsidiary corporation and a plan of reorganization based upon the compromise ....

The petitioners are a committee for the protection of preferred stockholders. The respondents are the trustee of the debtor, Deep Rock Oil Corporation ... and Standard Gas and Electric Company, which owns practically all of the common stock of the debtor, claiming as a creditor.

The debtor was organized in 1919 to take over the properties then being operated by one C.B. Shaffer. Standard Gas & Electric Company ... then had investments in various utility properties but had never been interested in oil. [Standard bought Deep Rock from Shaffer for] ... $15,580,000 ... of cash, a note, and [new] preferred and [new] common stock of [Deep Rock] ....

... From its organization Deep Rock was, most of the time, "two jumps ahead of the wolf," as one of Standard's officers testified ....

Thenceforward the debtor was under the complete control and domination of Standard through ownership of the common stock. Standard's officers, directors, and agents always constituted a majority of the Board. The remaining directors were operating officers or employees of Deep Rock who had been employed on behalf of Deep Rock by Standard [or an affiliate] or were under the complete control of Standard. A majority of Deep Rock's officers were officers or directors of Standard or [an affiliate]. The officers of the debtor, who were chosen for their technical or business experience in the oil industry, although allowed some discretion in the matter of development and operation of the oil properties, reported to and were always subject to the direction of officers and directors of Standard. All of the fiscal affairs of the debtor were wholly controlled by Standard, which was its banker and its only source of financial aid.

Deep Rock was placed in the hands of a receiver in March 1933 and the present proceeding under § 77B of the Bankruptcy Act was instituted in June 1934. Standard filed a claim as a creditor ... , which the receivers and the trustee resisted .... The basis of claim was an open account which embraced transactions between Standard and Deep Rock from the latter's organization in 1919 to the receivership in 1933. The account consists of thousands of items of debit and credit ....

The account contains debits to Deep Rock in excess of $52,000,000 and credits of approximately $43,000,000 leaving a balance shown to be due Standard of $9,342,642.37, which was the amount of the claim presented. Cash payments by Standard to Deep Rock, or to others for its account, as shown by the books, total $31,804,145.04. Management and supervision fees paid or credited to [an affiliate of Standard] amount to $1,219,034.83. Interest charges by Standard to Deep Rock on open account balances total $4,819,222.07. Rental charges upon a lease to Deep Rock of oil properties owned by a Standard subsidiary but claimed by petitioners to belong, in equity, to Deep Rock, amount to $4,525,000. Debits by Standard to Deep Rock of the amounts of dividends declared by Deep Rock to Standard, but not paid, reached the sum of $3,502,653. In addition there are hundreds of debits and credits representing other intercompany items.

Two preferred stockholders were permitted to intervene in the proceedings and they joined in the trustee's objections to [Standard's] claim [on Deep Rock]. Many transactions entered in the account were attacked as fraudulent and it was asserted that as Standard had made Deep Rock its mere agent or instrumentality it could not transmute itself from the status of the proprietor of Deep Rock's business to that of creditor .... Standard proposed a compromise of its claim.

... The trustee ... recommended the approval of the compromise, which involved the allowance of Standard's claim at $5,000,000 [not $9 million] ... [and] Standard's claim to the extent of $3,500,000 was to stand on a parity with the debtor's notes [with the remainder of Standard's claim on Deep Rock presumably subordinated].

\* \* \*

Months later the reorganization committee presented an amended plan which, as modified by the Court, contemplated the compromise of Standard's claim at $5,000,000, as before, and the organization of a new company [with more cash distributed to the noteholders and more stock to the old preferred stockholders]. The District Court permitted the petitioners to intervene and, over their objections, approved the compromise and the plan. A majority of the Circuit Court of Appeals examined the record only to the extent of determining that it was possible that Standard might establish its claim in whole or in part, and concluded that the District Court had not exceeded the bounds of reasonable discretion in granting its approval. One judge thought that the instrumentality rule was applicable; that, under the rule, Standard had no provable claim; and that it was an abuse of discretion to approve the compromise and the reorganization plan. We agree with the conclusion of the dissenting judge, but for different reasons.

* * *

Without going into the minutiae of the transactions between the two companies, enough may be stated to expose the reasons for our decision. As has been stated, Standard came into complete control of Deep Rock in 1921. From the outset Deep Rock was insufficiently capitalized, was top heavy with debt and was in parlous financial condition. Standard so managed its affairs as always to have a stranglehold upon it.

At organization Deep Rock had cash working capital of only about $6,600,000 and a mortgage indebtedness of $12,000,000, the interest and sinking fund requirements of which were nearly $2,000,000 a year. Its assets at that time were appraised at about $16,000,000 .... So inadequate was Deep Rock's capitalization that, in the period from organization to 1926, the balance due on open account to Standard grew to more than $14,800,000. Standard determined to place some of this indebtedness of Deep Rock with the public. In order to do so it had to improve Deep Rock's balance sheet. This it did by purchasing 80,000 shares of preferred stock for which it credited Deep Rock $7,223,333.33. It then bought $7,500,000 face value two year six percent notes for $7,273,750, which were sold to the public .... Deep Rock's requirements of additional capital persisted and, by the spring of 1928, *the open account and a note which Deep Rock had given Standard for advances totaled over $11,000,000.* As the two-year notes held by the public were maturing, Standard found it necessary to make a new offering. There still remained nearly $2,000,000 of first mortgage bonds outstanding which had to be retired to make an unsecured note issue saleable. Standard, therefore, determined that Deep Rock's balance sheet must again be put in such shape that notes could be sold. *It accordingly purchased common stock from Deep Rock to the amount of the then open balance and commuted 90,000 shares of the preferred stock, which it held, into common.* It caused Deep Rock to issue $10,000,000 of six percent notes ... and applied the proceeds to the redemption of the two-year notes and the outstanding mortgage bonds. This financing, however, merely changed the character of Deep Rock's funded indebtedness and gave it no new working capital. This $10,000,000 note issue is the one now outstanding. As before, Deep Rock's resources were wholly insufficient for its business and the open account began again to build up so that between February 1928 and February 1933, the date of receivership, the account had grown to $9,342,642.37.

No dividends were paid on preferred stock until 1926. In that and the following year existing arrearages were paid by Standard, for Deep Rock's account, in the amount of $1,435,813. Between 1928 and 1931 Standard advanced Deep Rock, for payment of preferred dividends, $1,106,706.

During the period between 1926 and 1929 Deep Rock declared dividends on its common stock in a total of $3,064,685.50. Of these dividends $1,946,672 was charged by Standard, as owner of common stock, against Deep Rock in the open account. Standard took new common stock for dividends to the amount of $1,015,437.50 and advanced Deep Rock cash to pay dividends to outside holders of common stock in the sum of $102,576. Against the total of $2,645,095 advanced by Standard to pay Deep Rock's dividends, Standard credited payments received from Deep Rock in the open account in the sum of $927,500.

These dividends were declared in the face of the fact that Deep Rock had not the cash available to pay them and was, at the time, borrowing in large amounts from or through Standard.

\* \* \*

[Standard caused Deep Rock to buy various properties for Deep Rock's business. Many of the purchases were done by Standard employees. Some of the properties were held in the name of Standard employees.]

During the whole period from 1919 to the receivership, Standard charged Deep Rock interest at the [annual] rate of seven per cent ... [on] the open account. During the entire period [Standard's affiliate] charged Deep Rock with round annual sums for management and supervision of Deep Rock's affairs which totaled $1,219,034.83, all of which Standard assumed and charged into the open account.

It is impossible within the compass of this opinion to detail the numerous other transactions evidenced by the books of the two companies many of which were to the benefit of Standard and to the detriment of Deep Rock. All of them were accomplished through the complete control and domination of Standard and without the participation of the preferred stockholders who had no voice or vote in the management of Deep Rock's affairs.

The suggested basis of compromise of Standard's claim needs comment. As has been said, when, in 1928, it became necessary to refinance Deep Rock's note obligations, Standard had to wipe out the enormous and threatening credit balance in its favor on Deep Rock's books. It, therefore, took common stock in payment of the balance. It is said that the compromise figure is reached by disregarding all transactions prior to February 24, 1928, when Standard commuted its then claim, starting fresh from that date, and considering only the items in the account thenceforward to the date of receivership .... It is said that this computation of the claim eliminates debits to Deep Rock made since 1928 for the fees of Management Corporation, for dividends on preferred and common stock held by Standard, and for every other questionable item; and that there can be no just criticism of the recognition of Standard's claim in the amount represented by the compromise offer.

Petitioners invoke the so-called instrumentality rule, —under which, they say, Deep Rock is to be regarded as a department or agent of Standard, —to preclude the allowance of Standard's claim in any amount. The rule was much discussed in the opinion below. It is not, properly speaking, a rule, but a convenient way of designating the application in particular circumstances of the broader equitable principle that the doctrine of corporate entity, recognized generally and for most purposes, will not be regarded when so to do would work fraud or injustice. This principle has been applied in appropriate circumstances to give minority stockholders redress against wrongful injury to their interests by a majority stockholder. It must be apparent that the preferred stockholders of Deep Rock assert such injury by Standard as the basis of their attack on the decree below. We need not stop to discuss the remedy which would be available to them if § 77B of the Bankruptcy Act had not been adopted for we think that, by that section, the court, in approving a plan, was authorized and required, as a court of equity, to recognize the rights and the status of the preferred stockholders arising out of Standard's wrongful and injurious conduct in the mismanagement of Deep Rock's affairs.

The section contains a provision new in bankruptcy legislation with respect to the standing of stockholders in corporate reorganization. Subsection (b) provides: "A plan of reorganization ... (2) may include provisions modifying or altering the rights of stockholders generally, or of any class of them, either through the issuance of new securities of any character or otherwise; ...." In the present case there remains an equity after satisfaction of the creditors in which only the preferred stockholders and Standard can have an interest. Equity requires the award to preferred stockholders of a superior position in the reorganized company. The District Judge, we think, properly exercised his discretion in refusing to approve the first offer of compromise and concomitant plan because it partly subordinated preferred stockholders to Standard. The same considerations which moved him to reject that plan required the rejection of the new offer and the amended plan.

Deep Rock finds itself bankrupt not only because of the enormous sums it owes Standard but because of the abuses in management due to the paramount interest of interlocking officers and directors in the preservation of Standard's position, as at once proprietor and creditor of Deep Rock. *It is impossible to recast Deep Rock's history and experience so as even to approximate what would be its financial condition at this day had it been adequately capitalized and independently managed and had its fiscal affairs been conducted with an eye single to its own interests.* In order to remain in undisturbed possession and to prevent the preferred stockholders having a vote and a voice in the management, Standard has caused Deep Rock to pay preferred dividends in large amounts. Whatever may be the fact as to the legality of such dividends judged by the balance sheets and earnings statements of Deep Rock, it is evident that they would not have been paid over a long course of years by a company on the precipice of bankruptcy and in dire need of cash working capital. This is only one of the aspects in which Standard's management and control has operated to the detriment of Deep Rock's financial condition and ability to function. Others are apparent from what has been said and from a study of the record.

If a reorganization is effected the amount at which Standard's claim is allowed is not important if it is to be represented by stock in the new company, provided the stock to be awarded it is subordinated to that awarded preferred stockholders. No plan ought to be approved which does not accord the preferred stockholders a right of participation in the equity in the Company's assets *prior to that of Standard*, and at least equal voice with Standard in the management. Anything less would be to remand them to precisely the status which has inflicted serious detriment on them in the past.

Reversed.

## ¶803: *Deep Rock* problems

1. Was the parent company's claim disallowed? Does it matter financially whether it was disallowed or subordinated?
2. Was the parent's claim affected only to the extent of the mismanagement and inadequate capitalization of the subsidiary? How is (or can) the extent be measured? Did the court simply conclude that the dividends declared by the subsidiary were illegal under local corporate law?
3. What if the advances that the parent made to the subsidiary were those that a third-party lender might have made? How can you tell? If a third-party lender would have made them, why didn't the parties go to a third-party lender? Could the insiders have had informational or other transactional advantages?
4. Companies that fail often will in retrospect appear to have been undercapitalized. The problem of undercapitalization is one of judging the risks as perceived by reasonable business people at the time of the (under) investment. Is this a task easily done by a judge, or for that matter by anyone? See generally Robert Clark, *The Duties of the Corporate Debtor to Its Creditors*, 90 Harv. L. Rev. 505, 520 n.49 (1977), and sources cited therein.
5. Is there any difference between equitable subordination and recovery of a fraudulent conveyance? Professor Clark suggests that the two doctrines deal with similar transactions and reach similar results. Why the two then? He speculates that equitable subordination arose because of the bankruptcy court's incomplete jurisdiction. To recover a fraudulent conveyance, the bankruptcy trustee would have to go into state or federal district court to sue for recovery. (The bankruptcy judge may indeed have had the requisite jurisdiction, but mistakenly thought he did not, or was uncertain whether he did.) However, by subordinating a claim, the bankruptcy court could achieve the same financial result without going outside the bankruptcy court. See id. at 528–29.

Fraudulent conveyance doctrine required precise analysis of terms, evidence and values transferred. Equitable subordination cut through the complexity and uncertainty to simply make the claimant wait until the others were paid. Id. at 530–31. But it'd be fortuitous that the amount owed (and therefore subordinated) was the amount that would have been due if the presumably fraudulent conveyances were precisely analyzed.

6. Is control via stock ownership crucial? If control was obtained via contract (bond covenants, management contract, or other veto over strategy and action), could *Deep Rock* liability be triggered? Cf. infra *American Lumber*, *W.T. Grant*, *Farah Manufacturing*.

## ¶804: *Deep Rock* and corporate planning

1. Subsidiary, an oil company, is worth $1000. Parent company owns all of the subsidiary's common stock. The subsidiary has $1000 (face amount) of preferred stock outstanding with the public. The dividend rate is ordinary. There is no expectation that (absent the considerations noted below) the preferred will be redeemed soon.

| Subsidiary | |
|---|---|
| $1000 | $1000 Preferred |
|  | Common stock |

2. The oil company is drilling for oil. The well will be fully evaluated in the next few months. The best guess now is that the well will be worth either $2000 (for which there is a 50% prospect) or nothing (for which there is also a 50% chance). How much should the preferred trade at in the marketplace? How much should the common stock trade at? (Ignore present value adjustments.)

|  | Outcomes | | | Expected Values | | |
|---|---|---|---|---|---|---|
|  | Company | Preferred | Common | Company | Preferred | Common |
| .5 x 0 | 0 | 0 | 0 | 0 | 0 | 0 |
| .5 x 2000 | 2000 | 1000 | 1000 | 1000 | 500 | 500 |

3. Management of the parent company approaches you, as counsel to the corporate group. Management informs you that the oil engineers have said that with a $1000 investment by the parent in the subsidiary, the expected value of the subsidiary can be increased by $1250. The investment will make certain at least a $1000 return (i.e., no dry well) and will increase the value of the good outcome (the "gusher") by more than $1000, to $3500.

# Ch. 8  EQUITABLE SUBORDINATION  291

4. Would management of the parent company, if properly representing the interests of their stockholders, make the investment by buying $1000 of common stock of the subsidiary? What would the values be of the common stock and the preferred stock after the investment?

| (1) | Outcomes | | | Expected values | | |
|---|---|---|---|---|---|---|
| | Company | Preferred | Common | Company | Preferred | Common |
| .5 x 1000 | ? | ? | ? | ? | ? | ? |
| .5 x 3500 | ? | ? | ? | ? | ? | ? |
| | Total expected value: | | | ? | ? | ? |

5. Could the common stockholders make a deal with the preferred stockholders? Should the preferred be willing to accept payment of between $500 and $750 for the company to buy back the preferred? Should the common stockholders be willing to buy back the preferred for between $500 and $750?

6. Consider the company's alternatives if the preferred and the common cannot make a deal. Could the parent company lend the $1000 to the subsidiary? What are the respective values even if the capital structure is respected? What are the *Deep Rock* risks? If the top row ($1000) is the result, would the company appear in retrospect to have been badly managed? Would it appear in retrospect to have been undercapitalized?

| (2) | Outcomes | | | | Expected values | | | |
|---|---|---|---|---|---|---|---|---|
| | Company | Loan | Preferred | Common | Company | Loan | Preferred | Common |
| .5 x 1000 | ? | ? | ? | ? | ? | ? | ? | ? |
| .5 x 3500 | ? | ? | ? | ? | ? | ? | ? | ? |
| | Total expected value: | | | | ? | ? | ? | ? |

7. This last table shows *Deep Rock* debilitating a worthwhile project. But aren't the numbers loaded? Isn't the problem that parent companies will make such loans and take equity-like risks, because the equity risks redound to their benefit as stockholders? For instance, assume that the original profile for the $1000 company was $1800 or $200, each with equal likelihood:

| (3) | Outcomes | | | Expected values | | |
|---|---|---|---|---|---|---|
| | Company | Preferred | Common | Company | Preferred | Common |
| .5 x 200 | 200 | 200 | 0 | 100 | 100 | 0 |
| .5 x 1800 | 1800 | 1000 | 800 | 900 | 500 | 400 |
| | Total expected value: | | | ? | ? | ? |

The company could increase the value of the entire firm to $1975, with a $1000 investment, with a $1000 loan with an expected value of $975, but whose proceeds would be used to make a risky investment that redounds to the stockholders' benefit:

| (4) | Outcomes | | | | Expected values | | | |
|---|---|---|---|---|---|---|---|---|
| | Company | Loan | Preferred | Common | Company | Loan | Preferred | Common |
| .5 x 950 | 950 | 950 | 0 | 0 | 475 | 475 | 0 | 0 |
| .5 x 3000 | 3000 | 1000 | 1000 | 1000 | 1500 | 500 | 500 | 500 |
| | Total expected value: | | | | ? | ? | ? | ? |

What was the value of the parent company's investment before the loan? What was the total value of the parent company's investment after the loan? Is the loan beneficial to the company as a whole? I.e., does the company's value go up by an amount equal to the amount loaned? If not, why would the parent company make the loan?

The loan is a slight loser from a company-wide perspective, but it enables the stockholder to take extra risk with the preferred, extra risk which is expected to lower the value of the preferred and shift value down to the common. The lender-parent is willing to make the risky loan, because it gets the upside on the stock; it maximizes the value of its common stock stick in the firm's bundle of sticks, at the price of a slightly bad loan. Its willingness to lend is due to its combining of the loan outcomes with the stock outcomes, making this scenario an excellent one for equitable subordination. The problem in putting together an efficient and fair financial system is thus: Can a court distinguish this set of expected outcomes in [4] from the previous set in [2]? The previous set, [1]–[2], is a bad one for justifying equitable subordination; the second set, [3]–[4], is a good one for justifying it. If one concluded that the court was as likely to get it wrong as to get it right, and if firms in such condition have few worthwhile projects, how would you generalize?

8. Can we extricate the holding company from the inefficiencies by using a third-party, arms-length lender? That is, if the third-party lender would make the loan, and doesn't benefit as stockholder, does that "prove" to the judge that the loan should not be equitably subordinated?[1] Third party lenders would not make the

---

[1] Actually, it shouldn't. The loan might just enable the parent company to shift value to itself. But properly understood, this would be attacked as parent company mismanagement of the subsidiary.

| | Outcomes | | | Expected values | | |
|---|---|---|---|---|---|---|
| | Company | Preferred | Common | Company | Preferred | Common |
| .5 x 200 | 200 | 200 | 0 | 100 | 100 | 0 |
| .5 x 1800 | 1800 | 1000 | 800 | 900 | 500 | 400 |

loan outlined above, but they would make the loan in the footnote. Using a third-party loan standard is inadequate if the loan allows the controlling stockholder to shape the risk profile of the subsidiary.

9. And would a bank lend the $1000 in the first hypothetical? See the Posner excerpt, at ¶706. Are there any informational or monitoring disadvantages for the bank? Even if the bank lends, would the prospect of a claim for mismanagement or undercapitalization be avoided? Is the damage claim (or state law veil piercing) less threatening to the parent company than *Deep Rock* subordination?

10. How do you remedy the bank's reluctance to lend? Can it be done in any way that presents no legal risks to the parent company? Consider the values that would be distributed if the subsidiary sold off the oil property *before* the investment. Would a guarantee from a solvent parent of the debt of a shaky subsidiary represent anything different than a loan to the parent by the bank and then a re-lending of the funds by the parent, as a conduit, to the subsidiary? *If* so, then does a guarantee fully shield the parent from *Deep Rock* damage? Is the bank necessarily damaged? Is the bank relying on the creditworthiness of the subsidiary? Or of the parent?

If the bank were relying on the creditworthiness of the guaranteeing parent, shouldn't the same facts that would lead to subordination of a parent company's direct loan lead to subordination of the bank's loan and the parent's subrogation rights?

## ¶805: Partnership liability

Ordinary partners are liable for the partnership's debts. If the creditor has become a partner with the debtor, then the results would be similar to those obtaining under equitable subordination doctrines. Without giving effect to equitable subordination, all creditors would claim on the enterprise and share pro rata. Then the non-partner creditors would claim against the creditor that is deemed to be a partner of the debtor.

Expected value is $1000, with a new loan of $1000, the value will be $1950, but the risk-taking will be worthwhile for the stockholders:

|  | Outcomes | | | | Expected values | | | |
|---|---|---|---|---|---|---|---|---|
|  | Company | Loan | Preferred | Common | Company | Loan | Preferred | Common |
| .5 x 1000 | 1000 | 1000 | 0 | 0 | 500 | 500 | 0 | 0 |
| .5 x 2900 | 2900 | 1000 | 1000 | 900 | 1450 | 500 | 500 | 450 |

The loan and its deployment lowers total company value and reduces the preferred value by $100, but increases equity's value by $50.

## J. William Callison, Partnership Law and Practice: General and Limited Partnership 5-2, 5-26 through 5-30 (1997)

\* \* \*

Uniform Partnership Act (UPA) § 6(1) defines the term *partnership* as "an association of two or more persons to carry on as co-owners a business for profit."

\* \* \*

### [Profit Sharing in Creditor-Debtor Relationships]

Although profit sharing is prima facie evidence that a partnership exists, this is not the case if the profits are received in payment of "a debt by installments or otherwise."[2] It is clear under Uniform Partnership Act (UPA) § 7(4) that a person who loans money to a business and receives a profit share in consideration for the loan does not necessarily become a partner in the business.[3] When a creditor participates in business profits, the greatest legal risk lies in blurring the lines between investing in, and lending to, the debtor or the project being financed.[4] Creditors generally are entitled to repayment of the amount loaned regardless of whether profits exist. However, creditors may at times, particularly in the case of troubled businesses, agree that principal payments will be required only if the business has profits. In such a case, the issue of whether a creditor has become a partner, and is thereby liable to other creditors who extend credit while he or she is a partner is important. For example, assume that Bank A makes a large loan to Partnership XY, which subsequently encounters financial trouble and is unable to make principal payments as required by the note. If Bank A were to work out an arrangement with Partnership XY whereby note payments would equal 75 per cent of Partnership XY's net profits, it would be critical to Bank A that it not be considered a partner in Partnership XY. If Bank A were a partner, creditors of Partnership XY that extend credit while Bank A is a partner would be able to assert that Bank A is jointly liable for partnership obligations ....

The protected relationship under UPA § 7(4)(a) extends to loans which will be repaid from business profits pursuant to their terms. If a debtor-creditor relationship can be shown, the person asserting the partnership's existence will have the burden of

---

[2] UPA § 7(4)(a).

[3] [Section 7(4) of the Uniform Partnership Act states that although "[t]he receipt by a person of a share of the profits of a business is prima facie evidence that he is a partner in the business, ... no such inference shall be drawn if the profits were received in payment ... as interest on a loan, though the amount of payment var[ies] with the profits of the business ...."—Roe.]

[4] See, e.g., In re Washington Communications Group, Inc., 18 Bankr. 437 (Bankr. DDC 1982); Cohen v. Orlove, 190 Md. 237, 57 A.2d 810 (1948).

proving that all elements of the UPA § 6(a) definition are met.[5] UPA § 7(4)(a) only eliminates the evidentiary inference arising from profit sharing and does not protect creditors from being considered partners if the elements of partnership can be proven. Although loan agreements often contain provisions describing the parties' intention to create a loan rather than a partnership,[6] the parties' characterization of their relationship is not controlling ....

If the normal formalities and terms of a loan transaction are absent, the courts are more likely to hold that the purported lender is a partner. For example, in *Minute Maid Corp. v. United Foods, Inc.*,[7] Minute Maid Corporation argued that United Foods, a direct purchaser from Minute Maid, was engaged in a partnership with Cold Storage Corporation, thereby making Cold Storage jointly liable for the unpaid purchase [orders of] commodities [that Minute Maid had] sold to United Foods. In concluding that a partnership existed, the court relied in part on the fact that the transaction between United Foods and Cold Storage did not take the form of a ... loan ....

In addition, the courts have emphasized the degree of control exerted by the purported lender over the business in determining the existence of partnership. For example, in *Minute Maid*, the court held [that the] borrower and the lender jointly exercised ... control over the business enterprise:

> There can be no question but that the parties had joint control over this enterprise. This follows from the fact that United initially determined how much to buy but such determination was subject to Cold Storage's right to determine whether the proposed collateral would be "acceptable." Also it was provided that in case of pending price increases, which the court found would offer the opportunity to speculate on inventory, the parties would agree on the volume to be purchased. In point of fact the responsible officer for United testified that, "they [Cold Storage] could have stepped in and written me [United] off pretty dammed fast ...." [W]e think the operation heretofore outlined was clearly within the joint control of the parties.[8]

On the other hand, *In re Washington Communications Group, Inc.*,[9] the court held that a passive creditor who did participate in management was not a partner. Creditors are frequently given the power to approve or to disapprove significant transactions which might impair their ability to be repaid. Courts have held that lenders are permitted

---

[5] [Section 6 of the UPA says: "a partnership is an association of two or more persons to carry on as co-owners a business for profit."—Roe.]

[6] Careful drafters will include such provisions in their agreements if only to prevent the parties from arguing inter se that they entered into a partnership ....

[7] 291 F.2d 577 (5th Cir.), *cert. denied,* 368 U.S. __ (19__).

[8] Id. at 583.

[9] 18 Bankr. 437 (Bankr. D.DC 1982).

those controls which are necessary to protect the loan, and that the exercise of such controls does not create a partnership with the debtor.[10] To avoid partnership status, the lender should not participate in day-to-day management of the borrower's business, and the loan documentation should be drafted to avoid any implication that the lender has any power to participate in ordinary business management.

The case law indicates that courts allow extensive lender control in "salvage" or "distress" situations. In the landmark English case of *Cox v. Hickman*,[11] the creditors of a financially troubled ironworks exerted substantial, if not complete, control over the debtor's business. The court stated that the creditors ran the business strictly as creditors for the debtor's benefit and not as co-owners, and held that a partnership was not created. The *Cox* decision, and the American cases that have followed,[12] indicate that more control may be exercised by a creditor in a troubled business setting than would otherwise be permitted.

If the percentage of profits allocated to the purported creditor is abnormally high, or if there is no cap on the amount of profits which can be received by the purported creditor, courts have found a partnership between the creditor and the debtor. In *Minute Maid Corp. v. United Foods, Inc.*,[13] where a partnership was found to exist, the purported lender had a continuing interest in business profits beyond the amount required to repay its loan. Further, in *In re Krau*,[14] the court held that there was a partnership where the purported creditor's share of profits would not end when its loan was recouped. Where the creditor's share of profits is limited to a specified dollar amount, courts have held that there is no partnership.[15]

If loan repayment is entirely contingent on the existence of profits, courts are more likely to hold that a partnership exists between the purported lender and the borrower. For example, in *Parker v. Northern Mixing Co.*[16] the court held that although "an agreement to share profits alone is not conclusive evidence of the existence of a partnership," a lender's receipt of profits is evidence of a partnership where repayment is contingent on profits:

---

[10] See, e.g., Meechan v. Valentine, 145 U.S. 611 (1892); Spier v. Lang. 4 Cal. 2d 711, 53 P.2d 138 (1935); Martin v. Peyton, 246 N.Y. 213, 158 N.E. 77 (1927) (lender permitted to veto speculative ventures but not to initiate any transaction).

[11] 11 Eng. Rep. 431 (1860).

[12] See, e.g., Martin v. Peyton, 246 N.Y. 213, 158 N.E. 77 (1927).

[13] 291 F.2d 577 (5th Cir.), cert. denied, 368 U.S. 928 (1961).

[14] 37 Bankr. 726 (Bankr. E.D. Mich. 1984).

[15] See, e.g., Martin v. Peyton, 246 N.Y. 213, 158 N.E. 77 (1927); Cox v. Hickman, 11 Eng. Rep. 431 (1860).

[16] 756 P.2d 881, 887 (Alaska 1988).

In general, an advance of funds is a loan (and thus does not indicate the creation of a partnership relation) if its repayment is not contingent on the profits of the enterprise; if repayment is contingent on profits, it tends to demonstrate the existence of a partnership because the funds are at risk in the business rather than being made the personal responsibility of the borrower.[17]

## C. Subordination of securities law claims

### ¶806: Oppenheimer v. Harriman National Bank & Trust Co., 301 U.S. 206 (1937)

For some years prior to the occurrences out of which this litigation arose the defendant bank was doing business in New York City. Being unable to meet current demands, it closed March 3, 1933. March 13 a conservator was appointed; October 16 the comptroller declared it insolvent and appointed a receiver ... May 31, Oppenheimer brought this action in the federal court for the southern district of New York to recover damages upon an executed rescission of a sale to him of stock of the bank by means of fraudulent representations made by its president and vice president .... The Circuit Court of Appeals ordered that judgment for the amount demanded in the complaint be entered against the bank collectible out of assets of the receivership after payment in full of all who were creditors when the bank became insolvent ....

Plaintiff applied for a writ of certiorari, contending that the Circuit Court of Appeals erred in holding that his judgment is not entitled to rank with other unsecured creditors' claims and that its ruling conflicts with decisions of other Circuit Courts of Appeals ....

November 1, 1930, plaintiff purchased 10 shares of the bank's stock for $15,120. He was induced to buy the stock by false and fraudulent representations of the president and vice president of the bank .... Later, on May 6, 1933, he gave the bank notice of rescission [and] tendered it the certificate .... The bank rejected his demand; he brought this suit for $12,187 with interest and costs ....

[Is the] plaintiff's judgment ... entitled to share equally in the receivership estate with other unsecured creditors' claims[?]

In 1930 when the bank by false representations sold him the stock and by that means obtained the price out of his deposit it immediately became bound to make restitution. The fraudulent sale was subject to rescission by the plaintiff at any time before the bank closed. Neither lapse of time while plaintiff remained ignorant of the fraud nor insolvency of the bank detracted from its liability. We assume that after March 3, 1933, the bank was without means sufficient to meet current demands and that its debts exceeded the value of its assets plus the statutory liability of its stockholders. After the appointment of a conservator, but some months before the comptroller declared the bank insolvent, the plaintiff rescinded and brought this suit. He

---

[17] Id. at 887.

claims no lien, preference, or priority but merely seeks to share in the estate as do other unsecured creditors.

\* \* \*

[P]laintiff's judgment is entitled to rank on a parity with other unsecured creditors' claims.

---

### ¶807: John Slain & Homer Kripke, The Interface Between Securities Regulation and Bankruptcy—Allocating the Risk of Illegal Securities Issuance Between Securityholders and the Issuer's Creditors, 48 N.Y.U. L. Rev. 261 (1973)[18]

[Synopsis]

Securityholders who assert rescission claims against their issuer are presently afforded special treatment in bankruptcy [under *Oppenheimer* and subsequent cases]. Despite the fact that they are conscious risk-takers, these claimants are allowed to share equally with, or to take before, general creditors. Professors Slain and Kripke argue that this treatment gives inadequate recognition to interests which ought to be, and are in other contexts, protected in a bankruptcy distribution. Applying traditional concepts of reliance and laches, the authors propose a system which more nearly harmonizes securities law policies with those of the Bankruptcy Act.

Not many doctrines have passed more fully into the collective consciousness of the legal and commercial communities than the absolute priority rule, which states this prohibition: in bankruptcy, stockholders seeking to recover their investments cannot be paid before provable creditor claims have been satisfied in full. Nevertheless, there is a class of cases not subject to this rule under current practice. In these cases a dissatisfied investor may rescind his purchase of stock or subordinated debt by proving that the transaction violated federal or state securities laws. Under such circumstances, it is currently held that the investor's claim ... shares pari passu with ... claims of general creditors.

While rescission cases arise in a wide variety of factual contexts, they all have two characteristics in common: First, they disappoint the general creditor's expectation that in bankruptcy his claims will be paid out ahead of equity claims; secondly, they assume that the interests protected by federal and state securities regulation should take precedence over all other interests normally taken into account when dealing with claims against a distressed enterprise.

\* \* \*

In this article, we question the basic wisdom of treating rescission claims any differently from equity claims in bankruptcy cases. It is our thesis that the present ap-

---

[18] Copyright, 1973, New York University Law Review. Reproduced with permission.

proach is wrong and that the problem should be reconceptualized as one of risk allocation. In our view, in any such allocation one interest should be weighted far more heavily than at present: the reliance interest of persons having the normal expectation that equity investment and junior debt will bear the first losses of the enterprise.

# I

## The Mis-en-Scene

The inequity of allowing rescinding shareholders to share equally in bankruptcy with general creditors can be demonstrated by use of a hypothetical. Assume XYZ, Inc., having just been organized to engage in the widget business, requires an additional $300,000 of capital to start up. XYZ's management, either directly or through investment bankers, searches for a group of substantial investors prepared to provide the $300,000 and accept equity risks. They locate one such investor, H, who has a personal investment portfolio of several million dollars. Prior to his retirement, H was employed as a portfolio manager for a financial business and is concededly a "sophisticated investor." H meets the principals in XYZ, investigates the affairs and prospects of the company to the extent he deems necessary, calls for and receives financial statements, and purchases 30,000 shares of XYZ's common stock for $180,000. Mr. H recognizes that the widget business provides both high risk and high return and is, in short, speculative. Another 20,000 shares are sold for $120,000 to others less sophisticated, who are impressed by the information that the sophisticated Mr. H is participating.

XYZ begins operations and for six months after H's stock purchase conducts an active business. The corporation quickly incurs $1,000,000 in liabilities to unsecured lenders and open-account vendors who have advanced money or credit in reliance on the general knowledge that XYZ has sold $300,000 of stock. XYZ does not prosper. Seven months after H's purchase, the corporation files a petition under Chapter XI of the Bankruptcy Act, and the reorganization quickly ripens into a straight bankruptcy proceeding. In this proceeding, H asserts a claim for rescission of his $180,000 stock purchase, alleging that the issuer violated § 5 of the Securities Act of 1933. (Securities Act.) XYZ's trustee in bankruptcy attempts to show that the issue was exempted as a nonpublic offering under § 4(2) of the Act, but fails when he is unable to demonstrate that all the persons to whom the $300,000 in stock had been offered were "sophisticated" and had access to the same information that would have been available had the stock been registered under the Securities Act.

As will be demonstrated, it is probable that H has a claim entitled to share pari passu with the claims of general creditors ....

The claim asserted by H in our hypothetical is unusual: a knowledgeable buyer does not often use an issuer's Securities Act violation to opt out of his investment if he has not actually been prejudiced by the violation. More commonly, a stockholder seeking to rescind will assert some claim of misrepresentation (or nondisclosure) of material information in connection with his purchase. Yet from the general creditor's point of view, the injustice of assigning to him a status merely equal to ... that of a rescinding shareholder does not depend on the basis of the shareholder's claim. In extending credit, he has relied on the operation of the absolute priority rule in case of bankruptcy. Furthermore, in shifting his priority position, the courts impose upon him the burden of a risk he has never assumed and should not be made to assume—the possibility of a defective stock issue.

To avail himself of the present exception to the absolute priority rule, the shareholder may base his rescission claim on one or more of several federal and state statutes and common law rules. A transaction may violate the Securities Act in two respects: it may be an unregistered nonexempt public offering of securities or it may be effected through the use of a deceptive prospectus. Section 12(1) of the Securities Act allows rescission by the purchaser in the first situation, and Section 12(2) allows rescission in the second. Alternatively, Section 12 of the Act affords a claim for damages to the stockholder who has sold his shares and thus cannot retender them to the corporation. An issuer's conduct may also violate other sections of federal securities law, most obviously the antifraud provisions of Section 17(a) of the Securities Act or rule 10b-5 under the Securities Exchange Act of 1934 (Exchange Act). Each of these may be the predicate of a private action in which either rescission or damages are claimed by a continuing stockholder or damages are claimed by a former stockholder.

\* \* \*

We are only incidentally concerned with the precise predicate of a disaffected stockholder's efforts to recapture his investment from the corporation. For present purposes it suffices to say that when the basis of the stockholder's disaffection is either the issuer's failure to comply with registration requirements or the issuer's material misrepresentations, one or more state or federal claims may be made. Our purpose is to consider the impact of such claims on the distribution of the corporation's assets in bankruptcy and the development of a plan of reorganization under Chapter X.

... Typically ... two classes of investors benefit most dramatically from the availability of securities law remedies in bankruptcy: stockholders and subordinated lenders such as the holders of [a] ... subordinated debenture.

Some securityholders may not benefit from their securities law rights, since their contracts with the issuer often provide for equal or superior remedies. For example, the note evidencing a bank loan made to an issuer is a security, and if the loan has been obtained by misrepresentation, securities law remedies may be available to the bank. Since, however, the bank is already a creditor, these remedies will not ordinarily improve the bank's position vis-a-vis the issuer's general creditors. Assuming it holds documents in reasonably conventional form, the bank may demand its money by reason of an acceleration clause and may have a security interest in some assets of the issuer .... Except in a rare case, it is unlikely that the availability of securities law remedies will add significantly to the bank's bundle of rights.

By contrast, investors in stock or in subordinated debentures may be able to bootstrap their way to parity with ... general creditors even in the absence of express contractual rights. This unexpected result is the product of the unthinking application of the policies underlying the securities laws at the expense of policies underlying bankruptcy distribution. Since this favored treatment is clearly outside the original contemplation of both the securityholders and the general creditors affected, it is with securities of this type that we are concerned. Hereafter, the discussion is focused upon the rescinding stockholder. Mutatis mutandis, the discussion is equally applicable to holders of subordinated debentures and to other creditors whose debt securities are contractually subordinated ....

### C. Classification of Creditors—Reliance

[A] distinction [ought to] be drawn between general creditors who have relied upon the stockholder's undertaking and those who have not. The strongest reliance case would thus be made by parties who became creditors after the stockholder's investment and after viewing a financial statement which reflected the stockholder's investment in equity accounts.

\* \* \*

If a contract law reliance test is applied between the rescinding stockholder and the post-investment general creditor, we suggest that the burden of proving non-reliance be placed on the stockholder. Creditor reliance may often be genuine but not susceptible of easy proof. Consider the case of the supplier who does not see a balance sheet and is unaware of a particular stock issue. Such a creditor may, in fact, rely derivatively on the stockholder's investment. Credit managers talk to one another. Any creditor who follows an issuer's affairs with any degree of regularity, by, for example, drawing Dun & Bradstreet reports or by reviewing financial statements, is likely to reveal his impressions to fellow credit suppliers. A stockholder's failure to seek rescission thus becomes an important part of a misleading picture seen vicariously. Reliance of this kind, while difficult to demonstrate, is nonetheless real.

If reliance is to be the touchstone between creditor and rescinding stockholder, a distinction should be drawn between credit obligations incurred before and after the stockholder's investment. An occasional case may arise in which a prior creditor can demonstrate that he later changed his position in reliance on the stockholder's investment. For example, a creditor may release a security interest, renew a term loan or waive an event of default upon learning of an apparent improvement in the debtor's equity position. In general, however, it is unlikely that a prior creditor will be able to show even derivative reliance. Consequently, while subsequent creditors should be presumed to have relied on the rescinding stockholder's investment, prior creditors should be required to sustain the burden of proving their detrimental reliance ....

## VI
## Recommended Solution

We propose that a new approach be taken to the competition in bankruptcy between rescinding stockholders and general creditors. There are three aspects to our formulation:

1. We propose that each creditor of a distressed enterprise be presumed to have relied upon each prior investment in equity and junior debt. The corollary is that the rescinding investor should be barred from competition with any subsequent creditor unless, and to the extent that, the investor can prove nonreliance by the subsequent creditor.
2. As to prior creditors, we would shift the burden of proof, permitting the rescinding investor to share pari passu with each prior creditor unless, and to the extent that, the prior creditor can prove detrimental reliance upon the investor's participation.
3. We propose that a rescinding shareholder be barred by the doctrine of laches from competing with any creditor, prior or subsequent, if the investor has failed to assert his claim within a reasonable time after learning of its existence.

## VII
## Conclusion

The absolute priority rule mandates the complete subordination of equity claims against a bankrupt to the claims of general creditors. Yet, under present law, a shareholder can escape the effects of the rule if he can prove a right to rescind his purchase. Establishment of such a claim will give him equality with or perhaps priority over general creditors. Although it is arguable that such treatment accords with policies of the securities acts, it takes no account of the rules and policies of bankruptcy distribution.

In particular, the present exception allocates to the general creditor risks of business insolvency and illegal stock offering which should be borne by the equity investor. The exception does not acknowledge the fact that the general creditor relies on the existence of an equity cushion in case of his debtor's bankruptcy. The exception allows a shareholder with a known rescission claim the option of retaining his interest if an enterprise prospers or reclaiming his investment if it fails. In sum, the exception gives full recognition to the interests of shareholders, but neglects the interests and expectations of laborers, lenders and trade creditors. We suggest that the exception be reconsidered in light of these interests.

\* \* \*

The policies of state and federal securities regulation are important; they are not transcendental. In case of corporate bankruptcy, the public interest favoring private remedies for the violation of these laws must be balanced against other interests worthy of protection—notably the reliance interests of laborers, lenders and trade creditors. Adoption of the rules we have suggested would strike a more equitable balance among these interests.

## ¶808: Bankruptcy Code, § 510

In 1978, Congress reacted, enacting § 510, whose subsection (b) subordinates securities law claims against the bankrupt debtor. In its entirety, § 510, as subsequently amended, reads:

**§ 510. Subordination**

(a) A subordination agreement is enforceable in a case under this title to the same extent that such agreement is enforceable under applicable nonbankruptcy law.

(b) For the purpose of distribution under this title, a claim arising from rescission of a purchase or sale of a security of the debtor or of an affiliate of the debtor, for damages arising from the purchase or sale of such a security, or for reimbursement or contribution allowed under section 502 on account of such a claim, shall be subordinated to all claims or interests that are senior to or equal the claim or interest represented by such security, except that if such security is common stock, such claim has the same priority as common stock.

(c) Notwithstanding subsections (a) and (b) of this section, after notice and a hearing, the court may—
> (1) under principles of equitable subordination, subordinate for purposes of distribution all or part of an allowed claim to all or part of another allowed claim or all or part of an allowed interest to all or part of another allowed interest; or
> (2) order that any lien securing such a subordinated claim be transferred to the estate.

## ¶809: *Oppenheimer*, Slain & Kripke, § 510, rescission and fraud

1. Does § 510(b) overturn *Oppenheimer*?
2. What is the policy basis for subordinating rescission and fraud claims of lower level claimants and interests to all higher level claimants and interests? Is it the financial fact that creditors have knowledge of, and rely upon, bankruptcy law's absolute priority rule? What does such a relying creditor know about the securi-

ties laws? Can these creditors get legal advice on the consequences of bankruptcy law but be unable to find lawyers who can advise them about securities law?

3a. Is there a sound policy basis to disallow ranking a tort claim arising from a fraudulently-induced investment as a general creditor's claim? Where does the reliance interest lie? Why shouldn't the defrauded securityholder be allowed to rely on the integrity of the prospectus and financial statements he or she reviewed before buying the security?

3b. Does § 510(b) undermine the policies of the securities laws just at the moment in a company's life when those policies become critical, i.e., protecting securities claimants against deceit or irregularity in the issuance of stock of shaky companies?

3c. Who makes bankruptcy law? Institutional creditors, like banks, insurers and finance companies, see the virtues of their being repaid. Debtors, managers, and employees see the virtues of rehabilitation and of the firm not being liable on securities law claims. These two groups—debtors, their managers, and institutional creditors (and lawyers for each)—are acutely interested in bankruptcy law. Securities issuers, underwriters, institutions holding public debt and equity bump into bankruptcy less often. Hence, they are less acutely concerned with bankruptcy results.

4a. XYZ Corp. sells a Magic Pill at $1,000 each to 1,000 customers, guaranteeing that it will cure baldness. A class action for fraud results in a judgment of $1 million against XYZ. In the subsequent bankruptcy, how does the class split up the $1 million in cash left in XYZ with XYZ's $1 million creditor?

4b. XYZ Corp. sells 1,000 shares of stock to new shareholders at $1,000 per share, under a prospectus that states, "Our new product, the Magic Pill will cure baldness." A securities class action brings in a judgment of $1 million against XYZ and in favor of the defrauded stock purchasers. In the subsequent bankruptcy, how does the stock class split the $1 million in cash left in XYZ with XYZ's $1 million creditor?

4c. Distinguish ¶4b from ¶4a, if that is possible.

4d. On what did the creditor rely? What is reasonable? For an informed institutional creditor could reliance depend on the bankruptcy rule? Or should the Bankruptcy Code depend, as § 510(b)'s content and Slain and Kripke's analysis suggest, on what creditors might think before they learned of the Bankruptcy Code's and the securities law's provisions?

5a. Company A sells stock to X for $50. A defrauded X. Had X known the true facts, he would have paid $20.

5b. A goes bankrupt before the proceeds of the stock sale are dissipated. A owed $50 to creditor C, but its only assets are from the stock sale. (I.e., A is insolvent.) If X were allowed to rescind, wouldn't X have avoided both the fraud loss and the business risk loss it would have willingly accepted for $20? What result under § 510(b)?

6a. Same numbers as in 5a. In addition, A, after the stock sale, is worth $100 and owes $50 to D. X sues in fraud and recovers $30, thereby reducing A's value to $70. A dissipates $40 in the next year or so, then goes bankrupt. Summarize the distributional results.

6b. Same numbers as 5a and 6a. However, while X is suing for fraud, A dissipates $40, defaults under a covenant in the loan agreement with D, and voluntarily files for bankruptcy. What distributional result?

6c. Same numbers. The stock sale by A to X was underwritten by Z, the investment banking firm, which was aware of the fraud. A and Z go bankrupt. X asserts securities law fraud claims against A and Z. A has contract debt of $50 and the company had a value of $48 at the time of bankruptcy. What distributional result?

6d. Same as 6c. A agreed to indemnify Z for any claims arising under securities laws. If such an agreement were enforceable, cf. *BarChris*, what distributional result? What does § 510(b) say about claims for reimbursement and contribution relating to securities law claims? See generally Kenneth Davis, *The Status of Defrauded Security Holders in Corporate Bankruptcy*, 1983 Duke L.J. 1 (1983).

7a. Does § 510(b) always render a securities issuance claim valueless to the defrauded investor? Could it conceivably increase the *amount* of the claim, even if it could not affect the claim's priority? Cf. §§ 1124, 1129(b).

7b. Could it give cause for a separate class? What if some subordinated creditors were defrauded, but others not? Should there be a separate class for the fraud claims? Do they then get at least the nuisance value needed to purchase their consent? Cf. § 1129(a)(8).

---

### ¶810: Does subordination make the rescission or damages claim useless, always?

The bankrupt company is worth $2000, with $1000 of senior debt, $1000 of subordinated debt, and an issue of preferred stock. The subordinated debt has a low interest rate. If § 1124 were successfully invoked against them, the market value of their claim would be $500. The subordinated bondholders were defrauded in the issuance of their securities.

| $2000 | $1000 Senior |
|---|---|
| | 1000 Subordinated at 7%, worth $500 if § 1124(2) used |
| | Preferred stock |
| | Common stock |

The 7% debentureholders would like to assert a fraud claim for $1000 as a general creditor of the bankrupt, but they can't because of § 510(b). And § 1124 hurts them further.

Is this the balance sheet of the bankrupt company after invocation of § 1124 and subordination of the debentureholders' fraud claim under § 510(b)?

| $2000 | $1000 Senior |
| | 1000 [Contractually] Subordinated at 7%, worth $500 if § 1124(2) used |
| | 500 fraud claim (subordinated due to § 510(b)) |
| | Preferred stock |
| | Common stock |

## ¶811: Reranking

End of story? Can the damaged securities buyers sue the underwriter, the accountants, and management for their acts in the securities violations? Can these third parties then assert contractual claims for indemnification against the issuer? Will the indemnification claims be subordinated?

Rarely do courts stay proceedings against co-defendants of a bankrupt, even though § 362 stays proceedings against the bankrupt. Melvyn Weiss, William Lerach & Jan Adler, *Obtaining Adequate Monetary Relief for Shareholders of Bankrupt Public Companies: The Nearly Impossible Dream, in* Complex Litigation in the Context of the Bankruptcy Laws 11, 16-24 (Michael Perlis ed. 1984) (Practicing Law Institute) (collecting authorities).

Consider a suit against an investment bank for fraud in the issuance of a security. Outside of bankruptcy, the investment bank would usually have a claim, if the underlying plaintiff's suit for fraud is successful, for contribution or indemnity against the bankrupt corporation. Although some bankruptcy courts have decided that the claim for indemnity may only be asserted to the extent of the underlying claim (which would be subordinated under § 510(b)), does the statute explicitly cover indemnity claims?

In 1984 Congress amended the original form of § 510, adding the phrase "or for reimbursement or contribution ... on account of such a claim [for rescission or damages in the purchase or sale of a security]." See § 510 in its entirety at ¶808. In Christian Life Center Litigation Defense Comm. v. Silva, 821 F.2d 1370 (1987), deciding a case that arose before the phrase "for reimbursement or contribution" was added in 1984, claims for contractual indemnity for litigation expenses—but not for liability—were reimbursable. Similarly-situated creditors failed after 1984. Official Committee of Unsecured Creditors v. PaineWebber Inc., D.C.C.Cal., No. CV90-3663

(WJR Feb. 21, 1991) (claims for contractual indemnity for litigation expenses not reimbursable). See also In re Investors Funding Corp., 8 Bankr. 260, 264 (S.D.N.Y 1980); In re Georgian Villa Inc., 9 Bankr. 969, 9732 (N.D.Ga. 1981).

---

### ¶812: Transition problem

Bank lends to Corporation, a publicly-held firm. Corporation's fortunes then decline to an extent greater than is publicly known. Bank informs the management of Corporation that, absent an increase in their equity cushion, Bank will call its loan (or fail to renew the credit upon its maturity).

Thereafter Corporation issues common stock to the public under a prospectus that fails to disclose the full extent of its ill-fortune. In the subsequent bankruptcy the defrauded stock purchasers seek to assert a claim other than as stockholders. What result under § 510(b)? Under § 510(c)? Cf. *W.T. Grant* and *American Lumber*, next chapter.

## CHAPTER 9

# MORE ON CREDITORS' CONDUCT

**A. Equitable subordination of a creditor's claim**
**B. Lender liability**

•••••••••••••••••••••••••••••••••••••••••••••••••••••••••••••••••••••••••••••••••••••••••••••

Must the creditor have a stock interest to justify equitably subordinating the creditor? The legislative history to § 510(c) says:

> Section 510(c)(1) of the House amendment represents a compromise between similar provisions in the House bill and Senate amendment. After notice and a hearing, the court may, under principles of equitable subordination, subordinate for purposes of distribution all or part of an allowed claim to all or part of another allowed claim or all or part of an allowed interest to all or part of another allowed interest. ... It is intended that the term "principles of equitable subordination" follow existing case law and leave to the courts development of this principle. To date, under existing law, a claim is generally subordinated only if the holder of such claim is guilty of inequitable conduct, or the claim itself is of a status susceptible to subordination, such as a penalty or a claim for damages arising from the purchase or sale of a security of the debtor. The fact that such a claim may be secured is of no consequence to the issue of subordination. However, it is inconceivable that the status of a claim as a secured claim could ever be grounds for justifying equitable subordination.

Senate Report No. 95-989, 95th Cong., 2d Sess. 74 (1978).

## A. Equitable subordination of a creditor's claim

### ¶901: In re American Lumber Co., 7 Bankr. 519 (1979)

[American Lumber was formed in January 1975. It obtained its financing largely from defendant bank.]

7. After January 17, 1975, ALC [American Lumber Company] commenced operation of a wholesale lumber business. It purchased lumber, held it in inventory and sold it to residential and commercial buildings. The building and lumber business climate in the summer and fall of 1975 was unfavorable and ALC suffered losses in the following amounts:

| | | |
|---|---|---|
| May | 1975 | $27,144.00 |
| June | 1975 | $31,380.00 |
| July | 1975 | $102,360.00 |
| August | 1975 | $42,380.00 |

* * *

9. On September 19, 1975, defendant loaned ALC $100,000.00, evidenced by a demand promissory note. The loan was made because ALC was short of cash.

* * *

11. On October 17, 1975, the three principals of ALC met with ... officers of defendant, and advised them that the loan was in default and ALC was acutely short of cash, and proposed a "cut-back" plan designed to improve the financial stability of ALC.

* * *

13. On October 21, 1975, a meeting was held at the office of defendant-bank. It was attended by bank officers Shepley and Dingman, two of its counsel, Jerome Simon, Esq. and Charles Bans, Esq., ALC officers Lilja, Kulas and Peterson, and ALC counsel Leo Stern. Shepley announced at the outset that defendant was calling all of the indebtedness of ALC. There was discussion concerning foreclosure of defendant's security interests in the assets of ALC. *Simon learned that defendant had no security interest in the inventory of ALC*, a discussion ensued between defendant's officers and its counsel, and Simon remarked in substance that he had an idea whereby a security interest could be taken on the inventory of ALC, *funds could be advanced by defendant to ALC to increase the value of certain accounts receivable on projects that were not completed and in which defendant had [a] security interest*, and the general creditors could be "screwed." No accommodation was reached during this meeting. Approximately $400,000.00 of unsecured creditors other than defendant existed at that time. Defendant considered placing ALC in bankruptcy.

14. On October 22, 1975, another meeting was held attended by Lilja, Kulas and Peterson of ALC and Shepley and Dingman of defendant. Discussion centered around the value of the interest of ALC in a housing project known as Lame Deer, Montana, in which ALC had made a substantial investment which would be seriously jeopardized if it were not completed. Again, no resolution of the situation occurred. *Plaintiff's officers refused to execute security agreements covering the inventory and equipment of ALC.*

15. On October 23, 1975, Shepley and Dingman of defendant advised Lilja of plaintiff that no further funds would be advanced to ALC, that defendant was declaring ALC in default on its promissory notes and the demand promissory note of September 19, 1975, and that defendant was offsetting all funds in the accounts of ALC with defendant. Such offsets were then made.

16. On October 24, 1975, Dingman hand-delivered a letter from Shepley to Lilja of ALC. The letter recited all the existing defaults, including the failure to pay the ESOT installment due on October 15, 1975 [to the Employee Stock Ownership Trust] and detailed what the bank had done and proposed to do. *Security Agreements describing inventory and equipment of ALC and corresponding financing statements were executed and delivered to defendant.*

17. On October 24, 1975, the liquidation of the business of ALC under the supervision of defendant began.

18. All cash and amounts collected on accounts receivable were given by ALC to defendant, which deposited them into a "collateral" or "dominion" account which was opened at Mr. Dingman's instruction and on which he was the sole signatory. On October 24, 1975, defendant foreclosed upon its security interests in accounts receivable and contract rights and at no time thereafter relinquished its control over the collection of accounts receivable.

19. On October 24, 1975, ALC's obligation on its Guaranty of the $1,000,000.00 loan obligation of ESOT to defendant was unconditional. The only assets of ESOT on that date were 10,000 shares of common stock of ALC which had been pledged to defendant and $93.47 in its general checking account. The common stock of ALC had no value.

20. On October 24, 1975, the fair market value of the assets of ALC were approximately as follows [in thousands of dollars]:

| | |
|---|---:|
| Cash | [—] |
| A/R ... | 1,262 |
| Inventories | 771 |
| Prepaid | 20 |
| Fixed Assets | 512 |
| | 2,566 |

21. On October 24, 1975, the liabilities of ALC were [in thousands of dollars] as follows:

|  |  |
|---|---:|
| Accounts Payable | $570 |
| Accrued Liabilities | 50 |
| Salaries | 30 |
| Long Term Debt | 1,587 |
| Mortgage | 167 |
| Indebtedness on Guaranty to ESOT | 938 |
|  | 3,332 |

22. On October 24, 1975, the liabilities of ALC substantially exceeded the fair and reasonable value of its assets, by $766,500.00 more or less, and ALC was insolvent.

23. Prior to October 24, 1975, ALC had employed Park Detective Agency, Inc. a security guard service, to guard its lumber yard in Minneapolis. On October 24, 1975, defendant contacted Mr. Pavey, President of Park Detective Agency, Inc., and informed him that defendant wished to contract with his firm to secure the premises of ALC. A contract was entered into between Park Detective Agency and defendant on October 25, 1975. Thereafter, defendant instructed Park as to whom could be admitted to the premises and in effect took control over access to said premises. Defendant instructed Park that [bank officers] were to be contacted in emergency situations and gave Park their home telephone numbers. Defendant advised Park it would pay all fees of Park. It paid fees for those services rendered from October 25, 197[5], to March 1, 1976, at which time it discharged Park. Park during this time period received instructions either by telephone or notes from defendant when admitting individuals to the ALC lumber yard.

24. On October 24, 1975, all employees of ALC were terminated. On or about October 31, 197[5], effective October 28, 197[5], ALC rehired a skeleton crew for the year and truck driver employees, an accounts receivable clerk, an accounts payable clerk, two city desk clerks, and a receptionist. Its entire sales force of approximately four employees was not rehired because further sales were not contemplated. Before rehiring those employees identified above, in accordance with instructions from defendant, ALC advised Dingman who in its view were necessary to conduct an orderly liquidation and defendant approved of their rehiring and agreed to honor payroll checks for them .... This conduct was only consistent with orderly liquidation of ALC.

25. On or about October 24, 1975, defendant, by and through Dingman, began receiving and opening the incoming mail at the office of ALC and at all material times thereafter continued doing so on nearly a daily basis. All checks and cash so received were taken by Dingman and deposited into the collateral (dominion) account described in paragraph 18. This conduct was consistent with orderly liquidation of ALC.

26. On and after October 24, 1975, defendant, by and through Dingman, reviewed ALC checks prepared by ALC which had not been delivered to payees and ALC checks presented for payment by payees, and determined whether they respectively would be released or paid. Defendant made such determinations based upon its understanding and belief as to whether or not such payment would likely enhance the value of one or more of the accounts receivables in which defendant had a perfected security interest. When defendant believed there would be such an increase, the check was released or paid; when it believed the contrary, the release or payment was not authorized. General unsecured creditors were not paid unless that test was satisfied. On and after October 24, 1975, defendant did not intend to pay general unsecured creditors. Sales taxes incurred were not approved for payment by defendant. This conduct was only consistent with orderly liquidation of ALC.

27. During the course of meetings between October 17, 1975, and October 24, 1975, much discussion between representatives of ALC and defendant centered on a project known as Lame Deer, Montana which was a government-financed housing development for Indians on and around the Cheyenne Indian Reservation. Defendant was advised that ALC had been awarded a subcontract by G.R. Construction Co., dated July 1975, which had a contract price of $1,026,365.00 payable to ALC if entirely completed. The terms of payment were stated in the subcontract. Under the subcontract ALC had the duty to furnish construction supplies and materials, fabricate them into panels, furnish all of the labor related to fabrication and construction, and construct residences. Payment to be made as residence[s] were completed and accepted. Prior to October 24, 1975, only one payment had been made [to] ALC by G.R. Construction Co. That payment was in an approximate sum of $34,000.00 and ALC anticipated receiving more funds as the project continued. Virtually all materials and supplies required for completion of the project had been delivered to the Lame Deer project site prior to October 24, 1975[.] [H]owever, some additional materials and substantial amounts of labor were necessary. ALC had contracted with Aetna Oak-Mak Construction Co. to furnish all labor on the project. Defendant was advised about the status of the subcontract and decided that the potential high value of the G.R. Construction account receivable of ALC would be in serious jeopardy if the project were not completed and that such jeopardy justified the infusion of more funds for materials, supplies, and labor. This decision was only consistent with an orderly liquidation of ALC.

* * *

37. [In October and November, the bank advanced about $440,000 to the debtor. The advances] were used to pay suppliers, materialmen and laborers in connection with the Lame Deer, Montana project, other projects where failure to pay suppliers, materialmen or laborers would jeopardize the value of an account receivable in which defendant had a security interest or for ALC payroll for personnel critical to the handling of the orderly liquidation of ALC. At least $127,000.00 of said advances were used on or about November 18, 1975, to pay materialmen and

suppliers in connection with the Lame Deer project, and $33,783.78 of said advances were used to pay Aetna Oak-Mak laborers working on said Lame Deer project between October 17, 1975, and December 7, 1975.

\* \* \*

39. On October 24, 1975, defendant decided to not pay general unsecured creditors and at all material times thereafter adhered to that decision.

\* \* \*

45. On or about October 30, 1975, ALC was operating under the supervision of defendant. ALC referred a telephone inquiry made by R.J. Long of the American Lumbermen's Credit Association, a trade credit organization, to defendant's officer Dingman. Dingman told Long that the business of ALC was continuing to the extent of fulfilling current contracts where it was necessary to supply additional material in order to protect the investment already made. Dingman advised Long that ALC was not in a bankrupt situation. Dingman advised Long that it was defendant's intention to run the liquidation on a completely orderly basis and that defendant did not view it as a fire sale situation.

46. On or about November 19, 1975, Dingman again received a telephone inquiry from Long of the American Lumbermen's Credit Association. At that time, *Dingman said ALC was not insolvent on the books,* that ALC continued to operate, was still delivering material on uncompleted contracts, and that defendant was paying cash for a little material necessary to complete such contracts.

47. During this conversation, Dingman represented that defendant was doing everything possible to salvage something for the unsecured creditors, and that the best evidence of this was the fact that defendant was giving ALC enough support to liquidate slowly, rather than on a quick sacrifice basis.

48. *The American Lumbermen's Credit Association disseminated the information received from defendant to one creditor.*

49. On or about November 21, 1975, defendant gave written notice to ALC that it was foreclosing its security agreement obtained on October 24, 1975.

50. On November 3 and 4, 1975, Dingman of defendant-bank and Timothy Peterson of ALC visited Lame Deer, Montana, for the purpose of inspecting the project to determine whether defendant should advance additional funds to complete the project. Dingman determined that the value of the account receivable which could be recovered by completing the contract was substantially in excess of the financial investment it would require. Any value realized would under the then circumstances have redounded solely to the benefit of the defendant.

\* \* \*

52. On or about December 1, 1975, defendant had employed James Haney, formerly construction superintendent with ALC in charge of the Lame Deer project, to

watch the inventory at the construction site. First National agreed to pay Haney for his services, employed him through January 8, 1976, and paid him according to its agreement.

* * *

58. On or about October 24, 1975, defendant advised Lilja, Kulas and Peterson that it was not prepared to finance the salaries which each had been receiving from ALC .... Those salaries had been established at $300,000.00 in the aggregate .... On or about October 24, 1975, defendant told them it was prepared to pay lesser annualized salaries of approximately $30,000.00, $20,000.00, and $20,000.00, respectively, for their services. This was accepted and was a part of the orderly liquidation of ALC.

59. Checks were drawn about December 1, 1975 on the general checking account of ALC payable to Lilja in the sum of $2,190.00, Kulas in the sum of $2,190.00, and Peterson in the sum of $2,190.00. At defendant's demand, each was endorsed to defendant and applied by it to reduce the personal loans of the three principals of ALC. Defendant approved the payment.

60. After October 23, 1975 neither ALC nor its officers or directors had control over the moneys of ALC or have any sources of funds with which to pay suppliers or general unsecured creditors. Defendant exercised absolute control over the use of the funds resulting from its advances to ALC as reflected by promissory notes given between October 24, 1975, and December 2, 1975.

61. Between October 24, 1975, and December 2, 1975, defendant advanced an aggregate of $442,810.74 to ALC. Between October 24, 1975, and December 10, 1975, defendant had received and credited to the indebtedness of ALC the aggregate sum of $410,092.34. By December 11, 1975, such credits totaled $466,187.81. Such credits reflected the collection of ALC accounts receivable.

62. An Involuntary Petition in Bankruptcy against ALC was filed on February 11, 1976, and ALC was subsequently adjudicated bankrupt.

63. Defendant filed its Proof of Claim No. 37 for $1,781,382.69 in the resulting bankruptcy case. The claim included claimed indebtedness of $937,500.00 of ALC resulting from Guaranty of the ESOT indebtedness to defendant.

64. By receiving the proceeds of sales of inventory and equipment of ALC, defendant received proceeds which otherwise would have been available for payment of general unsecured creditors of ALC.

65. When the principals resigned on December 5, 1975, all the books and records of ALC were intact. Defendant changed locks and had sole and exclusive use of the offices of ALC and sole and exclusive access to and control over such records. To the extent any existent records of ALC were not available at trial, such resulted from defendant's failure to properly maintain custody of such books and records.

CONCLUSIONS OF LAW

1. On October 24, 1975, ALC transferred security interests in inventory and equipment to defendant.
2. Said transfers occurred within four (4) months [the pre-1978 ordinary preference period] of the filing of the Involuntary Petition in Bankruptcy against ALC. [Ninety days is the preference period under § 547 of the subsequently-enacted 1978 Bankruptcy Code.]
3. Said transfers were made to secure an antecedent debt of ALC to defendant.
4. Said transfers allowed defendant to obtain a higher percentage of the obligation of ALC to it than other creditors of the same class.
5. Such transfers occurred at a time that ALC was insolvent within the meaning of the Bankruptcy Act.
6. Defendant knew and had reasonable grounds to know of such insolvency.
7. Said transfers constituted voidable preferences under § 60 of the Bankruptcy Act[, the predecessor to § 547 of the 1978 Bankruptcy Code].
8. Said transfers were made without fair consideration.
9. Said transfers were part of a design to liquidate ALC.
10. ALC and defendant knew ALC would incur debts which ALC would be unable to pay as they matured.
11. Said transfers were made with the intent to hinder, delay and defraud existing and future creditors of ALC.
12. Said transfers are recoverable by plaintiff under § 67(d)(2) of the Bankruptcy Act[, which was the old Bankruptcy's Act's fraudulent conveyance provision].
13. Said transfers were fraudulent as to existing and future creditors.
14. Said transfers were made in contemplation of the liquidation of ALC.
15. Said transfers were made with the intention to use the purported considerations therefor, to wit: future advances to enable defendant to obtain a greater portion of the indebtedness of ALC to it than other creditors of the same class.
16. ALC and defendant knew and believed that ALC and defendant intended to make such use of the purported consideration.
17. Said transfers are recoverable by plaintiff [as a fraudulent conveyance].
18. Plaintiff is entitled to judgment in the sum of $488,744.65; representing the aggregate of $346,753.88 received by defendant from the sale of ALC Minneapolis inventory, the $94,554.00 fair and reasonable value of Montana inventory which defendant took into possession on or about December 5, 1975, and the $47,436.77 received by defendant from the sale of equipment, together with interest thereon according to law from January 1, 1976, to the present.

19. On October 24, 1975, and at all material times thereafter, defendant had and exercised control over all aspects of the finances and operations of ALC including the following: payment of payables and wages, collection and use of accounts receivable and contract rights, purchase and use of supplies and materials, inventory sales, the lumber yard in Minneapolis, the salaries of the principals, the employment of employees, and receipt of payments for sales and accounts receivable.

\* \* \*

21. By reason of its exercise of control over ALC and its operation defendant had a duty and an obligation to deal fairly and impartially with ALC and its other unsecured creditors.

22. Defendant breached its duty by undertaking a course of liquidation that was designed solely to preempt from general unsecured creditors any portion of the value of the inventory and equipment of ALC and to thereby enhance the value of defendant's previously existing security interest in the accounts receivable and contract rights of ALC.

23. By reason of said breach of fiduciary duty to the creditors of ALC, defendant's claim shall be subordinated to the claims of general unsecured creditors in the interest of equity.

ORDER FOR JUDGMENT

Let judgment be entered accordingly.

---

### ¶902: Questions on *American Lumber*

1. What were the Bank's business problems in dealing with the failing American Lumber? First, it didn't have a security interest in the company's inventory. Second, it faced a problem generally encountered by creditors of a declining firm. The value of accounts receivable deteriorates when a firm liquidates. When the firm liquidates (as opposed to reorganizing but staying in business), customers have one less incentive to pay the bill on time or in full. One crucial incentive for a customer to pay on time is that the customer wants to deal with the firm again; if the customer fails to pay on time in full, the supplier is less likely to ship the next batch of goods to the customer. But when it becomes known that the supplier is going out of business (i.e., not just in trouble and reorganizing, although sometimes even then, but closing up its shop), some customers find fault with the delivery, state that the supplier breached the contract, or in some cases just do not pay:

> While it is true that under the stress of financial difficulties ordinarily honest debtors do things to their creditors that they would not do in the absence of financial stress, it is also true that financially disabled debtors have things done to them by ordinarily honest persons which would not be attempted if they enjoyed apparently good financial health. When word of financial difficulty spreads, the debtor's own creditors [e.g., its trade creditors] often decline to pay as they

would have in the ordinary course, suddenly reporting that the dresses were the wrong size, were the wrong color, or were not ordered. The more formal the recognition of the debtor's plight, the greater the pressure on it, and the greater the damages through the debtor, to its creditors.

Peter Coogan, Richard Broude & Herman Glatt, *Comments on Some Reorganization Provisions of the Pending Bankruptcy Bills*, 30 Bus. Law. 1149, 1155 (1974).

2. What did the Bank do wrong? Was its taking a security interest in the inventory a basis for equitably subordinating its entire claim? Why isn't that a preference on the eve of bankruptcy? The remedy would usually be the return of the seized security for the benefit of all unsecured creditors (including the Bank, to the extent unsecured). In fact, didn't the court invoke and apply preference law? (Incidentally, don't be confused by the four month preference period in the case, which arose under pre-1978 bankruptcy law. In 1978 Congress changed the basic preference period to 90 days.)

3. What then did the Bank do wrong? Did it "control" American Lumber? How? What implications are there to control? If control put the Bank in a position analogous to that of a controlling shareholder, what analysis? Was the controlling shareholder engaged in an interested party transaction?

4. The Bank misrepresented American Lumber's condition to the trade creditors' credit association. Did that hurt trade creditors as represented on the October 24 balance sheet? Did it hurt new trade creditors? To whom should the Bank be equitably subordinated? To what extent?

5. On October 24 what distribution in bankruptcy to trade creditors and the Bank? Use the balance sheets the court provides.

6. Why the remedy in the final paragraph of the opinion? What did the Bank do wrong? Cf. § 510(c) ("under principles of equitable subordination, [the court may] subordinate ... all or part of an allowed claim"). Administrative convenience? Punishment? Deterrence?

7. Does *American Lumber* follow directly from *Deep Rock*?

8. Consider a comment on an earlier batch of equitable subordination cases:

> The lure of equitable subordination doctrine [is] ... the erroneous but understandable belief of judges that any imprecision in the corrective function of the doctrine typically bears down on and punishes a transferee who was ... at fault ....

Robert C. Clark, *The Duties of the Corporate Debtor to Its Creditors*, 90 Yale L.J. 505, 532 (1977).

9. In the district court affirmation, In re American Lumber Co., 5 Bankr. 470, 478 (D. Minn. 1980), the affirming court said:

> While defendant [bank] argues that subordination will cause members of the financial community to feel they cannot give financial assistance to failing companies, but must instead foreclose on their security interests and collect debts swiftly, not leaving any chance for survival, the Court is singularly unimpressed.

10. A word or two about the interaction between preferences under § 547 and floating liens on inventory or accounts receivable: A business that sells goods, say lumber, will get regular shipments in and regularly sell the product. The Uniform Commercial Code allows "floating" liens, in which a secured creditor has a lien in the "pool" of lumber, although the contents of the "pool" might change daily. Each new receipt of lumber by the debtor is a transfer that benefits the secured creditor and accordingly *could* be viewed as a preference (if the other criteria were met). That is, all the lumber shipped into the debtor in the 90 days before bankruptcy benefits the secured creditor, setting up a preference situation. The lumber may be worth, say, $100,000 90 days before the bankruptcy and the total value may stay more or less constant for the 90 days, but the actual physical lumber on the day of bankruptcy may differ completely from the lumber in the lumberyard 90 days before: Lumber was sold to customers and new lumber came in from the suppliers and, over 90 days, all the original lumber could have been replaced. Is each new shipment from a supplier a potential preference?

    The Code excepts floating liens in § 547(c)(5) from preference attack: If the creditor did not improve his or her aggregate position during the 90 day period before bankruptcy (one-year for insiders), there's no preference. If new shipments made the value of the lumber in inventory higher on the date of petition than it was 90 days before the petition, then the increase might be preferential (if the other criteria are met).

    (Note that if the creditor improves in position due to the market value of the inventory rising, that increase is not preferential. For a preference to arise, there must be a *transfer* under § 547.)

11. Ironically when set next to *American Lumber*, the Bankruptcy Code allows some security interests to be filed *after* the date the bankruptcy petition is filed and for this taking of security *not* to be a voidable preference. This may not be important in practice, and it requires some statutory parsing to see how this result could arise.

    Section 547 gives a "safe harbor" for some preferences, the most important of which is the ordinary course of business exception (§ 547(c)(2)). In addition, there's a safe harbor for security interests taken in reasonably contemporaneous purchase money loans used by the debtor to buy new property. That is, suppose lender lends to the debtor for the debtor to buy new property. Lender and debtor both intend that the creditor will take a security interest. But the lender files the security interest later. Without an exception or "safe harbor," the lender would then be getting a preference, if the debtor files for bankruptcy within 90 days after the lender got the security interest. (That's because the final filing of the security interest would be a transfer of property on an *antecedent* debt, even though the antecedent debt was only, say, 20 days old.)

Section 547(c)(3) pulls such late filed security interests out from preference attack, as long as the parties intended that the security interest be given at the time of the loan and the secured lender gets its act together and files within 20 days of the actual loan:

### § 547. Preferences

(c) The trustee *may not* avoid under this section a transfer—

\* \* \*

(3) that creates a security interest in property acquired by the debtor—
 (A) to the extent such security interest secures new value that was—
  (i) given at or after the signing of a security agreement that contains a description of such property as collateral;

\* \* \*

  (iii) given to enable the debtor to acquire such property; and
  (iv) in fact used by the debtor to acquire such property; and
 (B) that is perfected on or before 20 days after the debtor receives possession of such property[.]

Could the lender file the security interest *after* the debtor filed for bankruptcy, as long as the 20-day period hasn't run out? The creditor faces a steep problem, namely the bankruptcy stay in § 362, which bars all collection activities and which we've noted a number of times.

In addition, the creditor faces another problem, namely § 544, which gives the trustee the rights of a judgment creditor on the date of bankruptcy. Judgment creditors (usually) beat unfiled security interests. Hence, as of the date of the petition in bankruptcy, § 544 would give the bankruptcy trustee the right to beat the creditor with an unfiled security interest. (This section is a bankruptcy aficionado's favorite because it creates intricate statutory construction, such as the one we're about to get into. But it rarely is critical for the practicing financial lawyer.)

### § 544. Trustee as lien creditor ...

(a) The trustee shall have, as of the commencement of the case ... the rights and powers of, or may avoid any transfer of property of the debtor or any obligation incurred by the debtor that is voidable by—

(1) a creditor that extends credit to the debtor at the time of the commencement of the case, and that obtains, at such time and with respect to such credit, a judicial lien on all property on which a creditor on a simple contract could have obtained such a judicial lien, whether or not such a creditor exists;

(2) a creditor that extends credit to the debtor at the time of the commencement of the case, and obtains, at such time and with respect to such credit, an execution

against the debtor that is returned unsatisfied at such time, whether or not such a creditor exists; ....

Thus the Bankruptcy Code as a general rule both bars filing the subsequent security interest (§ 362) and gives the trustee authority to set aside unfiled security interests (§ 544). (The debt exists, but the trustee need not respect the unfiled security interest.)

*However,* the creditor can surmount these two barriers in some states, because there's an interplay between state law and the Bankruptcy Code here. Here's how:

Section 546 denies the trustee power to avoid some transfers that it could otherwise avoid under § 544 (the section that allows the trustee to set aside incomplete security interests). Section 546 says that the trustee *cannot* set aside an incomplete security interest *if* state law allows subsequent completion of the security interest to beat creditors that lent before the security interest was completed. So if the secured creditor is lending in a *state* that gives the secured creditor a 20-day grace period for filing, then § 546(b) says the trustee *can't* use § 544 to set aside the security interest. (Many states give ten days via U.C.C. § 9-301(2); some give more.)

### § 546. Limitations on avoiding powers

(b)(1) The rights and powers of a trustee under section[] 544 ... are subject to any generally applicable [state] law that—

(A) permits perfection of an interest in property *to be effective against an entity that acquires rights in such property before* the date of perfection ....

This exception would get the trustee past § 544 *if* the trustee were free to file the security interest after the bankruptcy petition were filed. But so far we haven't gotten the creditor past the § 362 stay. Section 546 only says that the secured creditor wins under § 544 *if* state law gives a grace period, but neither § 544 nor § 546 lifts the stay.

But another exception lifts the stay if the creditor's priority would be shielded by § 546:

### § 362. Automatic stay

(b) The filing of a petition ... does *not* operate as a stay—

\* \* \*

(3) ... of any act to perfect ... an interest in property *to the extent that the trustee's rights and powers are subject to such perfection under section 546(b)* ...

So, if underlying state law gives a 20-day grace period, then the trustee can't set aside the incomplete security interest under § 544 (because of the § 546(b) exception to the trustee's avoiding powers) and the stay is lifted (via the § 362(b)(3) exception to the stay), allowing the creditor to rush to file within the 20 days even if there's an intervening bankruptcy.

## ¶903: Note re Washington Plate Glass Co., 27 Bankr. 550 (D.D.C. 1982), 3 Bankruptcy News Letter (WGL), No. 6 (June 1986), at 1

*Equitable Subordination Applied.* In Washington Plate Glass Co., 27 [Bankr.] 550 (D.D.C. 1982), one of two owners withdrew from the business and sold his stock to the corporation, receiving in return a note secured by the assets of the corporation. The transaction was not undertaken either with a fraudulent intent or in anticipation of bankruptcy. Three years later, the company defaulted on the note and, some months later, became insolvent.

In affirming the finding of the bankruptcy court, District Judge Gerhard A. Gesell did not apply Section 548[, the Bankruptcy Code's fraudulent conveyance section,] but, rather, applied Section 510(c). He found that enforcement of the security interest held by the former shareholder as of the date of bankruptcy would be manifestly unfair to the general unsecured creditors of the debtor corporation and that, accordingly, the doctrine of equitable subordination should be applied.

*Prejudice to Creditors Must Be Avoided.* In the view of the court, the corporation did not acquire anything of a value equivalent to the depletion of its assets when it acquired the stock. Instead, the transaction was devised to achieve a distribution of the corporate assets to the stockholder. Since assets of a corporation are to be available first to creditors, the stockholders were not entitled to receive any part of the assets until the creditors were first paid in full. The court concluded that even in cases where no intent to defraud the creditors is present and the transaction is entered into in good faith, the transaction will not be upheld unless there is sufficient surplus available at the time that payment is made out of assets to retire the stock without prejudice to creditors.

[The issue of whether a court needed to see bad conduct in order to invoke equitable subordination has been litigated, with courts indicating generally that bad conduct isn't necessary. In many instances equitable subordination was invoked to favor the United States as a tax claimant (with the court equitably subordinating other creditors to the United States).]

## ¶904: The collapse of W.T. Grant Company

The following case, Gosoff v. Rodman (In re W.T. Grant Co.), 699 F.2d 599 (2d Cir. 1983), is the circuit court's final opinion on the settlement of the complex litigation surrounding the collapse of W.T. Grant Co. Grant's bankruptcy was, at the time (October, 1975), both the largest failure of a retailer and the largest bankruptcy under the Bankruptcy Act that reigned from 1938 through 1978.

Prior to July 1973, Grant relied on its finance subsidiary, W.T. Grant Financial Corporation, for the majority of its short-term cash financing needs. Grant Financial obtained financing by selling commercial paper. Commercial paper is a short-term I.O.U. running directly from the borrower to the lender, usually without a bank as intermediary. There is no indenture, loan agreement, or trustee. The lender relies on the high creditworthiness of the borrower and the short duration of the loan.

Later, Grant converted a portion of its outstanding commercial paper to long-term debt. (This may have been because short-term interest rates were unusually high at the time; however, as Grant deteriorated it was going to lose access to the commercial paper market anyway.) Morgan Guaranty Trust Company became the "lead bank" in the structuring and financing of Grant's long term debt. A summary of the complex financial transactions that preceded the bankruptcy filing follows:

1. January 31, 1973: Grant has $380,033,500 of outstanding commercial paper and $10,000,000 in outstanding bank debt.
2. July 5, 1973: The Term Loan—Grant Financial borrows $100,000,000 from eight banks as a five year term loan. The banks include Chase Manhattan, which also was the indenture trustee for Grant's $92,507,000 of 4¾% unsecured subordinated debentures, and Citibank, which also was the indenture trustee for Grant's $834,000 of 4% unsecured subordinated debentures.
3. Late 1973 and early 1974: Grant's financial performance declines; the credit rating agencies lower their rating for Grant's commercial paper.
4. December 1973: Grant Financial has $400,000,000 in outstanding commercial paper.
5. March 5, 1974: Moody's, the bond and credit rating agency, withdraws Grant's commercial paper rating and further lowers long-term debt rating.
6. March 12, 1974: Eight banks re-establish Grant's lines of credit and advance funds; total outstanding loans to Grant Financial reach $415,000,000; $132,000,000 used to pay off commercial paper.
7. June 1974: Outstanding commercial paper has been reduced to $1,000,000.
8. Early August 1974: Secured Demand Loan—Morgan, Chase and Citibank advance $5,000,000 to Grant secured by accounts receivable.
9. Late August 1974: Interim Loan and Guaranty Agreement—Grant Financial becomes indebted to 11 banks for $44,000,000; Grant Financial assumes Grant's obligation to repay $15,000,000 of Secured Demand Loans and incurs $29,000,000 of new loans. Grant guarantees the $44,000,000 and secures the guaranty by granting a security interest in accounts receivable from sales of goods. Total outstanding borrowings from term loans and short term borrowings to 12 banks reach $517,000,000.
10. September 16, 1974 (effective October 8, 1974): Loan and Guaranty Agreement—Grant Financial and Grant as guarantor receive additional advance from banks of $66,587,500. Banks agree to extend maturity of $44,000,000 and all other short term loans to June 2, 1975. Banks receive security for total outstanding loans of $600,000,000 and $100,000,000 term loan. Security is all of Grant's accounts re-

ceivable and a pledge of stock in a Grant Canadian subsidiary. Loan is to be junior to inventory liens to certain suppliers and senior to unsecured debentureholders.

11. April 1, 1975 (executed June 2, 1975): Loan Extension Agreement—Grant pays 116 banks owed less than $5,000,000 each a total of $56,931,665 from sale of inventory. Remaining banks extend maturity of short-term loans to March 31, 1976. Short-term outstanding bank loans now total $560,916,978.

12. May 15, 1975: To obtain inventory to sell in stores, Grant gives certain vendors and suppliers a lien on inventory.

13. August 6, 1975 (effective September 15, 1975): Amended Loan Extension Agreement—Maturity of $540 million of short-term loans extended to July 30, 1976. Under a Trade Subordination Agreement, $300 million of $540 million is subordinated to certain trade obligations. Under an Intercorporate Subordination Agreement, Grant Financial's loans to its parent of $819,887,663 are subordinated to bank claims against Grant under the various guaranty and loan agreements of $640,916,978.

14. October 2, 1975: Grant files for bankruptcy.

15. During the settlement negotiations, the trustee argued that the banks dominated and controlled Grant. A director of Morgan Guaranty, the lead bank, sat on Grant's Board and was a member of Grant's Executive Committee and Audit Committee. The banks agreed to settle the debentureholders' equitable subordination suit, with the settlement reflecting the banks' expectation that they might fail to persuade the court that they did not control Grant or that, if they did, their priority should not be altered. The subordinated debentureholders get 19 cents on each dollar of their claim, although the banks aren't paid back in full. Dissenting subordinated debentureholders sued, and the appellate opinion for their suit appears next.

See Cosoff v. Rodman, 699 F.2d 599, 601-04 (2d Cir. 1983); In re W.T. Grant Co., 4 Bankr. 53 (Bankr. S.D.N.Y. 1981); *Investigating the Collapse of W.T. Grant*, Bus. Week, July 19, 1976, at 60-62; M. Douglas-Hamilton, *ALI-ABA Resource Materials: Banking and Commercial Lending Law—1980, in* Some Problems Associated with Creditor Control of Debtor Companies 330-57 (1980).

### ¶905: In re W.T. Grant Co., 699 F.2d 599 (1983)

Friendly, Circuit Judge:

These appeals arise from the mammoth bankruptcy proceedings of W.T. Grant Co. Grant filed under Chapter XI on October 2, 1975 .... The present appeals concern the last of a series of compromises and settlements designed to avoid what would necessarily have been extremely protracted litigation with the various claimants.

\* \* \*

## The Proceedings in the Bankruptcy Court and the District Court

After Grant had been ordered into liquidation, the banks and Charles G. Rodman, as Trustee, asserted a multitude of claims against each other .... [S]ettlement negotiations were instituted. These resulted in an agreement which, in addition to settling the claims of the banks, encompassed what [the trial judge] termed a "global settlement," i.e., a "framework for the further administration of the bankrupt estate and the satisfaction of claims filed against such estate." 4 Bankr. Ct. Dec. at 602 .... [T]he settlement provided that the bank claimants were to receive an initial cash distribution of $165,700,000, or approximately 25% of their allowed claims. More was to be paid when and if funds became available. The Trustee agreed not to sue the 116 banks whose loans of $56,931,665.59 were paid in June, 1975 [although these repayments might have been preferential.] Finally, the agreement created a fund of $95,378,373, the full amount of the claims of subordinated debentureholders, pending resolution of their dispute with the bank claimants as to whether the subordination clauses of their indentures should be given effect so as to subordinate the debentureholder's claims to the bank claims. The Bankruptcy Judge approved the banks' settlement on July 20, 1978 .... There was no appeal of this "global settlement" to the district court.[1]

Having thus provided the necessary framework, the Trustee, the bank claimants, United States Trust Company (U.S. Trust) as indenture trustee replacing Chase under the Indenture for the 4¾% Subordinated Debentures, and representatives of these debentureholders entered into negotiations for the settlement of the latter's claims. The rights of the debentureholders depended on the interpretation and application of a clause in their indentures subordinating their claims to "Senior Indebtedness" of Grant. The Indenture under which the 4¾% Debentures were issued defined this as stated in the margin;[2] the Indenture [governing] the small amount of outstanding 4% Debentures was to the same effect. If the bank claims were and remained enforceable as Senior Indebtedness to which the debentureholders were subordinated, the latter would receive nothing. However, [the debentureholders' trustee] alleged that ... the conduct of the banks might require that the contractual subordination provisions be

---

[1] An Ad Hoc Protective Committee of 4¾% Convertible Subordinated Debentures of W.T. Grant Company ... raised objections to the bank's settlement at the hearing. The [Ad Hoc Committee's] failure ... to pursue its objections by appealing [all issues] forecloses some of the issues raised in the present appeal [,including whether there should be a] re-opening of the question whether the Trustee properly agreed not to question the [potentially preferential] June 1975, payments of $56,931,665.59 to the 116 other bank creditors of Grant.

[2] The term "Senior Indebtedness" shall mean the principal of and premium, if any, and interest on (a) indebtedness ... of the Company for money borrowed from or guaranteed ... evidenced by notes or similar obligations, (b) indebtedness of the Company evidenced by notes or debentures ... issued under the provisions of an indenture or similar instrument between the Company and a bank or trust company ...; *unless, in each case, by the terms of the instrument by which the Company incurred, assumed or guaranteed such indebtedness is not superior in right of payment to the Debentures* ....

disregarded and even that the subordinated debentureholders be accorded a status prior to that of the banks. These reasons, stated in detail in [the trial judge's] opinion approving the settlement, ... were as follows:

> (a) At the time of the Initial Security Agreement of September 16, 1974, the bank claimants knew or had reasonable cause to believe that Grant was insolvent and that the granting of security interests would discourage further extensions of trade credit to Grant and substantially reduce the flow of merchandise into Grant stores, thereby impairing the prospects for a successful reorganization of Grant.
> (b) By forcing Grant into the Inventory Security Agreement and Trade Subordination Agreement the bank claimants increased the amount of Senior Indebtedness to which the junior debentureholders were subordinated.
> (c) In the summer of 1974, the bank claimants directed Grant not to proceed with a proposed sale of $100,000,000 of customer accounts receivable to Beneficial Finance Corporation and the use of some undetermined portion of the proceeds to purchase 4¾% debentures at 25 cents on the dollar.
> (d) The bank claimants used their position of control over Grant's management to prevent Grant from promptly seeking relief under the Bankruptcy Act, feeding it just enough money to keep its head above water while strengthening their security position, allowing the passage of the four months period for avoiding preferences under [the predecessor to § 547] and hoping to allow the passage of the one year provision of [the predecessor to § 550] for the avoidance of liens and fraudulent transfers.

The bank claimants made a variety of responses. They denied having had any fiduciary relationship to Grant, asserted that they had made loans in the belief fostered by Grant's management that Grant remained viable, contended that Grant's management itself had abandoned the proposed sale of accounts receivable, and denied that they had prevented Grant from seeking rehabilitation under the Bankruptcy Act. They asserted, moreover, that as to many of U.S. Trust's claims, the remedy, even if the claim were made out, would be invalidation of the banks' security interests rather than subordination to the debentureholders. U.S. Trust also raised claims of conflict of interest and derelictions of duty against Chase, its predecessor trustee ....

The settlement originally provided for the payment of 14% of the claims of the accepting subordinated debentureholders ....

At a hearing before Judge Galgay objections were made by eleven debentureholders .... The [eleven] objectors asserted principally that the ... bank claims should be equitably subordinated to the debentures because of the control and dominion over Grant allegedly exercised by the banks .... Judge Galgay ... concluded that the original settlement represented a fair compromise, taking into account the strengths and weaknesses of the claims of both sides and the delay and expense incident to litigation, and approved ....

Timely appeals were taken ....

\* \* \*

Before the appeals could be heard, negotiations looking toward an improvement of the offer were begun.... These resulted in an amended offer. The amount payable to the debentureholders was raised from a floor of 14 cents on the dollar to one of 19 cents on the dollar ....

\* \* \*

### Discussion

\* \* \*

In undertaking an examination of the settlement, we emphasize that this responsibility of the bankruptcy judge, and ours upon review, is not to decide the numerous questions of law and fact raised by appellants but rather to canvass the issues and see whether the settlement "fall[s] below the lowest point in the range of reasonableness" ...

### [The structure of the loans and substantive consolidation]

We start with appellants' argument that, quite apart from the banks' conduct, part or all of the banks' claims are not "Senior Indebtedness," see note [2], supra, to which alone the claims of debentureholders are subordinated .... Appellants ... argue that until Grant's guaranty of August 21, 1974, the banks' claims did not qualify as Senior Indebtedness of Grant since their loans were not to Grant but to Grant Financial. Judge Galgay thought a sufficient answer to be that Grant's indebtedness to Grant Financial was evidenced at the time of the filing of the Chapter XI petition by an Intercorporate Demand Note in the amount of $819,887,663, more than the amount of the banks' loans to Grant Financial, and that this would qualify as Senior Indebtedness if the corporate entities are respected; if they are not, as well might be proper, the loans to Grant Financial, all evidenced by notes, would qualify even more directly [as Senior Indebtedness].[3] ...

### [Grant's guarantee as a fraudulent conveyance?]

Finally, under the Loan and Guaranty Agreement all loans to Grant Financial were guaranteed by Grant. While this did not become effective until October 8, 1974, which fell 6 days short of a year of the Chapter XI petition, there is no showing that the trustee could have established lack of fair consideration for the guaranty under [the predecessor to § 548]; the legal standard in a situation such as this, which is governed

---

[3] [To see why they "would qualify even more directly" as Senior Indebtedness, read the italicized last clause of the subordinated debentures' designation clause in the previous footnote. Compare it to the designation clause in the Drum Financial indenture. See p. 184.—Roe.]

by [the predecessor to § 548] of the Bankruptcy Act, is whether "the economic benefit ... that accrued to [the] bankrupt as a result of the third person's indebtedness" was "'disproportionately small' when compared to the size of the security that that bankrupt gave and the obligations that it incurred," Rubin v. Manufacturers Hanover Trust Co., 661 F.2d 979, 993 (2d Cir. 1981). Through its subsidiary, Grant received the full benefit of the extended maturity of some $490,000,000 in short-term loans and additional loans up to the total amount of $600,000,000 in return for its guaranty and for security interests, estimated by the Bankruptcy Judge to amount to $288,000,000. We thus conclude that while the subordinated debentureholders have some arguments that the larger part of the bank debt would not qualify as Senior Indebtedness because the loans initially were made to Grant Financial rather than to Grant, these did not have much chance of prevailing.

[The defective prospectus]

Appellants contend that, however things might otherwise stand, the banks are estopped from claiming that Grant's indebtedness to Grant Financial constituted Senior Indebtedness because the prospectus under which the 4¾% Debentures were issued showed Senior Indebtedness of only $28,775,000 whereas Grant then owed Grant Financial $246,420,216 .... *Appellants[] argu[e] ... [that] Grant, allegedly with the banks' knowledge,*[4] acted in such a way as to make it inequitable for the banks to rely on [anything more than what the prospectus showed as outstanding]. Yet even if this were upheld—and we find no proof of the banks' complicity in Grant's prospectus, the point remains that the prospectus goes on to define Senior Indebtedness as, inter alia, "indebtedness ... for money borrowed from or guaranteed to persons, firms or corporations evidenced by notes or similar obligations" (emphasis supplied). Grant's fresh guaranty of the indebtedness of Grant Financial to the banks in 1975 would itself therefore qualify as Senior Indebtedness even if some principle of estoppel were to prevent the banks from claiming that the ... intercorporate loans from Grant Financial ... in 1971 [were senior].

[Equitable subordination for collecting on a loan?]

Once it is concluded that there was a strong probability that all of the bank debt would be deemed Senior Indebtedness and a certainty that some of it would be appellants' other claims lose much of their force. It is true, as appellants urge, that the contractual subordination of the debentures to the bank debt would not prevent the bankruptcy court, as a court of equity, from placing the debentures on a plane of equality with or even ... of superiority to all or part of the Senior Indebtedness if the banks had engaged in inequitable conduct. However, what appellants disregard is that in judging the equity of the banks' conduct their position as creditors prima facie sen-

---

[4] [Emphasis supplied.—Roe.]

ior to the debentureholders must be taken into account. We see no reason to quarrel with the substance of Judge Galgay's summary of the law of equitable subordination, 4 [Bankr.] at 74–75, although every judge would probably state his own version differently. We entirely agree with his conclusion that "[a] creditor is under no fiduciary obligation to its debtor or to other creditors of the debtor in the collection of its claim," 4 [Bankr.] at 75. *The permissible parameters of a creditor's efforts to seek collection from a debtor are generally those with respect to voidable preferences and fraudulent conveyances proscribed by the Bankruptcy Act; apart from these there is generally no objection to a creditor's using his bargaining position, including his ability to refuse to make further loans needed by the debtor to improve the status of his existing claims.*

... [T]he gravamen of [the next] charge is that Grant management, apparently in the summer of 1974, contemplated taking action to place Grant in a Chapter XI proceeding, which might have enabled Grant to survive as a reduced operation with lower administrative expenses, but that the banks prevented this, making specious explanations but acting in reality to improve their preferred position. For this appellants cited passages from two depositions neither of which supports the contention they advance. In the first of appellants' references, John P. Schroeder, Morgan Guaranty's officer in charge of the Grant credit, merely agreed with questions suggesting that in the late summer of 1974 the banks wished "to recoup the most amount of money as possible on the Grant loans," an understandable and permissible desire, and that for this reason they "did not opt for liquidation at that time." In the second passage cited, Robert Dannenbaum of the Bank of New York stated that *at some unspecified time the banks would have liked an "unofficial reorganization program," by which he meant not a Chapter XI proceeding but rather nothing more than "general monitoring of the Company's affairs by the banks."* No suggestion is found in any passage of these witnesses' testimony reproduced by appellants that Grant itself actively contemplated undergoing voluntary liquidation or reorganization under the Bankruptcy Act in the summer of 1974. We also note that after July 1974, the banks increased their loans [and] subordinated $300,000,000 on their debt to trade obligations. While a sinister interpretation is possible, this is not demanded; considering that the fresh money provided by the banks after July 1974, amounted to some $226,000,000 as against $95,378,373 principal amount of the debentures, the banks would have been paying a rather high price to obtain whatever legal advantages [they obtained when Grant] invok[ed] the Bankruptcy Act.

**[Control, or influence as creditor?]**

With respect to [the equitable subordination claim], the Bankruptcy Judge was warranted in attaching little importance to general statements by Grant officials that the banks were "running" Grant. There is no doubt that, at least from March of 1974, the banks kept careful watch on what was going on at Grant; they would have been derelict in their duty to their own creditors and stockholders if they had not. *It is not uncommon in such situations for officers whose companies have been brought to the verge of disaster to think that they still have better answers than do the outsiders.* In order to establish their claims *the appellants must show not simply that the banks proffered advice to Grant that was unpalatable to management, even advice gloved with an implicit threat that, unless it were taken, further loans would not be forthcoming.* They must show at least that the banks acted solely for their own benefit, taking into account their reasonable belief that their claims constituted Senior Indebtedness vis-a-vis the debentureholders, and adversely to the interest of others.

**[Causation vis-a-vis the sale of accounts receivable]**

The allegation most discussed by appellants is that ... Harry Pierson, the acting president of Grant and Robert Luckett, the controller, made a report to a meeting of the Grant board of directors in June of 1974 proposing a transaction wherein $100,000,000 of customer accounts receivable would be sold to Beneficial Finance Company (Beneficial) at a discount of up to 27% and some undetermined portion of the proceeds would be used to purchase on the market 4¾% subordinated debentures which were then selling at about 25 cents on the dollar. Pierson reported that two of the major banks, Morgan Guaranty and Chase, were opposed to the transaction .... Their reasons were that proceeds of one of Grant's most valuable assets would be used to pay junior debt and that trade creditors would be upset. According to Luckett, Pierson had nevertheless determined to sign the contract with Beneficial and apparently persisted in that intention after a meeting at Morgan Guaranty where the banks' opposition was strongly conveyed. [Negotiations over the sale broke down, apparently for other business reasons.] ...

... [I]t would have been surprising if the banks had not objected to the portion of the transaction which involved use of proceeds of quick assets to purchase long-term subordinated debt. The banks reasonably thought that their claims were senior to the debentures. True, the purchase of debentures at 25 cents on the dollar would have meant a saving of interest of some 19% on the purchase price. But Grant's immediate problem was short term; what it needed was to conserve resources and obtain short-term loans in order to stay afloat until the tide turned. Even if we should assume the evidence went so far, we see nothing inequitable in the banks taking the position that if Grant wished to use quick assets to redeem subordinated long-term debt, even on an advantageous basis, it could expect no further help from them.

\* \* \*

We conclude by reemphasizing that the task of the bankruptcy judge was not to determine whether the settlement was the best that could have been obtained, something that neither he nor we can ever know, but whether it "fall[s] below the lowest point in the range of reasonableness." If we take the Trustee's estimated realization of

$600,000,000, and deduct the estimated $143,000,000 of administration and ... priority claims, the $76,000,000 owing to secured suppliers, and the $24,000,000 owing to senior debentureholders, there would be a balance of $357,000,000 available for distribution among $650,000,000 of bank claims, $95,000,000 of Subordinated Debentures and $82,000,000 of general unsecured claims. If the banks could sustain their claims of subordination, let alone their claims of lien protection for $288,000,000 of their debt, the subordinated debentureholders would take nothing. Even if the banks' claims to secured creditor status and subordination of the debentures were rejected but the banks were not subordinated to them, all of which was highly problematical, the debentureholders would receive only 43 cents on the dollar, after much further expense. After considering the strengths and weaknesses of the claims of the debentureholders a settlement assuring them of 19 cents can hardly be regarded as below the lowest point in the range of reasonableness.

We therefore affirm the judgment of the district court on the merits.

## ¶906: Questions on *W.T. Grant*

1. Do the best you can to construct a balance sheet for the parent company and the finance subsidiary. Does it make any distributional difference if the companies are consolidated in bankruptcy?
2. Can you find four different ways that the financial structure of W.T. Grant and Grant Financial would lead to the banks coming first, ahead of the subordinated debentureholders? For the parent company and the finance subsidiary, specify which company owed what to whom. Who guaranteed what? Which loans and guarantees were senior?
3. Did the banks ever "control" Grant? Does that make any difference?
4. By what mechanism is debt designated as senior under Grant's subordinated debenture indenture? How is it designated as senior under the Drum Financial indenture? Does it make any difference which designation clause was used in the event of consolidation of Grant with its subsidiary? Would the debt be senior if the Drum Financial clause had been used? Would the guarantee merge with the debt?
5. The Restatement (Second) of Agency (1958) states:

    ### § 14 O. Security Holder Becoming a Principal

    A creditor who assumes control of his debtor's business for the mutual benefit of himself and his debtor, may become a principal, with liability for the acts and transactions of the debtor in connection with the business.
    Comment:
    a. A security holder who merely exercises a veto power over the business acts of his debtor by preventing purchases or sales above specified amounts

does not thereby become a principal. However, if he takes over the management of the debtor's business either in person or through an agent, and directs what contracts may or may not be made, he becomes a principal, liable as any principal for the obligations incurred thereafter in the normal course of business by the debtor who has now become his general agent. The point at which the creditor becomes a principal is that at which he assumes de facto control over the conduct of his debtor, whatever the terms of the formal contract with his debtor may be.

6. Why did Grant switch from commercial paper financing to bank financing? What could banks do that buyers of commercial paper couldn't? The banks might have eventually charged more in interest (adjusting for the term of their loan), but that couldn't by itself explain why Grant switched to them (or more properly, why the commercial paper buyers abandoned Grant). Surely, commercial paper buyers, when they saw that Grant was deteriorating and becoming riskier, could have raised their interest rate. But could the commercial paper buyers efficiently meet with Grant's officers, gather information, and monitor Grant's operations? In a reorganization, in or out of bankruptcy, could they organize easily to renegotiate the loans?

7. The subordinated noteholders' settlement (at $.19 for each dollar of obligation) suggests what about the banks' fears of equitable subordination? How easy is it to look at the facts and determine whether they warrant equitable subordination? Hence, how easy is it to determine the settlement value of an equitable subordination claim? Where and when does a creditor cross the line from permissible protection of its contract position over to impermissible control and pursuit of its own interests. Consider the Fifth Circuit's difficulties in dealing with the facts in the next case.

## ¶907: In re Clark Pipe & Supply Co., Inc., 870 F.2d 1022 (5th Cir. 1989)

Before POLITZ and JOLLY, Circuit Judges, and HUNTER, District Judge.

E. GRADY JOLLY, Circuit Judge:

... [W]e are presented with three issues arising out of the conduct of the bankrupt's lender during the ninety days prior to the bankrupt's filing for protection from creditors. The first is whether the lender ... received a voidable transfer. If so, the second question is whether the lender engaged in inequitable conduct that would justify subordination of the lender's claims to the extent that the conduct harmed other creditors. If so, we must finally determine whether avoiding the transfer and equitable subordination are duplicative or complementary.

## I

Clark Pipe and Supply Company, Inc., ("Clark") was in the business of buying and selling steel pipe used in the fabrication of offshore drilling platforms. ... Associates Commercial Corp. ("Associates") [made a] revolving loan[ to Clark,] secured by an assignment of [its] accounts receivable and an inventory mortgage. ... The agreements provided that Associates could reduce the ... advance[s] at any time at its discretion. When bad times hit the oil fields in late 1981, Clark's business slumped. In February 1982 Associates began reducing [its] percentage advance[s] so that Clark would have just enough cash to pay its direct operating expenses. Clark used the advances to keep its doors open and to sell inventory, the proceeds of which were used to pay off the past advances from Associates. Associates did not expressly dictate to Clark which bills to pay. Neither did it direct Clark not to pay vendors or threaten Clark with a cut-off of advances if it did pay vendors. But Clark had no funds left over from the advances to pay vendors or other creditors whose services were not essential to keeping its doors open. [When Clark's unpaid vendors began foreclosure proceedings] and seized the pipe it had sold Clark ... Clark sought protection from creditors by filing for reorganization under Chapter 11 of the Bankruptcy Code.

... The trustee sought the recovery of alleged preferences and equitable subordination of Associates' claims. ... The [bankruptcy] court required Associates to turn over $370,505 of payments found to be preferential and subordinated Associates' claim. The district court affirmed ... .

## II

... Clark, by selling its inventory and thereby converting the inventory to accounts receivable that had been assigned to Associates, made a preferential transfer to Associates that [is avoidable] in accordance with sections 547(b) and (c)(5) of the Bankruptcy Code. It is undisputed that the reduction of pipe to accounts receivable was in effect a transfer of the pipe to Associates. ... [T]he bankruptcy court correctly determined the existence of a voidable preference and the amount of the preference.

## III

The second issue before us is whether the bankruptcy court was justified in equitably subordinating Associates' claims. The Fifth Circuit has enunciated a three-pronged test to determine whether and to what extent a claim should be equitably subordinated: (1) the claimant must have engaged in some type of inequitable conduct, (2) the misconduct must have resulted in injury to the creditors of the bankrupt or conferred an unfair advantage on the claimant, and (3) equitable subordination of the claim must not be inconsistent with the provisions of the Bankruptcy Code.

A

The courts have recognized three general categories of conduct as sufficient to satisfy the first prong of the three-part test: (1) fraud, illegality or breach of fiduciary duties; (2) undercapitalization; and (3) a claimant's use of the debtor as a mere instrumentality or alter ego.

... [T]he bankruptcy court found that once Associates realized Clark's desperate financial condition, Associates asserted total control and used Clark as a mere instrumentality to liquidate Associates' unpaid loans ... , to the detriment of ... Clark's other creditors. Associates contends that its control over Clark was far from total. Associates says that it did no more than determine the percentage of advances as expressly permitted in the loan agreement; it never made or dictated decisions as to which creditors were paid. Thus, argues Associates, it never had the "actual, participatory, total control of the debtor" required to make Clark its instrumentality ... .

\* \* \*

... [W]e look to equitable subordination cases for the applicable law. The case most directly on point is In re American Lumber Co., 5 B.R. 470 (D. Minn.1980). In that case the bank was a formerly unsecured creditor that took a security interest in the inventory and accounts receivable. It began liquidation of the debtor by commencing a foreclosure on its security interests. The debtor's employees were all fired and a new skeleton crew was subsequently hired. The bank instituted a depository system into which all the debtor's collections were deposited and it determined who would be paid. The bank refused to pay general unsecured creditors or sales taxes while seeing to it that accounts receivable were enhanced.

... [T]he court said:

> [I]t was the Bank's use of its control over [the debtor's] operations in a manner detrimental to the unsecured creditors which constitutes the inequitable conduct. The purposeful exercise of that control to implement its plan is amply demonstrated, not merely by [an attorney's] comments as to the plan he had to disadvantage the general creditors by taking security interests in inventory and equipment, but also by the Bank's actions in following through with conduct designed to obtain for the Bank a greater percentage of the debt owed to it by [the debtor] than owed to other general creditors.

... Associates used its control in a manner detrimental to the unsecured creditors. As a de facto insider, ... Associates knew that Clark was headed for bankruptcy and sought to defer it as long as possible in order to recoup its investment at the expense of the suppliers. Knowing that Associates would be grossly undersecured if Clark went under immediately, Fred Slice, Associates' loan officer responsible for the Clark account, devised a plan that would allow Clark to keep its doors open to generate accounts receivable by liquidating as much inventory as possible. Slice testified as to what he had in mind:

> I just kept on trying to get out of the loan, you know. My attitude was bankruptcy is inevitable. I want to get in the best position I can prior to the bankruptcy; i.e., I want to get the absolute amount of dollars as low as I can by hook or crook. And, you know, worry [about] preferences and all of that at a later date which, you know, I was aware there was a danger, but I don't know all of the legal ramifications.
>
> ....
>
> ... As long as they were selling my pipe, collecting my receivables and turning my inventory from something that was highly illiquid into something more liquid, yeah. As long as I could—it was in my interest for Clark to keep operating. And, yeah, I personally would have preferred that to bankruptcy. But it was inevitable. It was going to happen in my opinion. I was trying to get in—the ship was going down. I just wanted to get myself on a life raft with a few provisions so we could cut our losses.

Associates used its loan agreement and advances not merely to protect its investment, as it claims, but to leverage its recovery at the expense of other creditors. Because of Associates' policy, suppliers were forced to bear the cost of Associates' liquidation of Clark. ... The unfairness to inventory vendors was especially egregious. Every time Clark sold pipe, Associates improved its position to the detriment of the vendor of that pipe. ... The moment the pipe was sold, ... Associates took priority by virtue of its security interest in receivables. Thus, Associates' strategy was apparently to convert inventory into receivables as fast as possible without alerting the vendors to what was happening. ... Associates reduced advances so that Clark received only enough to keep selling its inventory; any income from the sales was sent directly to Associates in Dallas. Thus, Associates' reduction of advances forced Clark to defer payments to its vendors and trade creditors, sell inventory out from under the vendors' privileges, and send the cash to Associates. Associates' intent is demonstrated by the following testimony:

> If he [the comptroller of Clark] had had the availability [of funds to pay a vendor or other trade creditor] that particular day, I would have said, "Are you sure you've got that much availability, Jim," because he shouldn't have that much. The way I had structured it, he wouldn't have any money to pay his suppliers.
>
> ... .
>
> But you know, the possibility that—this is all hypothetical. I had it structured so that there was no—there was barely enough money—there was enough money, if I did it right, enough money to keep the doors open. Clark could continue to operate, sell the inventory, turn it into receivables, collect the cash, transfer that cash to me, and reduce my loans. And, if he had ever had availability for other things, that meant I had done something wrong, and I would have been surprised. To ask me what I would have done is purely hypothetical I don't think it would happen. I think it's so unrealistic, I don't know.

... [T]he bankruptcy court and the district court correctly concluded that Clark was an instrumentality of Associates for the limited purpose of equitable subordination. Moreover, they correctly held that Associates used that control to engage in the type of overreaching and spoliation to the detriment of the rights of fellow creditors that amounts to inequitable conduct. ...

* * *

IV

The final issue is whether, by setting aside the preference and equitably subordinating Associates' claim to the claims of the other creditors, the bankruptcy court has awarded duplicate remedies. We think not. ...

AFFIRMED.

...................................................................................................................................

**In re Clark Pipe & Supply Co., Inc., 893 F.2d 693 (5th Cir. 1990).**

ON SUGGESTION FOR REHEARING EN BANC

Before POLITZ and JOLLY, Circuit Judges, and HUNTER, District Judge.

E. GRADY JOLLY, Circuit Judge:

Treating the suggestion for rehearing en banc filed in this case by Associates Commercial Corporation ("Associates"), as a petition for panel rehearing, we hereby grant the petition for rehearing. After re-examining the evidence in this case and the applicable law, we conclude that our prior opinion was in error. We therefore withdraw our prior opinion and substitute the following:

... [W]e decide that equitable subordination is an inappropriate remedy .... [W]e need not decide whether avoiding the transfer and equitable subordination are duplicative or complementary remedies.

* * *

III

[Was] the bankruptcy court ... justified in equitably subordinating Associates' claims[?] ...

... [T]he bankruptcy court found that once Associates realized Clark's desperate financial condition, Associates asserted total control and used Clark as a mere instrumentality to liquidate Associates' unpaid loans ... to the detriment of the rights of Clark's other creditors. Associates contends that its control over Clark was far from total. Associates says that it did no more than determine the percentage of advances as expressly permitted in the loan agreement; it never made or dictated decisions as to which creditors were paid. Thus, argues Associates, it never had the "actual, participatory, total control of the debtor" required to make Clark its instrumentality .... If it did not use Clark as an instrumentality or engage in any other type of inequitable conduct ... , argues Associates, then it cannot be equitably subordinated.

A

... In our prior opinion, we agreed with the district court and the bankruptcy court that, as a practical matter, Associates asserted total control over Clark's liquidation, and that it used its control in a manner detrimental to the unsecured creditors. Upon reconsideration, we have concluded that we cannot say that the sort of control Associates asserted over Clark's financial affairs rises to the level of unconscionable conduct necessary to justify the application of the doctrine of equitable subordination.

We ... cannot [now] escape the salient fact that, pursuant to its loan agreement with Clark, Associates had the right to reduce funding, just as it did, as Clark's sales slowed. We now conclude that ... Associates [did not] exceed[] its authority under the loan agreement, [n]or [did] Associates act[] inequitably in exercising its rights under that agreement.

* * *

... The agreement provided that Associates could reduce the ... advance rates at any time in its discretion. When Clark's business began to decline ... Associates ... reduce[d its] advance[s] .... Clark prepared a budget at Associates' request that indicated the disbursements necessary to keep the company operating. The budget did not include payment to vendors for previously shipped goods. Associates' former loan officer, Fred Slice, testified as to what he had in mind:

> If he [the comptroller of Clark] had had the availability [of funds to pay a vendor or other trade creditor] that particular day, I would have said, "Are you sure you've got that much availability, Jim," because he shouldn't have that much. The way I had structured it, he wouldn't have any money to pay his suppliers.
>
> ....
>
> But you know, the possibility that—this is all hypothetical. I had it structured so that there was no—there was barely enough money—there was enough money, if I did it right, enough money to keep the doors open. Clark could continue to operate, sell the inventory, turn it into receivables, collect the cash, transfer that cash to me, and reduce my loans. And, if he had ever had availability for other things, that meant I had done something wrong, and I would have been surprised. To ask me what I would have done is purely hypothetical[;] I don't think it would happen. I think it's so unrealistic, I don't know.

Despite Associates' motive, which was, according to Slice, "to get in the best position I can prior to the bankruptcy, i.e., I want to get the absolute amount of dollars as low as I can by hook or crook," the evidence shows that the amount of its advances continued to be based on the applicable funding formulas. Slice testified that the lender did not appreciably alter its original credit procedures when Clark fell into financial difficulty.

In our original opinion, we failed to focus sufficiently on the loan agreement, which gave Associates the right to conduct its affairs with Clark in the manner in which it did. In addition, we think that in our previous opinion we were overly influenced by the negative and inculpatory tone of Slice's testimony. Given the agreement he was working under, his testimony was hardly more than [boasting] about the power that the agreement afforded him over the financial affairs of Clark. Although his talk was crass (e.g., "I want to get the absolute dollars as low as I can, by hook or crook"), our careful examination of the record does not reveal any conduct on his part that was inconsistent with the loan agreement, irrespective of what his personal motive may have been.

*Through its loan agreement, every lender effectively exercises "control" over its borrower to some degree.* A lender in Associates' position will usually possess "control" in the sense that it can foreclose or drastically reduce the debtor's financing. The purpose of equitable subordination is to distinguish between the unilateral remedies that a creditor may properly enforce pursuant to its agreements with the debtor and other inequitable conduct such as fraud, misrepresentation, or the exercise of such total control over the debtor as to have essentially replaced its decision-making capacity with that of the lender. The crucial distinction between what is inequitable and what a lender can reasonably and legitimately do to protect its interests is the distinction between the existence of "control" and the exercise of that "control" to direct the activities of the debtor. ...

In our prior opinion, we drew support from In re American Lumber Co., 5 B.R. 470 (D.Minn. 1980), to ... equitably subordinate ... [Associate's claim]. Upon reconsideration, however, we find that the facts of that case are significantly more egregious than we have here. ...

Associates exercised significantly less "control" over the activities of Clark than did the lender in American Lumber. ... Associates did not ... interfere with the operations of the borrower to an extent even roughly commensurate with the degree of interference exercised by the bank in American Lumber. Associates made no management decisions for Clark, such as deciding which creditors to prefer with the diminishing amount of funds available. At no time did Associates place any of its employees as either a director or officer of Clark. Associates never influenced the removal from office of any Clark personnel .... Associates did not expressly dictate to Clark which bills to pay, nor did it direct Clark not to pay vendors or threaten a cut-off of advances if it did pay vendors. Clark handled its own daily operations. The same basic procedures with respect to the reporting of collateral, the calculation of availability of funds, and the procedures for the advancement of funds were followed throughout the relationship between Clark and Associates. Unlike the lender in American Lumber, Associates did not mislead creditors to continue supplying Clark. Cf. American Lumber, 5 B.R. at 474. Perhaps the most important fact that distinguishes this case from American Lumber is that Associates did not coerce Clark into executing the security agreements after Clark became insolvent. Instead, the loan and security agreements between Clark and Associates were entered into at arm's length prior to Clark's insolvency, and all of Associates' activities were conducted pursuant to those agreements.

Associates' control over Clark's finances, admittedly powerful and ultimately severe, was based solely on the exercise of powers found in the loan agreement. Associates' close watch over Clark's affairs does not, by itself, however, amount to such control as would justify equitable subordination. In re W.T. Grant, 699 F.2d 599, 610 (2d Cir.1983). "There is nothing inherently wrong with a creditor carefully monitoring his debtor's financial situation or with suggesting what course of action the debtor ought to follow." In re Teltronics Services, Inc., 29 B.R. 139, 172 (Bankr. E.D.N.Y. 1983). Although the terms of the agreement did give Associates potent leverage over Clark, that agreement did not give Associates total control over Clark's activities. At all material times Clark had the power to act autonomously and, if it chose, to disregard the advice of Associates; for example, Clark was free to shut its doors at any time it chose to do so and to file for bankruptcy.

Finally, on reconsideration, we are persuaded that the rationale of In re W.T. Grant Co., 699 F.2d 599 (2d Cir.1983) should control the case before us. In that case, the Second Circuit recognized that

> a creditor is under no fiduciary obligation to its debtor or to other creditors of the debtor in the collection of its claim. The permissible parameters of a creditor's efforts to seek collection from a debtor are generally those with respect to voidable preferences and fraudulent conveyances proscribed by the Bankruptcy Act; apart from these there is generally no objection to a creditor's using his bargaining position, including his ability to refuse to make further loans needed by the debtor, to improve the status of his existing claims.

699 F.2d at 609-10. Associates was not a fiduciary of Clark, it did not exert improper control over Clark's financial affairs, and it did not act inequitably in exercising its rights under its loan agreement with Clark.

B

... We therefore conclude that the district court erred in affirming the bankruptcy court's decision to subordinate Associates' claims.

## IV

... Because we have held that equitable subordination is inapplicable in this case, we do not address the question whether avoiding the transfer and equitable subordination are duplicative or complementary remedies.

\* \* \*

### ¶908: Cross-collateralization

1. Similar to creditors' conduct in *W.T. Grant* and *American Lumber* are the efforts by lenders advancing funds in bankruptcy to request or insist upon collateral not only for the new loan but for the pre-bankruptcy loans as well. In effect, the creditor insists upon, as a price for the new funds, enhanced repayment terms (seniority) on the old loans. Such a creditor request was made in In re Texlon Corp., 596 F.2d 1092 (2d Cir. 1979).

2. In *Texlon*, the debtor and creditor requested cross-collateralization ex parte; that is, they made the request without a hearing where other creditors could object. While cross-collateralization was not prohibited, the appellate court held the ex parte hearing to be inadequate. Judge Friendly noted that the debtor in possession was hardly neutral; the debtor was giving away the bankruptcy claim of the unsecured creditors. Accordingly, a hearing was required to "determine [whether] other sources of financing are available; [whether] other creditors would like to share in the financing if similarly favorable terms are accorded them; or [whether] the creditors do not want the business continued at the price of preferring a particular lender." Although the procedural requirement might be onerous if the loan were needed immediately, the judge saw no obvious alternative solution. Of course, the extent of the burden would depend on the differential capacity of the pre-bankruptcy creditor to act quickly and cheaply. If third-party lenders (i.e., without pre-bankruptcy loans) would be just as good, there's no reason for the debtor to go to the pre-bankruptcy lender and offer cross-collateralization. (Management presumably wants to "buy" the money as cheaply as possible when the "purchase" will be made with the bankrupt enterprise's funds. But when the payment will be made with the pre-existing creditors' funds, it is less concerned with keeping the loan cheap.)

3. The Eleventh Circuit struck down cross-collateralization as barred by § 364, § 507 and, indirectly, the preference provisions. Shapiro v. Saybrook Mfg. Co., 963 F.2d 1490 (11th Cir. 1992). Pre-petition, the bank lent the debtor $34 million, secured by $10 million of collateral. Post-petition, the bank lent an additional $3 million. The bankruptcy court allowed the debtor to offer all of its assets to secure the total $37 million in bank loans.

Section 364 allows a court to "authorize the obtaining of credit or the incurring of debt." The Circuit Court said this section allowed collateralization only of the *new* debt, not the old. The bank argued the bankruptcy court's inherent and wide equitable powers authorized cross-collateralization. The court believed that such a wide grab of equitable powers would violate § 507, which fixes priorities and contemplates equal treatment among the priorities. Cross-collateralization would create super-priorities not allowed by § 507, making the previously unsecured (but now cross-collateralized) claim superior to other unsecured claims. If undertaken by an insolvent company *before* bankruptcy, cross-collateralization would be a preference. For a court to sanction cross-collateralization would thereby violate central principles of bankruptcy.

4. Note incidentally that § 364 allows the court to "over-ride" a negative pledge clause in a bond. That is, a firm outside of bankruptcy might be unable to get new financing without giving the new financiers priority. Negative pledge clauses in pre-existing debt could preclude new priority debt. Section 364 substitutes the court's judgment for the contractual limitation of a negative pledge clause.

## B. Lender liability

### ¶909: Sources of lender liability

There are other sources of lender liability in substantially similar circumstances to equitable subordination. Recall from *Deprizio* that an insider must return to the estate preferential payments or preferential increases in collateral obtained within one year of the debtor's filing of the bankruptcy petition. Insiders include any person in control of the bankrupt. Bankruptcy Code, §§ 101(31), 547(b)(4); James Koch, *Bankruptcy Planning for the Secured Lender*, 99 Banking L.J. 788, 798–807 (1982); Morris Macey, *No Fault Subordination of Loans in Bankruptcy*, 85 Com. L.J. 44 (1980).

Apart from § 510 of the Bankruptcy Code, controlling persons can be held more directly liable for violations of the securities laws. Securities Act of 1933, § 15, 15 U.S.C. § 77o; Securities Exchange Act of 1934, § 20, 15 U.S.C. § 78t.

### ¶910: State National Bank of El Paso v. Farah Mfg. Co., 678 S.W.2d 661 (Tex. Ct. App. 1984)

[William Farah was the chief executive officer of Farah Manufacturing Company. After a bitter labor dispute, during which the company lost a great deal of money, Farah left as CEO. The labor dispute was settled. FMC's banks agreed to extend new loans of about $22 million to FMC only on condition that Farah not return to FMC. Farah attempted to return to FMC; the banks blocked him. FMC's losses continued. Eventually Farah did succeed and returned as CEO. The company prospered, and Farah had the company sue the banks, resulting in a jury verdict of $19 million against the banks. The decision on appeal follows.]

CHARLES R. SCHULTE, Associate Justice

This case centers around a management change clause contained in a $22,000,00.00 loan agreement [between Farah Manufacturing ("FMC")] and the banks. The jury found Appellant bank, acting alone or in conspiracy with any of the other lenders, committed acts of fraud, duress and interference, proximately resulting in damages to Appellee, and set damages at $18,947,348.77. We reform and affirm.

[The creditors had implied that they would declare an Event of Default under the loan agreement, accelerate the maturity of the principal amount, and demand repayment in full if Farah, the debtor's former CEO, returned to manage the company; in fact, the trial court concluded, the creditors were uncertain about their intentions if he returned, or they intended not to call the loan.]

**[The management clause]**

The management change clause set forth in Section 6.1(g) of the February 14, 1977, loan agreement made it an event of default if there occurred:

> Any change in the office of President and Chief Executive Officer of Farah [Manufacturing Company, Inc.] or any other change in the executive management of Farah [Manufacturing Company, Inc.] which any two Banks shall consider, for any reason whatsoever, to be adverse to the interests of the Banks.

\* \* \*

... FMC began in 1919 as a family owned apparel manufacturer. Farah became CEO in 1964. In 1967 FMC went public. By 1970, the company had plants in Texas and overseas with annual sales of $136,000,000.00. Beginning in 1972, the firm suffered a strike and a nationwide boycott. The strike was settled in 1974. During the period 1972–1976 FMC experienced a pre-tax loss of $43,965,000.00. On July 9, 1976, the FMC Board named one of its members, Leone, as CEO of FMC replacing Farah. On February 14, 1977, a preexisting loan agreement between FMC [and the banks] was amended and included the management change clause previously set forth. [As the following paragraphs detail, over the opposition of the banks, several of whom had directors on the FMC board, Farah eventually returned to FMC as CEO.]

[The banks] characteriz[e] the case as one arising out of warnings issued to FMC in March, 1977, by [the banks] in reliance on the management change clause above set forth. Appellant's position is that when Farah attempted to persuade FMC's board to elect him CEO, the banks stated their intent to enforce their right under the loan agreement to treat Farah's election as a default and call their loan. Appellant insists that the warnings of the banks did not exceed their legal rights under the change clause (and otherwise) and further that FMC failed to adduce evidence to establish a cognizable cause of action. [The banks] maintai[n] that the banks made the loan to FMC in reliance upon FMC's assurances in 1976 that the company was under new management and that the banks would be protected by the management change clause against any future change in management .... [The banks also maintain] that the covenant was a provision freely given by FMC, that it was undisputedly lawful, and that the subsequently strengthened and amended clause was approved by the entire FMC board with the clear understanding that the covenant could be used to resist an effort by Farah to return as CEO.

On the other hand, FMC, plaintiff below and Appellee here, asserts the general position that under the management change clause, when it became apparent that Farah was about to regain control of FMC, which was unacceptable to the banks, that the banks had two legitimate options ... They could attempt to call the loan or elect not to and live with Farah as CEO. Instead, Appellee maintains, the banks chose a third option and unlawfully prevented Farah's election and installed directors and officers to keep Farah out of management. The claim is made that the "hand picked minions" mismanaged the company and stripped it of valuable assets for unnecessary loan prepayments. Further, Appellee asserts, when the banks defrauded and coerced FMC's directors to prevent Farah's return to management, they defrauded and coerced FMC itself. When they installed their own choice of management, stacked the FMC board and undertook the actions to exclude Farah from management, the banks interfered with FMC's management and corporate governance rights through an unlawful course of conduct marked with deception and coercion. These alleged wrongful acts are stated to have proximately caused damages to FMC in two respects. First, the incompetent management installed and perpetuated by the banks resulted in losses and auction sale damages [when a mill was sold at auction]. Second, their preventing the election of competent management caused losses and lost profits. Appellee finally contends Farah fought his way back into control, saved the company from bankruptcy and restored it to profitability.

\* \* \*

Following the strike and boycott of 1972–1974, and substantial losses, on March 3, 1976, the FMC Board unanimously elected Leone, an FMC director since 1973 and chosen by Farah to succeed him, as president and COO. Farah retained his positions as board chairman and CEO. Farah assigned to Leone nearly all executive responsibility in expectation that Leone would offer a different style of management. The lenders had no input in Leone's election. On the same day, Farah's son, J. Farah, was elected as a director. The board then consisted of Farah, J. Farah, Conroy, Leone, Gordon Foster, Frost, Kozmetsky and Lerner.

At its meeting on July 9, 1976, the board demanded that Farah resign as CEO. A resolution, introduced by Farah and naming Leone as new CEO, was passed. Farah retained the title of board chairman, a ceremonial position with no management responsibilities. His resignation as CEO was demanded on the basis that he was the cause of FMC's management problems and poor financial condition.

Farah later deemed Leone incapable of properly managing the company and unable to quickly adjust to changes in market demand for fashions. Under Leone, FMC's sales and profits declined. Farah urged Leone to change his practices. Both Leone and the board viewed this as unwarranted interference.

In the spring of 1976, FMC had begun to seek a $30,000,000.00 loan to survive losses. An interim agreement was arrived at to be followed in October, 1976, by a finalized loan agreement. Both contained management change clauses. On February 14, 1977, a restructured collateralized loan agreement was reached. FMC maintains that the appraised value of the collateral was $72,000,000.00 which amount is disputed by State National. This latest agreement had the strengthened management change clause earlier set forth in this opinion.

At a shareholders' meeting on March 7, 1977, Farah sought to have a new board of directors elected to insure his return to management .... Several factors induced him to change his mind and to vote for the incumbent board which he believed would elect him CEO anyway. Because of the management change clause, the board declined absent a statement of position from the lenders. The lenders initially refused to assert a position. The board suggested Farah personally present his management proposal to the lenders. He did so at [one of the banks] in Dallas on March 14, 1977, stressing his return as CEO was the only way to save FMC. After his presentation, Farah was asked to leave the meeting so the lenders could discuss the matter. [One bank] voiced opposition to Farah. No decision was reached. Farah was informed of their indecision and that a change in CEO could constitute a violation of the management change clause ....

On March 16, Farah talked to ... the senior loan officer of [a bank] on a flight to New York and repeated the proposal he had made to all the lenders in Dallas two days before. Farah testified, "[h]e (Bunten) said he felt that we ought to disregard the covenant as being boiler plate, they had it in all of their agreements, and run the business and get the thing back in shape." Farah began planning his return to management. [A bank candidate for CEO also emerged. When it appeared that Farah had the support of a majority of the board, the banks considered what to do.]

The lenders analyzed the ramifications of FMC's bankruptcy, should a default be declared, and their exposure to liability for changes in FMC management. According to the testimony of Daugherty, President of State National, the lenders felt that their only legitimate options, should Farah become CEO, were to either call the loan or let Farah hold office unmolested. Daugherty testified that neither choice was acceptable to the banks. They were adverse to the bankruptcy of FMC. As FMC was not otherwise in default on the loan at the time, State National was unwilling to put El Paso's largest private employer into bankruptcy.

\* \* \*

Then on March 22, Donahue drafted a letter conveying the lenders' position to the board. The letter approved by all the lenders was signed by Tom Foster and delivered to Gordon Foster prior to the board meeting to be held that day. Farah testified that at the time of the board meeting he was unaware of the lenders' meeting of the previous day. He anticipated he would be elected CEO and that his election would be approved by Bunten of Republic, to whom he had spoken on the plane trip to New York. The letter of March 22 read in part:

> The Banks wish to advise the Board that a change of executive management which includes the election of Mr. William Farah as chief executive of the Company or results in his being the power to generally supervise and control the operations and affairs of the Company is unacceptable to the Banks, and the Banks will not grant any waiver of default based thereon. The Banks are, however, willing to consider a waiver of the default clause ... if the Board decides that a change in the office of the Chief Executive of the Company (involving others than Mr. Farah) is in the best interests of the Company. The Banks do not intend hereby and do not waive any default based on the developments in the Company constituting a material adverse change of circumstances .... The Banks are still considering their position regarding the events which have and are coming to their attention.

Tom Foster testified that the lenders did not want to call the loan and create a default which would result in FMC's bankruptcy. He admitted that, if Farah were elected, the lenders had a choice of either doing nothing or attempting to call the loan. Although the interpretation of the letter was left to the board, he conceded that the statement of the lenders, that they would not waive a default, could have created an impression that there would be a default if Farah were elected ....

[At the board meeting at which Farah expected to named CEO, the letter was presented to the board. Some directors were concerned that election of Farah as CEO would put FMC in default, the loan would be accelerated, and the company would then be closed or bankrupt.] The meeting was recessed without an election of new directors or CEO.

[Thereafter, the bankers continued to oppose the return of Farah as CEO.] [T]he lenders then met with [FMC directors early in the day of the next board meeting, on March 23. One director,] Azar described Donahue as the spokesman for the lender group and said Donahue opened the meeting by saying that "Willie [Farah] was not acceptable as a chief executive officer and president." Azar said he told Donahue that Farah was the only one who could turn the company around. When asked what else Donahue had said, Azar responded, "[w]ell, it got to the point where if Willie Farah was elected president of the company, why, he would automatically bankrupt the company and he would padlock it the next day." Azar said that after talking to [the company's] attorney ... on the phone he came back and told Donahue that "he could take his loan agreement and shove it up his ass." Azar explained he did that "trying to determine how serious they were about bankrupting and closing the company, what was his intent. I intended to push him to the very brink and very edge and find out." Azar said Donahue's response was "[w]e will." Azar said he then believed Donahue would bankrupt and padlock the company if the board elected Farah. He said as a result of the meeting, "I was fearful of putting the company in bankruptcy. So I agreed to talk to Mr. Farah and ask him to stand down and not stand for election." ...

Also, at the Azar meeting, J. Farah criticized his father's views on management of FMC and indicated he could not support him for CEO, expressing emotional pressure and danger from the management change clause .... Azar also testified that the lenders never told him that they would not, in fact, bankrupt FMC if Farah were elected. Several of those in attendance at the Azar meeting testified that Donahue did not make any statement regarding bankrupting and padlocking the company. Tom Foster admitted that Azar was not informed of the lenders' meeting of March 21 [at which lenders tentatively concluded] that a default would be declared only after Farah's election or that a default might never be declared.

* * *

In accordance with his representation that he would talk to Farah, Azar met with Farah prior to the board meeting [scheduled for later that day]. Azar testified he told Farah that the lenders wanted Farah to resign as board chairman and to elect in his stead Gordon Foster (an employee of El Paso National Bank) and Conroy (a director of State National) as CEO. Azar asked Farah to stand down and told him of assurances by the lenders that they would bankrupt and padlock the company. Azar said he (Azar) believed there was no other way to save FMC and that the election of Gordon Foster and Conroy was the only way to prevent FMC's bankruptcy. Farah testified he believed what Azar and Donahue had told him and that after talking to Azar, "I went to the board meeting, nominated Mr. Conroy to be chief executive officer and Mr. Gordon Foster to be Chairman."

Gordon Foster and Conroy were unanimously elected as nominated. Azar testified that his feelings for Conroy [as not capable of running FMC] had not changed. Gordon Foster testified that in his opinion, in spite of reservations, Conroy was the only one available who could assume the position. The lenders agreed not to deem Conroy's election as an event of default.

* * *

[FMC continued its financial decline. Conroy was replaced as CEO by Galef, who had] proposed to the lenders in June that he replace Conroy as CEO. He indicated to them his plan to make sizable loan prepayments during the next several months by selling company assets. The lenders approved of his becoming CEO. Galef presented his proposal to the board and expressed that he could have FMC "in the black in 90 days." ... Galef's projection for profitability never materialized. Galef also proposed that Farah be used as a consultant in manufacturing and management. At the July 30 board meeting, Galef was unanimously elected as CEO. Farah testified he supported

Galef in order to save FMC from Conroy and because Galef had asked him (Farah) to serve as a consultant. Farah viewed this as the only way he could return to management.

Azar testified he supported Galef because Galef had agreed to use Farah and because of the continued existence of the management change clause.

State National had expressed opposition to Farah as a consultant. Unable to determine whether Galef's election was adverse to their interests, the lenders did agree to waive the management change clause in favor of Galef's election.

The consternation caused by Galef's suggestion to use Farah, according to Tom Foster, was reported to him by Gordon Foster. Once elected, Galef did not use Farah as a consultant.

[While Conroy was CEO,] FMC lost production contracts because it was unable to timely deliver quality goods. As Conroy continued to miss his budget and sales projections, FMC's sales and order rates continued to decline. Conroy resigned from the board on September 24, 1977.

FMC also maintains that the evidence shows Galef was inexperienced in the men's apparel business. Galef failed to make improvements in the 1977 fall line and was responsible for introducing the 1978 spring line which was too expensive, poorly priced and contrary to market demand. The spring line, although heavily advertised, received poor public response. As a result thereof, many orders were canceled and excess inventory accumulated. With FMC losing much of its market to competitors by early 1978, Farah testified that Galef introduced the 1978 fall line with the dominant theme the same as that in the previously unsuccessful spring line.

FMC presented evidence showing that [FMC's condition deteriorated while Galef was CEO.]

While Galef was CEO, assets of FMC were sold at internationally publicized auctions. The net proceeds from the sales were used to make prepayments on FMC's loan. FMC points to the evidence that the auctions stripped it of valuable assets and that its competitors purchased much of the machinery and equipment for use in competition with FMC and that State National financed the purchase of certain auctioned assets by one of FMC's competitors .... It is State National's position that the machinery and equipment sold were in excess of FMC's operating needs. The lenders requested FMC to sell the assets pursuant to a promise made by FMC in June, 1976, that it would do so. Such promise had been an inducement for the lenders to make the loan.

\* \* \*

On November 10, 1977, the board passed a resolution calling for Farah's resignation as a director. Although Farah and Azar dissented, they both soon resigned. In January, 1978, Farah gave notice of a proxy fight that he was preparing in order to elect a slate of directors at the March board meeting whereby he could be reinstated as

CEO. Clifford and Virginia Farah responded with a suit to remove Farah as trustee under the trust holding their stock. This was viewed by Farah as a measure to force his vote for the incumbent board.

There is evidence that the lenders took an active interest to oppose Farah in his proxy fight and in his suit with Clifford and Virginia. Farah prevailed in the suit. This ultimately meant success for him in his proxy fight.

In January, 1978, FMC's financial condition was critical. At this time, the lenders determined that they were no longer willing to finance FMC's day-to-day operations although they did want to maintain some type of a long-term loan. FMC's short-term debts were soon to be due. Prior to Farah's return, the lenders had decided that the loan would be restructured whereby the management change clause would be deleted if: (1) FMC repaid the short-term debt by the middle of February, 1978; and (2) the long-term debts were substantially reduced and prepaid through third party accounts receivable financing. These conditions were met and the way was paved for Farah's return as CEO. The restructuring document originally contained a release for lender liability. When discovered by FMC, it was deleted.

\* \* \*

On April 4, 1978, the FMC board approved the restructured loan agreement. Although FMC failed to make several payments that were due in the spring of 1978, those payments were made in July. By July of 1979, FMC had refinanced and then repaid the loan in full.

FMC cites to considerable testimony regarding Farah's abilities and the high regard in which he is now held by others in the apparel industry for his success in turning FMC around after his return. After his return, he reduced selling and administrative costs, disposed of unusable inventory to generate working capital, expanded international sales and regenerated employee, supplier and retailer confidence in FMC and its products. Since Farah's return to management, FMC has consistently experienced an increase in sales and profits and has regained its position as an effective competitor with other manufacturers of apparel.

\* \* \*

### [Fraud]

FMC's cause of action for fraud focuses upon the March 22 letter and the statements made by Donahue to Farah and other board members on March 23 of bankruptcy and padlocking if Farah were elected as CEO. The evidence is legally and factually sufficient, albeit conflicting, that on March 21 the lenders had either decided not to declare a default which would result in FMC's bankruptcy or reached no decision on the matter. Neither position was conveyed to the board. Regardless of the position taken, the "warnings" (representations) made in the letter and by Donahue are characterized by FMC as false threats constituting fraud.

Fraud may be effected by a misrepresentation .... A representation consists of words or other conduct manifesting to another the existence of a fact, including a state of mind. It may be made directly to the other or by a manifestation to third persons intended to reach the other. A misrepresentation is a representation which, under the circumstances, amounts to an assertion not in accordance with the facts .... A representation literally true is actionable if used to create an impression substantially false ....

**[Good faith]**

FMC maintains that the lenders were required to exercise good faith in their representations made to FMC on March 22 and 23 .... In regard to good faith, the Texas Business and Commerce Code (Vernon 1968) provides:

> Sec. 1.203. Every contract or duty within this title implies an obligation of good faith in its performance or enforcement.
> Sec. 1.201(19). "Good faith" means honesty in fact in the conduct or transaction concerned.

FMC also maintains that once the lenders voluntarily conveyed information which was false or misleading (the March 22 letter and the representations attributed to Donahue) and which would influence Farah and other board members, then the lenders were under a duty to disclose the whole truth regarding any decision on default ....

[The bank] maintains that fraud cannot arise from a warning of an intention to enforce legal rights. It argues that the issue is not whether the lenders had yet to commit to do what they had warned. Rather, the issue is whether they had a legal right to do it.

... The representations that a default would be declared and the company bankrupted and padlocked if Farah were elected as CEO concern a material fact and amount to more than a mere opinion, judgment, probability or expectation on the part of the lenders .... The March 22 letter and representations created a false impression regarding the lenders' decision (or lack of decision) to declare a default.

\* \* \*

As a matter of law, FMC has established a cause of action for fraud. The evidence is legally and factually sufficient to support the jury's finding thereon ....

**[Duress]**

[Next is the question of] the legal and factual sufficiency of the evidence to support the jury's finding of duress .... Dale v. Simon, 267 S.W. 467, 470 (Tex. Comm'n

App. 1924, judgement adopted) is the leading case as to the elements of and the limitations upon a cause of action for duress. It was there held:

> There can be no duress unless [1] there is a threat to do some act which the party threatening has no legal right to do. [2] Such threat must be of such character as to destroy the free agency of the party to whom it is directed. It must overcome his will and cause him to do that which he would not otherwise do, and which he was not legally bound to do. [3] The restraint caused by such threat must be imminent. [4] It must be such that the person to whom it is directed has no present means of protection.

\* \* \*

Even where an insecurity clause is drafted in the broadest possible terms, the primary question is whether the creditor's attempt to accelerate stemmed from a reasonable, good-faith belief that its security was about to become impaired. Acceleration clauses are not to be used offensively such as for the commercial advantage of the creditor. They do not permit acceleration when the facts make its use unjust or oppressive.

\* \* \*

Economic duress (business coercion) may be evidenced by forcing a victim to choose between distasteful and costly situations, i.e., bow to duress or face bankruptcy, loss of credit rating, or loss of profits from a venture.

There is evidence that the loan to FMC was not in default at the time the warnings were given by the lenders on March 22 and 23. There was then no impaired prospect of repayment but for the perpetuation of FMC's alleged poor financial condition or perhaps for the possibility of Farah's election as CEO (in view of his past performance). Admittedly, his election could have constituted a default under the management change clause thereby enabling the lenders to legitimately enforce their legal rights.

However, there was no circumstance to authorize the manner in which the warnings to declare default were made. This is particularly true when given the evidence that the lenders previously had either decided not to declare a default which would result in FMC's bankruptcy or reached no decision on the matter....

FMC did undertake a new obligation to the lenders under duress. By virtue of the warnings made on March 22 and 23, it became specifically and absolutely obligated not to have Farah elected as CEO. Under the management change clause, however, Farah could have been elected. The board had been under no obligation to see that such would not occur. In the "event" that it did, then it was the legitimate option of the lenders to determine whether or not it should be viewed as a default. Instead, they chose to issue warnings designed to force the board to elect someone other than Farah.

It is argued that the management change clause was approved by the entire FMC board with the clear understanding that the clause could be used to resist an effort by Farah to return as CEO. It is true that use of the management change clause had been perceived by the board in context with the legitimate options available to the lenders. However, the evidence reflects that there was no anticipation of the manner in which it was ultimately used.

\* \* \*

As a matter of law, FMC has established a cause of action for duress. The evidence is legally and factually sufficient to support the jury's finding thereon....

\* \* \*

**[Damages]**

Actual losses were awarded in the amount of $2,668,000.00. Generally, State National contends that there is no evidence that it caused such damages to be incurred or that the losses were attributable to the alleged mistakes of FMC's management during the year in controversy (April, 1977 through March, 1978) or to any lender action as distinguished from circumstances existing or events occurring prior to that time.

\* \* \*

The evidence is legally sufficient to support the jury's finding of $2,668,000.00. Cases cited by [the banks] pertain to situations wherein there was no evidence to support a recovery of damages. The evidence is also factually sufficient to support the finding ....

[Next is the question of] the legal and factual sufficiency of the evidence to support the jury's finding of lost profits .... [The banks allege] that the trial court erroneously rendered judgment on such finding because as a matter of law FMC is not entitled to a recovery [and] that the evidence is factually insufficient to support the finding.

In contrast to the jury's finding of $15,482,500.00, Killman testified that FMC lost profits totaling $51,232,000.00 (by use of the base period of 1959 through 1971). His calculations derived from the base period of 1959 through 1975 reflect lost profits totaling $24,377,000.00.

Numerous reasons are advanced by State National in support of its position that FMC has no legal basis for recovery. First, it is argued that the evidence does not distinguish between the effects of the lenders' alleged conduct and other known factors affecting FMC's profits ....

Numerous reasons are raised which, when construed together, allege that FMC's lost profits cannot be intelligently estimated. [FMC's expert used a base period of 1959 through 1975, not the most recent period of staggering losses.] ...

\* \* \*

FMC was an established business despite the fact that it had sustained these losses in the several years preceding the damage period. The omission of the year 1976 from either base period would not affect its ability to recover lost profits ....

State National argues that ... [unpredictable] market fluctuations in the men's apparel business ... render the projection of lost profits conjectural. Admittedly, the men's apparel business is volatile in nature due to the changes in market demand ....

\* \* \*

[However, FMC's expert nevertheless] utilized a satisfactory methodology to calculate lost profits.

\* \* \*

As a matter of law, FMC is entitled to the recovery of lost profits. The evidence is legally and factually sufficient to support the jury's finding thereon ....

... [T]he trial court's judgment is reformed to award Appellee judgment in the total sum of $18,647,243.77 ....

... [A]ffirmed.

---

### ¶911: Questions on lender liability in *Farah*

1. To the extent that Farah did (or could) control the Board of Directors, could Farah have obtained a loan from another bank, without the management clause and presumably at a higher rate of interest? Could he then have defaulted on the first loan and repaid it with the proceeds of the new loan without the control clause?

2. To the extent that Farah could not control a majority of stock before January 1978, was it his family and not the banks who were critical in keeping him out of management?

3. During 1972–1976, when Farah was CEO, the company lost $44 million. The company was not well-known for smooth labor relations. Farah resigned in July 1976. The management clause was put into the loan agreement by the banks in February 1977. Could the FMC board have sensibly agreed to the management clause to assure lenders that the company was not about to return to the 1972–1976 labor tensions?

4. Is it surprising that the lenders were uncertain whether they would declare a default if Farah returned? Why wouldn't the lenders bluff, threatening a default, but wait until Farah actually returned before finally deciding whether to declare one? Was the bank statement a form of notice of probable intention to declare a default if Farah returned?

5. Damages were based on losses of $2.6 million and lost profits of $15.5 million. These damages were caused, concludes the court, by lenders that lent FMC $22 million, a sum not much larger than the damages found. Again, if Farah and FMC

thought that the banks were causing such damage to FMC, were they under any duty to mitigate? That is, should they have found another lender who (at a higher interest rate) would have lent money to FMC with Farah as CEO? Would the company's damage claim then have been the difference between the interest rate on the El Paso loan and the higher rate on the new loan, presumably 2% or 3% on $22 million for a few years until FMC's profits stabilized at the (expected) high level?

6. Should the lenders have been more circumspect in their letter to the Board? What result if they wrote: "Under the loan agreement, a return of Farah as CEO could constitute an event of default, which could lead to FMC's bankruptcy and the padlocking of the company's factories. While the lenders have not yet reached any decision on whether a default will be declared, we point out that the clause was inserted for the purpose of preventing the return of Mr. Farah as CEO, that the banks have consistently opposed the return of Mr. Farah as CEO, and that the banks now oppose the return of Mr. Farah as CEO."

7. On the duress theory, what did the bankers get from FMC beyond that which they were entitled to get under the management clause? That is, did the bankers threaten to invoke the management clause and thereby extract from FMC a higher interest rate, better security, or other benefits? Or did the bankers threaten to invoke the management change clause solely to prevent a change in management?

8. Did the bankers threaten to invoke the management change clause to get more than a veto over the return of Farah? Did they use it to get particular people they wanted as managers? Divide the duress analysis into three parts: (1) keeping Farah out, (2) getting the banker's preferred managers, associated with the banks, in, and (3) selling FMC assets.

Banks usually get interest for their loan. What if a debtor doesn't pay and the banks threaten to sue under the loan agreement? Does the debtor have a claim for duress if the debtor under threat of suit pays up?

9. Had the lenders been directors, would the business judgment rule have protected their actions in a suit by the shareholders? Which actions? Sale of the machinery? Mistakes in running the business?

10. Subsequent history: The Texas supreme court granted a hearing, suggesting some possibility of revision or reversal. The winners in *Farah* decided to settle, rather than take a chance.[5]

11. Would or should the analysis of the banks' actions differ if the banks owned stock in FMC? Realistically, most creditors would not want to own stock, but one could imagine that a "lead" bank would own some stock in the company, with the other

---

[5] 105 Harv. L. Rev. 1780, 1789 (1992).

creditors not owning stock. For example, imagine this as FMC's balance sheet when the loans were first made:

| $50M | $40 M loans, | $8M held by El Paso Nat'l |
|---|---|---|
|  | $10 M stock, | $2M held by El Paso Nat'l |
|  |  | $3M held by Farah family |
|  |  | $5M publicly-held, or held by other banks |

This is purely imaginary for an American bank. American banks are generally not allowed to own any stock in industrial firms; they can affiliate with companies that do own stock, but the affiliates themselves can own no more than 5% of the voting stock of an industrial firm, and bank regulators have interpreted the banking law prohibitions as barring the affiliate from being active in the industrial company. So use your imagination here.[6]

Were this financial scenario in play, should El Paso be entitled to business judgment deference? Would this kind of structure indeed undermine much of the justification for the automatic stay and chapter 11? Would it be distinguishable from *Deep Rock*? If the lead bank foreclosed and sold some of the firm's assets (as FMC did), would the financial structure support a court's deference to the business judgment of the lead bank?

## ¶912: A comparative note

These doctrines and incentives are not the only ones imaginable. Consider how Japanese banks have been said to act when a client was in trouble:

> The bank will send a director to an ailing firm. If the director succeeds in revitalizing the firm, he or she is a hero and is guaranteed a top position in the bank. If one bank pulls out its person before the company is rejuvenated, another bank will step in. If this director concludes that changes are necessary for the corporation's management practices, he or she will recommend them. The perspective as an objective third party who is not involved in daily affairs of the company lets this director perceive necessary changes better. The bank might also recommend that a supplier make certain changes that are necessary to revitalize the company
> ....

---

[6] The ban on bank ownership of stock originates in the 19th century National Bank Act and was reconfirmed in the more famous Glass-Steagall Act in 1933. In 1999 Congress repealed the Glass-Steagall Act in general, but not the ban on stock ownership.

William Ouchi, The M-Form Society 88 (1984). Mainstream scholarship here has seen the main bank as crisis epicenter, making managerial, strategic and financial changes when the first-line team failed.[7] This practice might have succeeded often when corporate failures were isolated, and their causes clear (such as poor management of a known technology). But when crises are economy-wide (as they became in Japan in recent years), and when the information needed to transform the firm is not likely to be within the bank's knowledge, then the system would presumably work less well (as it seems to have in recent years).

Practices like lender liability and equitable subordination played a role in Japan, but in inducing bank involvement, not deterring it. Anecdotes say Japanese practice had the "main" bank—the largest stockholder with 5% of the firm's stock and a big chunk of the bank lending—subordinating its loan to the other financiers' loans. The bank could not avoid subordination by forsaking involvement, as the American bank can. Rather, the bank could improve its position by improving the value of the failing firm. It became the residual claimant, both formally through its stock holding and informally through the expectation of "voluntary" subordination.

---

[7] Masahiko Aoki, Ex Post Monitoring by the Main Bank (1992); Masahiko Aoki & Paul Sheard, The Role of the Japanese Main Bank in the Corporate Governance Structure in Japan (1991); Robert Reich and John Donahue, New Deals: The Chrysler Revival and the American System 81–85 (1985) (Mazda rescue).

# CHAPTER 10

# REJECTING PRE-BANKRUPTCY CONTRACTS

**A. The trustee's right to reject or assume**
**B. Social costs**
**C. Specific performance**
**D. Labor**
**E. Assignment**
**F. Environmental clean-up obligations**

...........................................................................................................

A bankrupt company has contracts on which its performance is due. The type of contract we have examined thus far has been the financial contract: the bankrupt company is obligated to repay money it has borrowed, and bankruptcy adjusts the rights of those on the other side of a bankrupt's financial contracts.

## A. The trustee's right to reject or assume

How about a bankrupt's other contracts? Are those left unadjusted? The Bankruptcy Code allows the bankrupt to affirm or to reject executory contracts—those contracts for which neither side has substantially performed its obligation under the contract. Upon rejection, the nonbankrupt party obtains a claim in bankruptcy, and shares with the bankrupt's other creditors.

### § 365. Executory contracts and unexpired leases

(a) ... the trustee, subject to the court's approval, may assume or reject any executory contract or unexpired lease of the debtor.

(b) (1) If there has been a default in an executory contract or unexpired lease of the debtor, the trustee may not assume such contract or lease unless ... the trustee—

(A) cures ... ;

(B) compensates ... ; and

(C) provides adequate assurance of future performance ....

(2) Paragraph (1) of this subsection does not apply to a default that is a breach of a provision relating to—

(A) the insolvency or financial condition of the debtor at any time before the closing of the case;

(B) the commencement of a case under this title;

(C) the appointment of ... a trustee ...; or

(D) the satisfaction of any penalty rate or provision relating to a default arising from any failure by the debtor to perform nonmonetary obligations under the executory contract or unexpired lease.

### § 502. Allowance of claims or interests

(g) A claim arising from the rejection, under section 365 ... of an executory contract ... of the debtor that has not been assumed shall be determined, and shall be allowed ... or disallowed ... , the same as if such claim had arisen before the date of the filing of the petition.

This "right" of the bankrupt to assume or reject an uncompleted contract is no different than the "right" of any contracting party to perform or to default. But because the contracting party's claim for damages is treated as a *pre-bankruptcy* default of the bankrupt, this power of the bankrupt gives it a head's-the-bankrupt-wins, tails-the-other-party loses quality: the bankrupt contracting party can pay damages in discounted "bankruptcy dollars." If the bankrupt contracts before bankruptcy with A, for A to deliver 100 widgets at $10 each, and the market price rises to $15 each by the time of the bankruptcy, then the bankrupt assumes the contract and pockets the $500 gain (to be shared ultimately by all of the bankrupt's creditors). But if the market price declines to $5, then the bankrupt would reject the contract. A has a claim in bankruptcy for $500, which ordinarily would be paid (in essence by the unsecured creditors or the stockholders) at less than $500.

For "spot" transactions, the analysis is easy. For more complex, relational contracts, the analysis is only a little harder. If the bankrupt's and A's contract for the widgets is part of a larger deal, of say, a requirements contract, or a contract for A to build a factory for the bankrupt, part of which requires that it deliver widgets to A, then the Bankruptcy Code takes an all-or-nothing approach: the bankrupt must assume the burdens of the contract along with its benefits. Once it affirms the entire contract, it must pay any of the missed partial installments.

Section 365 has three principal exceptions to the all-or-nothing approach: First, the nonbankrupt cannot take advantage of an ipso facto clause, i.e., a clause that allows it, the nonbankrupt, to opt out of a contract just because the bankrupt has filed for bankruptcy. Once the debtor assumes the contract, it need not cure the breach of an ipso facto clause. Second, if the contract has penalty rates that arise from a bankrupt's failure to perform, the penalty is not enforceable against the bankrupt.[1] Third, the bankrupt can assign contracts and leases, notwithstanding that the contract or lease bars assignment. (This allows the bankrupt to profit from contracts or leases that it cannot itself use as it consolidates its operations. It can still "profit" from these unusable contracts and leases if they have better-than-market rates for the bankrupt.)[2]

We've seen that a typical large bankruptcy takes two or three years until the court confirms a plan of reorganization. When must the bankrupt decide whether to reject or assume its contracts and leases?

Generally the bankrupt gets until the confirmation of the plan to assume or reject. (Once assumed, the bankrupt's obligation becomes an administrative expense of the estate; once rejected, the contract claim is an ordinary creditor's claim, usually unsecured.) One major exception to the debtor's authority to wait to decide whether to confirm is for commercial leases, which the bankrupt must decide on within sixty days of the bankruptcy filing.

But as a business matter the bankrupt might not be able to wait to decide. Imagine an irate supplier shipped goods in before bankruptcy under a long-term supply contract. The bankrupt needs another delivery, but the supplier won't ship until it's paid on the old shipment and the bankrupt assumes the entire contract, so that the supplier knows that it has a long-term deal.

Could the bankrupt "force" a delivery—i.e., get specific performance—before it decides whether to assume or reject? Case law is mixed. But as a practical matter when dealing with suppliers, it may have to assume the contract to get satisfactory deliveries under the contract. (Note that the bankrupt can always reject the contract and buy elsewhere—and will usually do so if the contract price has become unfavorable to the bankrupt.)

Note the bankruptcy difference between a long-term supply contract, with multiple delivery dates, and a series of "spot" contracts. Contrast (1) a supplier who has a contract to deliver the bankrupt, say, 100 pairs of jeans weekly for the next year with (2) a dress manufacturer who has a few separate, discrete orders from the bankrupt. In case (1), the bankrupt must assume or reject the entire contract. If assumed, the bankrupt must pay for everything; if rejected the jean-maker has a claim for damages as a general, pre-bankruptcy creditor. In case (2), the dress-manufacturer ships the first order to the bankrupt Barney's fashion store a month before its bankruptcy. The dress manufacturer is unpaid when the petition is filed. The dress manufacturer will wait until plan confirmation to be paid, and usually will not be paid in full for that ship-

---

[1] This provision was rushed through Congress in 1994. It applies only to the bankrupt's failure to perform nonmonetary obligations under the contract.

[2] Also, the bankrupt can assign these contracts or leases without keeping liability if the assignee breaches the lease or contract. And if the bankrupt has a "profitable" lease to assign, but the lease restricts the bankrupt's use of the premises, both the bankrupt and the assignee can ignore the use-restriction clause of the lease.

ment. The same dress manufacturer whose pre-bankruptcy order was open when the petition was filed, and who ships into Barney's after the filing, and after the bankrupt assumes the contract, will be paid in full, usually on time, as an administrative expense entitled to priority. And, if the dress manufacturer gets Barney's next order for dresses *after* Barney's files its petition in bankruptcy, that order will be an administrative expense and, even if rejected, would yield the dress manufacturer a claim for damages, a claim usually paid in full as an administrative expense.

### § 507. Priorities

(a) The following expenses and claims have priority in the following order:
(1) First, administrative expenses allowed under section 503(b) ....
....

### § 503. Allowance of administrative expenses

(a) ...
(b) After notice and a hearing, there shall be allowed, administrative expenses ... including—
(1)(A) the actual, necessary costs and expenses of preserving the estate ...
(2) ... .

## B. Social costs

Consider a firm that contracts for widgets at $100 before bankruptcy. The seller will produce these at a cost of $60. Before the seller delivers, the buyer files for bankruptcy, during which the trustee can assume or reject the delivery contract.

What will the trustee's calculations be? Let's assume that the widgets are now worth only $80 to the buyer (but still would cost the seller $60 to make). The bankrupt in retrospect regrets having promised to buy the widgets at $100; the contract is a $20 burden. Outside of bankruptcy if it rejected or breached the contract, it would be liable for $40 in damages, so it would want to take delivery, despite the burden. But if the trustee rejects the contract under § 365, then it is obliged under § 502(g) to pay up on the $40 damage claim, but *only as if* the supplier's claim had arisen *before* bankruptcy. The $40 will be paid in "bankruptcy dollars" at the rate of distribution to the unsecured creditors. If that rate is only 10%, the trustee will pay only 4 "real" dollars in damages to get out of a contract that the bankrupt regrets.

The trustee would tend to reject in this hypothetical as long as the payout ratio on unsecured claims is 50% or less. You should be able to figure out why this is so.

As shown in detail in Jesse Fried, *Executory Contracts and Performance Decisions in Bankruptcy,* 46 Duke L.J. 517 (1996), and summarily in George G. Triantis, *The Effects of Insolvency and Bankruptcy on Contract Performance and Adjustment,*

43 U. Toronto L.J. 679 (1993), this scenario creates a potential inefficiency. The social cost of producing the widgets is $60 and the widget's value to the bankrupt is $80, yielding a social gain of $20. But because the bankrupt unburdens itself of $20 (the decrease in market value) at a private cost of only $4, the bankrupt will reject the contract, and accordingly $20 of social value, of GNP, of produced goods could be lost.

Some of this lost value can be recovered. After the trustee rejects the contract, it could place a new order for widgets at $80, which the seller would presumably still fulfill because they would cost $60 and the new widget order would be entitled to an administrative priority under § 507. With an administrative priority, the seller would usually be paid in full. The seller loses $16 (a $40 loss from the original contract, a $4 bankruptcy damage payment, and a $20 profit on the second contract). But the social loss is avoided.

Similarly, it's possible that the bankrupt and seller could renegotiate after the rejection to make the deal still happen; price would change but the widgets would still change hands. The social loss then is the sum of the transaction costs of the renegotiation and the lost production when these renegotiations fail.

The bankrupt's power to reject contracts during bankruptcy and pay damages as if on a pre-bankruptcy claim is one of the disruptions that induces suppliers and customers to be leery of dealing with a near bankrupt.

## C. Specific performance

Thus far we've been looking at basic contracts for the delivery of goods. Contracts are of course more complex, and § 365 has special rules for technology licensing contracts, real estate, and (via § 1113) labor. Case law confronts more unusual business deals that debtors wish to avoid under § 365. In one, an actress filed for bankruptcy to reject a performance contract, so that she could switch and perform on another show.

In another, a Burger King franchisee who did poorly filed for chapter 11 and rejected the franchise contract. As to the franchisee's obligation to pay royalties to Burger King, the analysis and case were unexceptionable. Controversy arose over the franchisee's non-competition obligation under the franchise agreement. After it filed, it rejected under § 365, then pursued a hamburger business at the same location, but not as a Burger King franchisee. Burger King argued that the contract wasn't executory (and therefore not rejectable), because Burger King, having performed, had no further obligations. The court concluded that Burger King had sufficient continuing ancillary obligations that the contract remained executory on both sides and was rejectable. Burger King Corp. v. Rovine Corp., 6 Bankr. 661 (Bankr. W.D. Tenn. 1980).

But what to do about the franchisee's obligation not to compete, which it breached by competing anyway?

### § 502. Allowance of claims or interests

> (c) There shall be estimated for purposes of allowance under this section [502]—
>
> (1) any contingent or unliquidated claim, the fixing or liquidation of which ... would unduly delay the administration of the case; or
>
> (2) any right to payment arising from a right to an equitable remedy for breach of performance.

The legislative history to § 502 is more specific:

> Subsection (c) requires the estimation of any claim liquidation of which would unduly delay the closing of the estate, such as ... any claim for which applicable law provides only an equitable remedy, such as specific performance. This subsection requires that all claims against the debtor be converted into dollar amounts.

Thus claims that state law judges find so speculative that they award specific performance are susceptible to estimation by the (more skillful?!) bankruptcy judges. So the bankrupt Burger King franchisee in *Rovine* rejected the franchise agreement and its non-competition clause under § 365, and the value of Burger King's claim against the franchisee for specific performance had to be estimated under § 502(c), coming in as a "pennies for dollars" prebankruptcy claim under § 502(g).

*Rovine* is carefully analyzed in Jay Westbrook, *A Functional Analysis of Executory Contracts*, 74 Minn. L. Rev. 227 (1989).

---

## D. Labor

The Bankruptcy Code limits the bankrupt's authority to reject one type of long-term supply agreement, that for labor under union contracts. For ordinary executory agreements, the trustee or debtor-in-possession exercises its business judgment on whether to reject or assume, and the court approves (or doesn't). For labor contracts, the bankrupt must first negotiate with the union, by proposing "those necessary modifications ... [to the employees'] benefits and protections that are *necessary* to permit the reorganization of the debtor and assures that all creditors, the debtor, and all of the affected parties are treated fairly and equitably." Section 1113(b)(1) (emphasis supplied). The bankrupt must provide the union with the information needed for the union to evaluate whether the bankrupt's proposal meets § 1113's standards. If the union rejects the proposal, the court may allow the bankrupt to reject the union contract, if it concludes that the union rejection was without good cause and "the balance of the equities clearly favors rejection ...." Presumably if the court allows the bankrupt to reject the contract, the bankrupt's terms of rejection can go beyond rejecting only those terms necessary to permit reorganization.

Section 1113 was placed in the Code as a "pro-"labor measure, to reverse prior court decisions allowing the bankrupt to unilaterally reject a collective bargaining agreement without getting a court to approve the rejection and without complying with labor law's standards for modifying or rejecting a union contract. (The principal decision that § 1113 overruled was NLRB v. Bildisco & Bildisco, 465 U.S. 513 (1984).)

### E. Assignment

The bankrupt may assign a contact, even if the contract bars assignment:

**§ 365. Executory contracts and unexpired leases**

(f) (1) ... [N]otwithstanding a provision in an executory contract or unexpired lease of the debtor ... that prohibits, restricts, or conditions the assignment of such contract or lease, the trustee may assign such contract or lease ....

(2) The trustee may assign an executory contract or unexpired lease of the debtor only if—

(A) ...

(B) adequate assurance of future performance by the assignee of such contract or lease is provided ....

Sections 1124(2), 365(a), and 365(f) all have a similar financial effect: They give the bankrupt "heads the bankrupt wins, tails the other party loses" powers in long-term financial contracts and in executory contracts. If the terms are, taken all together, favorable to the bankrupt because of, say, interim changes in interest rates or prices of the underlying commodity, the bankrupt reinstates, assumes, or assigns the contract. But if the underlying interest rate or product price is unfavorable to the bankrupt, the bankrupt doesn't have to live with the unfavorable contracts and declines to reinstate or rejects them.

..................................................................................................

To reiterate, at least in non-labor settings, when an executory contract is rejected, the contract creditor normally then has a claim for damages. That claim, usually an unsecured claim, would share pro rata with other unsecured claims.

### F. Environmental clean-up obligations

Environmental laws require firms to clean up some of the messes that they make. How are these obligations treated in bankruptcy? While not usually a contractual obligation, these pre-bankruptcy obligations are analogous to pre-bankruptcy contract obligations and, hence, we briefly discuss them here.

Suppose a firm spills toxins into the river and thereafter goes bankrupt. Downstream homeowners sue for damages done to them by the pollution. If damages can't be calculated, they seek to get an order against the bankrupt to clean up the mess. Presumably though the court would estimate damages, and the homeowners would be paid in "bankruptcy dollars," thereby having to foot the clean-up bill themselves, or bear the costs of the pollution. (Post-bankruptcy spills would presumably be actionable and paid as an administrative expense.)

Now suppose that the pollution violated an environmental law and the *Environmental Protection Agency* sued the firm under one of Congress' environmental laws, to clean up the mess caused before the bankruptcy and to stop polluting in the future.

The Bankruptcy Code awards no special explicit priority here to the government, and what's worse for the government, their suit for pre-bankruptcy pollution seems clearly stayed under § 362(a):

### § 362. Automatic stay

> (a) ... [A bankruptcy petition] operates as a stay ... of—
>
> (1) the commencement or continuation, ... of a judicial, administrative, or other action or proceeding against the debtor that was or could have been commenced before the commencement of [the bankruptcy];
>
> (2) the enforcement, against the debtor or against property of the estate, of a judgment obtained before the commencement of the case under this title;
>
> (3) any act to obtain possession of [the bankrupt's] property ... or to exercise control over property of the estate;
>
> (4) any act to create, perfect, or enforce any lien against property of the [bankrupt];
>
> (5) any act to create, perfect, or enforce against property of the debtor any lien to the extent that such lien secures a claim that arose before the commencement of the [bankruptcy];
>
> (6) any act to collect, assess, or recover a claim against the debtor that arose before the [bankruptcy];
>
> ...

Sections (1) and (2) clearly stop the government from pursuing the litigation for pre-bankruptcy pollution. Before October 1998, the government lawyer could only turn to subsection (b), the exceptions to the stay provisions:

### § 362. Automatic stay

> (b) The filing of a petition ... does *not* operate as a stay—
>
> * * *
>
> (4) under subsection (a)(1) ... , of the commencement or continuation of an action or proceeding by a governmental unit ... to enforce such governmental unit's ... *police or regulatory power* ... ;

(5) under subsection (a)(2) ... of the enforcement of a judgment, other than a money judgment, obtained in an action by a governmental unit to enforce such governmental unit's *police or regulatory power* ... .

These allowed (and still allow) the EPA to pursue its lawsuit against the bankrupt firm to clean up the pre-bankruptcy pollution, despite (a)(1) and (a)(2). Courts have so held.

Note that the effect is to make the clean-up obligation prior to the bankrupt's other obligations. This may be sensible from several perspectives, including that of inducing the other players in the firm to monitor the debtor more carefully in making sure it's not a gross polluter.

But were the court holdings though really consistent with the statute? Those courts ignored subsections (a)(3) and (a)(6) of the stay provisions. Subsection (a)(3) stays all actions in which the plaintiff is trying to exercise control over the property of the estate; presumably a clean-up order, especially if the spill is on the debtor's property represents the EPA's effort to control the debtor's property and accordingly such action is stayed. Subsection (b) had *no* government police power exception to (a)(3).

And subsection (a)(6) stays any act to collect, assess, or recover a claim that arose prior to the bankruptcy. The government would seem to be trying to recover on a pre-bankruptcy claim.

Courts ignored (a)(3) and (a)(6), perhaps believing that the government should not be stopped by the stay because pollution is policy not a mere debt. Perhaps the courts thought that the drafters of subsection (b) simply forgot to extend the (b)(4) and (b)(5) exceptions to (a)(3) and (a)(6). See Kathy Heidt, *The Automatic Stay in Environmental Bankruptcies*, 67 Am. Bankr. L.J. 69 (1993); Robert Rasmussen, *Bankruptcy and the Administrative State*, 42 Hastings L.J. 1567 (1991). But a literalist judge would have had trouble here, as the words would have stayed the government's EPA suit. The issue now though is moot. In October 1998, Congress extended the (b)(4) exception beyond (a)(1) to (a)(2), (a)(3) and (a)(6). It repealed (b)(5), presumably because it was superfluous.

Notice the policy basis for allowing the government to proceed. The policy basis isn't so much that when the debtor is in bankruptcy the only alternative would be more pollution: the government can clean it up (as it often does) and then bill the company. The government's bill would then come in as a general creditor's claim. When seen in this way, the post-bankruptcy issue is "merely" one of priority: who will pay for the clean-up, the polluting debtor's creditors or the American taxpayer? (An order to stop *post*-bankruptcy pollution is different: post-bankruptcy pollution is an operation of the bankrupt estate and subject to any applicable regulation.)

The pre-bankruptcy policy issues are more substantial. If the government isn't stayed and is accordingly effectively prior to the firm's other creditors, then imagine how the firm's other creditors will act pre-bankruptcy. If they conclude that the debtor is a high-risk for bankruptcy and is a heavy polluter, the creditors either will not lend or insist on a clean-up. If the creditor won't lend, then a polluter has fewer assets and presumably the social good is improved by diminishing the debtor's assets, and hence usually its capacity to pollute. If the lender induces the debtor to clean up the toxins, by, say, insisting on EPA-compliance certificates from an environmental engineer, then the result is also good, in that the creditor then enforces environmental policy. (This analysis assumes that the environmental policy is in fact correct and does not over- or under-enforce environmental clean-ups.)

Note two issues here: First, the same sort of analysis applies to tort claimants. If tort policy is correct, then priority for tort claimants would make creditors enforce tort policy.

Second, the only way for the government to get its *effective* priority is to sue and not accept the stay; it has no formal priority, i.e., the government cannot do the clean-up and then bill the company. If it cleans up the toxins itself and sends the bankrupt a bill, it would be a mere general creditor, not a priority creditor. But for those (few?) firms that are viable even when they stop polluting, the government's suit to force a clean-up could force the piecemeal liquidation of the firm. If the premise that chapter 11 holds the firm together long enough for a scientific decision on whether to liquidate or keep the firm going is correct, then a better way for the EPA to get its priority would not be surreptitiously (through an exception to the automatic stay) but directly (via priority).

# CHAPTER 11

# INTEREST

A. The statute
B. Creditors versus stockholders
C. Seniors versus juniors
D. Guarantors versus guaranteed
E. Secured versus unsecured
F. What rate?
G. General and miscellaneous

........................................................................................................

## A. The statute

### ¶1101: Interest accruals and nonaccruals in bankruptcy for unsecured creditors

#### a. § 502(b). Allowance of claims or interest

[T]he court, after notice and a hearing, shall determine the amount of such *claim as of the date of the filing of the petition*, and shall allow such claim in such amount, except to the extent that—

\* \* \*

(2) *such claim is for unmatured interest*[.]

#### b. § 362. Automatic stay

(a) ... [A bankruptcy petition] operates as a stay ... of—
(1) the commencement or continuation, ... of a judicial, administrative, or other action or proceeding against the debtor that was or could have been commenced before the commencement of [the bankruptcy];
(2) the enforcement, against the debtor or against property of the estate, of a judgment obtained before the commencement of the case under this title;

(3) any act to obtain possession of [the bankrupt's] property ...;

(4) any act to create, perfect, or enforce any lien against property of the [bankrupt];

(5) any act to create, perfect, or enforce against property of the debtor any lien to the extent that such lien secures a claim that arose before the commencement of the [bankruptcy];

(6) any act to collect, assess, or recover a claim against the debtor that arose before the [bankruptcy];

...

### c. § 1129. Confirmation of plan

...

(b) (2) ... [T]he condition that a plan be fair and equitable ... includes the following requirements:

...

(B) With respect to a class of unsecured claims—

(i) ... each holder ... receive[s] ... property of a value, as of the effective date of the plan, *equal to the allowed amount of such claim* ...; or

(ii) [claims and interests junior to the dissenting class are eliminated.]

### d. § 726. Distribution of property of the estate [in chapter 7, which deals with liquidation]

(a) ... [P]roperty of the estate shall be distributed—

(1) first, in payment of [administrative and priority] claims ...;

(2) second, in payment of any allowed unsecured claim ...;

(3) third, in payment of any allowed unsecured claim proof of which is tardily filed ...;

(4) fourth, in payment of [certain fines];

(5) fifth, *in payment of interest at the legal rate from the date of the filing of the petition*, on any claim paid under paragraph (1), (2), (3), or (4) of this subsection; and

(6) sixth, to the debtor.

---

## ¶1102: Interest accruals

Time is money. The Bankruptcy Code stays the creditors' attempts to seize collateral or bring their unsecured claim to judgment and collect on the claim. While the stay is in place, the debtor attempts to reorganize, and that reorganization usually takes a few years. Because creditors can't collect on their security or their debt, whether or not interest must be paid in a multi-year chapter 11 proceeding is a critical financial issue. Do the creditors get interest on their claims while their collection efforts are stayed?

The answer is not a simple yes or no. The Bankruptcy Code's interest rate results come from a cross-current of policy issues, leading to overlapping and sometimes contradictory statutory provisions.

At least five interest payment contests are embedded in bankruptcy:

1. All creditors versus stockholders: Do creditors of a solvent company get interest before the stockholders get anything?
2. For an insolvent company, seniors versus juniors: do senior creditors get interest before juniors get principal?
3. Secured versus unsecured: Do secured creditors get interest before unsecured get principal? Does it make a difference whether the secured creditor is over- or under-secured?
4. High-interest creditors versus low-interest creditors: For insolvent bankrupts, do creditors with a high rate of interest do better than creditors with a low rate of interest?
5. Guarantors versus the guaranteed: Do guarantors have to make good on a creditor's claim for interest, even when the Code disallows the claim for interest?

To see these in problem form, recall the Dieglom problem at ¶413, p. 116. A summary balance sheet based on the firm's market value looks about like this when the petition in bankruptcy is filed:

Dieglom

| $50M | Current liabilities: | $20M |
|---|---|---|
| | 7% senior debentures: | 20M |
| | 3½% mortgage bonds: | 20M |
| | 14% subordinated debentures: | 30M |
| | | $90M |

When the petition is filed what are the allowed amounts of the claims? While interest payments due *before* the bankruptcy are surely legitimate claims, what about *post-petition* claims for interest? See § 502(b)(2). Do the allowed claims include interest that has not yet matured as of the date of the petition for reorganization?

Assume that reorganization takes five years or more, a longer than normal bankruptcy. During that time the firm has about $10 million income annually. After five years with some compounding, the firm will have retained about $60 million:

Dieglom

| $110M | Current liabilities: | $20M+interest |
|---|---|---|
| | 7% senior debentures: | 20M+$7M interest |
| | 3½% mortgage bonds: | 20M+$3.5M interest |
| | 14% subordinated: | 30M+$21M interest |
| | | $90M+$31.5M more in interest |

The stockholders propose that the creditors be paid their full principal amount, and that the stockholders get the $20 million excess beyond the $90M needed to pay the creditors their principal amount.

Stockholders' Plan of
Reorganization for Dieglom

| $110M | Current liabilities: | $20M |
|---|---|---|
| | 7% senior debentures: | 20M |
| | 3½% mortgage bonds: | 20M |
| | 14% subordinated: | 30M |
| | Stockholder: | 20M |
| | | $110M |

The financial creditors reject the shareholders' plan, which would not give any accumulated interest to the creditors. The trade creditors consent. The shareholders seek cram-down. (For now, ignore the fact that one of the creditors, the mortgagee, has security.) Who wins? See Bankruptcy Code §§ 502(b)(2) and 1129. Does cramdown under § 1129(b)(2) tie to the *allowed amount* of the claim, an amount determined on the *date of the bankruptcy petition?* Isn't the statute constructed as if bankruptcy were nearly instantaneous, as if the debtor filed the petition in the morning, proposed the plan at lunch-time, and had the plan confirmed in the afternoon?

Do the creditors have room to maneuver and argue by using the predicate to § 1129(b)(2), that the requirement that the plan be fair and equitable *includes* payment of the allowed amount of the claim or wipe-out of the juniors?

..........................................................................................................................

If the creditors fail to convince the bankruptcy court that the concept of fair and equitable requires that interest be paid by bankrupt debtors that are solvent by the time a plan is confirmed, can they turn to another section of the Bankruptcy Code for support? What if the firm were liquidated? See Bankruptcy Code, § 726(a)(5). (Note that until the 1994 amendments, § 1124(3) deemed a claim unimpaired if, on the confirmation date, the claimants were paid in cash equal to the allowed amount of their claim. What relevance? If a creditor is unimpaired, is § 1129(a)(7) available to it? Section 1124(3) was repealed in 1994. Any guess as to why? Were creditors happy with it?) Does § 726(a) give the creditors an incentive to move the firm from chapter 11 to chapter 7? Could the creditors import § 726 into chapter 11 via § 1129(a)(7)?

## B. Creditors versus stockholders

### ¶1103: Chaim Fortgang & Lawrence King, The 1978 Code: Some Wrong Policy Decisions, 56 N.Y.U. L. Rev. 1148 (1981)[1]

Postpetition Interest

A routine principle that was developed under the case law construing the Bankruptcy Act of 1898 was that interest on claims ceased to accrue as of the date a bankruptcy petition was filed .... [T]here was no specific provision in the statute dealing with [any significant] postpetition interest. The courts, however, developed a policy that the accrual of interest should cease as a matter of convenience and efficiency in the administration of bankrupt estates: cessation avoided the necessity for recomputation of interest each time a distribution of dividends was made to creditors. In cases in which the assets of the debtor were insufficient to pay all of the claims of creditors, cessation did not change the actual amounts paid to creditors, since claims were paid on a pro rata basis. This principle of convenience was a deviation from the more general principle that a creditor was entitled to be paid the full amount of the debt, including the principle amount owed and interest accrued to the date of payment.

The drafters of the new Bankruptcy Code were not content to permit the judicially developed principle of convenience to continue. Instead, several sections of the Code explicitly deal with postpetition interest in technical detail. Specifically, § 502(b)(2) of the Code provides that a claim for unmatured interest is not allowable. The House and Senate committee reports accompanying the Code make clear that this provision requires disallowance of interest unmatured at the date of the filing of the petition, *including postpetition interest not yet due* .... Postpetition interest under the Code ... explicitly is made a nonallowable part of a creditor's claim.

The nonallowability of such claims has important ramifications under the Bankruptcy Code, just as it did under the Bankruptcy Act. Nonallowed claims are not entitled to any distribution in a case, whether it be a chapter 7 liquidation case or a chapter 11 reorganization case. Section 726 of the Code, which establishes the order of distribution of property of the estate for liquidation cases, includes as the second rung of the payment ladder "any allowed unsecured claim." In chapter 11, only holders of allowed claims are entitled to accept or reject plans. Pursuant to the "cramdown" provisions of § 1129(b)(2)(B), an unaccepting class of unsecured claims may be forced to accept a plan even if a class lower than it is to receive a distribution, as long as the unaccepting class receives property under the plan "equal to the allowed amount" of the claims of that class. These sections are not exhaustive of the provisions that refer to the concept of allowability[;] the concept is one that permeates the entire Code.

---

[1] Copyright, 1981. Reproduced with permission of New York University Law Review.

Moreover, the concept of allowability is inflexible. Under the Bankruptcy Act, courts would invoke the general principle that a creditor is entitled to full payment if the convenience factor was not present. If an estate proved to be solvent, the notion that it would be inconvenient to recompute interest was not invoked. The rationale was that, in this instance, the nonpayment of postpetition interest would permit the return of property to the debtor while creditors were not being paid in full—a patently unjust result. Section 502(b)(2), on the other hand, appears absolute on its face. Section 502, read simply and applied exclusively, provides that postpetition interest is not an allowable part of a claim. This appears to be so even if the debtor's assets have a value in excess of all its liabilities including postpetition interest.

### A. Chapter 7 Liquidation Cases

Under chapter 7, there is one exception, in section 726(a)(5), to the absolute rule of section 502(b)(2): If an estate is solvent, before the debtor is entitled to retain any property of the estate, creditors are required to receive postpetition interest in an amount computed at the "legal rate."

\* \* \*

### B. Reorganization Cases

Postpetition interest issues are of even greater significance and the problems created by the Code appear to be exacerbated in chapter 11 reorganization cases. A fundamental underpinning of new chapter 11 is that a successful arrangement should be the result of informed negotiations between the interested parties culminating in a consensually arrived at chapter 11 plan. The whole premise of new chapter 11 is its voluntary and consensual nature. Nevertheless, there are inevitably situations in which creditors cannot agree on a plan. This generally occurs when there are disparate views as to the enterprise value of the debtor or as to the type of plan that is in the best interests of the creditors. If a dissenting view is held by a creditor that is in a class by itself, in control of a class, or in a position to influence the voting of a class, acceptance of the plan may not be achievable on a voluntary basis. Thus, chapter 11 provides for the treatment of recalcitrant classes of creditors.

The new chapter 11 contains in a modified form the cramdown mechanism which permits a plan to be confirmed despite nonacceptance by a class of creditors, provided that the plan pays the class that to which it is entitled .... [F]or a plan to be confirmed by the court, it must either be accepted by all "impaired" classes of creditors and equity security holders, or it must be capable of being crammed down pursuant to section 1129(b) of the code. This has serious implications for the recovery of postpetition interest.

1. [Best interests test under Section 1129(a)(7)]

\* \* \*

Another interesting question that has arisen in this regard concerns the applicability of section 1129(a)(7)(ii) .... Under that subsection, the confirming court must find that each holder of a claim or interest in a given class will receive or retain under the plan property having a value not less than that which such holder would have received or retained on account of such claim or interest had the case been administered under the liquidation provisions of chapter 7. This provision has the effect of bringing into play the distribution scheme set forth in section 726 as a minimum standard. That requirement needs to be satisfied, even if the class has accepted the plan, as long as there is a dissenting holder in the class. In other words, it cannot be waived by a class vote unless it is unanimous.[2]

\* \* \*

2. Cramdown

Pursuant to section 1129(b) of the Code, when any impaired class of creditors or equity security holders does not accept the plan ... the plan may nevertheless be confirmed by the court if (i) the proponent of the plan requests confirmation, and (ii) the court finds that the plan is "fair and equitable" as to the dissenting class ....

[S]ection 1129(b)(2) provides that the phrase "fair and equitable ... includes the following requirements" with respect to a class of unsecured claims: The court must find either that the plan provides the holders of a class of unsecured claims with property having a value at least equal to the allowed amount of their claims or that no class junior to the dissenting class will receive any distribution under the plan.

The operation of this provision can be seen in the following hypothetical case. Assume a situation in which a plan proposes to distribute to a class of unsecured creditors property having a value equal to the principal amount of their claims plus interest up to the date of the filing of the petition. Assume further that the plan provides for the equity holders to retain an interest in the debtor. May this plan be confirmed over the objection of the class of unsecured creditors on the ground that the dissenting class is receiving property equal to the full amount of its allowed claim? The allowed amount of the claim would not, by reference to section 502(b)(2), include postpetition interest; thus, there would appear to be compliance with the statutory standards .... Thus, the cramdown provisions of section 1129(b) may produce the same inequitable result that has been alluded to previously: The debtor may retain an inter-

---

[2] [Is there a better way to understand § 1129(a)(7) here? Is it that it cannot be waived by a class vote unless it is unanimous? Or is it that dissenters cannot be bound by the class vote? Those who assent are bound, despite that they do not get interest; the assenters though cannot bind the dissenters under § 1129(a)(7).—Roe.]

est, or shareholders of the debtor may retain an interest in the debtor, while creditors of a concededly senior class are not receiving the full amount dictated by their contractual rights.

\* \* \*

## C. Significance of the Problem

It is not an adequate response to contend that because there will be few cases of solvency, the issue of postpetition interest has no practical significance. In the context of very large chapter 11 cases, depending on the length of the proceedings, solvency may not be terribly unlikely. Moreover, the way the new Code is written, the number of solvent debtors is likely to increase [because insolvency is not a prerequisite to filing for chapter 11]. If the statute is not amended, there is a substantial potential for abuse by recalcitrant debtors in out-of-court workouts and by debtors going out of business who might seek to liquidate their businesses under the aegis of the Bankruptcy Code. Conceivably, solvent debtors could begin to use the Bankruptcy Code strictly for the purpose of reducing their debt service. This could be accomplished by extending a case over a protracted length of time, during which the debtor would obtain a direct subsidy from its creditors either through the complete forgiveness of postpetition interest or through a reduction in the rate of interest from the contractual rate to the statutory rate.

\* \* \*

One solution may be for courts and creditors to exercise some control over the duration of cases. However, such control is impossible in most instances, particularly in large cases. Other possible remedies, such as allowing creditors to file their own plan after the lapse of the exclusivity period set forth in section 1121, allowing the appointment of a trustee to terminate the exclusivity period, or allowing interim distributions prior to a plan, are equally unrealistic. This is because of the historical predilection of bankruptcy courts to view debtors in a paternalistic manner—to routinely accept the positions propounded by frail debtors, especially when confronted with contested issues that may adversely affect the debtors' future viability. It is not at all unusual for a bankruptcy judge to permit delaying tactics so long as the debtor provides some reasonable justification. For example, debtors can easily stretch arguments about the amount of time and information they need to propose a plan and to negotiate with creditors. In short, there often is a built-in delay in the reorganization process that is compounded by the delays that ordinarily occur during all court proceedings. Because of the reduced postpetition interest rate, such delay could give solvent debtors the benefit of reduced debt service—a result that is not only unjust, but contrary to the aims of the Bankruptcy Code.

\* \* \*

¶1104: **Case law, and then Congress acts**

Fortgang & King note that "solvent debtors could begin to use the Bankruptcy Code strictly for the purpose of reducing their debt service." While that kind of problem does not seem to be common in the dozen years since their article came out, a similar one has been. The bankruptcy occurs for legitimate operating reasons. For the year or two before bankruptcy, managers faced creditors who were trying to collect, managers felt harassed trying to come up with the cash to meet interest and principal payments, and managers' negotiations with creditors had the over-hanging cloud of foreclosure threatening the managers. Once the firm entered chapter 11, these clouds cleared and the managers saw some spots of sunshine: no creditor could harass the managers (due to the bankruptcy stay in § 362), managers did not usually have to scramble to come up with the cash to meet interest and principal payments, and life for the managers became much more comfortable. Even if interest had to be paid eventually (still perhaps an uncertain matter), it would be paid later. Even if the time value of the delay were accounted for financially, managers breathed easier if they could delay payment. Review ¶418, at p. 125 (Blum & Kaplan reading re delay and the Cotton Belt Railroad).

Notwithstanding the statutory structure before 1994, some courts labored to give interest to creditors of solvent firms when shareholders would take something under the plan. Some thought that plans that gave creditors no interest while stockholders got something couldn't be proposed in good faith. Others said that the plan would not be fair and equitable if a creditor were left less than fully compensated and funds were to be returned to the debtor or its shareholders. So unsecured creditors could be given post-petition interest (to the extent enforceable under applicable law), notwithstanding the structure of §§ 502(b)(2), 1124(3) [repealed in 1994], and 1129. See, e.g., In re Manville Forest Prods. Corp., 43 Bankr. 293, 299-300 (Bankr. S.D.N.Y. 1984) (solvent bankrupt must pay unsecured, as well as secured, creditors enforceable post-petition interest).

Other courts tried to import § 726 into chapter 11, via § 1129(a)(7). But in In re New Valley Corp., 168 Bankr. 73 (Bankr. D.N.J. 1994), the court refused to so labor, pointing to the old, pre-1994 impairment section (§ 1124(3)), which said that a claim wasn't impaired if the claimant received cash on the effective date of the bankruptcy plan equal to that of the allowed amount of the claim, which as we know from § 502, does not include interest accruing after the petition in bankruptcy was filed. Because Congress explicitly said such creditors weren't impaired, despite that they received no post-petition interest, the court wouldn't labor to find a way to give such creditors post-petition interest.

In 1994 Congress repealed § 1124(3). While the repeal removes a roadblock to the creditors receiving interest, it does not itself affirmatively grant post-petition interest. True, a creditor that doesn't receive interest could be impaired and, as such, could invoke § 1129(a)(7) to import § 726(a) into chapter 11. But recall that (a)(7)'s standard is liquidation value and the judge might well conclude that liquidation value is the company's scrap value, which is usually much less than its reorganization value. Hence repeal of § 1124(3) doesn't with certainty give the creditors interest accruing during the multi-year reorganization.

What else is in play? Remember that § 502(b) does not include post-petition interest in the allowed claim and that § 1129(b)(2) uses the allowed amount of the claim as the value that must be given to a dissenting class (if lower ranking claims and interests are not wiped out). Congress in 1994 amended neither § 502(b)(2) nor § 1129(b). But it did say in the legislative history to the 1994 changes:

> As a result of this change [repeal of section 1124(3)], if a plan proposed to pay a class of claims in cash in the full allowed amount of the claims, the class would be impaired[,] entitling creditors to vote for or against the plan of reorganization. If creditors vote for the plan ..., it can be confirmed [over] the vote of a dissenting class of creditors only if it complies with the "fair and equitable" test under section 1129(b)(2) ....
>
> The words "fair and equitable" are terms of art that have a well established meaning under the case law of the Bankruptcy Act as well as under the Bankruptcy Code. Specifically, courts have held that where an estate is solvent, in order for a plan to be fair and equitable, unsecured and undersecured creditors' claims must be paid in full, including postpetition interest, before equity holders may participate in any recovery. [Citation to *Consolidated Rock*.]

Bankruptcy Reform Act of 1994, Section-By-Section Description, 140 Cong. Rec. H10752 (1994). If Congress wanted creditors to receive post-petition interest, why would it do so in such a convoluted way, by using legislative history and by referring to pre-Code cases? Wouldn't a simple addition to the Bankruptcy Code have resolved the issue definitively? What could explain why an easy-to-draft concept found its way into the legislative history, but not into the statute?

## C. Seniors versus juniors

### ¶1105: Subordination

Thus the creditors strongest claim for post-petition interest against the debtor resides in interpretation of the open-ended phrase, "fair and equitable," against the specific bar of a claim for "post-petition" interest in § 502(b)(2). More bankruptcy courts give post-petition interest to creditors of solvent bankrupts than don't give it, but as of now no appellate court has definitively resolved the issue.

Most bankrupts are not solvent at the time a plan of reorganization is confirmed. So for now put aside the question of whether the debtor must pay interest if the bankrupt turns out to be slightly solvent at the end of the bankruptcy proceeding. This then raises several contests for interest *between* creditor classes. The first that we shall examine is the contest between seniors and juniors. What if the debtor's assets allow it to pay the seniors in full, with a little more spilling over to the juniors? Do the seniors get interest paid to them before the juniors get any principal repaid? The second setting is that of a guarantor of repayment: The creditor cannot get interest from the debtor (§ 502(b)). Does the guarantor have to pay the interest even though the Bankruptcy Code has said the claim for interest is not allowed? The third contest to consider is whether a secured creditor gets interest during the period it is stayed from seizing its security.

To exemplify the first contest, that between seniors and juniors, return to the Dieglom interest accrual problem, ¶1102. All creditor classes, except the senior debentureholders, now consent to foregoing their post-petition interest. The seniors dissent and turn to their bond indenture. See Drum Financial "Description of Debentures—Subordination of Debentures," ¶603, at p. 180. Under the Drum Financial indenture and the American Bar Foundation subordination provisions, can senior creditors obtain post-petition interest out of the subordinated creditors' principal? Would the court's requiring that the juniors turn over their principal to make good on the seniors' claim for interest surprise the juniors? See *In re King Resources*, next; Bankruptcy Code § 510(a).

### ¶1106: In re King Resources, Inc., 528 F.2d 789 (10th Cir. 1976)

The issue here to be resolved is whether the trial court erred in its determination that certain so-called senior lenders to King Resources Company, the debtor, were not entitled to interest from and after the date an involuntary petition was filed against the debtor under Chapter X of the Bankruptcy Act. Our study of the record leads us to conclude that the trial court did not err, and we therefore affirm.

\* \* \*

The precise question posed in the present appeal has been before both the Second and Third Circuits, and each circuit held that there was no error on the part of the trial court in refusing to allow such a senior lender post-petition interest .... We agree with both the reasoning and result reached in those cases.

The senior lenders in the present proceeding agree with the general proposition that in a bankruptcy proceeding an unsecured creditor, such as the senior lenders, cannot recover post-petition interest on a claim against the bankrupt. To escape the effect of this general rule the senior lenders emphasize that here they are not seeking post-petition interest from the debtor, and that should post-petition interest be allowed it would be at the expense of the debenture holders and not the debtor. Such result should obtain in the instant case, according to the senior lenders, because of certain subordinating language contained in the indenture agreement. The subordination provisions in the indentures in the present case read as follows:

Upon any distribution of assets of the Company upon ... reorganization of the Company ... (a) The holders of all Senior Indebtedness shall first be entitled to receive payment in full of the principal thereof (and premium, if any) and interest due thereon before the holders of the Debentures are entitled to receive any payment on account of the principal of (or premium, of any) or interest on the Debentures ....

... [T]he subordination provisions make no specific reference to the question of post-petition interest .... [W]here the subordinating provisions are unclear or ambiguous as to whether post-petition interest is to be allowed a senior creditor, the general rule that interest stops on the date of filing of the petition in bankruptcy is to be followed. In [one prior case] appears the following pertinent comment:

> The district court's conclusion that the subordination provision contained in the debenture notes did not appropriately apprise the debenture note holders that their claims against the bankrupt would be subordinated to [the senior]'s demand for post-petition interest is not incorrect and, thus, is adequate to sustain its order denying [the senior]'s claim for post-petition interest. Certainly, in light of this conclusion of the district court, we cannot say that its refusal to allow post-petition interest constituted an abuse of the discretion it has with regard to the exercise of its equitable power.[10] If a creditor desires to establish a right to post-petition interest and a concomitant reduction in the dividends due to subordinated creditors, the agreement should clearly show that the general rule that interest stops on the date of the filing of the petition is to be suspended, at least vis-a-vis these parties. 491 F.2d at 844.

Footnote 10 in the above quotation from [a prior case] reads as follows:

> [10] "It is manifest that the touchstone of each decision on allowance of interest in bankruptcy, receivership and reorganization has been a balance of equities between creditor and creditor or between creditors and the debtor." Vanston Bondholders Protective Committee v. Green, 329 U.S. 156, 165 (1946).

In the instant case the indentures do not "clearly show" that the senior lenders are entitled to post-petition interest at the expense of the debenture holders. Hence, ... the trial court did not err or in any case abuse its discretionary powers in following the general rule that interest stops on the date of the filing of a petition in bankruptcy.

Judgment affirmed.

---

### § 510. Subordination

(a) A subordination agreement is enforceable in a case under this title to the same extent that such agreement is enforceable under applicable nonbankruptcy law.

Must the indenture "clearly show" that the seniors get post-petition interest from the juniors after 1978, when § 510(a) became law? For the first twenty years of § 510(a)'s life, bankruptcy courts continued the pre-Code rule of explicitness, looking for a clear statement in the indenture that the junior's principal was subordinated to the senior's post-petition interest, and several courts read the indenture at issue as not being sufficiently clear. In re Ionosphere, 134 Bankr. 528 (Bankr. S.D.N.Y. 1991); In re Southeast Banking, 188 Bankr. 452 (Bankr. S.D. Fla. 1995).

One circuit court recently interpreted § 510(a) as clearly on its face requiring that the subordination contract be enforced as it read, but nevertheless concluded the issue of what level of notice to juniors was necessary was an issue of state law, even as to post-petition matters, and thus certified the question of contract interpretation to the New York Court of Appeals. Chemical Bank v. First Trust, No. 97-4436 (11th Cir. Sept. 28, 1998). The New York court answered that New York law "would require specific language in a subordination agreement to alert a junior creditor to its assumption of the risk and burden *of allowing the payment of a senior creditor's post-petition interest* demand." In re Southeast Banking Corp., 93 N.Y.2d 178 (Apr. 29, 1999). The court seemed to feel itself to be a bit out-of-place, as they were answering, as they expressed it, an "unusually intermingled Federal State law question."

If the Circuit Court had run with its initially logical reading of § 510 with blinders on, would it have certified the question as what New York law was *post-petition*, or what New York law was *in the absence* of a bankruptcy? Perhaps the courts were deferring to practice, as both courts partly implied: financial parties expected explicitness post-petition, partly due to pre-Code decisions like *King Resources* and the no-interest rule of § 502(b)(2), and the courts were loathe to upset financiers' expectations, whatever Congress may have said in § 510(a).

Is the result simply a trap for the unwary, for senior creditors lacking counsel up-to-date on the bankruptcy decisions? Consider this provision from the ABA's Model Simplified Indenture (available for only $3 when it was originally published from ABA's Section of Corporation, Banking and Business Law, 1155 E. 60th St., Chicago, IL 60637):

### ARTICLE 11
### SUBORDINATION
\* \* \*

**Section 11.03.** *Liquidation; Dissolution; Bankruptcy.* Upon any distribution to creditors of the Company in a liquidation or dissolution of the Company or in a bankruptcy, reorganization, insolvency, receivership or similar proceeding relating to the Company or its property:

(1) holders of Senior Debt shall be entitled to receive payment in full in cash of the principal of and interest *(including interest accruing after the commencement of any such proceeding)* to the date of payment on the Senior Debt before [the Subordinated Debentureholders] shall be

entitled to receive any payment of principal of or interest on [their Subordinated] Securities; and

\* \* \*

Is the seniors' claim for interest extinguished under § 502(b)(2)? Need the subordinated make the seniors whole on a claim that Congress has destroyed? That is, could the juniors argue that for them to be subordinated to something, that something, namely "Senior Indebtedness" of the debtor company, must exist. But, say the juniors, § 502(b)(2) *extinguished* the seniors' claim for post-petition interest. The seniors have no claim for post-petition interest against the debtor; therefore, there's nothing left to which the juniors can be subordinate. The seniors' interest claim is gone and, hence, so is the juniors' obligation to subordinate themselves to it.

Could you reconceive of the subordinated debentureholders as nonrecourse guarantors of the seniors' interest and use the guarantee cases, where similar arguments have been made? That is, can we view the subordinated as having guaranteed the seniors repayment, but with the guarantee limited to the proceeds that the subordinated get from the debtor? See *In re Bruno*, next.

## D. Guarantors versus guaranteed

### ¶1107: In re Bruno, [1984 Transfer Binder] Bankr. L. Rep. (CCH) ¶70,084 (1st Cir. Nov. 2, 1984)

Plaintiff United States ... loaned a sum of money ... to the debtor[.] Plaintiff received a note in the principal amount of the loan, with a stated rate of interest. It also, as consideration for making the loan, received personal guarantee agreements from defendants herein, the debtor's principal officers. In August 1981 the debtor filed a Chapter XI bankruptcy reorganization proceeding. Thereafter the fishing vessel, its principal asset, sank. The note, and accrued interest except for certain post filing interest, was ultimately paid from the hull insurance proceeds. Plaintiff sues defendants for the interest unpaid. The facts being agreed upon, both sides moved for summary judgment. The district court held for plaintiff, and defendants appeal. We affirm.

It might not surprise even a legally uninformed person who lent money on a note to learn that interest might no longer accrue after the debtor filed in bankruptcy, even though the note called for interest until the principal was paid. This is, in fact, the law. 11 U.S.C. § 502(b)(2). He might be surprised, however, to learn that one of the reasons given is that interest is a "penalty" for non-payment of the principal, and that there should not be a penalty when, by law, a bankrupt is forbidden to make payments. Vanston v. Green, 329 U.S. 156, 163 (1946). He would have wondered why interest was regarded as consideration for the loan, and did not become a penalty when the debtor's lack of assets prevented payment, but did become such when the lack of assets served as a basis for a petition in bankruptcy. He might wonder even more when, as here, guarantors used the penalty reasoning to assert that "it is unjust to make ... guarantors pay a penalty for a detention of funds for which they are not to blame." Guarantors are never to "blame" for the debtor's lack of assets. Their liability is a matter of contract, not fault. Nor did the bankruptcy court forbid them to pay.

Apart from alleged "unjustness," defendants advance two arguments why they should not be liable. The first is that as the bankruptcy filing terminated the debtor's obligation for future interest, and the guarantors only undertook to guarantee the debtor's obligations, there had been no default. For this they cite Salitan v. Magnus, 62 N.J. Super. 323, 162 A.2d 883 (1960). It is not at all clear that Salitan goes that far. The debtor's obligation is not unconditionally terminated; claims for post filing interest may sometimes be recognized if secured. 11 U.S.C. § 506(b).... . But even if we accept defendants' contention that a simple guaranty is coextensive with the debtor's ultimate obligation, theirs was not a simple guaranty. Their agreement guaranteed payment in accordance with the note's original terms regardless of future events.

In addition to the general provision guaranteeing the obligor's performance (¶2), the guaranty contained further provisions.

> 3. The obligations, covenants, agreements and duties of the Guarantor under this Guaranty Agreement shall in no way be affected or impaired by ...
>
> (c) the modification or amendment (whether material or otherwise) of any of the obligations of the Obligor ...
>
> (f) the voluntary or involuntary ... bankruptcy, assignment for the benefit of creditors, reorganization ... or other similar proceedings affecting the Obligor or any of its assets; and
>
> (g) the release of the Obligor ... from the performance or observance of any of the agreements, covenants, terms or conditions contained in ... such instrument(s) by the operation of the law.

We have quoted more than is necessary in order to show the general breadth of defendants' undertaking. Nothing, however, could be more specific than the provisions of paragraph 3(g). One of the debtor's agreements was that interest was due until the principal was paid. While "the operation of law" relieved the debtor-obligor, the guaranty agreement expressly provided that it did not release the guarantors.

Defendants say that this undertaking, and the consequences, are, and would be, contrary to the provision of the bankruptcy act designed to prevent depletion of the funds available for other creditors by the payment of post-filing interest, for, if plaintiff recovers from defendants, defendants will claim over against the bankrupt estate. Thus there would be accomplished indirectly what cannot be accomplished directly. This contention is a perfect example of assuming the point. Nor does it wash. The debtor did not agree to repay the guarantors; it was not even a party to the guaranty agreement. A guarantor recovers from an obligor simply as a matter of being subrogated to the creditor's claim. In this case, quite apart from the fact that defendants' claim against the obligor would not arise until after bankruptcy, plaintiff, as defendants themselves vigorously assert, has no claim against the debtor for the post filing interest. Hence, when the guarantors paid such, there would be nothing for them to be subrogated to, and the bankruptcy proceedings could not be affected.

In sum, defendants promised that plaintiff would be paid in accordance with the terms of the note, "in no way ... affected or impaired by ... bankruptcy ... [or] by the operation of law." They are liable on their contract, even though, because of bankruptcy, the debtor itself was relieved. Even if this were a matter of equity, which it is not, we see no reason why they should not be liable.

Affirmed.

---

## ¶1108: The lawyers

Can lenders chart their way through the interest minefield without a lawyer?

---

## E. Secured versus unsecured

## ¶1109: Adequate protection for secured creditors

We have not yet examined how the Bankruptcy Code governs interest payments to secured creditors. Are secured creditors entitled to better treatment than unsecured creditors as to interest accruing during a reorganization?

### § 506. Determination of secured status

(b) To the extent that an allowed secured claim is secured by property the value of which, after any recovery under subsection (c) of this section, is greater than the amount of such claim, there shall be allowed to the holder of such claim, interest on such claim, and any reasonable fees, costs, or charges provided for under the agreement under which such claim arose.

(c) The trustee may recover from property securing an allowed secured claim the reasonable, necessary costs and expenses of preserving, or disposing of, such property to the extent of any benefit to the holder of such claim.

...........................................................................................................................

Section 506(b) benefits the oversecured creditor. And what about the secured creditor who is not oversecured? Section 506(b) is unhelpful.

Do other sections of the Bankruptcy Code protect the undersecured creditor? Does the policy underlying, or the explicit words of these sections, demand that interest be paid the secured creditor, even if the secured creditor is not oversecured? Section 362 of the Code requires that secured creditors who are stayed from seizing their security are entitled to adequate protection:

## § 362. Automatic stay

(a) ... [A bankruptcy petition] operates as a stay ... of—

...

(3) any act to obtain possession of [the bankrupt's] property ...;

(4) any act to create, perfect, or enforce any lien against property of the [bankrupt];

(5) any act to create, perfect, or enforce against property of the debtor any lien to the extent that such lien secures a claim that arose before the commencement of the [bankruptcy];

(6) any act to collect, assess, or recover a claim against the debtor that arose before the [bankruptcy];

...

(d) On request of a party in interest and after notice and a hearing, the court shall grant relief from the stay ...—

(1) for cause, *including the lack of adequate protection of an interest in property of such party in interest* ....

Section 362(d) assures the secured creditor of adequate protection. And if not adequately protected, the secured creditor is entitled to "relief from the stay," i.e., the court should, if the secured creditor is not adequately protected, allow the secured creditor to seize the security.

But what protection is the secured creditor entitled to? Is the creditor entitled to protection from deterioration of the collateral? Is the secured creditor entitled to the time value of money, because the secured creditor could, were it not for the automatic stay, seize the collateral, sell it, and reinvest the proceeds at market rates of interest?

In early cases under the Code, secured creditors argued that their bargain entitled them to seize the security and that they should be protected from the loss they would incur due to the Code's delay in realization of the security. The court should order that the debtor compensate them for that delay, presumably by paying them what the undersecured creditor would otherwise get in interim interest payments.

## § 361. Adequate protection

When adequate protection is required under section 362 ... , such adequate protection may be provided by—

(1) requiring the trustee to make a cash payment or *periodic cash payments ... to the extent that the stay ... results in a decrease in the value of [the protected entity's] interest in such property*;

...

(3) granting such other relief ... as will result in the realization by such entity of the indubitable equivalent of such [protected] entity's interest in such property.

In 1984, the Ninth Circuit held for the secured creditor in In re American Mariner Indus., Inc., 734 F.2d 426 (9th Cir. 1984). The holding was not without some difficulties. In pre-Code cases, such as *Yale Express* and *Bermec*, the Second Circuit had held that the protection that must be afforded secured creditors who could seize their collateral was protection only against deterioration in the value of the collateral. So consider the Ninth Circuit's statement:

> The secured creditor's right to take possession of and sell collateral on the debtor's default has substantial measurable value. The secured creditor bargains for this right when it agrees to extend credit to the debtor and both parties consider the right part of the creditor's bargain.

This argument has a surface appeal. But putting contract together with the Bankruptcy Code makes the argument more complex: Does it make sense to consider the right a part of the creditor's bargain if Congress or the courts will not enforce that right? Does it make sense to think of the right to interest as part of the bargain if creditors know full well (under *Bermec* and *Yale Express* or interpretation of the Bankruptcy Code) that they *won't* get interest? If they know they won't, the creditors will adjust elsewhere: by not making loans to some supplicants or by charging a slightly higher interest rate to those to whom they do make the loans.

That is, the Ninth Circuit seemed to be making an expectations argument. But for institutional creditors, aren't expectations formed with reference to clear legal rules? If knowledgeable creditors understand that adequate protection means protection of the value of the collateral only (the pre-Code understanding from *Bermec* and *Yale Express*) then isn't *that* the bargain they get?

Presumably in the world of *Bermec* and *Yale Express,* secured creditors took into account the inability to get interest in bankruptcy. So they either charged a premium to reflect that risk or ignored that inability as insignificant to their return. Or businesses hovering near bankruptcy were swept out from credit markets as bad credit risks (because creditors did not want to take the risk of bankruptcy and the consequent interest failure, if they could not readily get compensation from a pre-bankruptcy interest premium). A poorly functioning credit market for companies on the verge of bankruptcy might be the policy consequence of rules that mandate nonpayment of interest, and there might be good reason to change those rules. But this is not an *expectations* argument.

Second, would § 506(b) add anything to the *over*-secured creditor's entitlement once the Ninth Circuit interpreted § 361 as it did in *American Mariner?*

The Circuits split, with some following *American Mariner* and giving interest as part of adequate protection under § 361, and others following the pre-Code cases, *Bermec* and *Yale Express*. The Supreme Court granted certiorari from the Fifth Circuit in *Timbers*, excerpted next. Notice the (lack of) finance and policy arguments as to whether a decision one way or another would encourage delay in reorganization, help or hinder pre-bankruptcy reorganizations, facilitate pre-bankruptcy financing, or facilitate reorganizations that could not be financed with new investors. Are those who drafted the Code really likely to have parsed the implication of every section of the Code, or at least have parsed the interplay between § 361, § 362 and § 506(b)?

## ¶1110: United Savings Ass'n v. Timbers of Inwood Forest Assoc., 484 U.S. 365 (1988)

SCALIA, J., delivered the opinion for a unanimous Court.

Petitioner United Savings Association of Texas seeks review of an en banc decision of the United States Court of Appeals for the Fifth Circuit, holding that petitioner was not entitled to receive from respondent debtor, which is undergoing reorganization in bankruptcy, monthly payments for the use value of the loan collateral which the bankruptcy stay prevented it from possessing. In re Timbers of Inwood Forest Assoc., 808 F.2d 363 (1987). We granted certiorari to resolve a conflict in the Courts of Appeals regarding application of §§ 361 and 362(d)(1) of the Bankruptcy Code ....

On June 29, 1982, respondent Timbers of Inwood Forest Associates, Inc. executed a note in the principal amount of $4,100,000. Petitioner is the holder of the note as well as of a security interest created the same day in an apartment project owned by respondent in Houston, Texas. The security interest included an assignment of rents from the project. On March 4, 1985, respondent filed a voluntary petition under Chapter 11 of the Bankruptcy Code, in the United States Bankruptcy Court for the Southern District of Texas.

On March 18, 1985, petitioner moved for relief from the automatic stay of enforcement of liens triggered by the petition, see 11 U.S.C. § 362(a), on the ground that there was lack of "adequate protection" of its interest within the meaning of 11 U.S.C. § 362(d)(1). At a hearing before the Bankruptcy Court, it was established that respondent owed petitioner $4,366,388.77, and evidence was presented that the value of the collateral was somewhere between $2,650,000 and $4,250,000. The collateral was appreciating in value, but only very slightly. It was therefore undisputed that petitioner was an undersecured creditor. Respondent had agreed to pay petitioner the postpetition rents from the apartment project (covered by the after-acquired property clause in the security agreement), minus operating expenses. Petitioner contended, however, that it was entitled to additional compensation. The Bankruptcy Court agreed and on April 19, 1985, it conditioned continuance of the stay on monthly payments by respondent, at the market rate of 12% per annum, on the estimated amount realizable on foreclosure, $4,250,000—commencing six months after the filing of the bankruptcy petition, to reflect the normal foreclosure delays. The court held that the postpetition rents could be applied to these payments. Respondent appealed to the District Court and petitioner cross-appealed on the amount of the adequate protection payments. The District Court affirmed but the Fifth Circuit en banc reversed.

We granted certiorari to determine whether undersecured creditors are entitled to compensation under 11 U.S.C. § 362(d)(1) for the delay caused by the automatic stay in foreclosing on their collateral.

II

When a bankruptcy petition is filed, § 362(a) of the Bankruptcy Code provides an automatic stay of, among other things, actions taken to realize the value of collateral given by the debtor. The provision of the Code central to the decision of this case is § 362(d), which reads as follows:

> "On request of a party in interest and after notice and a hearing, the court shall grant relief from the stay provided under subsection (a) of this section, such as by terminating, annulling, modifying, or conditioning such stay—
> 
> "(1) for cause, including the lack of adequate protection of an interest in property of such party in interest; or
> 
> "(2) with respect to a stay of an act against property under subsection (a) of this section, if—
> 
> "(A) the debtor does not have an equity in such property; and
> 
> "(B) such property is not necessary to an effective reorganization."

The phrase "adequate protection" in paragraph (1) of the foregoing provision is given further content by § 361 of the Code, which reads in relevant part as follows:

> "When adequate protection is required under section 362 ... of this title of an interest of an entity in property, such adequate protection may be provided by—
> 
> "(1) requiring the trustee to make a cash payment or periodic cash payments to such entity, to the extent that the stay under section 362 of this title ... results in a decrease in the value of such entity's interest in such property;
> 
> "(2) providing to such entity an additional or replacement lien to the extent that such stay ... results in a decrease in the value of such entity's interest in such property; or
> 
> "(3) granting such other relief ... as will result in the realization by such entity of the indubitable equivalent of such entity's interest in such property."

It is common ground that the "interest in property" referred to by § 362(d)(1) includes the right of a secured creditor to have the security applied in payment of the debt upon completion of the reorganization; and that that interest is not adequately protected if the security is depreciating during the term of the stay. Thus, it is agreed that if the apartment project in this case had been declining in value petitioner would have been entitled, under § 362(d)(1), to cash payments or additional security in the amount of the decline, as § 361 describes. The crux of the present dispute is that petitioner asserts, and respondent denies, that the phrase "interest in property" also includes the secured party's right (suspended by the stay) to take immediate possession of the defaulted security, and apply it in payment of the debt. If that right is embraced by the term, it is obviously not adequately protected unless the secured party is reimbursed for the use of the proceeds he is deprived of during the term of the stay.

The term "interest in property" certainly summons up such concepts as "fee ownership," "life estate," "co-ownership," and "security interest" more readily than it does the notion of "right to immediate foreclosure." Nonetheless, viewed in the isolated context of § 362(d)(1), the phrase could reasonably be given the meaning petitioner asserts. Statutory construction, however, is a holistic endeavor. A provision that may seem ambiguous in isolation is often clarified by the remainder of the statutory scheme—because the same terminology is used elsewhere in a context that makes its meaning clear, or because only one of the permissible meanings produces a substantive effect that is compatible with the rest of the law. That is the case here. Section 362(d)(1) is only one of a series of provisions in the Bankruptcy Code dealing with the rights of secured creditors. The language in those other provisions, and the substantive dispositions that they effect, persuade us that the "interest in property" protected by § 362(d)(1) does not include a secured party's right to immediate foreclosure.

Section 506 of the Code defines the amount of the secured creditor's allowed secured claim and the conditions of his receiving postpetition interest. In relevant part it reads as follows:

> "(a) An allowed claim of a creditor secured by a lien on property in which the estate has an interest ... is a secured claim to the extent of the value of such creditor's interest in the estate's interest in such property, ... and is an unsecured claim to the extent that the value of such creditor's interest ... is less than the amount of such allowed claim ....
>
> "(b) To the extent that an allowed secured claim is secured by property the value of which ... is greater than the amount of such claim, there shall be allowed to the holder of such claim, interest on such claim, and any reasonable fees, costs, or charges provided for under the agreement under which such claim arose."

In subsection (a) of this provision the creditor's "interest in property" obviously means his security interest without taking account of his right to immediate possession of the collateral on default. If the latter were included, the "value of such creditor's interest" would increase, and the proportions of the claim that are secured and unsecured would alter, as the stay continues—since the value of the entitlement to use the collateral from the date of bankruptcy would rise with the passage of time. No one suggests this was intended. The phrase "value of such creditor's interest" in § 506(a) means "the value of the collateral." H.R. Rep. No. 95-595, pp. 181, 356 (1977); see also S. Rep. No. 95-989, p. 68 (1978). We think the phrase "value of such entity's interest" in § 361(1) and (2), when applied to secured creditors, means the same.

Even more important for our purposes than § 506's use of terminology is its substantive effect of denying undersecured creditors postpetition interest on their claims—just as it denies oversecured creditors postpetition interest to the extent that such interest, when added to the principal amount of the claim, will exceed the value of the collateral. Section 506(b) provides that "*[t]o the extent* that an allowed secured claim is secured by property the value of which ... is greater than the amount of such claim, there shall be allowed to the holder of such claim, interest on such claim." (Emphasis added.) Since this provision permits postpetition interest to be paid only out of the "security cushion," the undersecured creditor, who has no such cushion, falls within the general rule disallowing postpetition interest. See 11 U.S.C. § 502(b)(2). If the Code had meant to give the undersecured creditor, who is thus denied interest on his claim, interest on the value of his collateral, surely this is where that disposition would have been set forth, and not obscured within the "adequate protection" provision of § 362(d)(1). Instead of the intricate phraseology set forth above, § 506(b) would simply have said that the secured creditor is entitled to interest "on his allowed claim, or on the value of the property securing his allowed claim, whichever is lesser." Petitioner's interpretation of § 362(d)(1) must be regarded as contradicting the carefully drawn disposition of § 506(b).

Petitioner seeks to avoid this conclusion by characterizing § 506(b) as merely an alternative method for compensating oversecured creditors, which does not imply that no compensation is available to undersecured creditors. This theory of duplicate protection for oversecured creditors is implausible even in the abstract, but even more so in light of the historical principles of bankruptcy law. Section 506(b)'s denial of postpetition interest to undersecured creditors merely codified pre-Code bankruptcy law, in which that denial was part of the conscious allocation of reorganization benefits and losses between undersecured and unsecured creditors. "To allow a secured creditor interest where his security was worth less than the value of his debt was thought to be inequitable to unsecured creditors." Vanston Bondholders Protective Committee v. Green, 329 U.S. 156, 164 (1946). It was considered unfair to allow an undersecured creditor to recover interest from the estate's unencumbered assets before unsecured creditors had recovered any principal. See id. at 164, 166. We think it unlikely that § 506(b) codified the pre-Code rule with the intent, not of achieving the principal purpose and function of that rule, but of providing oversecured creditors an alternative method of compensation. Moreover, it is incomprehensible why Congress would want to favor undersecured creditors with interest if they move for it under § 362(d)(1) at the inception of the reorganization process—thereby probably pushing the estate into liquidation—but not if they forbear and seek it only at the completion of the reorganization.

\* \* \*

Section 362(d)(2) ... belies petitioner's contention that undersecured creditors will face inordinate and extortionate delay if they are denied compensation for interest lost during the stay as part of "adequate protection" under § 362(d)(1). Once the movant under § 362(d)(2) establishes that he is an undersecured creditor, it is the burden of the debtor to establish that the collateral at issue is "necessary to an effective reorganization." See § 362(g). What this requires is not merely a showing that if there is conceivably to be an effective reorganization, this property will be needed for it; but that the property is essential for an effective reorganization that is in prospect. This means, as many lower courts, including the en banc court in this case, have properly said, that there must be "a reasonable possibility of a successful reorganization within a reasonable time." 808 F.2d, at 370–371, and nn.12–13, and cases cited therein. The cases are numerous in which § 362(d)(2) relief has been provided within less than a year from the filing of the bankruptcy petition.

### III

#### A

\* \* \*

[P]etitioner contends that failure to interpret § 362(d)(1) to require compensation of undersecured creditors for delay will create an inconsistency in the Code ... when the debtor proves solvent. When that occurs, 11 U.S.C. § 726(a)(5) provides that postpetition interest is allowed on unsecured claims. Petitioner contends it would be absurd to allow postpetition interest on unsecured claims but not on the secured portion of undersecured creditors' claims. It would be disingenuous to deny that this is an apparent anomaly, but it will occur so rarely that it is more likely the product of inadvertence than are the blatant inconsistencies petitioner's interpretation would produce. Its inequitable effects, moreover, are entirely avoidable, since an undersecured creditor is entitled to "surrender or waive his security and prove his entire claim as an unsecured one." United States Nat. Bank v. Chase Nat. Bank, 331 U.S. 28, 34 (1947). Section 726(a)(5) therefore requires no more than that undersecured creditors receive postpetition interest from a solvent debtor on equal terms with unsecured creditors rather than ahead of them—which, where the debtor is solvent, involves no hardship.

#### B

Petitioner contends that its interpretation is supported by the legislative history of §§ 361 and 362(d)(1), relying almost entirely on statements that "[s]ecured creditors should not be deprived of the benefit of their bargain." H.R. Rep. No. 95-595, at 339; S. Rep. No. 95-989, at 53. Such generalizations are inadequate to overcome the plain textual indication in §§ 506 and 362(d)(2) of the Code that Congress did not wish the undersecured creditor to receive interest on his collateral during the term of the stay. If it is at all relevant, the legislative history tends to subvert rather than support petitioner's thesis, since it contains not a hint that § 362(d)(1) entitles the undersecured creditor to postpetition interest. Such a major change in the existing rules would not likely have been made without specific provision in the text of the statute; it is most improbable that it would have been made without even any mention in the legislative history.

* * *

The Fifth Circuit correctly held that the undersecured petitioner is not entitled to interest on its collateral during the stay to assure adequate protection under 11 U.S.C. § 362(d)(1) .... Accordingly, the judgment of the Fifth Circuit is Affirmed.

## F. What rate?

### ¶1111: Unsecureds with high interest rates versus those with low rates

1. In a multi-year reorganization does value shift among claimants?
    a. Debtor owes the bank $10 million, at prime (17%) plus 3% per annum. Debtor owes on debentures of $10 million, due 2005, at 5% per annum. At bankruptcy debtor has $12.5 million in value.
    b. What are the allowed amounts of the claims?
2. a. If post-petition interest accrued at the pre-default contract rate, what would happen to the distribution proportions in a plan confirmed two years after the filing of the petition?
    b. Would accrual at the contract rate systematically favor short-term creditors that renegotiate their interest rate shortly before the bankruptcy filing?

Fortgang and King, supra, after noting that § 726(a)(5) provides creditors in liquidations with interest at the "legal rate," discuss alternatives to the standard notion (the post-judgment rate of interest): contract rate and market rate:

> ... [N]either the statute nor the legislative history defines "legal rate." Legal rate may mean (i) the rate set statutorily by each state to be paid on judgments of its courts; (ii) the rate agreed to contractually by the parties (as long as it is not usurious) or, if no rate has been agreed to, the rate set forth in (i) above; or (iii) the market rate of interest at the particular time.
>
> Some courts have assumed that "legal rate" means the statutory rate applied by each state to the payment of judgments. If that assumption ultimately is given judicial sanction, then the Code will [yield] inequitable results. For instance, assume that a creditor's claim is based on a loan agreement that provides for the payment of interest at the rate of 15% per annum, that the statutory rate applied to the payment of judgments in that particular state is 7%, and that the estate turns out to be solvent. If there were more than sufficient value to provide for the liabilities set forth in the first four levels of priority in section 726, then, under section 726(a)(5), the creditor's claim would be allotted 7% interest from the date of the filing of the petition until the date of payment, instead of the 15% interest for

which the creditor has bargained. The allowed portion of the creditor's claim would also include the principal unpaid balance plus interest at the rate of 15% up to the date of the filing of the petition. But even if the bankruptcy case had been pending for eighteen months, the creditor would be entitled to recover interest of only 7% for the entire period after the date of filing.

Thus, the debtor would be permitted to retain value directly at the expense of the creditor. Ordinarily, bankruptcy laws and rules affect the rights of creditors in favor of or at the expense of other creditors by changing the rules that would prevail outside a bankruptcy court in order to more equitably allocate the value of the debtor among the creditors. The alteration of a valid, binding, and legal contractual obligation, so that the debtor retains nonexempt property prior to the payment of its valid debts, is a legally startling and somewhat appalling result. Under this "legal rate" theory, the Bankruptcy Code effectively states that the statutory rate of interest is preferred to the rate of interest to which the parties have themselves agreed and that the difference should be retained by the debtor. There does not appear to be any substantial policy consideration that would sanction this result.

Courts usually use the judgment rate as the legal rate. Does § 506(b) use the contract rate for oversecured creditors? (Careful readers will note that the (lack of) placement of a comma in § 506(b) creates some ambiguity, an ambiguity that some lawyers will exploit.[3])

## G. General and miscellaneous

### ¶1112: Interest on interest

Although the main battle for creditors here is to get post-petition interest (or to prevent competing creditors from getting it), keep in mind that getting post-petition interest at the end of a proceeding is not the same as getting it on time. Interest on interest is a matter of concern to financiers, and not just under §§ 1129(b), 726, and 362.

Under § 1124(2), you'll recall, a creditor is deemed nonimpaired if its claim is reinstated and damages paid for missed payments. Must interest on interest be paid for a reinstatement to be valid?

In 1994, Congress added this to the Bankruptcy Code (as § 1123(d)), thinking of it as a consumer bankruptcy issue:

> Notwithstanding [section 1123(a), about the contents of a plan of reorganization] and sections 506(b), 1129(a)(7), and 1129(b) of this title, if it is proposed in a

---

[3] In U.S. v. Ron Pair Enterprises Inc., 489 U.S. 235 (1989), the Supreme Court held that the phrase "interest on such claim" in § 506(b) was independent of the statute's phrase allowing payment for fees "provided for under the agreement." Afterward, the Fifth Circuit, in Crozier v. Bradford, 958 F.2d 72 (1992), relying *not* on the statute but on pre-Bankruptcy Code practice, looked to the contract rate. The Supreme Court denied certiorari in Crozier v. Bradford, 506 US 917 (1992).

plan to cure a default the amount necessary to cure the default shall be determined in accordance with the underlying agreement and applicable nonbankruptcy law.

Congress explained why it sought to overrule a 1993 Supreme Court decision, Rake v. Wade, 508 U.S. 464 (1993):

> In that case, the Court held that the Bankruptcy Code required that interest be paid on mortgage arrearages paid by debtors curing defaults on their mortgages. Notwithstanding State law, this case has had the effect of providing a windfall to secured creditors at the expense of unsecured creditors by forcing debtors to pay the bulk of their income to satisfy the secured creditors' claims. This had the effect of giving secured creditors interest on interest payments, and interest on the late charges and other fees, even where applicable law prohibits such interest and even when it was something that was not contemplated by either party in the original transaction. This provision ... will limit the secured creditor to the benefit of the initial bargain with no court contrived windfall. It is the Committee's intention that a cure pursuant to a plan should operate to put the debtor in the same position as if the default had never occurred.

Bankruptcy Amendments of 1994, H.R. Rep. 103-835, at 55 (1994). Did Congress succeed in its goal of putting the debtor, and presumably the secured creditor, in the same position as if the default had never occurred? That is, if under applicable state law the mortgagee could seize the mortgaged assets, wouldn't it *in effect* and as a matter of business reality get interest on interest?

## ¶1113: **A relational theory of bankruptcy?**

One might argue that the policy of stopping most interest payments in the 1978 Code via § 502(b) (a policy that might have been amended or reversed by the legislative history to the 1994 amendments and the repeal of § 1124(3)) forced the debtor and creditor into a tighter relationship than they otherwise would have had.[4] When the firm deteriorates, they are both in the mess together. Even if there's enough money to pay back the creditor's principal and interest, the creditor's incentive to avoid bankruptcy is enhanced if it won't get interest. The creditor hence has an enhanced incentive to monitor the debtor and keep the debtor from making big, bankruptcy-producing mistakes.

This incentive mitigates efficiency costs of nonpayment rules (such as the enhanced incentive of debtors when in bankruptcy to delay). But this "relationship benefit" is unlikely to reverse the efficiency costs. Why? Because the creditor and debtor could always have *written* their own relational contract. They could have provided that interest would not be due in such and such a circumstance. Or the creditor could become a partial equity holder. Or part of the interest could be fixed and part of the

---

[4] Thomas Jackson & Robert Scott, *On the Nature of Bankruptcy*, 75 Va. L. Rev. 155 (1989).

creditor's return could be tied to the firm's performance, disappearing when the firm did poorly. If the creditors could have, but didn't, write their own private relational contract, then there's reason to suspect that bankruptcy, by imposing a relational contract, is imposing terms that the private parties didn't want and that usually would, net, be inefficient.

The relational theory has another problem. To work well it would require that relational creditors roll up their sleeves and get involved in the enterprise, especially as the enterprise slips toward bankruptcy. But the equitable subordination and lender liability cases give the creditor strong *dis*incentives to get involved with debtor. The relational result from the combination thus seems that we get most of the costs of relational contracts without the benefits.

What then can explain the hodge-podge of interest rules?

## ¶1114: Oscillations: Roe, Bankruptcy, Priority and Economics, 75 Va. L. Rev. 219, 234-40 (1989)

Interest does not always accrue in bankruptcy. Secured creditors usually obtain interest only if they are oversecured; unsecured creditors do not ordinarily obtain interest at all.[5]

Those with an economics background might at first criticize the nonaccrual rule. Given the time value of money, if interest does not accrue assets might not be deployed effectively because the equity holder or a junior creditor will have an incentive to delay the proceedings.[6] In a Coasian world without transaction costs this would have no ex ante distributional effect. Anticipating nonaccrual, as at least institutional creditors must, the creditor would not lose anything on a portfolio-wide basis. Interest rates would rise for the firms at risk. Nor would the assets in bankruptcy be deployed improperly when interest did not accrue; the parties would bargain swiftly and effectively to the efficient result.[7]

But there are allocational costs in real-world bankruptcy cases. Uncertainty as to the distributional effect of the nonaccrual rule, due to uncertainty as to how long the bankruptcy will last and differing internal time values for the delay that cannot be communicated convincingly, increases the time needed for settlement.

---

[5] 11 U.S.C. §§ 502(b)(2), 506 (1982 & Supp. IV 1986). [But note that the new 1994 legislative history makes it more plausible that unsecured creditors would get interest against the debtor.]

[6] Douglas Baird & Thomas Jackson, *Corporate Reorganization and the Treatment of Diverse Ownership Interest: A Comment on Adequate Protection of Secured Creditors in Bankruptcy,* 51 U. Chi. L. Rev. 97 (1984).

[7] In a Coasian world the cost would lie in those loans that do not occur because the full priority contract is not permitted.

Law and economics analysis prior to Jackson and Scott's entry doubted the wisdom of nonaccrual rules. The law might not have been consistent with the rules suggested by economic analysis, but the economic prescription seemed clear.[8]

Jackson and Scott[, when they construct a relational justification for the interest-muting rules, might be suggesting that efficient risk sharing justifies these rules or explains them as something other than] bankruptcy anomalies. [But, if so, c]ould happenstance, institutional lags, misconception, and mistake be better historical explanations of the rules than relational efficiency? Jackson and Scott have not claimed that risk sharing was the original reason for adopting these rules, saying only that risk sharing is the best normative justification for their existence. As such they might not at all disagree that to get a richer understanding of the bankruptcy process we may have to examine noncontractarian paradigms. An efficiency explanation alone puts too fine a filigree on phenomena too crude to hold the detail.

Other analysts have explained the nonaccrual rules differently from Jackson and Scott. Some contend that they developed because, in a world of small business bankruptcies, judges thought it more trouble than it was worth to determine the various interest accruals. But because there was so little to distribute, and because most of the accruals would mean only slight adjustments in each creditor's return, courts did not bother with these calculations.[9] In today's world of instant adjustments on Lotus spreadsheets and personal computers, it is hard to believe that such a task once seemed too difficult to bother, but so it once was.

Thereafter, the nonaccrual rules became disembodied from their administrative justification and took on a life of their own.[10] Like painters in a hurry, these judges might just have missed a spot [because the time value of money isn't obvious to everyone.]

If our goal is to explain the nonaccrual rules historically as opposed to finding a mental construct that is consistent with its results, then we may have to consider non-rational explanations as well. Religious precepts once militated against interest.[11] Like persistent medieval rules against usury that had a religious or quasi-religious origin, the interest accrual rules may have persisted into modern times even though they might not have arisen in a modern commercial economy were they not already there.

---

[8] See Baird & Jackson, supra note [6].

[9] Chaim Fortgang & Lawrence King, *The 1978 Code: Some Wrong Policy Decisions,* 56 N.Y.U. L. Rev. 1148, 1149 (1981).

[10] See, e.g., 11 U.S.C. § 502(b)(2) (Supp. IV 1986).

[11] E.g., Leviticus 25:35–38 ("And if thy brother grow poor, and his means fail ... though he be a stranger ... [t]ake thou no usury of him, or increase[.] Thou shalt not give him thy money upon usury, nor lend him thy foodstuffs for increase.").

Secular analogues to this religious view exist. A persistent strain in American culture favors the underdog, hesitates to kick someone when he is down (even when he "has it coming to him"), and worships the comeback.

Or perhaps the nonaccrual rules can be seen as coming from the same cultural sentiments that lead us to put a dark sack on the head of the executioner, or to give one soldier in the firing squad a blank bullet so as to allow each of the squad's members an opportunity to believe he did not kill the prisoner. Not to give interest might indeed violate contract, express and implied, but the social structure may be unwilling to enforce the obligation and execute the debtor.

Moreover, once the rules were in place they may have persisted because the ideology continued to have some adherents, because they served administrative needs, or because at least until recently, they did not really matter in economic terms.

Many legal rules are analogous to noise: random motion that does little economic damage and little economic good.[12] They happen and persist because, like people, institutions are subject to Herbert Simon's bounded rationality.[13] We cannot focus on enough, so rules persist if they do not significantly harm the economy or those with influence.

A closer examination of the nonaccrual rule serves to illustrate this point. If untutored in the ways of bankruptcy, one might think the rule straightforward—either the creditor gets interest or he does not.... But the rules are very intricate—taken together they defy classification and economic explanation. They have all the precision of a Jackson Pollack randomized splashing of paint. They are oscillations, I suspect, between contrary tendencies [of forgiveness on the one hand and enforcing the full financial contract on the other].

First, interest accrues in liquidation against the debtor. But it does not accrue among unsecured creditors until all receive payment of their principal.[14] And then it accrues at the "legal rate," a term whose meaning has been subject to some controversy—is it the contract rate, judgment rate, or market rate?[15]

Second, for secured creditors, interest accrues only if there is excess security. If there is no excess, it does not accrue.

---

[12] I am speaking of aggregate wealth-maximization now, not counting the dispersed utility of letting someone off the hook so that we can be nice fellows, assuming that such a dispersed utility can be said to exist.

[13] See Herbert Simon, Models of Man: Social and Rational (1957); cf.Richard Nelson & Sidney Winter, An Evolutionary Theory of Economic Change 8 (1982) ("Never is such a theoretical actor confused about the situation or distracted by petty concerns; never is he trapped in a systematically erroneous view of the problem; never is a plain old mistake made.").

[14] 11 U.S.C. § 726 (Supp. IV 1986).

[15] Fortgang & King, supra note [9], at 1151–52 (arguing that the choice is an open question, although they favor a market or contract rate).

Third, as a general rule, interest does not accrue to unsecured creditors in reorganization. However, even unsecured creditors do, sometimes, get interest. The Bankruptcy Code provides that they should get no less than what they would receive in a liquidation, which as we have already noted provides that creditors should get interest before stockholders are paid.[16] [And perhaps unsecured creditors cannot fairly and equitably be deprived of interest if the stockholders receive anything in the chapter 11 proceeding.]

Fourth, the rules for interpreting an agreement that subordinates a bond's principal to the senior creditor's interest payment need to be parsed. ... If the agreement were interpreted literally, the senior creditor would get interest out of the bond's principal payment (if any) in the bankruptcy. Nevertheless, some courts say that a subordination provision is enforceable only if the agreement specifies postpetition interest.[17]

Finally, what about reinstatement? Under the Bankruptcy Code, a debt may be reinstated according to its terms.[18] If the debt is reinstated the interest payments missed during the reorganization proceeding must be paid. But what if the interest payments are offered at the end of the proceeding, without payment for the delay (i.e., without interest on interest)? If the case is in the Southern District of New York, there is some question whether the interest on the delayed payment is due. New York law prohibits the payment of interest on interest; this prohibition was incorporated—perhaps incorrectly—into the Bankruptcy Code's reinstatement provisions.[19]

Are these distinctions sensible? Do they comport with the relational theory? Indeed, do they comport with any theory? [Bankruptcy analysts have explicitly said they'd like to find a theory that would make the interest rules coherent; but this may be a] striving to make sense of an apparently incoherent system[, because] perhaps the incoherent is at base just that—incoherent and internally inconsistent. I suspect that interest accrual rules, as they now exist, cannot readily be brought within a grand theory based on a single explanatory rationale.

\* \* \*

---

[16] See 11 U.S.C. § 1129(a)(7) (1982 & Supp. 1986).

[17] In re King Resources, Inc., 528 F.2d 789 (10th Cir. 1976); In re Kingsboro Mortgage Corp., 514 F.2d 400 (2d Cir. 1975); In re Times Sales Fin. Corp., 491 F.2d 841 (3d Cir. 1974). These cases may be inconsistent with the Code's new mandate that subordination provisions be enforceable in bankruptcy to the same extent that they are enforceable under nonbankruptcy law. See 11 U.S.C. § 510(a) (1982).

[18] 11 U.S.C. § 1124(2) (1982 & Supp. IV 1986).

[19] In re Kizzac Management Corp., 44 Bankr. 496, 502-03 (Bankr. S.D.N.Y. 1984); see In re Manville Forest Prods. Corp., 43 Bankr. 293, 300-01 (Bankr. S.D.N.Y. 1984); In re Forest Hills Assocs., 40 Bankr. 410 (S.D.N.Y. 1984). [After 1989 New York allowed interest on interest on commercial loans larger than $250,000.—Roe.]

## B. Another Heuristic: The Regulators and the Bankers

When reading [Jackson and Scott's] article [for this symposium] a metaphor occurred to me about the muting of priority in bankruptcy. One can see bankruptcy's muting the priority rules as a game between the bankruptcy authorities on the one hand and debtors and creditors on the other. The game is similar to the rules that Charles Kindleberger discussed and recommended to govern the relationship between financial regulatory officials and the regulated.[20]

The regulatory officials must tell the regulated that the regulators will never intervene to save failing financial institutions, even if exogenous risks threaten the financial fabric, and especially if managerial mishap threatens a particular institution. But when the disaster strikes, the institutions must be saved, because failure threatens to rip the financial fabric. But then when saved, rational expectations will change in the future. So financial regulators warrant that there was something special about this intervention, that it will never happen again. (But when it does happen again, they intervene.)

Could business bankruptcy results be seen similarly? Could the regulatory paradigm sketch a more active, anthropomorphic role to the state in the bankruptcy contest than does the Jackson and Scott's passive contractarian paradigm? Priority is necessary to support a business credit system. It is crucial to sorting out good credits from bad. But when bankruptcy strikes the recapitalization costs are great and those costs would be diminished by muting priority. So priority is muted ex post. To dampen rational expectations in the next round outside of bankruptcy, the rules are made sufficiently complex that nonexperts do not fully grasp them and mistakenly believe that priority means priority.

I do not for one moment think that the system was consciously so designed or that it survived in its present form because it had such beneficial features. But it is a nice story. And I suspect the view that bankruptcy inconsistencies reflect an oscillation between contrary tendencies [of forgiveness on the one hand and contract enforcement on the other] has some weight to it.

\* \* \*

## CONCLUSION

... It may be that administrative justifications, deep-seated moral aversions to interest, or sentiments that favor giving losers another chance were the real reasons for the original adoption of these sharing rules. It is also possible that society wants a collective proceeding for bankruptcy but that the polity cannot ascribe the character of executioner to the bankruptcy system. The death of the enterprise must—if possible—

---

[20] See Charles Kindleberger, Manias, Panics and Crashes: A History of Financial Crises (1980).

take place off-stage. The bankruptcy system can do most of the credit collection work, but the coup de grace must be administered by the economy as the business is absorbed (or closes) after the proceeding.

Some sharing rules that soften the blow to the debtor may be just what they seem to be: a contest between judicial forgiveness for those who have lost financially and the desire of critics to see a more efficient, wealth-maximizing system. Sometimes forgiveness wins [and interest is disallowed]. The contest between forgiveness and contractarian efficiency cannot be resolved without one view dominating the other in a specific case; precedent and accident have forgiveness winning in some cases and claims enforcement winning in others. The results may well be inconsistent and irresolvable.

..................................................................................................................................

Oscillation might only have been symbolic under the Bankruptcy Code until the 1980s. Because interest rates were low, their treatment in bankruptcy was not essential. The incentive for delay is much stronger when interest rates are 15% than when they were 3%. If interest rates remain high, the efficiency costs become more prominent and those who pay have enhanced motivation to call for legislative reform. Perhaps rising interest rates help explain New York's reversal in 1989, making interest on interest enforceable on New York financial contracts.

CHAPTER 12

# WORKOUTS TO AVOID A BANKRUPTCY

**A. General**
**B. Modification of the indenture**
**C. Holding out and buoying up**
**D. Exit consents**

........................................................................................................................

## A. General

### ¶1201: Workouts to avoid bankruptcy

Bankruptcies are costly. Lawyers and bankers must be paid. The persistent proceedings divert the firm's managers to dealing with financial and legal matters at a time when their operations badly need attention. Customers, suppliers and employees frequently become uneasy and abandon the firm. If bankruptcy is costly, why don't the creditors and the debtor recapitalize the firm outside of bankruptcy and split up these saved costs?

Some firms try to recapitalize outside of bankruptcy and succeed. Some try and fail. Some try and fail because of the matters we shall examine in this chapter.

### ¶1202: Arthur S. Dewing, The Financial Policy of Corporations (5th ed. 1953)[1]

[The contents of the bond indenture can be summarized:]

This rather elaborate document has, ordinarily, six important sets of provisions, some of which are mere recapitulations or elaborations of statements made in the pri-

---

[1] As reproduced in Victor Brudney and Marvin Chirelstein, Corporate Finance (3d ed., 1987).

mary contract, the bond, and some provisions only indirectly referred to in the bond. There is, first, the set of provisions summarizing the amounts [and] future dates of payment, the interest rate and the time of interest payment-provisions which acknowledge that the bondholder is a creditor of the corporation entitled to the payment of his loan with interest. Furthermore, if the payment of the debt may be anticipated by the corporation, the fact will be clearly stated, together with the specific mechanism of prepayment which shall insure fairness to all the scattered bondholders .... *Fourthly, there is a set of provisions which defines with a high degree of precision the exact course the bondholders, acting individually or together, must pursue in order to levy on the corporation, as general creditors,* or to levy on the specific property, if any, set aside for the security of the bonds issued under the indenture. Again, fifthly, there are provisions describing the duties and the obligations of the trustee. These clauses define with precision what he can and what he cannot do, on behalf both of the corporation and of the individual and collective bondholders ....

## B. Modification of the indenture

### ¶1203: Aladdin Hotel Co. v. Bloom, 200 F.2d 627 (8th Cir. 1953)

GARDNER, Chief Judge.

As originally brought this was in form a class action in which Josephine Loeb Bloom as plaintiff sought for herself and other minority bondholders of the Aladdin Hotel Company similarly situated equitable relief. She named as defendants Aladdin Hotel Company, a corporation, Charles O. Jones, Inez M. Jones, Charles R. Jones, Kathryn Dorothea Jones, Barbara Ann Jones and Mississippi Valley Trust Company, a corporation. She alleged that the class whom she purported to represent consisted of approximately 130 members who were the owners of a minority in value of certain bonds issued by the Aladdin Hotel Company ...; that on September 1, 1938, the Aladdin Hotel Company executed and delivered a series of 647 bonds aggregating in principal amount the sum of $250,000.00. The bonds on their face were made payable September 1, 1948, with interest to that date at 5 per cent per annum payable only out of net earnings and with interest at the rate of 8 per cent per annum from maturity until paid ...; that the bonds and deed of trust contained provisions empowering the bondholders of not less than two-thirds principal amount of the bonds, by agreement with the Hotel Company, to modify and extend the date of payment of said bonds provided such extension affected all bonds alike. She then alleged that she was the owner of some of said bonds of the total ... principal amount of $3500; that the defendants, other than the Hotel Company ... were all members of the so-called Jones family and during the period from May 1, 1948 to the time of the commencement of this action they were the owners of a majority of the stock of the Hotel Company and controlling members of its Board of Directors and dominated and controlled all acts and policies of the Hotel Company; that they were also the owners and holders of more than two-thirds of the principal amount of said bonds, being the owners of more than 72 per cent thereof; that they entered into an agreement with the Hotel Company June 1, 1948 to extend the maturity date of said bonds from September 1, 1948 to September 1, 1958 .... It was alleged that ... the purported changes were made on application of the Hotel Company and with the consent of the holders of two-thirds in principal value of the outstanding bonds; that no notice of said application for change in the due date of the bonds was given to the mortgage bondholders and that plaintiff did not consent nor agree to the modification. She then alleged that the modifications were invalid because [they were] not made in good faith and were not for the equal benefit of all bondholders but were made corruptly for the benefit of the defendants and such modification deprived plaintiff and the other mortgage bondholders of their rights and property; .... Plaintiff prayed for a declaratory judgment declaring and holding that the purported modifications, waivers and certifications are illegal, inequitable and void; that she and all other bondholders of the defendant Aladdin Hotel Company have judgment against defendant Aladdin Hotel Company for the principal amount of the bonds held by each of them with interest thereon at 8 per cent per annum (allowing said defendant credit thereon, however, for the 5 per cent per annum interest paid thereon) from September 1, 1948 until the payment of such principal and interest.

On trial the court dismissed as to all individual defendants ... and made findings that the amendments benefitted the Hotel Company and the Joneses but did not benefit the bondholders; that all bondholders were entitled to notice of any proposed amendments; that the Joneses acting as the Hotel Company's officers and as majority bondholders, had a legal duty to exercise an honest discretion in extending the bonds; that the power to postpone the maturity date of the bonds could not be legally recognized in the majority bondholders under the facts of this case; that the decree, however, should be limited to a money judgment because that would grant plaintiff full relief .... The judgment was a money judgment for the amount due on plaintiff's bonds.

In seeking reversal the Hotel Company in substance contends: (1) that the modification of the provisions of the trust deed extending the time of maturity of the bonds was effected in strict compliance with the provisions of the contract of the parties and hence was binding on all the bondholders; ... (4) that if a cause of action resulted from the acts of the parties to the contract it could be prosecuted only by the Mississippi Valley Trust Company, named as trustee in the trust deed.

**[Modification clauses in the bond and indenture]**

The trust deed contained [a] provision that,

> "In the event the Company shall propose any change, modification, alteration or extension of the bonds issued hereunder or of this Indenture, such change, if approved by the holders of not less than two-thirds in face amount of the bonds

at the time outstanding, shall be binding and effective upon all of the holders of the then outstanding bonds, provided, however, that such modification, change, alteration or extension shall affect all of the outstanding bonds similarly."

The bonds, including those held by plaintiff, contained the following:

"The terms of this bond or of the Indenture securing the same may be modified, extended, changed or altered by agreement between the Company and the holders of two-thirds or more in face amount of bonds of this issue at the time outstanding. Any default under the Indenture may be waived by the holders of two-thirds or more in face amount of the bonds at the time outstanding."

The bonds also contained the following provision:

"For a more particular description of the covenants of the Company as well as a description of the mortgaged property, of the nature and extent of the security, of the rights of the holders of the bonds and of the terms and conditions upon which the bonds are issued and secured, reference is made to said General Mortgage Deed of Trust."

### [Joneses have no fiduciary duty to bondholders]

It appears without dispute that the modification here under consideration was made in strict compliance with the provisions contained in the trust deed and by reference embodied in the bonds. The Hotel Company made the application to the trustee and it was approved by the holders of more than two-thirds in face amount of the bonds at the time outstanding. When this application for modification was made to the trustee he was guided in his action by the terms of the contract between the parties. That contract made no provision for notice. It required that such application have the approval of those holding two-thirds or more in face value of the bonds. The only other limitation contained in the contract with reference to the power to modify its terms was to the effect that "such modification, change, alteration or extension shall affect all of the outstanding bonds similarly." The modification did affect all outstanding bonds similarly and it is important, we think, to observe that the contract does not require that such modification affect all bondholders similarly. What effect this change might have on various bondholders might depend upon various circumstances and conditions with which the trustee was not required to concern itself. The so-called Joneses were the controlling stockholders of the Hotel Company and were its officers and the court found that the alteration was advantageous to the Hotel Company. *It was doubtless effected primarily to benefit the financial standing and operating efficiency of the hotel.* It does not follow, however, that such modification was prejudicial to the bondholders. Their security was greatly improved in value by the management and *it is inconceivable that the Joneses should deliberately act to the prejudice or detriment of the bondholders when* they held and owned some 72 per cent of the entire outstanding bond issue. It is urged that because the Joneses were acting in a dual capacity they became trustees for the other bondholders and that as such it was incumbent upon them to do no act detrimental to the rights of the bondholders. The rights of the bondholders, however, are to be determined by their contract[,] and courts will not make or remake a contract merely because one of the parties thereto may become dissatisfied with its provisions, but if legal will interpret and enforce it. There is no question that the provision in the trust deed and bonds was a legal provision which violated no principle of public policy nor private right. The sole ground for holding the modification extending the time for payment void is that no notice was given the minority bondholders. If the Joneses had not been acting in a dual capacity, then, we assume, the modification, effected as it was with the approval of the holders of two-thirds of the face value of the outstanding bonds, would have been held good. It is conceded that under such circumstances no notice would have been necessary. We think the situation must be viewed realistically. No notice was required so far as the parties to the contract were concerned. Their rights must be determined by their contract and not by any equitable doctrine, and notice to the other bondholders could have served no possible purpose. Litigants have no standing in a court of equity where a remedy at law is available. The holders of more than two-thirds of the face value of the bonds could not have been prevented from approving the proposed change even had notice been given and the acts of the parties must be determined in relation to the terms of their contract. It follows that no prejudice could have been suffered by plaintiff or her grantors by the fact that notice of the proposed change or modification was not given them.

We have searched the record with great care and find no substantial evidence warranting a finding of bad faith, fraud, corruption or conspiracy of the Joneses. When Charles O. Jones became manager of the hotel properties in 1944 no interest had been paid on the bonds prior to that date. The Hotel Company paid the interest to all bondholders in 1944 and the interest has been paid each year since. Numerous improvements were made in the hotel property at an expense of over $300,000. At the time the Joneses took over the management in 1944 the Company had a deficit of $70,000 and a balance due of $24,000 on the first mortgage of $50,000, all of which has been paid off, and the gross income of the hotel has increased from $219,000 in 1944 to $600,000 in 1951, and the book value of the stock has increased from $384,000 in 1944 to $916,000 in 1951. The properties covered by the trust deed were at the time of the trial of the proximate value of $1,000,000.

\* \* \*

**[No-action clause in the bond indenture]**

It remains to consider the contention that plaintiff in her individual capacity could not maintain this action. The deed of trust provides that,

"No holder of any bond hereby secured shall have any right to institute any suit or other action hereunder unless the Trustee shall refuse to proceed within thirty (30) days after written request thereto of the holders of not less than twenty per cent (20%) in face value of the bonds then outstanding and after tender to it of indemnity satisfactory to the Trustee."

More than 20 per cent of the bonds were in the hands of the minority bondholders but no written request was made upon the trustee to bring this suit. The court has held that the trustee at all times acted in good faith and no reason appears why he was not requested to bring this suit. Plaintiff is the owner of only $3500 face value of a bond issue of $250,000. According to her complaint there are 130 other minority bondholders and if she can maintain this action individually then the defendant may be subjected to 130 other similar lawsuits. As stated by this court in Central States Life Ins. Co. v. Koplar, 80 F.2d 754, 758:

"The reason for the rule is not far to seek. If in a mortgage securing thousands of bonds every holder of a bond or bonds were free to sue at will for himself and for others similarly situated, the resulting harassment and litigation would be not only burdensome but intolerable."

We think plaintiff could not maintain this action in her individual capacity without first having complied with the provisions of the deed of trust which vests in the trustee the right to maintain such an action.

The judgment appealed from is therefore reversed and the cause is remanded to the trial court with directions to dismiss plaintiff's complaint.

### ¶1204: Questions on *Aladdin*

1. When representing Ms. Bloom in a future bond issuance, what clauses might you seek? Would you seek a rigid clause, such as no modifications at all? If you did, how might the company respond? Would you seek to have insiders barred from voting under a modification clause? Might you seek a super-majority modification clause, requiring that at least, say, two-thirds or three-quarters of all non-insider bondholders, or all voting non-insider bondholders, consent to any modification, compromise, extension, or change of interest rates? Would you seek that each bondholder have authority to institute suit? If so, how would the company respond?

2. Could the transactions in the *Aladdin* case have been accomplished under the Drum Financial indenture? See "Description of Debentures—Modification of Indenture," at ¶603.

3. Why is the Modification of Indenture provision in the Drum Financial indenture? Cf. Trust Indenture Act, § 316(b), ¶1205.

4. In the event of reorganization in chapter 11, what is the effect of the Drum Financial's (and § 316(b)'s) Modification of Indenture provision?

5. Modifying an indenture is more complex than modifying a loan from a single bank. The conventional wisdom as to renegotiation of public debentures is:

> In a private borrowing from an institutional lender, the debtor may be less concerned with the scope of restrictions on additional debt in the loan agreement than in the case of a public borrowing from scattered debenture holders. In the former case, not only is obtaining the lender's waiver, or consent to alteration, mechanically feasible, but the creditor is likely to be responsive to changes which it perceives will enhance the borrower's economic well being. In the latter case, the mechanics of consent to change are more cumbersome, and the scattered debenture holders are less likely to be able or willing to make the judgment that concessions are advantageous to themselves as well as to the debtor.

Victor Brudney & Marvin Chirelstein, Corporate Finance 175 note h (3d ed. 1987). Do institutional changes in recent decades make modification institutionally possible and plausible? See the Chrysler consent solicitation at ¶608; when Chrysler sought to renegotiate key provisions of its negative pledge clause, it discovered that a large portion of the bonds were owned by two or three junk bond mutual funds. Does the institutionalized debt market give reason to think that successful consent solicitation would be mechanically easier in the 1980s than in the 1920s, if it were legally facilitated?

## ¶1205: Trust Indenture Act of 1939, § 316(b) (15 U.S.C. § 77ppp)

### Directions and waivers by bondholders; prohibition of impairment of holder's right to payment

### (b) Prohibition of impairment of holder's right to payment

Notwithstanding any other provision of the indenture to be qualified, the right of any holder of any indenture security to receive payment of the principal of and interest on such indenture security, on or after the respective due dates expressed in such indenture security, or to institute suit for the enforcement of any such payment on or after such respective dates, shall not be impaired or affected *without the consent of such holder* ....

## C. Holding out and buoying up

### ¶1206: Collapse of a workout

A. The MGF Oil Story

In the 1970s MGF Oil Corporation explored for, developed and produced oil, principally in west Texas and nearby states. As the price of oil soared in the 1970s, its business expanded. It financed much of its expansion with bank and other debt. In 1981 it sold $75 million of junk bonds.[2]

In the early 1980s MGF's business declined. As the world price for oil fell, the demand for drilling activity declined and the value of finding oil decreased. Losing money, MGF stopped much of its drilling activity.[3] It owed several hundred million dollars to old junk bondholders, but it was worth much less than the face value of its debt. MGF was insolvent and headed for bankruptcy.

B. The Attempted MGF Workout

1. *Why are there bankruptcies?* Bankruptcies are thought to be expensive. Due to the bankruptcy, the bankrupt firm loses sales and profits on a scale beyond the economic decline that first drove it there. Consumers hesitate to buy from a shaky company that may not be around later to service its warranties and provide spare parts. Managers depart. Those that stay have their attention diverted from operations to guiding the firm through bankruptcy. Some operations are shut-down to satisfy creditor repayment requirements. Direct payments to lawyers and investment bankers are not trivial. The need to apply to court for approval of some decisions slows the firm down.

If bankruptcy is costly, why don't the owners and creditors of the firm negotiate a deal to avoid its cost? They can try to make a deal and split the gains from improved efficiency of the firm, or from the avoided bankruptcy costs.[4] The creditors could take a large stock position, or they could reduce their demand for current cash payments in return for a greater deferred return. In the workout, they could then split among themselves (and perhaps with stockholders) the savings in bankruptcy costs. Often creditors and stockholders make that attempt. Sometimes they succeed.

That's what MGF tried to do in August 1984.

2. *The MGF exchange offer.* MGF tried to eliminate two-thirds of its debt by getting the creditors to exchange their debt for stock. The maturity of the remaining debt would be extended for five years. Had the exchange offer succeeded, MGF still would

---

[2] Junk bonds are corporate bonds that lack an investment grade rating from Moody's or Standard & Poor, the organizations that rate the quality of bonds. The junk bonds have more than a trivial chance of default. Once junk bonds were primarily bonds that when issued were investment grade, but then declined in quality as the issuing firm's operations declined. These bonds were called "fallen angels." In the late 1970s and the 1980s junk bonds were issued that lacked an investment grade rating at the time of issuance. These were called (or its issuers hoped them to be) "rising stars." In the mid-1980s junk bonds made up one-quarter of the corporate bond market. Issuers and their bankers prefer to call the bonds high yield securities.

[3] MGF Oil Corporation, Exchange Offer Prospectus ["MGF Exchange Offer Prospectus"], Aug. 20, 1984, at 34–35, 37.

[4] Ronald Coase, *The Problem of Social Cost,* 3 J.L. & Econ. 1 (1960).

have been highly leveraged, but with much less debt, the firm would then have had assets exceeding liabilities and could then have been expected to pay its debts as they came due.

The secured bank creditors made their willingness to extend maturity and exchange one-quarter of their debt for stock contingent upon a minimum of 95% of the junk bondholders exchanging their bonds for stock. This high minimum condition is critical to understanding the problem of junk bonds in workouts.

3. *Holdouts and the buoying-up effect*. In brief: when the firm is shaky, those bondholders that do not exchange their bonds will be enriched at the expense of the exchanging bondholders. As long as that subsidy to the nonexchanging, overhanging bondholders is greater than the savings in avoided bankruptcy costs accruing to potentially exchanging bondholders, the potentially exchanging bondholders are better off holding fast, frustrating the workout. Recognizing this, those that want to exchange condition their willingness to participate on others also exchanging. These effects are neatly captured in the legal practitioners' simple admonition to creditors against "losing your priority" in a recapitalization.

We can use a metaphor: Think of ice cubes jammed in a cylinder partly filled with water. Vis-a-vis other substances in the cylinder, each substance is entitled to a pay-off dependent on its height in the cylinder. Vis-a-vis other ice cubes, each cube is entitled to a pay-off commensurate with its size. Most of the cubes voluntarily melt. The remaining few cubes then "float" on top. Since pay-off vis-a-vis other substances is dependent on height in the cylinder, the holdouts from melt-down see their pay-off increase. They are buoyed up.

Now with numbers. Let's simplify the MGF scenario by positing a firm worth $150 million, with a single bond issue that was worth $200 million upon issuance. The debt is held in equal-sized portions by five creditors. Stockholders cannot be eliminated outside of bankruptcy. Let's give them a hold-up value of $25 million; the debt is worth the remaining $125 million.

So MGF's simplified, market-oriented balance sheet looks like this:

MGF Balance Sheet 1

| $150M | $125M | Market value of debt ($200M face value) |
|---|---|---|
|  | $25M | Common stock[5] |

Arithmetic tells us that the bonds are worth $.625 on the dollar. Would four of the five bondholders agree to exchange their $.625-per-dollar debt for common stock? Before the exchange, their debt is worth $100 million (4/5 of the firm's $125 million).

---

[5] The $25 million could come from the stockholders' hold-up value or from the possibility the firm's oil prospects give it a .5 chance of being worth $250 million and a .5 chance of being worth $50 million.

They hope to put the firm on a sound footing and obtain some of the enhanced value for themselves. Let's tentatively say they'd exchange their bonds for X amount of stock.

What would happen to the residual bondholder, whose claim was worth $25 million before the proposed exchange?

Her bond would increase in real value to $40 million. Because the exchange by the four other bondholders would make a further workout unnecessary, the remaining creditor could then expect to be paid according to her bond's terms: after the exchange the company would have the wherewithal to pay the reduced level of debt. The holdout bondholder gains would come at the expense of the four exchanging bondholders (and the stockholder). The subsidy would cost them $15 million.

To see the subsidy, imagine MGF's balance sheet after the hypothetical exchange:

MGF Balance Sheet 2

| $150M + Y* | | |
|---|---|---|
| | $40M | Nonexchanging bondholder |
| | X+4/5Y | Four exchanging bondholders |
| | $25M+1/5Y | Old stockholders |

(*Y is the increase in MGF's operational value if the exchange offer succeeds.)

The exchanging bondholders and the old stockholders have $110 million (plus Y) among them. ($150 million in firm value, minus $40 million in debt value equals $110 million.) Imagine that the first deal offered is for each exchanging bondholder to get 100 shares of common stock, the same number of shares outstanding before the deal. If *all five* bondholders took the deal, each would get $25 million in stock, plus a share of Y, the efficiency gains, for their $25 million bond.

But what if only four of the bondholders took the exchange? Wouldn't the exchange then "cost" the exchanging bondholders (and the stockholders) $15 million (minus Y)? See supra MGF Balance Sheet 1, in which the four exchanging bondholders had 4/5 of $125 million before the exchange, but only 4/5 of $110 million after the exchange. The holdout bondholder was "buoyed up" by $15 million.

The exchanging bondholders have by the exchange turned their $100 million of debt into $88 million of stock. The stockholders would have found that their stock would decline in value by $3 million. (Again, we're ignoring Y, for the time being.) Charity of that kind is not big on Wall Street. Unless Y, the enhancement in firm's operational value, is expected to be greater than $15 million, the exchange will not take place.

........................................................................................................................

The buoying-up effect requires that all five bondholders go along with the proposed exchange of bonds for stock. Even an overwhelming majority of 80% can fail to get a deal done, because too much value would be shifted from the exchanging bondholders to the nonexchanging bondholders. The economics literature has developed another vocabulary dealing with this problem: the bondholders can be seen as locked in game theory's prisoners' dilemma. (The original form of the dilemma has a prosecutor offering each of two prisoners freedom if one testifies against the other; both draw weak sentences if neither testifies and severe jail sentences if they both testify.)

These problems are succinctly captured in the lawyers' maxims that a creditor should not lightly "give up its priority" and that the "principle of equality of sacrifice" ought to govern a workout. Creditor and bondholder self-protection will induce adherence to these maxims in serial form (i.e., do not give up your priority unless there's equality of sacrifice among creditors). Serial adherence will put the firm in the MGF bind: without (near) unanimity, a workout of a seriously troubled firm fails.

4. *Failure: MGF files as a bankrupt*. Eighty percent of MGF's bondholders tendered their bonds into the exchange offer. If MGF could have used (and chose to use) a majority action clause, a choice not open to it or its bondholders given the Trust Indenture Act prohibition, the workout would have succeeded. But some creditors had conditioned their agreement to exchange and extend maturity on 95% bondholder acceptance. Overwhelming bondholder acceptance is a usual and necessary condition to effectiveness of a distressed company recapitalization, Wall Street bond traders report.[6] The offer failed and MGF filed for bankruptcy.

One peculiarity to which we will return: MGF stated repeatedly in its exchange offer prospectus, starting with a bold face statement on the prospectus cover page, that if the exchange offer failed, it would file for bankruptcy and expected to "present as its plan of reorganization a plan substantially identical to the restructuring plan set forth in the [Exchange Offer] Prospectus." MGF did eventually present such a plan.[7]

Ironic? What procedure is needed to bind the class in bankruptcy? A vote? What happens to the holdouts? See Bankruptcy Code §§ 1125(b), 1126(b). Why was all of that necessary? Was the MGF bankruptcy inevitable?

## ¶1207: The economics of holding out

Why are there holdouts? And why do recapitalizations sometimes fail? If there is a gain to split—the avoided bankruptcy costs—then money can be made by having a deal.

---

[6] Fritz Wahl, A New Technique for Evaluating Exchange Offers (1986) (Morgan Stanley & Co. memorandum).

[7] MGF Exchange Offer Prospectus, at 1, 4, 9; Disclosure Statement Accompanying First Amended Plan of Reorganization of MGF Oil Corp., No. 7-84-02160-E-11, at 1 (Bankr. W.D. Tex. filed June 11, 1985).

1. *Single creditor bargains.* Even if MGF had had a single creditor, it is possible although unlikely that a deal might have failed. Disparate expectations, mutual mistrust and strategic action could still thwart a deal.

*Disparate expectations.* Disparate expectations can thwart the deal: The creditor thinks the firm is worth enough to pay themselves off, so it won't renegotiate the bonds. Moreover, if the stockholder thinks there is some chance that the firm will be worth more than it owes (if the oil market turns up), he or she will often find it worthwhile to take the gamble that the oil market will turn up and the firm will pull through without a recapitalization.

Even more subtle variations may thwart a deal. Creditor and stockholder may both believe the firm is worth $150 million. But if their dispersion estimates are different, a deal could be thwarted. Or the creditor may have the same estimate of dollar value in the dispersion, but may have different estimates than the stockholder of the probability of each outcome.

*Mutual mistrust.* On what informational base does the creditor assess the firm's value? True, most of the crucial information comes from outside the firm. MGF's value was critically dependent on the future price of oil. To form an estimate of future oil prices the creditor could go to oil consultants or just read the newspaper.

But how does the creditor estimate the size of the company's Permian Basin oil reserves? Again, a third party—an independent oil engineer—might be employed, by the creditor (or by the firm itself). But some packet of information is in the control of the firm. The creditor may fear receiving misleading information from the firm's managers and shareholders, which could induce the creditor to accept a disadvantageous deal.

The managers may never provide erroneous information, but the creditor will not know whether the information is slanted to the creditor's detriment. When that mistrust is present, completing the deal will be harder than otherwise.[8]

---

[8] Offering stock for debt can reduce the mutual mistrust problem. Bondholders might fear that the insider/stockholder would tell the bondholders the firm is on the brink of bankruptcy and only an exchange offer will avoid the firm's destruction, when the firm is in fact much healthier than that. But to the extent the stockholders paint an excessively grim picture to the bondholders to justify the exchange, they are saying that the firm is not worth much. Hence, they must offer a large portion of the common stock to the bondholders. The grim picture gets painted into the bonds and new common stock that the firm is trying to "sell" to the bondholders: the bondholders would undervalue both. Bondholders might mistakenly exchange undervalued bonds; but the exchange would be for undervalued stock. Furthermore, when the stockholders obtain a small percentage of the restructured common stock, the room for effective misrepresentation is reduced. For example, MGF stockholders planned to take only 7% of the stock of the recapitalized firm. Disclosure Statement Accompanying First Amended Plan of Reorganization of MGF Oil Corp., No. 7-84-02160-E-11, at 22 (Bankr. W.D. Tex. filed June 11, 1985). The prospect that a stock-for-debt exchange would reduce cheating is important, because the rationale behind the TIA for banning majority action was a belief that bondholders would be cheated. A stock-for-debt exchange reduces or eliminates one form of potential mulcting.

Presumably at least institutional bondholders sense the information problem and, when inside information seems possibly crucial, will evaluate proposals to exchange bonds for stock differently from

*Strategic action.* The parties have a gain to split—the avoided costs of bankruptcy and continuing financial stress—but they have no ready-made guide on where to cut that bargain. The parties are not truly in a marketplace setting, where a single acceptance from one out of many offerees will suffice. The debtor and creditor are mutually dependent. In an economist's terms they are bilateral monopolists. The operational gain—avoidance of bankruptcy costs—cannot be obtained unless both sides consent. But what if the other side asks for 90% of the gain as a precondition to consent? The parties may waste time thrashing out the bargain.

* * *

Disparate expectations, mutual mistrust, and strategic action are reasons why a single creditor and the firm might fail to reach a bargain that avoided bankruptcy.

2. *Multi-creditor bargains.* Multi-creditor bargains present more obstacles. The buoying-up effect is crucial to understanding why. Holdout creditors that do not agree to a recapitalization will be buoyed up; value will flow from agreeing creditors to the holdouts. Agreeing creditors cannot just strike their own deal and ignore those that do not go along.

The buoying-up effect in combination with any of the single creditor debilities can be deadly. If enough creditors have optimistic expectations, mistrust managerial or stockholder representations, or seek for themselves a greater portion of the gains of recapitalization, then the deal could well be unmarketable. And then other creditors—willing to go along if their fellow creditors do so—may recognize the buoying-up effect and to defend their own interests also hold back their consent.

Some bondholders—the few individuals left in the bond market—may be hard to find or fail to respond. Some may temporarily lack authority to act. Others—and this could be important—may react strategically to the buoying-up effect. They could try to use the effect offensively: by withholding their consent and hoping the others will recapitalize and buoy them, the holdouts, up.

*Unresponsive creditors.* Although few individuals today hold bonds directly (instead of through mutual funds and pension funds), just getting them to act could be hard. When a bondholder's holding is small in relation to her wealth, she sees the request for action as a nuisance. If the recapitalization is complex, the investment in time may not be worthwhile. If the bondholder is a doctor, not a lawyer or financial analyst, professional help may be necessary but expensive. A busy professional has other responsibilities. She could leave the mail unopened, the proxy solicitor's phone calls unreturned.

*Lack of authority.* Occasionally, some bondholders' authority to act on the recapitalization may be in flux. The bond may have been transferred; the new owner

---

stretch-out and reduction proposals. Cf. Robert Reich & John Donahue, New Deals: The Chrysler Revival and the American System 178, 253–55 (1985) (bank creditors insist upon receiving warrants in Chrysler recapitalization; warrants later become very valuable).

will get it in a week or two. Or some bonds may be tied up in a decedent's estate for which letters testamentary have yet to be issued by the court.

*Strategic action against other bondholders: seeking to be buoyed up.* Some bondholders will seek to use the buoying-up effect offensively. They see themselves as small holders who are unlikely to influence the outcome of the recapitalization effort. In a multi-million dollar recapitalization, their refusal to exchange their $25,000 face value of defaulted bonds will not in itself hold the deal up. But by withholding consent, they may see the economic value of their bonds go from $10,000 to $20,000. In the right circumstances that would look like a good bet to play. But if enough bondholders think the same way and act offensively, the deal cannot go through. Furthermore, even if only a few act offensively, their holdout combined with the unresponsive bondholders, the optimistic bondholders, and the mistrusting bondholders may induce others to act defensively to protect themselves from the buoying-up effect. Again, the deal collapses.

(A question worth pursuing is why so many of MGF's bondholders did not holdout. One explanation lies in the plausible size of each holding: because of the 95% minimum for effectiveness, anyone with 5% or more of a bond issue could never have been a buoyed-up holdout since by not tendering their entire holding, the large holder would have destroyed the deal. The holdout problem could not regularly be solved though by increasing the minimum needed percentage to, say, 98%. Although the increase will reduce the buoying-up problem (because more bondholders will know that their refusal to tender will kill the deal), the increase also will increase the chance that a single errant bondholder who thinks the deal is a bad one will kill the deal. Balancing these chances is part of the dilemma that investment bankers face when advising firms in workouts.)

These matters are discussed in excruciating detail in Mark J. Roe, *The Voting Prohibition in Bond Workouts*, 97 Yale L.J. 232 (1987).

...................................................................................................................

The Trust Indenture Act was part of a unified recapitalization framework that emerged at the end of the 1930s. The *Los Angeles Lumber* decision shows some of the thinking behind the hostility to recapitalization deal-making.

### ¶1208: Case v. Los Angeles Lumber Prods. Co., 308 U.S. 106 (1939) (Douglas, J.) (again)

MR. JUSTICE DOUGLAS delivered the opinion of the Court.

These cases present the question of the conditions under which stockholders may participate in a plan of reorganization under § 77B (48 Stat. 912) of the Bankruptcy Act where the debtor corporation is insolvent.

...

... The debtor's principal asset consists of the stock of Los Angeles Shipbuilding and Drydock Corporation which is engaged in shipbuilding and ship repair work in California. [The debtor] has fixed assets of $430,000 and current assets of approximately $400,000 [and] current debts of a small amount, not affected by the plan ....

The debtor's liabilities consist of principal and interest of $3,807,071.88 on first lien mortgage bonds issued in 1924 and maturing in 1944, secured by a trust indenture covering [its] fixed assets ....

In 1937 the management prepared a plan of reorganization to which over 80% of the bondholders and over 90% of the stock assented. This plan of reorganization, as we shall discuss hereafter, *provided for its consummation either on the basis of contract or in a § 77B proceeding, such election to be made by the board of directors.* In January 1938 the directors chose the latter course and the debtor corporation filed a petition for reorganization under § 77B of the Bankruptcy Act, with the plan attached and reciting, inter alia, that the required percentage of security holders had consented to it. This plan as filed was later modified by the debtor, as we point out later, in a manner not deemed by us material to the issues here involved. That plan as modified provides for the formation of a new corporation, which will acquire the assets of Los Angeles Shipbuilding and Drydock Corporation, and which will have a capital structure of 1,000,000 shares of authorized $1 par value voting stock. This stock is divided into 811,375 shares of preferred and 188,625 shares of common. The preferred stock will be entitled to a 5% non-cumulative dividend, after which the common stock will be entitled to a similar dividend. Thereafter all shares of both classes will participate equally in dividends. The preferred stock will receive on liquidation a preference to the amount of its par value. Thereupon the common will receive a similar preference. Thereafter all shares of both classes participate equally.

... 641,375 shares of the preferred are to be issued to the bondholders .... The Class A stockholders will receive the 188,625 shares of common stock, without the payment of any subscription or assessment. No provision is made for the old Class B stock ....

The plan was assented to by approximately 92.81% of the face amount of the bonds, 99.75% of the Class A stock, and 90% of the Class B stock. Petitioners own $18,500 face amount of the bonds. They did not consent to the so-called voluntary reorganization in 1930 whereby the trust indenture was amended. And throughout the present § 77B proceedings they appropriately objected that the plan was not fair and equitable to bondholders.

The District Court found that the debtor was insolvent both in the equity sense and in the bankruptcy sense[;] the total value of all assets of Los Angeles Shipbuilding and Drydock Corporation was $830,000, those assets constituting practically all of the assets of the debtor and of its various subsidiaries of any value to the estate. Yet in spite of this finding, the court, in the orders now under review, confirmed the plan. And the court approved it despite the fact that the old stockholders, who have no equity in the assets of the enterprise, are given 23% of the assets and voting power in the new company without making any fresh contribution by way of subscription or assessment ....

\* \* \*

[The lower court noted that because of the outstanding bond issue, bonding] companies are unwilling to assume the risk of becoming surety for the debtor or its principal subsidiary "because of the outstanding bond issue." The government's construction program will provide "valuable opportunities" to the debtor if it is prepared to handle the business. Hence, the value to the bondholders of maintaining the debtor "as a going concern, and of avoiding litigation, is in excess of the value of the stock being issued" to the old stockholders.

\* \* \*

[A]s a matter of law the plan was not fair and equitable.

[W]here a plan is not fair and equitable as a matter of law it cannot be approved by the court even though the percentage of the various classes of security holders required by § 77B(f) for confirmation of the plan has consented. It is clear from a reading of § 77B(f)[9] that the Congress has required both that the required percentages of each class of security holders approve the plan and that the plan be found to be "fair and equitable." The former is not a substitute for the latter. The court is not merely a ministerial register of the vote of the several classes of security holders. All those interested in the estate are entitled to the court's protection. Accordingly the fact that the vast majority of the security holders have approved the plan is not the test of whether the plan is a fair and equitable one .... The contrary conclusion in such cases would make the judicial determination on the issue of fairness a mere formality and would effectively destroy the function and the duty imposed by the Congress on the district courts under § 77B ....

Hence, in this case the fact that 92.81% in amount of the bonds ... have approved the plan *is* as *immaterial* on the basic issue of its fairness as is the fact that petitioners own only $18,500 face amount of a large bond issue.

\* \* \*

We come then to the legal question of whether the plan here in issue is fair and equitable within the meaning of that phrase as used in § 77B.

We do not believe it is, for the following reasons. Here the court made a finding that the debtor is insolvent not only in the equity sense but also in the bankruptcy sense. Admittedly there are assets not in excess of $900,000, while the claims of the

---

[9] It provides in part: "After hearing such objections as may be made to the plan, the judge shall confirm the plan if satisfied that (1) it is fair and equitable and does not discriminate unfairly in favor of any class of creditors or stockholders, and is feasible; ... (3) it has been accepted as required by the provisions of subdivision (e), clause (1) of this section; ...."

bondholders for principal and interest are approximately $3,800,000. Hence even if all of the assets were turned over to the bondholders they would realize less than 25 percent on their claims. Yet in spite of this fact they will be required under the plan to surrender to the stockholders 23 percent of the value of the enterprise.

\* \* \*

And there is a further reason why this result necessarily follows, if the will of the Congress as expressed in § 77B is not to be thwarted and if the integrity of such proceedings is to be maintained. As we have said, this plan had its origin in an endeavor on the part of the debtor in 1937 to effect a voluntary reorganization. A plan was proposed by the debtor which was the same as that here involved except for the amount and nature of the stock to be received by the bondholders.[10] That plan contained two methods for its consummation. *The first was by means of an amendment to the trust indenture and a recapitalization of the debtor, a method to be followed if the board felt that sufficient approvals had been obtained.* The second was by means of § 77B. Over 80% of the bondholders and over 90% of the stock approved the original plan. Thereupon the debtor filed its petition in § 77B. Thereafter, the debtor filed a modification of the plan to which the assents, here relied upon, were obtained.[11] Thus respondent argues that since the plan of reorganization was entered into between the bondholders and the stockholders before institution of the reorganization proceedings under § 77B, the consideration flowing from the stockholders had been furnished and the interests of the bondholders and stockholders in the assets of the debtor had been fixed prior to the filing of the petition. In fact, respondent frankly insists that the stockholders' "right of participation was secured by contract before, and as a condition precedent to, the institution of the 77B proceedings."

But the mere statement of this proposition is its own refutation. If the reorganization court were bound by such conventions of the parties, it would be effectively ousted of important duties which the Act places on it. Federal courts acting under § 77B would be required to place their imprimatur on plans of reorganization which disposed of the assets of a company not in accord with the standards of "fair and equitable" but in compliance with agreements which the required percentages of security holders had previously made. Such procedure would deprive scattered and unorganized security holders of the protection which the Congress had provided them under § 77B. The scope of the duties and powers of the Court would be delimited by the bargain which reorganizers had been able to make with security holders before they asked the intercession of the court in effectuating their plan. Minorities would have

---

[10] Under that plan the new company was to have an authorized capital of $1,000,000 consisting of 1,000,000 shares of a par value of $1.00 per share, the bondholders getting 590,065 of the shares and the old Class A stockholders getting 239,935 of the shares. Shares going to the bondholders were of the same class as those received by stockholders.

[11] These assents were apparently measured by the failure of the bondholders to withdraw their consents which had been given to the original plan, on receiving copies of the proposed modification.

their fate decided not by the court in application of the law of the land as prescribed in § 77B, but by the forces utilized by reorganizers in prescribing the conditions precedent on which the benefits of the statute could be obtained. No conditions precedent to enjoyment of the benefits of § 77B can be provided except by the Congress. To hold otherwise would be to allow reorganizers to rewrite it so as to best serve their own ends.

4. The holding of the District Court that the value to the bondholders of maintaining the debtor as a going concern and of avoiding litigation with the old stockholders justifies the inclusion of the latter in the plan is likewise erroneous .... Of course, this is not to intimate that compromise of claims is not allowable under § 77B. There frequently will be situations involving conflicting claims to specific assets which may, in the discretion of the court, be more wisely settled by compromise rather than by litigation. Thus, ambiguities in the wording of two indentures may make plausible the claim of one class of creditors to an exclusive or prior right to certain assets as against the other class in spite of the fact that the latter's claim flows from a first mortgage. Close questions of interpretations of after-acquired property clauses in mortgages, preferences in stock certificates, divisional mortgages and the like will give rise to honest doubts as to which security holders have first claim to certain assets. Settlement of such conflicting claims to the res in the possession of the court is a normal part of the process of reorganization. In sanctioning such settlements the court is not bowing to nuisance claims; it is administering the proceedings in an economical and practical manner. But that is not the situation here .... Consequently, these claims of the stockholders are, as we have said, entitled to no more dignity than any claim based upon sheer nuisance value.

\* \* \*

We therefore hold that the plan is not fair and equitable and that the judgment below must be and is

Reversed.

## ¶1209: Notes on *Los Angeles Lumber*

1. Once again, what is wrong with creditors agreeing in advance to decide whether to compromise their claim by a vote?

   Several elements of the absolute priority rule are inter-connected: (i) creditors have "absolute" priority over stockholders, i.e., they are to be paid in full before stockholders receive anything, (ii) creditor consent to deviation from that priority via a creditor vote is not dispositive, (iii) when there are intermediate creditors (as there do not seem to have been in *Los Angeles Lumber*, but were in other cases), creditors cannot skip over an intermediate class to consent to a lower class' participation.

2. Recall the fair and equitable standard, which is the statutory basis for the doctrinal result. Would it be relevant in determining whether the result was fair and equitable to note, as the lower court had, that the creditors took the bonds under a bond indenture that allowed a majority vote to compromise the claim of the bonds and that the bondholders had given an approving vote prior to the reorganization of Los Angeles Lumber? See In re Los Angeles Lumber Prods., 24 F. Supp. 501, 504 (S.D. Cal. 1938), rev'd sub. nom. Case v. Los Angeles Lumber Prods. Co., 308 U.S. 106 (1939).

3. Presumably a strong basis for strict priority is that priority is what the parties bargained for. See supra Drum Financial Prospectus: "Description of Debentures—Events of Default and Notice Thereof." Is that strong basis vitiated if the parties also bargained to allow a majority vote of the bondholders to recapitalize the bonds and the majority vote is obtained?

4. Is the hindrance value of the claim a persuasive reason to prohibit the creditors from giving the stockholders something? 308 U.S. at 129. A partnership agrees to take most actions by a 2/3 vote. A customer of the partnership defaults in payment for goods sold and delivered. The partnership votes to accept $900, because the litigation process is slow, uncertain and expensive. Could similar considerations have motivated the bondholders in *Los Angeles Lumber*?

5. *Los Angeles Lumber* was decided toward the end of the depression; markets were distrusted, administrators trusted. At the heart of the decision (and its later companion, *Consolidated Rock*) was a faith in the valuation process. Courts could quickly and accurately value the firm. Claims could then be compensated. That faith in the valuation process seems to have been misplaced. At least, Congress sought to avoid the valuation hearing in 1978. See infra Bankruptcy Code § 1129. How much of *Los Angeles Lumber* survives the new Bankruptcy Code? Compare § 1129(a)(7) with § 1126 & § 1129(a)(8).

6. Does a non-waivable rule give the bondholders a negotiating advantage? I.e., by being available to negotiate, they might give up something in the negotiation. Lack of availability can sometimes be advantageous in a negotiation. (Modern changes in the tax code require that bonds be registered, allowing the company to find all holders. In the 1930s, bonds were often not registered and were held in bearer form.)

7. The Los Angeles Lumber bond indenture, a pre-1939, non-TIA indenture, apparently allowed a majority of the bondholders to amend the payment terms of the indenture. Yet although the company got a super-majority to consent, it (i) had asked in its consent solicitation for bondholder consent also to use the bankruptcy law to confirm the plan, and (ii) did in fact use bankruptcy law to confirm the plan. The explanation for this action probably lies in the 1930s negotiability rules. In the 1930s for a bond to be negotiable (i.e., for a bondbuyer to take the bond free and clear of the company's defenses) it had to have a sum certain due on a

date certain. Some of LA Lumber's bonds may well have been negotiated to holders who had no notice of the recapitalization proceeding. These holders would be holders in due course, who could usually demand payment in full when the bond came due. They would have been buoyed up.

8. Consider the modern-day negotiability provisions of the Uniform Commercial Code, applicable today to checks and commercial paper, but not to bonds listed on a stock exchange:

### § 3-302. Holder in Due Course

(1) A holder in due course is a holder who takes the instrument
   (a) for value; and
   (b) in good faith; and
   (c) without notice that it is overdue or has been dishonored or of any defense against or claim to it on the part of any person.

\* \* \*

### § 3-305. Rights of a Holder in Due Course

To the extent that a holder is a holder in due course he takes the instrument free from

(1) all claims to it on the part of any person; and
(2) all defenses of any party to the instrument with whom the holder has not dealt except

\* \* \*

   (d) discharge in insolvency; and
   (e) any other discharge of which the holder has notice when he takes the instrument.

9. If holdouts cannot be bound by a vote, could the company induce a majority of the bondholders to change their bonds' terms in a nonbankruptcy workout? Could the change in terms affect the calculations of the holdout? See the next paragraph, which deals with exit consents, and *Katz*.

## D. Exit consents

### ¶1210: Exit consents

1. Reconsider the MGF hypothetical. One holdout destroys the plan to recapitalize into all common stock, because the four bondholders who were willing to exchange their bonds for stock anticipate the shift in value from them to the nonex-

changing bondholder. Anticipating the shift, they refuse to exchange without the fifth bondholder also exchanging.

The company now comes up with a more complex plan. The company's and its investment banker's lawyers read the bond indenture to find what terms the bondholders *can* modify by a vote. They find dividend, debt incurrence, and other covenants, all of which are can be modified by a vote. These covenants are similar to those that we've seen when looking at the Drum Financial indenture in ¶603, at p. 180. These covenants aren't covered by the individualized-consent provision of § 316(b), and Drum Financial's indenture allows bondholders to modify them by vote, see pp. 185–86.

The company and its investment bankers set up this as the deal: Moments before the four exchanging bondholders would exchange their bonds into stock, the four bondholders would vote to modify the indenture by eliminating the covenants. After the vote and modification, the four would exchange the bonds into stock.

2. What is the purpose and effect of the vote? With the bond stripped of covenants, the bond is worth less than its face value. If the "buoying"-up effect is so strong that no serious possibility of default would exist after the exchange, then the nonexchanging bond's value would be reduced only slightly. If the risk of default is, although reduced, still substantial, and the covenants were serious protections, then the vote stripping the bond indenture of covenants would be more damaging to the nonexchanging bondholder.

Sometimes this covenant-stripping alone could induce the holdout bondholder to go along with the deal. But because the junk bond indentures tend not to be filled with valuable covenants and because the "buoying"-up effect may often be much stronger than the small effect of stripping the covenants, voting to reduce the covenants would often not be enough to change incentives. (The validity of such a vote and exchange is at issue in *Katz*, below. For now though we are focusing on incentives, not validity.)

So the company and its investment bankers come up with a more complex plan, one targeted to further affect the holdout bondholder's incentives. They seek a post-exchange structure that would eliminate the buoying-up effect and, if possible, even *reduce* the value of any nonexchanging bondholder's bond. If they could reduce the value of the nonexchanging bondholder's bond, then they could induce unanimity and make the exchange work.

The investment bankers come up with a new, complex deal for the company. The company offers the holders of the bonds a package of new bonds and new stock. Each one of the five holders is offered a bond, with a face value of $26 million. The bond will be due in 2001. (The original MGF bonds are due in 2005.) The bonds will be secured and be senior to the old bonds.

If four bondholders take the deal, and one doesn't, what would the balance sheet look like?

## MGF Balance Sheet 3

| | |
|---|---|
| $150M+Y | $105M Market Value (?) of debt, due 2001, senior, secured |
| | $ 40M Face value of old debt (now subordinated) |
| | $ 25M Common stock |

Analyze the incentives of the holdout bondholder. If the holdout refuses to exchange and a bankruptcy ensues (when the firm declines in value below, say, $105 million), then the *exchanging* bondholders will get all of the value of the firm, because they will be made senior and they will have security. If there's a fifty-fifty chance of a decline in value of the firm below $105 million, then the holdout's value is $20 million (50% of $40 million + 50% of zero), plus whatever value the frictions of bankruptcy could give the holdout. If the frictions provide an expected value of less than $5 million, then the holdout is made *worse off* by refusing to exchange.

3. But the company and the stockholders have a problem in offering this plan. The bond indenture for these old bonds has a negative pledge clause and has no subordination clause. To remedy this problem, the company asks the old bondholders (before the exchange of new bonds for old) to vote to delete the negative pledge clause from the indenture and to add a subordination clause into the old indenture.

4. The company also realizes that with the debt so high, Y will be low. So it modifies the recapitalization plan to use a little less debt, by offering the bondholders a package of debt and stock in a more complex plan.

## MGF Balance Sheet 4

| | |
|---|---|
| $150M+Y | $80M Senior debt (face value) maturing in 2001, |
| [$80M or 240M] | a year earlier than original maturity |
| Y=$10M | $20M Real value of old debt (now subordinated), |
| | market value is $20M, although face is $40M |
| | $25M Stock issued to the four exchanging |
| | bondholders + 1/2Y |
| | $25M Common stock +1/2Y |

"Y," the increase in operational value from avoiding a bankruptcy, is $10 million because, although some debt is eliminated, not enough is. If the recapitalization succeeds, the company will have a 50% chance of being worth $80 million and a 50% chance of being worth $240 million, for an expected value of $160 million.

5. The company asks the bondholders to vote for the amendment and send their old bonds in to the company at the same time. Again, analyze the incentives of the holdout bondholder.

6. Four of the bondholders vote to amend the bond indenture, and send their old bonds in for new ones. The holdout sues to enjoin the vote and the exchange offer, as in *Katz*. What result?

### ¶1211: Katz v. Oak Industries, Inc., 508 A.2d 873 (Del. Ch. 1986) (Allen)

\* \* \*

Plaintiff is the owner of long-term debt securities issued by Oak Industries, Inc. ("Oak"), a Delaware corporation; in this class action he seeks to enjoin the consummation of an exchange offer and consent solicitation made by Oak to holders of various classes of its long-term debt. As detailed below that offer is an integral part of a series of transactions that together would effect a major reorganization and recapitalization of Oak. The [nonexchanging bondholder, the plaintiff, asserts] that the exchange offer is a coercive device and, in the circumstances, constitutes a breach of contract. This is the Court's opinion on plaintiff's pending application for a preliminary injunction.

I.

The background facts are involved ....

[Oak] has now entered into an agreement with Allied-Signal, Inc. for the sale of the Materials Segment of its business and is currently seeking a buyer for its Communications Segment.

Even a casual review of Oak's financial results over the last several years shows it unmistakably to be a company in deep trouble .... [T]he Company has experienced unremitting loses from operations; on net sales of approximately $1.26 billion during that period it has lost over $335 million .... [T]otal stockholders' equity has ... disappeared completely ( ... [and] there was a $62 million deficit in its stockholders' equity accounts). Financial markets, of course, reflected this gloomy history.[12] Unless Oak can be made profitable within some reasonably short time it will not continue as an operating company. Oak's board of directors, comprised almost entirely of outside directors, has authorized steps to buy the company time ....

In February, 1985, in order to reduce a burdensome annual cash interest obligation on its $230 million of then outstanding debentures, the Company offered to exchange such debentures for a combination of notes, common stock and warrants. As a result, approximately $180 million principal amount of the then outstanding debentures were exchanged. Since interest on certain of the notes issued in that exchange

---

[12] The price of the company's common stock has fallen from over $30 per share on December 31, 1981 to approximately $2 per share recently. The debt securities that are the subject of the exchange offer here involved ... have traded at substantial discounts.

offer is payable in common stock, the effect of the 1985 exchange offer was to reduce to some extent the cash drain on the Company caused by its significant debt.

About the same time that the 1985 exchange offer was made, [t]he Company announced its intention to discontinue certain of its operations and sell certain of its properties ... . [D]uring 1985 representatives of the Company held informal discussions with several interested parties exploring the possibility of an investment from, combination with or acquisition by another company. As a result of these discussions, the Company [agreed to sell,] and Allied-Signal, Inc. [agreed to buy,] for $15 million cash ... 10 million shares of the Company's common stock together with warrants to purchase additional common stock. The Stock Purchase Agreement provides as a condition to Allied-Signal's obligation that at least 85% of the aggregate principal amount of all of the Company's debt securities shall have tendered and accepted the exchange offers that are the subject of this lawsuit. Oak has six classes of such long term debt.[13]

If less than 85% of the aggregate principal amount of such debt accepts the offer, Allied-Signal has an option, but no obligation, to purchase the common stock and warrants contemplated by the Stock Purchase Agreement .... Thus, as part of the restructuring and recapitalization contemplated by the Acquisition Agreement and the Stock Purchase Agreement, the Company has extended an exchange offer to each of the holders of the six classes of its long-term debt securities. These pending exchange offers include a Common Stock Exchange Offer (available only to holders of the 9⅝% convertible notes) and the Payment Certificate Exchange Offers (available to holders of all six classes of Oak's long-term debt securities). The Common Stock Exchange Offer currently provides for the payment to each tendering noteholder of 407 shares of the Company's common stock in exchange for each $1,000 9⅝% note accepted. The offer is limited to $38.6 million principal amount of notes (out of approximately $83.9 million outstanding).

The Payment Certificate Exchange Offer is an any and all offer. Under its terms, a payment certificate, payable in cash five days after the closing of the sale of the Materials Segment to Allied-Signal, is offered in exchange for debt securities. The cash value of the Payment Certificate will vary depending upon the particular security tendered. In each instance, however, that payment will be less than the face amount of the obligation. The cash payments range in amount, per $1,000 of principal, from $918 to $655. These cash values however appear to represent a premium over the market prices for the Company's debentures as of the time the terms of the transaction were set.

---

[13] The three classes of debentures are: 13.65% debentures due April 1, 2001, 10½% convertible subordinated debentures due February 1, 2002, and 11⅞% subordinated debentures due May 15, 1998. In addition, as a result of the 1985 exchange offer the company has three classes of notes which were issued in exchange for debentures that were tendered in that offer. Those are: 13.5% senior notes due May 15, 1990, 9⅝% convertible notes due September 15, 1991 and 11⅝% notes due September 15, 1990.

The Payment Certificate Exchange Offer is subject to certain important conditions before Oak has an obligation to accept tenders under it. First, it is necessary that a minimum amount ($38.6 million principal amount out of $83.9 total outstanding principal amount) of the 9⅝% notes be tendered pursuant to the Common Stock Exchange Offer. Secondly, it is necessary that certain minimum amounts of each class of debt securities be tendered, together with consents to amendments to the underlying indentures.[14] Indeed, under the offer one may not tender securities *unless at the same time one consents to the proposed amendments to the relevant indentures.*

The condition of the offer that tendering security holders must consent to amendments in the indentures governing the securities gives rise to plaintiff's claim of breach of contract in this case. Those amendments would, if implemented, have the effect of removing significant negotiated protections to holders of the Company's long-term debt including the deletion of all financial covenants. Such modification may have adverse consequences to debt holders who elect not to tender pursuant to either exchange offer.

Allied-Signal apparently was unwilling to commit to the $15 million cash infusion contemplated by the Stock Purchase Agreement, unless Oak's long-term debt is reduced by 85% (at least that is a condition of their obligation to close on that contract). ... But existing indenture covenants ... prohibit the Company, so long as any of its long-term notes are outstanding, from issuing any obligation (including the Payment Certificates) in exchange for any of the debentures. Thus, in this respect, amendment to the indentures is required in order to close the Stock Purchase Agreement as presently structured.

Restrictive covenants in the indentures would appear to interfere with effectuation of the recapitalization in another way. Section 4.07 of the 13.50% Indenture provides that the Company may not "acquire" for value any of the 9⅝% Notes or 11⅝% Notes unless it concurrently "redeems" a proportionate amount of the 13.50% Notes. This covenant, if unamended, would prohibit the disproportionate acquisition of the 9⅝% Notes that may well occur as a result of the Exchange Offers; in addition, it would appear to require the payment of the "redemption" price for the 13.50% Notes rather than the lower, market price offered in the exchange offer.

In sum, the failure to obtain the requisite consents to the proposed amendments would permit Allied-Signal to decline to consummate both the Acquisition Agreement and the Stock Purchase Agreement.

\* \* \*

---

[14] The holders of more than 50% of the principal amount of each [class of notes and debentures] must validly tender such securities and consent to certain proposed amendments to the indentures governing those securities.

The Exchange Offers are dated February 14, 1986. This suit seeking to enjoin consummation of those offers was filed on February 27. Argument on the current application was held on March 7.

## II.

Plaintiff's claim that the Exchange Offers and Consent Solicitation constitutes a threatened wrong to him and other holders of Oak's debt securities[15] appear[s] to be summarized in paragraph 16 of his Complaint:

> The purpose and effect of the Exchange Offers is [1] to benefit Oak's common stockholders at the expense of the Holders of its debt securities, [2] to force the exchange of its debt instruments at unfair price and at less than face value of the debt instruments [3] pursuant to a rigged vote in which debt Holders who exchange, and who therefore have no interest in the vote, must consent to the elimination of protective covenants for debt Holders who do not wish to exchange.

As amplified in briefing on the pending motion, plaintiff's claim is that no free choice is provided to bondholders by the exchange offer and consent solicitation. Under its terms, a rational bondholder is "forced" to tender and consent. Failure to do so would face a bondholder with the risk of owning a security stripped of all financial covenant protections and for which it is likely that there would be no ready market. A reasonable bondholder, it is suggested, cannot possibly accept those risks and thus such a bondholder is coerced to tender and thus to consent to the proposed indenture amendments.

It is urged this linking of the offer and the consent solicitation constitutes a breach of a contractual obligation that Oak owes to its bondholders to act in good faith. Specifically, plaintiff points to [two] contractual provisions from which it can be seen that the structuring of the current offer constitutes a breach of good faith. Those provisions (1) establish a requirement that no modification in the term of the various indentures may be effectuated without the consent of a stated percentage of bondholders; [and] (2) restrict Oak from exercising the power to grant such consent with respect to any securities it may hold in its treasury[.]

---

[15] ... [A] high percentage of the principal value of Oak's debt securities are owned in substantial amounts by a handful of large financial institutions. Almost 85% of the value of the 13.50% Notes is owned by four such institutions (one investment banker owns 55% of that issue); 69.1% of the 9⅝% Notes are owned by four financial institutions (the same investment banker owning 25% of that issue) and 85% of the 11⅞% Notes are owned by five such institutions. Of the debentures, 89% of the 13.65% debentures are owned by four large banks; and approximately 45% of the two remaining issues is owned by two banks. [Could these bondholders alone have killed the deal? Could these larger bondholders have been coerced?—Roe.]

## III.

\* \* \*

I turn first to an evaluation of the probability of plaintiff's ultimate success on the merits of his claim. I begin that analysis with two preliminary points. The first concerns what is not involved in this case. To focus briefly on this clears away much of the corporation law case law of this jurisdiction upon which plaintiff in part relies. This case does not involve the measurement of corporate or directorial conduct against that high standard of fidelity required of fiduciaries when they act with respect to the interests of the beneficiaries of their trust. Under our law—and the law generally—the relationship between a corporation and the holders of its debt securities ... is contractual in nature. Arrangements among a corporation, the underwriters of its debt, trustees under its indentures and sometimes ultimate investors are typically thoroughly negotiated and massively documented. The rights and obligations of the various parties are or should be spelled out in that documentation. The terms of the contractual relationship agreed to and not broad concepts such as fairness define the corporation's obligation to its bondholders.[16]

Thus, the first aspect of the pending Exchange Offers about which plaintiff complains—that "the purpose and effect of the Exchange Offers is to benefit Oak's common stockholders at the expense of the Holders of its debt"—does not itself appear to allege a cognizable legal wrong. It is the obligation of directors to attempt, within the law, to maximize the long-run interests of the corporation's stockholders; that they may sometimes do so "at the expense" of others (even assuming that a transaction which one may refuse to enter into can meaningfully be said to be at his expense) does not for that reason constitute a breach of duty. It seems likely that corporate restructurings designed to maximize shareholder values may in some instances have the effect of requiring bondholders to bear greater risk of loss and thus in effect transfer economic value from bondholders to stockholders .... But if courts are to provide protection against such enhanced risk, they will require either legislative direction to do so or the negotiation of indenture provisions designed to afford such protection.

The second preliminary point concerns the limited analytical utility, at least in this context, of the word "coercive" which is central to plaintiff's own articulation of his theory of recovery. If, pro arguendo, we are to extend the meaning of the word coercion beyond its core meaning—dealing with the utilization of physical force to overcome the will of another—to reach instances in which the claimed coercion arises from an act designed to affect the will of another party by offering inducements to the

---

[16] To say that the broad duty of loyalty that a director owes to his corporation and ultimately its shareholders is not implicated in this case is not to say, as the discussion below reflects, that as a matter of contract law a corporation owes no duty to bondholders of good faith and fair dealing. See, Restatement of Law, Contracts 2d, § 205 (1979). Such a duty, however, is quite different from the congeries of duties that are assumed by a fiduciary. See generally, Bratton, The Economics and Jurisprudence of Convertible Bonds, 1984 Wis. L. Rev. 667.

act sought to be encouraged or by arranging unpleasant consequences for an alternative sought to be discouraged, then ... further refinement is essential. Clearly some "coercion" of this kind is legally unproblematic. Parents may "coerce" a child to study with the threat of withholding an allowance; employers may "coerce" regular attendance at work by either docking wages for time absent or by rewarding with a bonus such regular attendance. Other "coercion" so defined clearly would be legally relevant (to encourage regular attendance by corporal punishment, for example). Thus, for purposes of legal analysis, the term "coercion" itself—covering a multitude of situations—is not very meaningful. For the word to have much meaning for purposes of legal analysis, it is necessary in each case that a normative judgment be attached to the concept ("inappropriately coercive" or "wrongfully coercive," etc.). But, it is then readily seen that what is legally relevant is not the conclusory term "coercion" itself but rather the norm that leads to the adjective modifying it.

In this instance, assuming that the Exchange Offers and Consent Solicitation can meaningfully be regarded as "coercive" (in the sense that Oak has structured it in a way designed—and I assume effectively so—to "force" rational bondholders to tender), the relevant legal norm that will support the judgment whether such "coercion" is wrongful or not will, for the reasons mentioned above, be derived from the law of contracts. I turn then to that subject to determine the appropriate legal test or rule.

Modern contract law has generally recognized an implied covenant to the effect that each party to a contract will act with good faith towards the other with respect to the subject matter of the contract. See, Restatement of Law, Contracts 2d, § 205 (1981) .... The contractual theory for this implied obligation is well stated in a leading treatise:

> If the purpose of contract law is to enforce the reasonable expectations of parties induced by promises, then at some point it becomes necessary for courts to look to the substance rather than to the form of the agreement, and to hold that substance controls over form. What courts are doing here, whether calling the process "implication" of promises, or interpreting the requirements of "good faith," as the current fashion may be, is but a recognition that the parties occasionally have understandings or expectations that were so fundamental that they did not need to negotiate about those expectations. When the court "implies a promise" or holds that "good faith" requires a party not to violate those expectations, it is recognizing that sometimes silence says more than words, and it is understanding its duty to the spirit of the bargain is higher than its duty to the technicalities of the language. Corbin on Contracts (Kaufman Supp. 1984), § 570.

It is this obligation to act in good faith and to deal fairly that plaintiff claims is breached by the structure of Oak's coercive exchange offer. Because it is an implied contractual obligation that is asserted as the basis for the relief sought, the appropriate legal test is not difficult to deduce. It is this: *is it clear from what was expressly agreed upon that the parties who negotiated the express terms of the contract would have agreed to proscribe the act later complained of as a breach of the implied covenant of good faith—had they thought to negotiate with respect to that matter?* If the answer to this question is yes, then, in my opinion, a court is justified in concluding that such act constitutes a breach of the implied covenant of good faith.[17]

With this test in mind, I turn now to a review of the specific provisions of the various indentures from which one may be best able to infer whether it is apparent that the contracting parties—*had they negotiated with the exchange offer and consent solicitation in mind*—would have expressly agreed to prohibit contractually the linking of the giving of consent with the purchase and sale of the security.

IV.

Applying the foregoing standard to the exchange offer and consent solicitation, I find first that there is nothing in the indenture provisions granting bondholders power to veto proposed modifications in the relevant indenture that implies that Oak may not offer an inducement to bondholders to consent to such amendments. Such an implication, at least where, as here, the inducement is offered on the same terms to each holder of an affected security, would be wholly inconsistent with the strictly commercial nature of the relationship.

Nor does the second pertinent contractual provision supply a ground to conclude that defendant's conduct violates the reasonable expectations of those who negotiated the indentures on behalf of the bondholders. Under that provision Oak may not vote debt securities held in its treasury. Plaintiff urges that Oak's conditioning of its offer to purchase debt on the giving of consents has the effect of subverting the purpose of that provision; it permits Oak to "dictate" the vote on securities which it could not itself vote.

The evident purpose of the restriction on the voting of treasury securities is to afford protection against the issuer voting as a bondholder in favor of modifications that would benefit it as issuer, even though such changes would be detrimental to bondholders. But the linking of the exchange offer and the consent solicitation does not involve the risk that bondholder interests will be affected by a vote involving anyone with a financial interest in the subject of the vote other than a bondholder's interest. *That the consent is to be given concurrently with the transfer of the bond to the issuer does not in any sense create the kind of conflict of interest that the indenture's prohibition on voting treasury securities contemplates.* Not only will the proposed consents be granted or withheld only by those with a financial interest to maximize the return on their investment in Oak's bonds, but the incentive to consent is equally available to all members of each class of bondholders. Thus the "vote" implied by the consent solicitation is not affected in any sense by those with a financial conflict of interest.

---

[17] [Emphasis supplied.—Roe. Who wrote the relevant contract terms?]

In these circumstances, while it is clear that Oak has fashioned the exchange offer and consent solicitation in a way designed to encourage consents, I cannot conclude that that offer violates the intendment of any of the express contractual provisions considered or, applying the test set out above, that its structure and timing breaches an implied obligation of good faith and fair dealing.

* * *

Accordingly, I conclude that plaintiff has failed to demonstrate a probability of ultimate success on the theory of liability asserted.

V.

An independent ground for the decision to deny the pending motion is supplied by the requirement that a court of equity will not issue the extraordinary remedy of preliminary injunction where to do so threatens the party sought to be enjoined with irreparable injury that, in the circumstances, seems greater than the injury that plaintiff seeks to avoid.

Oak is in a weak state financially. Its board, comprised of persons of experience and, in some instances, distinction, have approved the complex and interrelated transactions outlined above. It is not unreasonable to accord weight to the claims of Oak that the reorganization and recapitalization of which the exchange offer is a part may present the last good chance to regain vitality for this enterprise. I have not discussed plaintiff's claim of irreparable injury, although I have considered it. I am satisfied simply to note my conclusion that it is far outweighed by the harm that an improvidently granted injunction would threaten to Oak.

For the foregoing reasons plaintiff's application for a preliminary injunction shall be denied.

IT IS SO ORDERED.

---

### ¶1212: *Katz* and the Trust Indenture Act

1. The type of transaction outlined in *Katz* is frequently used, although not always successfully.
2. Is there a qualitative difference between the nature of the consent given in *Los Angeles Lumber Products* and that given in *Katz*? Is one judge more solicitous of individualized consent than the other? Do both judges have the same view of bankruptcy and the judicial review inside bankruptcy as desirable or undesirable?
3. What does "intent of the parties" mean for a contractual provision that a statute required the parties to place in their contract?
4. Is § 316 of the Trust Indenture Act relevant to the *Katz* decision and the underlying transaction? Is it relevant as a matter of doctrine? Is it relevant to understanding why the transaction ever took place? If § 316 didn't exist what might the bond

indenture's modification clause have looked like? Could you imagine a different transaction than that used by Oak Industries, if § 316 didn't exist? I.e., wouldn't the debenture holders simply have voted?

**Trust Indenture Act of 1939, § 316 (15 U.S.C. § 77ppp)**

**Directions and waivers by bondholders; prohibition of impairment of holder's right to payment**

**(a) Directions and waivers by bondholders**

The indenture to be qualified—

(1) shall automatically be deemed (unless it is expressly provided therein that any such provision is excluded) to contain provisions authorizing the holders of not less than a majority in principal amount of the indenture securities ... at the time outstanding ... on behalf of the holders of all such indenture securities, to consent to the waiver of any past default and its consequences; ...

(2) may contain provisions authorizing the holders of not less than 75 per centum in principal amount of the indenture securities ... at the time outstanding to consent on behalf of the holders of all such indenture securities to the postponement of any interest payment for a period not exceeding three years from its due date.

For the purposes of this subsection in determining whether the holders of the required principal amount of indenture securities have concurred in any such direction or consent, indenture securities owned by any obligor upon the indenture securities, or by any person directly or indirectly controlling or controlled by or under direct or indirect common control with any such obligor, shall be disregarded, except that for the purposes of determining whether the indenture trustee shall be protected in relying on any such direction or consent, only indenture securities which such trustee knows are so owned shall be so disregarded.

5. Financial institutions, such as mutual funds, pension funds, and insurance companies, owned most of the Oak Industries' bonds. First, how much can the company coerce a bondholder owning 55% of the bonds? 15% of the bonds? Is it relevant that the offering company has conditioned the offer on getting 85% of the bondholders to exchange? Second, does this indicate who might get hurt in the exit-consent recapitalization used in *Katz?* Whom was Douglas trying to protect in *Los Angeles Lumber* and when pushing for passage of § 316?

6. Did § 316(b) of the Trust Indenture Act induce the company to use exit consents in *Katz*?

7. Could an issuing company give bondholders $35 for every $1000 face amount of bonds that the holders voted in favor of giving up an important protective financial covenant? The payment, although available to every assenting bondholder,

would not go to bondholders voting against the indenture amendment or to those that did nothing. Eastern Airlines did just that during its merger with Texas Air. Held (by the same court that wrote the *Katz* opinion): no violation of the Eastern Airlines indenture or of any implied contractual terms. Kass v. Eastern Air Lines, Civ. No. 8700, slip op. at 11-14 (Del. Ch. Nov. 14, 1986); accord, Pisik v. BCI Holdings Corp., No. 14593, slip op. (N.Y. Sup. Ct. June 25, 1987).

8. *Katz* was decided in 1986 in the midst of a merger boom. In the mid-1980s, two-tiered tender offers for a target company's stock became a serious issue for the Delaware courts. In a two-tiered tender offer, the offering company offers to pay, say, $75 for the first 51% of the shares tendered. With a majority of the stock in hand, the offering company will force a merger of the target with itself, and pay the dissenters, say, $60. These were seen to be coercive, because shareholders that feared being on the back end of the offer rushed to tender. Arguably they would rush to tender even if they thought the blended, average price ($67.50) was too low. They'd rush because they feared that if everyone else tendered and they held out, they'd get only $60. Managers at targets sought to deter takeovers and their counsel justified tactics such as poison pills as deterring the coercive effects of a two-tiered tender offer. Relevance to *Katz?*

9. The "coercion" of exit consents could reduce the value of the bonds if they don't participate in sharing any gains. The buoying-up effect might induce some issuers to give bondholders their "due." Which effect is greater? In the abstract one can't know whether buoying up is more important than the "coercive," value-reducing elements of an exit consent. Research suggests that bondholder returns around the time of an exit consent solicitation are, on average, positive. Marcel Kahan and Bruce Tuckman, *Do Bondholders Lose from Junk Bond Covenant Changes?*, 66 J. Bus. 499 (1993). Thus, on average, "buoying up" is more important than "coercion."

10. Could Oak Industries have used a "pre-packaged" bankruptcy? That is, could it have used the consents obtained outside of bankruptcy to bind all of the bondholders *inside* bankruptcy? Bankruptcy Code § 1126 says:

> [A] holder of a claim or interest that accepted or rejected the plan before the commencement of the case under this title is deemed to have accepted or rejected such plan, as the case may be, if—
>
>> (1) the solicitation of such acceptance or rejection was in compliance with any applicable nonbankruptcy law, rule, or regulation governing the adequacy of disclosure in connection with such solicitation; or
>>
>> (2) if there is not any such law, rule, or regulation, such acceptance or rejection was solicited after disclosure to such holder of adequate information ... .

11. Although before 1986 these "pre-packaged" bankruptcies were unpopular and apparently nonexistent, after the 1980s proliferation of junk bonds, "pre-

packaged" bankruptcies (sometimes engineered with exit consents) became more popular. In the first half of 1993, pre-packaged bankruptcies made up just under half of the bankruptcy filings of publicly-traded firms having assets of more than $100 million. They took an average of three months to complete after filing (but needed 18 months to negotiate before the filing). Elizabeth Tashjian, Ronald C. Lease, and John J. McConnell, Prepacks: An Empirical Analysis of Prepackaged Bankruptcies (unpublished manuscript) (April, 1994).

¶1213: **Fidelity Investments petition to the SEC**

Robert C. Pozen
General Counsel
Managing Director

November 16, 1990

FMR Corp.
82 Devonshire Street
Boston MA 02109
617-570-7703

Mr. Jonathan G. Katz
Secretary
United States Securities and Exchange Commission
450 Fifth Street, N.W., Mail Stop 6-9
Washington, D.C. 20549

Dear Mr. Katz:

FMR Corp., the parent of Fidelity Management & Research Company ("FMR"), respectfully petitions the Securities and Exchange Commission (the "Commission") ... to revise Securities Exchange Act Rule 14e-1 (the "Rule"). We are joined in this petition by The Prudential Insurance Company of America ("Prudential" and, together with FMR, the "Petitioners") and are supported by the institutions listed under Exhibit A to this petition. The Petitioners are proposing the Rule amendment in response to a manipulative and deceptive practice used by bidders in connection with tender offers for debt securities. Specifically, the proposal would address simultaneous tender offers/consent solicitations and would require the results of the consent solicitation to be disclosed before the tender offer could be closed.

Background

\* \* \*

Some of the high-yield debt obligations which the Petitioners hold on behalf of their clients have been the subject of issuer tender offers, coupled with the threat that investor protections in the indenture will be removed at the completion of the tender offer. If these protections are removed at the completion of the tender offer, the market value of any debt still outstanding will decline sharply. Thus, the holders of these debt obligations are effectively forced to tender before they know whether the indenture protections will remain after the tender offer.

Issuers have begun using this strategy with alarming frequency since the market for high-yield securities has weakened. Recent examples have included Mary Kay Corporation's September 28, 1990 offer for its 15% Discount Debentures due November 30, 2000 (the "Mary Kay Offer"); Armco Inc.'s August 1, 1990 offer for its 13½% Senior Notes (the "Armco Offer"); Dimola Pty. Ltd.'s June 5, 1990 offer for the 12⅝% Extendable Subordinated Debentures of Bond Brewing Holdings Limited (the "Bond Brewing Offer"); Ingersoll Newspapers, Inc.'s March 22, 1990 offer for Community Newspapers Inc.'s 13% Senior Subordinated Reset Notes and Subordinated Discount Debentures (the "Community Newspapers

Offer"); H.C. Crown Corp.'s February 6, 1990 offer for Univision Holdings, Inc.'s Senior Subordinated Discount Notes and 13⅜% Subordinated Debentures (the "Univision Offer"); and Beatrice Company's December 2, 1988 offer for its 11% Ten Year Senior Notes, 12½% Twelve Year Senior Subordinated Debentures and 12¾% Fifteen Year Subordinated Debentures (the "Beatrice Offer").

... [M]any issuers of high-yield debt want to eliminate certain restrictive provisions pursuant to which the debt was issued. During the 1980s, many of these issuers restructured through leveraged buyouts, acquisitions by third parties, or the assumption of massive debt as a takeover defense. As part of that restructuring, the companies agreed to incorporate certain debtholder protections (the "Protections") into their indentures in order to sell their debt to investors.

The Protections exist to help assure repayment of the debt, generally by prohibiting the issuer from taking any of a number of specified corporate actions. Protective covenants may prohibit an issuer from inter alia, incurring additional debt; declaring dividends to stockholders or affiliated companies; granting liens upon assets of the company; selling or otherwise disposing of assets of the company; or taking actions which would affect the seniority of the security holders. Other typical Protections might include providing collateral for the debt or a guarantee of the debt by a third party.

Issuers are obviously entitled to bargain with investors, and to persuade their security holders to part with value for fair value received. Collectively, the Petitioners have participated in hundreds of issuer tender offers on behalf of their clients.

However, issuers which couple a tender offer with a consent solicitation often do so to force security holders to tender. Realistically, investors are coerced into tendering their debt because they do not know the outcome of the consent solicitation. As is discussed in greater detail below, if the consent solicitation is successful, the value of the security may plummet.

Accordingly, without knowing the results of the consent solicitation, debt holders have no economic alternative to tendering their securities in these dual offers, regardless of the fairness of the price offered by the issuer.

The Petitioners believe that this strategy is a deceptive and manipulative practice in violation of the policies underlying Section 14(e) of the Securities Exchange Act of 1934. Under that Section, the Commission is given the responsibility to promulgate rules reasonably designed to prevent such practices. Therefore, we request that the Commission adopt a new section (e) to Rule 14e-1 as set forth below.

Structure of the Tender Offer

A dual tender offer/consent solicitation is generally structured as follows. A tender offer is made by the issuer (or an affiliate of the issuer) to purchase all or part of an outstanding class of debt obligations at a fixed price. However, in addition to the normal preconditions to consummation of the tender offer, the offer is made contingent on either or both of two unusual conditions. First, the bidder will not accept tendered securities from any security holder which does not also give its consent in the accompanying consent solicitation. Second, the bidder will not accept any securities at all unless a specified majority approves the accompanying consent solicitation.

The accompanying consent solicitation seeks security holder approval of one or more changes to the terms of the debt. Generally, approval is sought to strip all or some of the Protections from the debt's governing indenture. In some of these offers, the bidder provides a separate payment for a consent, in addition to the tender offer price. For example, an issuer might bid $600 to purchase a $1,000 face amount bond in the tender offer, and offer an additional $50 per $1,000 face amount as a payment for the consent. Alternatively, a single price might be offered for both consent and tender by a security holder. For example, in exchange for both a consent and tender, an issuer might offer $650 for each $1,000 face amount security. However, in either alternative the two offers are integrated, in that no tenders will be accepted unless the consent solicitation is successful.

A key feature of these offers is that debt holders do not know whether the consent solicitation will succeed before they must accept or reject the tender offer. Bidders are not required to disclose this information to security holders before completing the tender offer. Accordingly, investors do not know the ultimate terms of the security they are being asked to tender.

In the case of a partial tender offer, priority proration periods can be created to force bondholders to tender prior to the consent date, even though the tender offer remains open until after the consent date. For example, the Mary Kay Offer provided for a pro rata purchase if more bonds were tendered than the maximum principal amount specified in the offer. Bonds that were tendered prior to the consent date would be entitled to a pro rata share of the fund available to purchase the bonds prior to any of the bonds tendered after the consent date being entitled to such fund. Essentially, those bondholders who tendered prior to the consent date were much more likely to have all of their bonds purchased than those who tendered after the consent date. Additionally, those who tendered after the consent date would be left with securities with less Protections and value.

Manipulative and Deceptive Nature of the Tender Offer

In our view, a simultaneous tender offer/consent solicitation is usually designed to coerce debt holders into both tendering and consenting, regardless of whether the total compensation to be paid reflects the true value of the target security. Several aspects of these offers support our view.

First, unlike traditional consent solicitations, simultaneous tender offer/consent solicitations are inherently more likely to obtain consents to proposals which disadvantage security holders. Obviously, if the solicitation is successful, security holders who both tender and consent will no longer own the security and accordingly will have no interest left to protect. In contrast, investors who consent in traditional solicitations affect the terms of a security they will continue to hold. Because investors who consent will continue to bear the costs of the changed terms of a security, these investors have an interest in disapproving unfair or disadvantageous proposals.

Second, the issuer's offer invariably ties together the two decisions of security holders. As noted above, some issuers offer one price for both decisions. However, even if the prices are technically separate, it makes no economic sense for a security holder to tender and not consent, or consent and not tender.

For example, assume the price is $600 for tenders and $50 for consents per $1,000 face amount. A security holder which tenders for $600 would also consent: the gain would be an additional $50 and, because the holder would no longer own the debt, the holder would be unconcerned about the elimination of Protections on the debt. Conversely, a security holder would not consent without tendering, because the consent price would almost never compensate the holder for the decline in price attributable to the elimination of the Protections.

Accordingly, a security holder has no choice but to tender and consent, because the holder will not know whether the consent solicitation has been successful until it is too late to tender. If the holder does not tender and the consent solicitation is successful, the Protections will be eliminated and the holder's debt security will fall significantly in market value.

The adverse effect of a successful consent solicitation upon the market value of an investor's holding can be dramatic. Once the Protections have been stripped from the target securities, the issuer becomes free to take actions which may make repayment of the debt less likely, e.g., paying dividends, selling assets which once supported the debt, or incurring additional debt senior to the target securities. Obviously, the market revalues the stripped securities at a much lower price.

Simultaneous offers are not justified by the legitimate rights of an issuer to repurchase or renegotiate outstanding debt. If an issuer's board of directors determines in good faith that it is in the best interests of the company and its security holders to commence a tender offer for its own securities, the company may do so without simultaneously mounting a consent solicitation. If the company offers a fair price for the securities, security holders will tender, and the tender offer will be successful. If the company offers an unrealistically low price instead, security holders will be free to retain their debt.

Similarly, we understand that, from time to time, it may be in the best interest of an issuer and its security holders to amend the terms of the company's outstanding debt. Most indentures provide that the terms of the debt may be amended by the consent of the holders of either a majority or two-thirds in principal amount of the outstanding debt. The issuer is free to propose a restructuring of the terms of the debt, and to offer debt holders some incentive to consent to the restructuring. Debt holders can be provided the opportunity to decide for themselves whether to accept the new terms or retain the old terms.

Individually, a consent solicitation or a tender offer each can be structured to provide the security holder with a fair choice. However, when a tender offer is structured so that material information—i.e., whether the securities will retain their Protections—is withheld until the tender offer ends, it is clear to us that the offer is designed to foreclose any rational choice that security holders might exercise regarding the tender offer.

The Proposed Rule

We respectfully submit that the Commission adopt the following amendment to the Rule. New language is underlined:

Rule 14e-1. Unlawful Tender Offer Practices

As a means reasonably designed to prevent fraudulent, deceptive or manipulative acts or practices within the meaning of section 14(e) of the Act, no person who makes a tender offer shall:

... (e) During the course of a tender offer for any security, solicit the holders of such security to approve, by proxy, consent or otherwise, a material change in the terms of such security, or a material change in the terms of such security's governing instrument, unless such tender offer ... remains open until the expiration of ten business days

<u>after the results of the concluded solicitation of approval have been publicly disclosed. ...</u>

The proposed Rule amendment would require bidders to disclose whether a security's protections have been stripped before security holders decide whether or not to tender. It would apply to changes in the terms of the security itself, or to changes in the security's governing instrument, such as an indenture. It would impose a period of ten business days after disclosure of the results of the consent solicitation for the market to digest the information and possibly revalue the target security. ...

\* \* \*

The Petitioners believe that this amendment to the Rule is the least burdensome means of preventing issuers from using consent solicitations to force security holders to tender. Under the Rule as amended, issuers would still have the ability to solicit tenders. Security holders would determine for themselves whether the price offered for the security was fair, and would tender or not on that basis. Similarly, issuers would remain free to bargain with their investors for a change in the terms of the debt. The proposed Rule would only restrict the ability of issuers to coerce their debt holders into accepting an unfair price by withholding a decisive piece of material information.

Authority

The Commission has clear authority [under the Williams Act] to require disclosure of material information in connection with tender offers which would otherwise be deceptive and manipulative.[18] ...

The proposed amendment to the Rule is directed at precisely the type of deceptive and manipulative practice the Williams Act was designed to prohibit. "The purpose of the Williams Act is to insure that public shareholders who are confronted by a cash tender offer for their stock will not be required to respond without adequate information." Rondeau v. Mosinee Paper Corp., 422 U.S. 49, 58 (1975). Senator Williams further described the purpose of the Act in remarks relied upon by the Court in Schreiber v. Burlington Northern, Inc., 472 U.S. 1 (1985) ("Schreiber") at pp. 8–9:

> Today, the public shareholder in deciding whether to accept or reject a tender offer possesses limited information. No matter what he does, he acts without adequate knowledge to enable him to decide rationally what is the best course of action. This is precisely the dilemma which our securities laws are designed to prevent. 113 Cong. Rec. 24664 (1967).

---

[18] We are not suggesting that commission regulation should supplant the contractual rights of issuers and debt holders. We appreciate that two Delaware courts have considered, and rejected, breach of contract claims for similar dual offers. See Kass v. Eastern Air Lines, Inc., Civil Action Nos. 8700, 8711 (Del. Ch. 1986); Katz v. Oak Industries, Inc., 508 A.2d 873 (Del. Ch. 1986). However, those cases turned on whether such offers violated express or implied provisions of the debt's indenture. They did not address questions of federal tender offer regulation.

Debt holders in simultaneous tender offers/consent solicitations are put into precisely this dilemma by bidders. No information is provided to them regarding the most material fact involved in the decision to tender: the outcome of the consent solicitation. As explained above, this information generally is decisive in determining whether a security holder will tender or retain the target security.

* * *

Sincerely,

Robert C. Pozen

cc: Richard C. Breeden, Chairman
    Edward H. Fleischman, Commissioner
    Philip R. Lochner, Jr., Commissioner
    Richard Y. Roberts, Commissioner
    Mary L. Schapiro, Commissioner
    Richard G. Ketchum, Director
      Division of Market Regulation
    William R. McLucas, Director
      Division of Enforcement
    Linda C. Quinn, Director
      Division of Corporation Finance
    David A. Sirignano, Chief, Office of Tender Offers
      Division of Corporation Finance

## ¶1214: Questions on Fidelity application

1. How can the Fidelity application be reconciled with the *Katz* result?
2. Analyze exit consent offers in three settings: (i) institutions own big blocks of bonds of an insolvent company, (ii) institutions own small blocks of bonds of an insolvent company, (iii) the company is in good shape, but the company seeks exit consents to modify the bond indenture and restructure the core terms of the bonds. If the company is in good shape financially, then the bonds should not be highly discounted in the marketplace. If not highly discounted, then the buoying-up or debt overhang effect should be minimal. Thus for exit consent exchange offers for diffusely distributed bonds of healthy firms (setting iii, but not settings i or ii), the buoying-up effect could easily be less than the coercive effect.
3. Keep in mind that there are two trigger points. The first is the amount needed to amend the bond indenture, typically a simple majority or two-thirds. The second is the amount needed to effectuate an exchange offer, which for a distressed company is typically 80% or 90%. An institution holding a large block might be able to veto the second, but not the first.
4. Coordination among bondholders costs something. If the bonds are in ten blocks of 10% each, two bondholders can veto the exchange and five can veto the

## ¶1215: Exchange offer problem

In the 1980s, Debtor borrows $200 million in a junk bond offering. The bonds initially trade at face value.

XYZ Balance Sheet (before exchange)

| $250M | $200M Junk Bond Issue, due 2000 |
|---|---|
|  | Common stock |

A few years later, when XYZ was in trouble, its bonds traded at about 50 cents on the dollar and it successfully exchanged $160 million of the Junk Bond Issue for new bonds with an earlier maturity date and a lower interest rate. One holder of $40 million of the junk bonds refused to exchange.

XYZ Balance Sheet (after exchange)

| $150M+Y | $ 40M | Unexchanged bond, due 2000 at 10% |
|---|---|---|
| Y=25M | $110M | Exchanged bond A, due 1999, with 6% interest [value is $27.5M for each bond, with the exchanging bondholders capturing some of "Y"] |
|  | $ 25M | Common stock |

All of the debt continues to have an equal priority.

A few months after the exchange was completed, the company declines in value and goes bankrupt.

The following materials address these questions: What are the bondholders' allowed claims in the bankruptcy? Do the exchanging and nonexchanging bondholders have the same allowed claim in bankruptcy? See Burlington prospectus description of the *Chateaugay* decision. What would their allowed claims be after the appellate decision in *Chateaugay*? What should the exchanging bondholders have done? Should they just have extended the maturity of their bonds and changed their interest rate, without changing the face value of the debt?

Consider the possibility that, when bankrupt, XYZ is worth $100 million. Before the exchange, the nonexchanging bondholder would have gotten 40/200 of the assets in a bankruptcy. The exchangers would, before they exchanged, have gotten 160/200, or 80% of the firm. After the exchange, the nonexchanger would get 40/150 of the firm, and the exchangers would get 110/150, or 73% of the firm.

\* \* \*

# Ch. 12 WORKOUTS 439

The problem of the size of the claim in a bankruptcy is yet more complex when discounted bonds are used in the exchange. To see this, we must first understand how discounted bonds are treated in bankruptcy when there's been no exchange.

Suppose a firm issues a $1000 bond, which carries no interest. It'll mature in ten months. The creditor though turns over only $900 to the company. Obviously the difference between the price at which the bond is sold ($900) and is scheduled for repayment ($1000) represents the interest to the creditor. This difference is called "original issue discount."

If the issuer goes bankrupt in the afternoon of the day the $1000 bond was issued (or is it a $900 bond that day?), what should the allowed amount of the claim be in the bankruptcy? If the issuer goes bankrupt five months later, what should the allowed amount of the claim be?

The legislative history of the Bankruptcy Code says (at H.R. Rep. No. 595, 95th Cong., 1st Sess. 352-53, reprinted in 1978 U.S. Code Cong. & Admin. News 5963, 6307-08):

> Interest disallowed under [§ 502(b)(2)] includes postpetition interest that is not yet due and payable, and any portion of prepaid interest that represents an original [issue] discounting of the claim, yet that would not have been earned on the date of bankruptcy. For example, a claim on a $1,000 note issued the day before bankruptcy would only be allowed to the extent of the cash actually advanced. If the original discount was 10%, so that the cash advanced was only $900, then notwithstanding the face amount of the note, only $900 would be allowed. If $900 was advanced under the note some time before bankruptcy, the interest component of the note would have to be pro-rated and disallowed to the extent it was for interest after the commencement of the case.

Consider this sequence:

1. Issuer issues a $1000 bond in the morning and is paid $900 in cash. It files for bankruptcy in the afternoon. What is the allowed amount of the claim in bankruptcy?
2. Issuer issues a $1000 bond in the morning for $900 worth of gold. It files in the afternoon. What is the allowed amount of the claim?
3. Issuer issues a $1000 bond in the morning for $900 worth of IBM's bonds. It files in the afternoon. What is the allowed amount of the claim?
4. Issuer issues a $1000 bond in the morning *for $900 worth of its own bonds, which an old bondholder turns in for the new bonds*. The old bonds were originally issued for $900 and were worth $900 on the morning of the exchange. The issuer files in the afternoon. What is the allowed amount of the bondholder's claim?
5. Issuer issues a $1000 bond in the morning *for $900 worth of its own bonds, which an old bondholder turns in for the new bonds*. The old bonds were originally issued years ago for $2000, but are worth only $900 on the morning of the exchange. The issuer files in the afternoon. What is the allowed amount of the bondholder's claim?

¶1216: **Exchange offer prospectus (the *Chateaugay* problem)**

Prospectus and Consent Solicitation

### BURLINGTON NORTHERN RAILROAD COMPANY

**Offers to Exchange and Solicitation of Consents
The Dealer Manager for the Exchange Offers is:**

**Merrill Lynch & Co.**

**The Date of this Prospectus and Consent Solicitation is November 8, 1990**

Burlington Northern Railroad Company ("BNRR" or the "Company") hereby offers, upon the terms and subject to the conditions set forth in this Prospectus and Consent Solicitation (the "Prospectus") and the applicable accompanying Letters of Transmittal and Consents and Letters of Transmittal (collectively, the "Letters of Transmittal," together with the Prospectus, the "Exchange Offers"), to exchange the following new securities of BNRR to be issued under the Company's Consolidated Mortgage dated March 2, 1970 between the Company and Morgan Guaranty Trust Company of New York and W.A. Johnson, Trustees, as supplemented and amended (the "Consolidated Mortgage"), in connection with the Exchange Offers (the "New Bonds") for the following publicly held outstanding securities of BNRR (the "Old Debt Securities") as set forth below:

\* \* \*

... If the Proposed Amendments are approved and become effective, the Company will make a payment at the rate of $10.00 for each $1,000 principal amount of SL-SF Securities consenting to the Proposed Amendments (the "Consent Payment"), regardless of whether the holder of SL-SF Securities so consenting tendered such SL-SF Securities into the applicable Exchange Offer. The Proposed Amendments with respect to each issue of the SL-SF Securities are being presented as one proposal. If a holder of SL-SF Securities wishes not to consent to one or more of the Proposed Amendments, such holder must not tender or otherwise deliver a consent.

Each of the Exchange Offers is subject to certain conditions as specified herein, including, in the case of the Exchange Offers to holders of SL-SF Securities, that there have been received on or prior to the applicable Expiration Date (as defined herein) valid and unrevoked consents to the Proposed Amendments by the holders of at least 66⅔% of the outstanding aggregate principal amount of the SL-SF Bonds and the SL-SF Debentures, respectively.

\* \* \*

## Certain Effect of the Exchange Offers on Non-Tendering Holders of Old Debt Securities

Holders of All Old Debt Securities

To the extent that other holders of each issue of Old Debt Securities exchange for New Bonds, holders of the same issue who do not so exchange will experience an increase in the Book Value Coverage Ratio relating to such issue. The amount of such increase will depend upon the principal amount of Old Debt Securities exchanged.

The market price for untendered Old Debt Securities may be affected adversely to the extent that the principal amount of Old Debt Securities tendered pursuant to the Exchange Offers reduces the principal amount available for trading. A debt security with a smaller outstanding principal amount available for trading (a smaller "float") may command a lower price than would a comparable debt security with a greater float. The reduced float may also tend to make the market price of untendered Old Debt Securities more volatile.

In addition, if after the expiration of the Exchange Offers the aggregate principal amount or market value of each issue of Old Debt Securities publicly held is less than $1,000,000, the NYSE under its current published guidelines may delist such issue of Old Debt Securities. The Company intends to have the Old Debt Securities delisted from the NYSE and deregistered under the Exchange Act upon successful completion of the Exchange Offers, if the conditions for such delisting and deregistration are satisfied.

\* \* \*

In the event of delisting of any Old Debt Securities there might be no viable market for such Old Debt Securities or, if publicly traded, such Old Debt Securities would likely be traded in the over-the-counter market. Trading in an issue of Old Debt Securities in the over-the-counter market may be subject to higher commission rates for executing trades and greater uncertainty with respect to such matters as eligibility for margin borrowing and the probable execution price of trades than is currently the case for Old Debt Securities listed on the NYSE.

If, after the expiration of the Exchange Offers, any issue of Old Debt Securities is delisted from the NYSE and deregistered under the Exchange Act, any further solicitations of consents from holders of such Old Debt Securities would not be subject to the provisions of the Exchange Act.

\* \* \*

Holders of SL-SF Bonds and SL-SF Debentures

If the Requisite Consents are obtained, supplemental indentures amending both the SL-SF Mortgage and the SL-SF Debenture Indenture will be executed upon the completion of the Exchange Offers. If the Proposed Amendments are effected, holders of SL-SF Bonds and SL-SF Debentures who do not tender such securities in the Exchange Offers will [be subject to the amended indentures] whether or not such non-tendering holders have consented to the Proposed Amendments. See "The Proposed Amendments."

If the Proposed Amendments become effective, the rights of non-exchanging holders of SL-SF Securities will be adversely affected. The Proposed Amendments to the SL-SF Mortgage would (i) eliminate the requirement that the Company maintain a Special Reserve Fund, with the effect of reducing the collateral securing the SL-SF Bonds by approximately $5.5 millions, the amount in the Special Reserve Fund, (ii) eliminate the prohibition against the Company's paying dividends on common stock or purchasing its common stock for purposes of retirement while the amount in the Special Reserve Fund is less than $500,000, and (iii) [otherwise reduce the] collateral securing the SL-SF Bonds ....

The Proposed Amendment to the SL-SF Debenture Indenture would (i) eliminate a provision permitting the SL-SF Indenture Trustee to declare a default on the SL-SF Debentures simply because of a default of the Company under any other debt instrument to which it is a party, (ii) eliminate a [negative pledge] provision prohibiting the Company ... from creating or permitting any new mortgage or lien to be created on the property or assets then owned by or leased to the Company ... unless the SL-SF Debentures are secured by such mortgage or lien equally or ratably with the bonds or other obligations issued under or secured by such new mortgage or lien ....

**Amount of Claim in Bankruptcy**

In general, a bond or debenture represents a potential bankruptcy claim equal to its face amount plus accrued and unpaid interest as of the date a bankruptcy is commenced. Unmatured interest, including original issue discount, generally is not allowable as a claim under the Bankruptcy Code. Therefore, if a bond or debenture is issued with original issue discount, a holder's claim in respect of such bond or debenture will be reduced by the amount of unamortized original issue discount at the date a bankruptcy is commenced. A claim in respect of the New Bonds in a bankruptcy of the Company (unlike a claim outside of bankruptcy) could be reduced below the stated principal amount of such New Bonds by the amount of unamortized original issue discount, if any, with respect thereto at the date such bankruptcy is commenced. It is unclear whether and to what extent the issuance of bonds in an exchange transaction should be determined to involve original issue discount for the purpose of fixing the claim of a holder of such bonds in a subsequent bankruptcy, although it is likely that a bankruptcy court would compare the face amount of the New Bonds to the value of the consideration received by the Company in the Exchange Offers to make such a determination. Under one possible formula, the value of the consideration received by the Company would be equal to the principal amount of the Old Debt Securities less any unamortized original issue discount of such securities plus accrued interest relating thereto. A bankruptcy court adopting this view would likely determine that there was no additional original issue discount on the New Bonds and allow a bankruptcy claim for their full face amount, less any unamortized original issue discount attributable to the Old Debt Securities.

In contrast, a bankruptcy court that chose to follow the recent bankruptcy court decision in In re Chateaugay Corporation, 109 Bankr. 51 (Bankr. S.D.N.Y. 1990) ("Chateaugay"), might reach a contrary result. Under Chateaugay, a bankruptcy court would likely determine that the value of the consideration received by the Company would be equal to the fair market value of the Old Debt Securities on the date the exchange occurred. In Chateaugay, the court determined that holders of old unsecured debentures of LTV Corporation ("LTV") who elected to accept in exchange therefor an equal face amount of new unsecured debentures and shares of common stock of LTV were not entitled to a claim for unamortized original issue discount under the applicable provisions of the Bankruptcy Code, and the amount of such unamortized original issue discount was equal to the face amount of the new unsecured debentures less the fair market value of the old debt securities on the exchange date, calculated under the constant interest method ..., thereby limiting the claims of the holders of unsecured [claims] to the fair market value of the old debt securities on the exchange date plus that amount of original issue discount which is amortized prior to the date of bankruptcy.

## ¶1217: **Original issue discount**

If a $40 million bond is exchanged for a $25 million bond and the company then goes bankrupt, is the allowed claim in bankruptcy $40 million or $25 million?

Begin first with the problem of original issue discount. If the debtor *issues* a new $40 million bond and the creditor pays only $25 million for the bond (presumably because the interest rate is low), what is the allowed amount of the claim in the bankruptcy that shortly follows, $40 million or $25 million?

Again, the legislative history of the Bankruptcy Code helps (at H.R. Rep. No. 595, 95th Cong., 1st Sess. 352-53, reprinted in 1978 U.S. Code Cong. & Admin. News 5963, 6307–08):

> Interest disallowed under [Section 502(b)(2)] includes postpetition interest that is not yet due and payable, and any portion of prepaid interest that represents an original [issue] discounting of the claim, yet that would not have been earned on the date of bankruptcy. For example, a claim on a $1,000 note issued the day before bankruptcy would only be allowed to the extent of the cash actually advanced. If the original discount was 10%, so that the cash advanced was only $900, then notwithstanding the face amount of the note, only $900 would be allowed. If $900 was advanced under the note some time before bankruptcy, the interest component of the note would have to be pro-rated and disallowed to the extent it was for interest after the commencement of the case.

The legislative history thus answers one question clearly: If the new $40 million bond were issued for $25 million in cash, and the debtor quickly went bankrupt, the allowed amount of the claim would be $25 million.

The next issue, one that the exchanging bondholders in Burlington and Chateaugay would worry about, is whether the amount of the claim would similarly be $25 million if the creditor paid for that very same bond not with a check for $25 million, but with property worth $25 million. The property is, however, not gold or real estate or securities of other companies, but an *old* bond of the debtor company, a bond originally issued for $40 million, but whose value had declined to $25 million.

Same answer? $25 million? Or should the old $40 million amount be carried over to the new bond as the claim allowed under § 502(b)(2)? The first opinion in *Chateaugay,* the one from the bankruptcy court, which the Burlington prospectus referred to, clearly concluded that the fair market value of the bonds tendered was the amount from which the discounted interest should start accreting.

The *Chateaugay* bankruptcy court opinion was controversial, with critics claiming that the result would induce more bankruptcies and fewer out-of-court workouts. The bondholders appealed, and the appellate decision follows.

## ¶1218: Subsequent developments (*Chateaugay* on appeal)

### In re Chateaugay Corp., 961 F.2d 378 (2d Cir. 1992)

PRIOR HISTORY: Appeal from a judgment of the United States District Court for the Southern District of New York, Shirley Wohl Kram, Judge, affirming a judgment of the United States Bankruptcy Court for the Southern District of New York, Burton R. Lifland, Chief Judge, granting partial summary judgment in favor of the debtor, disallowing bondholders' claims in bankruptcy to the extent of unamortized original issue discount, both on original debt and on new debt issued pursuant to an exchange offer. Affirmed in part and reversed in part.

Judges: Before: Oakes, Chief Judge, Pratt and Miner, Circuit Judges.

Opinion: OAKES, Chief Judge:

[The indenture trustee] and intervenors appeal from a judgment of the United States District Court for the Southern District of New York, Shirley Wohl Kram, Judge, affirming a judgment of the United States Bankruptcy Court for the Southern District of New York, Burton R. Lifland, Chief Judge. The bankruptcy court granted partial summary judgment in favor of the debtor, the LTV Corporation ("LTV"), disallowing [the indenture trustee's] claims to the extent they included unamortized original issue discount ("OID"). On this appeal, [the indenture trustee] argues that the bankruptcy court and district court erred by holding (1) that new OID arose on an exchange of debt securities performed as part of LTV's failed attempt to avoid bankruptcy through a consensual workout, and (2) that amortization of OID should be calculated by the constant interest method, rather than by the straight line method. For the reasons set forth below, we reverse in part and affirm in part. We hold first that while claims must be disallowed to the extent of unamortized OID, no new OID arose on LTV's debt-for-debt exchange, and second, that OID amortization should be calculated by the constant interest method.

FACTS

In July 1986, LTV, a steel company that makes defense and industrial products, filed for Chapter 11 reorganization .... LTV filed objections in September 1989 to two proofs of claim, numbers 20,069 and 20,067, filed in November 1987 by [the Trustee] on behalf of the holders of two securities, the "Old Debentures" and the "New Notes." ...

The Old Debentures are 13⅞% Sinking Fund Debentures due December 1, 2002, of which LTV had by December 1, 1982 issued a total face amount of $150,000,000 [for $133,000,000]. The proceeds received for the Old Debentures thus amounted to 88.67% of their face value.

The New Notes are LTV 15% Senior Notes due January 15, 2000. In May 1986, LTV offered to exchange $1,000 face amount of New Notes and 15 shares of LTV common stock for each $1,000 face amount of Old Debentures. As of June 1, 1986, $116,035,000 face amount of Old Debentures had been exchanged for the same face amount of New Notes and LTV Common Stock.

In its proofs of claim, [the Indenture Trustee] did not deduct any amount for unamortized OID. LTV objected to the claims and moved for partial summary judgment, seeking an order disallowing unamortized OID. LTV argued that unamortized OID is unmatured interest which is not allowable by virtue of section 502(b)(2) of the Bankruptcy Code, 11 U.S.C. § 502(b)(2) (1988), and that therefore the claims must be reduced by the amount of unamortized OID ....

The bankruptcy court granted partial summary judgment for LTV .... The court held that unamortized OID is not allowable under section 502(b)(2) ....

... The district court affirmed the bankruptcy court's decision in its entirety.

DISCUSSION

I. Original Issue Discount and Section 502(b)(2)

A

Original issue discount results when a bond is issued for less than its face value. The discount, which compensates for a stated interest rate that the market deems too low, equals the difference between a bond's face amount (stated principal amount) and the proceeds ... received by the issuer. OID is amortized, for accounting and tax purposes, over the life of the bond, with the face value generally paid back to the bondholders on the maturity date. If the debtor meets with financial trouble and turns to the bankruptcy court for protection, as in the present case, then OID comes into play as one of the factors determining the amount of the bondholder's allowable claim in bankruptcy.

Section 502 of the Bankruptcy Code, the framework for Chapter 11 claim allowance, provides that a claim shall be allowed "except to the extent that ... such claim is for unmatured interest." The first question we face is whether unamortized OID is "unmatured interest" within the meaning of section 502(b)(2). We conclude that it is. As a matter of economic definition, OID constitutes interest. Moreover, the Bankruptcy Code's legislative history makes inescapable the conclusion that OID is interest within the meaning of section 502(b)(2). The House committee report on that section explains:

> Interest disallowed under this paragraph includes postpetition interest that is not yet due and payable, and any portion of prepaid interest that represents an original discounting of the claim, yet that would not have been earned on the date of bankruptcy. For example, a claim on a $1,000 note issued the day before bankruptcy would only be allowed to the extent of the cash actually advanced. If the original issue discount was 10% so that the cash advanced was only $900, then notwithstanding the face amount of [the] note, only $900 would be allowed. If $900 was advanced under the note some time before bankruptcy, the interest component of the note would have to be pro-rated and disallowed to the extent it was for interest after the commencement of the case.

H. Rep. No. 595, 95th Cong., 1st Sess. 352-53 (1977), reprinted in 1978 U.S.C.C.A.N. 5963, 6308-09.

... [U]nder section 502(b)(2) ... unamortized OID is unmatured interest and therefore unallowable as part of a bankruptcy claim.

Applying this [concept] ... to the case at hand, we conclude, as did the bankruptcy and district courts, that OID on the Old Debentures, to the extent it was unamortized when the bankruptcy petition was filed, should be disallowed. We now turn to the main issue in dispute: the applicability of section 502(b)(2) to the New Notes, which were issued in a debt-for-debt exchange offer as part of a consensual workout.

B

A debtor in financial trouble may seek to avoid bankruptcy through a consensual out-of-court workout. Such a recapitalization, when it involves publicly traded debt, often takes the form of a debt-for-debt exchange, whereby bondholders exchange their old bonds for new bonds. The debtor hopes that the exchange, by changing the terms of the debt, will enable the debtor to avoid default. The bondholders hope that by increasing the likelihood of payment on their bonds, the exchange will benefit them as well. The debtor and its creditors share an interest in achieving a successful restructuring of the debtor's financial obligations in order to avoid the uncertainties and daunting transaction costs of bankruptcy.

An exchange offer made by a financially troubled company can be either a "fair market value exchange" or a "face value exchange." See Marc S. Kirschner, et al., *Prepackaged Bankruptcy Plans: The Deleveraging Tool of the '90s in the Wake of OID and Tax Concerns*, 21 Seton Hall L. Rev. 643, 645–47 (1991). In a fair market value exchange, an existing debt instrument is exchanged for a new one with a reduced principal amount, determined by the market value at which the existing instrument is trading. By offering a fair market value exchange, an issuer seeks to reduce its overall debt obligations .... A face value exchange, by contrast, involves the substitution of new indebtedness for an existing debenture, modifying terms or conditions but not reducing the principal amount of the debt ....

The question is whether a face value exchange generates new OID. The bankruptcy court, in an opinion endorsed by the district court, held that it does. The court reasoned that, by definition, OID arises whenever a bond is issued for less than its face amount, and that in LTV's debt-for-debt exchange, the issue price of the New Notes was the fair market value of the Old Debentures. The court therefore concluded that the New Notes were issued at a discount equaling the difference between their face value and the fair market value of the Old Debentures.

The bankruptcy court's reasoning leaves us unpersuaded. *While its application of the definition of OID to exchange offers may seem irrefutable at first glance, we believe the bankruptcy court's logic ignores the importance of context, and does not make sense if one takes into account the strong bankruptcy policy in favor of the speedy, inexpensive, negotiated resolution of disputes, that is an out-of-court or common law composition.* See H.R. Rep. No. 95–595, 95th Cong., 1st Sess. 220 (1977), reprinted in 1978 U.S.S.C.A.N. 5963, 6179–80; see also In re Colonial Ford, Inc., 24 B.R. 1014, 1015–17 (Bankr. D. Utah 1982). ("Congress designed the Code, in large measure, to encourage workouts in the first instance, with refuge in bankruptcy as a last resort.") If unamortized OID is unallowable in bankruptcy, and if exchanging debt increases the amount of OID, then creditors will be disinclined to cooperate in a consensual workout that might otherwise have rescued a borrower from the precipice of bankruptcy. We must consider the ramifications of a rule that places a creditor in the position of choosing whether to cooperate with a struggling debtor, when such cooperation might make the creditor's claims in the event of bankruptcy smaller than they would have been had the creditor refused to cooperate. The bankruptcy court's ruling places creditors in just such a position, and unreversed would likely result in fewer out-of-court debt exchanges and more Chapter 11 filings. Just as that ruling creates a disincentive for creditors to cooperate with a troubled debtor, it grants a corresponding windfall both to holdouts who refuse to cooperate and to an issuer that files for bankruptcy subsequent to a debt exchange.

The bankruptcy court's decision might make sense in the context of a fair market value exchange, where the corporation's overall debt obligations are reduced. In a face value exchange such as LTV's, however, it is unsupportable. LTV's liability to the holders of the New Notes was no less than its liability to them had been when they held the Old Debentures. The bankruptcy court, by finding that the exchange created new OID, reduced LTV's liabilities based on an exchange which, because it was a face value exchange, caused no such reduction on LTV's balance sheet.

We hold that a face value exchange of debt obligations in a consensual workout does not, for purposes of section 502(b)(2), generate new OID. Such an exchange does not change the character of the underlying debt, but reaffirms and modifies it.

In the absence of unambiguous statutory guidance, we will not attribute to Congress an intent to place a stumbling block in front of debtors seeking to avoid bankruptcy with the cooperation of their creditors. Rather, given Congress's intent to encourage consensual workouts and the obvious desirability of minimizing bankruptcy filings, we conclude that for purposes of section 502(b)(2), no new OID is created in a face value debt-for-debt exchange in the context of a consensual workout. Thus, OID on the new debt consists only of the discount carried over from the old debt, that is, the unamortized OID remaining on the old debt at the time of the exchange.

... The [bankruptcy] court found support for its conclusion by looking to tax cases, because under the Internal Revenue Code, for purposes of determining taxable income, an exchange offer generates new OID. The tax treatment of a transaction, however, need not determine the bankruptcy treatment. The tax treatment of debt-for-debt exchanges derives from the tax laws' focus on realization events, and suggests that an exchange offer may represent a sensible time to tax the parties. The same reasoning simply does not apply in the bankruptcy context.

\* \* \*

II. Calculating OID Amortization

We now turn to the methodology for calculating OID amortization. [The Indenture Trustee] argues that the proper method for calculating unamortized OID under the Bankruptcy Code is the straight line method, by which the amount of the discount is spread equally over the duration of the maturation of the note. Under the straight line method, the same amount of interest accrues during each day of the instrument's term. LTV argues, in contrast, that the constant interest method—which also goes by the names yield-to-maturity, effective interest, or economic accrual—should be used. The constant interest method calculates OID amortization on the assumption that interest is compounded over time. Under the constant interest method, the amount of interest that accrues each day increases over time.

The bankruptcy court and district court opted for the constant interest method, and we agree. The constant interest method comports more closely than the straight line method with economic reality.

\* \* \*

One further point must be addressed regarding the calculation of OID amortization. Our holding today that, for purposes of section 502(b)(2), no new OID is created by a face value debt-for-debt exchange in a consensual workout, means that the old OID is carried over to the new debt. In other words, when the Old Debentures were exchanged for the New Notes, the New Notes carried a discount equaling the amount of OID remaining on the Old Debentures after amortization by the constant interest method. The amount of OID remaining must then be amortized, again employing the constant interest method, over the life of the New Notes. Thus, a creditor's claim in bankruptcy may differ depending on whether the creditor participated in a workout; that difference, however, derives not from any new OID created by the exchange, but from the logical necessity of an amortization schedule that concludes on the maturity date. In the present case, because the New Notes carried an earlier maturity date than the Old Debentures, those bondholders who cooperated with the debtor find themselves with a slightly larger claim in bankruptcy, after the disallowance of unamortized OID, than those who did not.

Accordingly, the judgment of the district court is affirmed in part and reversed in part, and the matter remanded to the district court for remand to the bankruptcy court for further proceedings consistent with this opinion.

### ¶1219: Exchange offers and original issue discount

1. What is original issue discount?
2. If a $1000 bond, maturing ten months from now, is issued for $900 in cash, and the debtor goes bankrupt tomorrow, what is the allowed claim in bankruptcy? If the debtor goes bankrupt in five months, about how much is the allowed claim?
3. If instead of bankruptcy, the $1000 bond is exchanged five months from now in an exchange offer for a new bond worth $500 and having a face value of $500 (the firm deteriorates badly in the intervening five months), what is the allowed claim in a subsequent bankruptcy the next day (five months and one day after the original issuance)?
4. If the bond is exchanged five months from now for a $1000 face value bond with different terms, at a time when the trading value of the bond was $500 (and the new bond is worth $500) what is the allowed claim in the bankruptcy the next day? If the firm issues brand new $1000 face value bonds five months from now,

for $500, what is the allowed amount of the new issue claim in the bankruptcy occurring the next day?

5. Look at the hypothetical exchange in ¶1215 again. In that exchange, the exchanging bondholders' claim in bankruptcy goes from $40 million per bond before the exchange, to $27.5 million per bond after the exchange, a decrease of about one-third. Isn't that the import of *Chateaugay*, both in the bankruptcy court and on appeal?

6. If the exchanging bondholders in ¶1215 thought that the exchange would leave the company vulnerable to a bankruptcy, with the chance of bankruptcy reduced but not eliminated, what kind of exchange should they have opted for? What result under the *Chateaugay* appeal had they used the following alternative?

XYZ Balance Sheet (after face value exchange)

| | | |
|---|---|---|
| $150M+Y | $ 40M | Unexchanged bond, due 2005 at 10% interest |
| Y=25M | $110M | Exchanged bond A, due 2004, with zero coupon, i.e., no interest, but face value of $160M (the original face value) [the market value of the exchanged bond is $27.5 for each bond]. Each gets a promise of a $40 million balloon ($12.5 million more than was "paid" for the bond at the time of the exchange) when the bond matures in 2004. The exchanging bondholders still capture some of "Y." |
| | $ 25M | Common stock |

7. If zero coupon and interest bearing securities can be made financially equivalent, which one will exchanging bondholders prefer after the Second Circuit decision? The court seems to think that face value exchanges are used by relatively healthy companies and that fair value exchanges are used by companies on their death beds. Is that necessarily so? After the *Chateaugay* holding on appeal do some exchanging bondholders and companies have an incentive to use a face value exchange?

The court thought that the face value exchange was usually an exchange of one bond for another approximately equal bond. And in fact the LTV exchange did involve roughly the same interest rate, roughly the same maturity date, and exactly the same face value. But do all face value exchanges have to fit this mold? Could a face value exchange involve a radical alteration of the other terms of the bond?

The court concludes: "We hold that a face value exchange of debt obligations ... does not generate new OID." That would seem to apply to bonds that gave up all their interest and covenants, and grossly altered the maturity date. If the face value rule is followed scrupulously—that rule is, after all, the formal holding—would it

8. Is there a cost in the *Chateaugay* result? Consider two scenarios. In one, the bondholders prefer a cash payment from the company, because they fear that management of the company will waste the money unless it's paid out. In fact, the original rationale for the leveraging of this debtor company was to force the cash payout. The parties to that recapitalization just over-estimated the company's ability to come up with cash. A down-sizing of the debt is in order, but the parties prefer (absent *Chateaugay*) to have the down-sizing still bind the company to pay out cash, but just to pay less cash out. What effect does *Chateaugay* have?

   In the second scenario, consider the informational problems the bondholders face. They fear that the company is lying to them, that the company is even in worse shape than it is. Incumbent managers just want to push the day of reckoning off into the future, hoping that a stroke of luck might arise. Even if that stroke of luck doesn't come, these managers hope to be working somewhere else (or retired) when the debacle and the bankruptcy occurs. Or so some bondholders fear. If those are their fears, would they prefer some cash payout between the moment of the exchange and the scheduled maturity date? What effect does *Chateaugay* have on the exchange's structure?

   Could the bondholders often get the *Chateaugay* face value carryover, but with interim payments, by requiring the debtor to pay a sinking fund to a trustee, who'll hold the funds until maturity?

9. What is the conceptual difference between the straight-line method of accreting interest and the constant interest method? Isn't it just that the constant interest method is another phrase for compounding of interest?

---

## ¶1220: On the possible inability to raise capital during financial stress: Chrysler on the verge of shut-down, 1978–1979

Could a firm in financial stress but with a profitable project be denied the capital for that project by an otherwise efficient capital market? Could good operational bets not be taken because the preexisting creditors would take too much of the winning outcome? (Usually we have seen stockholders get the upside of the winning bets. In this chapter, we have been examining such bets when the firm is insolvent. The payoffs have been different: *creditor* gains, not stockholder gains, distort the operational decision.) These distortions from overhanging debt affect the heavily-indebted firm's ability to recapitalize, to raise new capital, and to merge.

Consider XYZ Corp., a large manufacturing company that borrowed several billion dollars to finance production of a product that, due to massive shifts in consumer preferences, no longer is profitable. It verges on bankruptcy, although its book value indicates solvency:

(1)

| | XYZ Corp. (Book value) |
|---|---|
| $6.4 billion | $3.4 billion bank, trade and other debt |
| | $1 billion junk bonds |
| | $2 billion common stock |

In market terms the company's balance sheet is gruesome. Creditors are no longer sure of fully being paid back. The publicly-traded debt is valued at 50 cents on the dollar. The bank and other debt is similarly discounted.

(2)

| | XYZ Corp. (Market-oriented balance sheet) |
|---|---|
| $2.6 billion | $2.2 billion debt ($4.4 billion face value) |
| | $400 million common stock |

(As a realistic matter, the common stock will have a positive value even if the firm is insolvent. The stock will have hold-up value for two major reasons: First, deals cannot commence without their consent. And second, they get value from the prospect of an unusually good outcome, because the $2.6 billion comes from a bell curve of expected values, some exceeding $4.4 billion. These have been considered earlier; let's put these problems aside for now to isolate the new capital problem for insolvent firms.)

Let's suppose the firm has a unique opportunity to sell a new product that people expect will have good marketplace acceptance. However, it needs $1.6 billion to tool-up its factories, to advertise, to pay employees until the cash starts flowing in. The expected value of the project is $2.8 billion, making it clearly worth pursuing.

Common stock offering?

Could the firm raise the money via a common stock offering?

Clearly not. Imagine new stockholders pay $1.6 billion for new stock and the company's operating value increases by $2.8 billion. But $2.2 of that $2.8 billion would go to the preexisting creditors. The cash from the $1.6 billion stock offering would enhance the stock level by only $600 million. Anticipating immediate enhancement to the creditor layers, Wall Street investors could be expected not to make the investment *even if they believed the project was a billion-dollar-plus winner.*

New borrowing?

Could the firm raise the money via new debt?

The answer is also no, but getting to the answer for debt is more complicated than getting there for stock. If the debt came in at the same level as the preexisting debt, what resultant distribution of value?

(3)

XYZ Corp.
Market balance sheet (assets), with book value
of liabilities after $1.6 billion debt infusion

| $5.4 billion | $4.4 billion face value old debt |
| | $1.6 billion face value new debt |
| | $400 million common stock |

Obviously the firm would still be insolvent. The expected value of the debt will be about 5/6 of its face value. The new $1.6 billion creditor would not have a liability worth the amount pumped into the company. The new creditor's liability would be worth about $1.4 billion, although the creditor provided $1.6 billion. The deal cannot go through, despite that it produces extraordinary operational value. The problem again is that a disproportionate amount of the value is not produced for the investor.

Other priority techniques?

What must be done? One of the priority techniques *might* work: If the firm could offer the new project (or preexisting assets) as security, or if the preexisting overhanging creditors allow themselves to be subordinated, or if the firm could develop the new project in a subsidiary *and* insulate the subsidiary from the claim of the preexisting overhanging debt, then the capital could flow in for the project.

Many times these separation techniques will work. It's the lawyers' job, as transaction cost engineers, to find the technique that will work. But when the priority techniques still fail (or often in order to make them succeed), the preexisting creditors must be dealt with. That is, the creditors must, in the simplest separation scenario, agree to subordinate themselves to the new debt. The difficulty with this is that we now have a multi-party workout, subject to the chancy prospects of deadlock and delay. The new funding is not impossible, but requires renegotiation.

How real can this hypothetical be?

In 1979 Chrysler had a project it wanted to pursue: tooling of automotive plants to produce the K-car, a fuel-efficient, front-wheel drive car that the American public seemed to demand. It had factories to produce large rear-wheel drive, inefficient cars that the consumer did not want. It also had a lot of debt, incurred to produce the large cars made unmarketable by an unexpected shift in consumer preferences due to the rise in oil prices. That old debt did not permit its subordination. That debt had negative pledge clauses, prohibiting security that would make a new creditor senior (see supra ¶¶608–609, discussing Chrysler's negative pledge clause).

At the end of 1979, Chrysler had a book value of $6.6 billion. Obviously the market value of its factories and inventory was much lower. Consider the liabilities shown on Chrysler's balance sheet, reproduced next:

## *CHRYSLER CORPORATION*

|  | (In millions of dollars) |
|---|---:|
|  | 1979 |
| **LIABILITIES AND SHAREHOLDERS' INVESTMENT:** |  |
| **Current Liabilities:** |  |
| Accounts payable | $1,530.4 |
| Accrued expenses | 807.9 |
| Short-term debt (Notes 3 and 4) | 600.9 |
| Payments due within one year on long-term debt (Notes 3 and 11) | 275.6 |
| Taxes on income | 16.8 |
| **TOTAL CURRENT LIABILITIES** | **3,231.6** |
| **Other Liabilities and Deferred Credits:** |  |
| Deferred employee benefit plan accruals | 301.4 |
| Deferred taxes on income | 83.0 |
| Unrealized profits on sales to unconsolidated subsidiaries | 47.7 |
| Other noncurrent liabilities | 134.9 |
| **TOTAL OTHER LIABILITIES AND DEFERRED CREDITS** | **567.0** |
| **Long-Term Debt** (Notes 3 and 11): |  |
| Notes and debentures payable | 880.7 |
| Convertible sinking fund debentures | 96.0 |
| **TOTAL LONG-TERM DEBT** | **976.7** |
| **Obligations Under Capital Leases** (Note 9) | **15.4** |
| **Minority Interest in Net Assets of Consolidated Subsidiaries** | **38.3** |
| Preferred Stock—no par value (Note 12) | 218.7 |
| Common Stock—par value $6.25 a share (Note 13) | 416.9 |
| Additional Paid-In Capital (Note 15) | 692.2 |
| Net Earnings Retained (Note 16) | 496.3 |
| **TOTAL LIABILITIES AND SHAREHOLDERS' INVESTMENT** | **$6,653.1** |

See notes to financial statements.

Vastly simplifying Chrysler's balance sheet (and ignoring that Chrysler had an unconsolidated finance subsidiary), we come up with a balance sheet of:

(4)

| | Chrysler |
|---|---|
| Book value | $3.4 billion bank, trade and other debt |
| | $1 billion junk bonds |
| | Common stock |

The bonds traded at *34* cents on the dollar. Using a higher 50% figure for simplicity, we can reconstruct a simple market-oriented balance sheet. Since the debt was not subject to intercreditor priorities, we can apply the 50% discount to all of the debt. A market value of the common stock—presumably a result of its holdout value and the prospect of government funding—comes from taking the stock's trading price at the time and multiplying the price by the shares outstanding.

(5)

| | Chrysler |
|---|---|
| $2.6 billion | $2.2 billion debt ($4.4 billion face value) |
| | $400 million common stock |

Chrysler's market-oriented balance sheet looks quite a bit like balance sheet 3; the only difference is the reality of including the common stockholders.

New debt or equity would have had to provide an unusually good return. Even if the project would yield a good risk-adjusted return on a $1.6 billion inflow, buoying up would require that it provide a value of at least *$3.8* billion. (If the old creditors refuse to subordinate themselves, and if the old stockholders insist on getting stock that after the transaction would be worth at least $400 million, then the total value of the company would have to be $4.4 billion+$1.6 billion+$400 million, or $6.4 billion, after the transaction. To be worth $6.4 billion, the project would have to be a $3.8 billion winner. Anything less and a priority technique would be needed, but might fail.)

The intuition behind this is simple: the new money would have buoyed up the preexisting debt. When the buoying-up effect is small, or when the previously-negotiated covenants allow senior debt (and the interim outflow of interest to preexisting creditors does not stymie the deal), or a transactional alternative, such as separate incorporation for, or sale of, the new opportunity, then such deals can be worked out. But eventually these techniques can be used up. Often they are barred by preexisting financial arrangements (loan agreements with negative pledge clauses or clauses requiring the buyer to assume the seller's debts, for example) that would have to be renegotiated.

To be sure, Chrysler's position was so complex—and perhaps operationally untenable without informal import quotas on cars—that even if the risky debt effects were absent, the financial market would still have viewed the investment as not worthwhile. Buoying up was sufficient but not necessary to thwart financing of the K-car; operational debilities were *also* sufficient to thwart the project.

Keep in mind that firms in financial stress do not usually have worthwhile new opportunities. Oftentimes they should be shrinking not expanding. But when they do have good opportunities that require new cash, a merger, or sale of most of their assets, they cannot readily take them. When the lawyers' separation techniques are exhausted, only a renegotiation with preexisting creditors—a workout or a bankruptcy—will do.

*Atlas Pipeline* again. This analysis of Chrysler helps us understand a central point in *Atlas Pipeline*. Recall that the SEC thought that Atlas could not be renewed. Once its facilities wore out, it would not have access to new financing, assumed the SEC. This led to a double count, as the SEC seemed to increase the discount rate for the years *before* new financing was needed. A critique of the SEC's view could also revolve around the potential efficiency of the marketplace: *If* Atlas had a good project, why shouldn't it be able to raise money to finance it? Companies with too much overhanging debt might not be able to finance worthwhile projects, because of the buoying-up effect.

The bankruptcy apparatus can help the bankrupt firm get future access to capital markets: The court can help the firm avoid the Chrysler scenario by making sure that the firm is not top-heavy with debt when it emerges from bankruptcy.

## ¶1221: Mergers

"[Donald Dewey] has argued [in Dewey, *Mergers and Cartels: Some Reservations about Policy*, 51 Market Econ. Rev. 257 (1961)] that most mergers ... are merely a civilized alternative to bankruptcy or the voluntary liquidation that transfers assets from falling to rising firms. ... If, as Dewey suggests, mergers are superior to bankruptcy as a method of 'shifting assets from falling to rising firms,' and if mergers were completely legal, we should anticipate relatively few actual bankruptcy proceedings in any industry which was not itself contracting. The function so wastefully performed by bankruptcies and liquidations would be economically performed by mergers at a much earlier stage of the firm's life." Henry Manne, *Mergers and the Market for Corporate Control*, 73 Journal of Political Economy 110, 111–12 (1965).

A vexing question asked in the merger and tender offer literature is why failing firms are so infrequently the subject of hostile tender offers. The answer is important because a central goal worth preserving has been use of the hostile tender offer as a means for disciplining unimaginative target firm management. Why, it is sometimes asked, wasn't Chrysler in the late 1970s the target of a hostile offer? While the firm's problems were not of management's doing—demand shifts, an oil crisis, and a depressed economy did the company in—incumbent managers were criticized as unimaginative in responding to the deteriorating environment. Substantial changes in management in time were made, but they were made through internal governance mechanisms, not through a tender offer or the explicit threat of one.

Several good explanations are available: offering firm managers do not want to take on the burden of a near-bankrupt. The target firm was too far gone; money could not be expected to be made by managing the target firm any better. Antitrust barriers would have thwarted those most interested in the acquisition. Chrysler was unique.

The buoying-up effect is another (sufficient but not necessary) explanation: the offering firm would have seen a disproportionate share of the returns from superior management going to the preexisting, overhanging creditors. For the offer to be worth pursuing, a deal with creditors (as well as stockholders and managers) would have been necessary. And, with reorganizations of public firms requiring two years or more, that might have been too complex to pursue and succeed quickly.

Although the inability to merge was less important to Chrysler than its inability to get private financing for the K-car, the inability to merge probably is more important for the ordinary bankrupt firm. Why?

It's plausible that bankrupt firms are drawn disproportionately from industries that are contracting. As technologies and markets change, some industries just have to contract, because the demand for their product isn't there, or because competitors can make the same product more cheaply with new technology. As these technologies and markets change, the incumbent firms lose money. They either sell less product at a lower price, or face high costs on their old technologies (or both). They lose money. If they lose enough money they become candidates for bankruptcy.

In fact, bankruptcies sometimes come in industry waves—oil firms in the 1980s, retailers in the 1990s. The policy consequence here is that often the best disposition for some firms in a contracting industry is to merge. The merged entity can preserve the strong parts of each constituent firm and close-down the weak parts. The cost then of the buoying-up effect, of recapitalizations, of deadlocks, and of slow, multi-year chapter 11 proceedings, is that American society cannot get the benefit of quick, low-cost mergers in these kinds of industries. Note that after a long delay, Chrysler was eventually acquired by a foreign automaker, a result discussed during 1979 and 1980 as an alternative to a government loan or a bankruptcy.

CHAPTER 13

# DUTIES TO CREDITORS?

**A. The trustee**
**B. Duties of the company**
**C. Contract theory**

━━━━━━━━━━━━━━━━━━━━━━━━━━━━━━━━━━━━━━━━━━━━━━━━━━━━━━━━━━━━━━━━━━━━━

**A. The trustee**

**¶1301: <u>Trustees under the Trust Indenture Act</u>**

The Trust Indenture Act governs the standards for behavior by the trustee. Trust indentures have several justifications. For secured bonds, any mechanism that would give each bondholder a security interest directly in the debtor's property would be prohibitively complex, because each bondholder would have to write, file, and police an individualized mortgage or its own UCC filing. Instead, a single trustee takes the security interest on behalf of all bondholders. In addition to the transaction costs of the bondholders taking security, the bondholders were distant from the enterprise and, at least in the first decades of the bonds' use until holdings concentrated, scattered as well. Thus there would be extensive free-riding among bondholders, who would collectively "under" monitor the debtor. A single trustee, operating under a bond indenture would, in theory, police the debtor, be sure that it was complying with the bond indenture's covenants, and if need be sue the debtor company. (In addition, the bondholders' original underwriters sometimes took on the "policing" function, at least after a default. The Morgan bank did so for bondholders of the many railroads that defaulted at the end of the 19th century.)

Problems arose in implementation. As documented in a massive 1930s study begun by William O. Douglas, the bondholders' collective action problem extended back to the negotiation of the bonds. Frequently the bond issue had clauses that exculpated the indenture trustee, usually a bank, from all kinds of wrong-doing and watered down the trustee's obligation to actively check the debtor. Few bondholders were thought to read through the indenture to see the extent of the exculpation and adjust their bond price accordingly. (Since few did so, it's possible that in the aggregate the exculpatory clauses were not a fundamental economic problem, but a secondary one.) Douglas and the SEC proposed the Trust Indenture Act to reduce these problems.

The Trust Indenture Act's original (and to some extent, its continuing) structure was (and is) unusual, differing from that of the other securities laws. Rather than establishing statutory standards (or, via SEC regulation, regulatory standards), the TIA established *contractual* requirements for judicial enforcement. It requires that before a debtor issues bonds in the United States, it must have the bond indenture "qualified" under the Trust Indenture Act. The company's lawyers "qualify" the bond indenture by inserting into the indenture the terms that the TIA requires and by assuring themselves that the terms that the TIA bars are not in the indenture. The SEC declares that the bond indenture qualifies under the TIA, the underwriters sell the bonds, and thereafter the SEC disappears from the TIA enforcement. (This disappearance was formal until 1990, because the SEC lacked statutory authority to act after the bond indenture was qualified; after the 1990 amendments to the TIA, the SEC has more authority, but in the first years after the change, it did not use it.) Congress also amended the TIA in 1990 to require that the TIA's standards control, even if the lawyers forgot to put them into the bond indenture. 15 U.S.C. § 77rrr(c).

The TIA seeks to control the trustee's conflicts and duties: it provides whether the indenture can allow the trustee to be under the control of, or under common control with, the debtor (it can't); whether the indenture can exculpate the trustee from investigating possible defaults or can conclusively rely on the company's certificates (it can, if the indenture so provides, TIA § 315(a), 15 U.S.C. § 77ooo(a)); the minimum capital required of a qualifying trustee; whether the trustee shall have access to any lists of bondholders that the company maintains; whether the trustee shall have to examine certificates from the debtor about the debtor's compliance with the trust indenture; whether the trustee must give the bondholders notice once the trustee learns of the debtor's default; whether the indenture can relieve the trustee of liability to the bondholders for the trustee's own willful misconduct; whether the trustee who is simultaneously a lender must return payments it receives within 90 days of the debtor's default (it must), in a return analogous to the Bankruptcy Code's preference provisions. Collectively it yields one of the most boring statutes conceivable.

Can the trustee, which is usually a bank, also simultaneously lend to the debtor company? One might have thought that this setting was so fraught with danger that Congress might have barred a trustee from simultaneously being a lender. Congress, however, did not. The *Morris* case, the Fleischman memo, and the 1990 TIA amendments show the history of the problem.

## ¶1302: The depression-era SEC investigation into trustees

During the 1930s, the SEC conducted a multi-year investigation into corporate reorganizations and produced a massive report, some of which touched on the conflicts of interest facing bond trustees.

Securities and Exchange Commission, Report on the Study and Investigation of the Work, Activities, Personnel and Functions of Protective and Reorganization Committees—Part VI, at 2-6 (1936):

> Under modern trust indentures securing issues of corporate bonds, debentures and notes, important powers are vested in the trustee. The security holders themselves are generally widely scattered and their individual interest in the issue is likely to be small. The trustee, on the other hand, is usually a single bank. By virtue of the broad discretionary powers vested in it under the typical trust indenture it is in a position to take immediate action in a variety of ways to protect or enforce the security underlying the bonds, debentures and notes .... Theoretically, the result should be beneficial to all concerned: to the security because of increased efficiency, expedition and economy; to the issuer because a trustee is a convenient legal device for conveying title, and because the presence of the trustee relieves the issuer of possible suits and supervision by many individual security holders.
>
> But as a matter of fact, this arrangement has resulted in injury to thousands of investors. They have bought securities and have retained no effective control over the issuer's performance of its obligations in respect of them. Such control has been surrendered to or assumed by the trustee. It has been invested with power to certify securities; to supervise the deposit and withdrawal of collateral and application of funds; to take action upon default; and, in short, to do everything upon which the protection and enforcement of the security of a bondholder depends.
>
> \* \* \*
>
> ... [A]n examination of the provisions of modern trust indentures and their administration by trustees will show that this reliance [on the trustee] is unfounded. It will show that typically the trustees do not exercise the elaborate powers which are the bondholders' only protection; that they have taken virtually all of the powers designed to protect the bondholders, but have rejected any duty to exercise them; and that they have shorn themselves of all responsibilities which normally trusteeship imports. The "so-called trustee" which is left is merely a clerical agency and a formal instrument which can be used by the bondholders when and if enough of them combine as specified in the indenture.
>
> \* \* \*
>
> The basic problem is to refashion the trust indenture for the purpose of according greater protection to investors. That entails prescribing certain minimum standard specifications for the conduct of trustee and issuer thereunder. As in the case of the other contracts involving persons not capable nor in a position to protect themselves, the contents of the trust indenture can no longer be left to the conventions of the issuer, the trustee or the underwriter.

This means that a more proper balance between interests of investors and requirements of issuers can be had only by enlarging the definition of the trustee's duties in those cases where its failure to take swift and positive action leaves the investors without effective protection of their interests. The contrary desires of issuer, trustee and underwriter must be made to bow to the insistent demands of investors and of the public interest in such cases.

---

The SEC report's images are of thousands of bondholders, ignorant of the indenture and perhaps of finance and corporate events as well. In today's financial markets, the bondholders are overwhelmingly institutional investors—banks, pension funds, mutual funds, and insurance companies—institutions that make these investments for a living. (Nor is it altogether clear how different the ownership structure was for bonds back in the 1930s. It seems to have already been overwhelmingly institutional then.) However, Douglas and the framers at the SEC may have picked up the image of scattered owners from Berle & Means, The Modern Corporation and Private Property (1932), which described the scattered owners of the corporation, who typically were in fact individuals, often distant from the firm and ill-informed about it. That image for stockholders may have carried over to the image for bondholders.

## ¶1303: The notion of trustee: fiduciary or contracted-for agent? (from Brudney & Chirelstein, Corporate Finance 148-49 (3d ed. 1987))

Notwithstanding the title, "trustee," the norms determining the care and fidelity to which indenture trustees were held prior to enactment of the Trust Indenture Act of 1939 derived more from the terms of the indenture (and its exculpatory clauses) than from any legally imposed fiduciary obligations. The breadth and effectiveness of the exculpatory language of the indenture in relieving the trustee of fiduciary obligations was demonstrated in Hazzard v. Chase National Bank of the City of New York, 159 Misc. 57, (Sup.Ct. N.Y.C., 1936), aff'd, 257 App. Div. 950, (1st Dept.1939), aff'd, 282 N.Y. 652 (1940) which raised the question whether the bank serving as trustee for an issue of debentures of a public utility holding company was to be liable for permitting withdrawal of valuable collateral securing the issue and accepting, in substitution thereof, worthless collateral at a time when the obligor was also a direct borrower from the bank. The plaintiffs predicated their claim upon the propositions that (1) the bank's tolerance of withdrawal and substitution of collateral breached its fiduciary duty because it enabled the obligor to obtain the wherewithal to continue to pay interest on the outstanding debentures and thus to stave off inevitable default, and during the time thus "bought," to repay the outstanding bank loan, and (2) the bank was guilty of the "gross negligence" which the indenture established as the trustee's norm, in appraising the adequacy of the new collateral. In rejecting the suggestion that the trustee should be held "to fiduciary's duty in spite of the various verbal devices used to free it from such responsibility ..." the Court said: "Irrespective of holdings or tendencies in other jurisdictions, it is now the well-settled doctrine of this state that so long as the trustee does not step beyond the provisions of the indenture itself, its liability is measured, not by the ordinary relationship of trustee and cestui, but by the expressed agreement between the trustee and the obligor of the trust mortgage. Where the terms of the indenture are clear, no obligations or duties in conflict with them will be implied .... The question is, therefore, whether gross negligence ... has been committed under the terms of the indenture." The Court answered the question in the negative.

The dominance of the "contract" over the "trust" aspects of the indenture trustee's duties at common law, which is reflected in the *Hazzard* case, has not been uniformly accepted.

## ¶1304: Morris v. Cantor, 390 F.Supp. 817 (S.D.N.Y. 1975)

Robert J. Ward, District Judge:

Plaintiffs Robert G. Morris, Israel Patents Corporation and Patents Management Corporation, calling themselves the "Protective Committee of 4% Convertible Subordinated Debentures of Interstate Department Stores, Inc.," bring this action on behalf of themselves and all others similarly situated ("the bondholders"). The complaint alleges that the several defendants violated provisions of the Trust Indenture Act of 1939, 15 U.S.C. § 77aaa et seq. ("the Act") ... in connection with various loans to defendant Interstate Department Stores, Inc. ("the Company") during 1972.

The Bankers Trust Company ("the Bank") which is charged with violations of the Trust Indenture Act ... moves pursuant to Rule 12(b), Fed. R. Civ. P., to dismiss the complaint against itself for failure to state a claim upon which relief can be granted. For the reasons discussed below, the motion is denied.

The Company issued $20,000,000 in 4% convertible subordinated debentures under an indenture agreement dated August 1, 1967, in which the Bank was named Trustee. The indenture agreement was duly registered with the Securities and Exchange Commission ("the Commission"), and its terms conformed to the requirements of the Act. The debentures were by their terms unsecured and subordinated to all "senior indebtedness" of the issuer, as that term was defined in the indenture agreement, including any which might be later acquired. The indenture agreement provided that should the indenture trustee be or become a creditor of the issuer, the trustee would be entitled to the benefit of the subordination provisions of the indenture with respect to senior indebtedness to the same extent as any other holder of such indebtedness.

The complaint alleges that the Bank, while Trustee, acted as lead bank in negotiating the extension of a $900,000,000 line of credit to the Company, which qualified as senior indebtedness with respect to the debentures. The Bank thus became a ... secured creditor of the Company, with priority over the bondholders, in the event of bankruptcy. Plaintiffs concede that the loan was not consummated until after the Bank resigned as Trustee, and in any event, not even negotiated within four months prior to a default in payment of the principal or interest under the indenture. They contend, however, that the Bank's action constituted "willful misconduct" within the meaning of § 315(d) of the Act, 15 U.S.C. § 77ooo(d).

This Court's jurisdiction of the controversy between plaintiffs and the Bank is based exclusively upon the Trust Indenture Act, 15 U.S.C.§ 77vvv, which provides:

> "Jurisdiction of offenses and violations under, and jurisdiction and venue of suits and actions brought to enforce any liability created by, this subchapter, or any rules or regulations or orders prescribed under the authority thereof, shall be as provided in section 77v(a) of this title [the Securities Act of 1933]."

A threshold question therefore is whether the Act by its terms creates any liability for violation of the provisions of indentures qualified thereunder, or more generally for willful misconduct on the part of a trustee appointed according to the Act's provisions [or whether the question is solely one of contract law]. ...

The unique structure of the Act creates the [threshold] question, whether by its terms it imposes any obligations upon the indenture trustee. The Act requires that any indenture agreement under which [debt] is offered to the public be registered with the Commission and contain certain terms which the Act carefully specifies. Thus, section after section of the Act begins with the language, "The indenture to be qualified shall provide ..." or "shall require ..." or "shall contain provisions requiring ...." and continues with detailed and often technical terms pertaining to the naming of the trustee, qualifications of eligible trustees, required reports to bondholders or from the obligor to the trustee, duties of the trustee both prior to and in the event of default, or in the event of its acquiring conflicting interests. Other sections are permissive in language, substituting the language "... may require ... ."

The particular section at issue here reads:

> "The indenture to be qualified shall not contain any provisions relieving the indenture trustee from liability for its own negligent action, its own negligent failure to act, or its own willful misconduct ...." 15 U.S.C. § 77ooo(d).

\* \* \*

Prior to the Act's passage, indenture agreements, as private contracts, had been governed by the common law of contracts and fiduciary obligations, articulated primarily in the state courts ... . But trustees under such indenture agreements had developed a widespread practice of contractually limiting their liability for performance of their trust functions, and courts enforced these terms of limitation in many instances.

Thus, the scheme of the Act is to regulate in a limited fashion by taking a type of private contract, requiring that it contain certain terms and be registered with the Commission ... .

* * *

Thus, the legislative history suggests that Congress considered the existing body of common law sufficient to protect investors, so long as the trustee was precluded from contractually limiting the duties it imposed upon fiduciaries, and so long as he explicitly assumed particular duties. As the House Report, at 26, stated, " ... the deficiencies in corporate trust practice are largely due to deficiencies in the trust indenture itself ..." and the remedy Congress chose was simply to state precisely which terms were required, permitted and prohibited in the contract. It viewed the problem as nationwide in scope and sought a nationwide solution. The format it chose, by which the indenture agreement remained a contract between the parties, the rights and obligations it set forth enforceable only by the parties in the courts, simultaneously limited the degree of Commission intrusion into the everyday or business aspects of the indentures. Accordingly, this legislation must be viewed as an indirect method of imposing nationally uniform and clearly defined obligations upon those associated with the issuance of corporate debt ....

* * *

The Bank [also] argues that ... plaintiffs have not stated a claim upon which relief can be granted. It contends that the Act addresses the situation of the trustee-creditor in clear terms in 15 U.S.C. § 77kkk, and that if a trustee's actions as creditor of the obligor on the bonds do not violate that section, they cannot be considered willful misconduct within the meaning of § 77ooo. The parties agree that the Bank's action does not constitute a violation of § 77kkk.

The Act requires that qualified indenture agreements contain provisions for disqualification of the institutional trustee upon the occurrence of certain enumerated conflicts of interest, thus in effect prohibiting those conflicts. § 77jjj. Its creditor relationship to the obligor on the bonds is not among these conflicts. Rather, the Act requires merely that the indenture provide that the trustee who is also a creditor within four months prior to any default on the bonds, or at any time thereafter, and who receives any preferential payment as a creditor, shall hold the proceeds for distribution to the bondholders. § 77kkk. The Bank reads this requirement as an implied permission for it to be simultaneously trustee under the indenture agreement and creditor of the obligor, and further, for it to become even a preferred creditor of the obligor while it is trustee.

The legislative history supports the Bank's interpretation, revealing that Congress explicitly considered the problems of conflicting interest that might arise in such a circumstance. The S.E.C. Report condemned the practice of a bank simultaneously acting as trustee and creditor, Report, e.g. at 84, 90, 98, 107, while, however, noting that the period of greatest danger to the interests of the bondholders was immediately prior to a default. Id. at 98. But spokesmen for several banks testified before the House Committee, emphasizing that it was often in the interest of a company and its bondholders that credit be available to sustain the company as a going concern, and that frequently the bank most familiar with the affairs of the company and most willing to advance credit was also the indenture trustee. See, e.g., Hearings, at 159–60, 170–71, 268–9. Congress determined to protect the interests of the bondholders, without prohibiting such a dual relationship, by providing that any preferential collection which the trustee as creditor should make in the four months prior to default, when it should have a clear idea of the precarious position of the company, be held for the benefit of the bondholders. As the House Report described the effect of this provision:

> And, where the trustee is also a creditor of the obligor, section 311 of both bills prevents the trustee from improving its own creditor position at the expense of the bondholders, within 4 months prior to a principal or interest default under the indenture, or after such a default. House Report, supra at 34.

The Court therefore concludes that the mere existence or creation of a dual relationship, as trustee under the indenture and as preferred creditor of the obligor on the bonds, although there may be an inherent conflict of interest, does not of itself constitute a violation of § 77ooo(d). Congress specifically dealt with this inherent conflict when drafting the bill, in such a way as to permit it, with certain named protections for the interests of the bondholders. Having so prescribed contract terms addressed to this subject, it removed this conduct from the area of residual liability which could not be limited by contract, set forth in § 77ooo(d).

That area of residual liability, however, is defined by the common law as it had developed prior to the statute and has developed since. Willful misconduct encompasses knowing, intentional action in flagrant disregard of the interests of the bondholders. See Notes 1-4, supra. While the mere making of a loan to the Company, protected under § 77kkk, cannot be such willful misconduct as the statute contemplates, it is possible that in the circumstances known to the Bank, to negotiate such a loan did constitute knowing, intentional action in flagrant disregard of the interests of the bondholders. Were these facts developed during discovery and at trial, plaintiffs would have stated a claim upon which relief can be granted under the statute. Accordingly, the Court considers it premature to dismiss the complaint.

Defendant Bankers Trust Company's motion to dismiss the complaint is denied.

It is so ordered.

---

### ¶1305: Passage of the Trust Indenture Act

From Joel Seligman, The Transformation of Wall Street 196 (1982):

> Enactment of the Trust Indenture Act of 1939 was facilitated by policy differences between the two principal bank lobby organizations, which Douglas skillfully exploited. Soon after [the SEC's study,] 'Trustees Under Indentures[,]' was published, [the chair] of an ad hoc committee of the American Bankers Association, the commercial bankers' lobbying organization, wrote his fellow commercial

bankers that the report was 'most drastic' and 'astonishingly unfair to corporate trustees as a class' .... Douglas and the American Bankers Association [then] negotiated the provisions of what ultimately became the Trust Indenture Act. Because commercial bankers' concern with the bill was for the most part limited to preserving the power of trustee banks to lend money to a corporate debt issuer and to limiting trustees' exposure to negligence liability, the SEC won pledges that the commercial banks would not oppose the trust indenture bill, with relatively few concessions. This isolated the Investment Bankers Association in opposition and undermined many of their arguments against the bill, because they no longer could claim that most bankers found the bill impractical.

### ¶1306: Broad v. Rockwell Int'l Corp., 642 F.2d 929-30 (5th Cir. 1981)

The first significant activities of the Trust Company, other than its performance of routine administrative duties as substitute Trustee under the Indenture, came in the fall of 1973 when the Trust Company was called upon to consider whether the terms of a proposed supplemental indenture to be executed by Rockwell, as successor by merger to the obligations of Collins under the Indenture. Under that supplemental indenture, Rockwell would assume in full all of the obligations of Collins under the Indenture, including the obligation to pay interest, and eventually to repay the principal, on the outstanding Debentures until they either were redeemed or matured in 1987. With regard to the conversion feature of the Debentures, the proposed supplemental indenture provided that each holder of a Debenture would have the right to convert his Debenture into the amount of cash that would have been payable to him under the Merger Plan had he converted his Debenture into Collins Common Stock immediately prior to the merger. In other words, a holder of Debentures could, at any time while his Debentures were outstanding, choose to convert them into exactly that which he would have received had he converted immediately before the merger and participated therein as a holder of Collins Common Stock. Because the holders of Collins Common Stock received no common stock in the merger, the holders of Debentures would have no right to convert into common stock—either of Collins (who would have no more common stock) or of Rockwell—after the merger. Rockwell's view of its post-merger obligations under the Indenture was shared by its counsel (the New York firm of Chadbourne, Parke, Whiteside & Wolff), and by Collins and Collins' counsel (the Los Angeles firm of Gibson, Dunn & Crutcher).

In order to determine whether the proposed terms of the supplemental indenture complied with the terms of the Indenture, the Trust Company engaged the New York law firm of Curtis, Mallet-Prevost, Colt & Mosle. Two partners in that firm—John P. Campbell and John N. Marden—undertook a review of the Indenture and the applicable law. Campbell and Marden took the position in September 1973 that a court might in the future find that the intent of the parties at the time the Indenture was executed was that the right to convert into common stock would survive a merger of Collins into another company, and that every holder of Debentures would have the right to convert his Debentures into common stock of the surviving company as long as the Debentures remained outstanding. Since the Indenture required that Rockwell assume all of Collins' obligations under the Indenture in the event of a merger, Campbell and Marden contended that Rockwell would be bound to agree in a supplemental indenture with terms providing for a conversion right of the Debentures into the common stock of Rockwell ("Rockwell Common Stock"), unless Rockwell could obtain the consent of each holder of Debentures that such a right could be extinguished. Furthermore, they contended, Rockwell's voting control of Collins prior to the merger imposed upon Rockwell and the directors of Collins a fiduciary obligation to the holders of Debentures.

The record indicates that discussions and exchanges of memoranda and drafts of opinions between counsel for Rockwell and Collins on the one hand, and counsel for the Trust Company on the other hand, continued for several weeks, and their disagreement was heated. There is also evidence in the record indicating that Rockwell exerted considerable pressure on the Trust Company to change its position, threatening the withdrawal of certain other business from the Trust Company and possible litigation if the Trust Company blocked the merger by refusing to execute a supplemental indenture. At something of an impasse with counsel for Rockwell, Campbell advised the Trust Company on September 18, 1973, that it could follow any of four alternative courses of action: (1) the Trust Company could decline to execute a supplemental indenture (thus blocking the Collins-Rockwell merger) unless the supplemental indenture provided for a right to convert into Rockwell Common Stock; (2) the Trust Company, as a policy decision, could refuse to take a position as to the rights of the holders of the Debentures after the merger, relying on the provisions in the Indenture and in the supplemental indenture by which Rockwell would indemnify the Trust Company from liability in any lawsuits that might later be brought; (3) the Trust Company could resign as Trustee under the Indenture; or (4) the Trust Company could seek a declaratory judgment with respect to the conversion rights of the holders of Debentures after the merger. Campbell recommended alternative (2), and the Trust Company ultimately followed that recommendation.

## ¶1307: Questions on *Rockwell*

1. Since Rockwell was willing to assume Collins' obligations under the indenture and was willing to offer the debentureholders the right to convert into the consideration offered to all Collins' stockholders (cash), what explains the reluctance of the debentureholders?

2. If Collins' stock disappeared, into what would the convertible debentureholders be convertible?

3. If the trustee's choices outlined by Campbell, counsel to the Trust Company, were always available to trustees, how would the trustee serve as centralized protector of the debentureholders, as the agency through which the debentureholders' free-

## Ch. 13 DUTIES TO CREDITORS? 469

rider problems are overcome? Would the purposes of the Trust Indenture Act be facilitated by having such a range of choices available?

4. Is the case a hard one? Could the merger transaction have still been overall good for the bondholders? Consider the possibility of any buoying-up benefits that offset the loss of the conversion feature?

---

## ¶1308: Excerpt from *Grant* opinion

The following is an excerpt from the *Grant* opinion, portions of which were provided earlier:

> The appellants raise a special point concerning Chase. As previously stated, Chase, one of the three lead banks, had been Indenture Trustee for the 4¾% debentureholders until August 1974, when it resigned and was succeeded by U.S. Trust. A debentureholder accepting the offer of settlement releases his claim against both. Despite the limited duties of a trustee for debentureholders, as distinguished from a trustee holding property as security, it is settled in this circuit that he owes a duty "not to profit at the expense of his beneficiary," Dabney v. Chase Nat'l Bank, 196 F.2d 668, 670 (2 Cir.1952) (L. Hand, J.). See also Broad v. Rockwell Int'l Corp., 642 F.2d 929, 959-60 (5th Cir.) (en banc) (construing New York law), cert. denied, 454 U.S. 965, (1981); Morris v. Cantor, 390 F.Supp. 817, 824 (S.D.N.Y. 1975). When an indenture trustee assumes the role of a lender, it takes the risk that, in the event of insolvency of the issuer, its acts will be subject to special scrutiny. Here the Bankruptcy Trustee conducted an examination of Chase's files covering its activities as indenture trustee, and [one of the] objector[s] deposed a Chase vice president concerning its decision to resign as indenture trustee and other matters. Neither the deposition nor any of the exhibits ... were offered in evidence at the hearing on objections. In their briefs in this court objectors rely on Chase's having played a principal role in the opposition to the sale of accounts receivable to Beneficial Finance Co. and having participated in the negotiation and drafting of the agreements of the summer and fall of 1974.
>
> At first blush the argument that Chase helped to thwart a plan whereby at least some of the debentureholders would have received partial payment might seem to have possible merit. However, it falls on the rock of so much of our previous discussion as shows that Grant would not have consummated the Beneficial deal [even if] the banks [were not opposed, because Beneficial and Grant could not work out terms]. The second argument falters on the fact that the $44,000,000 of secured loans covered by the Interim Loan and Guaranty Agreement [was] new money, $12,480,000 of which was supplied by Chase. Even if the facts showed that Chase participated in negotiation of the October 8, 1974, Loan and Guaranty Agreement while still indenture trustee, which is not at all clear, this also involved $66,587,500 of new money, $17,973,000 of which was supplied by Chase. This is some distance from the acts of "[a] creditor who accepts payment of part of a loan before it is due, from a debtor known to be 'fighting for its life,' and who insists upon security for the balance [of unsecured debt] when it is due," of which Judge Hand wrote in Dabney, supra, 196 F.2d at 672. As the Fifth Circuit en banc recently concluded, New York authority runs contrary to the assertion "that an in-

denture trustee has a duty, fiduciary or otherwise, to seek for the holders of debentures any benefits that are greater than those contractually due them," Broad v. Rockwell Int'l Corp., supra, 642 F.2d at 959 (emphasis in original). In short, while Chase might have been better advised to resign at an earlier date we see little prospect of a recovery against it as indenture trustee on the facts before us.

## ¶1309: Edward Fleischman,[1] Proposed Amendments to the Trust Indenture Act of 1939 (SEC memorandum Aug. 10, 1987)

The Trust Indenture Act of 1939 ... regulates terms of most non-governmental debt securities offered and sold in interstate commerce .... [A]spects of the Trust Indenture Act have become obsolete, and [the SEC], in an open meeting on July 9, 1987, has authorized its staff to draft specific proposals designed to modernize the TIA generally and to ensure its future adaptability to market developments. The proposals are to cover the following subjects: qualification procedures; exemptive authority; conflicts of interest; eligibility of foreign persons to act as indenture trustees; and miscellaneous technical matters.

What follows is an analysis and a description of the several legislative proposals, as presented to and approved by the Commission in its open meeting ... .

I. Qualification Procedures

A. The present requirements for qualification of debt securities [include] ... conformity to sections 310 through 318 of the TIA (the "mandatory provisions"), description of the terms of the debt, and eligibility of the indenture trustee. (As for the absence of conflicts described in section 310(b), a further condition, see infra III.–V.)

B. Qualification under the Trust Indenture Act is tied to effectiveness under the Securities Act. Under section 305(b) of the TIA, the SEC is directed to issue an order prior to the effective date of a registration statement refusing to permit the registration statement to become effective if it finds that the requirements of the TIA have not been met .... When a registration statement does become effective, however, the related indenture is "deemed to have been qualified" pursuant to section 309 of the TIA. The Commission's authority ends abruptly at that moment.[2] See section 309(e) of the TIA (forbidding "an investigation or other proceeding for the purpose of determining whether the provisions of [a qualified] indenture ... are being complied with, or to enforce such provisions") ... .

---

[1] Commissioner, Securities and Exchange Commission; member New York bar. The Securities and Exchange Commission, as a matter of policy, disclaims responsibility for any private publication or statement by any of its members or employees. The views expressed herein are those of the author and do not reflect the views of the Commission, the other Commissioners, or the Commission's staff.

[2] [The SEC's authority "ended abruptly" for the first fifty years of the statute, but then was extended when the Fleischman proposals amended the TIA.]

C. The Trust Indenture Act assumes, therefore, that the terms of the debt will be fixed at the moment of effectiveness and qualification ... .

D. ...

E. ... [T]he best way to ensure compliance with the Trust Indenture Act is to make the mandatory provisions self-executing ... . This can be done in a fairly straightforward way. What is required, essentially, is a new provision in the TIA to the effect that those provisions of sections 310 to 318, inclusive, that are required to be included in an indenture are a part of and govern every qualified indenture, whether or not they are physically contained therein, while those provisions of such sections that may be included at the option of the obligor are not a part of such an indenture unless they are specifically included. (It must be remembered, in this regard, that certain of the provisions in sections 310 through 318 are optional.) Obviously, this approach would eliminate the need for any lawyer, either inside or outside the SEC, at whatever time of day or night, to review indentures for compliance with the mandatory provisions. Printing and related costs also would be saved as indentures would become much shorter.

* * *

III. Conflicts of Interest

    A. Conflict as Disqualification Only at Time of Default

        1. Despite the SEC's urging, see VI Securities and Exchange Commission, Report on the Study and Investigation of the Work, Activities, Personnel and Functions of Protective and Reorganization Committees 110 (1937),[3] Congress enacted section 315(a) of the TIA in a form that permits indentures to limit the trustee's liability to duties "specifically set out" in the indenture and to permit well-nigh "conclusive" reliance on certificates and opinions of compliance. As a result, trustees are not bound to perform real duties of guardianship prior to default.

           a. The statute requires the trustee, prior to default, to preserve lists of debt holders, act as a medium for communications among them, and receive reports and certificates from the obligor. While these functions are important, they are also ministerial.

           b. In addition, the section 315(a) "option" is always elected, with the uniform result that the trustee, unless directed by debt holders, is under no duty to investigate the existence of an event of default. The trustee does not follow the obligor closely; its knowledge of the obligor's operations and condition, and of the obligor's compliance with financial covenants, is ordinarily limited to what the obligor reports. A contrary

---

[3] [Douglas' massive report.—Roe.]

position was considered by the Reporter for the Federal Securities Code, who concluded: "It has been persuasively urged that extension of the 'prudent man' test for purposes of ascertaining the occurrence of a default ... would be impracticable and prohibitively expensive in terms of increased trustees' fees." Loss, Introduction to I Federal Securities Code, supra, at xl (emphasis in original). [If the trustee had such a duty it would be a lightening rod for lawsuits when problems arose. Anticipating this, the trustee would raise its fees.]

c. On the other hand, section 315(d) forbids exculpatory terms as to trustee negligence or willful misconduct. The trustee is thus held to a general standard of due care in the performance of its administrative duties.

d. A conflict of interest cognizable under section 310(b) should not cause a trustee, with limited pre-default duties and a minimal standard of care, to withhold performance or to perform unfaithfully. To insist on an absolute standard of independence prior to default appears unnecessary under the circumstances.

2. Adoption of a post-default conflict provision [is sought by the banker-trustees].

* * *

c. Bearing in mind the ministerial quality of a trustee's duties prior to default, it therefore appears to the author that nothing would be lost, and something would be gained, by moving to a post-default conflicts standard. Under that standard, a trustee would not be prohibited by the Trust Indenture Act from engaging or having engaged in underwriting activities except in the case of a default. At the time of default, any underwriting or other present "conflict" by the trustee or any of its affiliates within the preceding twelve months would constitute a disqualifying conflict of interest. (The period chosen by the Commission is not sacrosanct.)

3. Moving to a post-default standard might trigger concerns about untimely trustee resignations. Trustees will resign, it may be said, just when they are really needed. Yet, that has *always* been the case. The obligor's customary debtor-creditor relationship with its trustee bank has not heretofore been treated *by the TIA* as a prohibited conflict of interest. But see infra. Trustees themselves, however, have been rather more practical. They routinely resign upon a default, or even earlier when default is anticipated, ... passing the trustee's hat to another eligible institution that has no lending relationship with the obligor .... Revising the law should not be expected to affect these bankers' decisions.

B. Debtor-Creditor Relationship as a Proscribed Conflict
1. Strange as it may seem to the uninitiated, the Trust Indenture Act does *not* treat a debtor-creditor relationship between the obligor and the trustee as a disqualifying conflict of interest. The SEC recommended that treatment when the Act was written, see VI Protective Committee Study, supra, at 107, but Congress decided the issue in favor of the banks.
2. That decision has been subject to vehement criticism on the ground that no conflict of interest possibly could be clearer ... . The proposed amendment, accordingly, would require creditor-trustees, at the time of a default, to do what they have always done anyway—resign. Since conflicts of interest would matter only once a default occurs ... . [T]he banks should not be troubled by this particular development.

\* \* \*

V. Technical Amendments

\* \* \*

B. Since obligors are generally in the best position to determine whether or not they are meeting their obligations, they should be under a duty to certify annually the absence of incipient defaults.

## ¶1310: Amendments to the Trust Indenture Act

At the end of 1990, most of the proposals in the Fleischman memo were adopted. The SEC can grant exemptions from the TIA, either by exempting an individual transaction or a class of transactions. 15 U.S.C. § 77ddd(d).

## ¶1311: The Trust Indenture Act's new conflicts provision

Section 310, as amended in 1990 and codified at 15 U.S.C § 77jjj, provides:

**(b) Disqualification of trustee**

If any indenture trustee has or shall acquire any conflicting interest as hereinafter defined—

(i) then, within 90 days after ascertaining that it has such conflicting interest, and if the default (as defined in the next sentence) to which such conflicting interest relates has not been cured or duly waived or otherwise eliminated before the end of such 90-day period, such trustee shall either eliminate such conflicting interest or ... resign ... ;

\* \* \*

(iii) ... any security holder who has been a bona fide holder of indenture securities for at least six months may, on behalf of himself and all others similarly situated, petition any court of competent jurisdiction for the removal of such trustee ...

... an indenture trustee shall be deemed to have a conflicting interest if the indenture securities are in default (as such term is defined in such indenture ...) and—

(1) such trustee is trustee under another indenture ... of an obligor upon the indenture securities ...

* * *

(10) ... the trustee shall be or shall become a creditor of the obligor.

## B. Duties of the company

### ¶1312: MetLife v. RJR Nabisco

```
UNITED STATES DISTRICT COURT
SOUTHERN DISTRICT OF NEW YORK

------------------------------------------X
METROPOLITAN LIFE INSURANCE COMPANY        :
and JEFFERSON-PILOT LIFE INSURANCE COMPANY,:
                                           :
                   Plaintiffs,             :
                                           : 88 Civ. 8266
                                           : (JMW)
     -against-                             :
                                           : FIRST AMENDED
                                           : COMPLAINT
RJR NABISCO, INC. and F. ROSS JOHNSON,     :
                                           :
                   Defendants.             :
                                           :
------------------------------------------X
```

Plaintiffs Metropolitan Life Insurance Company ("MetLife") and Jefferson-Pilot Life Insurance Company ("Jefferson-Pilot") ... allege upon knowledge as to themselves and upon information and belief as to all other allegations:

1. MetLife and Jefferson-Pilot Life bring this action for a declaratory judgment and permanent injunction to protect their rights as holders of long-term debt securities of Defendant RJR Nabisco, Inc. ("RJR Nabisco" and the "Company"). These rights are threatened by the proposed "buy-out" of the Company's shareholders that has been agreed to between the Company and Kohlberg Kravis Roberts & Co. ("Kohlberg Kravis").

2. The "buy-out" was initiated by RJR Nabisco's top management, and will result in stripping the Company of substantially all the value of its assets and distributing it to the Company's shareholders. To finance the "buy-out," RJR Nabisco will be burdened by $19 billion of additional debt, without one new product or asset added to its balance sheet.

3. RJR Nabisco sold the bonds held by MetLife and Jefferson-Pilot expressly on the basis that the bonds represented investment grade debt of one of America's strongest companies. In the "buy-out," the Company intends not to redeem the existing $5 billion of blue chip bonds but instead

to misappropriate their value by using this investment grade debt to help finance the high risk "buy-out." The public bond market immediately recognized this impact by reducing the value of RJR Nabisco's outstanding long-term debt, on the day following management's "buy-out" proposal, by almost $1 billion.

4. This action seeks relief before the Company incurs substantial liabilities and liquidates assets in implementing the "buy-out," and thereby irreparably injures Plaintiffs' investments. The transaction is imminent and, if consummated, would jeopardize Plaintiffs' ability to collect a judgment. Plaintiffs' remedies at law are inadequate.

The Parties

5. Plaintiff MetLife is a life insurance company organized and existing under the laws of the State of New York ....

\* \* \*

7. Defendant RJR Nabisco is one of America's premier companies, and the owner of such diverse businesses and product lines as Del Monte canned fruits and vegetables, LifeSavers candy, Shredded Wheat cereal, Nabisco cookies and Winston cigarettes. In the diversity of its products and the strength of its balance sheet, RJR Nabisco stands at the highest tier of corporate America ....

8. Defendant F. Ross Johnson is the Chief Executive Officer .... Johnson is, and has been at all relevant times, a "controlling person" for purposes of Section 20 of the Securities Exchange Act of 1934 (the "1934 Act").

\* \* \*

Plaintiffs' Purchase of the Company's Investment Grade Debt

\* \* \*

12. MetLife and a wholly-owned subsidiary own $340,542,000 in principal amount of the notes and debentures of Defendant RJR Nabisco .... MetLife also owns approximately 186,000 shares of RJR Nabisco common stock.

13. RJR Nabisco actively solicited "investment grade" ratings for its debt, which are forecasts of the future creditworthiness of the Company. As a result, RJR Nabisco and its shareholders received the benefits of fixed rate, long-term debt with interest rates at only a modest spread above comparable maturity United States Treasury obligations ...

14. Plaintiffs agreed to invest in RJR Nabisco based upon the Company's blue chip business; upon its descriptions

of a strong capital structure and earnings record that include prominent display of its ability to pay the interest obligations on its long-term debt several times over; upon express and implied representations of the Company concerning its future creditworthiness; and upon implied representations that it would not deliberately deplete or dissipate its assets. Plaintiffs also relied upon the good faith of RJR Nabisco and its management, both at the times of purchase and thereafter.

15. The Company's long-term bonds were issued in a market environment in which "leveraged buy-outs" of $25 billion were not expected. RJR Nabisco's investment grade rating did not reflect the possibility that management of one of America's leading companies would, in order to amass personal fortunes, put the Company's future at risk and strip the Company of substantially all the value of its assets in a "leveraged buy-out," and, as part of the scheme, would deliberately misappropriate the investment grade value of the long-term debt. Such a transaction is contrary to RJR Nabisco's express and implied representations, and undermine the foundation of the investment grade debt market which the Company knowingly availed itself of and upon which the Company and Plaintiffs have relied for decades.

16. The indentures under which the securities were issued are typical of indentures used by blue chip issuers at the times of issuance of the securities. The indentures include covenants protecting the first priority position of bondholders and assuring assumption of the Company's obligations in the event of mergers or similar events. As is common with blue chip debt of America's largest companies, however, the indentures do not purport to limit dividends or debt; nor do they contain other express covenants, found in indentures for weaker companies, that are intended to guard against financial deterioration. Such covenants were believed unnecessary with blue chip companies. Such covenants would have also unnecessarily added to transaction costs and could have unduly restricted the management of blue chip companies acting in good faith during the long term of blue chip debt. The prospect of a blue chip company deliberately stripping the value of its assets through a "buy-out" of all its shareholders was not contemplated.

The Events Leading to the "Buy-out" Agreement

17. On October 20, 1988, the Company announced that its Chief Executive Officer, F. Ross Johnson, had proposed to "buy-out" all of the Company's shareholders at $75 per

share. Subsequent disclosures indicated that, for more than a year before this announcement, Johnson and other members of management were ... developing a "buy-out" proposal ....

18. While top management pursued the possibility of a "buy-out" of the shareholders, RJR Nabisco continued to issue its investment grade debt securities. In 1988 alone, the Company issued $1.4 billion in blue chip debt. The Company solicited an investment grade rating for this debt, which projects creditworthiness and low risk into the future, and confirms the appropriateness of investment by insurance companies, pension funds and other institutional savers.

### The "Buy-Out" Proposals

19. Johnson initially offered to purchase all of the outstanding shares of RJR Nabisco for $75 per share, for a total price of $17 billion. A key motive was huge personal profit: if successful in his bid, Johnson expected to make at least $100,000,000. If a competing bidder acquired the Company for a higher price, Johnson's personal interest in the Company would appreciate dramatically. As the loser in the auction, Johnson will profit personally by approximately $18 million.

20. Kohlberg Kravis almost immediately countered Johnson's bid with a $90 per share proposal, and Johnson thereafter increased his offer to the shareholders by $3.8 billion, to $92 per share. A special committee of the directors of RJR Nabisco announced that it would put the Company on the auction block.

21. All of the proposals were premised upon replacing the shareholders' equity with high-interest, high-risk debt. Rather than redeeming and refinancing the existing blue chip debt to reflect the deliberate depletion of the value of the Company's assets, the Company permitted the proposals to assume that the existing blue chip debt, with low-risk interest rates, could be used to help finance the "buy-out." The investment grade debt previously issued by RJR Nabisco would be transformed into "junk bonds," but with investment grade interest rates.

22. On December 1, 1988, the special committee recommended Kohlberg Kravis's bid, nominally valued at $109 per share, and the Company and Kohlberg Kravis signed a merger agreement.

## Outline of the Proposed Transaction

23. Under the agreement, Kohlberg Kravis states that it is paying $25 billion for the Company .... The cash payment to shareholders totals $18.4 billion. Another $700 million will be paid in fees and "transaction costs."

24. To raise the necessary funds, Kohlberg Kravis entities will borrow, and the Company will guarantee, about $19 billion in addition to the $5 billion of existing debt. As a result, the Company, which currently earns about $2 billion before taxes and interest, and is obligated on $5 billion of debt, will be required to service or repay an additional $19 billion of debt ....

25. The new debt by itself exceeds the total assets of the Company before the "buy-out." Part of this additional debt will be paid off by dismemberment of the Company and the sale of divisions. The proceeds from the sale of assets will be used primarily to repay new debt, which has a shorter maturity than the original investment grade debt.

26. The success of the plan, and the future solvency of the Company, depend upon the continuation of favorable interest rates and the absence of business or economic downturns. The success of the plan also depends upon obtaining a high enough price for the divisions that are sold to make it possible for the remaining pieces of the Company to service both the $5 billion of existing debt and the additional debt not repaid out of the sale of divisions. The plan consequently subjects existing debtholders to dramatically greater risk of non-payment, and the Company to a significant risk of insolvency.

27. If successful, the participants in the "buy-out," having achieved private ownership of the common stock of RJR Nabisco, have the potential for tremendous profits.

28. If the plan is unsuccessful, even to a minor degree, RJR Nabisco will face default on its debt obligations and possible bankruptcy.

29. This is the gamble of the "buy-out" proponents, with their downside minimized [due to the] over $700 million in fees reported to be immediately paid by RJR Nabisco to the participants and lenders to the "buy-out." The lenders of the $19 billion of additional debt will also receive either a high interest rate or a chance to participate in future profits, or both.

30. A major portion of the risk will be borne by parties who will have no share of the reward and who will be irreparably damaged: the holders of RJR Nabisco's existing blue chip debt. The $1 billion decline in value on the day fol-

lowing the announcement of the initial "buy-out" proposal, without any outside adverse event, reflects the market's understanding that, under the proposals considered, RJR Nabisco would deliberately convert its investment grade debt into "junk." ...

### Nature of the Complaint

31. This complaint is based upon, inter alia, (i) the contractual obligations that RJR Nabisco undertook when it sold its long-term debt; (ii) fraud; (iii) violations of securities laws; ... and (vi) the requirements of state fraudulent conveyance and other laws for the protection of creditors.

### Count I
### Breach of Implied Covenant of Good Faith and Fair Dealing
### (Against RJR Nabisco)

33. At the time MetLife and Jefferson-Pilot acquired these securities, each rated issue of the Company had an "A" credit rating or better. The Company actively solicited these ratings, which project the future financial security of the Company, in order to induce their purchase by MetLife .... The liquidations of substantially all the value for the Company's assets -- more that quadrupling the debt and distributing the proceeds to the shareholders -- is not an event that was contemplated at the time MetLife ... invested in RJR Nabisco's investment grade debt. The transaction contradicts the premise of the investment grade market and invalidates the blue chip rating that the Company solicited and took the benefit from.

34. Under common law and the Uniform Commercial Code, Defendant RJR Nabisco owes a continuing duty of good faith and fair dealing in connection with the contracts through which it borrowed money form MetLife ... and other holders of its debt, including a duty not to frustrate the purpose of the contract to the debtholders or to deprive the debtholders of the intended object of the contracts -- purchase of investment-grade securities.

35. In the "buy-out," the Company breaches the duty of good faith and fair dealing by, inter alia, destroying the investment grade quality of the debt and transferring that value to the "buy-out" proponents and to the shareholders.

Count II
Fraud
(Against Both Defendants)

37. The proposed "buy-out" of RJR Nabisco wrongfully and fraudulently seeks to expropriate the investment grade value of Plaintiffs' securities. The deliberate effort to use the blue chip bonds to finance a high-risk "buy-out" is contrary to the express and implied representations made by RJR Nabisco when offering the securities.

38. The conduct of the Defendants in connection with the proposed acquisition of RJR Nabisco is knowing, intentional and fraudulent, and is designed for the personal benefit of the Defendants, to Plaintiffs' damage and detriment.

Count III
Violations of Section 10(b) of the 1934 Act
(Against both Defendants)

40. In documents and statements disseminated to the public (including annual reports and statements to securities analysts), and in statements made to the entities responsible for rating the quality of its debt securities, Defendants made or caused to be made untrue statements of material facts, or omitted to state material facts required to be stated or necessary to make its statements not misleading, in connection with RJR Nabisco's offering of its long-term debt to the public. For example, the RJR Nabisco Annual Report, issued in February 1988, states that one of the Company's "strategies for growth is to continu[e] to maximize our balance sheet strength," and makes numerous other similar statements. In an address on November 12, 1987 to the New York Society of Security Analysts, Johnson emphasized the same point:

> "Our strong balance sheet is a cornerstone of our strategies. It gives us the resources to modernize facilities, develop new technologies, bring on new products, and support our leading brands around the world."

The prospectuses for debt securities issued by the Company contain or incorporate similar statements and representations.

41. Defendants acted willfully or recklessly in making these untrue statements of material facts, and omitting to state material facts regarding the "buy-out."

42. By reason of the foregoing, Defendants violated Section 10(b) of the 1934 Act, 15 U.S.C § 78j, and Rule 10b-5 promulgated thereunder, 17 C.F.R. § 240.10b-5.

43. MetLife and Jefferson-Pilot relied on Defendants' misrepresentations and misleading statements, and upon the credit ratings for RJR Nabisco debt, in deciding whether to purchase the Company's long-term debt securities.

44. As a result of Defendants' misrepresentations and omissions to state material facts, MetLife and Jefferson-Pilot have been damaged.

\* \* \*

Count IX
Fraudulent Conveyance Act
(Against RJR Nabisco)

63. Upon information and belief, the "buy-out" will be a fraudulent conveyance because: (a) it will be a conveyance made or obligation incurred without fair consideration or reasonably equivalent value by a person that: (i) is or will thereby be rendered insolvent; (ii) is engaged or is about to engage in a business or transaction for which the property remaining in its hands after the conveyance constitutes an unreasonably small capital; or (iii) intends or believes that it will incur debt beyond its ability to pay as they mature; or (b) it will be a conveyance made or obligation incurred with actual intent to injure present creditors.

64. The "buy-out" constitutes a fraudulent conveyance, among other reasons, because the post "buy-out" equity in the Company will consist mainly of overstated goodwill created by the transaction, because transfers will be made out of, and obligations will be incurred on behalf of, the stockholders without any consideration benefiting the Company, and because the solvency appraisal upon which the transaction is conditioned will not involve an appraisal of the Company's largest contingent liability -- tobacco-related diseases.

WHEREFORE, MetLife and Jefferson-Pilot demand judgment as follows:

> (i) A declaration that the "buy-out" constitutes a breach of the implied covenant of good faith and fair dealing owed to Plaintiffs;
>
> (ii) A declaration that the "buy-out" constitutes fraud upon Plaintiffs;
>
> \* \* \*
>
> (iv) A declaration that Defendants violated the securities laws by their misstatements and omissions;

\* \* \*

   (vii) A declaration that the transfers made and debt incurred in the "buy-out" may be avoided by Plaintiffs under applicable fraudulent conveyance statutes;

OR, if Defendant RJR Nabisco seeks to consummate the "buy-out" before a final judgment declaring the rights of the parties, MetLife and Jefferson-Pilot demand judgment as follows:

   (viii) For restitution or damages for violations of the rights and duties set forth in the above First Amended Compliant;

   (xi) For preliminary and permanent injunctions requiring RJR Nabisco to hold in trust for MetLife and Jefferson-Pilot an amount sufficient to ensure that restitution or damages can be paid as demanded above.

AND FURTHER, awarding Plaintiffs pre-judgment and post-judgment interest, and the costs and expenses of the action, including attorney's fees, together with such further relief as the Court deems just and proper.

Plaintiffs demand a trial by jury.

Dated: New York, New York  
December 8, 1988

HOWARD, DARBY & LEVIN

By:_____  
A Member of the Firm

10 East 53rd Street  
New York, New York 10022  
(212) 751-8000

Attorneys for Plaintiffs  
Metropolitan Life Insurance Company and  
Jefferson-Pilot Life Insurance Company

. . . . . . . . . . . . . . . . . . . . . . . . . . . . . . . . . . . . . . . . . . . . . . . . . . .

The MetLife complaint was disposed of in Metropolitan Life Ins. Co. v. RJR Nabisco, Inc., 716 F.Supp. 1504 (S.D.N.Y. 1989): The parol evidence rule barred the bondholders from trying to include Ross Johnson's speeches as part of the contract; the court refused to imply a financial ratio covenant; 10b-5 securities fraud requires a purchase or sale, not refraining from purchasing or selling.

What exactly was MetLife's financial complaint? Its priority wasn't altered, its covenants weren't stripped. Unlike in *Katz*, nothing was done to its indenture. It had the same obligation from the same company as it had before the transaction. But after the transaction, the obligation to repay MetLife comes from a financially different company. Before the buyout of the stock, which was financed with new debt, RJR Nabisco's balance sheet in very round numbers looked like this:

| RJR Nabisco | |
|---|---|
| $20 billion<br>[$10B or $30B] | $ 5 billion [due to MetLife and others<br>    at 8% interest per annum]<br>$15 billion common stock |

Although RJR Nabisco, a company in the tobacco business, faced risks (of, say, being worth either $10 billion or $30 billion), in all normally foreseeable circumstances the company could re-pay MetLife and the other lenders. Even if the company declined in value to $10 billion, it would readily be able to pay off MetLife and the other creditors.

Then the buyout organizers buy-back a large portion of RJR's common stock, financing the buy-back with new debt. The company's overall operations are made more valuable. But look at what happens to the preexisting bondholders.

| RJR Nabisco | |
|---|---|
| $22 billion<br>[$12B or $32B] | $ 5 billion [due to MetLife and others,<br>    at 8% interest per annum, with a<br>    market value now of about $4B]<br>$10 billion new debt at 12% interest<br>    [with $10B market value]<br>$ 8  billion common stock |

The new debt could have a market value equal to its face value because it carries an interest rate commensurate with its riskiness. The MetLife debt, however, carries an interest rate meant for a low-risk borrower that can in all foreseeable circumstances pay back the debt. But after the buyout transaction, if the low-end results come about, $15 billion of debts will seek satisfaction from a company worth $10 billion, and the MetLife bondholders will get only about 33 cents on the dollar. And because the new debt matures earlier than the old, previously-investment grade debt, there's some chance that a noticeable portion of the new debt would be paid back in full, and then, if the company goes bankrupt, the old creditors would be paid from an even further shrunken pie.

Financial alchemy? The company has stock worth $15 billion before the transaction. It borrows $10 billion to buy-back the stock, and the residual common stockholders (the buyout organizers) put in $5 billion, but end up with stock worth $8 billion. How could the organizers subtract $15 billion in stock, then add $15 billion in new financing, and have $3 billion left over?

Well, $1 billion of the value should be clear now: It came from the preexisting bondholders. But $2 billion is still to be accounted for. The best explanations come from taxes and operations. The new capital structure is taxed more favorably than the old one. (See Chapter 14.) And the new capital structure could make managers run the company more effectively: Managers usually want to ward off bankruptcy. With bankruptcy a more serious risk after the recapitalization, they could be motivated to work harder. And with a large portion of the company's cash flow dedicated to debt repayment, the managers have less discretion to expand the company. So, if this company were one for which expansion was unwarranted (but managers wanted to expand anyway), the new capital structure would tend to deter managers from ill-advisedly expanding the company.

That then is the bondholders' financial complaint and the core motivations of organizers and managers for the transaction.

How would you, were you the judge, handle MetLife's contractual complaint, knowing, as you do, about the terms of the Drum Financial indenture?

---

¶1313: **Gary Hector, The Bondholders' Cold New World, Fortune, Feb. 27, 1989**

The talk of the securities world these days is Metropolitan Life Insurance Co.'s lawsuit against RJR Nabisco. Since 1984 the hapless holders of blue-chip corporate bonds have seen their securities devalued as issuers fell prey to leveraged buyouts or other debt-laden deals. Now staid Met Life is fighting mad and banging on the courthouse door, says John J. Creedon, the insurer's chief executive: "You deal fairly with the people who lend you money. You don't embark on a course of action that purposely hurts bondholders, that purposely depreciates the value of the outstanding bonds and takes that value and gives it to somebody else."

Oh, you don't? Cynics might wonder just where Creedon has been for the past five years. And some of his fellow players in the $460 billion market for industrial bonds are asking a variant on that question: What do we do when we lose the Met Life suit?

[Taking from the old] bondholders is the very stuff that LBO's are made of. In that notorious RJR deal, the hit—albeit on paper—was about $1 billion on $5.4 billion of outstanding debt....

Between 1984 and 1988 there were 254 downgrades of industrial debt by Moody's Investors Service as a result of takeovers, buyouts, or defensive maneuvers by companies borrowing heavily to avoid a raid. The rating agency estimates that $160 billion worth of bonds have been downgraded, clipping bondholders for at least $13 billion. Not surprisingly, these creditors are talking about "theft."

As exercised as bondholders may be about their losses, they haven't attracted much sympathy. That may be because the average bondholder is an institutional investor, a pro, even though the money he is managing in a pension fund, a mutual fund, or the general account at a life insurance company comes from small investors. The losses are mostly on paper and will be negligible, if the bonds are paid off in full at maturity. If debt-heavy corporations begin to topple in droves, the damage could be huge ....

One mystery is why the professionals have been mouthing off instead of withholding more of their money ....

\* \* \*

Most of the suits are carefully aimed at a specific deal or company. The Met Life suit also tries to advance a broader principle, the notion that management has a responsibility to treat bondholders fairly. Right now all you get when you buy a bond is a promise that the company will make regular interest payments, repay the bonds in the future at face value and, in the event of bankruptcy, put you near the head of the line to be paid off. Any other protection must be spelled out in detailed covenants in the contract between lender and borrower. Fairness isn't necessarily part of the deal.

Shareholders, on the other hand, are owners of the company, and management has a fiduciary obligation to them. In case after case, courts have affirmed this obligation ....

The most adamant bond advocates want more than fairness; they think they should have equal footing with shareholders. "It's time to establish a fiduciary responsibility between management and the bondholders," says Morey McDaniels, chief finance counsel for Union Carbide.

If Met Life doesn't win its suit, disgruntled bondholders had better not look to Washington for remedy. Treasury Secretary Nicholas Brady wants to cool the corporate ardor for debt. But the Federal Reserve chairmen and Treasury secretaries have been complaining for years about the level of corporate indebtedness, to little effect. There won't be much help from the Securities and Exchange Commission either. Chairman David S. Ruder, disturbed by LBO's effects on outstanding bonds, has asked his staff to look into disclosures to bondholders. But he says flatly: "I am of the school of thought that the fiduciary obligations of the board of directors and the officers of the corporation run to the shareholders and not to the bondholders. Most of the holders of corporate bonds in today's markets are sophisticated institutional investors. They are quite able to take care of themselves."

Just how to do that Ruder leaves to the bondholders themselves. They could demand stricter covenants. Twenty years ago most bond indentures included restrictions on a corporation's right to pay special dividends, add debt, or sell assets. But with blue-chip borrowers able to borrow overseas or tap short-term markets, traditional covenants on long-term bonds disappeared. Says Met Life's Creedon: "People thought they didn't need them." Eastman Kodak, for example, managed to sell $300 million of 16-year securities in October, just days after the RJR announcement, without any special restraints.

So-called super poison puts have gained a following. They are triggered by the purchase of a big block of shares, an unusually large dividend payout, or a hostile takeover. Happenings of this kind have come to be known in the bond market as "event risks." If they result in a downgrading of the issuer's debt, management must buy the securities back at par ....

* * *

Short of abandoning the industrial bond market, investors can buy more selectively. One approach is to shorten maturities. Prudential Insurance Co. estimated that losses due to event risk in its intermediate bond portfolio, where the longest maturity is ten years, have averaged about 4%. Portfolios with maturities of 20 years or longer have lost 15% to 20% of their value. Other portfolio managers are constructing sophisticated screens to identify potential takeover targets or candidates for restructuring. Just one whiff of a rumor that Company X is date bait for a raider, and they dump the bonds. Still another strategy is to hedge the bonds by buying stock in the same company. Met Life, which lost $40 million on paper in its RJR bonds, made $11 million in the stock. That didn't satisfy Creedon, but it may be enough to pay his legal bills.

---

### ¶1314: When is there a fiduciary duty? In re MortgageAmerica Corp., 714 F.2d 1266 (5th Cir. 1983)

RANDALL, Circuit Judge:

This case comes to us upon a final order of the district court concerning the scope of the automatic stay provided for in section 362 of the Bankruptcy Code. The district court held that the stay extends far enough to prevent the American National Bank of Austin from asserting various state-law causes of action in state court against Joe R. Long, who had controlled the MortgageAmerica Corporation before its descent into bankruptcy under chapter 7 ... . For the reasons given below, we affirm.

This dispute began in April, 1981, when the bank obtained a jury verdict in state court against MortgageAmerica for $192,554.40. The present case follows from the various efforts the bank has made to collect on that judgment from Long personally, rather than from his insolvent company. Although the parties vigorously disagree about whether Long was an officer or director of MortgageAmerica, neither Long nor his company has challenged the district court's assertion that "[i]t is undisputed ... that Long owned all of the issued and outstanding stock of RJF, Inc., which owned all the issued and outstanding stock of MortgageAmerica Corporation." The essential fact that Long controlled MortgageAmerica thus seems beyond dispute ....

The bank's principal collection effort consists of a suit filed against Long in state court in July, 1981. The gist of all three claims in the suit is that because Long deliberately stripped MortgageAmerica of assets in order to benefit himself while defrauding the company's creditors, he is personally liable to one of those creditors, i.e., the bank, for the company's obligations. The suit is based on three allegedly wrongful transfers, all of which occurred in May and June, 1981: the bank claims, first, that Long caused MortgageAmerica to transfer without consideration $200,000 to RJF, which used the money to make a payment on one of its own loans that Long had personally guaranteed; second, that Long caused MortgageAmerica to transfer $100,000 directly to him, personally, also without consideration; and third, that Long caused MortgageAmerica to transfer approximately $2,000,000 to another bank in order partially to repay another loan on which he was personally liable. Long vigorously denies all of these charges.

Meanwhile, business for MortgageAmerica apparently continued to worsen, and the company was forced into involuntary bankruptcy in August, 1981. (Various motions in connection with the bankruptcy court's granting of final relief on November 22, 1982, are still pending in the bankruptcy and district courts.) As far as the present appeal is concerned, the only relevant issue before the bankruptcy court was whether the section 362 automatic stay applied to prevent the bank from pursuing its state-court action against Long. After a combined preliminary and final hearing under section 362, the bankruptcy court determined in January, 1982, that the three state-law causes of action against Long were "property of the [bankrupt's] estate" and that the stay therefore applied. The district court agreed, and ruled that section 362 prohibited the bank from "usurp[ing] causes of action" that rightfully belonged to the bankrupt's estate. The bank appeals from that ruling.

I

The bank's principal argument on this appeal is that under state law the three causes of action in issue all accrue solely to creditors in their individual capacities, not to the company, and that these particular causes of action thus cannot be considered "property of the estate" as that term is defined in the Bankruptcy Code. We therefore pause to examine the state-law causes of action and the protective and rehabilitative scheme established by the new Bankruptcy Code before going on in Part II to determine how the two laws—state and federal—fit together.

A

The three causes of action asserted in the state-court suit are based upon the "corporate trust fund" doctrine, the "denuding the corporation" theory, and the Texas Fraudulent Transfers Act, Tex. Bus. & Com. Code Ann. §§ 24.02–.03 (Vernon 1968).

Although the "corporate trust fund" doctrine is the theory that has been the most thoroughly studied by both courts and commentators, it is nonetheless often poorly understood. It was first established in 1824 by Chief Justice Story sitting alone as a Circuit Justice on the Circuit Court for the District of Maine, see Wood v. Drummer, 30 F.Cas. 435 (Story, Circuit Justice 1824) (No. 17,944), and, since then, has become such a source of confusion that a leading commentator has introduced his forty-page treatment of the subject with the warning that "[p]erhaps no concept has created as much confusion in the field of corporate law as has the 'trust fund doctrine.'" 15A W. Fletcher, Cyclopedia of the Law of Private Corporations § 7369 (rev. perm. ed. 1981). The doctrine does not, in fact, involve the application of any actual "trust" at all.

When a court of equity does take into its possession the assets of an insolvent corporation, it will administer them on the theory that they in equity belong to the creditors and stockholders rather than to the corporation itself. In other words, and that is the idea which underlies all these expressions in reference to "trust" in connection with the property of a corporation, the corporation is an entity, distinct from its stockholders as from its creditors. Solvent, it holds its property as any individual holds his, free from the touch of a creditor who has acquired no lien; free also from the touch of a stockholder who, though equitably interested in, has no legal right to, the property. Becoming insolvent, the equitable interest of the stockholders in the property, together with their conditional liability to the creditors, places the property in a condition of trust, first, for the creditors, and then for the stockholders.

Whatever trust there is arises from the peculiar and diverse equitable rights of the stockholders as against the corporation in its property and their conditional liability to its creditors. It is rather a trust in the administration of the assets after possession by a court of equity than a trust attaching to the property, as such, for the direct benefit of either creditor or stockholder.

Although any controlling person who breaches this "trust" is personally liable for the damage he does, the trust fund doctrine was established principally to permit a court of equity to marshal and distribute a corporation's assets upon its insolvency and dissolution in much the same way as would a modern bankruptcy court. See Wood, supra, at 436–37. Born of necessity in 1824 when federal bankruptcy and state corporation laws were as yet ill-established, the doctrine is rarely resorted to today.

The Texas courts have upon a number of occasions discussed the nature and scope of the doctrine in Texas. For our purposes, the Texas version of the theory has three significant aspects—the relationship of the doctrine to the dissolution provisions of the Texas Business Corporation Act, (corresponding to Model Bus. Corp. Act §§ 82-105 (1980)), the identity of those who have standing to bring the action (whether creditors or shareholders), and the distribution of funds recovered under the theory (whether on a pro-rata or first-come-first-served basis).

The Texas Supreme Court undertook an analysis of the first issue just two years ago in Hunter v. Fort Worth Capital Corp., 620 S.W.2d 547 (Tex.1981), when it was presented with the question whether a tort action arising eleven years after a defendant corporation's statutory dissolution could proceed under the trust fund theory despite the three-year limitation in section 7.12 of the Business Corporation Act. See Tex. Bus. Corp. Act Ann. art. 7.12 (corresponding to MBCA § 105). The court's language is worth reproducing in full:

> As early as 1879, the Texas legislature began enacting remedial statutes which embodied the trust fund theory .... These statutes were carried forward by subsequent legislation, with only minor changes, until repealed in 1955 with the enactment of Article 7.12 [and most of the rest of the Model Business Corporation Act] .... Under these remedial statutes, the legislature had given creditors of a dissolved

corporation "the same broad measure of relief which equity would have afforded in the absence of legislation." ... The effect of these statutes was to supplant the equitable trust fund theory by declaring a statutory equivalent. In Texas, recognition of the trust fund theory, as applied to dissolved corporations, did not exist apart from these statutes.

620 S.W.2d at 550 (citations omitted).

The court cited extensively, and ultimately adopted the solution recommended by, a law review article, see Norton, and concluded that actions brought after the limitation period in the state dissolution statute are time-barred. Hunter and the law review article—which extensively discussed Justice Story's opinion in Wood v. Drummer—make it unmistakably clear that the trust fund theory and the Texas statutory dissolution procedures are intimately related. We therefore think it significant (if not necessarily determinative) that under both section 97 of the Model Business Corporation Act and under sections 7.05(A) and 7.06(A)(3) of the Texas Act creditors and shareholders may bring actions to dissolve a failing corporation, and that any moneys recovered in that action are then distributed, according to section 98 of the Model Act and section 7.09 of the Texas Act, first to creditors and then to shareholders. The action is clearly in the right of the corporation, and creditors and shareholders participate in its proceeds in accordance with the usual priority rules.

A more direct analysis of the trust fund doctrine reinforces this conclusion. In the days before Erie Railroad v. Tompkins, 304 U.S. 64, 58 S.Ct. 817, 82 L.Ed. 1188 (1938), the federal courts concluded that both shareholders and creditors had an interest in the "trust," which necessarily meant that both had standing to bring the action. The Texas courts follow this rule. The supreme court has stated that Texas "follow[s] the general equitable rule that ... [the corporation's] assets constitute a trust fund for the benefit of its stockholders and creditors ...." Liquidating Trustees; 510 S.W.2d at 312–13. Although the action is usually brought by creditors, there is nothing in the Texas cases to suggest that a shareholder could not also bring the suit. A Texas court has even held that if the action is to be brought at all, it must be brought on behalf of all those similarly situated, and that a single creditor, acting on its own behalf, does not have standing to bring the suit. See 405 S.W.2d at 834–35.

Any money collected in the action is distributed pro-rata to all creditors and shareholders. Those who control an insolvent corporation that can no longer be considered a true going concern are, in the words of the Texas Supreme Court, "charged with the duty of seeing that the creditors of the corporation [are] either paid in full or that they [are] paid pro-rata out of the funds received from the assets of the corporation." Waggoner, 120 Tex. at 615, 40 S.W.2d at 5; accord, Nevitt, 595 S.W.2d at 143 ("ratable distribution" required) (emphasis in original) .... At least insofar as the Texas corporate trust fund cases are concerned, the principle of first-come-first-served simply does not exist. In short, a suit under the theory is brought in the right of the corporation for the benefit of first the creditors, and second the shareholders, and all like-situated claimants are treated equally.

What we have said about the corporate trust fund doctrine applies equally well to the denuding the corporation theory. The denuding theory is actually little more than a restatement of the corporate trust fund doctrine in slightly different terms .... Justice Brandeis summarized the doctrine in the following terms:

> The law which sends a corporation into the world with the capacity to act imposes upon its assets liability for its acts. The corporation cannot disable itself from responding by distributing its property among its stockholders, and leaving remediless those having valid claims. In such a case the claims, after being reduced to judgments, may be satisfied out of the assets in the hands of the stockholders.

... The trust fund and denuding doctrines state essentially the same theory. Each involves the imposition of personal liability upon the "trustees," that is, upon those who use their power of control for their personal benefit rather than for that of the corporation.

\* \* \*

II

As already noted above, the bank's three Texas claims state essentially only two causes of action, one under the corporate trust fund (or denuding the corporation) theory, and one under the Texas Fraudulent Transfers Act.

---

In Geyer v. Ingersoll Publications Co., Del. Ch., Civ. No. 12406, (Chandler, Vice Chancellor) (June 18, 1992), the court said that fiduciary duties are due creditors at the time of insolvency in fact, irrespective of whether a bankruptcy or state insolvency proceeding had begun. The court said that the "fiduciary duties at the moment of insolvency may cause directors to choose a course of action that best serves the entire corporate enterprise rather than any single group interested in the corporation at a point in time when shareholders' wishes should not be the directors' only concern." Any tension between the quoted standard and fiduciary duties to creditors? Can maximizing the value of the enterprise be bad for creditors? How?

¶1315: **Credit Lyonnais Bank Nederland, N.V. v. Pathe Communications Corporation, 1991 Del.Ch. LEXIS 215 at n.55 (Dec. 30, 1991)**

[In evaluating the actions of the controlling stockholder and the board of directors of an LBO company, Judge Allen said: "At least where a corporation is operating in the vicinity of insolvency, a board of directors is not merely the agent of the residual risk bearers, but owes its duty to the corporate enterprise."]

ALLEN, Ch.: The possibility of insolvency can do curious things to incentives, exposing creditors to risks of opportunistic behavior and creating complexities for directors. Consider, for example, a solvent corporation having a single asset, a judgment for $51 million against a solvent debtor. The judgment is on appeal and thus subject to modification or reversal. Assume that the only liabilities of the company are to bondholders in the amount of $12 million. Assume that the array of probable outcomes of the appeal is as follows:

| [Outcome] | Expected Value |
|---|---|
| 25% chance of affirmance ($51mm) | $12.75 million |
| 70% chance of modification ($4mm) | $ 2.8 million |
| 5% chance of reversal ($0) | $ 0 |
| Expected Value of Judgment on Appeal | $15.55 million |

Thus, the best evaluation is that the current value of the equity is $3.55 million. ($15.55 million expected value of judgment on appeal [minus] $12 million liability to bondholders.) Now assume an offer to settle at ... $17.5 million.[4] By what standard do the directors of the company evaluate the fairness of [this settlement offer]?

The creditors of this solvent company would be in favor of accepting ... [the offer to] avoid the 75% risk of insolvency and default. The stockholders, however, ... very well may be opposed to acceptance of the $17.5 million offer [even though] the residual value *of the corporation* would increase from $3.5 to $5.5 million. This is so because the litigation alternative, with its 25% probability of a $39 million outcome to them ($51 million [minus] $12 million = $39 million) has an expected value *to the residual risk bearer* of $9.75 million ($39 million x 25% chance of affirmance), substantially greater than the $5.5 million available to them in the settlement.[5]

---

[4] [Actually, because the debt is only paid off if the judgment is affirmed, the value of the equity is much higher, as Allen recognizes in the next paragraph. A better way to analyze the situation is to conclude the operational value of an appeal is $15.55 million and the operational value of a settlement is $17.5 million, but, due to risk, the stockholders prefer an appeal.—Roe.]

[5] [To use Allen's chart from above, deduct the $12 million due to the bondholders before the expected values are summed up:

| [Outcome] | Expected Value to Stockholders |
|---|---|
| 25% chance of affirmance ($51mm minus $12mm) | $9.75 million |
| 70% chance of modification ($4mm minus $12mm) | $ 0 |
| 5% chance of reversal ($0) | $ 0 |
| Expected Value to Shareholders of Judgment on Appeal | $9.75 million |

[—Roe.]

... [I]t seems apparent that one should in this hypothetical accept the best settlement offer available providing it is greater than $15.55 million, and one below that amount should be rejected. *But that result will not be reached by a director who thinks he owes duties directly to shareholders only. It will be reached by directors who are capable of conceiving of the corporation as a legal and economic entity.* Such directors will recognize that in managing the business affairs of a solvent corporation in the vicinity of insolvency, circumstances may arise when the right (both the efficient and the fair) course to follow for the corporation may diverge from the choice that the stockholders (or the creditors, or the employees, or any single group interested in the corporation) would make if given the opportunity to act. Thus, *the option perspective can support a rule that gives directors' fiduciary duties to debtholders when a firm approaches insolvency.*

### ¶1316: Questions on *Credit Lyonnais*

1. What standard for the board does Allen articulate? When does it apply?
2. Courts usually say that the board's duties shift to creditors when the company becomes insolvent. Was the company in Judge Allen's hypothetical insolvent?
3. Is the judge's standard that in the vicinity of bankruptcy, the company must maximize the value of its creditors' claims? The stockholders' value? The value of the corporation? Or must the board of directors balance stockholders against creditors? Or is the standard something else?
4. Reconcile the last two sentences of the decision with the following possibility.

| [Outcome] | Expected Value to Stockholders |
|---|---|
| 25% chance of affirmance ($80mm) | $20.00 million |
| 70% chance of modification ($4mm) | $ 2.80 million |
| 5% chance of reversal ($0) | $ 0 |
| Expected SH Value of Judgment on Appeal | $22.80 million |

Should the directors take a settlement at $17.5 million? Doesn't the formulation of the duty (to shareholders, to creditors, to the corporation as a whole) make a difference here? If, because the firm is in the vicinity of insolvency, the board's duties shift from shareholders to creditors, what should the board do, appeal or settle? If the board's duty is to maximize the value of the firm, what should the board do, appeal or settle?

5. When the expectations and probabilities are unclear, does Allen's standard face difficulties? Are they the kind of difficulties that support corporate law's business judgment rule? And if the business judgment rule would be applied to a new standard (of, presumably, maximizing the corporation's value), then would the board's work continue to be unreviewable?

6. The tough case under Allen's standard: The expected value of the appeal is $15.55 million, just as it is in Allen's opinion. The settlement offer though is also for $15.55 million.[6] Does Allen's standard tell us what to do? Or, if in the problem in paragraph 4, the settlement offer was at a risk-adjusted $22.8 million, would Judge Allen's opinion guide the board of directors?

   The setting here resembles that in one of the hypotheticals following *Atlas Pipeline,* in which the judge, listening to the First's and the Second's valuation and views on whether to liquidate or keep the firm going, cannot readily rely on either party.

7. The conventional view is that creditors are "outside" the corporation and they get the contractual covenants that they bargain for, but usually no more. Occasionally contractual gaps have to be filled in, and the debtor does owe a duty of good faith. See generally Steven L. Schwarcz, *Rethinking a Corporation's Obligations to Creditors,* 17 Cardozo L. Rev. 647 (1996). A reason for the conventional view is that financial creditors could bargain for lower risk, and then pay for it. A reason not to imply terms is that if the court implies a term, then if later parties find a better way to deal with the problem, they may not use that better way, because the court has already decided how the parties will deal with the problem.

8. Perhaps a potential justification for a fiduciary duty (or aggressive gap-filling) might come from the feed-back effects of chapter 11: The creditors *would* in this or that setting have bargained for a covenant that would allow them to quickly seize the firm if the debtor defaulted. The firm would default in the morning, but by the afternoon the creditors would have seized and sold their collateral, or seized the board of directors, installed their own people, and displaced the old stockholders with themselves. The new board's duties would continue to run to stockholders, but the stockholders would, by the afternoon, be the old creditors. The corporation's duties could then *always* run to shareholders; upon default the identity of the shareholders would (nearly) instantaneously change. Chapter 11, however, the argument would run, disallows this kind of contractual seizure and instantaneous shift in shareholder identity; in its place (advocates of fiduciary duties to creditors might argue) should be fiduciary duties.

## ¶1317: Fiduciary theory: Andrew Bogen, David Kennedy & Bradley Schwartz, Landmarks on an Unmapped Terrain: Defining the Rights of Debtholders, 5 Insights, Jan. 1991, at 19

Even cases which reject a general fiduciary duty to debtholders frequently acknowledge an exception in the case of insolvency. While extraordinarily ill-defined, the existence of such an exception—at least in principle—seems widely recognized.

---

[6] Ignore risk for this problem, or if one cannot ignore risk, assume that the settlement offer is at the certainty equivalent of the appeal's expected value. I.e., you can assume that the certainty equivalent is $15 million and that's the settlement offer.

The case law is not clear as to whether insolvency for this purpose is to be determined on the basis of a balance sheet test or the corporation's inability to pay its debts as they mature (sometimes referred to as the equity insolvency test).[7] It is also uncertain whether this fiduciary duty to creditors implicates the same duties of care, loyalty and independence that directors owe to shareholders prior to insolvency. Moreover, notwithstanding language in some cases suggesting that this duty arises upon insolvency, other cases suggest that it arises only if a receivership or bankruptcy proceeding is initiated or the corporation ceases operating as a going concern. Finally it is unsettled to what extent this "springing" fiduciary duty to creditors overrides the continuing fiduciary duties to shareholders and how conflicting duties to creditors and shareholders can be reconciled.

The source of the fiduciary duty to debtholders in the event of insolvency is often said to be in the "trust fund doctrine ... . Those who control an insolvent corporation that can no longer be considered a true going concern are ... charged with the duty of seeing that the creditors of a corporation [are] either paid in full or they [are] paid pro rata out of the funds received from the assets of the corporation."[8]

## C. Contract theory

### ¶1318: Charles Goetz & Robert Scott, Principles of Relational Contracts, 67 Va. L. Rev. 1089-91, 1149-50 (1981)

[A] significant proportion of private contracts [are relational contracts, which] do not easily fit the presuppositions of classical legal analysis. One reason for this is the pivotal role played in conventional legal theory by the concept of the complete contingent contract. Parties in a bargaining situation are presumed able, at minimal cost, to allocate explicitly the risks that future contingencies may cause one or the other to regret having entered into an executory agreement. Under these conditions, the role of legal regulation can be defined quite precisely. Once the underlying rules policing the bargaining process have been specified, contract rules serve as standard or common risk allocations that can be varied by the individual agreement of particular parties. These rules serve the important purpose of saving most bargainers the cost of negotiating a tailor-made arrangement. If the basic risk allocation provided by a legal rule fails to suit the purposes of particular parties, then bargainers are free to negotiate an alternative allocation of risks. All relevant risks thus can be assigned optimally—

---

[7] [Note that in the Credit Lyonnais hypothetical, the company taking the appeal renders the company 75% likely to be unable to pay its debts as they come due. In the MetLife hypothetical, the recapitalization renders the company 50% likely to be unable to pay its debts as they come due. And in the real MetLife recapitalization, the deal made it more likely, but to an uncertain degree, that RJR Nabisco would be unable to pay its debts to MetLife and the other bondholders as the debts came due.—Roe.]

[8] [In re MortgageAmerica Corporation, 714 F.2d 1266 (5th Cir. 1983).]

either by legal rule or through individualized agreement—because future contingencies are not only known and understood at the time the bargain is struck, but can also be addressed by efficacious contractual responses.

In a complex society, however, many contractual arrangements diverge so markedly from the classical model that they require separate treatment. Parties frequently enter into continuing, highly interactive contractual arrangements. For these parties, a complete contingent contract may not be a feasible contracting mechanism. Where the future contingencies are peculiarly intricate or uncertain, practical difficulties arise that impede the contracting parties' efforts to allocate optimally all risks at the time of contracting.[9] Not surprisingly, parties who find it advantageous to enter into such cooperative exchange relationships seek specially adapted contractual devices. The resulting "relational contracts" encompass most generic agency relationships, including distributorships, franchises, joint ventures, and employment contracts.

Although a certain ambiguity has always existed, there has been a tendency to equate the term "relational contract" with long-term contractual involvements. We here adopt a very specific construction of the term that is based more precisely on the contrast with the classical contingent contract. A contract is relational to the extent that the parties are incapable of reducing important terms of the arrangement to well-defined obligations. Such definitive obligations may be impractical because of inability to identify uncertain future conditions or because of inability to characterize complex adaptations adequately even when the contingencies themselves can be identified in advance. [L]ong-term contracts are more likely than short-term agreements to fit this conceptualization, but temporal extension per se is not the defining characteristic. The contracts that we actually observe are, of course, neither perfectly contingent nor entirely relational. Legal theory has merely tended to concentrate on agreements that fall close to [being completely contingent], while our focus in this article is directed toward the other end of the continuum, [at relational contracts].

Conventional doctrine has failed to explain adequately the nature and function of these relational contracts and how they differ from more standard contracts. The resulting incomplete understanding is a prime source of costly litigation over the meaning and enforceability of key provisions of such agreements. Much of the litigation has centered on two doctrinal linchpins of relational contracts: the obligation of one party (the "agent") to use its "best efforts" to carry on an activity beneficial to the other (the "principal"), and the concomitant right of the principal to terminate the relationship.

---

[9] The limits of human capacity to respond optimally to the external conditions of uncertainty and complexity are explained by the concept of "bounded rationality." Simon defines bounded rationality as behavior that is "intendedly rational, but only limited[ly] so." H. Simon, Administrative Behavior xxviii (3d ed., 1976). Thus, when transactions are conducted under conditions of uncertainty and complexity, it becomes extremely costly—if not literally impossible—for parties constrained by bounded rationality to describe the complete decision tree at the time of bargaining.

\* \* \*

Executory contracts allocated the risk of various contingencies whose occurrence would influence the costs or benefits of a contemplated activity. By in effect selling a risk to the other party, who presumably anticipates a lower cost of bearing that risk, each bargainer reduces the costs of his own risk portfolio. This article has examined the behavior of contracting parties when the relevant contingencies are deemed too uncertain or too complex to permit the associated risks to be identified, described, and assigned appropriately at the time of contracting. Although such circumstances render relational contractors unable to exchange risks in precise, conventional ways, the process of negotiating such an executory contract is nonetheless motivated by cost-minimizing incentives.

This cost-minimizing hypothesis is confirmed by examining two terms commonly found in relational contracts: a broadly defined "best efforts" standard of performance and a discretionary termination privilege. The vague concept of best efforts can most sensibly be construed as requiring the level of effort necessary to maximize the joint net product flowing from the contractual relationship. This joint-maximization criterion is a plausible norm for all cooperative contractual relationships where the parties have not specified a precise standard of required performance; it produces the largest possible net product for ultimate division between the parties. Unfortunately, the gains from this cooperative objective can be realized fully only if the parties are able to provide an appropriate monitoring/bonding package—perhaps incorporating a discretionary termination provision—that induces the optimal output. Although such provisions often appear to give one party an unfettered opportunity to exploit the other, they also serve as a risk-allocating mechanism designed to reduce the agency costs of relational exchange. The tension between the monitoring function and the exploitation opportunity is an inevitable consequence of many business environments.

The decisions reached by courts interpreting best efforts and termination agreements are generally consistent with the kinds of tradeoffs that we ascribe to parties motivated by cost-minimization. Standard legal doctrine, however, has failed to articulate any explicit rationalization or explanation of these intuitively plausible outcomes. The consequence has been a level of uncertainty and ambiguity in the case law that blunts the social utility of the legal rules involved. A reconciliation of doctrine and result in these cases may serve two purposes: to facilitate the understanding of those legal counsel who attempt to craft appropriate mechanisms for allocating risks under exceptionally complex and uncertain conditions, and also to sharpen the courts' perception of the tensions inherent in the mechanisms chosen and the policies designed to regulate them.

¶1319: **Allan Farnsworth, Disputes Over Omission in Contracts, 68 Colum. L. Rev. 860, 891 (1968)**

Introduction

It is a commonplace that, absent some overriding public policy, courts are to enforce contracts in accordance with the "expectations of the parties." Usually the parties will have aided the court by expressing at least some of their expectations in contract language, oral or written. Even so, disputes will arise. Sometimes, because of vagueness or ambiguity in the language they have used, the parties will disagree over the meaning of what they said or over how their language applies to a situation for which they have provided. Such disputes will be referred to here as disputes over expression; the process by which they are resolved is interpretation of language. Sometimes, however, the parties will disagree over what they did not say, over the effect of their contract on a situation for which they have failed to provide. These disagreements will be referred to here as disputes over omission. They may reflect an understatement of expectation and pose the question: What should a court do when a party had expectations that he failed to reduce to contract language? Or they may reflect an absence of expectation and pose the question: What should a court do when a party failed to foresee the situation and so had no expectation as to it? This article is concerned with such disputes over omission, with what the parties did not say.

Characteristically, common law courts have dealt with problems arising out of what the parties did not say about a situation by purporting to determine what the parties would have said if they had said something about it. What the court decides they would have said is then called an "implied term" and is "read into" the contract.

* * *

The traditional approach to disputes over omission in contracts had disguised the role played by the courts. It has referred to a fictional "intention" of the parties which is in turn supposed to take the form of fictional "terms" of the contract. The result has been to create an extensive framework of implied terms to deal with omissions. It has been suggested here that it is more realistic to assume that the parties form their expectations in connection with a limited number of significant situations, selected from a much larger number of foreseeable ones. As to those situations that are excluded by this process of selection, there is an absence of expectation. When they reduce their expectations to contract language, a second process of selection takes place, and they use their language only in connection with a limited number of the significant situations with respect to which they formed their expectations. As to the rest, there is an understatement of expectation.

A situation that does not survive these two processes of selection is a casus omissus. The process of determining whether there is a casus omissus is that of interpretation. The process of resolving the casus omissus is that of inference, based either on actual expectations or on general principles of fairness and justice. So where a dispute over omission concerns the qualification of a duty that has been expressed without qualification, a court must first determine by the process of interpretation whether the case at hand was one of the significant situations with respect to which the language was used. If it was not, then it is a casus omissus and the court should recognize that it is within its power to extend the duty by analogy to the case at hand, to refuse to extend it, or to reach an adjustment that lies between these extremes. In making these kinds of judgments it is sometimes helpful to view a dispute over omission in terms of the burden of expression.

The suggested analysis is also helpful in determining the application of the parol evidence rule. Where the agreement is integrated, it may nevertheless be shown that there is, with respect to the writing, a casus omissus, and since this is a matter of interpretation, evidence of prior negotiations may properly be used to this end. Such evidence should not, however, be admitted to resolve the casus omissus, for this would add to or vary the written agreement, and run counter to the purpose of the rule. Linguistic analysis, especially an understanding of the concepts of vagueness and ambiguity, is useful in defining the limits of interpretation for this purpose.

CHAPTER 14

# FINANCE THEORY AND DEBT: MODIGLIANI-MILLER, BANKRUPTCY COSTS AND TAXES

**¶1401: Why then debt?**

Debt causes intractable problems. Reorganizations work poorly. Risks, stress, and foregone opportunities afflict the firm with too much debt. Contracting and negotiating debt covenants—the loan agreement or the bond indenture—is not always an easy task. Some financial economists suggest that the aggregate level of these costs is quite substantial. See Roger Gordon & Burton Malkiel, *Corporation Finance, in* How Taxes Affect Economic Behavior 161, 171 (Henry Aaron & Joseph Pechman eds., 1981). Detailed studies show that highly leveraged firms lose market share and contract more rapidly than their competitors during industry-wide downturns.[1]

If debt presents problems, what offsetting advantages induce its use?

*Risk aversion*. One's first instinct is to turn to risk aversion as the answer. Debt is safer for the creditor, so it's cheaper for the borrower. Some investors prefer to avoid risk. They take debt; those who can handle (or prefer) risk, take common stock. That answer was the conventional wisdom for quite some time. But in a series of deductive proofs, Franco Modigliani and Merton Miller demonstrated that perspective's fallacies. Their work is at the center of modern thinking of finance economists; the Nobel committee cited Modigliani's contribution when awarding him the Nobel Prize in 1985 as helping to lay the foundation for the field of corporate finance. Miller

---

[1] Tim C. Opler and Sheridan Titman, *Financial Distress and Corporate Performance*, 49 Journal of Finance 1015 (1994).

shared the Nobel Prize in 1990. Much of the remaining material of this section outlines the Modigliani-Miller Hypothesis, its necessary assumptions, and its ramifications.

Two economic features render risk packaging unconvincing as an explanation for corporate debt: First, its advantages can be replicated by individuals, who can use personal leveraging as a substitute. The examples in the following paragraphs demonstrate this. Second, competition among issuing corporations should have eroded risk packaging's big advantages, if it had any, long ago. The problem then, after one understands that risk packaging can't explain debt, is to explain it otherwise.

*Taxes.* If risk packaging fails to explain the use of costly debt, taxes may. The borrower may deduct interest from taxable income, but may not deduct dividend payments. Does that make debt a cheaper source of capital?

So it would at first seem. But once again the finance economists show that the tax story is complicated, because although corporate taxation favors debt over equity (interest is deductible, dividends are not) at the corporate level, at the personal level the tax rates favor equity over debt. (And once again, individual firms may not be able to profit from debt's tax advantages, although the whole business system may prefer debt to equity. That is, competition among corporate issuers should also have eroded any big tax advantages long ago, by issuing debt until its disadvantages finally equaled its tax advantages. From then on, new issuers wouldn't profit from choosing debt or equity.)

Moreover, even if the basic corporate tax story—interest on debt is deductible, dividends to common stockholders are not—were complete, it could not completely explain business's use of debt. The history of corporate taxation suggests why: Debt was widely used *prior* to any meaningful taxation of corporate income, which began during World War II, and indeed was widely used prior to the 20th century income tax.

*Information.* Information disparities might help explain debt. Insiders know more about the firm than the outsiders. Investors might more precisely evaluate a loan's value than a stock's value; because the $1 million loan from the $3 million or $4 million firm returns the first $1 million of the firm's value to the creditor, the creditor need not assess the probabilities of the firm being worth $3 million or $4 million. In contrast, a prospective stockholder would be very concerned with whether the firm is worth $3 million or $4 million.

Insiders and outsiders may evaluate the same information differently. Those who are optimistic about the firm's prospects take common stock; those who are most pessimistic do not invest; those who think the firm has decent but not compelling prospects take debt.

But information costs cannot universally explain debt in the public corporation. Public common stockholders are usually in the *worst* position to evaluate the firm's value. Indeed institutional creditors probably could do better. Banks and insurers often get deep into a company before they make their loan. But institutional creditors seem likely to need less information than institutional stockholders; and public creditors would seem to need less information than public stockholders. All creditors would seem to need less information than insider-stockholders.

The experience in raising new capital supports the information rationale: stock is the least preferred method, new debt the next preferred, and retained earnings the most preferred.

*Agency costs.* Managers might not manage well. Passive investors understand that they will bear some of the costs of managerial shirking. Investing via debt means that the managers will eat through the common equity account first. Creditors incur less in the way of agency costs; sometimes they need not monitor the firm as much as common stockholders.

Those who take a managerial perspective of the firm make a related point. Managers prefer not to go to the capital markets for new funds, because that effort will impinge upon their independence. Investment bankers will investigate the firm prior to a public offering; documents will have to be produced; the inquiries might trigger unwanted news articles. If the firm must go to the capital markets, the managerial theorists assert, the managers will prefer debt, because it intrudes less into managerial affairs: The investment banker investigation is less intrusive for debt than for stock; the documents are not as consequential.[2]

*Control.* The original entrepreneur may wish to maintain working control of the enterprise and expand the scope of the enterprise's operations. To issue new stock might cause the entrepreneur to lose his or her majority (or working) control of the enterprise. Debt could solve the ambitious entrepreneur's dilemma. The creditors' influence is substantially limited to the effects of the covenants they negotiate for the loan agreement or bond indenture.[3]

*Bonding advantages.* Managers could shirk. Or they may take on low-value projects that enhance the size of their firm, and hence managerial prestige and salary, but at the costs of shareholder profitability. The value of shares may decline. Debt may act as a "bond" between managers and the firm's own capital-providers. Debt increases the risk of turmoil in which the managers could be thrown out, making managers work harder to avoid that turmoil. They "bind" themselves to work hard, to avoid the

---

[2] Institutional debt (debt owed directly to a bank syndicate or insurance company consortium) could decrease managerial insulation. The institutional creditor could breathe down managers' collective necks more often than the public creditor. But the managerial perspective is still plausible. Institutional creditors intrude more than public creditors, but public creditors intrude less than public stockholders. And institutional creditors intrude less than institutional stockholders.

[3] Furthermore, as the discussion of Chrysler's risky debt in ¶1220 shows, lots of debt may pose a barrier to a merger or hostile takeover of the company's public stock. The buoying-up effect arises when the firm uses much debt.

turmoil, not to shirk. Debt could be a pre-commitment by managers to work hard or to refuse to take low-value (but easy to handle) projects.

An example might illustrate. In the mid-1980s several oil firms were takeover targets. Offerors said that the target firms were spending too much money on oil exploration when the stock market consensus was that the price of oil was declining. These expenditures (spending $18 to find a barrel of oil that the stock market thought they would eventually only sell for $14) may have resulted from mistake, differing assessments of the future price of oil, an inability of engineer-managers to fire their friends in the exploration department, or a sense among the engineer-managers that exploration was the task of oil companies. Some firms—notably Phillips Petroleum—beat back takeover attempts by recapitalizing with debt. The firm bought much of its common stock with the proceeds of newly-issued debt. By promising such a high cash payout to its new "owners"—the new creditors—the firm had to cut current expenditures to the bone, such as oil exploration. Debt "bound" the firm to a low-exploration operating strategy.

This analysis looks at the agency cost problem from the perspective of motivating the managers. Debt can also bring new players into the firm, some of whom can provide specialized information to management, and some of whom have skills in monitoring managers and reducing the chances that the firm, their debtor, would make egregious mistakes.

*Regulation.* Regulated utilities, such as electrical power and gas companies, telecommunications companies, and (at one time) railroads and airlines have (or had) their prices set by government agencies. The prices allowed by the regulatory agencies are based on the regulated companies' costs. Debt has been considered a cost, for some purposes, and put into the expense base upon which the rates were charged.

*Signaling costs.* Related to information costs and bonding advantages are signaling costs. The managers know best how much the firm is worth, note the signaling theorists. Common stock could easily be over-priced. The managers (if they also own some stock) will be reluctant to issue new stock if they think the capital markets are under-valuing the company's stock. They turn to debt. What's more, more debt will signal that managers believe their firm's value is higher than if they use more equity. Why? The more debt, the greater the chance of turmoil and bankruptcy. Since that's so costly to managers (and maybe stockholders), the market believes that managers won't issue a lot of debt unless they believe the chances of bankruptcy are low. A low chance of bankruptcy ought to go along with profitable future projects. Lots of debt thus means managers think the firm is worth a lot.

\* \* \*

These explanations are hypothetical, partially inconsistent with one another, and unproven as general explanations. Debt may not have a single explanation. Each factor may explain one firm's use of debt but not another's. The next reading describes

Modigliani and Miller's famous arbitrage proof, which showed how under some basic restrictions (a world without taxation, bankruptcy costs, and perfect investor information about the firm's business), the risk-splitting rationale for choosing between debt and equity was false.

**¶1402: <u>Richard Brealey & Stewart Myers, Principles of Corporate Finance 473-91 (6th ed. 2000)</u>**

**Does Debt Policy Matter?**

A firm's basic resource is the stream of cash flows produced by its assets. When the firm is financed entirely by common stock, all those cash flows belong to the stockholders. When it issues both debt and equity securities, it undertakes to split up the cash flows into two streams, a relatively safe stream that goes to the debtholders and a more risky one that goes to the stockholders.

The firm's mix of different securities is known as its *capital structure*. The choice of capital structure is fundamentally a marketing problem. The firm can issue dozens of distinct securities in countless combinations, but it attempts to find the particular combination that maximizes its overall market value.

Are these attempts worthwhile? We must consider the possibility that *no* combination has any greater appeal than any other. Perhaps the really important decisions concern the company's assets, and decisions about capital structure are mere details—matters to be attended to but not worried about.

Modigliani and Miller (MM) ... showed that financing decisions don't matter in perfect markets.[4] Their famous "proposition I" states that a firm cannot change the *total* value of its securities just by splitting its cash flows into different streams: The firm's value is determined by its real assets, not by the securities it issues. Thus capital structure is irrelevant as long as the firm's investment decisions are taken as given.

MM's proposition I allows complete separation of investment and financing decisions. It implies that any firm could [invest, manufacture, and build] ... without worrying about where the money for capital expenditures comes from ....

We believe that in practice capital structure *does* matter, but we nevertheless devote all of this chapter to MM's argument. If you don't fully understand the conditions under which MM's theory holds, you won't fully understand why one capital structure is better than another. The financial manager needs to know what kinds of market imperfection to look for.

---

[4] [MM's paper is] F. Modigliani and M.H. Miller, "The Cost of Capital, Corporation Finance and the Theory of Investment," American Economic Review 48 (June 1958), pp. 261–297[.]

... [T]he imperfections that are most likely to make a difference [are] taxes, the costs of bankruptcy, and the cost of writing and enforcing complicated debt contracts. We will also argue that it is naive to suppose that investment and financing decisions can be completely separated.

But in this chapter we isolate the decision about capital structure by holding the decision about investment fixed ....

**The Effect of Leverage in a Competitive Tax-free Economy**

We have referred to the firm's choice of capital structure as *a marketing problem*. The financial manager's problem is to find the combination of securities that has the greatest overall appeal to investors—the combination that maximizes the market value of the firm. Before tackling this problem, we ought to make sure that a policy which maximizes firm value also maximizes the wealth of the shareholders.

Let D and E denote the market values of the outstanding debt and equity of the Wapshot Mining Company. Wapshot's 1000 shares sell for $50 apiece. Thus

$$E = 1000 \times 50 = \$50,000$$

Wapshot has also borrowed $25,000, and so V, the aggregate market value of all Wapshot's outstanding securities, is

$$V = D + E = \$75,000$$

Wapshot's stock is known as *levered equity*. Its stockholders face the benefits and costs of *financial leverage*, or *gearing*. Suppose that Wapshot "levers up" still further by borrowing an additional $10,000 and paying the proceeds out to shareholders as a special dividend of $10 per share. This substitutes debt for equity capital with no impact on Wapshot's assets.

What will Wapshot's equity be worth after the special dividend is paid? We have two unknowns, E and V:

| | | | |
|---|---|---|---|
| Old debt | $25,000 } | | |
| New debt | $10,000 } | $35,000 | = D [Value of Total Debt] |
| Equity | | ? | = E [Value of Equity] |
| Firm value | | ? | = V [Total value of the firm] |

If V is $75,000 as before, then E must be V − D = 75,000 − 35,000 = $40,000. Stockholders have suffered a capital loss which exactly offsets the $10,000 special dividend. But if V *increases* to, say, $80,000 as a result of the change in capital structure, then E = $45,000 and the stockholders are $5000 ahead. In general, any increase or decrease in V caused by a shift in capital structure accrues to the firm's stockholders ...

* * *

**Enter Modigliani and Miller**

Let us accept that the financial manager would like to find the combination of securities that maximizes the value of the firm. How is this done? MM's answer is that the financial manager should stop worrying: In a perfect market any combination of securities is as good as another. The value of the firm is unaffected by its choice of capital structure.

You can see this by imagining two firms that generate the same stream of operating income and differ only in their capital structure. Firm U is unlevered. Therefore the total value of its equity $E_U$ is the same as the total value of the firm $V_U$. Firm L, on the other hand, is levered. The value of its stock is, therefore, equal to the value of the firm less the value of the debt:

$$E_L = V_L - D_L$$

Now think which of these firms you would prefer to invest in. If you don't want to take much risk, you can buy common stock in the unlevered firm U. For example, if you buy 1 percent of firm U's shares, your investment is $.01V_U$ and you are entitled to 1 percent of the gross profits:

| Dollar Investment | Dollar Return |
|---|---|
| $.01V_U$ | .01 Profits |

Now compare this with an alternative strategy. This is to purchase the same fraction of both the debt and the equity of firm L. Your investment and return would then be as follows:

| | Dollar Investment | Dollar Return |
|---|---|---|
| Debt | $.01D_L$ | .01 Interest |
| Equity | $.01E_L$ | .01 (Profits-interest) |
| Total | $.01(D_L+E_L)$ $= .01V_L$ | .01 Profits |

Both strategies offer the same payoff: 1 percent of the firm's profits. In well-functioning markets two investments that offer the same payoff must have the same cost. Therefore $.01V_U$ must equal $.01V_L$: The value of the unlevered firm must equal the value of the levered firm.

Suppose that you are willing to run a little more risk. You decide to buy 1 percent of the outstanding shares in the *levered* firm. Your investment and return are now as follows:

| Dollar Investment | Dollar Return |
|---|---|
| $.01E_L$ <br> $= .01(V_L - D_L)$ | .01 (Profits−interest) |

But there is an alternative strategy. This is to borrow $.01D_L$ on your own account and purchase 1 percent of the stock of the *unlevered* firm. In this case, your borrowing gives you an immediate cash *inflow* of $.01D_L$, but you have to pay interest on your loan equal to 1 percent of the interest that is paid by firm L. Your total investment and return are, therefore, as follows:

|  | Dollar Investment | Dollar Return |
|---|---|---|
| Borrowing | $-.01D_L$ | −.01 Interest |
| Equity | $.01 V_U$ | .01 Profits |
| Total | $.01(V_U - D_L)$ | .01 (Profits − interest) |

Again both strategies offer the same payoff: 1 percent of profits after interest. Therefore, both investments must have the same cost. The quantity $.01(V_U - D_L)$ must equal $.01(V_L - D_L)$ and $V_U$ must equal $V_L$.

It does not matter whether the world is full of risk-averse chickens or venturesome lions. All would agree that the value of the unlevered firm U must be equal to the value of the levered firm L. As long as investors can borrow or lend on their own account on the same terms as the firm, they can "undo" the effect of any changes in the firm's capital structure. This is the basis for MM's famous proposition I: "The market value of any firm is independent of its capital structure."

### The Law of the Conservation of Value

MM's argument that debt policy is irrelevant is an application of an astonishingly simple idea ....

... We can slice a cash flow into as many parts as we like; the values of the parts will always sum back to the value of the unsliced stream ....

This is really a *law of conservation of value*. The value of an asset is preserved regardless of the nature of the claims against it. Thus proposition I: Firm value is determined on the *left-hand* side of the balance sheet by real assets—not by the proportions of debt and equity securities issued by the firm.

* * *

The law also applies to the *mix* of debt securities issued by the firm. The choices of long-term versus short-term, secured versus unsecured, senior versus subordinated, and convertible versus nonconvertible debt all should have no effect on the overall value of the firm.

Combining assets and splitting them up will not affect values as long as they do not affect an investor's choice. When we showed that capital structure does not affect choice, we implicitly assumed that both companies and individuals can borrow and lend at the same risk-free rate of interest. As long as this is so, individuals can undo the effect of any changes in the firm's capital structure.

In practice corporate debt is not risk-free and firms cannot escape with rates of interest appropriate to a government security. Some people's initial reaction is that this alone invalidates MM's proposition. It is a natural mistake, but capital structure can be irrelevant even when debt is risky.

If a company borrows money, it does not *guarantee* repayment: It repays the debt in full only if its assets are worth more than the debt obligation. The shareholders in the company, therefore, have limited liability.

Many individuals would like to borrow with limited liability. They might, therefore, be prepared to pay a small premium for levered shares *if the supply of levered shares was insufficient to meet their needs*.[5] But there are literally thousands of common stocks of companies that borrow. Therefore it is unlikely that an issue of debt would induce them to pay a premium for *your* shares.[6]

* * *

Suppose that corporations can borrow more cheaply than individuals. Then it would pay investors who want to borrow to do so indirectly by holding the stock of levered firms. They would be willing to live with expected rates of return that do not fully compensate them for the business and financial risk they bear.

Is corporate borrowing really cheaper? It's hard to say. Interest rates on home mortgages are not too different from rates on high-grade corporate bonds.[7] Rates on

---

[5] Of course, individuals could *create* limited liability if they chose. In other words, the lender could agree that borrowers need repay their debt in full only if the assets of company X are worth more than a certain amount. Presumably individuals don't enter into such arrangements because they can obtain limited liability more simply by investing in the stocks of levered companies.

[6] Capital structure is also irrelevant if each investor holds a fully diversified portfolio. In that case he or she owns *all* the risky securities offered by a company (both debt and equity). But anybody who owns *all* the risky securities doesn't care about how the cash flows are divided between different securities.

[7] One of the authors once obtained a home mortgage at a rate one-half percentage point *less* than the contemporaneous yield on long-term AT&T bonds.

margin debt (borrowing from a stockbroker with the investor's shares tendered as security) are not too different from the rates firms pay banks for short-term loans.

There are some individuals who face relatively high interest rates, largely because of the costs lenders incur in making and servicing small loans. There are economies of scale in borrowing. A group of small investors could do better by borrowing via a corporation, in effect pooling their loans and saving transaction costs.

But suppose that this class of investors is large, both in number and in the aggregate wealth it brings to capital markets. Shouldn't the investors' needs be fully satisfied by the thousands of levered firms already existing? Is there really an unsatisfied clientele of small investors standing ready to pay a premium for one more firm that borrows?

Maybe the market for corporate leverage is like the market for automobiles. Americans need millions of automobiles and are willing to pay thousands of dollars apiece for them. But that doesn't mean that you could strike it rich by going into the automobile business. You're at least 50 years too late.

### Where to Look for Violations of MM's Propositions

MM's propositions depend on perfect capital markets. Here we are using the phrase *perfect capital markets* a bit loosely, for scholars have argued about the *degree* of perfection necessary for proposition I. ...

We believe capital markets are generally well-functioning, but they are not 100 percent perfect 100 percent of the time. Therefore, MM must be wrong some times in some places. The financial manager's problem is to figure out when and where.

That is not easy. Just finding market imperfections is insufficient.

Consider the traditionalists' claim that imperfections make borrowing costly and inconvenient for many individuals. That creates a clientele for whom corporate borrowing is better than personal borrowing. That clientele would, in principle, be willing to pay a premium for the shares of a levered firm.

But maybe it doesn't *have* to pay a premium. Perhaps smart financial managers long ago recognized this clientele and shifted the capital structures of their firms to meet its needs. The shifts would not have been difficult or costly to make. But if the clientele is now satisfied, it is no longer willing to pay a premium for levered shares. Only the financial managers who *first* recognized the clientele extracted any advantage from it.

### Today's Unsatisfied Clienteles Are Probably Interested in Exotic Securities

So far we have made little progress in identifying cases where firm value might plausibly depend on financing. But our examples illustrate what smart financial managers look for. They look for an *unsatisfied* clientele, investors who want a particular kind of financial instrument but because of market imperfections can't get it or can't get it cheaply.

MM's proposition I is violated when the firm, by imaginative design of its capital structure, can offer some *financial service* that meets the needs of such a clientele. Either the service must be new and unique or the firm must find a way to provide some old service more cheaply than other firms or financial intermediaries can.

Now, is there an unsatisfied clientele for garden-variety debt or levered equity? We doubt it. But perhaps you can invent an exotic security and uncover a latent demand for it.

\* \* \*

However, while inventing these new securities is easy, it is more difficult to find investors who will rush to buy them.

\* \* \*

**Summary**

At the start of this chapter we characterized the firm's financing decision as a marketing problem. Think of the financial manager as taking all of the firm's real assets and selling them to investors as a package of securities. Some financial managers choose the simplest package possible: all-equity financing. Some end up issuing dozens of debt and equity securities. The problem is to find the particular combination that maximizes the market value of the firm.

Modigliani and Miller's (MM's) famous proposition I states that no combination is better than any other—that the firm's overall market value (the value of all its securities) is independent of capital structure. Firms that borrow do offer investors a more complex menu of securities, but investors yawn in response. The menu is redundant. Any shift in capital structure can be duplicated or "undone" by investors. Why should they pay extra for borrowing indirectly (by holding shares in a levered firm) when they can borrow just as easily and cheaply on their own accounts?

MM agree that borrowing increases the expected rate of return on shareholders' investments. But it also increases the risk of the firm's shares. MM show that the risk increase exactly offsets the increase in expected return, leaving stockholders no better or worse off.

Proposition I is an extremely general result. It applies not just to the debt-equity trade-off but to *any* choice of financing instruments. For example, MM would say that the choice between long-term and short-term debt has no effect on firm value.

The formal proofs of proposition I all depend on the assumption of perfect capital markets. MM's opponents, the "traditionalists," argue that market imperfections make personal borrowing excessively costly, risky, and inconvenient for some investors. This creates a natural clientele willing to pay a premium for shares of levered firms. The traditionalists say that firms should borrow to realize the premium.

But this argument is incomplete. There may be a clientele for levered equity, but that is not enough; the clientele has to be *unsatisfied*. There are already thousands of levered firms available for investment. Is there still an unsatiated clientele for garden-variety debt and equity? We doubt it.

Proposition I is violated when financial managers find an untapped demand and satisfy it by issuing something new and different. The argument between MM and the traditionalists finally boils down to whether this is difficult or easy. We lean toward MM's view: Finding unsatisfied clienteles and designing exotic securities to meet their needs is a game that's fun to play but hard to win.

## ¶1403: Leverage, value and Modigliani-Miller

The prior reading illustrates the "irrelevance" proposition with text and simple algebra. This paragraph illustrates the proposition with balance sheets and income statements.

Two companies, XYZ and TUV, are operational clones of one another, operating in a world of perfect markets, no taxes, and no bankruptcy costs. The expected annual income of each is $100,000 if they can put their project onstream. The project will cost $1 million to set up. Each project is identical.

Mr. A is the promoter of XYZ. He finances the project by selling its common stock to the public for $1 million. Buyers of XYZ's stock demand an expected return of 10% on their investment (i.e., they demand a 10x capitalization rate).

XYZ

| $1 million project (cost) <br> Expected income: $100,000/yr. | C/S 1 million |
|---|---|

Ms. B is the promoter of TUV. She finances the project by seeking common stock from risk-preferring potential stockholders. She gets a loan commitment for TUV of $500,000 from The Bank at 5% interest. The Bank commits to provide these funds to TUV upon TUV's having received at least $500,000 in common equity for The Project. Ms. B states to her prospective investors that because The Project's operations are expected to yield $100,000 per year and, because the first $25,000 of income will be devoted to debt service, the investors could expect $75,000 per year. If the investors demand the same 10x capitalization rate (i.e., they expect a 10% return, on average), they should be willing to pay $750,000 in total for the stock. If Ms. B succeeds in promoting TUV, she will have made the value of TUV's securities total up to $1,250,000, more than the total value of XYZ's securities. (Before Modigliani and Miller came along, financiers believed they could package securities to create this extra value.)

Ms. B though concedes that the increased risk associated with that income stream might not justify using the same 10x earnings capitalization rate of XYZ. But, she says, the risk-return trade-off leads to a suggested 8x earnings capitalization rate. That capitalization rate, she says, leads to a stock price of $600,000.

### TUV

| $1 million project (cost) | Bank debt $500,000 at 5% |
|---|---|
| Expected income: $100,000/yr. | C/S $600,000 (8x capitalization rate) |

```
TUV's expected earnings from operations: ......................... $100,000
Debt service ............................................................... (25,000)
Net ......................................................................... 75,000
```

Advise the prospective buyers of TUV stock on a cheaper way to achieve Ms. B's offered return.

In perfect, untaxed capital markets where many projects have an expected return close to that of these two projects what should the value of the aggregate capital of XYZ be? And that of TUV? Should or could "packaging" the operational income enhance the firm's value?

## ¶1404: With risk

Does risk make a difference? Assume that both XYZ's and TUV's operations have an expected return of $100,000, based on a 1/3 chance of earning $25,000, a 1/3 chance of earning $100,000, and a 1/3 chance of earning $175,000.

```
Earnings from operations:    .33 x $ 25,000
                             .33 x   100,000
                             .33 x   175,000
```

For TUV, $25,000 of interest must be paid each year. After paying the interest to the creditor, this is what is left for the owners:

```
.33 x [$25,000 – $25,000]  =  .33 x        0  =       0
.33 x [100,000 – 25,000]   =  .33 x   75,000  =  25,000
.33 x [175,000 – 25,000]   =  .33 x  150,000  =  50,000
```

Can't the same return with the same riskiness be achieved by buying XYZ with money borrowed personally? If it can, shouldn't the total value of securities issued by TUV converge with the total value of securities issued by XYZ?

## ¶1405: With corporate taxes

Do corporate taxes make a difference? Assume that both XYZ's and TUV's operations are expected to earn $100,000 annually, and that corporate income is taxed at a 33% tax rate. Doesn't the corporate tax and the deductibility of interest income increase the total return to TUV's owners over the total return to XYZ's owners?

| | |
|---|---:|
| **XYZ:** | |
| Earnings from operations: | 100,000 |
| Corporate income tax: | (33,333) |
| After-tax income to SH of XYZ: | 67,000 |
| Income to creditors of XYZ: | 0 |
| Total income to XYZ's owners: | 67,000 |
| **TUV:** | |
| Earnings from operations: | 100,000 |
| Deductible interest: | (25,000) |
| Net income before corp. taxes: | 75,000 |
| Corporate income tax: | (25,000) |
| Income to SH of TUV: | 50,000 |
| Income to creditors of TUV: | 25,000 |
| Total income to TUV's owners: | 75,000 |

TUV, the levered firm, returns $8,000 more to its owners, because TUV's debt partially "shields" its income stream from corporate taxation. More income, all other things being equal, should create more value. The value of TUV's stock and debt should, again all other things being equal, exceed that of XYZ, if the corporate tax story is the only missing piece here.

## ¶1406: With owner-level taxes

Do the owners' taxes offset debt's tax advantage at the corporate level? If owners are taxed favorably on equity, but unfavorably on debt, we may find ourselves with a system with offsetting and contrary tilts, one toward debt at the corporate level and toward equity at the ownership level.

Assume again that both XYZ's and TUV's operations are expected to earn $100,000 annually, and that corporate income is taxed at a 33% tax rate. The corporate tax and the deductibility of interest income increase the total return to TUV's owners over the total return to XYZ's owners. Do individual taxes change the balance? Assume an individual rate of 40%. Assume, for now, that all corporate income is paid out in dividends.

XYZ:
| | |
|---|---:|
| Earnings from operations: | 100,000 |
| Corporate income tax: | (33,333) |
| After-tax income to SH of XYZ: | 67,000 |
| Income tax to creditors of XYZ: | 0 |
| Total, pre-personal tax, to XYZ's owners: | 67,000 |
| Personal taxation: | (26,800) |
| After-tax to XYZ's owners: | 40,200 |

TUV:
| | |
|---|---:|
| Earnings from operations: | 100,000 |
| Deductible interest: | (25,000) |
| Net income before corp. taxes: | 75,000 |
| Corporate income tax: | (25,000) |
| After-tax income to SH of TUV: | 50,000 |
| Income to creditors of TUV: | 25,000 |
| Total after-tax income to TUV's owners: | 75,000 |
| Personal taxation: | (30,000) |
| After-tax to TUV's owners: | 45,000 |

Again the leveraged firm has an advantage, and that advantage derives from the tax "shield" at the corporate level. Again, the value of TUV's stock and debt should, again all other things being equal, exceed that of XYZ.

XYZ's stockholders *cannot* recreate this tax shield at the individual level when both they and creditors are taxed at the same rate. XYZ's shareholders might deduct something, but because their creditors would pay an equal and offsetting tax, the personal level tax "shield" doesn't shelter as much of the firm's cash flow from the IRS as does the corporate tax "shield."

### ¶1407: With individual taxes and long-term capital gains

But tax rates are not the same. True, *if* a corporation pays out all its income as dividends, then personal taxation of corporate distributions leads owners and the corporation to prefer that the borrowing be at the corporate level: The IRS takes two bites out of corporate income, once at the corporate level and again at the personal level. By reducing taxable income at the first level, the aggregate bite is reduced. That's the import of the example in ¶1406.

But what if the firm retains its income, so that it's not taxed as a dividend to the holder? Then the IRS would not tax corporate income at the personal level at ordinary rates. Dividends are taxed at ordinary rates and when received; capital gains, which typically result when the corporation retains its earnings, are taxed favorably. And, empirically, a large portion of corporate income is *not* paid out as a dividend, but is retained by the corporation. If invested in worthwhile projects, the retention ought to be reflected in an enhanced stock price. When individual shareholders sell the stock they are taxed on the resultant gain. I.R.C. § 1202. Because the individual investor chooses the timing of the tax event, if circumstances permit, the investor can perpetually defer realizing the gain for tax purposes. This deferral makes the effective rate considerably below the normal rate. If the stock with an unrealized gain is inherited, the heirs need not pay capital gains upon disposition of the inherited stock. I.R.C. § 1014.

To illustrate, assume now that the firm retains all of its earnings, that retention induces the value of the underlying stock to rise, and that the effective tax rate on long-term capital gains is low. Cf. Merton Miller, *Debt and Taxes*, 32 J. Fin. 261 (1977).[8] The corporate tax shield is thereby offset by the favorable personal-level taxation of equity. If the rates break "right" the two tax effects offset one another, and corporate level debt provides no net tax advantage for corporate owners.

So, assume again that both XYZ's and TUV's operations are expected to earn $100,000 annually, and that corporate income is taxed at a 33% tax rate. Now assume that returns to stockholders are taxed favorably, via long-term capital gains rates. Assume the *effective* rate on long-term gains is 10% (accounting for delay, timing choice, and stepped-up basis), and that all returns to equity are via long-term capital gains. Then:

```
XYZ:
Earnings from operations:                              100,000
Corporate income tax:                                 (33,333)
After-tax income to SH of XYZ:                         67,000
Income to creditors of XYZ:                                 0
Total pre-individual income to XYZ's owners:           67,000
Personal taxation (cap. gains, 10% effective rate):   ( 6,700)
After-tax to XYZ's owners:                             60,300

TUV:
Earnings from operations:                              100,000
Deductible interest:                                  (25,000)
Net income before corp. taxes:                         75,000
Corporate income tax:                                 (25,000)
Income to SH of TUV:                                   50,000
Income to creditors of TUV:                            25,000
Total pre-personal income to TUV's owners:             75,000
Personal taxation of SH (cap. gains)                   (5,000)
Personal taxation of creditor:                         (8,333)
After-tax to TUV's owners:                             61,667
```

---

[8] This is the example in ¶1406. And what if bankruptcy costs—lost customers, suppliers and worthwhile investment opportunities—are significant and, contrary to the assumption of Miller's Model, vary from firm to firm?

The favorable taxation of equity at the individual level roughly offsets the unfavorable taxation of equity at the corporate level. With competition among issuers, the advantage would even out as the tax-favored securities get issued first, and their price bid up.

## ¶1408: With tax-favored institutions

Now let's reverse direction: Some owners of capital, such as pension plans, charitable institutions and some forms of insurance plans, are not taxed (or forever defer taxation) no matter what the form is by which they receive their income. What if they dominate the market for provision of capital? Cf. Merton Miller & Myron Scholes, *Dividends and Taxes*, 6 Journal of Financial Economics 333 (1978). Then, as in ¶1405, the corporate tax shield dominates the tax analysis and corporations, again all other things being equal, will want to use corporate debt to shield their income from the IRS.

Assume again that both XYZ's and TUV's operations are expected to earn $100,000 annually, and that corporate income is taxed at a 33% tax rate. But this time assume that both debt and equity are owned by institutions that are untaxed. This assumption is not fully realistic. But critical and growing financial institutions fit this mold. Pension funds now account for about 30% of the stock market and they are not taxed on their earnings.

| | |
|---|---:|
| **XYZ:** | |
| Earnings from operations: | 100,000 |
| Corporate income tax: | (33,333) |
| After-tax income to SH of XYZ: | 67,000 |
| Income to creditors of XYZ: | 0 |
| Total income, pre-owner level tax to owners: | 67,000 |
| Owner-level tax: | 0 |
| After-tax to XYZ's owners: | 67,000 |
| **TUV:** | |
| Earnings from operations: | 100,000 |
| Deductible interest: | (25,000) |
| Net income before corp. taxes: | 75,000 |
| Corporate income tax: | (25,000) |
| Income to SH of TUV: | 50,000 |
| Income to creditors of TUV: | 25,000 |
| Total income, pre-owner level tax to owners: | 75,000 |
| Owner-level tax: | 0 |
| After-tax to TUV's owners: | 75,000 |

When institutions are (or become) the dominant owners, and are untaxed, the offset of the favorable personal-level tax on equity is (or will be) eliminated, and, as in the first tax example, the corporate-level tax shield dominates the balance again. The value of the two only equals out after (and if) competition bids up the price of debt and bids down the price of equity.

## ¶1409: Some stages of analysis

Finance theory concerning the trade-off of bankruptcy costs for debt's tax deduction has gone through four stages, corresponding roughly to the examples in the prior paragraphs. In the first stage, the theorists ignored taxation, by assuming it away. Risk-packaging was all there was and individual arbitrage could create whatever the corporation could create.

In the second stage, the theorists attended to taxes, but only at the corporate level. At the corporate level the interest deduction makes debt more valuable than equity, all other things being equal.

In the third stage, the theorists focused on taxes at the personal level. The stage breaks down into several sub-categories: If the shareholder obtains all of her equity returns in dividends, personal taxation does not upset the investor/corporate preference for debt. Dividends and interest payments are taxed at the same rate; but the interest deduction at the individual level is not as valuable as that at the corporate level. (Less is shielded from the tax collector at the personal level than at the corporate level.) But if equity is taxed favorably at the individual level via capital gains, while interest income is taxed unfavorably, then the net advantages of debt over equity at the corporate level will be mitigated at the individual recipient level, with receipts from equity having a net advantage. (Putting the debt incurrence at the individual level doesn't change the private return.)

In the fourth stage, institutional investors are seen as dominating the market (which they don't quite yet do) and they do not pay taxes (which is true only for some institutions). (That is, individuals in this model do not invest directly but invest through intermediaries such as pension funds, life insurance companies and banks.) More importantly, the corporate sector as a whole obtains a tax advantage from debt's tax deduction. (But eventually competition leads firms to bid away the advantage of the deduction, and then no particular corporation obtains much of an advantage.)

Debt in this synthesis is a trade-off of tax advantage against stress costs.

## ¶1410: Perspectives on the firm, capital structure, and some policy implications

The modern synthesis on financial structure sees the firm deciding on how much debt to take on by trading off tax advantages to the firm against the bankruptcy risks to the firm. Does that lead to any tax policy suggestions?

The tax advantages to the firm are foregone tax benefits to the public treasury. The bankruptcy risks have no obvious offsetting benefit. On a net basis the system's economy seems to lose.

Eliminating the deduction for interest (or taxing returns on equity similar to the way returns on debt are taxed) should lead to less debt, if one agrees with the modern synthesis. That should induce a lower risk of bankruptcy. A tax change that only eliminated the interest deduction would by itself increase corporate taxation. But it would not be hard to construct a revenue-neutral change. For example, corporate tax rates could be lowered to offset the corporate sector's loss of the interest deduction.

Perhaps the perspective of debt as capital provided by outsiders is too deeply part of conceptualization of the corporation. The entrepreneur borrows from an outsider. The cost of "renting" capital is a cost of doing business as much as the cost of renting the factory. Changing that perspective to, say, that of managers "hiring" capital in a variety of forms—debt, equity, convertible debentures—may be too strange. When the image of debt as an expense is strong, tax changes—especially if the benefits are attenuated, abstract, and dispersed—do not stand much of a chance. When the deduction for corporate interest is closely-related to popular tax deductions, such as that for interest on the home mortgage, the task is yet harder.

What if the body politic conceived of the large public firm in this way: managers "rent" capital, as they might rent a factory. Call that capital "debt," and then the rent—the interest payment—is deductible from the firm's tax bill. But call that capital "stock," and then the rent—dividends—is not deductible from the firm's taxes, because it's the return to the firm's owners. As we have seen, this tax differential creates a systematic preference for debt in a large firm's capital structure. Debt has costs compared with equity: The cost (A) is the prospect that debt could stymie future operations if a downturn puts the firm in a sticky position; the benefit (B) is the tax deduction on the interest paid.

Once again, we can see a social problem when we examine these costs and benefits. The costs (A) are real and, in a sense, public. Unnecessary factory shut-downs can occur. Unnecessary layoffs can occur. These external costs are borne not by financial parties but by people who don't own the firm.

On the other hand, (B) is a private benefit that is exactly offset by a public "cost." Tax revenues are reduced by an amount exactly equal to the private benefit.

\* \* \*

Some mergers, restructuring and leveraged buyouts are related to the taxation of debt. Many of these transactions result in firms that have substituted for much of their equity a lot of debt. Oftentimes the "value" that is created by the transaction is a private value without public benefit. After a leveraged buyout, the firm's tax bill is reduced because tax-deductible debt has been substituted for the safer equity that yielded no tax deduction.

It is possible, but not yet provable, that the reduction of frictions (legal and otherwise) inhibiting mergers contributed to the use of debt. When takeovers were more difficult, managers could afford to "rent" capital in the form of equity, which the managers found comfortable, but which was costly to the owners. After all, managers are often losers in a bankruptcy: they often lose their jobs; even if the job is not lost it surely becomes more stressful. Managers might well have been willing, if not otherwise constrained, to forego the shareholders' profit in the form of a tax reduction by using more debt in the capital structure.

But in the 1980s, managers may have feared that a takeover was more likely if they failed to take full advantage of the interest deduction on business debt. Takeovers—either if the offeror won or if the target firm retrenched and recapitalized—often yielded a heavily-indebted firm.

*Reservations and details: the benefits of debt.* Business debt has non-tax benefits. The fixed repayment can focus managers better: The managers know they must come up with enough cash by this or that deadline, or their lives will become uncomfortable. But there is no reason to think that managers need a tax advantage (compared with using equity) to achieve this disciplinary focusing. Presumably the tax skewing of debt makes managers and financiers over-shoot the mark in using debt to discipline the firm.

## ¶1411: Tax consequences of recapitalizations in bankruptcy

The bankruptcy lawyer should know of two "technical" tax consequences of recapitalizing in bankruptcy.[9]

First, the recapitalizing firm will usually create for itself a tax cost if creditors discharge debt by "forgiving" it (when the creditor either accepts less, or takes stock for the debt); the debt forgiven generates income to the debtor. U.S. v. Kirby Lumber, 384 U.S. 1 (1931).[10] Second, the firm could lose a tax "asset" because the I.R.C. requires that net operating loss carryforwards be reduced when ownership changes.[11]

---

[9] This section reflects tax law as of April 1998. Several of the underlying sections have been notably unstable, changing every few years, perhaps because of tension between tax policy and those who wish to help bankrupt firms through the tax code.

[10] That is, if a creditor "forgives" its debtor and no longer requires that the debtor repay the loan, the creditor has a loss and the debtor has income.

[11] And, when a firm loses money, it can carry the loss back several years to offset recent income. Once the firm exhausts recent earnings, it can carry the loss forward to offset future income. These are net operating loss carryforwards or N.O.L.'s.

Bankrupt corporations often have run losses for several years and have big N.O.L.'s. One might think that the value of the N.O.L. is small, because the firm could be expected to have anemic earnings for some time. But several bankrupt firms emerged and then "acquired" the earnings against which they could use their N.O.L. That is, the surviving bankrupt bought other companies with high current earnings,

But if the firm's ownership changes during a recapitalization, the new owners cannot use the old N.O.L.'s.

What are the pitfalls and policy considerations in avoiding forgiveness of indebtedness income and preserving N.O.L. carryforwards?

**Forgiveness of indebtedness**

As a general rule, a firm that exchanges its old debt for new stock whose fair market value is less than the original issuance value of the debt will produce taxable discharge-of-indebtedness income equal to the difference between the debt's original value and the stock's market value.

When the firm is bankrupt several exceptions are available. When a bankrupt exchanges old debt for new stock, there is no discharge-of-indebtedness income.[12] But the corporate taxpayer has to reduce beneficial tax attributes, such as net operating loss carryforwards. I.R.C. § 108(e). The net effect, because most bankrupts usually have large N.O.L.'s, equals that of the basic rule, that discharge-of-indebtedness creates income for the debtor. Only when the discharge exceeds the N.O.L. does the exception have value for the debtor. In such cases the I.R.C. still requires the debtor to reduce its other valuable tax attributes, such as the debtor's basis in property it owns.[13]

This suggests now a disheartening scenario: Before a possible bankruptcy, a firm and its creditors sense trouble. The debt trades at, say, 70 cents on each $1.00 of face value, because the debt is riskier than it was when the firm originally issued it, or because the implicit interest rate for the firm is higher than when the debt was issued. But if the firm and its creditors work out the problem immediately with a stock-for-debt exchange, the firm will incur 30 cents of discharge-of-indebtedness income for every $1.00 of debt exchanged.[14]

---

turning each $.66 of post-tax acquired earnings into $1.00 of post-tax earnings through use of their N.O.L.

[12] This exception has come and gone from the tax code several times.

[13] The I.R.C. allows the debtor to choose whether to reduce basis before using up N.O.L.'s.

[14] Recall that a firm can have risky debt trading at below its original value, even while the stock has significant value:

| 100 | 100 Original value of debt, trading at 70 |
|     | 30 Common stock |

For example, the company's project is worth either 160 or 40, each with equal chances. Or in recognition of the hold-out value of the stock, the market gives it a positive value.

In this setting a workout is worthwhile to avoid the nastier costs of recapitalization if the low value turns up. But the company is technically not insolvent: assets equal liabilities (at face value); in fact, assets exceed liabilities at market value.

That tax cost might induce the firm's managers to wait. The firm might pull out of the trouble, making the tax expenditure wasteful (from a private perspective). Or the problems might be seen by the managers as potentially needing a bankruptcy for resolution.

**Debt-for-debt?**

Debt-for-debt exchanges are subject to an analogous rule. The 1990 Tax Reform Act provided that the company will have discharge-of-indebtedness income equal to the difference between the fair market value of the debt exchanged and the original issue price of the debt. So: (1) the company issues debt of $100, then (2) falls on hard times, with the debt trading at $40. The company exchanges the old debt for new debt with better terms (e.g., extended maturity, payment-in-kind). The company realizes $60 of discharge-of-indebtedness income.[15] This is so even if the new debt has a face amount of $100 (or $90 or $75). (Prior to the 1990 tax revision, the difference between the face amount of the new debt and the face amount of the old debt (which could often be the same) controlled the discharge-of-indebtedness (and if they were the same, the company incurred no discharge-of-indebtedness income).)

**Net operating loss carryforwards**

In general, a corporation debtor loses its net operating loss carryforwards if ownership of the corporation changes.[16] However, if the firm's ownership changes in chapter 11, the N.O.L. is not lost as long as prior shareholders and historic creditors (not including financial creditors who became creditors within 18 months of the bankruptcy petition) continue to own 50% or more of the bankrupt's stock. I.R.C. § 382(l)(5).[17] (The saving of the loss is not completely free; the carryover is reduced by the interest deductions taken on the debt exchanged for stock during the three-year period prior to the ownership change.)

---

When the company is not just solvent but in good shape, the exchange is not likely to generate a lot of discharge-of-indebtedness income. Why? The creditors have no reason to accept stock with a market value less than the market value of the debt. Only when the market value of the debt declines for extraneous reasons—a rise in long-term interest rates, for example—is *Kirby Lumber* likely to bite.

[15] See I.R.C. § 108(e)(11), added by the Tax Reform Act of 1990, Pub. L. No. 101-508, § 11325(a)(1).

[16] The "loss" of the N.O.L. is not straightforward. It is more a "cap" than an elimination. If ownership changes, the debtor's annual use of the N.O.L.'s is capped at a percentage of the debtor's post-chapter 11 equity. The cap percentage is the "long-term tax exempt rate," an item defined in the Internal Revenue Code to approximate the return on long-term state and municipal bonds.

[17] Creditors that became creditors within the 18-month window can be counted as continuing owners if they became creditors in the ordinary course of trade or business with the debtor and the debt was held by these ordinary course creditors continuously until exchanged for stock.

Because ownership changes imperil the N.O.L., the tax code gives an incentive for the parties to avoid a full house-cleaning by recapitalizing with stock-for-debt. It also discourages a sale of the firm in its entirety to a new management group, because changes in control imperil the N.O.L.'s, often a bankrupt firm's most valuable "asset."

Moreover, the chapter 11 exception, which views the firm's ownership as not having been changed if long-term creditors become stockholders, can be lost if ownership changes after the bankruptcy is completed. Section 382 has a "look-back" provision that eliminates the post-chapter 11 carryforward if ownership changes during the two years after the plan is confirmed.

\* \* \*

The convoluted institutional structure governing risky debt is ironic. The favored tax status of debt (interest is deductible, dividends are not) encourages widespread use of debt, fixing application of a portion of the firm's cash flow. If the firm falls into trouble and attempts an early renegotiation to modify those fixed charges, the firm incurs tax penalties (increased taxable income, decreased tax benefits). But if it waits until the eve of bankruptcy, non-tax considerations become more difficult than they were well before a bankruptcy, due to the holdout and buoying-up problems discussed in Chapter 12. Moreover, because the firm would often lose its N.O.L.'s in a sale, tax policy discourages what often might be the best disposition of a failing firm, namely sale to another company.

---

## ¶1412: Could the market produce a bankruptcy-avoiding security?

So debt increases the chance of a bankruptcy or financial distress. The modern synthesis after Modigliani and Miller is that a firm's capital structure is a trade-off of the private tax savings of the interest deduction against increased bankruptcy costs. Can the bankruptcy costs be reduced by better financial planning?

If bankruptcy costs are high (a plausible but not proven statement), then why don't bankers and lawyers try to write bankruptcy-avoiding securities? That is, why is there little effort to precook a recapitalization? If the prospect of a decline in the firm will create deadlocks, could the recapitalization be pre-planned to avoid the costs of deadlock? If there are bankruptcy costs, as the financial models posit and practical observation confirms, why don't firms—in the manner prescribed in a different context by Ronald Coase[18]—precook a recapitalization to avoid these costs?

A simple numerical example will illustrate. The firm contracts with a creditor for a loan of $500. To avoid the costly haggle if the firm declines, the two agree that in

---

[18] Ronald Coase, *The Problem of Social Cost*, 3 J.L. & Econ. 1 (1960); Jeremy Bulow & John Shoven, *The Bankruptcy Decision*, 9 Bell J. Econ. 437, 438 (1978) (bankruptcy costs raise "primary question [of] why bankruptcy should ever occur").

the event that the firm's stock price falls to $2 per share (from its current $10 per share), the debt will be exchanged into 25 shares of stock. No bankruptcy, no recapitalization, no deadlock.

We are beginning to see securities that have similar features that automatically allow the firm to alleviate some financial stress. In recent junk bond recapitalizations, the recapitalizing firms, creditors and investment bankers are often providing that interest may be paid by the firm in shares of stock or other "payments-in-kind" having a market value equal to the interest payment.

A full inquiry requires an extended treatment elsewhere.[19] But we have covered enough similar terrain here that a summary answer can be usefully given.

1. Rejection in bankruptcy. A security that would accomplish an "automatic" recapitalization would be rejectable in bankruptcy. A bankrupt firm may reject executory contracts—contracts whose performance is incomplete under § 365. Contracts to deliver stock in exchange for debt would be likely candidates to be classified as executory contracts in bankruptcy. Similar contingent contracts have been canceled in bankruptcy, rejected under § 365. Although rejection gives rise to a claim for damages, once rejected, an exchangeable bond would be useless as a means of avoiding financial stress.

How would the exchange feature be rejected? Shareholder-managers, fearful of losing control of the firm, might launch a preemptive strike by filing for bankruptcy and seeking to reject the exchange feature. Even though the firm would decline in value because of the enhanced stress, the managers or shareholders might think that they would get a bigger slice of the diminished firm, thereby making the bankruptcy worthwhile for them.[20]

---

[19] Some of these ideas are developed in Note, *Distress-Contingent Convertible Bonds: A Proposed Solution to the Excess Debt Problem*, 104 Harv. L. Rev. 1857 (1991); Barry Adler, *Financial and Political Theories of American Corporate Bankruptcy*, 45 Stan. L. Rev. 311 (1993).

[20] However, this possibility could be reduced. The exchange feature could be structured so that bankruptcy could not easily be obtained before the exchange was complete. By having the exchange occur when the firm was still solvent, the potential to use bankruptcy in a preemptive strike would be doubtful. While insolvency is no longer a formal prerequisite to a voluntary bankruptcy, Bankruptcy Code § 301, good faith is. Bankruptcy Code § 1129(a)(3). (To be precise, the good faith requirement attaches to the plan confirmation prerequisites, not the petition prerequisites. Courts and commentators have viewed a bad faith petition as justifying a dismissal of a voluntary proceeding, since a plan arising from such a tainted petition usually could not be confirmed. In re Johns-Manville Corp., 36 Bankr. 727, 737 (Bankr. S.D.N.Y. 1984); Gaffney, *Bankruptcy Petitions Filed in Bad Faith: What Actions Can Creditor's Counsel Take?*, 12 U.C.C. L. J. 205, 210–11 (1980).) If the exchange were to occur before the stress of insolvency or near-insolvency was manifest, good faith would be in doubt. Indeed even if the firm were insolvent, if the exchange feature would eliminate the financial stress, the good faith of the bankruptcy petition would be in doubt. And, the fully managerial firm would not necessarily seek to advance shareholder interests when they as managers would incur some of the stress costs.

2. <u>Discharge-of-indebtedness income</u>. The firm's tax liability might be increased.[21] Generally when a creditor forgives a debtor of repayment, the debtor has taxable income to the extent debt is forgiven. Moreover, drafters would have to contemplate the instability of these forgiveness sections. Four structural changes have occurred in these sections since the early 1980s; and recent changes have grandfathered completed recapitalizations but not future recapitalizations involving securities outstanding. In addition, N.O.L.'s are lost for some categories of change in ownership. Those crafting exchangeable bonds would have to fear that the tax rules would affect them unfavorably.[22]

Moreover, the exchange feature might induce the IRS to view the security as really an equity security, for which the corporation would not be entitled to any interest deductions.

3. <u>Historical non-negotiability</u>. As an historical matter, negotiability frictions could well have impeded using such securities until recent years. When negotiability was governed by the Negotiable Instruments Law, the bond obligation had to represent a sum certain, maturing on a date certain. The prospect of automatic exchange into stock would have undermined the bond's negotiability until the 1960s, when the Uniform Commercial Code replaced the Negotiable Instruments Law, replacing the sum-certain, date-certain standard for bonds. Inertia may well have impeded a change from tradition unless the change offers important improvement. When the negotiability friction was lifted in the 1960s, the potential bankruptcy of the public firm just was not an especially pressing problem.

4. <u>First-mover disadvantages</u>. In today's world the first mover to use an exchangeable bond would incur costs. Lawyers' fees would be higher than normal. Securities' analysts might have some difficulty following the firm's securities, due to the unusual feature. Special tax rulings might have to be sought and paid for.[23] Furthermore, and this may be significant, the first-mover might seem odd. The atypical bond

---

[21] See I.R.C. § 108(e).

[22] Forgiveness of indebtedness income might be avoided if the deal structure gave the creditors stock with a value equal to that of the amount originally loaned. Thus the deal might have the creditors lend $500, and take 250 shares of stock if and when the stock price declined to $2 per share, from its current $10.

[23] To some extent the first firm might not bear these direct transactions costs. The underwriter of the bonds might be willing to bear all these costs. If a new instrument can be created that solves some financial problems, the underwriter can expect to have some repeat business from other issuers. See generally Van Horne, *Of Financial Innovations and Excesses,* 40 J. Fin. 621, 626 (1985). ("Nowadays, almost any proposal gets a receptive ear, unlike the past when proposed changes were viewed with innate skepticism. Never has the time been riper for new ideas.") The first underwriter will still bear a disproportionate share of these start-up costs, since if the innovation works other underwriters will enter the market. But since the underwriter expects to do many exchange financings if the first one works, it will more willingly bear some of the initial costs than will the issuing firm. The underwriter could also expect to gain some first-mover *advantages* from a reputation for financial innovation.

clause—such as the exchange feature would surely be at first—would attract special attention. Potential buyers would wonder whether there is some special reason to expect an issuer decline into financial stress or to expect especially costly stress if it occurs. This adverse signal, even if a false one, might be costly for the potential first issuer. In that case, it may decline to use the feature and take the chance of potentially costly financial stress. One might thus expect something short of a complete move to exchangeable bonds. If plausible hybrids were available, the first step might be to use them.[24]

Signaling theory may be relevant. Insiders have a better idea of the firms prospects than outsiders. The way the firm's capital structure is formed signals the firm's prospects. Debt, for example, signals good opportunities under one scenario, because the firm's managers would be reluctant to use excessive debt if it would measurably increase the chance of bankruptcy and disruption to the firm and the managers' careers. The effort to precook a recapitalization would be taken as an adverse signal. Similarly, some have argued that debt enhances agency benefits: managers scramble to best assure repayment. A precooked recapitalization reduces the incentives to scramble.

5. Benefits to nonbargain creditors. The precooked recapitalization would work only if all creditors participated or compensated other creditors for their nonparticipation. (I.e., nonparticipants would benefit because they would be better assured of being paid off in full after the participating financial creditors took stock. To make such a security work, nonparticipants would have to compensate participants ex ante.) But such compensation is sometimes difficult. Not all potential creditors readily bargain over such matters. (Tort claimants, some trade creditors, and labor creditors come to mind.)

6. Securities regulation. The 1930s regulators *wanted* a regulatory structure that would reduce the prospect of contractual reorganization. They instituted regulatory structures that would thwart out-of-court workouts. Some of those structures are still in place. For example, the SEC proposed and successfully shepherded through Congress a requirement that no bondholder could be bound to a recapitalization outside of bankruptcy without that bondholder's individual consent.[25] That is, votes among bondholders that would bind all are prohibited. Whether bondholders would *want* such a reorganizable security is one question; now they are simply prohibited from having one. Arguably the individual consent provision requires that the consent to a recapitalization be given at the time of the recapitalization (otherwise the requirement

---

[24] Troubled companies have been attempting to use bonds with the interest payable in common stock of the company. If the company suffers cash flow difficulties it can then be relieved of the obligation to use up whatever cash it has left. In essence, although the principal amount of the bond is not exchangeable into common stock at the then-current market price, the obligation to pay interest *is* exchangeable into common stock.

[25] Trust Indenture Act of 1939, § 316(b); 15 U.S.C. § 77ppp (1982).

that there be consent has no bite). If so, then such a reorganizable security would run afoul of the Trust Indenture Act.

7. <u>Agency benefits of debt</u>. By relieving financial stress, the agency benefits (of creating turmoil if managers fail to produce) would be foregone.

8. <u>Conservative skepticism.</u> Such a security would be new. A natural skepticism and conservatism might reduce the incentive for a radical departure from existing practice.

CHAPTER 15

# CHAPTER 11 AS A MECHANISM OF CORPORATE GOVERNANCE

In chapter 11, the parties' goals conflict. When trying to maximize their own stick in the corporate bundle, a party could diminish the value of the bundle as a whole. Some bankruptcy rules can be seen as rules designed for, or having the effect of, reducing the distortions from this conflict. Thus, principles of equitable subordination can be understood as efforts to control creditor over-reaching before bankruptcy. Other features of chapter 11 can be seen as efforts to control managerial and stockholder over-reaching. Each control is incomplete.

Several of these "controls" we've seen. This chapter reviews them and adds the major ones we haven't already seen in these materials.

## ¶1501: Operating the business in general

Business continues after the company enters chapter 11. It'll typically be two or three years before the bankruptcy is over. During that time the trustee can run the business as it deems fit, unless it collides with another bankruptcy provision. Section 1108 says so explicitly. Because a typical reorganization has the company's management stay in place with the rights and duties of the trustee, the bankrupt's pre-bankruptcy management typically runs the company (§ 1107).

After the bankruptcy petition is filed, a creditors' committee is formed, usually from among the company's largest creditors. The committee hires a law firm to represent it (and be paid ordinarily by the bankrupt company). Usually the committee meets regularly with the bankrupt's management and reviews confidential financial information such as interim income statements, balance sheets, and financial projections. The creditors can seek a court order for the bankrupt to take specific business actions (§ 1108). Although such orders are rare, the possibility of such an order allows the creditors' committee to negotiate a business plan with the debtor. The bankruptcy court could itself intervene (presumably if it felt that creditors were not diligent enough in protecting their own interests). Because the Code's provision for the court to intervene without motion from a party in interest is new (dating from 1994), it's too early to know how activist courts will be in supervising the business. One guesses that with heavy dockets, courts will act rarely without a motion from a creditor.

## ¶1502: Operating the business, getting inventory

Most businesses need to buy something, transform that something, and sell that something at a profit. A retailer needs to buy merchandise; an airline needs to buy fuel and food. Vendors usually ship such goods in on credit, expecting to be paid in a few days or a few weeks. Vendors frequently insist to weak customers that the customers pay cash on (or sometimes before) delivery. But the bankrupt will usually be cash-strapped. The Code strengthens the bankrupt company's ability to buy.

Sections 503(b) and 507(a)(1) make the expenses of administering the bankruptcy a priority expense, coming before most (but not all) other creditors. Credit obtained in the ordinary course of business, such as when a vendor ships goods to the bankrupt and expects to be paid within a few weeks, is entitled to this administrative expense priority (§ 364(a)). This priority usually makes it safe for vendors to ship goods to a bankrupt customer. The administrative priority also creates a peculiarity: the vendor who shipped goods into, say, Bloomingdales a few weeks before its bankruptcy waited a couple of years for repayment and in many chapter 11 proceedings such a vendor is not repaid in full; the same vendor could have shipped identical goods to Bloomingdales a week after the bankruptcy and would have been paid promptly and in full.

Why isn't the administrative priority absolutely safe, absolutely assuring that the vendor will be repaid in full? First off, the priority does not allow the vendor to jump ahead of secured creditors. If the bankrupt loses money before the vendor is to be repaid, there might not be enough in the bankrupt company to pay the vendor's administrative claim. Second, if secured creditors were offered "adequate" protection (when they were stopped from seizing their security) and that "adequate" protection turns out to be inadequate, then the inadequately protected secured creditor's "administrative" expense claim comes ahead of the ordinary vendor's administrative expense claim. Third, the vendor's shipment must be an ordinary course business event. Fancy terms may deny the vendor administrative expense treatment (and the court may let the claim sink to a run-of-the-mill pre-petition unsecured claim). Fourth, some creditors, usually those providing new financing, can get a "super-priority" claim that must be paid before other administrative expenses.

## ¶1503: Credit outside the ordinary course of business

The bankrupt might need to buy goods under unusual circumstances, subject to unusual terms. It might have to borrow money in a new, special loan facility. The credits will be outside the ordinary course of business—and hence not entitled to administrative priority, but the bankrupt needs them—and without administrative priority will not get them. The creditor can get administrative expense priority, but only after notice and a hearing (§ 364(b)). Unusual transactions give the bankrupt the opportunity to take unusual risks that gamble with other creditors' money; the notice provisions allow the affected creditors to object and try to convince the court not to allow the bankrupt to take the out-of-ordinary course action.

What if the bankrupt is cash-strapped, but could salvage value out of its operations if it could get some new financing? A new creditor insists on priority; the bankrupt's lawyers point to §§ 364 and 507 as providing administrative expense priority. But this potential creditor says the company is in such sad shape that it won't lend unless it gets a super-priority above all other administrative expenses, such as the expense of making secured creditors whole if their "adequate" protection proves to be inadequate, the amounts due vendors who shipped ordinary course merchandise into the stores, and the amounts due vendors who (after court order) made out-of-the-ordinary course extensions of credit. Section 364(c) allows the court to give a creditor a super-priority over "any or all" administrative expenses. Section 364(d) goes further, allowing the court when § 364(c) financing isn't available, to give the creditor priority over pre-bankruptcy secured creditors, but only as long as the court believes that those pre-bankruptcy secured creditors will be adequately protected.

..................................................................................................

### § 364. Obtaining credit

(c) If the trustee is unable to obtain unsecured credit allowable under section 503 (b) (1) of this title as an administrative expense, the court, after notice and a hearing, may authorize the obtaining of credit or the incurring of debt—

(1) with priority over any or all administrative expenses of the kind specified in section 503 (b) ... of this title;
(2) secured by a lien on property of the estate that is not otherwise subject to a lien; or
(3) secured by a junior lien on property of the estate that is subject to a lien.

### § 503. Allowance of administrative expenses

(b) After notice and a hearing, there shall be allowed, administrative expenses ... including—

(1)(A) the actual, necessary costs and expenses of preserving the estate, including wages, salaries, or commissions for services rendered after the commencement of the case ... ;

### § 507. Priorities

(a) The following expenses and claims have priority in the following order:

(1) First, administrative expenses allowed under section 503(b) ...

### § 1129. Confirmation of plan

(a) The court shall confirm a plan only if all of the following requirements are met:

* * *

(9) Except to the extent that the holder of a particular claim has agreed to a different treatment of such claim, the plan provides that—

(A) with respect to a claim of a kind specified in section 507(a)(1) ... on the effective date of the plan, the holder of such claim will receive on account of such claim cash equal to the allowed amount of such claim; ... .

### § 364. Obtaining credit

(d) (1) The court, after notice and a hearing, may authorize the obtaining of credit or the incurring of debt secured by a senior or equal lien on property of the estate that is subject to a lien only if—

(A) the trustee is unable to obtain such credit otherwise; and

(B) there is adequate protection of the interest of the holder of the lien [that is made junior].

---

### ¶1504: Cross-collateralization

A pre-bankruptcy creditor might be ready to extend credit *if* the court will grant it security not only on the new, § 364 debtor-in-possession loan, but also on its pre-petition loan. That is, it might want to cross-collateralize, getting security for the new debt and its old pre-petition debt at the same time.

What if the bankrupt debtor and the new creditor seek cross-collateralization, arguing that it's the only chance to save the bankrupt from liquidation? The potential new creditor says it needs not just statutory super-priority but it needs to have its other pre-petition loans to the bankrupt secured by the bankrupt's remaining free assets. The debtor has approached other creditors and they won't make even a super-priority loan. The judge finds the evidence of creditor refusal to be credible: no one will lend with just super-priority, and without new financing the enterprise is doomed to switching over to chapter 7 for liquidation. Only super-priority with cross-collateralization has a chance. Should the judge permit cross-collateralization?

The Eleventh Circuit held that the Bankruptcy Code does not authorize cross-collateralization under § 364 and, given the extensive specification of priorities in the Code, a bankruptcy court should not imply a power to authorize cross-collateralization. Shapiro v. Saybrook Mfg. Co., 963 F.2d 1490 (11th Cir. 1992). Other courts have granted cross-collateralization.

Should the judge be wary if creditors won't make loans even with super-priority? With whose money would the bankrupt and the cross-collateralizing creditor be gambling?

## ¶1505: Using cash to operate the business

Sometimes the bankrupt is healthy enough so that it generates some cash from its operations because it no longer has to pay back creditors.

When a company issues secured debt covering, say, its inventory and accounts receivable, it will sell inventory. When it collects from its customer, it will have cash. Typically it will outside of bankruptcy have to pay some or all of that cash over to its financing creditor.

The bankrupt company doesn't as a general rule have to pay over that cash to its creditor. The general rule comes from the bankruptcy stay in § 362, barring all creditors from collecting on their debts. When the cash is generated from a secured asset, the cash is called "cash collateral."

The governance problem now is obvious: when stockholder-managers run their business riskily, they could maximize the upside chance and ignore the downside, because they'll be gambling with creditors' money, not with their own money.

The Code doesn't allow the bankrupt to spend this "cash collateral" automatically. The bankrupt must either get the consent of the affected secured creditor or must apply to the court. (§ 363(c).) The court would normally allow the bankrupt to spend the cash collateral only if the court believes that the secured creditor is adequately protected otherwise (usually because the other secured property is more than enough to be sure that the secured creditor will be paid back).

What if the bankrupt comes into cash that's not cash collateral? What if it wants to sell a major (unsecured) facility and then begin another business? Section 363 says that if the bankrupt will use, sell or lease its property out of the ordinary course of business, it shall do so only after notice and a hearing.[1]

---

[1] Bankruptcy Rules curtail the hearing as an automatic occurrence. They require notice, but only require a hearing if a creditor requests one. Bankruptcy Rules 2000(a)(2) and 6004.

## ¶1506: Displacing management with a trustee

While lawyers consider replacing the debtor-in-possession management with a trustee to be unusual, data on managerial turnover show that *informal* replacement *isn't* unusual. Nearly half of the directors of public bankrupts are gone by the end of the proceeding and common stock ownership becomes more concentrated. Stuart C. Gilson, *Bankruptcy, boards, banks, and blockholders: Evidence on changes in corporate ownership and control when firms default*, 27 Journal of Financial Economics 355 (1990). The turnover of CEO's of public firms that go into chapter 11 is even higher. Lynn M. LoPucki & William C. Whitford, *Corporate Governance in the Bankruptcy Reorganization of Large, Publicly Held Companies*, 141 U. Pa. L. Rev. 669, 751 (1993). Multiple explanations are available: the directors may be disgusted with failure, they may find a better company, etc. But the possibility of creditor pressure must also be a partial explanation.

CHAPTER 16

# THE LBO

A. The leveraged buyout
B. Margin regulations

..................................................................................................................

## A. The leveraged buyout

### ¶1601: LBO's and the prospect of fraudulent conveyance liability

Leveraged buyouts come in several transactional types, having common features: Cash from outside lenders (the leverage) is used to buy up equity from the existing stockholders of the company (the buyout). Sometimes the firm's own managers initiate the buyout; other times outsiders initiate the buyout. Either way, the firm's post-buyout managers usually hold a large portion (or all) of the firm's stock. In one usual financial structure, institutional lenders obtain a security interest in the firm's assets and the firm issues junk bonds for additional financing.

In one form of LBO, a new, empty company is formed by the target company's managers, with little in the way of assets contributed by the managers. The new company then borrows from the lender. The cash is used to buy up the stock of the target company, which becomes a subsidiary of the new company. The target company is then merged into the new company. The assets of the target company, when moved into the new company, are given as security to the original lenders. The steps need not occur in any particular order.

In a leading 1980s case applying the Uniform Fraudulent Conveyance Act, the court collapsed a complex leveraged buyout: the conveyance of the security was intended to hinder and delay creditors when it was knowable that the target firm would have little cash after the transaction, with the target firm probably rendered insolvent. That was sufficient to establish a fraudulent conveyance under § 7 of UFCA. United States v. Tabor Court Realty Corp., 803 F.2d 1288 (3d Cir. 1986), cert. denied sub nom. McClellan Realty Co. v. United States, 107 S.Ct. 3229 (1987). See generally *Fraudulent Conveyances and Leveraged Buyouts*, 43 Bus. Law. 1 (1987).

The organizers of the LBO expect the total value of the firm's securities, post-buyout, to exceed the pre-buyout value. How can the substance of the LBO—a purchase of a company's stock with a loan secured by the company's assets—be reconciled with efficient market theory and the Modigliani-Miller irrelevance hypotheses? Consider taxes, information, managerial incentives, and control.

The explanations for LBO's are several. The main ones are:

- Inside managers may understand that public markets are under-valuing the company. They buy when the price is low. In some cases, it's been alleged, they conditioned the market to value the firm low, because they released the most pessimistic information possible about the firm's prospects.
- By substituting debt with tax deductible interest for equity, the company reduces its tax bill, thereby increasing its private value.
- Some firms reinvest too much of their cash in expanding despite that they lack good new opportunities. An LBO, with its enormous debt obligation, inhibits the managers from unwarranted over-expansion.
- The managers, fearing an outside attack via a hostile takeover offer, launch a preemptive strike, taking the company private (and in their control), thereby eluding the grasp of the hostile offeror.
- The managers with a big equity stake in the LBO will work harder or, more plausibly since they already work long hours, make the tough but necessary decisions that they avoided when they weren't working for themselves.

How can the substance of an LBO be made doctrinally to be a fraudulent conveyance, which under § 9 of the UFCA allows the offended creditors to annul the obligation to the creditor who received a fraudulent conveyance? Pre-existing creditors of the LBO company (such as the bondholders in MetLife) face greater risks of not being paid. But how can they succeed in having the obligations of the firm under the new loans viewed as fraudulent conveyances? The doctrinal difficulty is that the objective, non-intentional, constructive fraud sections (§§ 4 and 6) require that (i) either the LBO company be insolvent or rendered insolvent by the transaction (§ 4) or have incurred debts beyond the debtor's ability to pay, *and* (ii) that there not be fair consideration in the transaction. One can readily imagine one or the other of the *first* standards being met in an LBO, because LBO's entail insolvency sometimes and lots of debt usually. But both sections *also* require that the transaction not involve fair consideration, and the new lender would seem to be giving fair consideration. The new lender after all writes out a big check when it lends the debtor, the LBO firm, the money.

Section 3 of UFCA says something about fair consideration:

**Fair consideration.** Fair consideration is given for property, or obligation,
 (a) When in exchange for such property, or obligation, as a fair equivalent therefor, and in good faith, property is conveyed or an antecedent debt is satisfied, or
 (b) When such property, or obligation is received in good faith to secure a present advance or antecedent debt in amount not disproportionately small as compared with the value of the property, or obligation obtained.

An LBO lender writes a check to the company in return for the company's obligation to re-pay the lender. This check seems to be fair consideration, thereby taking the transaction out from the objective, constructive UFCA sections. Thus at first it would seem that those seeking to characterize the LBO as a fraudulent conveyance would have to turn to the subjective, actual fraud section, § 7, which doesn't require fair consideration, but does require actual intent to hinder, delay or defraud.

### ¶1602: United States v. Tabor Court Realty Corp., 803 F.2d 1288 (3d Cir. 1986)

We have consolidated appeals from litigation involving one of America's largest anthracite coal producers .... Ultimately, we have to decide whether the court erred in entering judgment in favor of the United States in reducing to judgment certain federal corporate tax assessments made against the coal producers, in determining the priority of the government liens, and in permitting foreclosure on the liens. To reach these questions, however, we must examine a very intricate leveraged buy-out and decide whether mortgages given in the transaction were fraudulent conveyances within the meaning of the constructive and intentional fraud sections of the Pennsylvania Uniform Fraudulent Conveyance Act (UFCA) ... and if so, whether a later assignment of the mortgages was void as against creditors. [We so hold.]

... We are told that this case represents the first significant application of the UFCA to leveraged buy-out financing.

We will address [these] issues presented by the appellants and an amicus curiae, the National Commercial Finance Association, and by the United States and a trustee in bankruptcy as cross appellants:

- whether the court erred in applying the UFCA to a leveraged buy-out;
- whether the court erred in "collapsing" two separate loans for the leveraged buy-out into one transaction;
- whether the court erred in holding that the mortgages placed by the guarantors were invalid for lack of fair consideration;

\* \* \*

We will summarize a very complex factual situation and then discuss these issues seriatim.

### I.

These appeals arise from an action by the United States to reduce to judgment delinquent federal income taxes, interest, and penalties assessed and accrued against Raymond Colliery Co., Inc. and its subsidiaries (the Raymond Group) for the fiscal years of June 30, 1966 through June 30, 1973 and to reduce to judgment similarly assessed taxes owed by Great American Coal Co., Inc. and its subsidiaries for the fiscal year ending June 30, 1975.

* * *

Raymond Colliery, [at first a family-owned corporation], owned over 30,000 acres of land in Lackawanna and Luzerne counties in Pennsylvania and was one of the largest anthracite coal producers in the country ... . Lurking in the background of the financial problems present here are two important components of the current industrial scene: first, the depressed economy attending anthracite mining in Lackawanna and Luzerne Counties, the heartland of this industry; and second, the Pennsylvania Department of Environmental Resources' 1967 order directing Blue Coal to reduce the amount of pollutants it discharged into public waterways in the course of its deep mining operations, necessitating a fundamental change from deep mining to strip or surface mining.

[Durkin was Raymond's president. He acquired an option to buy stock from the owners of Raymond. But] Durkin had trouble in raising the necessary financing to exercise his option. He sought help from the Central States Pension Fund of the International Brotherhood of Teamsters and also from the Mellon Bank of Pittsburgh. Mellon concluded that [Raymond] was a bad financial risk. Moreover, both Mellon and Central States held extensive discussions with Durkin's counsel concerning the legality of encumbering Raymond's assets for the purpose of obtaining the loan, a loan which was not to be used to repay creditors but rather to buy out Raymond's stockholders.

After other unsuccessful attempts to obtain financing for the purchase, Durkin incorporated a holding company, Great American, and assigned to it his option to purchase Raymond's stock. Although the litigation in the district court was far-reaching, most of the central issues have their genesis in 1973 when the Raymond Group was sold to Durkin in a leveraged buy-out through the vehicle of Great American.

A leveraged buy-out is not a legal term of art. It is a shorthand expression describing a business practice wherein a company is sold to a small number of investors, typically including members of the company's management, under financial arrangements in which there is a minimum amount of equity and a maximum amount of debt. The financing typically provides for a substantial return of investment capital by means of mortgages or high risk bonds, popularly known as "junk bonds." The predicate transaction here fits the popular notion of a leveraged buy-out. Shareholders of the Raymond Group sold the corporation to a small group of investors headed by Raymond's president [Durkin]; these investors borrowed substantially all of the purchase price at an extremely high rate of interest secured by mortgages on the assets of the selling company and its subsidiaries and those of additional entities that guaranteed repayment.

To effectuate the buy-out, Great American obtained a loan commitment from Institutional Investors Trust on July 24, 1973, in the amount of $8,530,000. The 1973 interrelationship among the many creditors of the Raymond Group, and the sale to Great American—a seemingly empty corporation which was able to perform the buy-out only on the strength of the massive loan from IIT—forms the backdrop for the relevancy of the Pennsylvania Uniform Fraudulent Conveyance Act, one of the critical legal questions presented for our decision.

Durkin obtained the financing through one of his two partners in Great American.[1] [Many of the assets of Raymond and its subsidiaries were given as security for the buy-out loan from IIT.] We must decide whether the borrowers' mortgages were invalid under the UFCA and whether there was consideration for the guarantors' mortgages.

\* \* \*

[IIT lent money to Raymond, but t]he exchange of money and notes did not stop with IIT's advances to [Raymond]. Upon receipt of the IIT loan proceeds, [Raymond] immediately transferred a total of $4,085,000 to [Durkin's company,] Great American. In return, Great American issued to each borrowing company an unsecured promissory note with the same interest terms as those of the IIT loan agreement. In addition to the proceeds of the IIT loan, Great American borrowed other funds to acquire the purchase price for Raymond's stock[, which Raymond's other stockholders sold to Great American].

When the financial dust settled after the closing on November 26, 1973, this was the situation at Raymond: Great American paid $6.7 million to purchase Raymond's stock, the shareholders receiving $6.2 million in cash and a $500,000 note; at least $4.8 million of this amount was obtained by mortgaging Raymond's assets.

Notwithstanding the cozy accommodations for the selling stockholders, the financial environment of the Raymond Group at the time of the sale was somewhat precarious. At the time of the closing, Raymond had multi-million dollar liabilities for federal income taxes, trade accounts, pension fund contributions, strip mining and

---

[1] Durkin owned 40% of Great American, Hyman Green owned 10%, and James R. Hoffa, Jr. owned the remaining 50%. Durkin and Green concealed Hoffa's ownership interest in Great American from IIT. Hoffa apparently came into the picture when Durkin attempted to borrow money from the Central States Pension Fund of the International Brotherhood of Teamsters to finance the purchase.

back-filling obligations, and municipal real estate taxes. The district court calculated that the Raymond Group's existing debts amounted to at least $20 million on November 26, 1983.

Under Durkin's control after the buy-out, Raymond's condition further deteriorated. Following the closing the Raymond Group lacked the funds to pay its routine operating expenses, including those for materials, supplies, telephone, and other utilities. It was also unable to pay its delinquent and current real estate taxes. Within two months of the closing, [its] deep mining operations ... were shut down; within six months of the closing, the Raymond Group ceased all strip mining operations. Consequently, the Raymond Group could not fulfill its existing coal contracts and became liable for damages for breach of contract. The plaintiffs in the breach of contract actions exercised their right of set-off against accounts they owed the Raymond Group. Within seven months of the closing, the Commonwealth of Pennsylvania and the Anthracite Health & Welfare Fund sued the Raymond Group for its failures to fulfill back-filling requirements in the strip mining operations and to pay contributions to the Health & Welfare Fund. This litigation resulted in injunctions against the Raymond Group companies which prevented them from moving or selling their equipment until their obligations were satisfied ... .

[Raymond's properties were later sold, but the central question in the subsequent lawsuit by the United States was whether the first loans by IIT were fraudulent conveyances.]

This, then, constitutes a summary of the adjudicative facts that undergird the litigation below and the appeals before us.

## II.

The instant action was commenced by the United States on December 12, 1980 to reduce to judgment certain corporate federal tax assessments made against the Raymond Group and Great American. The government sought to assert the priority of its tax liens and to foreclose against the property that Raymond had owned at the time of the assessments as well as against properties currently owned by Raymond. The United States argued that the IIT mortgages executed in November 1973 should be set aside under the Uniform Fraudulent Conveyance Act and further that the purported assignment of these mortgages to [the new purchasers] should be voided because at the inception [they] had purchased the mortgages with knowledge that they had been fraudulently conveyed.

... [T]he district court ... concluded, inter alia, that the mortgages given by the Raymond Group to IIT on November 26, 1973 were fraudulent conveyances within the meaning of the constructive and intentional fraud sections of the Pennsylvania Uniform Fraudulent Conveyance Act ....

[Raymond] appealed. As heretofore stated, all these mortgages, subsequently invalidated by the district court, had been granted to IIT on November 26, 1973 .... For the purpose of this appeal, we shall refer to the Raymond Group as "appellants," or "[the purchaser]."

* * *

### III.

[The purchaser] initially challenges the district court's application of the Pennsylvania Uniform Fraudulent Conveyance Act (UFCA) ... to the leveraged buy-out made by IIT to the mortgagors .... The district court determined that IIT lacked good faith in the transaction because it knew, or should have known, that the money it lent the mortgagors was used, in part, to finance the purchase of stock from the mortgagors' shareholders, and that as a consequence of the loan, IIT and its assignees obtained a secured position in the mortgagors' property to the detriment of creditors .... .

In applying section [3(a)] of the UFCA,[2] the district court stated:

> The initial question ... is whether the transferee, IIT, transferred its loan proceeds in good faith .... IIT knew or strongly suspected that the imposition of the loan obligations secured by the mortgages and guarantee mortgages would probably render insolvent both the Raymond Group and each individual member thereof. In addition, *IIT was fully aware that no individual member of the Raymond Group would receive fair consideration within the meaning of the Act in exchange for the loan obligations to IIT.* Thus, we conclude that IIT does not meet the standard of good faith under Section [3(a)] of the Act ....

565 F. Supp. at 574.

[The purchaser] argues that "the only reasonable and proper application of the good faith criteria as it applies to the lender in structuring a loan is one which looks to the lender's motives as opposed to his knowledge." Br. for appellants at 17. [It] argues that good faith is satisfied when "the lender acted in an arms-length transaction without ulterior motive or collusion with the debtor to the detriment of creditors." Id.

Section [4] of the UFCA is a "constructive fraud" provision. It establishes that a conveyance made by a person "who is or will be thereby rendered insolvent, is fraudulent as to creditors, without regard to his actual intent, if the conveyance is made ... without a fair consideration." [UFCA, § 4.] Section [3] defines fair consideration as an exchange of a "fair equivalent ... in good faith." Because section [4] excludes an examination of intent, it follows that "good faith" must be something other than intent; because section [4] also focuses on insolvency, knowledge of insolvency is a rational interpretation of the statutory language of lack of "good faith." [The purchaser] would

---

[2] [Citations are to the UFCA sections, not the court's citations to Pennsylvania's codification.— Roe.]

have us adopt "without ulterior motive or collusion with the debtor to the detriment of creditors" as the good faith standard. We are uneasy with such a standard because these words came very close to describing intent.

Surprisingly, few courts have considered this issue. [One] court held [in 1939] that because a transferee had no knowledge of the transferor's insolvency, it could not justify a finding of bad faith, implying that a showing of such knowledge would support a finding of bad faith. In [another, 1971 decision, a court] set forth a number of factors to be considered in determining good faith: 1) honest belief in the propriety of the activities in question; 2) no intent to take unconscionable advantage of others; and 3) no intent to, or knowledge of the fact that the activities in question will, hinder, delay, or defraud others. Where "any one of these factors is absent, lack of good faith is established and the conveyance fails."

We have decided that the district court reached the right conclusion here for the right reasons. It determined that IIT did not act in good faith because it was aware, first, that the exchange would render Raymond insolvent, and second, that no member of the Raymond Group would [when the entire set of contemplated transactions was completed] receive fair consideration. We believe that this determination is consistent with the statute and case law.

[The purchaser] and amicus curiae also argue that as a general rule the UFCA should not be applied to leveraged buy-outs. They contend that the UFCA, which was passed in 1924, was never meant to apply to a complicated transaction such as a leveraged buy-out. The Act's broad language, however, extends to any "conveyance" which is defined as "every payment of money ... and also the creation of any lien or incumbrance." [UFCA, § 1.] This broad sweep does not justify exclusion of a particular transaction such as a leveraged buy-out simply because it is innovative or complicated. If the UFCA is not to be applied to leveraged buy-outs, it should be for the state legislatures, not the courts, to decide.

In addition, although appellants' and amicus curiae's arguments against general application of the Act to leveraged buy-outs are not without some force, the application of fraudulent conveyance law to certain leveraged buy-outs is not clearly bad public policy.[3] In any event, the circumstances of this case justify application .... In

---

[3] A major premise of the policy arguments opposing application of fraudulent conveyance law to leveraged buy-outs is that such transactions often benefit creditors and that the application of fraudulent conveyance law to buy-outs will deter them in the future. See Baird and Jackson, Fraudulent Conveyance Law and Its Proper Domain, 38 Vand. L. Rev. 829, 855 (1985). An equally important premise is that creditors can protect themselves from undesirable leveraged buy-outs by altering the terms of their credit contracts. Id. at 835. This second premise ignores, however, cases such as this one in which the major creditors (in this instance the United States and certain Pennsylvania municipalities) are involuntary and do not become creditors by virtue of a contract. The second premise also ignores the possibility that the creditors attacking the leveraged buy-out (such as many of the creditors in this case) became creditors before leveraged buy-outs became a common financing technique and thus may not have anticipated such leveraged transactions so as to have been able to adequately protect themselves by contract. These possi-

the instant case, ... the severe economic circumstances in which the Raymond Group found itself, the obligation, without benefit, incurred by the Raymond Group, and the small number of shareholders benefitted by the transaction suggest that the transaction was not entered in the ordinary course, that fair consideration was not exchanged, and that the transaction was anything but unsuspicious. The policy arguments set forth in opposition to the application of fraudulent conveyance law to leveraged buy-outs do not justify the exemption of transactions such as this.

IV.

\* \* \*

E.

[The purchaser] next contends that the district court erred in not crediting [it] for that portion of the IIT loan that was not passed through to Raymond's shareholders: although "the District Court acknowledged that $2,915,000, or approximately 42 percent, of the IIT loan proceeds originally went for the benefit of ... [prior] creditors, IIT and McClellan received no credit therefor in regard to the partial validity of their liens." Br. for appellants at 28. [The purchaser] argues the district court determined that "the wrong committed upon the creditors ... [was] the diversion of some 58 percent of the loan proceeds from the IIT loan to [Raymond's] shareholders." Id. at 29. It concludes that to invalidate the entire mortgage would be to provide Raymond's creditors with a "double recovery." Id. at 28. We understand the dissent to agree with [the purchaser's] analysis when noting that "'creditors have causes of action in fraudulent conveyance law only to the extent they have been damaged.'" Dissenting typescript at ___ (citations omitted).

[The purchaser] and, by implication, the dissent mischaracterize the district court's findings and conclusions regarding the fraudulent nature of the IIT loans. The district court did not determine that the loan transaction was only partially—or, to use [the purchaser's] formulation, 58%—fraudulent. Nor did the district court conclude that Raymond's creditors had been wronged by only a portion of the transaction. Instead, the district court stated that:

> [The purchaser's] argument rests on the incorrect assumption that some portions of the IIT mortgages are valid as against the Creditors. In Gleneagles I, this Court found that IIT and Durkin engaged in an intentionally fraudulent transaction on November 26, 1973. The IIT mortgages are therefore invalid in their entirety as to creditors. In essence, the district court ruled that the aggregate transaction was

---

bilities suggest that Baird and Jackson's broad proscription against application of fraudulent conveyance law to leveraged buy-outs may not be unambiguously correct.

fraudulent, notwithstanding the fact that a portion of the loan proceeds was allegedly used to pay existing creditors.

This determination is bolstered by the fact that most of the $2,915,000 allegedly paid to the benefit of Raymond's creditors went to only one creditor—Chemical Bank. In Gleneagles I, the district court found that $2,186,247 of the IIT loan proceeds were paid to Chemical Bank in satisfaction of the mortgage that Raymond had taken to purchase ... [a Raymond subsidiary.] The purpose of this payment is of critical significance:

> [Raymond's selling shareholders] required satisfaction of the Chemical Bank mortgage as a condition of the sale of their Raymond Colliery stock at least in part because [one of the selling shareholders] had personally guaranteed repayment of that loan .... [The purchaser] does not challenge this finding on appeal. Thus, of the $2.9 million allegedly paid to benefit Raymond's creditors, $2.2 million were actually intended to benefit Raymond's shareholders and to satisfy a condition for the sale. The remaining amounts allegedly paid to benefit Raymond's creditors were applied to the closing costs of the transaction. See id. at 570 (finding 133).

On this record, the district court's characterization of the transaction as a whole as fraudulent cannot reasonably be disputed. The court's consequent determination that the "IIT mortgages are ... invalid in their entirety as to creditors" is supported by precedent ... .

The district court determined that "[t]he Creditors ... would not be placed in the same or similar position which they held with respect to the Raymond Group in 1973 merely by replacing the $4,085,500 of IIT loan proceeds that were misused on November 26, 1973." Gleneagles III, 584 F. Supp. at 681. We agree with the district court[.]

For the above reasons, therefore, we will not disturb the district court's determination that [the purchaser] is not entitled to a "lien superior to all other creditors" as the assignee of all or part of the IIT mortgages.

\* \* \*

## V.

[The purchaser], joined by the amicus, next argues that the district court erred "by collapsing two separate loans into one transaction." Br. for appellants at 30. The loan arrangement was a two-part process: the loan proceeds went from IIT to the borrowing Raymond Group companies, which immediately turned the funds over to Great American, which used the funds for the buy-out. [The purchaser] contends that the district court erred by not passing on the fairness of the transaction between IIT and the Raymond Group mortgagors ... .

Contrary to [the purchaser's] contentions, the district court did examine this element of the transaction, stating "[W]e find that the obligations incurred by the Raymond Group and its individual members to IIT were not supported by fair consideration. The mortgages and guarantee mortgages to secure these obligations were also not supported by fair consideration." Gleneagles I, 565 F. Supp. at 577 (emphasis supplied).

Admittedly, in the course of its determination that the IIT-Raymond Group transaction was without fair consideration under section [3(a)], the court looked beyond the exchange of funds between IIT and the Raymond Group. But there was reason for this. The two exchanges were part of one integrated transaction. As the court concluded: "[t]he $4,085,000 in IIT loan proceeds which were lent immediately by the borrowing companies to Great American were merely passed through the borrowers to Great American and ultimately to the selling stockholders and cannot be deemed consideration received by the borrowing companies." Id. at 575.

The district court's factual findings support its treatment of the IIT-Raymond Group-Great American transaction as a single transaction. For example, Durkin, president of Great American, solicited financing from IIT for the purchase. Id. at 566 (finding 70). The loan negotiations included representatives of all three parties. Id. at 567 (findings 83–87). The first closing was aborted by IIT's counsel because of, inter alia, concern about "unknown individuals" involved with Great American. Id. at 567–68 (finding 89(a)). The $7 million loaned by IIT to the borrowing companies was "immediately placed in an escrow account"; "simultaneously" with the receipt of the IIT proceeds, the borrowing companies loaned Great American the cash for the buyout and received in return "an unsecured note promising to repay the loans to the borrowing companies on the same terms and at the same interest rate as pertained to the loans to the borrowing companies from IIT." Id. at 570 (findings 127–29).

Appellant cannot seriously challenge these findings of fact. We are satisfied with the district court's conclusion that the funds "merely passed through the borrowers to Great American." This necessitates our agreement with the district court's conclusion that, for purposes of determining IIT's knowledge of the use of the proceeds under section [3(a)], there was one integral transaction.[4]

VI.

[The purchaser] next faults the district court's determination that the Raymond Group was rendered insolvent by "the IIT transaction and the instantaneous payment

---

[4] Admittedly, [the purchaser's] and amicus' arguments could have some validity where the lender is unaware of the use to which loan proceeds are to be put. This is not the case here. IIT was intimately involved with the formulation of the agreement whereby the proceeds of its loan were funneled into the hands of the purchasers of the stock of a corporation that was near insolvency. Try as they might to distance themselves from the transaction now, they cannot rewrite history.

to the selling stockholders of a substantial portion of the IIT loan in exchange for their stock." Gleneagles I, 565 F. Supp. at 580 ....

A reasonable construction of the ... statutory definition of insolvency indicates that it not only encompasses insolvency in the bankruptcy sense[,] i.e.[,] deficit net worth, but also includes a condition wherein a debtor has insufficient presently salable assets to pay existing debts as they mature ... .

We conclude that [the purchaser] has not demonstrated that this finding [of insolvency] was clearly erroneous ....

## VII.

[The purchaser] next argues that the district court erred in holding that the mortgages were invalid under section [7] of the UFCA ....

As distinguished from the "constructive fraud" sections of the UFCA discussed supra, section [7] invalidates conveyances made with an intent to defraud creditors: "Every conveyance made and every obligation incurred with actual intent, as distinguished from intent presumed in law, to hinder, delay, or defraud either present or future creditors, is fraudulent as to both present and future creditors." [UFCA, § 7.] Under Pennsylvania law, an intent to hinder, delay, or defraud creditors may be inferred from transfers in which consideration is lacking and where the transferor and transferee have knowledge of the claims of creditors and know that the creditors cannot be paid. Direct evidence is not necessary to prove "actual intent."

\* \* \*

### B.

Appellant also objects to the district court's statement that "[i]f the parties could have foreseen the effect on creditors resulting from the assumption of the IIT obligation by the Raymond Group ... the parties must be deemed to have intended the same." 565 F. Supp. at 581 ... . We are satisfied that this principle supports the district court's conclusion.

\* \* \*

---

## ¶1603: Questions on *Gleneagles*

1. When the lender made the LBO loan to Raymond, the borrower's obligations rose by the amount of the loan and its assets rose by the amount of the loan. The loan did *not* thereby render the debtor any more insolvent than it was before the loan. What then is the basic fraudulent conveyance problem?

2. Moreover, where is the unfair consideration for the loan? The lender lent, the debtor incurred an obligation, and the debtor received fresh cash. The consideration for the obligation to repay seems to be fair.

But what happens to the cash after the loan is made? Is the court collapsing the transaction?

    a. LBO lender lends to the company on fair terms.
    b. The lender gets a security interest in the company's property.
    c. Then the company buys back common stock with the loan proceeds.

Steps a and b are on fair terms. Is the court collapsing a and <u>c</u>? The bank lends, and money goes out to stockholders. Once a and c are collapsed, what is left is b, which standing alone suggests that the corporation failed to *receive* fair consideration, although the lender *gave* fair consideration.

Still, from the *lender's* perspective is the consideration unfair? Does the lender get a special, unfair deal? Or is it that from the *borrower's* perspective the entire deal (a *plus* c) yields the borrower unfair consideration?

3. Isn't the court making the LBO/lender the watchdog, the gatekeeper for the benefit of non-bargain creditors, such as the tax collector, trade creditors, tort claimants, and financial creditors who lent before the LBO became popular? Consider this description of one LBO:

> The buyout of Kaiser Steel Corporation in 1984 illustrates the potential significance of involuntary creditors. ... Payments to stockholders were financed with cash on hand and a new $100 million loan from Citibank, secured by substantially all the company's assets. However, at closing, the company had total liabilities of approximately $750 million, of which nearly $600 million (80%) was owed to retired employees for vested medical and pension benefits. Stockholders voted to approve the LBO. The approval of retired employees was not sought. Whether they had standing to challenge the transaction prior to closing was unclear in 1984, though other employee groups have since been allowed to mount such challenges ... .
>
> By the time Kaiser filed under Chapter 11 in 1987, Citibank had been repaid. The company's largest remaining creditors were retired employees and the Pension Benefit Guaranty Corporation ... . [They] had [not] approved the LBO, nor was the PBGC even a creditor at the time of the buyout.

Timothy A. Luehrman & Lance L. Hirt, *Highly Leveraged Transactions and Fraudulent Conveyance Law*, 6 J. App. Corp. Fin. 104, 109 (1993).

4. If you represent a lender in a future LBO, what do you want to do? Document the solvency of the company at the time of the loan? Document the company's ability to pay back its preexisting loans after the LBO transaction takes place? Document the fairness to the corporation of the entire transaction? Avoid some marginal, highly risky LBO's?

5. Will some stockholders be ready to engage in an LBO even if it's to the detriment of the corporation? Keep in mind that the net benefit to a stockholder differs from the benefit to a corporation. A stockholder may prefer that the firm declare a divi-

dend, even if the firm is worse off, because the dividend ends up in the stockholder's pocket. Thus the cashed-out stockholders have a reason to prefer dividends (and LBO's that buy them out) even if the company is made worse off.

But could new manager-stockholders sometimes have a similar motivation? If they prefer to run the new company, especially if they need put up little or no money of their own in the LBO, would they prefer the LBO result, even if the company is worse off? But then why would the LBO financiers participate? Would it be that with appropriate security, priority, and a high enough interest rate, their loan is expected to be profitable, but the firm would be made worse off?

But how can all of these people be better off and the firm worse off? Is it that more risk is put on the shoulders of the preexisting creditors? And isn't that just what fraudulent conveyance law is designed to regulate, some of the time?

Keep in mind that just because it's possible that the corporation is made worse off does not mean that it always is made worse off.

6. If a contract creditor anticipated the risk of an LBO that would make it worse off, what should it do in its loan agreement?

7. The proceeds of the LBO loan were partly used to pay off Chemical Bank, a preexisting creditor. To that extent, are the other preexisting creditors of Raymond harmed by the LBO loan?

8. Lender lends $3 million to Debtor when Debtor is insolvent. Debtor uses all the proceeds of the $3 million loan to pay off a preexisting creditor, Chemical Bank. Are other creditors of the Debtor harmed by the transaction? Under the theories in *Tabor Court* (sometimes called *Gleneagles*), is the loan a fraudulent conveyance? Does the Debtor receive fair consideration? If the Lender knew the Debtor would use the Lender's loan to pay $3 million to the preexisting creditor, would the new Lender be acting in good faith? If the theory of *Gleneagles* collapses the transactions, why shouldn't the court collapse the pay-off to a preexisting creditor as well?

9. If the new lenders wrote a check directly to Chemical Bank, which then assigned their note and security arrangement to the new lender, would that be a fraudulent conveyance? Under a "collapsed view" of the actual transaction, how would one view the new lender lending to the firm, with the firm then taking the proceeds to pay off Chemical? Isn't the "collapsed view" that the new lender is just buying the loan up from Chemical?

10. In related litigation, the IRS also sought to have the monies transferred to the old stockholders in the buyback found to be a fraudulent conveyance. (The IRS also sought to recover directly, and on behalf of the corporation apparently, on related theories of a breach of duty of care, an illegal dividend, and a breach of the duty of loyalty to creditors of an insolvent corporation.) The lawsuit was settled for $5 million. Should IIT's successors have received a "credit" for this $5 million settlement?

Many LBO's have the promoters buying back stock from public stockholders. How should the buyback from the public stockholders be analyzed under the fraudulent conveyance laws? The next decision deals with a public buyback.

11. Fraudulent conveyance law comes in three major flavors in the United States, each descending from the statute of 13 Elizabeth. The first, the Uniform Fraudulent Conveyance Act, has been around for decades. An updated version, the Uniform Fraudulent Transfer Act, is now making headway in some states. In bankruptcy, the trustee, under § 544, can use these state laws to annul fraudulently incurred corporate debts or recover fraudulently conveyed property. The trustee can also use the Bankruptcy Code's version of fraudulent conveyance law, which appears in § 548 and § 550 of the Code. Slight language differences exist among the three main versions. The typical reason for a trustee to use state law through § 544, instead of § 548 directly is that the state law statute of limitations is often longer than the one-year limit for § 548.

---

## ¶1604: Wieboldt Stores, Inc. v. Jerome M. Schottenstein, 94 Bankr. 488 (Bankr. N.D. Ill. 1988)

JAMES F. HOLDERMAN, District Judge:

Wieboldt Stores, Inc. ("Wieboldt") filed this action on September 18, 1987 under the federal bankruptcy laws, 11 U.S.C. §§ 101 et seq., the state fraudulent conveyance laws, Ill. Rev. Stat. ch. 59, § 4, and the Illinois Business Corporation Act, Ill. Rev. Stat. ch. 32, para. 1.01 et seq. Pending before the court are numerous motions to dismiss this action under Rules 9(b), 12(b)(2), 12(b)(6) and 19 of the Federal Rules of Civil Procedure.

### I. INTRODUCTION

Wieboldt's complaint against the defendants concerns the events and transactions surrounding a leveraged buyout ("LBO") of Wieboldt by WSI Acquisition Corporation ("WSI"). WSI, a corporation formed solely for the purpose of acquiring Wieboldt, borrowed funds from third-party lenders and delivered the proceeds to the shareholders in return for their shares. Wieboldt thereafter pledged certain of its assets to the LBO lenders to secure repayment of the loan.

The LBO reduced the assets available to Wieboldt's creditors. Wieboldt contends that, after the buyout was complete, Wieboldt's debt had increased by millions of dollars, and the proceeds made available by the LBO lenders were paid out to Wieboldt's then existing shareholders and did not accrue to the benefit of the corporation. Wieboldt's alleged insolvency after the LBO left Wieboldt with insufficient unencumbered assets to sustain its business and ensure payment to its unsecured creditors. Wieboldt therefore commenced this action on behalf of itself and its unsecured creditors, seeking to avoid the transactions constituting the LBO on the grounds that they are fraudulent under federal and state fraudulent conveyance laws.

## II. FACTS

### A. PARTIES

#### 1. Wieboldt

... In 1982 Wieboldt's business was operated out of twelve stores and one distribution center in the Chicago metropolitan area .... Its stock was publicly traded on the New York Stock Exchange.

During the 1970s, demographic changes in Wieboldt's markets, increased competition from discount operations, and poor management caused Wieboldt's business to decline ....

#### 2. Defendants

Wieboldt brings this action against 119 defendants. These defendants can be grouped into three non-exclusive categories: (1) controlling shareholders, officers and directors; (2) other shareholders of Wieboldt's common stock who owned and tendered more than 1,000 shares in response to the tender offer ("Schedule A shareholders"); and (3) entities which loaned money to fund the tender offer.

##### a. Controlling Shareholders, Officers and Directors

The individuals and entities who controlled Wieboldt in 1982 became controlling shareholders as a direct or indirect result of a 1982 takeover effort .... Jerome Schottenstein [and related parties acquired a major block of Wieboldt stock] (collectively referred to as the "Schottenstein interests") ... . [The] Schottenstein interests and [other connected parties] (collectively referred to as the "Trump interests" [not Donald—Roe]) each owned approximately 15 percent of Wieboldt's then outstanding shares and became Wieboldt's controlling shareholders.[5]

Wieboldt's Board of Directors consisted of nine individuals. In late 1982, Mr. Schottenstein became the Chairman of the Board [and nominated several directors, who were elected].

---

[5] The Trump brothers, MBT Corporation, Mr. Schottenstein and the Schottenstein affiliates are collectively referred to in this opinion as "controlling shareholders."

### b. Schedule A Shareholders

In addition to the Schottenstein and Trump interests, Wieboldt had a number of shareholders as of December 20, 1985 who owned more than 1,000 shares of Wieboldt's common stock. Wieboldt has listed these shareholders and the number of shares that they held on that date on a schedule which they have appended to their complaint ("Schedule A"). ...

### c. The LBO Lenders and Related Entities

On November 20, 1985 WSI commenced a tender offer for all outstanding shares of Wieboldt's common stock, for all of Wieboldt's outstanding shares of preferred stock, and for all outstanding options to purchase Wieboldt's stock. The tender offer was financed through three related financial transactions between Wieboldt and certain lenders and affiliated parties. These three transactions effected the LBO of Wieboldt.

[The plaintiffs have] included as defendants in this action four of the entities which were involved in these financial transactions [as lenders, including several banks, finance companies,] and General Electric Credit Corporation ("GECC").[6] ...

## B. THE TENDER OFFER AND RELATED TRANSACTIONS

By January, 1985 Wieboldt's financial health had declined to the point at which the company was no longer able to meet its obligations as they came due. On January 23, 1985 WSI sent a letter to Mr. Schottenstein in which WSI proposed a possible tender offer for Wieboldt common stock at $13.50 per share. The following day, Mr. Schottenstein informed Wieboldt's Board of Directors of the WSI proposal and the Board agreed to cooperate with WSI in evaluating the financial and operating records of the company. WSI proceeded to seek financing ... .

During 1985 it became apparent to Wieboldt's Board that WSI would accomplish its tender offer by means of an LBO through which WSI would pledge substantially all of Wieboldt's assets, including the company's fee and leasehold real estate assets, as collateral. Many of these real estate assets already served as collateral ... [to some of Wieboldt's] bank creditors. Wieboldt was at least partially in default on these obligations at the time of the LBO.

\* \* \*

... [B]y October, 1985 [the LBO lenders] had each agreed to fund WSI's tender offer, and each knew of the other's loan or credit commitments. These lenders were aware that WSI intended to use the proceeds of the financing commitments to (1) pur-

---

[6] These entities are collectively referred to in this opinion as "State Street defendants."

chase tendered shares of Wieboldt stock; (2) [to buy back Wieboldt's outstanding] Wieboldt stock options; or (3) eliminate [some of Wieboldt's bank] loan obligations.

The Board of Directors was fully aware of the progress of WSI's negotiations. The Board understood that WSI intended to finance the tender offer by pledging a substantial portion of Wieboldt's assets to its lenders, and that WSI did not intend to use any of its own funds or the funds of its shareholders to finance the acquisition. Moreover, although the Board initially believed that the tender offer would produce $10 million in working capital for the company, the members knew that the proceeds from the LBO lenders would not result in this additional working capital.

Nevertheless, in October, 1985 the Board directed ... Wieboldt's lawyers to work with WSI to effect the acquisition. During these negotiations, the Board learned that [one lender] would provide financing for the tender offer *only if Wieboldt would provide a statement from a nationally recognized accounting firm stating that Wieboldt was solvent and a going concern prior to the planned acquisition and would be solvent and a going concern after the acquisition.*[7] [However Wieboldt management] informed WSI that Wieboldt would only continue cooperating in the LBO if [the lender] agreed not to require this solvency certificate. [The lender] acceded to Wieboldt's demand and no solvency certificate was ever provided to [the lender] on Wieboldt's behalf.

On November 18, 1985 Wieboldt's Board of Directors voted to approve WSI's tender offer, and on November 20, 1985 WSI announced its offer to purchase Wieboldt stock for $13.50 per share.[8] By December 20, 1985 the tender offer was complete and WSI had acquired ownership of Wieboldt through its purchase of 99 percent of Wieboldt's stock at a total price of $38,462,164.00. All of the funds WSI used to purchase the tendered shares were provided by [the lenders]. After the LBO,

1. [Some of] Wieboldt's ... property was [sold];
2. Substantially all of Wieboldt's remaining real estate holdings were subject to first or second mortgages to secure the [LBO] loans; and
3. Wieboldt's customer credit card accounts were conveyed to GECC and Wieboldt's accounts receivable were pledged to GECC as security under the GECC accounts purchase agreement.

In addition, Wieboldt became liable to [an LBO lender] on an amended note in the amount of approximately $32.5 million. Wieboldt did not receive any amount of working capital as a direct result of the LBO.

---

[7] [Why would the lender so insist, even if the lender expected to get, say, good security? Could the lender's counsel have analyzed the *Gleneagles* situation carefully? If so, what advice would counsel give to LBO lenders?—Roe.]

[8] Approximately 1,900 shareholders held the 2,765,574 shares of Wieboldt common stock that were outstanding on that date. As a result of the offer, Mr. Schottenstein and his affiliates tendered at least 416,958 shares and received $5,628,933.00 from WSI. [The Trump interests] received $6,480,972.00 from WSI. ...

On September 24, 1986 certain of Wieboldt's creditors commenced an involuntary liquidation proceeding against Wieboldt under Chapter 7 of the United States Bankruptcy Code ("the Code"). On the same day, Wieboldt filed a voluntary reorganization proceeding pursuant to Chapter 11 of the Code ... .

C. THE COMPLAINT

In its complaint, Wieboldt alleges that WSI's tender offer and the resulting LBO was a fraudulent conveyance under the federal bankruptcy statute and the Illinois fraudulent conveyance laws. Counts I ... and V are based on Section 548(a)(1) of the Code, 11 U.S.C. § 548(a)(1). The essence of Count I is that the controlling and insider shareholders tendered their shares to WSI in response to WSI's offer with the actual intent to hinder, delay or defraud Wieboldt's unsecured creditors ... . Likewise, Count V, which names GECC as defendant, claims that the pledging of Wieboldt's customer charge card accounts and other accounts receivable violated Section 548(a)(1).

Counts II, IV, VI, and VII are based on Section 548(a)(2) ... . Counts II and VII allege that the tender offer to Wieboldt shareholders (including the Schedule A shareholders) was a fraudulent conveyance because it and the resulting LBO "rendered Wieboldt insolvent or too thinly capitalized to continue in the business in which it was engaged ... ." (Complaint Paras. 113, 139). Count IV claims that the sale of the One North State Street property violated Section 548(a)(2); Count VI claims that the pledging of Wieboldt's accounts receivable violated Section 548(a)(2).

Count VIII alleges that each of the three transactions (the tender offer, the sale of [the] property, and the pledging of the Wieboldt accounts receivable) violated the Illinois fraudulent conveyance law, § 4 ... . The essence of the claim in Count VIII is that *Wieboldt did not receive* fair consideration for the property it conveyed and was insolvent at the time of the conveyances. In each of Counts I through VIII, Wieboldt seeks to avoid the transfer of assets made to the named defendants as a result of the LBO.

\* \* \*

III. DISCUSSION

\* \* \*

C. RULE 12(b)(6) MOTIONS TO DISMISS

The controlling shareholders, insider shareholders, Schedule A shareholders, and the State Street defendants move to dismiss the complaint on the grounds that Wieboldt has failed to state a claim under either the federal or the state fraudulent conveyance laws ... .

\* \* \*

### 1. Applicability of Fraudulent Conveyance Law

Both the federal Bankruptcy Code and Illinois law protect creditors from transfers of property that are intended to impair a creditor's ability to enforce its rights to payment or that deplete a debtor's assets at a time when its financial condition is precarious. Modern fraudulent conveyance law derives from the English Statute of Elizabeth enacted in 1570, the substance of which has been ... enacted in American statutes prohibiting such transactions ... .

The controlling shareholders, insider shareholders, and some of the Schedule A shareholders argue that fraudulent conveyance laws do not apply to leveraged buyouts. These defendants argue (1) that applying fraudulent conveyance laws to public tender offers effectively allows creditors to insure themselves against subsequent mismanagement of the company; (2) that applying fraudulent conveyance laws to LBO transactions and thereby rendering them void severely restricts the usefulness of LBOs and results in great unfairness; and (3) that fraudulent conveyance laws were never intended to be used to prohibit or restrict public tender offers.

Although some support exists for defendants' arguments,[9] ... [t]he language of [the fraudulent conveyance] statutes in no way limits their application so as to exclude LBOs.

\* \* \*

### 2. The Structure of the Transaction

Although the court finds that the fraudulent conveyance laws generally [apply,] ... certain defendants argue ... that they are protected by the literal language of Section 548 of the Code and the "good faith transferee for value" rule in Section 550.[10] They contend, initially, that they did not receive Wieboldt property during the tender offer and, secondarily, that, even if they received Wieboldt property, they tendered their

---

[9] See, e.g., Baird & Jackson, "Fraudulent Conveyance Law and Its Proper Domain," 38 Vand. L. Rev. 829 (1985).

[10] While Section 548 defines the nature of the transactions that are avoidable by the debtor, Section 550 places limits on Section 548 by defining the kind of transferee from whom a debtor may recover transferred property. Section 550(a) permits a trustee to recover fraudulently transferred property from

1. the initial transferee;
2. the entity for whose benefit such transfer was made; or
3. an immediate or mediate transferee of such initial transferee (a "subsequent transferee").

11 U.S.C. § 550(a). Section 550(b) states that a trustee may not recover from

1. a subsequent transferee who takes the property for value, in good faith, and without knowledge of the voidability of the transfer; or
2. an immediate or mediate good faith transferee of such a transferee.

shares in good faith, for value, and without the requisite knowledge and therefore cannot be held liable under Section 550.

The merit of this assertion turns on the court's interpretation of the tender offer and LBO transactions. Defendants contend that the tender offer and LBO were composed of a series of interrelated but independent transactions. They assert, for example, that the transfer of property from [the LBO lenders] to WSI and ultimately to the shareholders constituted one series of several transactions while the pledge of Wieboldt assets to [the LBO lenders] to secure the financing constituted a second series of transactions. Under this view, defendants did not receive the debtor's property during the tender offer but rather received WSI's property in exchange for their shares.

Wieboldt, on the other hand, urges the court to "collapse" the interrelated transactions into one aggregate transaction which had the overall effect of conveying Wieboldt property to the tendering shareholders and LBO lenders. This approach requires the court to find that the persons and entities receiving the conveyance were direct transferees who received "an interest of the debtor in property" during the tender offer/buyout, and that WSI and any other parties to the transactions were "mere conduits" of Wieboldt's property. If the court finds that all the transfers constituted one transaction, then defendants received property from Wieboldt and Wieboldt has stated a claim against them.

Few courts have considered whether complicated LBO transfers should be evaluated separately or collapsed into one integrated transaction. However, ... [s]ee United States v. Tabor Court Realty, 803 F.2d 1288 (3rd Cir. 1986), cert. denied, McClellan Realty Co. v. United States, 107 S.Ct. 3229 (1987).

\* \* \*

[Although that case, *Gleneagles* or *Tabor Court*, did not involve] transactions which were identical to the WSI-Wieboldt buyout[, the *Gleneagles*] opinion [is] nonetheless significant .... Tabor Court found the LBO lender liable because it participated in the negotiations surrounding the LBO transactions and knew that the proceeds of its loan to Great American would deplete the debtor's assets to the point at which it was functionally insolvent under the fraudulent conveyance and bankruptcy laws .... [A] court should focus not on the formal structure of the transaction but rather on the knowledge or intent of the parties involved in the transaction.

Applying this principle to defendants' assertions, it is clear that, at least as regards the liability of the controlling shareholders, the LBO lenders, and the insider shareholders, the LBO transfers must be collapsed into one transaction. The complaint alleges clearly that these participants in the LBO negotiations attempted to structure the LBO with the requisite knowledge and contemplation that the full transaction, tender offer and LBO, be completed.[11] The Board and the insider shareholders knew that

---

[11] Although many of the allegations in the complaint refer to the state of mind and activities of the Board of Directors, these allegations may fairly be imputed to the controlling shareholders. The control-

WSI intended to finance its acquisition of Wieboldt through an LBO and not with any of its own funds. They knew that Wieboldt was insolvent before the LBO and that the LBO would result in further encumbrance of Wieboldt's already encumbered assets. Attorneys for Schottenstein Stores apprised the Board of the fraudulent conveyance laws and suggested that they structure the LBO so as to avoid liability. Nonetheless, these shareholders recommended that Wieboldt accept the tender offer and themselves tendered their shares to WSI.

Wieboldt's complaint also alleges sufficient facts to implicate the LBO lenders in the scheme. [They] were well aware of each other's loan or credit commitments to WSI and knew that WSI intended to use the proceeds of their financing commitments to purchase Wieboldt shares or options and to release certain Wieboldt assets from prior encumbrances. Representatives of the lenders received the same information concerning the fraudulent conveyance laws as did the Board of Directors. These LBO lenders agreed with WSI and the Board of Directors to structure the LBO so as to avoid fraudulent conveyance liability.

*The court, however, is not willing to "collapse" the transaction in order to find that the Schedule A shareholders also received the debtor's property in the transfer.* While Wieboldt directs specific allegations of fraud against the controlling and insider shareholders and LBO lenders, Wieboldt does not allege that the Schedule A shareholders were aware that WSI's acquisition encumbered virtually all of Wieboldt's assets. Nor is there an allegation that these shareholders were aware that the consideration they received for their tendered shares was Wieboldt property. In fact, the complaint does not suggest that the Schedule A shareholders had any part in the LBO except as innocent pawns in the scheme. They were aware only that WSI made a public tender offer for shares of Wieboldt stock. Viewing the transactions from the perspective of the Schedule A shareholders and considering their knowledge and intent, therefore, the asset transfers to the LBO lenders were indeed independent of the tender offer to the Schedule A shareholders.

This conclusion is in accord with the purpose of the fraudulent conveyance laws. The drafters of the Code, while attempting to protect parties harmed by fraudulent conveyances, also intended to shield innocent recipients of fraudulently conveyed property from liability. Thus, although Subsection (a) of Section 550 permits a trustee to avoid a transfer to an initial transferee or its subsequent transferee, Subsection (b) of that Section limits recovery from a subsequent transferee by providing that a trustee may not recover fraudulently conveyed property from a subsequent transferee who takes the property in good faith, for value, and without knowledge that the original transfer was voidable.[12] Subsection (b) applies, however, only to subsequent transferees.

---

ling shareholders nominated a majority of the directors to their positions on the Board. In addition, many of the individuals who served on the Board were "insiders" to Schottenstein['s or Trump's corporations].

[12] Section 550(b) also prohibits a trustee from recovering such property from a good faith transferee of such a transferee.

Similarly, the LBO lenders and the controlling and insider shareholders of Wieboldt are direct transferees of Wieboldt property. Although WSI participated in effecting the transactions, Wieboldt's complaint alleges that WSI was a corporation formed solely for the purpose of acquiring Wieboldt stock. The court can reasonably infer from the complaint, therefore, that WSI served mainly as a conduit for the exchange of assets and loan proceeds between LBO lenders and Wieboldt and for the exchange of loan proceeds and shares of stock between the LBO lenders and the insider and controlling shareholders. On the other hand, the Schedule A shareholders are not direct transferees of Wieboldt property. From their perspective, WSI was the direct transferee of Wieboldt property and the shareholders were merely indirect transferees because WSI was an independent entity in the transaction.

In sum, the formal structure of the transaction alone cannot shield the LBO lenders or the controlling and insider shareholders from Wieboldt's fraudulent conveyance claims. These parties were aware that the consideration they received for their financing commitments or in exchange for their shares consisted of Wieboldt assets and not the assets of WSI or any other financial intermediary. The Schedule A shareholders, on the other hand, apparently unaware of the financing transactions, participated only to the extent that they exchanged their shares for funds from WSI. Therefore, based on the allegations in the complaint, the court concludes that:

> 1. the motions to dismiss filed by the LBO lenders, insider shareholders, and controlling shareholders are denied at this point because these parties received Wieboldt property through a series of integrated LBO transactions; and
>
> 2. the Schedule A shareholders' motions to dismiss are granted because these defendants did not receive Wieboldt property through the separate exchange of shares for cash.

3. The Elements of a Fraudulent Conveyance

As discussed above, the transfers to and between the debtor and the LBO lenders, controlling shareholders, and insider shareholders are subject to the provisions in Section 548(a) of the Code and Section 4 of the Illinois statute. The court now must determine whether Wieboldt's complaint states sufficient facts to allege the elements of these causes of action.

   a. Section 548(a)(1)

In order to state a claim for relief under Section 548(a)(1) of the Code, a debtor or trustee must allege (1) that the transfer was made within one year before the debtor filed a petition in bankruptcy, and (2) that the transfer was made with the actual intent to hinder, delay or defraud the debtor's creditors. 11 U.S.C. § 548(a)(1) .... Although defendants do not dispute that the LBO transfers occurred within a year of the date on which Wieboldt filed for bankruptcy, they vigorously assert that Wieboldt has failed to properly allege "intent to defraud" as required by Section 548(a)(1).

"Actual intent" in the context of fraudulent transfers of property is rarely susceptible to proof and "must be gleaned from inferences drawn from a course of conduct." In re Vecchione, 407 F. Supp. 609, 615 (E.D.N.Y. 1976). A general scheme or plan to strip the debtor of its assets without regard to the needs of its creditors can support a finding of actual intent ... . In addition, certain "badges of fraud" can form the basis for a finding of actual intent to hinder, delay or defraud.

Counts I and III of Wieboldt's complaint state a claim under Section 548(a)(1). Count I, which Wieboldt brings against the controlling and insider shareholders, states that these defendants exchanged their shares with the actual intent to hinder, delay or defraud Wieboldt's unsecured creditors ... . The complaint also states generally that the LBO Lenders and the controlling and insider shareholders structured the LBO transfers in such a way as to attempt to evade fraudulent conveyance liability. These allegations are a sufficient assertion of actual fraud. Defendants' motion[] to dismiss Count[] I [is] therefore denied.

b. Section 548(a)(2)

Unlike Section 548(a)(1), which requires a plaintiff to allege "actual fraud," Section 548(a)(2) requires a plaintiff to allege only constructive fraud. A plaintiff states a claim under Section 548(a)(2) by alleging that the debtor (1) transferred property within a year of filing a petition in bankruptcy; (2) received less than the reasonably equivalent value for the property transferred; and (3) either (a) was insolvent or became insolvent as a result of the transfer, (b) retained unreasonably small capital after the transfer, or (c) made the transfer with the intent to incur debts beyond its ability to pay. 11 U.S.C. § 548(a)(2).

\* \* \*

Finally, defendants claim that Wieboldt cannot state a claim under Section 548(a)(2) because it received "reasonably equivalent value" in the transfer to the shareholders and the conveyance of the ... property. Wieboldt granted a security interest in substantially all of its real estate assets to [an LBO lender] and received from the shareholders in return 99 percent of its outstanding shares of stock.[13] This stock was virtually worthless to Wieboldt. Wieboldt received less than a reasonably equivalent value in exchange for an encumbrance on virtually all of its non-inventory assets, and therefore has stated a claim against the controlling and insider shareholders.

---

[13] Defendants argue that WSI (and not Wieboldt) received the outstanding shares of Wieboldt stock. However, a court analyzing an allegedly fraudulent transfer must direct its attention to "what the Debtor surrendered and what the Debtor received, irrespective of what any third party may have gained or lost." In re Ohio Corrugating Co., 70 Bankr. 920, 927 (Bkrtcy. N.D. Ohio 1987). As discussed in Section C.2. of this opinion, the court considers the tender offer and buyout transfers as one transaction for the purposes of this motion.

Likewise, the court need not dismiss Wieboldt's Section 548(a)(2) claim against the State Street defendants on the grounds that Wieboldt received reasonably equivalent value in exchange for its ... property. The effect and intention of the parties to the ... conveyance was to generate funds to purchase outstanding shares of Wieboldt stock. Although Wieboldt sold the property ... for $30 million, and used the proceeds to pay off part of the $35 million it owed ... , Wieboldt did not receive a benefit from this transfer. See Tabor Court, 803 F.2d at 1300. Defendants knew that the conveyance would neither increase Wieboldt's assets nor result in a net reduction of its liabilities. In fact, all parties to the conveyance were aware that the newly unencumbered assets would be immediately remortgaged to [an LBO lender] to finance the acquisition. According to the complaint, therefore, Wieboldt received less than reasonably equivalent value for the conveyance of the ... property and has stated a claim ... under Section 548(a)(2).

In sum, Counts II and IV of Wieboldt's complaint state a claim under Section 548(a)(2). Defendants' motions to dismiss these counts are denied.

### c. Illinois Fraudulent Conveyance Law

Under Section 544(b) of the Code, a trustee may avoid transfers that are avoidable under state law if there is at least one creditor at the time who has standing under state law to challenge the transfer. 11 U.S.C. § 544(b). Wieboldt utilizes this section to pursue a claim under [Section 4 of] the Illinois fraudulent conveyance statute ... .

The Illinois fraudulent conveyance statute is similar to Section 548 of the Code. The statute provides that:

> Every gift, grant, conveyance, assignment or transfer of, or charge upon any estate, real or personal, ... made with the intent to disturb, delay, hinder or defraud creditors or other persons, ... shall be void as against the creditors, purchasers and other persons.

\* \* \*

[For reasons similar to those used in analyzing the complaint under Section 548,] the court cannot dismiss Wieboldt's claim under Section 4 of the Illinois statute ... .

\* \* \*

## IV. CONCLUSION

The Schedule A shareholder defendants' motions to dismiss Count VIII against them are GRANTED. The other defendants' motions to dismiss the remaining counts of the complaint are DENIED.

## ¶1605: Questions on *Wieboldt*

1. What is the structure of the LBO transaction? A typical LBO has the organizers form a "shell" corporation. The shell corporation borrows money to acquire a majority of the stock of the "target" corporation. Once the "shell" acquires a majority of the stock, the LBO organizers merge the "target" with the "shell," and thereby eliminate the few remaining minority stockholders (by buying up their stock). The merged entity then has both the loan obligation (from the original "shell") and the assets (from the original "target"). The merged entity then often gives the assets as security to the LBO lenders. (The *Wieboldt* opinion doesn't state explicitly whether the merger occurred. Perhaps because the tender offer was unusually successful, with WSI getting 99% of Wieboldt's stock, the parties thought the merger not to be immediately necessary.)

    After the usual merger, the operating firm pledges its assets to the lender. Oftentimes the lenders, at the time they originally make the loan to the acquiring company, make it an event of default for the firm not to get control of the assets and give security interests and mortgages within a specified period of time.

    This seems to have roughly been the LBO transactional structure in *Wieboldt* (except that the formal merger seems not to have occurred; but this doesn't have any impact on the decision or the transaction).

2. The defendant stockholders claim that they never received any Wieboldt property. They didn't directly. They received a check from WSI. How then can the court conclude that the stockholders received Wieboldt property?

3. Why does the court state that the public stockholders (the Schedule A stockholders, as the court calls them) took property from Wieboldt indirectly, that the public stockholders were immediate transferees of WSI, the "shell," and not Wieboldt, the "target"? See § 550 (a)-(b):

    **§ 550. Liability of transferee of avoided transfer**

    (a)... the trustee may recover, for the benefit of the estate, the property transferred, or, if the court so orders, the value of such property, from—
    
    (1) the initial transferee of such transfer or the entity for whose benefit such transfer was made; or
    
    (2) any immediate or mediate transferee of such initial transferee.
    
    (b) The trustee may not recover under section (a)(2) of this section from—
    
    (1) a transferee that takes for value, including satisfaction or securing of a present or antecedent debt, in good faith, and without knowledge of the voidability of the transfer avoided; or
    
    (2) any immediate or mediate good faith transferee of such transferee.

4. How can the inside stockholders have taken directly from Wieboldt at all? Their cash came from WSI, not Wieboldt? True, the transaction could be collapsed: the

court could say that the last step, when Wieboldt transferred security to the lenders was "really" the first step, because the lenders would never have lent had they not been reasonably sure of getting the security. So the assets were "really" dividended up to WSI and pledged to the lenders. Then the lenders turned the assets (of Wieboldt) into cash, which WSI used to buy the stock. Therefore, the stockholders are indirect recipients of Wieboldt's property; if the transaction were collapsed, they could be viewed as direct recipients of Wieboldt's property.

But if the transaction is collapsed, so that the court concludes that the inside stockholders got their check directly from Wieboldt, how can the court simultaneously say that the public stockholders did not also get *their* check directly from Wieboldt? One can understand the policy basis why the court reaches this result, but what is the analytic, statutory basis?

5. Could the court have analyzed the setting more cleanly by concluding that *both public and nonpublic stockholders* took *indirectly* from Wieboldt, through WSI? Accordingly, they were both subsequent transferees under § 550(a)(2). But public stockholders could avail themselves of the good faith, lack of knowledge defense of § (b)(1), but the insider stockholders could not.

But, again, to go over the transaction once more, how could the stockholders be seen as indirect transferees from Wieboldt? Stay focused on the assets of Wieboldt. No LBO would happen, the Wieboldt trustee might have argued, unless Wieboldt's assets were transferred, ultimately into the hands of the shareholders. How did that happen, structurally? The assets were given to WSI. That was a fraudulent transfer. The bank lenders then got the assets, and then turned back cash to WSI. The bank lenders were subsequent transferees then of WSI, the initial transferee. WSI used the cash (from the asset pledge) to buy stock from Wieboldt's stockholders. The stockholders were subsequent transferees of the original asset transfer.

All of the shareholders, both insiders and public, accordingly were subsequent transferees. The outside, public stockholders can avail themselves of the good faith defense in § 550(b)(1): they are transferees who took "for value, ... , in good faith, and without knowledge of the voidability of the transfer ... ." The inside stockholders, with knowledge, cannot use § 550(b)(1) to defend themselves.

6. Rethink what it means for the courts in *Wieboldt* and *Gleneagles* to have "collapsed the transactions." Does "collapsing" the LBO clearly give us a fraudulent conveyance answer? When the buyout is done, the shareholders have cash and aren't shareholders anymore, the debtor owes a lot more money than before the transaction, and the creditor holds a note from the company. This "collapsing" tells us that the company is much weaker than before, but does it tell us who should be stuck with fraudulent conveyance liability? The "sequence" in which the court views the LBO to have happened can decide who is liable.

Consider the two alternative sequences, both resulting in the same "collapsed" transaction.

*Sequence 1:* Creditor buys up 99% of the stock from the target company's stockholders. Then the company buys back the stock *from the creditor*, giving the creditor a note and security for the buyback. The company never conveyed anything to the stockholders, hence they shouldn't be tagged with fraudulent conveyance liability. The company did convey a note and security to the stock-owning creditor; they presumably (if the other criteria were met) would have received a fraudulent conveyance. The Sequence 1 transaction "collapses" as above and the creditors are the obvious fraudulent conveyance target.

*Sequence 2:* Company buys back 99% of its stock from its stockholders, pro rata. It pays out all of its cash to pay the stockholders. Thereafter the cash-poor company contacts a lender, one who had never dealt with, or even heard of, the company before the CFO called up the lender. The lender lends to the company about as much as the company used to buy out the stockholders. The lender takes security with its note from the company. Presumably the creditor can't be tagged with fraudulent conveyance liability, but the stockholders (if the other criteria were met) could easily have received a fraudulent conveyance. The Sequence 2 transaction once again collapses as above, but this time the stockholders are the obvious target.

### ¶1606: A note on Kaiser Steel Corp. v. Charles Schwab

Section 546(e) of the Bankruptcy Code states that "notwithstanding sections 544, 545, 547, 548(a)(2), and 548(b)" a debtor may not avoid a transfer that is "a settlement payment, as defined in section 741(8) of this title, made by or to a ... stock broker, financial institution or securities clearing agency, that is made before the commencement of the case, except under section 548(a)(1)[.]"

Section 741(8) defines a settlement payment as "a preliminary settlement payment, an interim settlement payment, a settlement payment on account, a final settlement payment, or any other similar payment commonly used in the securities trade."

Kaiser Steel went through an LBO in 1983. It purchased its own stock from customers of Charles Schwab & Co., a securities broker. In essence, Schwab held stock in its name, for the benefit of its customers. Schwab forwarded securities held for it by a clearinghouse and a few days later credited its customers with $450,000 received from Kaiser.

Kaiser went bankrupt in 1987. The debtor brought a fraudulent conveyance action, seeking to recover payments made to stockholders, including Schwab. Schwab argued, first, that it was a "mere conduit" rather than a transferee and thus was not liable due to § 550(a). Second, it argued that § 546(e) exempted the LBO payments from the fraudulent conveyance sections, because the payments were settlement payments under § 546(e).

In Kaiser Steel Corp. v. Charles Schwab & Co., No. 90-1078 (10th Cir. Sept. 7, 1990), the Tenth Circuit held that the payments to Schwab were settlement payments, exempt from fraudulent conveyance liability under § 546(e).

Are payments to Schwab's customers also settlement payments? Could the *Wieboldt* result, which shielded public stockholders from fraudulent conveyance liability, be thus reached directly? Would this effectively make stockholders immune to fraudulent conveyance liability? From a policy perspective, is there a distinction between exempting settlement payments in the security industry from settlement payments to the ultimate risk-bearer? Did Congress make that distinction? Who is left holding the bag (of liability) after an LBO that leaves the firm insolvent?

If § 546 applies to the ultimate stockholder would the *Wieboldt* result as to the close stockholders, who were involved in the transaction, be reversed if the close stockholders held their stock through a broker?

Perhaps the 11th Circuit was unsettled by such questions when it held in 1996 that payments made to the bought-out company's one-time shareholders *could* be fraudulent conveyances, unprotected by § 546(e)'s securities settlement exception. The court said that even if near-final payment in the LBO was accomplished via settlement checks "made by or to a ... stockbroker, financial institution or securities clearing agency" (this is the language of § 546), when the stockbrokers turned the money over to the one-time stockholders, the ultimate recipients (the old stockholders) were not stockbrokers or clearing agencies acting as such, but regular ordinary stockholders. The purpose of § 546 was to protect the system of settling securities transactions, by exempting the intermediary institution from fraudulent conveyance liability; its purpose was *not* to exempt stockholders from fraudulent conveyance liability. Munford, Inc. v. Valuation Research Corp., 98 F.3d 604 (11th Cir. 1996).

---

### ¶1607: Benjamin Stein, Shooting Fish in a Barrel—Why Management Always Makes a Bundle in an LBO, Barron's, Jan. 12, 1987, at 6

The leveraged buyout has become the alchemist's stone of the 1980s. By its agency, worn-out, poorly regarded companies have been bought, often by their own managers, almost always at an improvement over current market price, and then "restructured," "rationalized," "down-sized," and generally put through the alchemy process. Invariably, the companies emerge from the LBO laboratory a few months or years later at values that endow the creators of the LBOs, the financiers of the deal and the managers involved, with spectacular profits.

By now, everyone in American must know about William E. Simon making profits of 100 times on his investments in Gibson Greetings and Anchor Hocking. There are rumors that the investors in Beatrice will make a profit measured around $5 billion on an equity investment by them in the millions. Rumors of multi-billion-dollar profit accruing to Ronald Perelman from his takeover of Revlon are also percolating.

There are smaller deals, too, such as the recent management LBO of Amsted Industries, a diversified pipe, air-coil and construction-goods company, in which managers reportedly were told that once they had taken the company private, they could expect a profit of about $5 million for every $100,000 they put in. There is the comparatively tiny recent takeover of Narragansett Capital by a joint venture of former management and Monarch Capital. Just consummated last week, that LBO promises to give former management, now designated as "advisers" to Monarch, 20% of the profits on the sale of Narragansett assets. These profits are estimated by Narragansett's former management to be about one and a half times the total cost of the company via a leveraged buyout from its hapless shareholders. (I am both a former shareholder and a present litigant against Narragansett, which denies any wrongdoing.) Profits to the former managers of Narragansett from the LBO will be in the tens of millions; yet these former managers put up no risk equity at all.

Then there is the LBO of Metromedia by its former CEO, John Kluge (Barron's, Aug. 18, 1986). That transaction yielded Kluge a profit of about $3 billion personally, making him one of the world's richest human beings, on his equity commitment in the millions. There also have been astonishingly successful LBOs of what were considered moribund corporations like Kaiser Aluminum, which yielded its principals profits of at least 40 times their investment within a few years ... .

The impending Viacom LBO by its senior managers offers hope of matching the "take" of the Metromedia deal. Its managers can confidently expect a gain in the nine-figure range for an equity investment in the seven-figure range.

The question that must occur to observers is basically this: Just how exactly do LBOs provide such immense returns to their investors? Of course, we know that part of the answer is that letter "L" in the initials LBO. There is so much debt and so little equity in the typical LBO that any profit commensurate with the magnitude of the transaction must result in large returns.

But beyond that superficial observation, why is there always a profit? Why do not at least some of the deals in which managers buy their own companies suffer small losses that completely wipe out the small amount of equity? Why do these deals, virtually alone among large financing transactions, always take companies at a total value of X and wind up turning them in short order into a multiple of X?[14]

How is it that the people who make LBOs are able to take companies which are sluggish and poorly regarded and make them miraculous fountains of money and esteem? Or, again, why do LBOs work?

One easy answer would be that managers and LBO financiers pay too little for the companies they buy. That is true as a matter of definition. But since the LBO groups usually pay more than the going stock price before the offer is announced, a more complex inquiry is required. Why is it that managers can pay more, often significantly more, than the market's valuation of a company, and still make it into something worth vastly more than the market's former valuation of the company?

---

[14] [Some LBO's do lose money. Some go bankrupt.—Roe.]

In the answer to why LBOs work are extremely fundamental facts about the value of time and money, the motivations of managers, the incompetence of securities analysts, and far more basic questions about ethics, duties to stockholders, and just how people get rich in contemporary America.

* * *

[Securities analysts look at the company's cash flow as it has been and as momentum would indicate it will be in the future.] Management [though] is free to rearrange operations such that they yield vastly more sensible and larger flow of cash. It can sell property, cut staff, stop capital spending, do anything at all that will yield value ....

... When an LBO is contemplated or takes place, the company's managers take the gloves off. They suddenly realize that they have a lot more value to play with for themselves than they did when they were working for the stockholders.

This is clear when one contemplates the history of LBOs. When Anchor Hocking went private, its management suddenly saw it could cut wage costs and sell off unneeded buildings. When Beatrice was taken over, its new owners saw that they could sell off literally dozens of divisions, revise their depreciation schedules, have billions in cash [from sales] and [still retain] virtually the pre-LBO cash flow. When Amsted's managers took it over from the stockholders (including me) they had the vision that Amsted has valuable real estate in Fontana, California, and in Illinois that was yielding virtually nothing but could be sold for tens of millions ... .

One suspects that Viacom's managers will "discover" that they can sell the syndicated rights to the Cosby TV series to a large limited partnership for close to a billion dollars, sell MTV for another billion, pay off most of their debt, have no stockholders, and still have a company with virtually the same cash flow as before the LBO, which they can then resell for their own benefit.

When management or new owners take over a company in an LBO, they suddenly stop managing so they can get to the country club by 3 p.m. Instead, they start to notice what the difference in the internal rate of return is if they sell a low-yielding parcel in Palm Springs tomorrow instead of earning 1% on its present value. When [the] management of [an] LBO[ ] go[es] into action, it suddenly starts to notice arbitrages between liquidation value and yield value. Out goes the three wood. In comes the HP-12.

Why do LBOs always work? Because those who are buying go into an LBO only when they know that they can redeploy assets [and] ... take the cash and then keep running the operation profitably. LBOs work because the people doing them command a huge advantage over the stockholders from whom they are buying the company: Stockholders and market analysts know only what the companies are worth when management is managing along the path of least resistance—or the path of obfuscation. Management or the new buyers know what the company would be worth if intelligence were applied to every single aspect of the company—correctly valuing physical assets instead of going by book or income, anticipating new developments in the field, knowing which workers are redundant and which are not, knowing when real interest rates are so high that liquidation makes more sense than operation. LBOs work because the people who do LBOs know the true value of assets of every kind in every different mode, from outright sale to heightened use, and the market doesn't.

And to some sad extent, LBOs work because management has willfully deceived the market about the true value of its assets. It is by now a commonplace of the pre-LBO management to tearfully announce lower earnings and anticipated lower earnings just before announcement and completion of an LBO. These forecasts are often based upon intangible charges such as new depreciation costs or reserves for various contingencies that never materialize. To see press releases from Metromedia announcing forecasts of drastically reduced earnings just before John Kluge took it over and reaped a $3 billion personal profit is bitter humor indeed. In the case of every LBO in which I have been personally involved—Amsted, Narragansett and Viacom—management has announced drastically lowered estimates of earnings just before the LBO was announced or completed. None of these three forecasts was based upon changed market conditions or changed profit margins. All were based upon mysterious charges and reserves and new depreciation schedules.

Occasionally the obfuscation is compounded by lowering earnings estimates because of real expenditures ... .

LBOs work, in other words, because management or the other LBO operators have figured out a way to use the company's assets, including earning power, far more efficiently than before. This calculation is never just a guess. It is worked out in dollars and cents so that the LBO practitioners know beforehand that they will be buying a company for far less than its new value when its assets are sold, cut back or used intelligently.

* * *

All of this raises some particularly important questions for a society that operates under the concept of law. This society, in fact, has a substantial body of law ostensibly protecting stockholders, requiring managers of companies to do their best for the stockholders—and requiring the highest possible standards of duty—fiduciary duty—on the part of managers.[15]

If managers can figure out a way to [reposition the company] and thereby boost cash and retain earnings, why doesn't management do that very thing for the benefit of the stockholder instead of for themselves? If Amsted's managers knew that they had surplus valuable real estate and a high eight-figure redundancy in their pension fund, why wait until the stockholders were out of the picture before realizing those sums? If Viacom's managers know—as they assuredly do—that the Cosby show will

---

[15] [Is Stein, the author, discovering that incentives are more powerful than fiduciary and legal duties?—Roe.]

be as valuable as East Texas, why doesn't management pass out the syndication proceeds to the stockholders instead of to themselves?

Why do managers seemingly only start to manage with an eye on the time value of money, discount to present value, market price vs. book price, recoupment of surplus property and conversion to cash once they have booted out the stockholders and are managing for themselves?

How can management rationalize at law or simple equity the use of stockholders' money to purchase assets that will be efficiently used only by the employees of the stockholders, the management? What is the legal rationale for allowing the corporate form to be used primarily as a way of accumulating value for management, rather than stockholders? Is this in any way what the securities laws or fiduciary-duty laws of this country contemplated?

LBOs always work because LBOs are methods of liquidating an arbitrage between stock price and real value of a company. But should this arbitrage be applied only for the managers and other new buyers, or should it be applied, as a matter of fiduciary duty and compliance with securities law, for the benefit of the stockholders? Are stockholders owners or lenders? If they are owners, are they not owed a duty to have management manage and value assets for the owner's benefit?

LBOs always work because the market has made large mistakes in valuing companies or because the market has been unable to perceive the range of options available to management. But should not those mistakes be capitalized upon for the stockholders as well as for management?

An LBO is another name for a correct evaluation of the assets of a company. Could not such an evaluation have other outcomes, such as a process of continuing liquidation in favor of the stockholders? Union Carbide has tried it, and the results have been spectacular for the large chemical company's stockholders. Every large, mature company has similar opportunities for ongoing liquidation of assets whose yield is not commensurate with their liquidation value. Mobil has been frequently named, and is a perfect example. Imagine if Mobil sold all of its gas stations and non-refinery real estate to a limited partnership and distributed the proceeds to the stockholders. Cash flow would hardly show a blip, and the stockholders would get a huge dividend. Imagine virtually any minerals company selling is less productive fields to investors with a longer time horizon and passing on the proceeds to stockholders. Imagine every company carefully assessing whether or not its pension plan was overfunded, then capturing the surplus—not for management, but for stockholders.

It is a sad commentary on the psyche of the American manager that most frequently he seems to aggressively manage only when the results go straight to him without the intermediation of stockholders.

There are further observations in order about LBOs. On a recent list of the nation's wealthiest men and women, several dozen got there either by managing an LBO of their former stockholders' companies or by financing such transactions. That is, a major avenue to wealth in America today is not making anything new or building up anything new, but rather taking away value from the people to whom one has a legal duty of protection ... .

* * *

## B. Margin regulations

### ¶1608: Margin regulations and other issues relating to debt

We have concerned ourselves largely with the problems arising from debt. The costs of debt lie largely in bankruptcy problems. Debt raises other issues worth examining, even if only briefly, although these other issues do not fit neatly in the materials thus far studied.

In October 1929, the stock market crashed. Political actors argued that the huge volume of margin debt—borrowings by individuals and others used to purchase common stock—was a pernicious influence in the crash. The costs of excessive margin debt were seen as twofold. First, individuals became, it was thought, overly optimistic and when the crash came individuals were especially damaged. To protect individuals from their optimism, it was thought necessary to impose limits on the degree to which they could finance stock purchases with borrowings. Second, excessive borrowing created a volatile system. A slight downturn in stock prices would be exacerbated by margin calls, liquidation of stock positions, which would lead to further downward price pressure, which in turn would lead to further margin calls. The cycle of margin calls (when many individuals had borrowed 90% of the value of their stock position) and stock liquidations exacerbated the crash, some thought.

In 1934 Congress enacted the Securities Exchange Act of 1934 which delegated to the Federal Reserve Board authority to set margin requirements. In rough measure the margin requirement in recent years has been at 50% of the value of stock purchased.

* * *

In the 1980s a wave of mergers, many hostile, came over the American economy. Some mergers, and certainly many of the mergers most prominent in the press, were financed with large borrowings by the offering company.

In 1985, Mesa Petroleum, a small company, nominally engaged in oil exploration and production, whose principal business was engaging in attempted takeovers of other companies, usually in the oil business, formed a subsidiary to acquire another oil firm, Unocal. Unocal's management bitterly resisted the offer. Among their resistance efforts was an attempt to persuade the Federal Reserve that the margin regulations applied to takeover efforts.

**¶1609: Federal Reserve Interpretive Rule: Securities Credit by Persons Other Than Banks, Brokers, or Dealers; Purchase of Debt Securities to Finance Corporate Takeovers, 12 C.F.R. Part 207 [Regulation G; Docket No. R-0562][16]**

I. Background

Section 7 of the Securities Exchange Act of 1934 provides that "[f]or the purpose of preventing the excessive use of credit for the purchase or carrying of securities, the Board ... shall ... prescribe rules and regulations with respect to the amount of credit that may be initially extended and subsequently maintained on any security ...." 15 U.S.C. 78g(a). The Board's Regulation G issued pursuant to this authority governs credit extended by a lender that is not a bank or a broker/dealer. Regulation G provides that no such lender shall extend credit for the purpose of buying or carrying a margin stock ("purpose credit"), secured directly or indirectly by margin stock in an amount that exceeds the maximum loan value of the collateral securing the loan.[17] 12 CFR 207(b). Regulation G further provides that the maximum loan value of any margin stock is 50 percent of its current market value. 12 CFR 207.7(a).

\* \* \*

In May 1985, the Unocal Corporation submitted a petition to the Board requesting a determination that the margin lending restrictions in Regulation G applied to debt securities issued by a shell corporation controlled by Mesa Petroleum Company to finance a tender offer for Unocal's stock. The shell corporation held substantially no assets other than the margin stock to be acquired. If the tender offer were successful, Mesa planned to merge the shell with Unocal, but even if successful, the tender offer would not have given Mesa the requisite number of shares of stock to complete a merger with Unocal immediately. Unocal argued that these securities would constitute purpose credit that would be indirectly secured by the margin stock of Unocal and thus subject to the lending restrictions of Regulation G. However, Mesa's acquisition attempt was terminated and no Board action was taken at that time on the issues raised by the petition.

In September 1985, a similar petition was filed with the Board by Revlon, Inc., seeking a determination that the lending restrictions in Regulation G applied to debt securities and other financing arrangements issued by Pantry Pride, Inc., as part of its attempt to acquire Revlon.[18] The Pantry Pride/Revlon transaction was structured dif-

---

[16] [In 1998, the substance of this interpretive rule was transferred to Regulation U, at 12 CFR § 221.124: Purchase of debt securities to finance corporate takeovers.—Roe.]

[17] "Margin stock" includes any equity security traded on a national securities exchange. 12 CFR 207.2(i).

[18] The GAF Corporation has recently announced a tender offer for the shares of Union Carbide Corp. GAF would control a shell acquisition vehicle, but all debt securities to be issued to finance the tender offer would be issued or guaranteed by the parent corporation itself, an operating company with

ferently from the Mesa/Unocal acquisition attempt. Pantry Pride, an operating company with substantial non-margin stock assets, would issue nominally unsecured debt securities to fund a tender offer for Revlon's stock, which was margin stock. In addition, Pantry Pride controlled a shell corporation that would be used as an acquisition vehicle and would obtain a bank loan that complied with the margin loan restrictions applicable to loans from banks (Regulation U, 12 CFR Part 221). Revlon's petition asserted that Pantry Pride proposed to obtain over $840 million in credit that could not be supported by Pantry Pride's existing assets (approximately $400 million) and net worth (about $145 million). The Board was made aware of the facts of the Pantry Pride/Revlon transaction but no action was taken on Revlon's petition.[19]

The Board has also received requests from a number of members of Congress that the Board specifically address the applicability of the margin lending restrictions to acquisition financing arrangements, especially nominally unsecured debt securities used in corporate takeover attempts.

The proposed interpretation gives the Board's views with regard to whether the debt securities involved in the kind of acquisitions at issue in the Unocal and Revlon situations could be indirectly secured by margin stock. The proposal is an interpretative rule that provides guidance to the financial community and to enforcement authorities as to a specific type of transaction that the Board believes, in its judgment, falls within the scope of lending transactions that are indirectly secured by margin stock. As such, this interpretation is not intended as an exercise of the Board's rulemaking authority conferred by statute or as binding upon reviewing courts, but as descriptive of those facts that indicate a secured transaction within the meaning of the margin requirement rules.

* * *

II. Basis of the Interpretative Rule

A. The Interpretative Rule

The interpretation provides that the Board is of the view that, absent other defined circumstances described below, debt securities issued by a shell corporation to finance the acquisition of the margin stock of a target company are indirectly secured by the margin stock for purposes of the restrictions on lending in the margin regula-

---

substantial non-margin stock assets. Together with its shell corporation, GAF, with assets of approximately $800 million and shareholders' equity of approximately $280 million, seeks to raise over $2.3 billion through issuance of debt securities.

[19] After the Revlon petition was filed, the terms of the Pantry Pride offer were altered several times. Recently, Pantry Pride completed its acquisition of Revlon after Revlon's attempt to accomplish a "friendly" leveraged buyout was invalidated by a Delaware court. MacAndrews & Forbes Holdings, Inc. v. Revlon, Inc. No. 8126 (Del.Ch. Oct. 23, 1985). The petition to the Board was withdrawn.

tions. Such a shell would have virtually no business operations, no significant business function other than to acquire and hold the shares of the target company, and substantially no assets or cash flow to support the credit other than the margin stock that it has acquired or intends to acquire.[20] The presumption that the debt securities are indirectly secured by margin stock would not apply if there is specific evidence that lenders could in good faith rely on assets other than margin stock as collateral, such as a guaranty of the debt securities by the shell corporation's parent company or another company that has substantial non-margin stock assets or cash flow. This presumption would also not apply if there is a merger agreement between the acquiring and target companies entered into at the time the commitment is made to purchase the debt securities or in any event before loan funds are advanced. In addition, the presumption would not apply if the obligation of the purchasers of the debt securities to advance finds to the shell corporation is contingent on the shell's acquisition of the minimum number of shares necessary under applicable state law to effect a merger between the acquiring and target companies without the approval of either the shareholders or directors of the target company. In these circumstances it is reasonable to assume that the lenders are looking to the target company's assets for repayment.

The interpretation applies only to shell companies. Thus the interpretation provides that debt securities issued by an operating company with substantial assets or cash flow to finance the acquisition of margin stock of a target company would not be presumed to be indirectly secured by margin stock.

B. Rationale for the Interpretative Rule

The purpose of the interpretative rule is to provide guidance in determining whether nominally unsecured debt securities issued to finance a tender offer for margin stock of a target company are subject to the existing margin lending restrictions in Regulation G in the situations presented in the Unocal and Revlon transactions. Regulation G describes two kinds of arrangements that are "include[d]" within the meaning of "indirect security"—restrictions on the disposition of margin stock and acceleration of the maturity of the credit if margin stock is disposed of—but further provides that these arrangements do not constitute indirect security if, among other things, the lender in good faith has not relied upon the margin stock as collateral in extending or maintaining the credit. Id. Sections 207.2(f)(1); (f)(2) (i)–(iv). However, since at least 1961 the Board has recognized that the meaning of indirect security as used in the Board's margin regulations encompasses a wide variety of arrangements as to collateral, other than a conventional direct security interest, that are not described in the

---

[20] Other forms of business organizations such as partnerships and business trusts with these characteristics would also be deemed to be shell corporations for the purpose of the interpretative rule.

Regulation, but that serve to some extent to protect the interest of the lender. Id. Section 221.113(f).[21]

It is clear that the debt securities issued by a shell corporation constitute "purpose credit" as defined in the Regulation. In addition, the purchasers of the debt securities may qualify as "lenders" for purposes of the Regulation because they purchase the debt securities in very large amounts. Although the debt securities issued by such a shell corporation are by their terms not directly secured by margin stock, the Board believes, for the reasons stated below, that in the limited situation described these debt securities would be "indirectly secured" by the margin stock to be acquired within the meaning of the provisions of Regulation G.

C. Lenders' Reliance on Margin Stock

As the interpretative rule set out at the end of the Notice points out, the Board is of the opinion that in the narrow situation described in the interpretation, the purchasers of the debt securities issued by the shell corporation to finance the acquisition of margin stock of the target can be viewed reasonably as relying on the margin stock as collateral for the credit, regardless of the lack of a conventional direct security agreement.

As the interpretative rule points out, under a prior interpretation of the margin regulations, loans to an investment company, the assets of which consist almost entirely of stock, are regarded as indirectly secured by that stock, since the lenders could not in good faith lend to the company without reliance on the stock. Federal Reserve Regulatory Service ¶5-917.12. The Board believes that the rationale of this prior ruling applies to the debt securities issued by the type of shell acquisition vehicle involved in the Mesa/Unocal transaction.

As described in the interpretative ruling, such a shell would have virtually no business operations, no significant business function other than to acquire and hold the shares of the target company, and substantially no assets or cash flow to support the credit other than the margin stock that it has acquired or intends to acquire. In this situation, the Board believes that the only significant asset available to support the credit is the margin stock and, therefore, the lender must be relying on that stock as collateral to secure repayment.

The fact that, as a number of comments point out, the shell corporation intends to vote its shares of the target company to merge with the target does not, in the Board's view, change the result. In the Mesa/Unocal transaction, which forms the basis for the interpretation, the tender offer would not have sought to acquire a sufficient number of shares of stock of the target company to permit a "short-form" merger between the target and the shell corporation. Nor was there a merger agreement between

---

[21] This interpretation construed the provisions in Regulation U (governing credit by banks) describing indirect security, which are the same as those in Regulation G.

Mesa and Unocal at the time the loans were committed or in any event before the loan funds were advanced. If the target company were to oppose the merger in this situation, the shell corporation may be unable to consummate the acquisition immediately or possibly at all and the shell may be forced to hold the margin stock for a significant period of time. During this time, the Board believes that the lenders could only rely on the margin stock, not the assets of the target, as security for the credit. Disclosures pursuant to the securities laws made by acquiring firms in these situations supports this view by stating that the proposed merger may not take place for an extended period of time or at all.[22]

For purposes of the margin regulations the Board regards the time a commitment to extend credit is entered into as the point at which a determination is made whether the margin lending restrictions apply. See Federal Reserve Regulatory Service ¶5-306. Accordingly, in the Board's opinion, at that time the lender can be viewed as relying on the margin stock as collateral for the credit. This position is supported by the fact that the lenders to the shell corporation described above will, at the time of commitment of their loan, be unable to predict the length of time during which the shell would hold no significant assets other than margin stock.

D. Practical Restriction on Disposition

The Board's presumption that in the shell corporation situation the lenders are relying for repayment on the margin stock is further supported by practical limitation on disposition of the margin stock by the shell corporation. Regulation G includes within the scope of "indirectly secured" any arrangement in which there is a restriction on the borrowers' legal right or practical ability to dispose of margin stock owned by the borrower during the life of the credit. 12 CFR 207.2(f)(1)(i). Where credit is extended to a shell corporation whose basic purpose is to acquire and hold margin stock of a particular company, as in the Mesa/Unocal transaction, the Board is of the view that there is a practical restriction on the ability of the shell corporation to dispose of that margin stock. The Board believes that it would be reasonable to assume that lenders would not extend credit to such a shell acquisition vehicle unless there were an understanding that it will hold the stock ... .

However, under Regulation G, even if there is a restriction on the disposition of margin stock or other evidence of indirect security, credit is not indirectly secured by margin stock if the lender in good faith did not rely on margin stock as collateral in extending credit. Accordingly, the presumption contained in the interpretation would not apply where there is specific evidence that the purchasers of the debt securities in

---

[22] See, e.g., Schedule 14D-1 filed by Mesa Partners II and Mesa Eastern, Inc. to acquire stock of Unocal Corp. at 21 (April 8, 1985); Offer by Coach Acquisition Inc. to Purchase Securities of MidCon Corp., at 28 (Dec. 16, 1985).

good faith have not relied on the margin stock to be acquired by the shell corporation as collateral.

\* \* \*

IV. Analysis of Comments

\* \* \*

A. Policy Considerations

Many commentators addressed policy issues relating to the advisability of regulating corporate acquisitions and debt generally. Some commentators supported the Board's interpretation on the grounds that the recent growth of debt financed corporate acquisitions should be curbed and the excessive debt for speculation in stock should be restrained. These commentators also argue that such financing diverts capital flows away from productive purposes and reduces credit available to such borrowers, results in excessive corporate debt that impairs the financial condition of the issuing corporations and increases the potential for major bankruptcies, results in corporate funds being diverted to repay debt rather than being used for productive growth, requires emphasis by management on short-term results to the detriment of sound corporate growth, results in higher cost of capital, which in turn is passed on to consumers, and results in distortions that impair the integrity and stability of the national securities markets.

On the other hand, many comments, including those of the Department of Justice, for itself and on behalf of a number of government agencies, and the Federal Trade Commission, opposed the interpretation, contending that governmental regulation of corporate acquisitions is not in the public interest. These comments state that corporate acquisitions have productive economic effects, such as removal of inefficient management and increases in the value of corporate stock, and that there is no evidence that the level of corporate debt is excessive or would be adversely affected by debt securities issued to finance corporate acquisitions. Among the other points raised in these comments are assertions that the interpretation frustrates the congressional objective of neutrality with regard to corporate takeovers expressed in the Williams Act and the Hart-Scott-Rodino Act, would have a disparate effect on competition for corporate control by shifting the balance that presently exists to favor large corporations over smaller ones, would discriminate in favor of foreign firms that may borrow abroad to finance the takeover of U.S. companies without being limited by the margin regulations, would increase acquisition costs, and will have an adverse effect on economic efficiency and financial markets.

A number of comments argue that the interpretation is not necessary to accomplish the basic objectives of the Board's authority to set margin requirements. Drexel Burnham Lambert Inc. and other commentators state that there is no regulatory need to protect the purchasers of the debt securities involved, who are financially sophisticated, and that the issuance of the debt securities neither diverts credit from other uses nor produces excessive price fluctuations in the market. Other commentators, however, believe that the interpretation will carry out the purposes for which the margin-setting authority was enacted. For example, a comment submitted by twelve members of the House of Representatives states that the interpretation addresses many of the same concerns that led Congress to enact the margin authority—"speculation leading to unstable markets and an undermined public confidence in the soundness of publicly traded" securities.

The comments also discuss a Federal Reserve Board staff study, transmitted to Congress in January 1985, which evaluated federal margin regulation and concluded that there are serious doubts about the need for continuing federal regulation to foster the objectives originally sought by Congress in enacting the legislation.[23] Drexel Burnham and other commentators assert that the extension of the margin regulations embodied in the interpretation is inconsistent with the Board's recognition of the general inefficiency of margin regulation. On the other hand, some members of Congress and others point out that whatever questions the Board has about the continuing need for margin requirement law and regulations, the existing margin law and regulations must be enforced and, unless the existing regulations are amended by the Board, they must apply equally to all transactions covered by their terms.

The Board recognized the conflicting public policy issues concerning highly leveraged mergers, and does not believe rulemaking or interpretations of margin regulations are appropriate means for settling such issues, which are properly matters for Congressional consideration. Moreover, the Board does not believe the interpretation set forth here is likely to substantially alter, in itself, the level of merger activity or the amount of debt created. Rather, the interpretation is intended to make clear the Board's view that a specific narrow class of acquisition financing transactions falls within the requirements of the margin regulations as currently written. The Board believes that the interpretation is consistent with the purposes of section 7 of the Securities Exchange Act of 1934. This conclusion is in no way undermined by the staff study which focuses on recommendations for legislative consideration for future action and not on administration of existing law so long as that law is in place.

In conjunction with Regulations T and U, Regulation G was adopted by the Board to carry out the purposes of section 7 of the Securities Exchange Act of 1934, to prevent inter alia, excessive use of credit for stock market speculation. The interpretative rule simply applies Regulation G to one kind of fact situation in a manner in which the Board believes is consistent with the purposes Congress had in mind in adopting the margin requirement legislation and which is covered by Regulation G. In doing so, the interpretation carries out the intention of Congress as embodied in section 7 and in the margin regulations. While the Board carefully considered the policy

---

[23] A Review and Evaluation of Federal Margin Regulation.

arguments made by the commentators and others that the margin requirements should not be applied to the facts covered by the interpretative rule, on balance the Board decided that fair and uniform administration of existing law requires that the margin regulations be applied in situations where it is reasonable to conclude that purpose credit is being extended that is indirectly secured by margin stock. Proposals for fundamental changes in the margin requirements are properly addressed to Congress, not to the Board, which must interpret the law as Congress has enacted it. As a number of comments and the Board's letter transmitting the proposed interpretation to Congress note, the Board would welcome such Congressional review.

CHAPTER 17

# MARKETS AND CHAPTER 11

¶1701: <u>Robert C. Clark, The Interdisciplinary Study of Legal Evolution, 90 Yale L.J. 1238 (1981)</u>[1]

\* \* \*

The fourth phase of [reorganization] development occurred ... when the equity receivership evolved to the point where ... the creditors of the insolvent business debtor [bought] ... the business ... using not cash as the means of payment, but their creditor claims, such as [their] notes, bonds, [and] debentures .... The creditors ... transform[ed] ... their debt holdings into ... new debt and stock, and at the same time [established] ... priorit[ies] among themselves and against the ... the old shareholders[] in a way that was just as definitive as a real liquidation sale to an outside buyer. *This procedure made economic sense whenever there were no or few potential outside buyers with accurate and timely information about the true state of affairs and the future prospects of the business, and when the process of searching for and informing outside buyers would itself be very expensive.*

\* \* \*

The [next] phase in ... corporate debtor-creditor law [established a formal,] ... structured version of the ... equity receivership ... with the ... Chandler Act in 1938. The ritual of the self-sale was dropped. All corporations in reorganization would presumptively be subjects of a reorganization plan that would primarily involve a reshuffling of the paper claims against the business assets. Furthermore, such restructuring of debt might be accomplished by a two-thirds majority vote within the classes of debtors, so that a good plan might be forced on otherwise obstreperous creditors.

---

[1] Reprinted by permission of The Yale Law Journal Company and Fred B. Rothman & Company from The Yale Law Journal, Vol. 90, pages 1238–1274.

These refinements, however, simply increased the need for careful judicial supervision of the valuation process.

[Why did these] phases ... of creditors' remedies occur[] so late in the history of trade and commerce[? Perhaps] lawyers in early times simply failed to think of the legal inventions and their advantages .... [T]he timing of [some] legal innovations is basically a random matter, and ... it takes time for ingenious persons to happen to be put in contact with situations that admit of improvement, and to see the solutions. An alternative, more idea-oriented explanation is that earlier lawyers were intellectually blinded by the influence of their modes of legal thought ....

... But the hypothesis that seems most powerful to me is more economic and institutional: only with the rise of very large business enterprises were there sufficiently frequent and sizable economies of scale in debt-enforcement proceedings to justify the legal innovations in question. Unless the surplus of going-concern value over liquidation value was substantial, as it might be for a large business, or the debtor business was so large and complex that it would have been impossible or quite expensive to find or to create a fair-sized pool of reasonably informed potential outside buyers, the efficiency benefits of a receivership or reorganization proceeding would not exceed the very substantial administrative, negotiating, and legal costs of the proceeding itself.[2]

## ¶1702: Mark J. Roe, Bankruptcy and Debt: A New Model for Corporate Reorganization (1983, 1987)[3]

[What if American capital markets are now so well developed that many outside investors can and do value large firms, and these investors buy and sell stock in such firms daily? And what if some of these investors buy and sell entire companies regularly?]

The core determinations made in a reorganization under chapter 11 of the Bankruptcy Code are simply stated: Who gets how much? What will the reorganized capital structure be? To resolve these simply stated questions, bankruptcy courts now loosely oversee *a lengthy bargaining process that is widely thought to be cumbersome, costly, and complex* ....

Three principal characteristics seem desirable for a corporate reorganization mechanism: speed, low cost, and a resulting sound capital structure. Other desirable characteristics are accuracy in valuation and compensation, predictability, and fairness. Accuracy and predictability diminish the uncertainty of the results of bankruptcy reorganizations, facilitating investment in risky but worthwhile enterprises before a

---

[2] These costs are high in the more advanced proceedings because of the greater need to consider valuation questions.

[3] Paper presented at a conference on bankruptcy at the University of Pennsylvania Law School, October 1987. I summarize here matters I dealt with more extensively in *Bankruptcy and Debt: A New Model for Corporate Reorganization*, 83 Columbia Law Review 527 (1983).

bankruptcy occurs. Speed and low cost help diminish the deadweight costs of the bankruptcy when it does occur.

Three ... mechanisms [can] ... accomplish a corporate reorganization: (1) a *bargain* among creditors and stockholders ...; (2) litigation in which the court imposes an *administered* solution and capital structure; and (3) ... use of *the market*. Since 1978, Congress has preferred that the parties first attempt a bargained-for solution, and if the bargain fails, that a judicial solution be imposed. Congress and the courts have assumed that marketplace valuation for bankrupts is too inaccurate to be viable .... [Would a sale be better?]

Anticipating an objective valuation of the firm [from a sale], the financial parties might, prior to any sale, more often than now fall into line with a settlement that would make the actual valuation sale unnecessary. If [a sale] could be successfully implemented, two major tasks of reorganization—valuation and restructuring—could take place not as now occurs over the course of years, but over a much shorter period.

... A market based reorganization has usually been rejected by courts and others because stigma, informational impediments, uncertainty, and institutional considerations all seem likely to distort the market's expectations of the firm's long-run value. These considerations have suggested to the reorganization decisionmakers (Congress and the courts) that the pinpoint accuracy (in terms of longer-run values) in a market-based reorganization is doubtful. Usually at this juncture analysis of market-based reorganization ends. Since a market-based approach would be less accurate than an ideal method of reorganization, it has thus far been cast aside as an unacceptable alternative.

Empirical work now suggests, however, that some of these feared inaccuracies are unlikely to exist in a market-based system .... On balance, the market value of a firm after reorganization seems likely to be more accurate than a judicial finding. This uncertain [increase in] ... accuracy would not necessarily in itself justify replacing the current devices with a market-based mechanism. Nevertheless, the additional possibility of quicker, cheaper reorganizations makes market-based mechanisms appropriate for serious consideration.

\* \* \*

## I. Current Doctrine and Some Game Theory: Bargaining Deadlocks and Reorganization Doctrine's Rejection of the Market

... [T]he bargaining process [in chapter 11] is likely to be a time-consuming effort to break an initial deadlock.

### A. Valuation and Bargaining in Bankruptcy

Corporate bankruptcy does not correspond to the financial economist's option model. In the simple option model, when the firm value slips below the debt's face value, then the creditors take the firm. If the firm's value were above the option price, then the stockholders buy back the firm from the creditors by paying off the debt. That, however, is not what happens in a two- or three-year corporate bankruptcy.

A crucial difficulty in bankruptcy seems to be the valuation process .... Which creditor and stockholder layers retain an interest in the reorganized firm depends on how much the firm is deemed to be worth. Judicial valuation uncertainties create an incentive for juniors to argue that markets do not value the firm accurately and an incentive for juniors to delay. The incentive to delay springs from several related sources. First, if the valuation (or settlement) today will wipe the juniors out, they have no desire to end the proceedings. Second, if there is an operational decline because of the delay, the seniors bear the brunt of that decline. On the other hand, third, if the company has an unusual upturn by the time a later settlement were negotiated then (after the upturn), the juniors would do better.

If that were all, corporate reorganization in bankruptcy would not take two or three years. Even if the judge picked an incorrect number, the distribution would occur and the bankruptcy would be over.

But the judge cannot readily value the firm, because he or she is inexpert at such tasks and will rarely be as well-informed as the firm's managers, creditors, or major stockholders about the firm itself. Even if expert, the judge mistrusts market valuation of bankrupt enterprises. Bankruptcy doctrine says that the market values the firm too low, because of uncertainties. Rarely do bankruptcy institutions recognize that the low value is principally a function of the bankrupt firm's poor opportunities.

In most reorganizations today, the judge does not formally value the firm or its constituent capital layers .... [T]he parties bargain to a solution. But what are they bargaining over? In large measure, they are bargaining over their guess as to what the judge would accept as a valuation number. That valuation dispute may be explicit or it may exacerbate other disputes. That is, some parties may dispute the validity of a lien, the interpretation of a subordination clause, the need for equitable subordination. These may be genuine disputes, but are exacerbated by uncertainty about the valuation result if the priority were more clearly established. I.e., whether the lien is worth invalidating for a particular party depends on what the valuation numbers look like. These disputes may in fact sometimes be the strategic arguments used—subconsciously or not—to wait for a valuation determination until the affected creditor is more likely to obtain a better pay-off.

\* \* \*

... While the legal process is unfolding, *the firm will incur costs: lost customers and suppliers [including skilled employees], unfinanced projects, diverted management time to dealing with the reorganization instead of the firm's operations.* Transaction costs are clear; and when the firm has unique opportunities, allocative costs may also be incurred.[4]

### B. Game Theory and Free-Riders

Although the particular party "causing" the deadlock incurs some of these costs, as a diminution in the value of that party's potential portion of the firm, most are borne by the other parties. The deadlock can be seen as a set of overlapping externalities. Each of the critical actors in reorganization can, by delaying, litigating, or rejecting a plan of reorganization, cause the firm and those with a claim on, or interest in, the firm to bear costs of delay. The decisionmaker bears only some of the costs that the decision triggers. A basic form of the prisoner's dilemma is at hand: the aggregation of individualistic, "rational" decisions leads to an inferior collective result.[5]

... [B]ecause the creditors' funds are already committed to the enterprise, the dependent relationship differs greatly from independent relationships that characterize the marketplace. The bargaining dynamic between and among dependent actors—those who must, because of continuing mutual commitments, deal with one another—provides enhanced opportunity for strategic behavior, threats, and appeals to nonmarket norms, all of which could lead to an unpredictable end to the negotiation [or to stalemates].

\* \* \*

Historically bankruptcy courts have mistrusted market valuations. Improperly so, for the public firm, I believe.

Why did [they mistrust market values]? Several hypotheses come to mind. Bankruptcy corporate reorganization legal doctrine first developed at the beginning of this century, when markets for bankrupt firms—and derivatively for their securities—were not highly developed. It might have made sense then to mistrust the market. The next push forward for legal doctrine in bankruptcy occurred during the Great Depression. The ideology of the time was mistrustful of the market; quick and expert valuation by the judge with the advice of the expert administrative agency, the SEC, seemed plausible.

Second, even today the overwhelming number of bankrupt firms are small, locally owned businesses. These firms probably do face an imperfect market; even if

---

[4] [For more ambiguous results on bankruptcy and recapitalization costs, see Robert H. Mnookin & Robert B. Wilson, *Rational Bargaining and Market Efficiency: Understanding Pennzoil v. Texaco*, 75 Va. L. Rev. 295 (1989) (high indirect costs); Gregor Andrade & Steven N. Kaplan, *How Costly is Financial (not Economic) Distress?—Evidence from Highly Leveraged Transactions that Became Distressed*, 53 J. Fin. 1443 (1998); Steven N. Kaplan, *Federated's Acquisition and Bankruptcy: Lessons and Implications*, 72 Wash. U. L.Q. 1103 (1994) (low indirect costs of pure financial stress).—Roe.]

[5] The process looks like the familiar common pool problem in oil recovery. Libecap & Wiggins, *Contractual Responses to the Common Pool: Prorationing of Crude Oil Production*, 74 Am. Econ. Rev. 87 (1984)[, excerpted supra ¶427].

not, judges are not sympathetic to putting the small business-owner out of business, a typical result of a market sale. The few large firm bankruptcies involve more assets, employees, and money than the aggregate of small business bankruptcies; but the legal mind adapts doctrines from the greater numbers to the fewer, but much more economically significant firms.[6]

## II. A New Reorganization Paradigm

### A. Using the Market

Whatever may be the reason, mistrust of the market in bankruptcy is the reality. Yet ... a quick method of valuation [would use the market to] end the multi-year contentiousness that corporate reorganization in bankruptcy now produces: *sell the firm in its entirety or use a stock float from which firm value is extrapolated.* One prospect is to sell the firm's operations, take the cash and distribute it to the creditors. And, if that seems too radical, disruptive or transactionally costly—for good reasons or bad—why not get the valuation number from a sale of, say, 10% of the firm's stock? From that sale, a value of the firm as a whole can be extrapolated. The extrapolated value will not be perfect; sometimes the whole is worth more than the securities parts. Whichever way the value is ascertained—extrapolated value or sale in its entirety—the resultant number allows for a distribution in bankruptcy. The highest ranking creditors get paid in full—in cash if there's a sale of the entire enterprise, in stock if there's a valuation sale of only 10% of the company's stock—and so on down the capital pecking order. That effort would make the bankruptcy reality correspond to the options models that finance economists use, but which are not readily implemented in corporate bankruptcy today.

### B. A Simple Illustration

Assume that the bankrupt firm has a capital structure consisting of $50 million of senior debt, $50 million of junior debt, and (old) common stock. There are no other creditors. Seniors argue the corporation is worth $50 million, juniors argue $100 million, (old) common stockholders argue $125 million. The court recapitalizes with a structure of 1,000,000 new common shares held for the parties, with the distribution

---

[6] A speculative additional reason: Use of market value would have compelled courts to validate an operational decision that as populist, semi-local officials they were loathe to validate. A fair market value of the firm would often reveal that the firm ought to [have been] liquidated: the firm was worth more if its parts were sold off than if it were reorganized. But if the bankruptcy judge—a product of local politics—were reluctant to liquidate, he or she faced the difficult task that a fair reorganization value was less than the cash sale value offered by those who would quickly liquidate the firm. To validate the reorganization decision—which would keep the judge from approving the closing of the local factory—a reorganization value had to be obtained that was higher than the cash sale, liquidation value. But that higher number was not obtainable in the market. Hence the market had to be rejected.

of these shares to be specified later. *Uncertain as to the ease of quickly marketing all 1,000,000 shares,* it has an underwriter sell 100,000 of the shares to the public. The underwriter obtains $100 per share, indicating an extrapolated enterprise value (with the proceeds of the offering) of $100 million. The $90 million in residual value ($100 million in total enterprise value minus $10 million owned by the purchasers of the 100,000 shares) is allocated among the seniors and juniors; the old common shareholders receive nothing. The remaining 900,000 shares are then distributed: 500,000 to the seniors, 400,000 to the juniors.

Such an approach would slash through the tangled bankruptcy knots of valuation, distributional conflicts, and recapitalization. The wisdom of replacing the current means of valuation in bankruptcy with this market-based approach is initially dependent on the relative accuracy, speed, and cost of market valuation when compared to the current mechanisms.

C. Efficient Markets?

In an efficient capital market, the price of a security will soundly reflect an informed estimate of the security's expected value. Investors will analyze the information available to them, and then purchase or sell securities at a price that reflects this information. The market will be efficient as long as both the information it receives is sufficiently complete and the analysis of that information is not systematically overly optimistic or overly pessimistic. If the number of analysts and potential buyers following a security is sufficiently large, efficient-capital-market theory suggests, they will compete to acquire sufficient publicly available information to analyze the security as accurately as possible given the available information .... Thus, the critical variables are information, analysis, and breadth of the market. Is the market for a bankrupt firm's securities efficient? More to the point, is a court better equipped than the capital market to value the public bankrupt and determine its capital structure?

1. *Data.* The few studies relevant to the direct question of the efficiency of the market for bankrupt securities indicate efficiency. In one, securities of firms entering bankruptcy were found to be effectively valued, in light of their subsequent returns. In another, a portfolio of income bonds, part of which had been issued in bankruptcy, was found to have been effectively valued.[7] In a third, the common shares of bankrupt firms were found to provide approximately the same return as a portfolio of all New York Stock Exchange securities.[8]

---

[7] Warner, Bankruptcy, *Absolute Priority and the Pricing of Risky Debt Claims*, 4 J. Fin. Econ. 239, 272 (1977); McConnel & Schlarbaum, *Returns, Risks and Pricing of Income Bonds, 1956–76,* 54 J. Bus. 33 (1981).

[8] Altman, *Bankrupt Firms' Equity Securities as an Investment Alternative,* Fin. Analysts J., July–Aug. 1969, at 129.

2. *Judicial Doctrine.* Bankruptcy institutions have usually assumed that a reorganized firm's securities and assets are systematically undervalued,[9] despite the evidence. The explanation may lie in a failure to distinguish the market faced by a publicly held firm with widely distributed securities and that faced by a bankrupt local barber shop ....

... Small enterprises, the bulk of business reorganizations as measured by the number of bankruptcy petitions filed, face a market so ineffective that judicial intervention appears to be warranted. Only a few large firms go bankrupt. They are included in the broad class for which the bankruptcy institutions reject the market and intervene as to value and capital structure, although the public firm's assets, liabilities, and satellite interests are so significant that separate consideration is worthwhile.

It seems natural that bankruptcy courts have not yet developed market-based doctrines. Only in recent decades, after completion of the major reorganizations of the 1930s and 1940s has such market-based thought been significant in other areas of corporate law. During the settling of the foundation of modern bankruptcy doctrine in the 1930s and 1940s, other significant legal institutions—including the National Recovery Administration and the Supreme Court, as reflected in important antitrust decisions—rejected the market as a basis for decisionmaking.[10] Several of the principal regulators had similar views of corporate bankruptcies. They wanted to thwart work-out bargains among financial creditors because they wanted a bankruptcy in which the judge would scrutinize the firm, its bankers, and its management. They wanted a judicially managed bankruptcy. Just as the New Deal was displacing markets in other contexts, they wanted a recapitalization decision made by New Deal expert regulators (the SEC with its advisory report to the court) and the judge.[11]

3. *Informational Impediments.* The publicly available information concerning bankrupts might be insufficient to allow many investors to gauge value accurately. As such, it might be argued, the court is better able than the market to search out and evaluate information that is not publicly dispersed and then use this information to value the firm .... A centralized information gatherer [would be] efficient ...; in the bankruptcy context it is the bankruptcy court. One might thus argue that judicial valuation would be warranted.

---

[9] E.g., Citibank, N.A. v. Baer, 651 F.2d 1341, 1347–48 (10th Cir. 1980) ("With a newly reorganized company coming from the throes of bankruptcy, the actual market value of a share of stock may be considerably less than the pro rata portion of the going concern value of the company represented by that stock.") ....

[10] See National Industrial Recovery Act, ch. 90, 48 Stat. 195 (1933); Parker v. Brown, 317 U.S. 341 (1943); Appalachian Coals, Inc. v. United States, 288 U.S. 344 (1933).

[11] See, e.g., W. Douglas, Democracy and Finance 189–90 (1940); Frank, *Some Realistic Reflections on Some Aspects of Corporate Reorganization*, 19 Va. L. Rev. 541, 568–69 (1933) (Douglas and Frank later became chairmen of the SEC) ....

... [But the] institution seeking the information need not also evaluate and act upon it. Efficient capital-market theory asserts that the market consensus represents the best guess as to value, other than the guess of insiders. To the extent the "buried" information is especially significant for bankrupts, the proper role of the court would then be to uncover it and make it public. The statute already provides the court with ample authority to do so.[12] If this were done, the market would have the missing information ....

Even if the courts were unable to transmit the better information to the market, courts would seem able to evaluate the information only with difficulty. It is not at all clear which a priori debility is more severe: less information or less skill ....

Furthermore, macro-economic, industry-wide and technological factors are now widely believed to be as significant in valuing a firm as company-specific information. To imagine a bankruptcy in the early 1980s of International Harvester (now Navistar): Its value depended at least as much upon guesses as to future economic conditions in the United States, Congressional policy toward farm prices, foreign policy as to American grain sales, decisions of Japanese manufacturers to expand or contract production of farm machinery, political decisions in major farming and food-importing nations abroad, and long-term weather trends, as it depended on guesses as to the future management, production, and technological capacity of Harvester itself. Such generalized, non-company-specific information is better understood and evaluated by the market (which is already making similar generalized judgments vis-a-vis other farm machinery companies) than by the court ....

D. The Uncertain Market Efficiency During Reorganization

Although the *post-reorganization* market seems in principle an accurate evaluator of enterprise value, serious problems would arise if the plausibly efficient market were thrust into *the midst of* reorganization. Use of a slice-of-common-stock sale and extrapolation of value could lead to significant distortions if there would be a residual block sufficiently large to control the enterprise, if the buyers in the valuation sale were those in the market who valued the bankrupt firm the highest, if parties to the reorganization attempted to manipulate the timing and terms of the valuation sale, or if parties to the reorganization strategically bid at the valuation sale to raise or lower the auction price to their own advantage.

1. *Control Blocks.* Creditors with large debts could obtain a block of stock sufficient to control the reorganized firm. This could skew the price offered by bidders in the valuation sale, who would anticipate the blocks. As such, the sale price and hence the compensation given creditors could be distorted, overcompensating large senior creditors because the bidders expected to be minority shareholders in the reorganized enterprise.

---

[12] Bankruptcy Code § 1125(b).

[But although] the marketing of large blocks of stock is often accompanied by a decline in price, some evidence indicates that the decline is not so much the result of the additional supply of the stock thrown onto the market as it is the result of the informational content of the sale.[13] The holder of a large block is often an insider. The market assesses the sale as an indication that one with ... superior information ... has concluded that the market currently overestimates the firm's value. But ... the post-reorganization desire of the former creditor to sell the block of common stock arises because of legal impediments ..., not [from] ... aversion to the particular bankrupt's security ....

[And] ... we are assessing market valuation against its practical alternatives, the bargain and judicial determination, not against an idealized system of valuation. Although reorganization courts that reject the market as a basis for valuation have initially recognized the control value of large blocks as having the potential to distort extrapolated value, they have at times cast aside or ignored this consideration when performing the task of valuation, because of the difficulty in surmising how to quantify the value of control. As such, the market extrapolation method discussed here is not necessarily less accurate than judicial valuation on this score.

2. *Strategic Delay and Manipulation of the Terms of the Valuation Sale.* Costly delay is one of the nasty side-effects of reorganization by bargain or litigation. Uncertainty as to valuation seems to be a focal point for some or much of that delay .... However, ... [e]liminati[ng] valuation disputes may only shift one of the focal points, not the result.

... [T]hose claimants likely to be hurt by a market valuation ... will seek to delay the time of a valuation sale if they see reasonable prospects for a market rise .... They [could] ... litigat[e] whatever preliminary questions had to be resolved—size of the offering, application of the proceeds (to pay off old creditors or to undertake new projects?), contents of the bankrupt estate, validity and priority of claims and security interests, and the means (or lack of means) to force dissipation of control blocks .... In a typical firm-commitment underwriting, the company negotiates a fixed price with the underwriters. If company management is controlled by common shareholders, conflicts could emerge as the shareholders, through management, attempt to maximize sale price, and thereby gain a large portion of the reorganized firm, perhaps by an attempt to market a very small number of shares at a high price. For example, the firm might overcompensate the investment banks with an abnormally high selling concession in order to induce placement of a few overpriced shares ....

The underwriting problem could be successfully managed. If the court is reasonably certain that the common stock is not under water, but uncertain as to how far above water it is, then it can tell the common shareholders (through management) that they must sell a specified minimum number of shares by a certain time at a "normal"

---

[13] Scholes, *The Market for Securities: Substitution versus Price Pressure and the Effects of Information on Share Prices*, 45 J. Bus. 179 (1972).

selling concession ... [If underwater, it would turn the sale over to representatives of the lowest ranking unsecureds.]

The difficulty here is again that the court might have to make preliminary determinations of value. (Is the firm possibly worth [enough to] warrant[] giving the first shot at marketing to the old common shareholders?) These determinations are subject to strategic manipulation and require the court to make determinations that ... it is unlikely to make particularly well.

Similar difficulties would arise from litigation about priority and liens. That is, the juniors might not concede the validity of (or extent of) their subordination agreement or might seek the equitable subordination of the seniors. But this need not stymie the valuation sale in its entirety. The sale could take place and shares reserved to be distributed after the subsequent determination of the subordination arrangements.

... Management, if acting for juniors, might force a reorganization as soon as it—armed with information better than that of the market—thought the market value was ... higher than longer run values. Limits would be needed to prevent all debt from effectively becoming convertible into stock at the option of management. Creditors with information superior to that of the market consensus could try to force a market-based reorganization when they sensed the market was undervaluing the firm. The effort to reduce these opportunities of creditors and shareholders to take value from another layer in the firm's capital structure could throw the firm into unneeded but costly litigation.

3. *Strategic Bidding.* The old common stockholders and juniors might want to bid high for the offered slice of the enterprise and thereby skew the valuation to their advantage ....

* * *

4. *Summary* .... [A]lthough the post-reorganization market might be better than a court, and quicker than the bargaining parties, in valuing the firm, bringing the market into an ongoing reorganization could introduce several distortions. As such, the simplicity of the market-based solution must be treated with skepticism. An administrative apparatus to control or assess the significance of the distortions would be necessary; the relevant choice is not simply among market, bargain, and judicial administration, but also among judicial administration of different matters .... [T]he question of the superiority of a market-based reorganization on this score is one of judgment ....

### III. More Problems

#### A. Other Valuation Problems

First, we have ignored secured creditors .... In a reorganization where the value of the property to which the security interest attaches is uncertain, the assets would have to be valued: litigation, bargaining and delay would to that extent become unavoidable. For similar reasons, the reorganization of complex holding company structures might require ... [judicial] valuation [anyway] .... Creditors of under-water [subsidiaries] would argue for a different valuation or [for] ... substantive consolidation ....

However, not all companies have a significant amount of secured debt or use complex holding companies. Of those that do, the secured party may be sufficiently secured such that there is no serious question that the value of the security covers the claim. Furthermore, some of these questions could be resolved after the valuation sale, with shares reserved to cover the contested amounts.

Second, for that rare reorganization of an operationally healthy firm in a healthy industry, it might be argued that a simple extension of maturities is all that is necessary to overcome the effects of a random, unlikely-to-be-repeated shock, such as an unusual strike or a natural disaster.

\* \* \*

B. Bankruptcy as Other Than a Bargain Among Financial Creditors

Reorganization is not always just a question of readjusting the financial capital structure. Executory contracts such as labor agreements may give rise to critical reorganization negotiations. Suppliers may have made informal investments in the firm (by committing equipment to production for that firm) that do not appear on the firm's balance sheet and that would not formally constitute a claim in bankruptcy. These suppliers (including labor and managerial claims) may be the real subject of some reorganizations, but would be untouched in a common-stock sale and recapitalization.

That is, financial creditors may stand-off against such claimants, offering to give up a few points in interest (or exchange debt into stock) in return for a reduction of the managerial workforce or a cut in wage rates from, say, $25 per hour to $18 per hour. [A market] sale would leave these claimants untouched, reducing their incentive to participate in the reorganization give-ups, effectively make them superior in right of payment to the financial claimants [because a further reorganization would no longer be necessary and the pressure for "give-ups" would subside]. Multi-party, deadlocking negotiations might have some use if they were more likely to produce an ethic under which everyone (creditors, suppliers, labor, and management) "chips in" something.

**Conclusion**

... Bankruptcy courts oversee a rambling bargain that implicitly assigns a value to bankrupt public firms and then provides a capital structure that often is high in debt. If the bargain fails, litigation results. Both these processes are lengthy, costly, and, if a rapid, objective basis to value the firm is available, unnecessary. Since the post-reorganization market seems likely to value the firm more accurately than does the court, the reasons offered by bankruptcy institutions for rejection of the market in favor of judicial valuation (when bargaining fails)—incomplete information, stigma, and insufficient buyers—seem unpersuasive .... It is true that incompleteness of available information, costliness of available information, ... and problems in the disparities between the value of a large block and the value of the few shares sold for purposes of extrapolating value all suggest that the post-reorganization market falls short as an *ideal* basis for accurate valuation. But judicial valuation (or the bargained-for result) faces some of these same debilities, as well as others; some debilities in the accuracy of market-based valuation can be eliminated or mitigated. More importantly, whatever the relative accuracy of the mechanisms, a market-based valuation and recapitalization via the slice-of-common-stock sale begins with the potential to be quicker *and cheaper* than the alternatives.

However, jamming the market valuation into the context of an ongoing reorganization would risk recreating the very problems that an objective market valuation might eliminate: delay and judicial inexpertise. A simple valuation sale would require determinations as to size, timing, price, and other terms .... While these problems are potentially resolvable, they could require judicial determinations similar to (although not as consequential as) those made in a valuation hearing. These determinations (and others, such as litigation of the validity of security interests or of contract liabilities) raise anew the specter of strategic delay by participants in the reorganizations. The question thus becomes one of judgement as to the relative severity of the defects in the three reorganization models, and the likely relative success of judicial control of the defects in each model. The choice cannot be made by economic deduction or statistical observation of market accuracy alone.

Furthermore, some bankrupt firms have substantial nonfinancial relationships with labor claimants, suppliers who have made investments specifically to sell to the bankrupt, and tort claimants. These may ... be informal claimants in that they would continue to obtain returns were there a successful reorganization. A swift marketplace valuation would eliminate the prospect of the firm rebargaining with them, effectively making such non-Code claimants superior in right of payment to the financial claimants. Either separate mechanisms would have to be developed for bankruptcies in which such claimants were significant (and means developed to swiftly distinguish the two types) or these claimants would be conceded as superior in payment rights to Code-defined claimants.

... [And e]ven a simple, purely financial reorganization would be difficult to implement. Complex reorganizations with secured debt, holding companies, labor claimants, and other non-Code "investors" and suppliers would be more difficult. Nevertheless, the prospect that corporate reorganizations in bankruptcy could be speeded up, so that the transactional time corresponds with that of a securities offering or a merger, instead of the two or three years a reorganization now takes, deserves continued scrutiny.

Because many of the problems with the slice-of-common-stock sale—such as secured credit, holding company structures, creation of other sources of delay, and uncertainty associated with anything new—are possible but not necessarily present in all reorganizations, a minimal response ought to be to add the suggested reorganization method as one of the possible means of valuation and restructuring, and to clear away as much of the inhibiting statutory underbrush as possible. For example, the market-based reorganization could at least be authorized as a judicial weapon if the bargain fails to produce a result after a specified period of time. The Code could be recast to allow the bankruptcy judge to intervene and force a market-based reorganization (with judicial administrative efforts to reduce the likely distortions) if negotiations became too complex and slow.

### ¶1703: Questions on Roe

1. If bankruptcy costs are low, is a market sale better than reorganization? See Frank Easterbrook, *Is corporate bankruptcy efficient?*, 27 J. Fin. Econ. 411 (1990). The direct costs of bankruptcy are about 3% of the firm's assets. Lawrence A. Weiss, *Bankruptcy resolution: Direct costs and violation of priority of claims*, 27 J. Fin. Econ. 285 (1990). Direct costs in mergers are not low. The MetLife transaction had $700 million in direct costs on a $25 billion transaction, or direct costs of about 2%. See MetLife complaint, ¶1312. If these are representative, the question is which transaction, sale or chapter 11, generates lower indirect costs; for that, there's no reliable hard evidence. Indirect costs would include the bankrupt's inability to make deals with uneasy contracting parties, the diversion of management time, the flight of high-quality employees and suppliers to other firms.

2. On the possibility of informal claimants that would effectively be made prior by a sale: Would the best resolution be to add a new section to chapter 11:

    **[Hypothetical] § 1195. Sale of debtor**

    After 120 days after the petition has been filed, the court may, upon motion of any party in interest, arrange for the sale of debtor in its entirety, or arrange for the sale of stock in the debtor, thereby fixing the value of the firm for purposes of § 1129.

    Would this provision, if added to the Code, tend to resolve the indirect priority problem, because creditors will not so move if the indirect priority problem is high? Would this also tend to resolve the high transaction cost problem, because the judge could deny the sale if the firm seems one ripe for a quick and low-cost renegotiation? (But would introducing a standard for allowing or disallowing the sale recreate some, maybe many, of the bargaining deadlocks the sale would be designed to prevent?)

**¶1704: Douglas Baird, The Uneasy Case for Corporate Reorganization, 15 Journal of Legal Studies 127 (1986)[14]**

... Even if some kind of collective proceeding is needed to prevent a destructive race to the firm's assets, [chapter 11] could be justified only if investors before the fact would (if they could) agree to a hypothetical sale of assets instead of a real one. I argue that, as a general matter, investors taken as a group would rarely prefer the hypothetical sale to an actual one. An actual sale eliminates the potential distortions from a fictive valuation of a firm. More important, *the costs of an actual sale are likely to be less than the cost of the procedures needed to prevent manipulation and game playing by the participants in a hypothetical sale.* I argue that for this reason the entire law of corporate reorganizations is hard to justify under any set of facts and virtually impossible when the debtor is a publicly held corporation.

\* \* \*

### III

The simplest collective proceeding is a sale of the firm for cash and the distribution of the proceeds to all the investors. The common objection to such sales is that they cannot preserve the value of a firm as a going concern. Under this view, finding a third party who is willing to buy the firm as a single unit is so time-consuming and so difficult that, without a mechanism to stay the rights of all creditors and force them to become owners of the firm, the firm would be broken into small pieces that are worth less than the firm as a single unit. Only a reorganization provides the necessary "breathing space" that gives all involved a chance to sort out their affairs.

Finding buyers for firms that in fact are worth preserving as going concerns may not be more difficult, more expensive, or more error prone than [a reorganization in chapter 11] ....

... A bankruptcy judge may be less able to cast a cold eye on an enterprise and make tough decisions than someone who has put his own money on the line. He may have no effective constraint analogous to the discipline a market imposes on competing buyers who make systematic errors. Like any other individual outside such constraints, he may tend to underestimate risks.

None of this, however, is to suggest that [a] going concern sale of a firm [is] without cost .... [A] sale of the firm's assets may be difficult to orchestrate. The sale should be conducted by the residual claimants to the firm's assets because they have an incentive to obtain the best price .... They also suffer the consequences if they devote insufficient resources to finding a buyer or buyers, or if they waste time and money trying to sell the assets for more than anyone is willing to pay.

---

[14] Copyright 1986 by the University of Chicago. All rights reserved.

Ensuring that residual claimants conduct the sale (or, more precisely, ensuring that those who conduct the sale are entitled to keep the excess) is not easy. For example, the identity of the residual claimants may be uncertain. If it is not clear whether the assets are worth more than is necessary to satisfy the claims of general creditors and those senior to them, a choice must be made between allowing the general creditors (or the trustee, as their representative) to conduct the sale alone and allowing those junior to them to participate. Either decision brings difficulties. If the general creditors act alone, they may not take account of the interests of those junior to them. On the other hand, if junior owners participate, they will tend to favor any tactic that might bring a higher price—such as costly searching or endless delay—that a sole owner would reject as unjustified. These junior claimants would have the correct set of incentives *only if* they bore the additional costs of searching for a buyer who would pay more than the total amount of claims senior to their own ....

In addition, there may be more than one residual claimant. A firm, for example, may have dozens or thousands of general creditors. Even if they can be identified easily, it may be difficult to fashion a set of rules that enables them to work together or to appoint someone to act on their behalf. Under current law, the bankruptcy trustee is charged with acting on behalf of the general creditors, but in practice it is hard for general creditors to monitor the trustee and ensure that he heeds his obligations to them. Problems of monitoring arise whenever one person acts as the agent of others ....

One should not, however, exaggerate the difficulties inherent in deciding who among the investors should conduct the sale. In the case of a large firm, the residual claimants would likely hire someone with the appropriate expertise (such as an investment banker) to run the sale. It may not much matter whether the decision to hire Goldman Sachs rather than Shearman Lehman Brothers rests in one investor rather than another.

IV

... In a liquidation, what various claimants are entitled to receive is relatively fixed. If a firm is sold outright, substantive nonbankruptcy entitlement[s] largely determine who gets what in what order. *There is often little to argue over because rights are fixed and payments are made in cash.* In a reorganization, on the other hand, many more issues are open. One must value shares in the reorganized company and allocate them to the old owners ....

A threshold question is whether the complications of reorganizations and the opportunities they provide for undercompensation and strategic game playing by creditors, shareholders, and managers are worth the benefits they bring. The justification for reorganizations usually begins with the observation that many firms are worth more if kept intact (or largely intact) than if sold piecemeal. The rationale for a reorganization, however, must not be simply that some firms are worth more as "going concerns" than if liquidated. Although not common under present law, a liquidation is consistent with keeping a firm intact as a going concern. The difference between a liquidation and a reorganization is that the first involves an actual sale of all the assets of a business to a third-party buyer and the second involves a hypothetical one. Under existing law, petitions filed under Chapter 7 usually lead to a piecemeal sale of the assets, and those under Chapter 11 involve attempts (many of which fail) to keep the firm intact as a going concern. Nothing in current law, however, prevents a sale of the firm as a going concern in Chapter 7, and Chapter 11 presently allows for a piecemeal sale of the assets of the firm. *The justification for a reorganization must focus on showing the higher costs of selling the firm to a third party.*

... The third party acquiring the assets can bargain with the managers and obtain their services by striking separate deals with each of them. If the managers will work only if given an equity interest in the firm, the new owners can offer it to them. In this respect, new owners are in the same position as investors who continue to own the firm after a reorganization.

\* \* \*

The owners of a firm might prefer a forced sale of assets to themselves (which a reorganization is, in effect) to an actual sale to one or more third parties *if it were cheaper* .... In a world in which information can be gathered and communicated quickly and in which many entrepreneurs specialize in acquiring firms in distress, the practical [business] obstacles (as opposed to the ones that are purely legal) seem quite surmountable ....

\* \* \*

V

... [T]he owners of a ... publicly held firm, would likely prefer a sale of the firm outright to whomever was willing to pay the most for it. A going-concern sale of assets is possible under the existing structure of Chapter 7 of the Bankruptcy Code. Such sales, however, run counter to the thinking of most bankruptcy judges and practitioners ....

\* \* \*

Even though Chapter 7 permits going-concern liquidations, it was not drafted with such sales in mind. The powers of the trustee have been conceived over the years as the powers of someone who would oversee the dismantling of a firm. Were the use of Chapter 7 to change, the powers of the trustee (and the ways in which his behavior would be monitored) would also change .... Some tax rules provide additional examples. Under existing law, a tax-loss carryforward disappears when there is a sale of the firm for cash, but it survives a sale of the firm for securities (even if they can be readily converted into cash), and it survives when a firm is reorganized under Chapter 11.[15] The rule governing tax-loss carryforwards should be independent of what kind of bankruptcy proceeding is involved and, indeed, whether there is any bankruptcy proceeding at all ....

This paper has suggested that the premise underlying Chapter 11 of the Bankruptcy Code may be unsound. But in making this observation, one should not overlook the virtues of the existing law. Existing rules of corporate reorganization are a vast improvement over what preceded them. The number of cases in which the bankruptcy process has done what it is supposed to do (readjust ownership interests while at the same time respecting substantive nonbankruptcy rights without interfering with the optimum deployment of the assets) is much greater now than it was before the Bankruptcy Reform Act was passed in 1978, and courts are more sensitive to the basic principles of bankruptcy law ....

## ¶1705: Questions on Baird

1. Again, what if the costs of reorganization are low? What if the transaction costs of a sale are substantial?

    Even if the transaction costs of a sale are substantial and the costs of reorganization low, one would want to know if many reorganized firms merge after the chapter 11 plans are confirmed; if so, they incur both costs and would be better off if they incurred only one.

2. Do most bankrupt firms have to be better off integrated into another firm in the industry for a bankruptcy sale to be worthwhile? Could bidders bid to keep the firm standing alone? Could management form a bidding group if managerial skills are especially valuable?

3. Would the sale alternative be seen as fair by the average voter (or average member of Congress)?

4. Must the sale be mandatory to be viable? If mandatory, what about the problem of "informal" priority for informal claimants?

5. Stockholders always can in theory overcome an under-valuation, by paying creditors off and keeping the firm for themselves. They would be impeded only by illiquidity (either directly or via an inability to convince financiers of the undervaluation) or their own poor information (which could lead them to abandon a valuable, but undervalued firm). Could these relationships be the foundation for a new model of reorganization, i.e., by giving the stockholders a short time in which to buy the firm back or be wiped out, after which the right to buy out the seniors would pass to the next highest ranking interest or claimant? The next read-

---

[15] See I.R.C. § 368.

ing, by Lucian Bebchuk, sets out an ingenious way to make this structure operational.

### ¶1706: Lucian Arye Bebchuk, A New Approach to Corporate Reorganizations, 101 Harv. L. Rev. 775 (1988)

II. THE DIVISION PROBLEM IN CORPORATE REORGANIZATION

Given the set of all claims by participants, each claim defined by its size and relative priority, how should the reorganization pie (that is, the value of the reorganized company) be divided among the participants?

... [T]his issue of division, although central, is not the only element in corporate reorganizations. *A reorganization inevitably must also include the preliminary process of determining the size and relative priority of the participants' claims.* For example, it might be necessary to determine the amount the company owes to the holders of a certain bond issue or to certain business partners, as well as the relative priorities of these debts. Although this preliminary, inevitable process of determining the size and ranking of claims often involves significant delay and litigation costs, I will not discuss it. Rather, I will focus on the division problem, and *to this end I will largely assume that the size and ranking of the participants' claims are already known.*

\* \* \*

III. THE PROPOSED METHOD

A. The Example

... Consider a publicly traded company that has three classes of participants. Class A includes 100 senior creditors, each owed $1. Class B includes 100 junior creditors, each owed $1. Class C includes 100 equityholders, each holding one unit of equity.

The company is now in bankruptcy proceedings and is to be reorganized. The Reorganized Company, which I will call RC, is going to have a capital structure that for now I will assume to be given. For any chosen capital structure, it is of course possible to divide the securities of RC into 100 equal units .... The question for the reorganization process is how to divide the 100 units of RC among the three classes of participants. [Each unit's value is $V$; the total value of RC is $100V$.]

\* \* \*

C. Participants' Entitlements as a Function of Reorganization Value

The question of division ... would pose no problem if we could measure $V$ with precision .... But even though we cannot identify precisely the value to which each participant is entitled, *we can precisely express this value as a function of V*, the reorganized company's per unit value.

Consider first the senior creditors .... [A] senior creditor is entitled to a value of V if V<=$1 and a value of $1 if V>$1. Alternatively put, a senior creditor is entitled to a value of $1 unless the reorganization value is less than $100, in which case the senior creditor is entitled to his pro rata share of the reorganization value (that is, to one unit of RC).

Consider next the junior creditors. A junior creditor, we have seen, is entitled to nothing if V<=$1, is entitled to V–$1 if $1<V<=$2, and is entitled to $1 if V>$2. Alternatively put, a junior creditor is entitled to a value of $1 unless the reorganization value is less than $200, in which case he is entitled to his pro rata share of the value that is left, if any, after the senior creditors are paid in full.

Finally, an equityholder is entitled to nothing if V<=$2, and to V–$2 if V>$2. Alternatively put, an equityholder is entitled to his pro rata share of the value that is left, if any, after the senior and junior creditors are paid in full.

Table 2 below summarizes these conclusions concerning participants' entitlements as a function of the reorganization value.

### D. The Proposed Approach

... Even though we do not know V and consequently do not know the value of participants' entitlements in terms of dollars or RC units, we do know precisely what participants are entitled to as a function of V .... With this knowledge, it is possible to design and to distribute to the participants a set of rights concerning RC's units such that ... these rights would provide participants with values perfectly consistent with their entitlements.

... I will assume below that the reorganized company will start its life and distribute the rights to participants on January 1; and that the exercise date for all the rights distributed will be four days later, on January 5.

Thus, on January 1, the reorganized company will start its life. But, under the proposed method, the units of RC will not be distributed at this point but rather will be retained by the company until January 5. Instead of receiving RC units, on January 1 the participants will get the following rights with respect to RC units.

1. *Senior Creditors.*—Each senior creditor will receive one type-A right. A type-A right may be redeemed by the company on January 5 for $1. If the right is not redeemed, its holder on January 5 will be entitled to receive one unit of RC.

To get some sense at this stage of the value to senior creditors of receiving type-A rights, consider a creditor that holds his type-A right until January 5. If the right is redeemed, then the creditor will be paid in full. If the right is not redeemed, then the creditor will receive a value of V. And indeed, the senior creditor is never entitled to receive more than either $1 or V (see Table 2).

2. *Junior Creditors.*—Each junior creditor will receive a type-B right. The company may redeem a type-B right on January 5 for $1. If the right is not redeemed, its holder will have the option on January 5 to purchase one unit of RC for $1. To exercise this option, the holder of the right must submit it to the company by January 5 accompanied by a payment of the $1 exercise price.

... [R]eceiving a type-B right will provide a junior creditor with the value to which he is entitled. If the creditor holds on to the type-B right and the right is redeemed, then the creditor will be paid in full. If the right is not redeemed, exercising it will provide the creditor with a value of V–$1. And indeed, the creditor is never entitled to receive a value higher than both $1 and V–$1 (see Table 2).

3. *Equityholders.*—Each equityholder will receive one type-C right. A type-C right may not be redeemed by the company. The holder of a type-C right will have the

### TABLE 2
### PARTICIPANTS' ENTITLEMENTS AS A FUNCTION OF V

|  | V≤$1 | $1<V≤$2 | V>$2 |
|---|---|---|---|
| Senior Creditor | V | $1 | $1 |
| Junior Creditor | 0 | V–$1 | $1 |
| Equityholder | 0 | 0 | V–$2 |
| TOTAL | V | V | V |

option to purchase one RC unit on January 5 for $2. To exercise this option, the holder must submit the right to the company by January 5 accompanied by a payment of the $2 exercise price.

Note that if an equityholder holds on to his right until January 5 and then chooses to exercise it, he will get a value V–$2. And indeed, the equityholder is never entitled to a positive value exceeding V–$2 (see Table 2).

These three types of rights will all be transferable. Thus, between January 1 and January 5, there will presumably be public trading in the rights. A participant that is given any one of the rights may thus either sell it on the market or retain it until the exercise date of January 5.

Table 3 below summarizes the terms of the rights ....

### E. The Exercise of Rights

Adding up the obligations that RC will have toward the holders of type-A, type-B, and type-C rights shows that the net obligation of RC is to distribute 100 RC units on January 5, which is exactly what is available for distribution. Thus, RC should have no problem meeting all its obligations toward the holders of the three types of rights ....

Suppose first that all of the holders of type-C rights wish to exercise their options to buy RC units and that they submit a total of $200 to the company. RC then will provide them with all 100 units of RC (one unit for each right submitted), and it will use the $200 received from them to redeem all of the type-A and type-B rights [from the creditors].

Suppose now that no type-C rights are submitted for exercise, but that all holders of type-B rights wish to exercise their options to buy RC units at $1 and therefore submit a total of $100 to the company. In this case, RC will give all of the RC units to the holders of these type-B rights, and it will use the $100 received from them to redeem all of the type-A rights.

Next, suppose that no type-B or type-C rights are submitted for exercise. The mechanics of this case will be simpler still: the 100 units of RC will be distributed to the holders of type-A rights (one RC unit per right).

## TABLE 3
### THE DISTRIBUTION OF RIGHTS

Senior Creditors

Each senior creditor receives one type-A right. A type-A right may be redeemed by the company on January 5 for $1. If the right is redeemed, on January 5 its holder will be entitled to receive one unit of RC.

Junior Creditors

Each junior creditor receives one type-B right. A type-B right may be redeemed by the company on January 5 for $1. If the right is not redeemed, on January 5 its holder will have the option to purchase one unit of RC for $1.

Equityholders

Each equityholder receives one type-C right. A type-C right may not be redeemed by the company. The holder of such a right on January 5 will have the option to purchase one unit of RC for $2.

Finally, it remains to consider situations in which only a fraction of the type-B or type-C rights are submitted for exercise. Such situations are unlikely to arise if there is public trading in the rights. But in any event, given the design of the rights—in particular, the fact that the total net obligation of the company toward all right holders is to distribute 100 units of RC—such situations will present no special problem for the execution process.

For example, suppose that only 50 type-B rights (and presumably no type-C rights) are submitted for exercise. Then, those who submitted type-B rights will receive 50 units of RC (one unit per submitted right). The $50 submitted by them will be used for pro rata redemption of type-A rights. Consequently, each holder of a type-A right will end up with $0.50 and 0.50 units of RC.

\* \* \*

## IV. CONSISTENCY WITH PARTICIPANTS' ENTITLEMENTS

... [T]he outcome of the proposed method of division will be perfectly consistent with the entitlements of the participants. As emphasized earlier, the problems of the division process arise from the difficulties involved in determining the monetary value of the reorganized company. The proposed method, however, makes no attempt to estimate this monetary value, nor does it require even a rough sense of the monetary value of the rights that the participants will receive. Although we may not know how much these rights are worth, we can be confident that whatever their worth is, they will provide the receiving participants with no less than the value to which they are entitled.

### A. The Significance of Not Relying on Accurate Market Pricing

The rights given to the participants will be traded on the market in the brief period between the issue date and the exercise date .... If the market does not underestimate the reorganized company's value, then the market price of any type of right will be no less than the value to which the participants receiving the right are entitled; consequently, the participants will be able to capture the value of their entitlement by immediately selling their rights on the market.

... It is therefore a significant advantage of the proposed method that an inaccurate market pricing of the rights will not provide participants with a basis for objecting to the method's outcome.

This feature of the method is the main reason why it is superior to the method of division put forward by Professor Roe five years ago.[16] Roe was the first to seek, as I do in this Article, a method of division that would not be based on the problematic process of bargaining among the various classes of participants. He proposed to estimate the value of the reorganized company by selling ten percent of the reorganized company's securities on the market and then extrapolating the company's value from the sale price for these securities. Although Roe's method is, in my view, superior to the existing process of bargaining among classes, the method's reliance on market pricing makes it, as Roe himself recognized,[17] substantially imperfect. First, the method does not address the concerns of those who believe that the market might not

---

[16] See Roe, [*Bankruptcy and Debt: A New Model for Corporate Reorganization*, 83 Colum. L. Rev. 527 (1983).]

[17] See id. at 575–80.

perceive accurately the value of companies in reorganization. Second, even if the market's perceptions are accurate, selling a sample of the company's securities might produce an inaccurate figure, because some participants will have an incentive to manipulate the sale price. Third, Roe's method is inapplicable to companies whose securities are not publicly traded. Because the method that I propose does not hinge on the existence of accurate market pricing, it does not suffer from any of these problems.

## ¶1707: Questions on Bebchuk

1. Surely the options proposal is the cleverest market-based alternative to chapter 11.
2. Should the transaction costs of the options-approach be high?
3. Can the options be distributed before the priorities are precisely determined? Must all equitable subordination (§ 510(c)), value of security (§ 506(a)), preference (§ 547), fraudulent conveyance (§ 548), lender liability, and other priority litigation be substantially completed first. If so, could parties seeking to delay use this litigation as a lever for delay?
4. The options mechanism is refined in Philippe Aghion, Oliver Hart & John Moore, *The Economics of Bankruptcy Reform,* 8 J. L. Econ. & Org. 523 (1992). One step farther along from auctions and options is to let the contracting financial parties decide at the time of contracting how they'd like to reorganize the firm. See Barry E. Adler, *A Theory of Corporate Insolvency,* 72 NYU L. Rev. 343 (1997); Michael Bradley & Michael Rosenzweig, *The Untenable Case for Chapter 11,* 101 Yale L.J. 1043 (1992); Robert K. Rasmussen, *Debtor's Choice: A Menu Approach to Corporate Bankruptcy,* 71 Tex. L. Rev. 51 (1992); Alan Schwartz, *Bankruptcy Workouts and Debt Contracts,* 36 J.L. & Econ. 595 (1993). And contra: Lynn M. LoPucki, *Strange Visions in a Strange World: A Reply to Professors Bradley and Rosenzweig,* 91 Mich. L. Rev. 79 (1992); Elizabeth Warren, *The Untenable Case for Repeal of Chapter 11,* 102 Yale L.J. 437 (1992).

## ¶1708: Advantages and disadvantages of each market-based alternative

Each market-based alternative has advantages and disadvantages. These fall into several general categories: transaction costs, susceptibility to delay, technical accuracy, and consistency with the ultimate disposition of the firm. Unfortunately, each one has advantages in one or two categories, but severe disadvantages in another.

The sale of the firm in its entirety is probably the highest in transaction costs, but is probably most consistent with the ultimate disposition of (many) bankrupt firms. Bankrupt firms come disproportionately from shrinking or restructuring industries (in recent years, first the oil industry, then the airline industry, then the retailing industry). These industries usually consolidate. Merging a weaker firm immediately into a stronger one might put the firm to its ultimate resting spot. Thus, the first-stage transaction costs are probably the highest of the three (mergers and auctions are expensive), but if the firm immediately moves to its ultimate disposition, the total transaction costs might be lower than the others (many of which after reorganization would still need to merge with stronger firms).[18]

The slice-of-stock sale is low in initial transaction costs, because stock sales are relatively cheap (compared to selling an entire firm). Like the sale of the firm, it also has a low propensity to delay, because the sale can proceed even while priority litigation is going on. But it is susceptible to inside manipulation and is possibly the least accurate, because investors have lower incentives to invest in valuation (because they can't move the firm immediately to a higher value use, and because they'd only be buying a slice of the firm, not its entirety). It also can't be used by non-public firms or firms too small to go public.

The options approach would probably also be cheap transactionally (not including the firm's later ultimate disposition). *At the time it would be* employed, it probably is accurate enough (because it piggy-backs on the information held by insiders). But it cannot proceed until priority litigation is resolved, because the judge cannot allocate the options until the judge knows which player comes first. Consider the possibility that security is insufficient to cover a secured claim. If so, the options approach may not work well until the security is valued. But such valuation is exactly what the market-based approaches are trying to avoid. As such this approach may sometimes be less viable than the other two. This should be seen in detail, not just because seeing the detail allows us to review the major topics of this course, but also because a principal reason to use the market is to kill the incentive of some reorganization players to delay a valuation of the firm. But because the options can't be allocated until one knows the priorities, the slowness of reorganization might not be ameliorated. Indeed, if parties who would benefit from delay can turn up the heat in priority litigation, nothing might be gained from the options approach. (Stated more positively, the options could be used to value the firm once the parties resolve priority. At that point it becomes a superior valuation method.)

This problem can be seen by reviewing what must be resolved before the option distribution can begin. The options cannot be distributed until the firm, or critical assets or subsidiaries of the firm are valued. At that time, will the central reorganization problems then have been already solved?

This recursive feature—to resolve the valuation problem, one distributes options, but one cannot know to whom to distribute the options without valuing the firm or its critical assets—is due to doctrinal uncertainty about priority, factual uncertainty about priority, and valuation uncertainty about the underlying assets of security interests and

---

[18] See Andrei Shleifer & Robert Vishny, *Liquidation values and debt capacity: A market equilibrium approach*, 47 J. Fin. 1343 (1992) (industry-wide distress); but see Gregor Andrade & Steven N. Kaplan, *How Costly is Financial (not Economic) Distress?—Evidence from Highly Leveraged Transactions that Became Distressed*, 53 J. Fin. 1443 (1998); Steven N. Kaplan, *Federated's Acquisition and Bankruptcy: Lessons and Implications*, 72 Wash. U.L.Q. 1103 (1994) (distress due to too much leverage).

claims on pieces of a holding company. Without resolving these uncertainties, rank-ordering of claims cannot proceed; and without rank-ordering of claims, the options cannot be distributed. Some of these problems could be reduced with a better bankruptcy law, but most will persist no matter how perfect the law is.

Take a simple example: Secured creditor is owed $100. Unsecured creditor is owed $100. Common stockholders get whatever is left. If the secured creditor comes first, it gets the option to pay for a share of stock with its $100 claim. Unsecured come next and get an option to buy a share of stock with $100 plus their claim. Common stockholders get an option to buy a share of stock for $200. This is the example most conducive to the options approach. (Everyone knows that the firm is worth $150. Thus the secured creditor will try to exercise the option, but when the unsecured exercise, the unsecured pay $100, which is used to buy out the secured creditor.)

*1. Uncertainty of the value of the underlying asset.* But suppose that the secured creditor's security is in a machine, *whose value is $50*. Hence the secured creditor's priority is only prior to the extent of $50. The secured creditor's claim must be divided into a $50 priority secured claim and a $50 unsecured claim under § 506. Thus the correct option distribution is a $50 option to the secured creditor, and a distribution of $150 in options to the *full* class of unsecured creditors ($100 of "pure" unsecured and $50 of the split claim). The unsecured would "split" their option with the "pure" unsecured, who would be entitled to buy 2/3 of the stock for $33 plus their claim. The split secured claim would be entitled to buy 1/3 of the stock for $17 plus the split-off unsecured half of the claim. When the dust settles, the $100 secured creditor would be bought out of the secured portion of its claim for $50 and own 1/3 of the stock, for which it would have paid $17. (Its net position will be $50+$50–$17, or $83.) The pure unsecured will own 67% of the stock, for which it will have paid $33. (Its net position will be $100–$33, or $67.)

Now the reader should see the problem. The option mechanism cannot proceed without a valuation authority knowing the value of the underlying asset. Valuing the machine is not avoided by using the options. What's more, if the underlying structural problem is that some parties use strategic delay to their advantage, uncertainty in valuing the underlying asset could be enough to make the option model a non-improvement. A secured credit system could avoid this problem by giving the secured creditor a "general charge" on *all* value in the firm; but this is not the American system.

Presumably a secured asset could be separately valued using an options approach analogous to the firm-level options. But then whether the result—multiple auctions, presumably going on simultaneously or sequentially for each secured asset—would sufficiently raise the transactions costs to render the approach unviable would be an issue. Perhaps firms and creditors would find ways to avoid security if its valuation were the only barrier to a speedy options-based reorganization.

*2. Uncertainty in the value of a subsidiary.* The machine is lodged in the firm's wholly-owned subsidiary. The $100 secured creditor lent to the subsidiary. The unsecured creditor lent to the parent company. The machine can be sold, or bought, for $25 (a value different from the prior example). Although the entire holding company is worth $150, one cannot ascertain the priority of the total $100 secured claim without valuing the subsidiary. But once the subsidiary is valued, there's no need (vis-a-vis the secured creditor) to deliver the options, because valuation and reorganization rights are then *already* known and one doesn't need the options to discover value and rights.

3. *Doctrinal uncertainty in whether the subsidiary should be respected.* If the parent company mismanaged the subsidiary, then an "asset" of the subsidiary is its claim against the parent company for mismanagement. *Deep Rock*, ¶802. It owns a machine and a legal cause of action. Even if one were going to distribute options on the parent company (unsecured financial claims of $100 and stockholders), one cannot do so until the court determines whether there's another unsecured claimant on the parent company, namely the subsidiary, suing for the parent's mismanagement. One cannot effectively distribute the options until this claim is resolved, and if a core purpose of the option mechanism is to avoid protracted litigation while the firm reorganizes, that purpose would not be met.

Similarly, if the intercorporate transactions (money and assets flowing back and forth between the two) are complex, some courts will collapse the holding company into a single firm for reorganization purposes ("substantive consolidation"). *Consolidated Rock*, ¶702, and *Commercial Envelope*, ¶708. If the firm were substantively consolidated, then the secured creditor's $75 unsecured claim could be asserted against the consolidated entity. Again, options wouldn't work well, or at all, until complex litigation was first resolved.

4. *Doctrinal uncertainty about equitable subordination.* Go back to the single firm without a subsidiary. All debt is lodged in the single firm. In the pre-bankruptcy attempts to revive the company, the secured creditor had a representative sit on the debtor's board of directors. The firm considered filing for bankruptcy when it was worth $150 and the security was worth less than $100, but management and the secured creditor thought the firm could turnaround and the value of the security would increase. It didn't. The unsecured creditor sues for equitable subordination, claiming that the entire value of the secured creditor's claim should be subordinated, because the secured creditor controlled the debtor and used that control to improperly advance the secured creditor's own interests. Options cannot be distributed until the claims are ranked, and that ranking cannot go forward until the equitable subordination litigation is resolved.

In recent years bankrupt firms have sued lenders acting in bad faith under loan covenants or for other misdeeds. Some of the theories are novel, and debtors have had several successes. Until that litigation is resolved, one doesn't know the net priority of all creditors.

5. *Preferences and the validity of the security interest.* The firm can recover some pre-bankruptcy preferential payments. Marshalling doctrines require that an

overly secured creditor with multiple pools of security must, if a junior lienor has recourse to only one of these pools, exhaust the pools available to him exclusively, so as to allow collection by the junior lienor. Not surprisingly, these doctrines are fuzzy at the edges and difficult in application. Until the disputes about preferences, fraudulent conveyances, compliance with local law, and the marshalling doctrines are resolved, one does not know how to distribute options.

* * *

The relative advantage of selling the firm (or a slice-of-stock) then is that the sale could occur and the priority litigation determined *afterward*. Operations could be severed from the mire of bankruptcy litigation and delay. Or could the options be distributed based on ostensible ownership, cleared, and then frozen while priority litigation proceeded, with the property received re-conveyed if priorities were altered? Would that be too complicated, and perhaps leave the firm rudderless while the priorities were determined?

(The sale-of-the-firm and the sale-of-a-slice face similar but less pernicious preliminary questions. For the sale-of-a-slice, an underwriter must be selected, the sale must be allocated as a secondary sale, with the proceeds going to prior owners, or as a primary sale, with the proceeds going into the firm. Deciding these preliminaries could be a lever for delay. Similarly, the means of selling the firm could be a lever for delay as the court decides whether the firm should be sold division-by-division or in its entirety, how long should bids be taken, and who should manage the sale.)

In the end, all the market-based alternatives have flaws, and the question of which one has the fewest flaws is, for now, one of judgment.

## ¶1709: General problems with using the market to replace chapter 11

By measuring each claim's value precisely, a sale will usually effectuate priority more effectively than a reorganization. The proponents of sale think this an advantage of a sale, but whether it is or is not depends on the value of absolute priority, which some see as costly and perhaps unfair. Absolute priority can exacerbate asset substitution incentives for equity-holders to put the firm on a risky path; on some configuration of numbers, muting absolute priority mutes the equity-holders incentives to take unwarranted risk. Absolute priority might similarly lead equity-holders to abandon the firm, because they have no realistic chance of an upside; muting presumably reduces their incentives to abandon.

But these costs of priority arise from creditors not having an efficient mechanism to seize the firm. If we did move to "true" absolute priority, chapter 11 might become a sword for creditors to seize the firm from equity-holders, rather than a shield for equity-holders and managers to prevent creditors from seizing the firm.

The sale proposals would, their spokesmen claim, facilitate quicker reorganizations by fixing a value quickly and objectively; a weakness of the options proposal is that it might not be able to function *until* priorities are determined. But do the proponents of sale need a sale to get most of what they believe to be valuable? Under the Code, § 1129, the court fixes the firm's value (directly or, by confirming a negotiated plan, indirectly) *after* priorities are determined. But what if the court *immediately* determined value upon the filing of a petition, with that value determining distributions under § 1129(b)(2)? Would that not do much of what the proponents of a sale think a sale would do?

Keep in mind also that the firm when sold (or when valued via options or a slice-of-stock sale) would *not* be worth the same as when continued. We have focused on the operational costs of chapter 11, but there are also gains, such as distributional gains that the insiders can obtain from outsiders. Tax benefits, like N.O.L. carry-forwards are often lost during chapter 11, but are more certain to be lost when there's a full ownership change. See ¶1411. The Bankruptcy Code itself shifts value from outsiders to insiders: the bankrupt can reject unprofitable contracts and assign profitable ones that it could not assign outside of bankruptcy. While looking at the total of dollars won and dollars lost to *everyone*, these rights may not add to America's *total* business value, but they are worth something to the players who would continue a chapter 11 rather than sell the firm so that they can exercise these rights.

How about perceived fairness and legitimacy? Commentators and citizens may see market-based reorganizations as too quickly shutting down firms and firing employees. Cf. Elizabeth Warren, *Bankruptcy Policy*, 54 U. Chi. L. Rev. 775 (1987); David Skeel, *Markets, Courts, and the Brave New World of Bankruptcy Theory*, 1993 Wisc. L. Rev. 465, 497–509. Consider this excerpt from Mark Roe, *Backlash*, 98 Colum. L. Rev. 217, 234–38 (1998):

> Suppose we know that a harsh chapter 11—say one facilitating the quick sale or liquidation of the bankrupt firm— ... best deployed capital and minimized Rawlsian pain[, because ... we kn[e]w that chapter 11 sales or liquidations end society's bad bets quickly. Capital moves to better uses and overall employment (both in raising the number of people employed and in raising salaries at the low end) is improved.
>
> But ... a rule of chapter 11 sale ... will make the employment losses [more] salient in the media. This media saliency [could] result ... eventually (or at least at a nontrivial level of probability) either in, say, debilitating, wealth-decreasing [other rules, or a retention of the current chapter 11] ....
>
> Lest the reader think I am adding a political reason to surreptitiously buttress a case against auctions in bankruptcy ..., I am not. I believe the best bankruptcy system, other than in the political sense of this Essay, would have some auction rule, probably as a default rule that would kick in on a creditor's motion after a few months of efforts to negotiate a reorganization plan for a public company ....
>
> * * *
>
> ... Imagine that the 1980s wave of hostile takeovers had continued undampened into the mid-1990s ... with continuing media saliency typified by mov-

ies like *Wall Street* and books like *Bonfire of the Vanities* and *Barbarians at the Gate*; imagine that financial operators like Michael Milken and Ivan Boesky were still front-page news; imagine a deeper militant populist tradition in the U.S. that was not assuaged and desiccated by a century of legislation that enact[ed] much of the form, and some substance, of the populist program; imagine that the gap between public opinion, which by a rate of 59% sees downsizings as bad for the economy, and economic opinion, which sees them as on balance good in the long run, widens and ossifies; and imagine rougher bankruptcy laws that immediately sold bankrupt firms into the takeover auction drama instead of sending them through two years of negotiation and reorganization. Imagine all this thrown into a heated political setting with media-salient downsizings and (contrary to fact in early 1996) a faltering economy in an election year. Fringe candidates might have become mainstream, or, to co-opt them, mainstream candidates might have adopted *trade protection or economically unwise (but politically astute) programs and made American society poorer.*

... One can believe in the local efficiency of this or that institution (freewheeling hostile takeovers, chapter 11 sales of public companies) and still doubt whether their persistence will maximize political efficiency. The dampening [antisale] rules [in bankruptcy] may enhance [the] system's adaptivity and stability, preserving the *core* efficiency tendencies of capitalism, private property, and competitive markets, by conceding a little economically unwise but politically astute regulation here and there. One could believe a set of legal institutions to be inefficient one-by-one—antitakeover rules, slow chapter 11 reorganizations, Glass-Steagall, old-style antitrust, and a list to which we could all add—and still one cannot conclude that the whole set is inefficient, because the inefficient fringe may preserve that efficient core of private property, mobility, and competition.

## APPENDIX A

# PRESENT VALUE

What is the value of a company's stock that will provide, with certainty, a perpetual stream of $100 per year dividends, if the investor demands a 10% rate of return? (There are no taxes or inflation.)

Intuitively one understands that $1000 will be paid. The formula for arriving at the answer is given by:

(1) PV = D/r

where PV = Present value of the perpetual stream,
D = the annual dividend,
r = the investor's demanded rate of return.

The method by which this formula is derived from the sum of annual discounts to present value is complex and not needed to see the basic formula, which can be intuitively-understood. However, since more complex present value problems cannot be solved by this—or any other—intuitively-understood formula, the method of derivation is set forth below.

The value of the dividend at the end of year 1 is given by:

(2) Value of first year's dividend = D/(1+r)

Second year:

(3) Value of second year's dividend = $D/(1+r)^2$

The nth year:

(4) Value of $n^{th}$ year's dividend = $D/(1+r)^n$

Thus the present value of the stream through year n:

(5) $$PV_n = \frac{D}{1+r} + \frac{D}{(1+r)^2} + \ldots + \frac{D}{(1+r)^n}$$

To simplify operations, let $x = 1/(1+r)$, then substitute:

(6) $$PV_n = Dx + Dx^2 + Dx^3 + \ldots + Dx^n$$

This is a convergent geometric series. There is a "trick" available to solve it. See G. Thomas, Calculus and Analytic Geometry 622–24 (4th ed. 1972).

Multiply each side of (6) by x:

(7) $$PV_n(x) = Dx^2 + Dx^3 + \ldots + Dx^n + Dx^{n+1}$$

Subtract (7) from (6) and most terms drop out:

(8) $$PV_n = Dx + Dx^2 + Dx^3 + \ldots + Dx^n$$

Grouping like terms:

(9) $$PV_n(x) = Dx^2 + Dx^3 + \ldots + Dx^n + D^{n+1}$$

(10) $$PV_n(1 - x) = D(x - x^{n+1})$$

Dividing by (1–x):

(11) $$PV_n(1 - x) = D\left[\frac{x - x^{n+1}}{1 - x}\right]$$

The number x, which equals $1/(1+r)$, is a fraction less than 1. As it is multiplied by itself again and again, the result becomes very small, approaching 0. (Think of it: ½ of ½ is ¼, ½ of ¼ is ⅛; $½^n$ gets closer to 0 as n gets larger.)

As n gets very large, $x^{n+1}$ gets closer to 0. Thus, if we value the perpetuity, we can ignore $x^{n+1}$ (i.e., treat it as 0).

(12) $$PV = Dx / (1 - x)$$

**App. A** PRESENT VALUE

Substituting back $x = 1/(1+r)$

$$(13) \quad PV = D \frac{\frac{1}{1+r}}{\left[1 - \frac{1}{1+r}\right]}$$

Multiplying numerator and denominator each by 1+r, which is equivalent to multiplying the fraction by 1 (i.e., (1+r)/(1+r)):

$$(14) \quad PV = D \cdot \frac{\frac{1}{1+r} \cdot (1+r)}{\left[1 - \frac{1}{1+r}\right] \cdot (1+r)}$$

Or:

$$(15) \quad PV = D \cdot \frac{1}{(1+r) - \frac{(1+r)}{(1+r)}}$$

**Finally:**

$$(16) \quad PV = \frac{D}{r}$$

# APPENDIX B

# THE STATUTES

## BANKRUPTCY ACT OF 1978
## (11 U.S.C. § 101 et seq.)

### § 101. Definitions

(5) "claim" means—

(A) right to payment, whether or not such right is reduced to judgment, liquidated, unliquidated, fixed, contingent, matured, unmatured, disputed, undisputed, legal, equitable, secured, or unsecured; ...

(10) "creditor" means—

(A) entity that has a claim against the debtor that arose at the time of or before the order for relief concerning the debtor; ...

(31) "insider" includes— ...

(B) if the debtor is a corporation—

(i) director of the debtor;
(ii) officer of the debtor;
(iii) person in control of the debtor;
...
(vi) relative of a general partner, director, officer, or person in control of the debtor;
...

(32) "insolvent" means ... financial condition such that the sum of such entity's debts is greater than all of such entity's property, at a fair valuation ...

(41) "person" includes individual, partnership, and corporation, but does not include governmental unit ....

(54) "transfer" means every mode, direct or indirect, absolute or conditional, voluntary or involuntary, of disposing of or parting with property or with an interest in property, including retention of title as a security interest and foreclosure of the debtor's equity of redemption; ...

## § 361. Adequate protection

When adequate protection is required under section 362 ... of this title of an interest of an entity in property, such adequate protection may be provided by—

(1) requiring the trustee to make a cash payment or periodic cash payments to such entity, to the extent that the stay under section 362 of this title ... results in a decrease in the value of such entity's interest in such property;

(2) providing to such entity an additional or replacement lien to the extent that such stay ... results in a decrease in the value of such entity's interest in such property; or

(3) granting such other relief ... as will result in the realization by such entity of the indubitable equivalent of such entity's interest in such property.

## § 362. Automatic stay

(a) ... [A bankruptcy petition] operates as a stay ... of—

(1) the commencement or continuation, ... of a judicial, administrative, or other action or proceeding against the debtor that was or could have been commenced before the commencement of [the bankruptcy];

(2) the enforcement, against the debtor or against property of the estate, of a judgment obtained before the commencement of the case under this title;

(3) any act to obtain possession of [the bankrupt's] property ... or to exercise control over property of the estate;

(4) any act to create, perfect, or enforce any lien against property of the [bankrupt];

(5) any act to create, perfect, or enforce against property of the debtor any lien to the extent that such lien secures a claim that arose before the commencement of the [bankruptcy];

(6) any act to collect, assess, or recover a claim against the debtor that arose before the [bankruptcy];

...

(b) The filing of a petition ... does not operate as a stay—

(3) ... of any act to perfect ... an interest in property to the extent that the trustee's rights and powers are subject to such perfection under section 546(b) ...

(4) under paragraph (1), (2), (3), or (6) of subsection (a) of this section of the commencement or continuation of an action or proceeding by a governmental unit ... to enforce such governmental unit's ... police and regulatory power, including the enforcement of a judgment other than a money judgment, obtained in an action ... by the governmental unit to enforce such governmental unit's ... police or regulatory power; ...

...

(d) On request of a party in interest and after notice and a hearing, the court shall grant relief from the stay provided under subsection (a) of this section, such as by terminating, annulling, modifying, or conditioning such stay—

(1) for cause, including the lack of adequate protection of an interest in property of such party in interest;

(2) with respect to a stay of an act against property under subsection (a) of this section, if—

(A) the debtor does not have an equity in such property; and
(B) such property is not necessary to an effective reorganization; ...

### § 363. Use, sale, or lease of property

(b)(1) The trustee, after notice and a hearing, may use, sell, or lease, other than in the ordinary course of business, property of the estate.

* * *

(c)(1) ... [U]nless the court orders otherwise, the trustee may enter into transactions, including the sale or lease of property of the estate, in the ordinary course of business, without notice or a hearing, and may use property of the estate in the ordinary course of business without notice or a hearing.

### § 364. Obtaining credit

(c) If the trustee is unable to obtain unsecured credit allowable ... as an administrative expense, the court, after notice and a hearing, may authorize the obtaining of credit or the incurring of debt—

(1) with priority over any or all administrative expenses ...
(2) secured by a lien on property of the estate that is not otherwise subject to a lien; or
(3) secured by a junior lien on property of the estate that is subject to a lien.

(d) (1) The court, after notice and a hearing, may authorize the obtaining of credit or the incurring of debt secured by a senior or equal lien on property of the estate that is subject to a lien only if—

(A) the trustee is unable to obtain such credit otherwise; and
(B) there is adequate protection of [the previously-secured creditor].

## § 365. Executory contracts and unexpired leases

(a) ... the trustee, subject to the court's approval, may assume or reject any executory contract or unexpired lease of the debtor.

(b) (1) If there has been a default in an executory contract or unexpired lease of the debtor, the trustee may not assume such contract or lease unless ... the trustee—

 (A) cures ...;

 (B) compensates ...; and

 (C) provides adequate assurance of future performance ....

(2) Paragraph (1) of this subsection does not apply to a default that is a breach of a provision relating to—

 (A) the insolvency or financial condition of the debtor at any time before the closing of the case;

 (B) the commencement of a case under this title;

 (C) the appointment of ... a trustee ...; or

 (D) the satisfaction of any penalty rate or provision relating to a default arising from any failure by the debtor to perform nonmonetary obligations under the executory contract or unexpired lease.

* * *

(f) (1) ... [N]otwithstanding a provision in an executory contract or unexpired lease of the debtor ... that prohibits, restricts, or conditions the assignment of such contract or lease, the trustee may assign such contract or lease ....

(2) The trustee may assign an executory contract or unexpired lease of the debtor only if—

 (A) ...

 (B) adequate assurance of future performance by the assignee of such contract or lease is provided ....

## § 501. Filing of proofs of claims or interests

(a) A creditor or an indenture trustee may file a proof of claim. An equity security holder may file a proof of interest.

## § 502. Allowance of claims or interests

(a) A claim or interest ... is deemed allowed, unless a party in interest ... objects.

(b) ... [T]he court, after notice and a hearing, shall determine the amount of such claim in lawful currency of the United States as of the date of the filing of the petition, and shall allow such claim in such amount, except to the extent that ... such claim is for unmatured interest;

(c) There shall be estimated for purposes of allowance under this section—

(1) any contingent or unliquidated claim, the fixing or liquidation of which ... would unduly delay the administration of the case; or

(2) any right to payment arising from a right to an equitable remedy for breach of performance.

(g) A claim arising from the rejection, under section 365 ... of an executory contract ... of the debtor that has not been assumed shall be determined, and shall be allowed ... or disallowed ... , the same as if such claim had arisen before the date of the filing of the petition.

### § 503. Allowance of administrative expenses

(a) ...

(b) After notice and a hearing, there shall be allowed, administrative expenses ... including—

(1)(A) the actual, necessary costs and expenses of preserving the estate ... .

### § 506. Determination of secured status

(a) An allowed claim of a creditor secured by a lien on property in which the estate has an interest ... is a secured claim to the extent of the value of such creditor's interest in the estate's interest in such property, or to the extent of the amount subject to setoff, as the case may be, and is an unsecured claim to the extent that the value of such creditor's interest or the amount so subject to setoff is less than the amount of such allowed claim. Such value shall be determined in light of the purpose of the valuation and of the proposed disposition or use of such property, and in conjunction with any hearing on such disposition or use or on a plan affecting such creditor's interest.

(b) To the extent that an allowed secured claim is secured by property the value of which, after any recovery under subsection (c) of this section, is greater than the amount of such claim, there shall be allowed to the holder of such claim, interest of such claim, and any reasonable fees, costs, or charges provided for under the agreement under which such claim arose.

(c) The trustee may recover from property securing an allowed secured claim the reasonable, necessary costs and expenses of preserving, or disposing of, such property to the extent of any benefit to the holder of such claim.

### § 507. Priorities

(a) The following expenses and claims have priority in the following order:
(1) First, administrative expenses allowed under section 503(b) ....
....

### § 510. Subordination

(a) A subordination agreement is enforceable in a case under this title to the same extent that such agreement is enforceable under applicable nonbankruptcy law.

(b) For the purpose of distribution under this title, a claim arising from rescission of a purchase or sale of a security of the debtor or of an affiliate of the debtor, for damages arising from the purchase or sale of such a security, or for reimbursement or contribution allowed under section 502 on account of such a claim, shall be subordinated to all claims or interests that are senior to or equal the claim or interest represented by such security, except that if such security is common stock, such claim has the same priority as common stock.

(c) Notwithstanding subsections (a) and (b) of this section, after notice and a hearing, the court may—

(1) under principles of equitable subordination, subordinate for purposes of distribution all or part of an allowed claim to all or part of another allowed claim or all or part of an allowed interest to all or part of another allowed interest; or

(2) order that any lien securing such a subordinated claim be transferred to the estate.

### § 544. Trustee as lien creditor ...

(a) The trustee shall have, as of the commencement of the case ... the rights and powers of, or may avoid any transfer of property of the debtor or any obligation incurred by the debtor that is voidable by—

(1) a creditor that extends credit to the debtor at the time of the commencement of the case, and that obtains, at such time and with respect to such credit, a judicial lien on all property on which a creditor on a simple contract could have obtained such a judicial lien, whether or not such a creditor exists;

(2) a creditor that extends credit to the debtor at the time of the commencement of the case, and obtains, at such time and with respect to such credit, an execution against the debtor that is returned unsatisfied at such time, whether or not such a creditor exists;

....

### § 546. Limitations on avoiding powers

(b) (1) The rights and powers of a trustee under section[] 544 ... are subject to any generally applicable [state] law that—

(A) permits perfection of an interest in property to be effective against an entity that acquires rights in such property before the date of perfection ....

\* \* \*

(e) Notwithstanding sections 544, ... , 547, 548(a)(1)(B), and 548(b) of this title, the trustee may not avoid a transfer that is ... a settlement payment, ... made ... to a ... stockbroker, financial institution, or securities clearing agency ....

### § 547. Preferences

(b) Except as provided in subsection (c) of this section, the trustee may avoid any transfer of an interest of the debtor in property—

(1) to or for the benefit of a creditor;

(2) for or on account of an antecedent debt owed by the debtor before such transfer was made;

(3) made while the debtor was insolvent;

(4) made—

    (A) on or within 90 days before the date of the filing of the petition; or

    (B) between ninety days and one year before the date of the filing of the petition, if such creditor at the time of such transfer was an insider; and

(5) that enables such creditor to receive more than such creditor would receive if—

    (A) the case were a case under chapter 7 of this title;

    (B) the transfer had not been made; and

    (C) such creditor received payment of such debt to the extent provided by the provisions of this title.

(c) The trustee may not avoid under this section a transfer—

(1) to the extent that such transfer was—

    (A) intended by the debtor and the creditor to or for whose benefit such transfer was made to be a contemporaneous exchange for new value given to the debtor; and

    (B) in fact a substantially contemporaneous exchange;

(2) to the extent that such transfer was—

    (A) in payment of a debt incurred by the debtor in the ordinary course of business or financial affairs of the debtor and the transferee;

    (B) made in the ordinary course of business or financial affairs of the debtor and the transferee; and

    (C) made according to ordinary business terms;

(3) that creates a security interest in property acquired by the debtor—

    (A) to the extent such security interest secures new value [in the nature of a purchase-money security interest] ...

        (i) given at or after the signing of a security agreement that contains a description of such property as collateral;

* * *

        (iii) given to enable the debtor to acquire such property; and

        (iv) in fact used by the debtor to acquire such property; and

    (B) that is perfected on or before 20 days after the debtor receives possession of such property[.]

(4) to or for the benefit of a creditor, to the extent that, after such transfer, such creditor gave new value to or for the benefit of the debtor ...

(5) that creates a perfected security interest in inventory or a receivable or the proceeds of either, except to the extent that the aggregate of all such transfers to the transferee caused a reduction ... to the prejudice of other creditors holding unsecured claims, of any amount by which the debt secured by such security interest exceeded the value of all security interests for such debt on [one of three defined dates] ...

(6) that is the fixing of a statutory lien that is not avoidable under section 545 of this title;

(7) ... or

(8) [aggregate transfers of less than $600 for an individual debtor].

...

(f) For the purposes of this section, the debtor is presumed to have been insolvent on and during the 90 days immediately preceding the date of the filing of the petition.

(g) For the purposes of this section, the trustee has the burden of proving the avoidability of a transfer under subsection (b) ..., and the creditor or party in interest against whom recovery or avoidance is sought has the burden of proving the nonavoidability of a transfer under subsection (c) ....

## § 548. Fraudulent transfers and obligations

(a)(1) The trustee may avoid any transfer of an interest of the debtor in property, or any obligation incurred by the debtor, that was made or incurred on or within one year before the date of the filing of the petition, if the debtor voluntarily or involuntarily—

(A) made such transfer or incurred such obligation with actual intent to hinder, delay, or defraud any entity to which the debtor was or became, on or after the date that such transfer was made or such obligation was incurred, indebted; or

(B) (i) received less than a reasonably equivalent value in exchange for such transfer or obligation; and

(ii) (I) was insolvent on the date that such transfer was made or such obligation was incurred, or became insolvent as a result of such transfer or obligation;

(II) was engaged in business or a transaction, or was about to engage in business or a transaction, for which any property remaining with the debtor was an unreasonably small capital; or

(III) intended to incur, or believed that the debtor would incur, debts that would be beyond the debtor's ability to pay as such debts matured.

...

(c) ... a transferee or obligee of such a transfer or obligation that takes for value and in good faith has a lien on or may retain any interest transferred or may enforce any obligation incurred, as the case may be, to the extent that such transferee or obligee gave value to the debtor in exchange for such transfer or obligation.

## § 549. Postpetition transactions

(a) ... the trustee may avoid a transfer of property of the estate—

(1) that occurs after the commencement of the case; and

(2) ... that is not authorized under this title or by the court.

## § 550. Liability of transferee of avoided transfer

(a) Except as otherwise provided in this section, to the extent that a transfer is avoided under section ... 547, 548 ... the trustee may recover, for the benefit of the estate, the property transferred, or, if the court so orders, the value of such property, from—

(1) the initial transferee of such transfer or the entity for whose benefit such transfer was made; or

(2) any immediate or mediate transferee of such initial transferee.

(b) The trustee may not recover under section (a)(2) of this section from—

(1) a transferee that takes for value, including satisfaction or securing of a present or antecedent debt, in good faith, and without knowledge of the voidability of the transfer avoided; or

(2) any immediate or mediate good faith transferee of such transferee.

(c) If a transfer made between 90 days and one year before the filing of the petition—

(1) is avoided under section 547(b) of this title; and

(2) was made for the benefit of a creditor that at the time of such transfer was an insider;

the trustee may not recover under subsection (a) from a transferee that is not an insider.

(d) The trustee is entitled to only a single satisfaction under subsection (a) of this section.

## § 726. Distribution of property of the estate

(a) Except as provided in section 510 of this title [providing for subordination of certain claims], property of the estate shall be distributed—

(1) first, in payment of [administrative and priority] claims ... ;

(2) second, in payment of any allowed unsecured claim ... proof of which is [in general] timely filed ... ;

(3) third, in payment of any allowed unsecured claim proof of which is tardily filed ... ;

(4) fourth, in payment of [certain fines];

(5) fifth, in payment of interest at the legal rate from the date of the filing of the petition, on any claim paid under paragraph (1), (2), (3), or (4) of this subsection; and

(6) sixth, to the debtor.

## § 1108. Authorization to operate business

Unless the court, on request of a party in interest and after notice and a hearing, orders otherwise, the trustee may operate the debtor's business.

## § 1112. Conversion or dismissal

(b) ... [O]n request of a party in interest ..., and after notice and a hearing, the court may convert [a chapter 11 proceeding to] chapter 7 ... for cause, including—

(1) continuing loss to or diminution of the estate and absence of a reasonable likelihood of rehabilitation;

(2) inability to effectuate a plan;

(3) unreasonable delay by the debtor that is prejudicial to creditors;

(4) failure to propose a plan under section 1121 ... within any time fixed by the court; [or]

(5) ....

### § 1121. Who may file a plan

(a) The debtor may file a plan with a petition commencing a voluntary case, or at any time in a voluntary case or an involuntary case.

(b) Except as otherwise provided in this section, only the debtor may file a plan until after 120 days after the date of the order for relief under this chapter.

(c) Any party in interest, including the debtor, the trustee, a creditors' committee, an equity security holders' committee, a creditor, an equity security holder, or any indenture trustee, may file a plan if and only if—

(1) a trustee has been appointed under this chapter;

(2) the debtor has not filed a plan before 120 days after the date of the order for relief under this chapter; or

(3) the debtor has not filed a plan that has been accepted, before 180 days after the date of the order for relief under this chapter, by each class of claims or interests that is impaired under the plan.

(d) On request of a party in interest made within the respective periods specified in subsections (b) and (c) of this section and after notice and a hearing, the court may for cause reduce or increase the 120-day period or the 180-day period referred to in this section.

### § 1122. Classification of claims or interests

(a) Except as provided in subsection (b) of this section, a plan may place a claim or an interest in a particular class only if such claim or interest is substantially similar to the other claims or interests of such class.

(b) A plan may designate a separate class of claims consisting only of every unsecured claim that is less than or reduced to an amount that the court approves as reasonable and necessary for administrative convenience.

### § 1123. Contents of plan

(a) Notwithstanding any otherwise applicable nonbankruptcy law, a plan shall—

(1) designate, subject to section 1122 of this title, classes of claims, other than claims of a kind specified in section 507(a)(1), 507(a)(2), or 507(a)(8) of this title, and classes of interests;

(2) specify any class of claims or interests that is not impaired under the plan;

(3) specify the treatment of any class of claims or interests that is impaired under the plan;

(4) provide the same treatment for each claim or interest of a particular class, unless the holder of a particular claim or interest agrees to a less favorable treatment of such particular claim or interest;

(5) provide adequate means for the plan's implementation, such as—

  (A) retention by the debtor of all or any part of the property of the estate;

  (B) transfer of all or any part of the property of the estate to one or more entities, whether organized before or after the confirmation of such plan;

  (C) merger or consolidation of the debtor with one or more persons;

  (D) sale of all or any part of the property of the estate, either subject to or free of any lien, or the distribution of all or any part of the property of the estate among those having an interest in such property of the estate;

  (E) satisfaction or modification of any lien;

  (F) cancellation or modification of any indenture or similar instrument;

  (G) curing or waiving of any default;

  (H) extension of a maturity date or a change in an interest rate or other term of outstanding securities;

  (I) amendment of the debtor's charter; or

  (J) issuance of securities of the debtor, or of any entity referred to in subparagraph (B) or (C) of this paragraph, for cash, for property, for existing securities, or in exchange for claims or interests, or for any other appropriate purpose;

(6) provide for the inclusion in the charter of the debtor, if the debtor is a corporation, ... of a provision prohibiting the issuance of nonvoting equity securities, ... including, in the case of any class of equity securities having a preference over another class of equity securities with respect to dividends, adequate provisions for the election of directors representing such preferred class in the event of default in the payment of such dividends; and

(7) contain only provisions that are consistent with the interests of creditors and equity security holders and with public policy with respect to the manner of selection of any officer, director, or trustee under the plan and any successor to such officer, director, or trustee.

(b) Subject to subsection (a) of this section, a plan may—

(1) impair or leave unimpaired any class of claims, secured or unsecured, or of interests;

(2) subject to section 365 of this title, provide for the assumption, rejection, or assignment of any executory contract or unexpired lease of the debtor not previously rejected under such section;

(3) provide for—

  (A) the settlement or adjustment of any claim or interest belonging to the debtor or to the estate; or

  (B) the retention and enforcement by the debtor, by the trustee, or by a representative of the estate appointed for such purpose, of any such claim or interest;

(4) provide for the sale of all or substantially all of the property of the estate, and the distribution of the proceeds of such sale among holders of claims or interests;

(5) modify the rights of holders of secured claims, other than a claim secured only by a security interest in real property that is the debtor's principal residence, or of holders of unsecured claims, or leave unaffected the rights of holders of any class of claims; and

(6) include any other appropriate provision not inconsistent with the applicable provisions of this title.

(c) In a case concerning an individual, a plan proposed by an entity other than the debtor may not provide for the use, sale, or lease of property exempted under section 522 of this title, unless the debtor consents to such use, sale, or lease.

(d) Notwithstanding subsection (a) of this section and sections 506(b), 1129(a)(7), and 1129(b) of this title, if it is proposed in a plan to cure a default the amount necessary to cure the default shall be determined in accordance with the underlying agreement and applicable nonbankruptcy law.

### § 1124. Impairment of claims or interests

[Unless a holder of a claim or interest agrees to less favorable treatment] a class of claims or interests is impaired under a plan unless, with respect to each claim or interest of such class, the plan [either]—

(1) leaves unaltered the legal, equitable, and contractual rights to which such claim or interest entitles the holder of such claim or interest; [or]

(2) notwithstanding any contractual provision or applicable law that entitles the holder of such claim or interest to demand or receive accelerated payment of such claim or interest after the occurrence of a default—

(A) cures any such default that occurred before or after the commencement of the case under this title, other than a default of a kind specified in section 365(b)(2) of this title; [and]

(B) reinstates the maturity of such claim or interest as such maturity existed before such default; [and]

(C) compensates the holder of such claim or interest for any damages incurred as a result of any reasonable reliance by such holder on such contractual provision or such applicable law; and

(D) does not otherwise alter the legal, equitable, or contractual rights to which such claim or interest entitles the holder of such claim or interest[.]

### § 1125. Postpetition disclosure and solicitation

(a) In this section—

(1) "adequate information" means information of a kind, and in sufficient detail, as far as is reasonably practicable in light of the nature and history of the debtor and the condition of debtor's books and records, that would enable a hypothetical reasonable investor typical of holders of claims or interests of the relevant class to make an informed

judgment about the plan, but adequate information need not include such information about any other possible or proposed plan; and ...

(b) An acceptance or rejection of a plan may not be solicited after the commencement of the case [unless] there is transmitted to such holder the plan or a summary of the plan, and a written disclosure statement approved, after notice and a hearing, by the court as containing adequate information. The court may approve a disclosure statement without a valuation of the debtor or an appraisal of the debtor's assets.

\* \* \*

(d) Whether a disclosure statement [under (b)] contains adequate information is not governed by any otherwise applicable nonbankruptcy law, rule, or regulation ...

(e) A person that solicits acceptance or rejection of a plan, in good faith and in compliance with the applicable provisions of this title ... is not liable, on account of such solicitation ... for violation of any applicable law, rule, or regulation governing solicitation of acceptance or rejection of a plan ....

### § 1126. Acceptance of plan

(b) ... a holder of a claim or interest that has accepted or rejected the plan before the commencement of the case ... is deemed to have accepted or rejected such plan ... if ... the solicitation ... was in compliance with any applicable nonbankruptcy law ... governing the adequacy of disclosure ....

(c) A class of claims has accepted a plan if such plan has been accepted by creditors ... that hold at least two-thirds in amount and more than one-half in number of the allowed claims of such class held by creditors, other than any entity designated under subsection (e) of this section, that have accepted or rejected such plan.

\* \* \*

(e) ... [T]he court may designate any entity whose acceptance or rejection of such plan was not in good faith, or was not solicited or procured in good faith ....

(f) Notwithstanding any other provision of this section, a class that is not impaired under a plan, and each holder of a claim or interest of such class, are conclusively presumed to have accepted the plan, and solicitation of acceptances with respect to such class from the holders of claims or interests of such class is not required.

(g) Notwithstanding any other provision of this section, a class is deemed not to have accepted a plan if such plan provides that the claims or interests of such class do not entitle the holders of such claims or interests to receive or retain any property under the plan on account of such claims or interests.

### § 1128. Confirmation hearing

(a) After notice, the court shall hold a hearing on confirmation of a plan.

(b) A party in interest may object to confirmation of a plan.

## § 1129. Confirmation of plan

(a) The court shall confirm a plan only if all of the following requirements are met:

(1) ...

(2) ...

(3) The plan has been proposed in good faith and not by any means forbidden by law.

(4) ...

(5) ...

(6) ...

(7) With respect to each impaired class of claims or interests

(A) each holder of a claim or interest of such class—

(i) has accepted the plan; or

(ii) will receive or retain under the plan on account of such claim or interest property of a value, as of the effective date of the plan, that is not less than the amount that such holder would so receive or retain if the debtor were liquidated under chapter 7 of this title on such date;

(B) ...

(8) With respect to each class of claims or interests—

(A) such class has accepted the plan; or

(B) such class is not impaired under the plan.

(9) Except to the extent that the holder of a particular claim has agreed to a different treatment of such claim, the plan provides that—

(A) with respect to a claim of a kind specified in section 507(a)(1) ... on the effective date of the plan, the holder of such claim will receive on account of such claim cash equal to the allowed amount of such claim; ... .

(10) If a class of claims is impaired under the plan, at least one class of claims that is impaired under the plan has accepted the plan, determined without including any acceptance of the plan by any insider.

(11) Confirmation of the plan is not likely to be followed by the liquidation, or the need for further financial reorganization, of the debtor ... unless such liquidation or reorganization is proposed in the plan.

(b) (1) ... if all of the applicable requirements of subsection (a) of this section other than paragraph (8) are met with respect to a plan, the court, on request of the proponent of the plan, shall confirm the plan notwithstanding the requirements of such paragraph if the plan does not discriminate unfairly, and is fair and equitable, with respect to each class of claims or interests that is impaired under, and has not accepted, the plan.

(2) For the purpose of this subsection, the condition that a plan be fair and equitable with respect to a class includes the following requirements:

(A) With respect to a class of secured claims, the plan provides—

(i) (I) that the holders of such claims retain the liens securing such claims, whether the property subject to such liens is retained by the debtor or transferred to another entity, to the extent of the allowed amount of such claims; and

(II) that each holder of a claim of such class receive on account of such claim deferred cash payments totaling at least the allowed amount of such claim, of a value, as of the effective date of the plan, of at least the value of such holder's interest in the estate's interest in such property;

(ii) for the sale ... of any property that is subject to the liens securing such claims, free and clear of such liens, with such liens to attach to the proceeds of such sale ...; or

(iii) for the realization by such holders of the indubitable equivalent of such claims.

(B) With respect to a class of unsecured claims—

(i) the plan provides that each holder of a claim of such class receive or retain on account of such claim property of a value, as of the effective date of the plan, equal to the allowed amount of such claim; or

(ii) the holder of any claim or interest that is junior to the claims of such class will not receive or retain under the plan on account of such junior claim or interest any property.

(C) With respect to a class of interests—

(i) the plan provides that each holder of an interest of such class receive or retain on account of such interest property of a value, as of the effective date of the plan, equal to the greatest of the allowed amount of any fixed liquidation preference to which such holder is entitled, any fixed redemption price to which such holder is entitled, or the value of such interest; or

(ii) the holder of any interest that is junior to the interests of such class will not receive or retain under the plan on account of such junior interest any property.

## § 1141. Effect of confirmation

(a) Except as provided in subsections (d)(2) and (d)(3) of this section, the provisions of a confirmed plan bind the debtor, any entity issuing securities under the plan, any entity acquiring property under the plan, and any creditor, equity security holder, or general partner in the debtor, whether or not the claim or interest of such creditor, equity security holder, or general partner is impaired under the plan and whether or not such creditor, equity security holder, or general partner has accepted the plan.

(b) Except as otherwise provided in the plan or the order confirming the plan, the confirmation of a plan vests all of the property of the estate in the debtor.

(c) Except as provided in subsections (d)(2) and (d)(3) of this section and except as otherwise provided in the plan or in the order confirming the plan, after confirmation of a plan, the property dealt with by the plan is free and clear of all claims and interests of creditors, equity security holders, and of general partners in the debtor.

(d) (1) Except as otherwise provided in this subsection, in the plan, or in the order confirming the plan, the confirmation of a plan—

(A) discharges the debtor from any debt that arose before the date of such confirmation, and any debt of a kind specified in section 502(g), 502(h), or 502(i) of this title, whether or not—

(i) a proof of the claim based on such debt is filed or deemed filed under section 501 of this title;

(ii) such claim is allowed under section 502 of this title; or

(iii) the holder of such claim has accepted the plan; and

(B) terminates all rights and interests of equity security holders and general partners provided for by the plan.

# TRUST INDENTURE ACT OF 1939
## (15 U.S.C. § 77aaa et seq.)

### § 310 (b) Disqualification of trustee

If any indenture trustee has or shall acquire any conflicting interest as hereinafter defined—

(i) then, within 90 days after ascertaining that it has such conflicting interest, and if the default (as defined in the next sentence) to which such conflicting interest relates has not been cured or duly waived or otherwise eliminated before the end of such 90-day period, such trustee shall either eliminate such conflicting interest or ... resign ...;

\* \* \*

(iii) ... any security holder who has been a bona fide holder of indenture securities for at least six months may, on behalf of himself and all others similarly situated, petition any court of competent jurisdiction for the removal of such trustee ...

... an indenture trustee shall be deemed to have a conflicting interest if the indenture securities are in default (as such term is defined in such indenture ...) and—

(1) such trustee is trustee under another indenture ... of an obligor upon the indenture securities ...

\* \* \*

(10) ... the trustee shall be or shall become a creditor of the obligor.

### § 316 (a) Directions and waivers by bondholders

The indenture to be qualified—

(1) shall automatically be deemed (unless it is expressly provided therein that any such provision is excluded) to contain provisions authorizing the holders of not less than a majority in principal amount of the indenture securities ... at the time outstanding ... on behalf of the holders of all such indenture securities, to consent to the waiver of any past default and its consequences; ...

(2) may contain provisions authorizing the holders of not less than 75 per centum in principal amount of the indenture securities ... at the time outstanding to consent on behalf of the holders of all such indenture securities to the postponement of any interest payment for a period not exceeding three years from its due date.

For the purposes of this subsection ... in determining whether the holders of the required principal amount of indenture securities have concurred in any such direction or consent, indenture securities owned by any obligor upon the indenture securities, or by any person directly or indirectly controlling or controlled by or under direct or indirect common control with any such obligor, shall be disregarded, except that for the purposes of determining whether the indenture trustee shall be protected in relying on any such direction or consent, only indenture securities which such trustee knows are so owned shall be so disregarded.

### (b) Prohibition of impairment of holder's right to payment

Notwithstanding any other provision of the indenture to be qualified, the right of any holder of any indenture security to receive payment of the principal of and interest on such indenture security, on or after the respective due dates expressed in such indenture security, or to institute suit for the enforcement of any such payment on or after such respective dates, shall not be impaired or affected without the consent of such holder ....

# UNIFORM FRAUDULENT CONVEYANCE ACT

### § 1. Definition of Terms

In this act "Assets" of a debtor means property not exempt from liability for his debts. To the extent that any property is liable for any debts of the debtor, such property shall be included in his assets.

"Conveyance" includes every payment of money, assignment, release, transfer, lease, mortgage or pledge of tangible or intangible property, and also the creation of any lien or incumbrance.

"Creditor" is a person having any claim, whether matured or unmatured, liquidated or unliquidated, absolute, fixed or contingent.

"Debt" includes any legal liability, whether matured or unmatured, liquidated or unliquidated, absolute, fixed or contingent.

### § 2. Insolvency

(1) A person is insolvent when the present fair salable value of his assets is less than the amount that will be required to pay his probable liability on his existing debts as they become absolute and matured.

(2) In determining whether a partnership is insolvent there shall be added to the partnership property the present fair salable value of the separate assets of each general partner in excess of the amount probably sufficient to meet the claims of his separate creditors, and also the amount of any unpaid subscription to the partnership of each limited partner, provided the present fair salable value of the assets of such limited partner is probably sufficient to pay his debts, including such unpaid subscription.

## § 3. Fair Consideration

Fair consideration is given for property, or obligation,

(a) When in exchange for such property, or obligation, as a fair equivalent therefor, and in good faith, property is conveyed or an antecedent debt is satisfied, or

(b) When such property, or obligation is received in good faith to secure a present advance or antecedent debt in amount not disproportionately small as compared with the value of the property, or obligation obtained.

## § 4. Conveyances by Insolvent

Every conveyance made and every obligation incurred by a person who is or will be thereby rendered insolvent is fraudulent as to creditors without regard to his actual intent if the conveyance is made or the obligation is incurred without a fair consideration.

## § 5. Conveyances by Persons in Business

Every conveyance made without fair consideration when the person making it is engaged or is about to engage in a business or transaction for which the property remaining in his hands after the conveyance is an unreasonably small capital, is fraudulent as to creditors and as to other persons who become creditors during the continuance of such business or transaction without regard to his actual intent.

## § 6. Conveyances by a Person About to Incur Debts

Every conveyance made and every obligation incurred without fair consideration when the person making the conveyance or entering into the obligation intends or believes that he will incur debts beyond his ability to pay as they mature, is fraudulent as to both present and future creditors.

## § 7. Conveyance Made With Intent to Defraud

Every conveyance made and every obligation incurred with actual intent, as distinguished from intent presumed in law, to hinder, delay, or defraud either present or future creditors, is fraudulent as to both present and future creditors.

\* \* \*

## § 9. Rights of Creditors Whose Claims Have Matured

(1) Where a conveyance or obligation is fraudulent as to creditor, such creditor, when his claim has matured, may, as against any person except a purchaser for fair consideration without knowledge of the fraud at the time of the purchase, or one who has derived title immediately or mediately from such a purchaser,

(a) Have the conveyance set aside or obligation annulled to the extent necessary to satisfy his claim, or

(b) Disregard the conveyance and attach or levy execution upon the property conveyed.

(2) A purchaser who without actual fraudulent intent has given less than a fair consideration for the conveyance or obligation, may retain the property or obligation as security for repayment.

## § 10. Rights of Creditors Whose Claims Have Not Matured

Where a conveyance made or obligation incurred is fraudulent as to a creditor whose claim has not matured he may proceed in a court of competent jurisdiction against any person against whom he could have proceeded had his claim matured, and the court may,

(a) Restrain the defendant from disposing of his property,
(b) Appoint a receiver to take charge of the property,
(c) Set aside the conveyance or annul the obligation, or
(d) Make any order which the circumstances of the case may require.

# INDEX

References are to Pages.

**ACQUISITIONS**
See also Consolidations and Mergers, this index
Creditors of target company, duties owed, 475 et seq.
Exit consents
    Generally, 418 et seq.
    Coercive tender offers to bondholders, 432 et seq.
Holding Companies, this index
Leveraged Buyouts, this index
Margin regulations, application to takeovers, 568
Net operating loss carryforwards, 520, 522
Two-tiered tender offers, 430 et seq.

**AGENCY PROBLEMS**
Generally, 226

**AGENT AND PRINCIPAL**
Security holder liable as principal, 331

**APPRAISAL**
See Valuation, this index

**ARBITRAGE**
LBOs, arbitrage analysis, 567

**ASSET SALES**
Generally, 145 et seq.
Best interests test, 159
Consolidations, bankruptcies resolved through, 600
Deteriorating assets, 153
Discretion of bankruptcy judge, 150
Earmarked sales, 157
Efficient sales, 591
Emergencies, 150
Market-based valuation proposals indicating, 582n
Mergers, bankruptcies resolved through, 600
Mock bids, 90
Perishable assets, 150
Public reactions to, 605
Reorganization pending, sales while, 147
Reorganization vs liquidation bankruptcy
    Generally, 1, 17, 591
    Best interests test, 159
    Criteria, 38 et seq.
    Fresh start philosophy and, 141
    Operating cash requirements, 47
    Transaction costs, 594
    Who decides, 45
Residual claimants as most efficient sellers, 591

**ASSET SALES**—Cont'd
Reorganization vs liquidation bankruptcy —Cont'd
Scrap value, 17
Section 363 sales
    Generally, 147
    All asset sales, 159
    Side deals, 157
Valuation determinations affecting, 24
Value, liquidation, 36
Wasting assets, 150, 156
Who conducts sale, 592

**ASSET SUBSTITUTION**
See Priority, this index

**ASSETS**
See Valuation, this index

**ASSUMPTIONS OF CONTRACTS**
Generally, 18
Adequate protection rights of secured creditors, 385
Co-defendants of bankrupts, 306
Controlling persons, actions against, 487
Definition, 10
Environmental damage claims, 363
Filing of security interests, 321
Interest accrual rights of secured creditors, 383
Waivers, 96

**ATTORNEYS AT LAW**
Dilatory practices, 129
Professional responsibility, 128
Rule 11 sanctions, 128

**AUTOMATIC STAYS**
Generally, 18
Adequate protection rights of secured creditors, 385
Co-defendants of bankrupts, 306
Controlling persons, actions against, 487
Definition, 10
Environmental damage claims, 363
Filing of security interests, 321
Interest accrual rights of secured creditors, 383
Waivers, 96

**AVOIDANCE**
Bankruptcy System, this index

**BALANCE SHEETS**
Generally, 15

INDEX

**References are to Pages.**

**BANKRUPTCY SYSTEM**
Generally, 9 et seq.
Administrative consolidation of related cases, 248
Administrative expenses, priority of, 124, 530
Alternatives to bankruptcy
    Generally, 399
    See also Workouts, this index
    Market-based valuation proposals, 577 et seq.
    Mergers, 456
    Securities, bankruptcy avoidance, 523
Avoidance
    Contract rejection, 11
    Preferential payments, 265
    Security interests, 215
    Settlement payments, 562
Cash flow problems of bankruptcy operations, 530, 533
Code
    Organization, 9
    Statutory text, 611
Common pool problem and bankruptcy law
    Generally, 135, 139
    Valuation delay, 581
Conflicts of interest, 80
Consolidation of related cases, 248
Contracts of bankrupts. See Contracts, this index
Corporate Governance, this index
Corporate trust fund doctrine, 488
Costs of bankruptcy, 590
Debtor-in-possession, 11
Defensive use, 10
Delay and valuation, 125
Delay costs, 131
Dilatory practices, 129
Efficiency analysis, 590
Equitable subordination
    See also Equitable Subordination, this index
    Settlement value of claim of, 332
Fraudulent Conveyances, this index
Fresh start philosophy of bankruptcy laws, 141
Good faith requirements for voluntary petitions, 524
Hybrid forms, 2
Indirect costs, 131
Insolvency and voluntary filings, 524n
Interest and Interest Accruals, this index
Labor, effect of reorganization on, 588
Liquidation. Reorganization vs liquidation, infra
Mergers as alternatives to bankruptcy, 456
Offensive use, 10

**BANKRUPTCY SYSTEM**—Cont'd
Ordinary course management decisions, 97
Ordinary course of business credit, 531
Preferences, this index
Pre-packaged bankruptcies, 430
Priority, this index
Reorganization mechanisms, reform of, 105
Reorganization v. liquidation, 1
Rule 11 sanctions, 128
Settlement psychology, 129
Social costs, 406
Stays. Automatic stay, supra
Substantive Consolidation, this index
Suppliers, effect of reorganization on, 588
Trust fund doctrine, 488
Trustees. See Trustees, this index
Valuation, this index
Voluntary petitions, good faith requirements, 524

**BANKS**
Financial intermediaries, roles as, 225

**BEST INTERESTS TEST**
Generally, 159

**BONDS**
Generally, 176
See also Creditors' Rights and Duties, this index
Bearer bonds, 417
Coercive tender offers, 421 et seq.
Covenant-stripping, 418
Debentures distinguished, 16, 176
Demands by bondholders, 403
Equity v. debt financing. See Finance Theory, this index
Event risks, 486
Exchange offers for bonds subject to original issue discount, 449
Fallen angels, 191, 406n
Fiduciary obligations of debtor companies, 486, 494
Fiduciary obligations to bondholders, 400
Hedging with equity investments, 487
High yield bonds
    Junk bonds, this index
Holdouts to renegotiation proposals, 407
Indentures, this index
Junk Bonds, this index
Low grade bonds, 190
Modifications
    Generally, 400
    See also Workouts, this index
    Bearer bonds, 417
    Covenant-stripping, 418
    Exit consents, 418
    Holdouts, 407

# INDEX

References are to Pages.

**BONDS**—Cont'd
Modifications—Cont'd
    Negative pledge provisions, 420
Monitoring of debtor's financial status, 226
Mortgage bonds
    Generally, 36
    Development of, 179
    Marketing ethics, 219
No-action restrictions on suits by bondholders, 403
Original issue discount
    Generally, 443
    Exchange offers, 449
Perpetuities, 28
Private vs public placement, 192
Rating systems
    Generally, 191
    Downgrading, corporate takeovers and, 485
    Event risks, 486
    Investment grade ratings, 477
    Misrepresentations to ratings agencies, 481
Regulated industries, debt financing advantages in, 504
Renegotiations, 400
Rising stars, 406n
SEC investigation of trustee practices, 461
Sinking funds, 182
Stock-for-bond exchanges, 406, 410n
Super-poison-puts, 486
Tax advantages of debt, 229
Trust Indenture Act. See Indentures, this index

**BROKERS**
See Securities Markets, this index

**BUOYING–UP**
Generally, 405, 455

**CAPITALIZATION AND RECAPITALIZATION**
See also Finance Theory, this index; Workouts, this index
Automatic recapitalization, 524
Capital structure defined, 505
Decapitalization, 78
Flat or varying rate capitalization, 74
Layers of capital, 74
Leveraged capitalization, 512
Multiplier, capitalization, 25
Net operating loss carryforwards, 520, 522
Perpetual income streams, 25
Precooked recapitalizations, 523
Rate, capitalization, 25, 42
Recapitalization generally, 78
Securities regulation restrictions, 526
Subsidiary, inadequately capitalized, 286
Supervision costs, 245
Tax consequences of recapitalization, 520
Top heavy capitalization, 66n
Undercapitalization, 289

**CAPITALIZATION AND RECAPITALIZATION**—Cont'd
Varying rate capitalization, 74

**CASH FLOW**
See Valuation, this index

**COLLATERAL**
See Security Interests, this index

**COMMON POOL PROBLEMS**
Generally, 135
Preferential payments, avoidance powers as to, 265
Valuation delay, 581

**CONFLICTS OF INTEREST**
Bankruptcy trustees, 80
Indenture trustees
    Indentures
Protective committees, 79

**CONSOLIDATIONS AND MERGERS**
Generally, 456
See also Acquisitions, this index
Bankruptcies resolved through, 600
Holding Companies, this index
Substantive Consolidation, this index

**CONTRACT SUBORDINATION**
See Subordination, this index

**CONTRACTS**
Bankrupts'
    Generally, 357 et seq.
    Assignments, 358, 363
    Avoidance powers generally, 11
    Efficiency and inefficiency in contract rejection, 360
    Environmental obligations of bankrupts, 363
    Executory vs executed contracts, 357, 361
    Financial and nonfinancial contracts, 357
    Ipso facto clauses, 358
    Labor contracts, 362
    Leases
        Time for acceptance or rejection, 359
        Use restrictions, 359n
    Obligees' rights on bankrupts' defaults, 357
    Penalty clauses, 358
    Redrafting of contracts in, 2
    Rejection of contracts in bankruptcy, 11
    Social costs of contract rejection, 360
    Specific performance by bankrupts, 359, 361
    Spot vs complex contracts, 358
    Trustees' rights to reject or assume, 357
Casus omissius, 498
Expectations, construction based on, 498
Relational contracts, 496
Risk allocation by, 495

**CONTROLLING PERSON LIABILITY**
Generally, 488

# INDEX
**References are to Pages.**

**CORPORATE CHARTERS**
Bankruptcy, redrafting in, 2

**CORPORATE GOVERNANCE**
Generally, 529 et seq.
See also Finance Theory, this index
Business judgment rule, 279, 281
Cash flow problems of bankruptcy operations, 530, 533
Creditors, outside status of, 494
Denuding the corporation, 488
Directors' duties, insolvency as affecting, 492
Equity stake levels, effect of on management, 536
Fiduciary obligations to bondholders, 486, 494
Intercorporate payments, fairness of, 278
Leveraged buyouts
    Generally, 535 et seq., 563
    Effect on management, 536
    Forecasts, gloomy, 566
Leveraged buyouts, duties owed senior creditors, 475 et seq.
Management change clauses in loan agreements, 341
Ordinary course of business transactions in bankruptcy
    Asset sales, 533
    Credit, 531
Outside status of creditors, 494
Shareholders, managers allied with in bankruptcy, 131
Springing duties on insolvency, 495
Trust fund doctrine, 488
Trustee as manager, 534
Turnaround managers, 131
Turnover of managers and directors, 534

**CORPORATE TRUST FUND DOCTRINE**
Generally, 488

**CORPORATE WASTE**
Common pool problems
    Generally, 135
    Valuation delay, 581
Denuding the corporation, 488
Junk bond issuance, 477
State law, 244
Trust fund doctrine, 488

**CRAM-DOWNS**
See Reorganization Plans, this index

**CREDITORS' RIGHTS AND DUTIES**
Lender liability
    Controlling creditors, 310 et seq.

**CREDITORS' RIGHTS AND DUTIES**
Generally, 459 et seq.
Acquisition activities, 475 et seq.
Adequate protection rights of secured creditors, 385
Bad faith, 348
Best interests test of reorganization plans, 122
Blue chip debt, 477
Bonds, this index
Buying of claims, 163
Collection efforts of powerful creditor, equitable subrogation based on, 329
Committees of creditors, 11
Common pool problems
    Generally, 135
    Valuation delay, 581
Conflicts of interest
    Generally, 79
    Indenture trustees, 460, 463
Control rights of creditors generally, 338
Controlling creditors, liabilities of, 310 et seq., 332 et seq.
Cooperation among creditors, bankruptcy laws as facilitating, 135, 581
Corporate trust fund doctrine, 488
Damages for tortious behavior, 351
Debt cascades, 22
Debtor companies, duties of, 475 et seq.
Deemed approvals of reorganization plans, 37
Definition, 36
Denuding the corporation, 488
Directors' duties, insolvency as affecting, 492
Discrimination, 112 et seq.
Duties to, 459 et seq.
Earmarked sales, 157
Equity interests, ownership of by banks, 354
Equity interests of individual creditors, misuse of, 283
Equity interests vs creditors, 97, 177
Fiduciary obligations of debtor companies, 486, 494
Fiduciary standards for indenture trustees, 462
Forgiveness of indebtedness, tax considerations of, 521
Fraudulent acts of lenders, 348
Fraudulent Conveyances, this index
Gap creditors, 125
Good faith obligations
    Generally, 348
    LBOs and senior creditors, 480
Grab rules of nonbankruptcy law, 137
Holding companies, 245
Indenture trustees. See Indentures, this index
Interest and Interest Accruals, this index
Interference actions against creditors, 341
Investment grade status of senior debt, LBO as impairing, 481
Junk Bonds, this index
Kinds of creditors, 13
Lender liability

# INDEX

References are to Pages.

**CREDITORS' RIGHTS AND DUTIES**
—Cont'd
Lender liability—Cont'd
  Generally, 341 et seq.
Leveraged buyouts, duties owed creditors, 475 et seq.
Management change clauses in loan agreements, 341
Marshalling doctrine, 218
Motive of creditor as equitable subordination factor, 338
Negative Pledges, this index
Open account credit, 211
Ordinary course of business credit, 531
Outside status of creditors, 494
Parent corporation as creditor of subsidiary, 283
Partnership liabilities of creditors, 293
Preferences, collection practices compared, 275
Priority, this index
Profit-sharing creditors, 293
Protective committees, 79
Relational theory of bankruptcy, 392
Rent assignment rights of secured creditors, 385
SEC investigation of indenture trustee practices, 461
Secured and unsecured creditors, 13
Senior creditors, LBO as impairing priority of, 481, 485
Subordination, this index
Substantive Consolidation, this index
Supervision of debtors, 245
Threats, 341
Tort liabilities of lenders, 341 et seq.
Trade creditors
  Generally, 36
  Administration expenses, priority of, 530
  Discrimination against, 111 et seq.
  Section 507(a) priority, 124
Trust fund doctrine, 488
Trust Indenture Act trustee standards, 459 et seq.
Types of creditors, 13
Undersecured creditors, 385
Unsecured and secured debt. See Security Interests, this index
Valuation affecting, 24
Veil piercing, 236
Voluntary vs involuntary creditors, protections afforded in LBOs, 542n, 547n

**CROSS–COLLATERALIZATION**
Generally, 532
Cash collateral, 533
Preference challenges, 340

**DEBENTURES**
See also Creditors' Rights and Duties, this index
Bonds distinguished, 16, 176
Definition, 16

**DEBTOR–IN–POSSESSION**
Generally, 11

**DEFINITIONS**
Absolute priority, 102
Agency problems, 226
Asset substitution, 144
Bankruptcy dollars, 360
Bankruptcy insolvency, 98
Beta, 34n
Blue chip debt, 477
Buoying-up, 407
Capital structure, 505
Capitalization rate, 43n
Casus omissius, 498
Common pool problems, 135
Contract rate of interest, 390
Cramdown, 11, 372
Debenture, 16, 176
Debtor-in-possession, 11
Deep Rock problem, 283
Discrimination, 112
Economic failure, 36
Efficient capital market hypothesis, 168
Equitable subordination, 11
Equity insolvency, 98
Equity receiverships, 4
Event of default, 185
Event risks, 486
Failure, 45
Fallen angel bonds, 191
Financial failure, 36
Floating liens, 319
Fraudulent conveyances, 11
Gap creditors, 125
Gearing, 506
Going concern value, 36
High yield bonds, 190
Holdouts, 407
Indenture, 16, 176
Indenture trustees, 36
Ipso facto clause, 358
Judgment rate of interest, 391
Legal rate of interest, 390
Leveraged equity, 506
Liquidation value, 36
Liquidity transformation, 226
Market rate of interest, 390
Marshalling, 218
M-form corporate organization, 259
Modigliani–Miller hypothesis, 505
Mode and median estimates of future income, 29
Mortgage bond, 36, 179
NOLs, 520
Option model, 579
Ordinary course management decisions, 97
Original issue discount, 443
Preferences, 11
Premium, risk, 32
Present value, 607

**References are to Pages.**

**DEFINITIONS—Cont'd**
Relational contract, 496
Secret lien, 207
Security interest, 387
Shell corporation, 255
Signaling costs, 504
Sinking fund, 182
Size transformation, 226
Strict priority, 101
Subordination, 175
Substantive consolidation, 236
Super poison puts, 486
Systemic and unsystemic risk, 34n
Trade creditor, 36, 124
Trustee, 16n, 37n
Unfair discrimination, 112
Value, 84
Veil piercing, 236

**DELAY**
Reorganization Plans, this index
Valuation, this index

**DEPRECIATION**
Straight line approach, 60
Valuation, effect of depreciation estimates on, 58

**DIMINISHING MARGINAL UTILITY**
Generally, 31

**DIRECTORS**
See Corporate Governance, this index

**DISCOUNTING**
See Valuation, this index

**DISCRIMINATION**
See Creditors' Rights and Duties, this index

**DIVIDENDS**
Equitable subordination, 284, 322
Intercorporate payments, 278
Liquidating, 236
State regulation, 244

**ECONOMIC FAILURE**
Generally, 35, 45

**EFFICIENT CAPITAL MARKET**
Generally, 165, 168
Market-based valuation proposals, 583

**ENVIRONMENTAL LAW**
Obligations of bankrupts, 363

**EQUITABLE SUBORDINATION**
Generally, 283 et seq., 322 et seq.
See also Creditors' Rights and Duties, this index; Subordination, this index
Bad conduct as element, 322

**EQUITABLE SUBORDINATION—Cont'd**
Bankruptcy Code provision, 303
Collection efforts of powerful creditor, 329
Conduct of creditors and, 309 et seq.
Contribution claims, 306
Controlling creditors, 310 et seq., 332 et seq.
Cross-collateralization, 340
Damage claims by shareholders, 297 et seq.
Defined, 11
Distributions to shareholders, 322
Dividends, claims based on rights to, 284
Fraudulent conveyances rule compared, 289
Holding company claims, 283 et seq.
Indemnification claims, 306
Instrumentality rule in parent-subsidiary claims, 286, 288
Misleading of other creditors, 318, 339
Mismanagement, 284
Parent corporations' claims, 283 et seq.
Partnership liabilities of creditors, 293
Reimbursement claims, 306
Relational theory of bankruptcy, conflict with, 392
Rescission claims by shareholders, 297 et seq.
Securities law claims
    Generally, 297 et seq.
    Controlling person liability, 341
    Reliance of creditors on equity investments, 301
    Rescission claims, 297 et seq.
Security interest demands by creditors, 310 et seq.
Stockholders' debt claims, 284
Three-pronged test, 333
Undercapitalization of subsidiary, 289

**EQUITY INTERESTS**
Banks, ownership of, 354
Common pool problems, 135
Creditors, profit-sharing by, 293
Creditors' misuse of equity control, 283
Creditors' rights vs, 97, 177
Debt vs equity financing. See Finance Theory, this index
Directors' duties, insolvency as affecting, 492
Dividends, this index
Equitable subordination of shareholders security act claims, 297 et seq.
Gearing, 506
History of equity financing, 4
Insolvency determinations affecting, 126
Junk bonds as disguised equity, 229
LBO conversion of to debt, 484
Leveraged Buyouts, this index
Leveraged equity, 506
Long-term capital gains, 515
Managers' as allied with equity, 131
Margin. See Securities Regulation, this index

## EQUITY INTERESTS—Cont'd
Reorganization plan, participation of stockholders in, 97
Rescission claims of shareholders, priority accorded, 297 et seq.
Securities Regulation, this index
Subordination of shareholders security act claims, 297 et seq.
Supervision costs, 245
Tax considerations, 515
Top heavy capitalization, deceptive securities resulting from, 66n
Valuation as affecting rights of, 24

## EQUITY RECEIVERSHIPS
Generally, 7
See also Receivers and Receiverships, this index
Definition, 4

## EXIT CONSENTS
Generally, 418 et seq.
Coercive tender offers to bondholders, 432 et seq.

## FAILURE
Generally, 35, 45

## FINANCE THEORY
Generally, 501 et seq.
Agency costs, 503
Automatic recapitalization, 524
Bankruptcy avoidance securities, 523
Bonding advantages, 503
Capital structure defined, 505
Conservation of value law, 508
Control considerations, 503
Debt and risk aversion, 501
Debt-for-debt exchanges, tax considerations, 522
Gearing, 506
Information disparities, 502
Leveraged capitalization, 512
Leveraged equity, 506
Modigliani–Miller Hypotheses
    Debt levels' effect on P/E ratios, 92n
Modigliani–Miller Hypothesis
    Development, 501
    Irrelevance proposition, 505, 512, 536
    LBOs considered, 536
    Leveraged capitalization, 512
    Leveraged investing, 507
    Risk considerations, 513
    Tax considerations, 514
Net operating loss carryforwards, 520, 522
Recapitalization, tax consequences of, 520
Regulated industries, debt financing advantages in, 504
Signaling costs, 504
Stages of analysis, 518
Tax considerations
    Discharge-of-indebtedness income, 525
    Modigliani–Miller Hypothesis, 514
    Net operating loss carryforwards, 520, 522

## FINANCE THEORY—Cont'd
Tax considerations—Cont'd
    Recapitalization, consequences of, 520

## FINANCIAL MARKETS
See Securities Markets, this index

## FINANCIAL STATEMENTS
See also Valuation, this index
Balance sheets, 15

## FINANCIERS
Creditors' Rights and Duties, this index
Equity Interests, this index

## FRAUDULENT CONVEYANCES
Generally, 253 et seq.
See also Bankruptcy System, this index
Avoidance of settlement payments, 562
Bankruptcy Code provisions, 256
Collapsing the LBO transaction, 561
Consideration for new loans, 536, 541, 547
Constructive fraud, 541
Controlling creditors, liabilities of, 310 et seq., 332 et seq.
Corporate trust fund doctrine, 488
Definition, 11
Denuding the corporation, 488
Development of law of, 257
Equitable subordination rule compared, 289
Fraud showings, 537
Good faith and constructive fraud, 541
Guarantee as, 327
Key triggers, 254
LBOs attacked as
    Public buybacks, 549 et seq.
    Senior creditors' remedies, 482
    Voluntary and involuntary creditors, 535 et seq.
Origins of laws, 549
Public stockholders, payments to, 562
Settlement payments by brokers, avoidance of, 562
State law, 244
Triggers, 254
Trust fund doctrine, 488
Uniform Fraudulent Conveyance Act
    Generally, 254
    Constructive fraud, 541
    LBO challenges under, 537
    Origins of fraudulent conveyance laws, 549
    Statutory text, 627
Uniform Fraudulent Transfer Act, 549

## FUTURE VALUE
See Valuation, this index

## GAME THEORY
Market based valuation, 579

## GEARING
Generally, 506

# INDEX
**References are to Pages.**

## GUARANTEES
Fraudulent conveyance law, application to, 327
Interest accruals, guarantors' liabilities for, 380
Preferences, guarantors as insiders, 264, 273
Workouts, guarantees in, 268

## HOLDERS IN DUE COURSE
Generally, 418

## HOLDING COMPANIES
Generally, 236
Business opportunities, appropriation of, 281
Creditors of subsidiaries, 259
Creditors' rights, 245
Effective seniority, 253
Equitable subordination of parents' claims, 283
Fair dealing between parent and subsidiaries, 280
Finance subsidiaries, 255
Fraudulent Conveyances, this index
Inadequately capitalized subsidiaries, 286
Instrumentality rule, 286, 288
Intercorporate debts, valuation of, 240
Intercorporate payments, 278
LBO holding companies, 535, 560
Margin regulations, application to takeovers by shell companies, 570
M-form organization, 259
Options proposal for market-based valuation, effect of claims against subsidiaries, 602
Parent creditors, equitable subordination of, 283
Person status within meaning of Bankruptcy Code, 263n
Preferences, this index
Priority control generally, 96
SEC disclosure regulations, 245
Shell corporations
    Generally, 255
    LBO, 560
Substantive Consolidation, this index
Veil piercing
    Generally, 236
    Unified operations of parent and subsidiaries, 241

## HOSTILE TAKEOVERS
See Acquisitions, this index

## INDENTURES
Generally, 176
Default provisions, 399
Definition, 16
Drafting considerations, 233
Financial ratio covenants, 477, 483
Forms
    American Bar Foundation, 187
    Junk bond, 180
Interest provisions, 379
Junk bond indenture form, 180
Levy provisions, 399

## INDENTURES—Cont'd
Modification provisions
    Generally, 180, 401
Negative Pledges, this index
No-action provisions, 403
Restrictive provisions in, 178
Traditional covenants, abandonment of, 486
Trust Indenture Act
    Generally, 428
    Amendments, 470
    Conflicts of interest amendments, 470
    Enactment, 466
    Exemptions, SEC, 473
    Purpose, 412, 460
    Statutory text, 626
    Trustees, standards, 459
Trustees
    Generally, 36, 37n
    Bankruptcy trustees distinguished, 16
    Conflicts of interest, 460, 463, 471
    Duties of, 459
    Fiduciary standards, 462
    SEC investigation of, 461
    Trust Indenture Act standards, 459

## INSOLVENCY
See Solvency and Insolvency, this index

## INTEREST AND INTEREST ACCRUALS
Generally, 367 et seq.
Absolute priority rule, 375, 396
Accrual generally, 140
Adequate protection rights of secured creditors, 385
Automatic stays and secured creditors' rights to interest, 383
Bankruptcy filing and, 140
Cramdown mechanism, 373
Efficiency costs of nonpayment rules, 392
Fair and equitable analyses of interest claims, 370
Guarantors' liabilities for unpaid interest, 380
Indenture drafting, 379
Interest on unpaid accruals, 391
Judgment rate of interest, 390
Legal rate of interest, 390
Liquidation bankruptcies, 372
Nonaccrual rule, criticisms, 393
Original issue discount, 443
Oversecured creditors, 382, 388
Penalty analysis of interest, 380
Policy questions, 369
Postpetition interest, 371
Priorities as to interest accruing during reorganization, 96
Priorities linked to interest rates, 16
Priority rights as between creditor classes, 376
Rate questions, 390
Reinstatement, interest rights on, 391
Relational theory of bankruptcy, 392

**INTEREST AND INTEREST ACCRUALS—Cont'd**
Rent assignment rights of secured creditors, 385
Reorganization bankruptcies, 372
Risk and interest premiums, 32
Secured and unsecured debt, 382
Solvent bankrupts, interest problems, 374, 389
Stays and secured creditors' rights to interest, 383
Subordination, 376
Undersecured creditors, 385, 388
Unpaid interest, right to interest on, 391

**INVOLUNTARY CREDITORS**
See Creditors' Rights and Duties, this index

**JUNIOR LENDERS**
See Priority, this index

**JUNK BONDS**
Generally, 175 et seq.
See also Creditors' Rights and Duties, this index; Leveraged Buyouts, this index
Bases for subordination, 229
Duties owed senior creditors, 475 et seq.
Equity nature of, 229
Fallen angels, 406n
Federally insured investors, 222
Form, indenture, 180
Growth in issuance of, 3, 223
Leveraged buyouts, duties owed senior creditors, 475 et seq.
Low priority, 225 et seq.
Marketing ethics, 219
Markets for, 190
Priorities and interest rates generally, 16
Private vs public placement of bonds, 192
Rising stars, 406n
Risk, 190
Savings and loan association investments, 222
Senior creditors, duties owed to, 475 et seq.
Stock for bond exchanges, 406, 410n
Subordination agreements by holders, 16
Tax advantages of debt, 229

**LABOR LAW**
Obligations of bankrupts under labor contracts, 362
Reorganizations, effect on workers, 588

**LENDER LIABILITY**
See Creditors' Rights and Duties, this index

**LEVERAGED BUYOUTS**
Generally, 535 et seq.
See also Junk Bonds, this index
Arbitrage analysis, 567
Collapsing the transaction, 561
Consideration for new loans, 536, 541, 547
Constructive fraud charges, 541
Corporate governance, effect on, 536

**LEVERAGED BUYOUTS—Cont'd**
Creditors, duties owed to, 475 et seq.
Equity interests in, 547
Explanations for, 536
Fiduciary duties of managers, 567
Forecasts by managers depressing stock values, 566
Fraud charges, 537
Fraudulent conveyance challenges
    Public buybacks, 549 et seq.
    Senior creditors' remedies, 482
    Voluntary and involuntary creditors, 535 et seq.
Good faith and constructive fraud, 541
Good faith obligations to senior creditors, 480
Holding company forms of, 535, 560
Injunctive relief by senior creditors, 475 et seq.
Insiders' valuations, 563 et seq.
Insolvency threats and fraudulent conveyance challenges, 535
Investment grade status of senior debt, impairment of, 481
Junk bond markets and hostile take overs, 219
Modigliani–Miller hypothesis and, 536
    See Finance Theory, this index
Preemptive strike LBOs, 536
Profits from, 563
Securities regulation violations, 481
Senior debt, impairment of, 481, 485
Shell corporations, 255
Shell holding companies, 560
Stockholders' attitudes towards, 547
Successful, 563
Tax advantages, 536
Transactional types, 535, 560
Valuation advantages of insiders, 563 et seq.
Voluntary vs involuntary creditors, protections afforded, 542n, 547n

**LEVERAGED EQUITY**
Generally, 506

**LIENS**
See Security Interests, this index

**LIQUIDATION**
See Asset Sales, this index

**MANAGERS**
See Corporate Governance, this index

**MARGIN REGULATIONS**
See Securities Regulation, this index

**MARKETS**
See Securities Markets, this index

**MARSHALLING DOCTRINE**
Generally, 218
Trust fund doctrine as rationale for, 489

**MERGERS**
See Consolidations and Mergers, this index

# INDEX

**References are to Pages.**

**MODIGLIANI–MILLER HYPOTHESIS**
See Finance Theory, this index

**MORTGAGE BONDS**
See Bonds, this index

**MORTGAGES**
See Security Interests, this index

**NEGATIVE PLEDGES**
Generally, 195 et seq.
Consent solicitations, 196
Enforcement, 203
Modification, deletion by, 420
Priority control generally, 96
Secret lien challenges, 207
Security interests compared, 217

**ORIGINAL ISSUE DISCOUNT**
See Bonds, this index

**PARENTS AND SUBSIDIARIES**
See Holding Companies, this index

**PAROL EVIDENCE RULE**
Generally, 499

**PARTNERSHIPS**
Creditors, profit sharing and partnership liabilities of, 293

**POOLING**
Substantive Consolidation, this index

**PREFERENCES**
Generally, 261 et seq.
See also Creditors' Rights and Duties, this index
Avoiding powers of trustees, 265
Benefitting insider, payment as, 261
Collection practices vs, 275
Controlling creditors, liabilities of, 310 et seq., 332 et seq.
Cross-collateralization, 340
Defenses, 270
Definition, 11
Elements, 270
Equitable concerns, 267
Equity control, misuse of by individual creditors, 283
Executions subject to, 276
Floating liens, 319
Guarantors, insider, 264, 273
Inside status of creditors, 261
Ordinary course payments, 270
Policy concerns, 267
Post-bankruptcy security interests, 319
Priority, this index
Recovery periods for insiders and outsiders, 266
Safe-harbor transactions, 319
Security interest demands by creditors as, 310 et seq.
Security interests subject to, 276
Third party payments, 277
Work out agreements, status of, 268, 273

**PRE–PACKAGED BANKRUPTCIES**
Generally, 430

**PRESENT VALUE**
See Valuation, this index

**PRINCIPAL AND AGENT**
Security holder liable as principal, 331

**PRIORITY**
Generally, 95 et seq.
See also Creditors' Rights and Duties, this index
Absolute
    Generally, 20, 95, 604
    Bankruptcy law changes, 106
    Expectations of creditors and, 124
    Interest accruals, 396
    Interest payments, 375
    Market-based valuation proposals and, 604
    Rationale for rule, 104
    Securities law claims, 298
    Workouts, 416
Administrative expenses, 124, 530
Anti-skipping rule, 104
Asset sales, residual claimants as most efficient sellers, 591
Asset substitution
    Generally, 144
    Risks of, 229
Bankruptcy system overview, 9
Best interests test of reorganization plans, 122
Blue chip debt, 477
Cash flow problems of bankrupt operations, 530 et seq.
Common pool problems, 135
Contractual control of, 96, 175
Creditors vs equity interests, 97, 177
Cross-collateralization
    Generally, 532
    Preference challenges, 340
Debt cascades, 22
Debtor-in-possession financing, 10
Deposits, purchasers,' 125
Discriminatory reorganization plans, 112 et seq.
Effective seniority, 253
Efficiency purposes, 142
Environmental cleanup claims, 365
Equalization across time, 275
Equitable Subordination, this index
Equity interests vs creditors, 97, 177
Fair and equitable standard for reorganization plans, 97, 112, 123
Indirect priority problem, 590
Interest and Interest Accruals, this index
Interest claims, 96, 376
Interest rates reflecting, 16
Junk Bonds, this index

**PRIORITY**—Cont'd
LBOs as impairing priority of senior creditors, 481, 485
Low priority of junk bonds, 225 et seq.
Market-based valuation affected by disputes re, 587
Marshalling doctrine, 218
Muting of in bankruptcy, 397
Negative Pledges, this index
New financing, 10
Options proposal for market-based valuation, effect of priority disputes on, 601
Ordinary course of business credit, 531
Ranking
    Determination of, 15
    Self ranking, 16
Relative priority doctrine, 105
Secret liens, 207
Section 507(a) priority, 124
Security Interests, this index
Senior creditors
    Determinations of seniority, 15
    Duties owed to, 475 et seq.
Statutory or contractual, 175
Strict priority, 101
Subordination, this index
Substantive consolidation affecting, 247
Super-priority claims, 530
Tax claims
    Generally, 125
    Equitable subordination, 322
Trade creditors
    Discrimination against, 111, 112 et seq.
    Section 507(a) priority, 124
True absolute priority, 604
Wage claims, 125
Waivers, 103

**PROFIT**
See Valuation, this index

**PROTECTIVE COMMITTEES**
Generally, 79

**RAILROADS**
Failures, importance of reorganization after, 6

**RANKING**
See Priority, this index

**RECAPITALIZATION**
Capitalization and Recapitalization, this index
Reorganization Plans, this index
Workouts, this index

**RECEIVERS AND RECEIVERSHIPS**
Generally, 6
Equity Receiverships, this index
Functions of receivers, 39n

**REJECTION OF CONTRACTS**
See Bankruptcy System, this index

**RELATED BUSINESS ENTITIES**
See Holding Companies, this index

**RELATIONAL CONTRACTS**
Generally, 496

**RELATIONAL THEORY OF BANKRUPTCY**
Generally, 392

**REORGANIZATION PLANS**
Generally, 96
Automatic recapitalization, 524
Bankruptcy law reform, 105
Best interests test, 122, 159
Buying of claims, 163
Capitalization levels and growth of, 3
Chandler Act, 577
Class acceptance, 163
Confirmation criteria, 110
Conflicts of interest, 79
Consolidation-based plans, 600
Corporate Governance, this index
Costs of reorganization, 134
Cramdowns
    Generally, 372
    Definition, 11
Criticisms of system, 578, 600
Debt-for-debt exchanges, tax considerations, 522
Deemed approvals of plans, 37
Discharge of indebtedness income, 525
Disclosure requirements, 140
Discriminatory plans, 112 et seq.
Earmarked sales, 157
Equity interests, participation in, 97
Equity Receiverships, this index
Exclusivity period, 11
Extrapolation valuation from partial sale, 582
Fair and equitable standard, determinations re, 97, 123, 417
Feasibility and fairness determinations, 65, 71
Forgiveness of indebtedness, tax considerations of, 521
Game theory and market based valuation, 579
Give-ups, 588
Growth of reorganization institutions, 4
Inability determinations, 146
Interest and Interest Accruals, this index
Labor, effect of plan on, 588
Liquidation vs reorganization
    Generally, 1, 17, 591
    Best interests test, 159
    Criteria, 38 et seq.
    Fresh start philosophy and, 141
    Operating cash requirements, 47
    Transaction costs, 594
    Who decides, 45
Managers' role in, 131
Market-based reorganization reform, 578, 600
Merger-based plans, 600
Mergers as alternatives to bankruptcy, 456

# Index

**References are to Pages.**

**RELATIONAL THEORY OF BANKRUPTCY**—Cont'd
Modification provisions in bond indentures, 405
Nonbankruptcy. See Workouts, this index
Pre-cooked recapitalizations, 523
Pre-packaged bankruptcies, 430
Priority, this index
Prisoner's dilemma theory, 164
Protective committees, 79
Railroad failures, importance to economy of continuing operations, 6
Reform proposals, 578, 600
Sales of assets while reorganization pending, 147
Section 363 sales
    Generally, 147
    All asset sales, 159
    Side deals, 157
    See Asset Sales, this index
Settlement psychology, 129
Shareholders, participation in, 97
Slice-of-stock sale valuation proposal, 578, 601
Solicitation requirements, 140
Suppliers, effect of plan on, 588
Tax consequences of recapitalization, 520
Tort claimants, effect of plan on, 588
Valuation, this index
Workers, effect of plan on, 588
Workouts, this index

**RESCISSION**
Equitable subrogation of shareholders' claims, 297

**RISK**
Allocation by contract, 495
Anticipated risk, 245
Asset substitution, 229
Beta, 34n
Bond rating systems, 191
Buying and selling risks, 497
Contract theory and, 495
Debt and risk aversion, 501
Diminishing marginal utility, 31
Diversification and variance, 32
Event risks in bond market, 486
Junk bonds, 190
Modigliani–Miller Hypothesis, risk considerations, 513
    See Finance Theory, this index
Packaging, 502
Premiums demanded by lenders, 32
Probability distributions, 30
Systemic and unsystemic, 34n
Valuation determinations, 29
Variance and diversification, 32

**SALES OF ASSETS**
See Asset Sales, this index

**SECURITIES**
See Equity Interests, this index

**SECURITIES MARKETS**
Generally, 577 et seq.
Agency problems, 226
Avoidance of settlement payments, 562
Bankruptcy valuation alternatives, 577 et seq.
Banks, competition with, 225
Buried information and market-based valuation, 585
Control blocks, valuation effects of, 585
Efficient market hypothesis
    Generally, 168
    Market-based valuation proposals, 583
Ethics of junk bond marketing, 219
Extrapolation valuation from partial sale, 582
Game theory analysis of market-based valuation of bankrupts, 579
Informational impediments, 584
Junk bond markets, 190
Leveraged investing, 507
Long term capital gains, 515
Macro-economic factors affecting valuation, 585
Margin. See Securities Regulation, this index
Modigliani–Miller Hypothesis, 507
    See Finance Theory, this index
Monitoring by investors, 226
Options proposal for market-based valuation, 595, 601
Private vs public placement of bonds, 192
Regulation. See Securities Regulation, this index
Settlement payments, avoidance in bankruptcy, 562
Strategic bidding and market-based valuation, 587
Subordination and priority disputes affecting market-based valuation, 587
Tax considerations, 515
Troubles with, 226
Valuation proposals, market-based, 577 et seq.

**SECURITIES REGULATION**
Controlling persons liability, 341
Equitable Subordination, this index
LBO violations, 481
Margin regulations
    Generally, 568 et seq.
    Purpose credit, 572
    Shell companies, 570
    Takeovers, application to, 568
Trust Indenture Act. See Indentures, this index
Workout restrictions, 526

**SECURITY INTERESTS**
Generally, 209 et seq.
See also Creditors' Rights and Duties, this index; Priority, this index
Adequate protection
    Generally, 385

INDEX

**References are to Pages.**

**SECURITY INTERESTS**—Cont'd
Adequate protection rights—Cont'd
    Administration expense claims, 530
Administration expenses vs, 530
After-acquired property provisions, 385
Attachment, 212, 214
Automatic stays, filing rights and, 321
Avoidance in bankruptcy, 215
Cash collateral, 533
Cross-collateralization
    Generally, 532
    Preference challenges, 340
Debentures and bonds distinguished, 176
Definition, 387
Determination of secured status, 118
Equitable subordination where creditors demand security protection, 310 et seq.
Filing and notice requirements, 16
Filing failures, 321
Finance theory applied to, 216
Floating liens, 319
Interest and interest accruals, 382
Market based valuation affecting, 587
Marshalling doctrine, 218
Mortgage bonds, 36
Negative pledges compared, 217
Oversecured creditors, 382, 388
Perfection, 214
Possessory and nonpossessory interests, 212
Post-bankruptcy interests as preferences, 319
Preferential grants of, 276
Principal, security holder as, 331
Priority control generally, 96
Purchase money, 212
Rights of secured creditors generally, 387
Secret liens, 207
Theft analysis, 217
UCC, applicability of, 213
Undersecured creditors, 388

**SENIORITY**
See Priority, this index

**SETTLEMENT**
See also Workouts, this index
Earmarked sales, 157
Equitable subordination claims, settlement value of, 332
Global settlement, 325
Negotiated vs judicial valuation generally, 161
Psychology of, 129

**SHARE HOLDERS**
See Equity Interests, this index

**SINKING FUNDS**
Definition, 182

**SOCIAL COSTS**
Generally, 406
Contract rejections in bankruptcy, 360

**SOLVENCY AND INSOLVENCY**
Generally, 126
See also Valuation, this index

**SOCIAL COSTS**—Cont'd
Accountants' solvency assurances, 552
Corporate trust fund doctrine, 488
Directors' duties, insolvency as affecting, 492
Equity and bankruptcy senses of, 98
Equity interests and insolvency determinations, 126
Fiduciary obligations to creditors, insolvency as affecting, 486 et seq.
Hearing procedure and delays, 126
Interest problems in solvency bankruptcies, 374, 389
LBO challenges alleging insolvency threats, 535
Solvency assurances by accountants, 552
Springing duties, 495
Voluntary bankruptcy, insolvency as requirement for, 524n

**STAYS**
See Bankruptcy System, this index

**STOCKHOLDERS**
See Equity Interests, this index

**SUBORDINATION**
See also Priority, this index
Asset substitution risks, 229
Bases for, 229
Contractual control of priority generally, 96, 175 et seq.
Costs to lenders of, 229
Definition, 175
Equitable Subordination, this index
Future subordination agreements, 229
Hybrid agreements, 17
Indenture provision form
    American Bar Foundation form, 188
    Junk bond, 184
Interest claims, 376
Junk Bonds, this index
Market-based valuation affected by disputes re priority, 587
Priority control generally, 96
Securities law claims, 297 et seq.
Senior debt definitions, 190
Voluntary, 355

**SUBSIDIARIES**
See Holding Companies, this index

**SUBSTANTIVE CONSOLIDATION**
Generally, 236
Administrative consolidation, 248
Commingling, 248
Creditors' rights, 247
State remedies, 244
Unified operations of parent and subsidiaries, 241

**TAKEOVERS**
See Acquisitions, this index
See Asset Sales, this index

**TAX CONSIDERATIONS**
Debt-for-debt exchanges, 522

INDEX
**References are to Pages.**

TAX CONSIDERATIONS—Cont'd
Discharge-of-indebtedness income, 525
Equity vs debt financing. See Finance Theory, this index
Forgiveness of indebtedness, 521
LBOs, tax advantages, 536
Long term capital gains, 515
Net-operating-loss carryforwards, 520, 522
Recapitalization, consequences of, 520

TORT CREDITORS
See Creditors' Rights and Duties, this index

TRADE CREDITORS
See Creditors' Rights and Duties, this index

TRUST FUND DOCTRINE
Generally, 488

TRUST INDENTURE ACT
See Indentures, this index

TRUSTEES
See also Bankruptcy System, this index
Avoiding powers, 265
Conflicts of interest, 80
Corporate governance, 534
Distinctions, 16n, 37n
Indenture
  Generally, 36
  Bondholders' demands on, 403
  Conflicts of interest, 460, 463, 471
  Duties of, 459
  Fiduciary standards, 462
  SEC investigation of, 461
  Trust Indenture Act standards, 459
Lien creditor status, 320
Management of bankrupt by, 534
Standards for appointment, 147
Standing, 81n

TRUSTS
Corporate trust fund doctrine, 488

TURNAROUND MANAGERS
Generally, 131

UNFAIR DISCRIMINATION
See Creditors' Rights and Duties, this index

UNIFORM FRAUDULENT CONVEYANCE ACT
See Fraudulent Conveyances, this index

UNSECURED AND SECURED DEBT
See Security Interests, this index

VALUATION
Generally, 13 et seq., 35 et seq., 166 et seq.
Absolute priority rule and, 107
Advantages of proposed alternatives to judicial valuation, 600
Bankruptcy law changes in hearing procedure, 106
Capitalization multiplier, 25
Capitalization rate, 42
Cash flow predictions, 19

VALUATION—Cont'd
Chandler Act, 577
Common pool analysis of delay motivations, 581
Costs of reorganization, 134
Criticisms of judicial process, 580
Definition of value, 84
Delay, effect of, 125
Delay incentives, 580
Depreciation, this index
Depreciation estimates affecting, 58
Diminishing marginal utility, 31
Disadvantages of proposed alternatives to judicial valuation, 600
Discounting, 24
Earning power, 20
Efficient capital market theory, 165
Experts, adversarial and appointed, 161
Extrapolation from partial sale, 582
Financial Statements, this index
Future cash flow predictions, 19
Future value, 24
Game theory and market based valuation, 579
Going concern value
  Generally, 36
  Recognition in valuation by sale, 591
  Unprofitable business, 45
Hearings
  Generally, 37
  Bankruptcy law changes, 106
Hypothetical sale approach, 591
Implications of, 24
Inflation distortions, 93
Informational impediments to market-based valuation of bankrupts, 584
Insiders,' 563 et seq.
Insolvency. See Solvency and Insolvency, this index
Intercorporate debts of related companies, 240
Intrinsic value, 167
LBOs by insiders, 563 et seq.
Liquidation decisions affected by, 24
Liquidation value, 36
Long-lived assets, 26
Macro-economic factors, 585
Market value vs reorganization value, 171
Marketable securities, 20
Market-based valuation proposals
  Generally, 577 et seq.
  Efficient market hypothesis, 583
Mock bids, 90
Mode and median estimates of future income, 29
Multipliers, times-earnings, 86
Negotiated vs judicial valuation, 161
Nonfinancial relationships of bankrupt, recognition of, 588
Option model, 579

**VALUATION**—Cont'd
Options proposal for market-based valuation, 595
Perpetual income streams, 25
Present value, 24 et seq., 607
Price-earnings ratios, 83, 88
Probability distributions, 30
Profit expectations, value as, 84
Reorganization value
    Generally, 166
    Market value vs, 23, 171
Replacement costs, 58
Risk determinations, 29
Rule 11 sanctions, 128
Sale-based valuation proposals, 577 et seq.
Scrap value, 17
Settlement psychology, 129
Slice-of-stock sale proposal, 578, 601
Solvency and Insolvency, this index
Stigma of bankruptcy as factor, 22, 168, 579
Stock and bond appraisal, 162
Subordination and priority disputes affecting market-based valuation, 587
Unprofitable concern, determining value of, 45
Varying rates of capitalization, 74

**VEIL PIERCING**
Generally, 236
Automatic stay protection of controlling person defendants, 487
State law, 244
Unified operations of parent and subsidiaries, 241

**VOLUNTARY CREDITORS**
See Creditors' Rights and Duties, this index

**WASTE**
See Corporate Waste, this index

**WORKOUTS**
Generally, 399 et seq.

**WORKOUTS**—Cont'd
See also Finance Theory, this index; Reorganization Plans, this index
Absolute priority rule and, 416
Bankruptcy alternatives generally, 399, 406
Bond modifications. See Bonds, this index
Buoying-up, 405, 455
Coercive recapitalization proposals, 421
Coercive tender offers to bondholders, 432 et seq.
Collapses, 405
Conflicts of interest of protective committees, 79
Discharge-of-indebtedness income, 525
Economics of holding out, 409
Exchange offer prospectuses, 440
Exchange offer for bonds subject to original issue discount, 449
Exit consents, 418 et seq.
Failures of, 409
Fair and equitable standard for reorganization plans, 417
Good faith requirements, 421
Guarantees in, 268
Holder-in-due-course negotiability rules, 418
Holding out, 405
Indenture provisions for levying on corporation, 399
Market-based reorganization reform, 578, 600
Mergers, 456
Multi-creditor bargains, 411
Preference avoidance policies, 268, 273
Pre-packaged bankruptcies, 430
Renegotiation of bonds, 400
Securities regulation restrictions, 526
Single creditor bargains, 410
Stock for bond exchanges, 406, 410n
Trust Indenture Act
    Generally, 428
    Purpose, 412, 460
    Trustees, standards, 459
Two-tiered tender offers, 430 et seq.

1-56662-966-7